COLORADO
REAL ESTATE MANUAL

DEPARTMENT OF REGULATORY AGENCIES

Patty Salazar, Executive Director

THE COLORADO DIVISION OF REAL ESTATE

Marcia Waters, Director

Eric Turner, Deputy Director

REAL ESTATE COMMISSION

Jarrod Nixon, Durango – Chair

Carolyn Ann Rogers, Colorado Springs –
Vice Chair

John Wendt, Carbondale

Lenee Koch, Golden

Michelle Espinoza, Henderson

BOARD OF REAL ESTATE APPRAISERS

Richard Shields, Centennial – Chair

Bonnie Deane Roerig, Denver – Vice Chair

Mickey Sanders, Denver

(Vacant Seat)

Kristy Ann McFarland, Crested Butte

Patrice Campbell, Grand Junction

Matthew Salazar, Centennial

BOARD OF MORTGAGE LOAN ORIGINATORS

Cindy Emerine, Evergreen – Chair

Dena Falbo, Westminster – Vice Chair

Charles "Buzz" Moore, Grand Junction

Bruce M. Jordan, Greenwood Village

Fred Joseph, Denver

PREFACE

The Colorado Division of Real Estate and LexisNexis have prepared this manual with assistance from members of the Real Estate Commission, the Board of Real Estate Appraisers, and the Board of Mortgage Loan Originators. We gratefully acknowledge the help of the many who have contributed their time and experience, especially Marcia Waters and the dedicated staff at the Division of Real Estate for their commitment to making this publication available to the industry.

We hope this manual will be helpful to new applicants for licensure and also a benefit to practicing real estate brokers, appraisers and mortgage professionals as a ready reference.

The information contained in this manual is fundamental to a sound introduction to the real estate industry. It is not intended as an all-inclusive real estate text; nor should it be relied upon as a source of legal advice.

For those who desire to increase their educational and professional competency, there are many classes and courses of instruction available throughout the State of Colorado and a number of colleges and universities that offer four-year programs leading to a degree in real estate and related fields. Suggestions, corrections and criticisms for and of this publication are solicited and will receive careful consideration.

Matthew Bender & Company, Inc.
Editorial Offices
701 E. Water Street
Charlottesville, VA 22902
800-446-3410
www.lexisnexis.com
Printers and Distributors

Print Edition ISBN: 978-1-5221-9173-5
Electronic Edition ISBN: 978-1-5221-9174-2

© 2019 **State of Colorado Department of Regulatory Agencies, Division of Real Estate**

TABLE OF CONTENTS

Chapter 1:
Real Estate Broker License Law

An * in the left margin indicates a change in the statute, rule, or text since the last publication of the manual.

I. Reason for Its Enactment

The Colorado Real Estate Broker License Law was passed to protect the people of the State of Colorado. Through licensing, the law seeks competency and integrity on the part of those engaged in the real estate business. The law has had the effect of raising the general standing of the real estate business and has helped to safeguard the interests of both the public and those engaged in the business.

II. What the Law Does Not Cover

The law does not dictate the ethical standards that should be observed in the real estate industry, or generally of any trade, business, or profession.

Codes of ethics have been voluntarily adopted by various real estate organizations as guiding standards of high moral and ethical practice. Adherence to such codes is recommended to all who are licensed to engage in real estate business, but is not regulated or enforced by the Colorado Real Estate Commission or the Division of Real Estate.

III. The Commission Office

* The Division of Real Estate has a five-member Commission that meets bi-monthly to conduct rulemaking hearings, make policy decisions, consider licensing matters, review complaints, and take disciplinary action against real estate brokers. Rules are promulgated after notice and public hearings at which all interested parties may participate. The five Commission members consist of three real estate brokers who have had not less than five years' experience in the real estate business in Colorado, one of whom has substantial experience in property management, and two representatives of the public at large. Members of the Commission hold office for a period of three years.

The Division of Real Estate is part of the Department of Regulatory Agencies and is responsible for budgeting, purchasing, and related management functions. The director of the Division is an administrative officer who executes the directives of the Commission and is given statutory authority in all matters delegated by the Commission.

The Division of Real Estate is the licensing, regulation, and enforcement agency for real estate brokers, appraisers, mortgage loan originators, and subdivision developers. Additionally, the Division registers HOAs and compiles regulatory statistics related to those HOAs. To become licensed, individuals must comply with education and/or experience requirements, qualify for reciprocity, and/or pass a general and/or state portion of the licensing exam.

The Division's objectives are to:

- Provide protection to consumers and other stakeholders.
- Promote consumer awareness throughout the State of Colorado.
- Enforce state and federal laws, rules, regulations, and standards and impose disciplinary action when recommended.
- License real estate brokers.
- License real estate appraisers.
- License mortgage loan originators.
- Register timeshares, raw land subdivisions developers and homeowners' associations.
- Investigate complaints.
- Enforce compliance with state and federal laws.
- Impose recommended disciplinary actions against licensees.
- Register HOAs and track and categorize complaints against those HOAs.

The Commission exercises its duties and authorities independently through the following programs or activities.

A. The Master File

The Division staff records the historical and day-to-day information concerning the licensing status of employers, employees, corporations, limited liability companies and partnership entities, trade names, office locations, and disciplinary actions.

B. Licensing

* The Licensing section's major responsibility is the data entry and upkeep of nearly 70,000 real estate broker, appraiser, and mortgage loan originator licensing records, as well as registration of subdivision/timeshare developers and homeowners' associations. The Licensing staff reviews and processes all incoming applications, which are screened for required qualifications, including education, experience, examinations, errors & omission (E&O) insurance, and criminal history background checks. The Licensing section also issues license histories to licensees who need to prove their credentials to other jurisdictions.

* Colorado recognizes real estate licenses issued by many other jurisdictions if the licensee in the other jurisdiction has held that license for 2 years or more. Licensing currently administers this program and offers a limited recognition program to these licensees. The Division also reciprocates with most other appraisal jurisdictions.

Applicants with a past civil judgment or criminal conviction may request a "preliminary advisory opinion" regarding the likelihood of receiving a license before completing the requirements to apply for a license (Commission Rule 3.8). The Commission/Board may issue either a favorable or unfavorable opinion.

* Both "preliminary advisory" applicants and license applicants are subject to pre-licensing investigations and fingerprinting to safeguard the statutory mandate for truthfulness, honesty, good moral character, and general fitness. (See §§ 12-10-202, -203(3), -606(6), and -711(1),

C.R.S.) All applications that disclose civil or criminal violations or any form of previous license discipline in any jurisdiction are reviewed and investigated thoroughly.

Licenses issued by the section include:

- Real estate broker
- Corporate/LLC real estate brokerage
- Partnership real estate brokerage
- Temporary real estate broker
- Ad Valorem appraiser
- Licensed appraiser
- Certified residential appraiser
- Certified general appraiser
- Temporary appraiser
- Mortgage loan originator

The Division also reviews and registers:

- Raw ground subdivision developers
- Timeshare and vacation club developers
- Condominium conversion developers
- Homeowners' associations

Information on licensing is located on the Division of Real Estate website at: http://dora.colorado.gov/dre

C. Enforcement Section

The Real Estate Commission has the power upon its own motion to investigate any licensee's real estate activities. If a written complaint alleging a potential license law violation is filed, the office is compelled to investigate.

If the complaint against the licensee is of such a serious nature that it may result in disciplinary action against a licensee, a hearing may be held before an administrative law judge. The judge is appointed by the Department of Personnel and Administration. The administrative law judge will make an initial decision of revocation, suspension, censure, or dismissal. Education courses, probation, and fines can also be mandated. If written objections are not filed with the Commission within 30 days, the initial decision becomes final. If written objections are filed, the Commission may adopt the findings and initial decision of the administrative law judge, modify the disciplinary action, or refer the matter back for rehearing. The Commission can also issue letters of admonishment in instances where conduct does not warrant formal disciplinary proceedings.

This program also includes:

- Investigation of applicants.
- Evaluation of complaints.
- Investigation of complaints.
- Routine and investigative audits.
- Recommendations for dismissal or disciplinary action.

- Preparation and execution of subpoenas, and other legal documents.
- Preparation of cases for formal hearing, restraining orders, injunctions, or complaints for filing with district attorneys and local law enforcement agencies.
- Working with federal agencies, *e.g.*, the Securities and Exchange Commission or Housing and Urban Development, the Federal Bureau of Investigation, or the Internal Revenue Service.

The Real Estate Commission should *not* be confused with the Colorado Association of REALTORS®, which is a private trade organization affiliated with the National Association of REALTORS® whose members are the only licensees authorized to use the registered trademark "REALTOR"®.

IV. License Law

A. Part 1 – Common Definitions

§ 12-10-101, C.R.S. Definitions.

Editor's note: Subsection (1) is similar to former §§12-61-702 (7) and 12-61-902 (3); subsection (2) is similar to former §§12-61-702 (8) and 12-61-902 (4); and subsection (3) is similar to former §§12-61-101 (1.2) and 12-61-401 (2.5), as those sections existed prior to 2019, and the former §12-10-101 was relocated to §12-110-101.

As used in this article 10, unless the context otherwise requires:

(1) "Director" means the director of the division of real estate.

(2) "Division" means the division of real estate.

(3) "HOA" or "homeowners' association" means an association or unit owners' association formed before, on, or after July 1, 1992, as part of a common interest community as defined in section 38-33.3-103.

B. Part 2 – Brokers and Salespersons

§ 12-10-201, C.R.S. Definitions.

Editor's note: This section is similar to former §12-61-101 as it existed prior to 2019; except that §12-61-101 (1.2) was relocated to §12-10-101 (3).

As used in this part 2, unless the context otherwise requires:

(1) "Commission" means the real estate commission created in section 12-10-206.

(2) "Employing real estate broker" or "employing broker" means a broker who is shown in commission records as employing or engaging another broker.

(3) "Limited liability company" shall have the same meaning as it is given in section 7-80-102 (7).

(4) "Option dealer" means any person, firm, partnership, limited liability company, association, or corporation that, directly or indirectly, takes, obtains, or uses an option to purchase, exchange, rent, or lease real property or any interest therein with the intent or for the purpose of buying, selling, exchanging, renting, or leasing the real property or interest therein to another or others, whether or not the option is in that person's or its name and whether or not title to said property passes through the name of the person, firm, partnership, limited liability company, association, or corporation in connection with the purchase, sale, exchange, rental, or lease of the real property or interest therein.

(5) "Partnership" includes, but is not limited to, a registered limited liability partnership.

(6)   (a)   "Real estate broker" or "broker" means any person, firm, partnership, limited liability company, association, or corporation that, in consideration of compensation by fee, commission, salary, or anything of value or with the intention of receiving or collecting such compensation, engages in or offers or attempts to engage in, either directly or indirectly, by a continuing course of conduct or by any single act or transaction, any of the following acts:

       (I)   Selling, exchanging, buying, renting, or leasing real estate, or interest therein, or improvements affixed thereon;

       (II)   Offering to sell, exchange, buy, rent, or lease real estate, or interest therein, or improvements affixed thereon;

       (III)   Selling or offering to sell or exchange an existing lease of real estate, or interest therein, or improvements affixed thereon;

       (IV)   Negotiating the purchase, sale, or exchange of real estate, or interest therein, or improvements affixed thereon;

       (V)   Listing, offering, attempting, or agreeing to list real estate, or interest therein, or improvements affixed thereon for sale, exchange, rent, or lease;

       (VI)   Auctioning or offering, attempting, or agreeing to auction real estate, or interest therein, or improvements affixed thereon;

       (VII)   Buying, selling, offering to buy or sell, or otherwise dealing in options on real estate, or interest therein, or improvements affixed thereon, or acting as an "option dealer";

       (VIII)   Performing any of the foregoing acts as an employee of, or on behalf of, the owner of real estate, or interest therein, or improvements affixed thereon at a salary or for a fee, commission, or other consideration;

       (IX)   Negotiating or attempting or offering to negotiate the listing, sale, purchase, exchange, or lease of a business or business opportunity or the goodwill thereof or any interest therein when the act or transaction involves, directly or indirectly, any change in the ownership or interest in real estate, or in a leasehold interest or estate, or in a business or business opportunity that owns an interest in real estate or in a leasehold unless the act is performed by any broker-dealer licensed under the provisions of article 51 of title 11 who is actually engaged generally in the business of offering, selling, purchasing, or trading in securities or any officer, partner, salesperson, employee, or other authorized representative or agent thereof; or

       (X)   Soliciting a fee or valuable consideration from a prospective tenant for furnishing information concerning the availability of real property, including apartment housing that may be leased or rented as a private dwelling, abode, or place of residence. Any person, firm, partnership, limited liability company, association, or corporation or any employee or authorized agent thereof engaged in the act of soliciting a fee or valuable consideration from any person other than a prospective tenant for furnishing information concerning the availability of real property, including apartment housing that may be leased or rented as a private dwelling, abode, or place of residence, is exempt from this definition of "real estate broker" or "broker". This exemption applies only in respect to the furnishing of information concerning the availability of real property.

   (b)   "Real estate broker" or "broker" does not apply to any of the following:

       (I)   Any attorney-in-fact acting without compensation under a power of attorney, duly executed by an owner of real estate, authorizing the consummation of a real estate transaction;

       (II)   Any public official in the conduct of his or her official duties;

(III)   Any receiver, trustee, administrator, conservator, executor, or guardian acting under proper authorization;

(IV)   Any person, firm, partnership, limited liability company, or association acting personally or a corporation acting through its officers or regularly salaried employees, on behalf of that person or on its own behalf as principal in acquiring or in negotiating to acquire any interest in real estate;

(V)   An attorney-at-law in connection with his or her representation of clients in the practice of law;

(VI)   Any person, firm, partnership, limited liability company, association, or corporation, or any employee or authorized agent thereof, engaged in the act of negotiating, acquiring, purchasing, assigning, exchanging, selling, leasing, or dealing in oil and gas or other mineral leases or interests therein or other severed mineral or royalty interests in real property, including easements, rights-of-way, permits, licenses, and any other interests in real property for or on behalf of a third party, for the purpose of, or facilities related to, intrastate and interstate pipelines for oil, gas, and other petroleum products, flow lines, gas gathering systems, and natural gas storage and distribution;

(VII)   A natural person acting personally with respect to property owned or leased by that person or a natural person who is a general partner of a partnership, a manager of a limited liability company, or an owner of twenty percent or more of such partnership or limited liability company, and authorized to sell or lease property owned by the partnership or limited liability company, except as provided in subsection (4) of this section;

(VIII)   A corporation with respect to property owned or leased by it, acting through its officers or regularly salaried employees, when the acts are incidental and necessary in the ordinary course of the corporation's business activities of a non-real-estate nature (but only if the corporation is not engaged in the business of land transactions), except as provided in subsection (4) of this section. For the purposes of this subsection (6)(b)(VIII), the term "officers or regularly salaried employees" means persons regularly employed who derive not less than seventy-five percent of their compensation from the corporation in the form of salaries.

(IX)   A principal officer of any corporation with respect to property owned by it when the property is located within the state of Colorado and when the principal officer is the owner of twenty percent or more of the outstanding stock of the corporation, except as provided in subsection (4) of this section, but this exemption does not include any corporation selling previously occupied one-family and two-family dwellings;

(X)   A sole proprietor, corporation, partnership, or limited liability company, acting through its officers, partners, or regularly salaried employees, with respect to property owned or leased by the sole proprietor, corporation, partnership, or limited liability company on which has been or will be erected a commercial, industrial, or residential building that has not been previously occupied and where the consideration paid for the property includes the cost of the building, payable, less deposit or down payment, at the time of conveyance of the property and building;

(XI)   (A)   A corporation, partnership, or limited liability company acting through its officers, partners, managers, or regularly salaried employees receiving no additional compensation therefor, or its wholly owned subsidiary or officers, partners, managers, or regularly salaried employees thereof receiving no additional compensation, with respect to property located in Colorado that is owned or leased by the corporation, partnership, or limited liability company and on which has been or will be erected a shopping center, office building, or industrial park when such shopping center, office building, or industrial park is sold, leased, or otherwise offered for sale or lease in the ordinary course of the business of the corporation, partnership, limited liability company, or wholly owned subsidiary.

(B)   For the purposes of this subsection (6)(b)(XI): "Shopping center" means land on which buildings are or will be constructed that are used for commercial and office purposes around or adjacent to which off-street parking is provided; "office building" means a building used primarily for office purposes; and "industrial park" means land on which buildings are or will be constructed for warehouse, research, manufacturing, processing, or fabrication purposes.

(XII) A regularly salaried employee of an owner of an apartment building or complex who acts as an on-site manager of such an apartment building or complex. This exemption applies only in respect to the customary duties of an on-site manager performed for his or her employer.

(XIII) A regularly salaried employee of an owner of condominium units who acts as an on-site manager of such units. For purposes of this subsection (6)(b)(XIII) only, the term "owner" includes a homeowners' association formed and acting pursuant to its recorded condominium declaration and bylaws. This exemption applies only in respect to the customary duties of an on-site manager performed for his or her employer.

(XIV) A real estate broker licensed in another state who receives a share of a commission or finder's fee on a cooperative transaction from a licensed Colorado real estate broker;

(XV) A sole proprietor, corporation, partnership, or limited liability company, acting through its officers, partners, or regularly salaried employees, with respect to property located in Colorado, where the purchaser of the property is in the business of developing land for residential, commercial, or industrial purposes;

(XVI) Any person, firm, partnership, limited liability company, association, or corporation, or any employee or authorized agent thereof, engaged in the act of negotiating, purchasing, assigning, exchanging, selling, leasing, or acquiring rights-of-way, permits, licenses, and any other interests in real property for, or on behalf, of a third party for the purpose of, or facilities related to:

(A)   Telecommunication lines;

(B)   Wireless communication facilities;

(C)   CATV;

(D)   Electric generation, transmission, and distribution lines;

(E)   Water diversion, collection, distribution, treatment, and storage or use; and

(F)   Transportation, so long as the person, firm, partnership, limited liability company, association, or corporation, including any employee or authorized agent thereof, does not represent any displaced person or entity as an agent thereof in the purchase, sale, or exchange of real estate, or an interest therein, resulting from residential or commercial relocations required under any transportation project, regardless of the source of public funding.

* **§ 12-10-202, C.R.S. License required.**

* ***Editor's note:*** *This section is similar to former §12-61-102 as it existed prior to 2019.*

It is unlawful for any person, firm, partnership, limited liability company, association, or corporation to engage in the business or capacity of real estate broker in this state without first having obtained a license from the commission. No person shall be granted a license until the person establishes compliance with the provisions of this part 2 concerning education, experience, and testing; truthfulness and honesty and otherwise good moral character; and, in addition to any other requirements of this section, competency to transact the business of a real estate broker in such manner as to safeguard the interest of the public and only after satisfactory proof of the qualifications, together with the application for the license, is filed in the office of the commission. In determining the person's character, the commission shall be governed by section 24-5-101.

* **§ 12-10-203, C.R.S. Application for license – rules – definition.**

* ***Editor's note:*** *(1) This section is similar to former §12-61-103 as it existed prior to 2019.*

* *(2) Before its relocation in 2019, this section was amended in HB 19-1166. Those amendments were superseded by the repeal and reenactment of this title 12, effective October 1, 2019. For those amendments to the former section in effect from April 18, 2019, to October 1, 2019, see HB 19-1166, chapter 125, Session Laws of Colorado 2019.*

* *(3) Section 78 of chapter 125 (HB 19-1166), Session Laws of Colorado 2019, provides that the act changing this section takes effect October 1, 2019, only if HB 19-1172 becomes law. HB 19-1172 became law and took effect October 1, 2019.*

(1) (a) All persons desiring to become real estate brokers shall apply to the commission for a license under the provisions of this part 2. Application for a license as a real estate broker shall be made to the commission upon forms or in a manner prescribed by the commission.

 (b) (I) Prior to submitting an application for a license pursuant to subsection (1)(a) of this section, each applicant shall submit a set of fingerprints to the Colorado bureau of investigation for the purpose of conducting a state and national fingerprint-based criminal history record check utilizing records of the Colorado bureau of investigation and the federal bureau of investigation. The applicant shall pay the fee established by the Colorado bureau of investigation for conducting the fingerprint-based criminal history record check to the bureau. Upon completion of the criminal history record check, the bureau shall forward the results to the commission. The commission shall acquire a name-based criminal history record check, as defined in section 22-2-119.3 (6)(d), for an applicant who has twice submitted to a fingerprint-based criminal history record check and whose fingerprints are unclassifiable or when the results of a fingerprint-based criminal history record check of an applicant performed pursuant to this subsection (1)(b)(I) reveal a record of arrest without a disposition. The applicant shall pay the costs associated with a name-based criminal history record check.

  (II) For purposes of this subsection (1)(b), "applicant" means an individual, or any person designated to act as broker for any partnership, limited liability company, or corporation pursuant to subsection (6) of this section.

(2) Every real estate broker licensed under this part 2 shall maintain a place of business within this state, except as provided in section 12-10-208. In case a real estate broker maintains more than one place of business within the state, the broker shall be responsible for supervising all licensed activities originating in the offices.

(3) The commission is authorized by this section to require and procure any such proof as is necessary in reference to the truthfulness, honesty, and good moral character of any applicant

for a real estate broker's license or, if the applicant is a partnership, limited liability company, or corporation, of any partner, manager, director, officer, member, or stockholder if the person has, either directly or indirectly, a substantial interest in the applicant prior to the issuance of the license.

(4) (a) An applicant for a broker's license shall be at least eighteen years of age. The applicant must furnish proof satisfactory to the commission that the applicant has either received a degree from an accredited degree-granting college or university with a major course of study in real estate or has successfully completed courses of study, approved by the commission, at any accredited college or university or any private occupational school that has a certificate of approval from the private occupational school division in accordance with the provisions of article 64 of title 23 or that has been approved by the commission or licensed by an official state agency of any other state as follows:

  (I) Forty-eight hours of classroom instruction or equivalent correspondent hours in real estate law and real estate practice; and

  (II) Forty-eight hours of classroom instruction or equivalent correspondent hours in understanding and preparation of Colorado real estate contracts; and

  (III) A total of seventy-two hours of instruction or equivalent correspondence hours from the following areas of study: *(Ed. Note: See also Rule A-17)*

   (A) Trust accounts and record keeping;

   (B) Real estate closings;

   (C) Current legal issues; and

   (D) Practical applications.

 (b) An applicant for a broker's license who has been licensed as a real estate broker in another jurisdiction shall be required to complete only the course of study comprising the subject matter areas described in subsections (4)(a)(II) and (4)(a)(III)(B) of this section.

 (c) An applicant for a broker's license who has been licensed as a real estate salesperson in another jurisdiction shall be required to complete only the course of study required in subsections (4)(a)(II) and (4)(a)(III) of this section.

(5) (a) The applicant for a broker's license shall submit to and pass an examination designated to determine the competency of the applicant and prepared by or under the supervision of the commission or its designated contractor. The commission may contract with an independent testing service to develop, administer, or grade examinations or to administer licensee records. The contract may allow the testing service to recover the costs of the examination and the costs of administering exam and license records from the applicant. The commission may contract separately for these functions and allow recovered costs to be collected and retained by a single contractor for distribution to other contractors. The commission shall have the authority to set the minimum passing score that an applicant must receive on the examination, and the score shall reflect the minimum level of competency required to be a broker. The examination shall be given at such times and places as the commission prescribes. The examination shall include, but not be limited to, ethics, reading, spelling, basic mathematics, principles of land economics, appraisal, financing, a knowledge of the statutes and law of this state relating to deeds, trust deeds, mortgages, listing contracts, contracts of sale, bills of sale, leases, agency, brokerage, trust accounts, closings, securities, the provisions of this part 2, and the rules of the commission. The examination for a broker's license shall also include the preparation of a real estate closing statement.

 (b) An applicant for a broker's license who has held a real estate license in another jurisdiction that administers a real estate broker's examination and who has been licensed for two or more years prior to applying for a Colorado license may be issued a broker's license if the applicant establishes that he or she possesses credentials and qualifications that are substantively equivalent to the requirements in Colorado for licensure by examination.

(c) In addition to all other applicable requirements, the following provisions apply to brokers that did not hold a current and valid broker's license on December 31, 1996:

(I) No such broker shall engage in an independent brokerage practice without first having served actively as a real estate broker for at least two years. The commission shall adopt rules requiring an employing broker to ensure that a high level of supervision is exercised over such a broker during the two-year period. *(Ed. Note: See Rule E-32)*

(II) No such broker shall employ another broker without first having completed twenty-four clock hours of instruction, or the equivalent in correspondence hours, as approved by the commission, in brokerage administration.

(III) Effective January 1, 2019, a broker shall not act as an employing broker without first demonstrating, in accordance with rules of the commission, experience and knowledge sufficient to enable the broker to employ and adequately supervise other brokers, as appropriate to the broker's area of supervision. The commission's rules must set forth the method or methods by which the broker may demonstrate the experience and knowledge, either by documenting a specified number of transactions that the broker has completed or by other methods.

(6) (a) Real estate brokers' licenses may be granted to individuals, partnerships, limited liability companies, or corporations. A partnership, limited liability company, or corporation, in its application for a license, shall designate a qualified, active broker to be responsible for management and supervision of the licensed actions of the partnership, limited liability company, or corporation and all licensees shown in the commission's records as being in the employ of the entity. The application of the partnership, limited liability company, or corporation and the application of the broker designated by it shall be filed with the commission.

(b) No license shall be issued to any partnership, limited liability company, or corporation unless and until the broker so designated by the partnership, limited liability company, or corporation submits to and passes the examination required by this part 2 on behalf of the partnership, limited liability company, or corporation. Upon the broker successfully passing the examination and upon compliance with all other requirements of law by the partnership, limited liability company, or corporation, as well as by the designated broker, the commission shall issue a broker's license to the partnership, limited liability company, or corporation, which shall bear the name of the designated broker, and thereupon the broker so designated shall conduct business as a real estate broker only through the partnership, limited liability company, or corporation and not for the broker's own account.

(c) If the person so designated is refused a license by the commission or ceases to be the designated broker of the partnership, limited liability company, or corporation, the entity may designate another person to make application for a license. If the person ceases to be the designated broker of the partnership, limited liability company, or corporation, the director may issue a temporary license to prevent hardship for a period not to exceed ninety days to the licensed person so designated. The director may extend a temporary license for one additional period not to exceed ninety days upon proper application and a showing of good cause; if the director refuses, no further extension of a temporary license shall be granted except by the commission. If any broker or employee of any such partnership, limited liability company, or corporation, other than the one designated as provided in this section, desires to act as a real estate broker, the broker or employee shall first obtain a license as a real estate broker as provided in this section and shall pay the regular fee therefor. *(Ed. Note: See Rule A-26)*

(7)   The broker designated to act as broker for any partnership, limited liability company, or corporation is personally responsible for the handling of any and all earnest money deposits or escrow or trust funds received or disbursed by the partnership, limited liability company, or corporation. In the event of any breach of duty by the partnership, limited liability company, or corporation as a fiduciary, any person aggrieved or damaged by the breach of fiduciary duty shall have a claim for relief against the partnership, limited liability company, or corporation, as well as against the designated broker, and may pursue the claim against the partnership, limited liability company, or corporation and the designated broker personally. The broker may be held responsible and liable for damages based upon the breach of fiduciary duty as may be recoverable against the partnership, limited liability company, or corporation, and any judgment so obtained may be enforced jointly or severally against the broker personally and the partnership, limited liability company, or corporation.

(8)   No license for a broker registered as being in the employ of another broker shall be issued to a partnership, a limited liability company, or a corporation or under a fictitious name or trade name; except that a married woman may elect to use her birth name.

(9)   No person shall be licensed as a real estate broker under more than one name, and no person shall conduct or promote a real estate brokerage business except under the name under which the person is licensed. *(Ed. Note: See also Rule C-18 and E-8)*

(10)   A licensed attorney shall take and pass the examination referred to in this section after having completed twelve hours of classroom instruction or equivalent correspondent hours in trust accounts, record keeping, and real estate closings. *(Ed. Note: Attorney may be licensed at any bar)*

*   ## § 12-10-204, C.R.S. Errors and omissions insurance required – rules.

*   ***Editor's note:** This section is similar to former §12-61-103.6 as it existed prior to 2019.*

(1)   Every licensee under this part 2, except an inactive broker or an attorney licensee who maintains a policy of professional malpractice insurance that provides coverage for errors and omissions for their activities as a licensee under this part 2, shall maintain errors and omissions insurance to cover all activities contemplated under parts 2 to 6 of this article 10. The division shall make the errors and omissions insurance available to all licensees by contracting with an insurer for a group policy after a competitive bid process in accordance with article 103 of title 24. A group policy obtained by the division must be available to all licensees with no right on the part of the insurer to cancel a licensee. A licensee may obtain errors and omissions insurance independently if the coverage complies with the minimum requirements established by the division.

(2)   (a)   If the division is unable to obtain errors and omissions insurance coverage to insure all licensees who choose to participate in the group program at a reasonable annual premium, as determined by the division, a licensee shall independently obtain the errors and omissions insurance required by this section.

        (b)   The division shall solicit and consider information and comments from interested persons when determining the reasonableness of annual premiums.

(3)   The division shall determine the terms and conditions of coverage required under this section based on rules promulgated by the commission. The commission shall notify each licensee of the required terms and conditions at least thirty days before the annual premium renewal date as determined by the commission. Each licensee shall file a certificate of coverage showing compliance with the required terms and conditions with the commission by the annual premium renewal date, as determined by the division.

(4)   In addition to all other powers and duties conferred upon the commission by this article 10, the commission shall adopt such rules as it deems necessary or proper to carry out the provisions of this section. *(Ed. Note: See Rule D-14)*

* ### § 12-10-205, C.R.S. Licenses – issuance – contents – display.

* *Editor's note: This section is similar to former §12-61-104 as it existed prior to 2019.*

The commission shall make available for each licensee a license in such form and size as the commission shall prescribe and adopt. The real estate license shall show the name of the licensee and shall have imprinted thereon the seal, or a facsimile, of the department and, in addition to the foregoing, shall contain such other matter as the commission shall prescribe.

* ### § 12-10-206, C.R.S. Real estate commission – created – compensation – immunity.

* *Editor's note: This section is similar to former §12-61-105 as it existed prior to 2019.*

(1)   There is hereby created a commission of five members, appointed by the governor, which shall administer parts 2 and 5 of this article 10. This commission is known as the real estate commission and consists of three real estate brokers who have had not less than five years' experience in the real estate business in Colorado, one of whom has substantial experience in property management, and two representatives of the public at large. Members of the commission hold office for a period of three years. Upon the death, resignation, removal, or otherwise of any member of the commission, the governor shall appoint a member to fill out the unexpired term. The governor may remove any member for misconduct, neglect of duty, or incompetence.

(2)   Each member of the commission shall receive the same compensation and reimbursement of expenses as those provided for members of boards and commissions in the division of professions and occupations pursuant to section 12-20-103 (6). Payment for all such per diem compensation and expenses shall be made out of annual appropriations from the division of real estate cash fund provided for in section 12-10-215.

(3)   Members of the commission, consultants, expert witnesses, and complainants shall be immune from suit in any civil action based upon any disciplinary proceedings or other official acts they performed in good faith.

(4)   No real estate broker's license shall be denied, suspended, or revoked except as determined by a majority vote of the members of the commission.

* ### § 12-10-207, C.R.S. Division of real estate – creation – director, clerks, and assistants.

* *Editor's note: This section is similar to former §12-61-106 as it existed prior to 2019.*

(1)   There is hereby created within the department the division of real estate. The executive director is authorized by this section to employ, subject to the provisions of the state personnel system laws of the state, a director of the division, who in turn shall employ such attorneys, deputies, investigators, clerks, and assistants as are necessary to discharge the duties imposed by parts 2 and 5 of this article 10. The division and the director shall exercise their powers and perform their duties and functions under the department as if they were transferred to the department by a **type 2** transfer.

(2)   It is the duty of the director, personally, or the director's designee to aid in the administration and enforcement of parts 2 and 5 of this article 10 and in the prosecution of all persons charged with violating any of their provisions, to conduct audits of business accounts of licensees, to perform such duties of the commission as the commission prescribes, and to act in behalf of the commission on such occasions and in such circumstances as the commission directs.

* ## § 12-10-208, C.R.S. Resident licensee – nonresident licensee – consent to service.

* *Editor's note: This section is similar to former §12-61-107 as it existed prior to 2019.*

(1) A nonresident of the state may become a real estate broker in this state by conforming to all the conditions of this part 2; except that the nonresident broker shall not be required to maintain a place of business within this state if that broker maintains a definite place of business in another state.

(2) If a broker has no registered agent registered in this state, the registered agent is not located under its registered agent name at its registered agent address, or the registered agent cannot with reasonable diligence be served, the broker may be served by registered mail or by certified mail, return receipt requested, addressed to the entity at its principal address. Service is perfected under this subsection (2) at the earliest of:

    (a) The date the broker receives the process, notice, or demand;

    (b) The date shown on the return receipt, if signed by or on behalf of the broker; or

    (c) Five days after mailing.

(3) All such applications shall contain a certification that the broker is authorized to act for the corporation.

* ## § 12-10-209, C.R.S. Record of licensees – publications.

* *Editor's note: This section is similar to former §12-61-108 as it existed prior to 2019.*

The commission shall maintain a record of the names and addresses of all licensees licensed under the provisions of parts 2 and 5 of this article 10, together with such other information relative to the enforcement of the provisions as deemed by the commission to be necessary. Publication of the record and of any other information circulated in quantity outside the executive branch shall be in accordance with the provisions of section 24-1-136.

* ## § 12-10-210, C.R.S. Compilation and publication of passing rates per educational institution for real estate licensure examinations – definition – rules.

* *Editor's note: This section is similar to former §12-61-108.5 as it existed prior to 2019.*

(1) The commission shall have the authority to obtain information from each educational institution authorized to offer courses in real estate for the purpose of compiling the number of applicants who pass the real estate licensure examination from each educational institution. The information shall include the name of each student who attended the institution and a statement of whether the student completed the necessary real estate courses required for licensure. The commission shall have access to such other information as necessary to accomplish the purpose of this section. For the purposes of this section, an "applicant" is a student who completed the required education requirements and who applied for and sat for the licensure examination.

(2) The commission shall compile the information obtained in subsection (1) of this section with applicant information retained by the commission. Specifically, the commission shall compile whether the student applied for the licensure examination and whether the applicant passed the licensure examination. The commission shall create statistical data setting forth:

    (a) The name of the educational institution;

    (b) The number of students who completed the necessary real estate course required for licensure;

    (c) Whether the student registered and sat for the licensure examination; and

    (d) The number of those applicants who passed the licensure examination.

(3) The commission shall publish this statistical data and make it available to the public quarterly.

(4)   The commission shall retain the statistical data for three years.

(5)   Specific examination scores for an applicant will be kept confidential by the commission unless the applicant authorizes release of the information.

(6)   The commission may promulgate rules for the administration of this section.

*   ## § 12-10-211, C.R.S. Change of license status – inactive – cancellation.

*   *Editor's note: This section is similar to former §12-61-109 as it existed prior to 2019.*

(1)   Immediate notice shall be given in a manner acceptable to the commission by each licensee of any change of business location or employment. A change of business address or employment without notification to the commission shall automatically inactivate the licensee's license.

(2)   A broker who transfers to the address of another broker or a broker applicant who desires to be employed by another broker shall inform the commission if the broker is to be in the employ of the other broker. The employing broker shall have the control and custody of the employed broker's license. The employed broker may not act on behalf of the broker or as broker for a partnership, limited liability company, or corporation during the term of the employment; but this shall not affect the employed broker's right to transfer to another employing broker or to a location where the employed broker may conduct business as an independent broker or as a broker acting for a partnership, limited liability company, or corporation.

(3)   In the event that any licensee is discharged by or terminates employment with a broker, it shall be the **joint duty of both** such parties to immediately notify the commission. Either party may furnish the notice in a manner acceptable to the commission. The party giving notice shall notify the other party in person or in writing of the termination of employment.

(4)   It is unlawful for any such licensee to perform any of the acts authorized under the license in pursuance of this part 2, either directly or indirectly, on or after the date that employment has been terminated. When any real estate broker whose employment has been terminated is employed by another real estate broker, the commission shall, upon proper notification, enter the change of employment in the records of the commission. Not more than one employer or place of employment shall be shown for any real estate broker for the same period of time.

*   ## § 12-10-212, C.R.S. License fees – partnership, limited liability company, and corporation licenses – rules.

*   *Editor's note: This section is similar to former §12-61-110 as it existed prior to 2019.*

(1)   Fees established pursuant to section 12-10-215 shall be charged by and paid to the commission or the agent for the commission for the following:

(a)   Each broker's examination;

(b)   Each broker's original application and license;

(c)   Each renewal of a broker's license;

(d)   Any change of name, address, or employing broker requiring a change in commission records;

(e)   A new application that shall be submitted when a licensed real estate broker wishes to become the broker acting for a partnership, a limited liability company, or a corporation.

(2)   The proper fee shall accompany each application for licensure. The fee shall not be refundable. Failure by the person taking an examination to file the appropriate broker's application within one year of the date the person passed the examination will automatically cancel the examination, and all rights to a passing score will be terminated.

(3)   Each real estate broker's license granted to an individual shall entitle the individual to perform all the acts contemplated by this part 2, without any further application on his or her part and without the payment of any fee other than the fees specified in this section.

(4)   (a)   (I)   The commission shall require that any person licensed under this part 2, whether on an active or inactive basis, renew the license on or before December 31 of every third year after issuance; except that an initial license issued under this part 2 on or after April 23, 2018, expires at 12 midnight on December 31 of the year in which it was issued.

            (II)   Renewal is conditioned upon fulfillment of the continuing education requirements set forth in section 12-10-213. For persons renewing or reinstating an active license, written certification verifying completion for the previous licensing period of the continuing education requirements set forth in section 12-10-213 must accompany and be submitted to the commission with the application for renewal or reinstatement. For persons who did not submit certification verifying compliance with section 12-10-213 at the time a license was renewed or reinstated on an inactive status, written certification verifying completion for the previous licensing period of the continuing education requirements set forth in that section must accompany and be submitted with any future application to reactivate the license. The commission may, by rule, establish procedures to facilitate such a renewal. In the absence of any reason or condition that might warrant the refusal of the granting of a license or the revocation thereof, the commission shall issue a new license upon receipt by the commission of the written request of the applicant and the appropriate fees required by this section. Applications for renewal will be accepted thirty days prior to January 1.

            (III)   A person who fails to renew a license before January 1 of the year succeeding the year of the expiration of the license may reinstate the license as follows:

                (A)   If proper application is made within thirty-one days after the date of expiration, by payment of the regular renewal fee;

                (B)   If proper application is made more than thirty-one days but within one year after the date of expiration, by payment of the regular renewal fee and payment of a reinstatement fee equal to one-half the regular renewal fee;

                (C)   If proper application is made more than one year but within three years after the date of expiration, by payment of the regular renewal fee and payment of a reinstatement fee equal to the regular renewal fee.

            (IV)   The commission may, by rule, establish procedures to facilitate the transition of the reinstatement license periods described in subsections (4)(a)(III)(A) to (4)(a)(III)(C) of this section from an anniversary expiration date to a December 31 expiration date.

    (b)   Any reinstated license shall be effective only as of the date of reinstatement. Any person who fails to apply for reinstatement within three years after the expiration of a license shall, without exception, be treated as a new applicant for licensure.

    (c)   All reinstatement fees shall be transmitted to the state treasurer, who shall credit the fees to the division of real estate cash fund, as established by section 12-10-215.

(5)   The suspension, expiration, or revocation of a real estate broker's license shall automatically inactivate every real estate broker's license where the holder of the license is shown in the commission records to be in the employ of the broker whose license has expired or has been suspended or revoked pending notification to the commission by the employed licensee of a change of employment.

*   ***Editor's note:*** *This section is similar to former §12-61-110.5 as it existed prior to 2019.*

(1)   A broker applying for renewal of a license pursuant to section 12-10-212 (4) shall include with the application a certified statement verifying successful completion of real estate courses in accordance with the following schedule:

     (a)   For licensees applying for renewal of a three-year license, passage within the previous three years of the Colorado portion of the real estate exam or completion of a minimum of twenty-four hours of credit, twelve of which must be the credits developed by the commission pursuant to subsection (2) of this section;

     (b)   For licensees applying for renewal of a license that expires less than three years after it was issued, passage within the license period of the Colorado portion of the real estate exam or completion of a minimum of twenty-four hours of credit, at least eight of which must be the credits developed by the commission pursuant to subsection (2) of this section.

(2)   The commission shall develop twelve hours of credit designed to assure reasonable currency of real estate knowledge by licensees, which credits shall include an update of the current statutes and the rules promulgated by the commission that affect the practice of real estate. If a licensee takes a course pursuant to rule 250 of the Colorado rules of civil procedure and the course concerns real property law, the licensee shall receive credit for the course toward the fulfillment of the licensee's continuing education requirements pursuant to this section. The credits shall be taken from an accredited Colorado college or university; a Colorado community college; a Colorado private occupational school holding a certificate of approval from the state board for community colleges and occupational education; or an educational institution or an educational service described in section 23-64-104. Successful completion of the credits shall require satisfactory passage of a written examination or written examinations of the materials covered. The examinations shall be audited by the commission to verify their accuracy and the validity of the grades given. The commission shall set the standards required for satisfactory passage of the examinations.

(3)   All credits, other than the credits specified in subsection (2) of this section, shall be acquired from educational courses approved by the commission that contribute directly to the professional competence of a licensee. The credits may be acquired through successful completion of instruction in one or more of the following subjects:

     (a)   Real estate law;

     (b)   Property exchanges;

     (c)   Real estate contracts;

     (d)   Real estate finance;

     (e)   Real estate appraisal;

     (f)   Real estate closing;

     (g)   Real estate ethics;

     (h)   Condominiums and cooperatives;

     (i)   Real estate time-sharing;

     (j)   Real estate marketing principles;

     (k)   Real estate construction;

     (*l*)   Land development;

     (m)   Real estate energy concerns;

     (n)   Real estate geology;

(o)   Water and waste management;

(p)   Commercial real estate;

(q)   Real estate securities and syndications;

(r)   Property management;

(s)   Real estate computer principles;

(t)   Brokerage administration and management;

(u)   Agency; and

(v)   Any other subject matter as approved by the commission.

(4)   A licensee applying for renewal of a license that expires on December 31 of the year in which it was issued is not subject to the education requirements set forth in subsection (1) of this section.

(5)   The commission shall promulgate rules to implement this section.

§ 12-10-214, C.R.S. Disposition of fees.

* *Editor's note: This section is similar to former §12-61-111 as it existed prior to 2019.*

All fees collected by the commission under parts 2 and 5 of this article 10, not including administrative fees that are in the nature of an administrative fine and fees retained by contractors pursuant to contracts entered into in accordance with section 12-10-203 or 24-34-101, shall be transmitted to the state treasurer, who shall credit the same to the division of real estate cash fund. Pursuant to section 12-10-215, the general assembly shall make annual appropriations from the fund for expenditures of the commission incurred in the performance of its duties under parts 2 and 5 of this article 10. The commission may request an appropriation specifically designated for educational and enforcement purposes. The expenditures incurred by the commission under parts 2 and 5 of this article 10 shall be made out of the appropriations upon vouchers and warrants drawn pursuant to law.

§ 12-10-215, C.R.S. Fee adjustments – cash fund created.

* *Editor's note: This section is similar to former §12-61-111.5 as it existed prior to 2019.*

(1)   This section applies to all activities of the division under parts 2, 5, 6, and 7 of this article 10.

(2)   (a)   (I)   The division shall propose, as part of its annual budget request, an adjustment in the amount of each fee that it is authorized by law to collect under parts 2, 5, 6, and 7 of this article 10. The budget request and the adjusted fees for the division must reflect direct and indirect costs.

(II)   The costs of the HOA information and resource center, created in section 12-10-801, shall be paid from the division of real estate cash fund created in this section. The division shall estimate the direct and indirect costs of operating the HOA information and resource center and shall establish the amount of the annual registration fee to be collected under section 38-33.3-401. The amount of the registration fee shall be sufficient to recover these costs, subject to a maximum limit of fifty dollars.

(b)   Based upon the appropriation made and subject to the approval of the executive director, the division shall adjust its fees so that the revenue generated from the fees approximates its direct and indirect costs incurred in administering the programs and activities from which the fees are derived. The fees shall remain in effect for the fiscal year for which the budget request applies. All fees collected by the division, not including fees retained by contractors pursuant to contracts entered into in accordance with section 12-10-203 or 24-34-101, shall be transmitted to the state treasurer, who shall credit the same to the division of real estate cash fund, which fund is hereby created. All money credited to the division of real estate cash fund shall be used as provided in this section or in section 12-

10-214 and shall not be deposited in or transferred to the general fund of this state or any other fund.

(c) Beginning July 1, 1979, and each July 1 thereafter, whenever money appropriated to the division for its activities for the prior fiscal year is unexpended, the money shall be made a part of the appropriation to the division for the next fiscal year, and the amount shall not be raised from fees collected by the division. If a supplemental appropriation is made to the division for its activities, its fees, when adjusted for the fiscal year next following that in which the supplemental appropriation was made, shall be adjusted by an additional amount that is sufficient to compensate for the supplemental appropriation. Funds appropriated to the division in the annual long appropriations bill shall be designated as a cash fund and shall not exceed the amount anticipated to be raised from fees collected by the division.

* ## § 12-10-216, C.R.S. Records – evidence – inspection.

* ***Editor's note:*** *This section is similar to former §12-61-112 as it existed prior to 2019.*

(1) The executive director shall adopt a seal by which all proceedings authorized under parts 2 and 5 of this article 10 shall be authenticated. Copies of records and papers in the office of the commission or department relating to the administration of parts 2 and 5 of this article 10, when duly certified and authenticated by the seal, shall be received as evidence in all courts equally and with like effect as the originals. All records kept in the office of the commission or department, under authority of parts 2 and 5 of this article 10, must be open to public inspection at such time and in such manner as may be prescribed by rules formulated by the commission.

(2) The commission shall not be required to maintain or preserve licensing history records of any person licensed under the provisions of this part 2 for any period of time longer than seven years.

* ## § 12-10-217, C.R.S. Investigation – revocation – actions against licensee or applicant – definition.

* ***Editor's note:*** *This section is similar to former §12-61-113 as it existed prior to 2019.*

(1) The commission, upon its own motion, may, and, upon the complaint in writing of any person, shall, investigate the activities of any licensee or any person who assumes to act in the capacity of a licensee within the state, and the commission, after holding a hearing pursuant to section 12-10-219, has the power to impose an administrative fine not to exceed two thousand five hundred dollars for each separate offense and to censure a licensee, to place the licensee on probation and to set the terms of probation, or to temporarily suspend a license, or permanently revoke a license, when the licensee has performed, is performing, or is attempting to perform any of the following acts and is guilty of:

(a) Knowingly making any misrepresentation or knowingly making use of any false or misleading advertising;

(b) Making any promise of a character that influences, persuades, or induces another person when he or she could not or did not intend to keep the promise;

(c) Knowingly misrepresenting or making false promises through agents, advertising, or otherwise;

(d) Violating any provision of the "Colorado Consumer Protection Act", article 1 of title 6;

(e) Acting for more than one party in a transaction without the knowledge of all parties thereto;

(f) Representing or attempting to represent a real estate broker other than the licensee's employer without the express knowledge and consent of that employer;

(g) In the case of a broker registered as in the employ of another broker, failing to place, as soon after receipt as is practicably possible, in the custody of that licensed broker-employer any deposit money or other money or fund entrusted to the employee by any person dealing with the employee as the representative of that licensed broker-employer;

(h) Failing to account for or to remit, within a reasonable time, any money coming into the licensee's possession that belongs to others, whether acting as real estate brokers or otherwise, and failing to keep records relative to the money, which records shall contain such information as may be prescribed by the rules of the commission relative thereto and shall be subject to audit by the commission;

(i) Converting funds of others, diverting funds of others without proper authorization, commingling funds of others with the broker's own funds, or failing to keep the funds of others in an escrow or a trustee account with some bank or recognized depository in this state, which account may be any type of checking, demand, passbook, or statement account insured by an agency of the United States government, and to keep records relative to the deposit that contain such information as may be prescribed by the rules of the commission relative thereto, which records shall be subject to audit by the commission;

(j) Failing to provide the purchaser and seller of real estate with a closing statement of the transaction, containing such information as may be prescribed by the rules of the commission or failing to provide a signed duplicate copy of the listing contract and the contract of sale or the preliminary agreement to sell to the parties thereto;

(k) Failing to maintain possession, for future use or inspection by an authorized representative of the commission, for a period of four years, of the documents or records prescribed by the rules of the commission or to produce the documents or records upon reasonable request by the commission or by an authorized representative of the commission;

(*l*) Paying a commission or valuable consideration for performing any of the functions of a real estate broker, as described in this part 2, to any person not licensed under this part 2; except that a licensed broker may pay a finder's fee or a share of any commission on a cooperative sale when the payment is made to a real estate broker licensed in another state or country. If a country does not license real estate brokers, then the payee must be a citizen or resident of the country and represent that the payee is in the business of selling real estate in the country.

(m) Disregarding or violating any provision of this part 2 or part 4 of this article 10, violating any reasonable rule promulgated by the commission in the interests of the public and in conformance with the provisions of this part 2 or part 4 of this article 10; violating any lawful commission orders; or aiding and abetting a violation of any rule, commission order, or provision of this part 2 or part 4 of this article 10;

(n) (I) Conviction of, entering a plea of guilty to, or entering a plea of nolo contendere to any crime in article 3 of title 18; parts 1, 2, 3, and 4 of article 4 of title 18; part 1, 2, 3, 4, 5, 7, 8, or 9 of article 5 of title 18; article 5.5 of title 18; parts 3, 4, 6, 7, and 8 of article 6 of title 18; parts 1, 3, 4, 5, 6, 7, and 8 of article 7 of title 18; part 3 of article 8 of title 18; article 15 of title 18; article 17 of title 18; section 18-18-404, 18-18-405, 18-18-406, 18-18-411, 18-18-412.5, 18-18-412.7, 18-18-412.8, 18-18-415, 18-18-416, 18-18-422, or 18-18-423; or any other like crime under Colorado law, federal law, or the laws of other states. A certified copy of the judgment of a court of competent jurisdiction of the conviction or other official record indicating that the plea was entered shall be conclusive evidence of the conviction or plea in any hearing under this part 2.

(II) As used in this subsection (1)(n), "conviction" includes the imposition of a deferred judgment or deferred sentence.

> *(**Editor's note:** The numbered articles in Title 18 of Colorado Revised Statute shown in this Part "n" refer to the following types of crimes:*
>
> *Article 3 is titled Offenses Against the Person and consists of six parts: homicide and related offenses, assaults, kidnapping, unlawful sexual behavior, human trafficking and slavery, and stalking.*
>
> *Article 4 deals with **offenses against property**, under which part 1 is arson, part 2 is burglary and related offenses, part 3 is robbery, and part 4 is theft.*
>
> *Article 5 consists of **offenses involving fraud**, including part 1 – forgery, simulation, impersonation, and related offenses (obtaining a signature by deception, offering a false instrument for recording, et al.), part 2 – fraud in obtaining property or services (dual contracts), part 3 – fraudulent and deceptive sales and business practices (unlawful activity concerning the sale of land), part 4 – bribery and rigging of contests, part 5 – offenses relating to the uniform commercial code, part 7 – financial transaction device crime act (ATM's, et al), part 8 – equity skimming and related offenses, and part 9 – identity theft and related offenses.*
>
> *Article 5.5 consists of **computer crime offenses**.*
>
> *Article 6 consists of **offenses involving family relations**.*
>
> *Article 7 consists of **offenses relating to morals**.*
>
> *Article 8 – part 3 refers to **governmental operations**, specifically bribery and corrupt influences.*
>
> *Article 15 deals with making, financing, or collection of **loans**.*
>
> *Article 17 is the Colorado **Organized Crime** Control Act.*
>
> *Article 18 is the Uniform Controlled Substances Act, and part 4 deals with **offenses and penalties**.)*

(o) Violating or aiding and abetting in the violation of the Colorado or federal fair housing laws;

(p) Failing to immediately notify the commission in writing of a conviction, plea, or violation pursuant to subsection (1)(n) or (1)(o) of this section;

(q) Having demonstrated unworthiness or incompetency to act as a real estate broker by conducting business in such a manner as to endanger the interest of the public;

(r) In the case of a broker licensee, failing to exercise reasonable supervision over the activities of licensed employees;

(s) Procuring, or attempting to procure, a real estate broker's license or renewing, reinstating, or reactivating, or attempting to renew, reinstate, or reactivate, a real estate broker's license by fraud, misrepresentation, or deceit or by making a material misstatement of fact in an application for the license;

(t) Claiming, arranging for, or taking any secret or undisclosed amount of compensation, commission, or profit or failing to reveal to the licensee's principal or employer the full amount of the licensee's compensation, commission, or profit in connection with any acts for which a license is required under this part 2;

(u) Using any provision allowing the licensee an option to purchase in any agreement authorizing or employing the licensee to sell, buy, or exchange real estate for compensation or commission, except when the licensee, prior to or coincident with election to exercise the option to purchase, reveals in writing to the licensee's principal or employer the full amount of the licensee's profit and obtains the written consent of the principal or employer approving the amount of the profit;

(v)   Effective on and after August 26, 2013, fraud, misrepresentation, deceit, or conversion of trust funds that results in the entry of a civil judgment for damages;

(w)   Any other conduct, whether of the same or a different character than specified in this subsection (1), that constitutes dishonest dealing;

(x)   Having had a real estate broker's or a subdivision developer's license suspended or revoked in any jurisdiction, or having had any disciplinary action taken against the broker or subdivision developer in any other jurisdiction if the broker's or subdivision developer's action would constitute a violation of this subsection (1). A certified copy of the order of disciplinary action shall be prima facie evidence of the disciplinary action.

(y)   Failing to keep records documenting proof of completion of the continuing education requirements in accordance with section 12-10-213 for a period of four years from the date of compliance with the section;

(z)   (I)   Violating any provision of section 12-10-218.

        (II)   In addition to any other remedies available to the commission pursuant to this article 10, after notice and a hearing pursuant to section 24-4-105, the commission may assess a penalty for a violation of section 12-10-218 or of any rule promulgated pursuant to section 12-10-218. The penalty shall be the amount of remuneration improperly paid and shall be transmitted to the state treasurer and credited to the general fund.

(aa)   Within the last five years, having a license, registration, or certification issued by Colorado or another state revoked or suspended for fraud, deceit, material misrepresentation, theft, or the breach of a fiduciary duty, and such discipline denied the person authorization to practice as:

        (I)   A mortgage broker or mortgage loan originator;

        (II)   A real estate broker or salesperson;

        (III)   A real estate appraiser, as defined by section 12-10-602 (9);

        (IV)   An insurance producer, as defined by section 10-2-103 (6);

        (V)   An attorney;

        (VI)   A securities broker-dealer, as defined by section 11-51-201 (2);

        (VII)   A securities sales representative, as defined by section 11-51-201 (14);

        (VIII)   An investment advisor, as defined by section 11-51-201 (9.5); or

        (IX)   An investment advisor representative, as defined by section 11-51-201 (9.6).

(2)   Every person licensed pursuant to section 12-10-201 (6)(a)(X) shall give a prospective tenant a contract or receipt; and the contract or receipt shall include the address and telephone number of the commission in prominent letters and shall state that the regulation of rental location agents is under the purview of the commission.

(3)   In the event a firm, partnership, limited liability company, association, or corporation operating under the license of a broker designated and licensed as representative of the firm, partnership, limited liability company, association, or corporation is guilty of any of the foregoing acts, the commission may suspend or revoke the right of the firm, partnership, limited liability company, association, or corporation to conduct its business under the license of the broker, whether or not the designated broker had personal knowledge thereof and whether or not the commission suspends or revokes the individual license of the broker.

(4)   Upon request of the commission, when any real estate broker is a party to any suit or proceeding, either civil or criminal, arising out of any transaction involving the sale or exchange of any interest in real property or out of any transaction involving a leasehold interest in the real property and when the broker is involved in the transaction in such capacity as a licensed broker, it shall be the duty of the broker to supply to the commission a copy of the

complaint, indictment, information, or other initiating pleading and the answer filed, if any, and to advise the commission of the disposition of the case and of the nature and amount of any judgment, verdict, finding, or sentence that may be made, entered, or imposed therein.

(5) This part 2 shall not be construed to relieve any person from civil liability or criminal prosecution under the laws of this state.

(6) Complaints of record in the office of the commission and commission investigations, including commission investigative files, are closed to public inspection. Stipulations and final agency orders are public records subject to sections 24-72-203 and 24-72-204.

(7) When a complaint or an investigation discloses an instance of misconduct that, in the opinion of the commission, does not warrant formal action by the commission but that should not be dismissed as being without merit, the commission may send a letter of admonition by certified mail, return receipt requested, to the licensee against whom a complaint was made and a copy thereof to the person making the complaint, but the letter shall advise the licensee that the licensee has the right to request in writing, within twenty days after proven receipt, that formal disciplinary proceedings be initiated to adjudicate the propriety of the conduct upon which the letter of admonition is based. If the request is timely made, the letter of admonition shall be deemed vacated, and the matter shall be processed by means of formal disciplinary proceedings.

(8) All administrative fines collected pursuant to this section shall be transmitted to the state treasurer, who shall credit the same to the division of real estate cash fund.

(9) Any application for licensure from a person whose license has been revoked shall not be considered until the passage of one year from the date of revocation.

(10) When the division becomes aware of facts or circumstances that fall within the jurisdiction of a criminal justice or other law enforcement authority upon investigation of the activities of a licensee, the division shall, in addition to the exercise of its authority under this part 2, refer and transmit the information, which may include originals or copies of documents and materials, to one or more criminal justice or other law enforcement authorities for investigation and prosecution as authorized by law.

* ### *§ 12-10-218, C.R.S. Affiliated business arrangements – definitions – disclosures – enforcement and penalties – reporting – rules – investigation information shared with the division of insurance.*

* *Editor's note: This section is similar to former §12-61-113.2 as it existed prior to 2019.*

(1) As used in this section, unless the context otherwise requires:

   (a) "Affiliated business arrangement" means an arrangement in which:

      (I) A provider of settlement services or an associate of a provider of settlement services has either an affiliate relationship with or a direct beneficial ownership interest of more than one percent in another provider of settlement services; and

      (II) A provider of settlement services or the associate of a provider directly or indirectly refers settlement service business to another provider of settlement services or affirmatively influences the selection of another provider of settlement services.

   (b) "Associate" means a person who has one or more of the following relationships with a person in a position to refer settlement service business:

      (I) A spouse, parent, or child of the person;

      (II) A corporation or business entity that controls, is controlled by, or is under common control with the person;

       (III)   An employer, officer, director, partner, franchiser, or franchisee of the person, including a broker acting as an independent contractor; or

       (IV)   Anyone who has an agreement, arrangement, or understanding with the person, the purpose or substantial effect of which is to enable the person in a position to refer settlement service business to benefit financially from referrals of the business.

   (c)   "Settlement service" means any service provided in connection with a real estate settlement including, but not limited to, the following:

       (I)   Title searches;

       (II)   Title examinations;

       (III) The provision of title certificates;

       (IV) Title insurance;

       (V)   Services rendered by an attorney;

       (VI) The preparation of title documents;

       (VII) Property surveys;

       (VIII) The rendering of credit reports or appraisals;

       (IX) Real estate appraisal services;

       (X)   Home inspection services;

       (XI) Services rendered by a real estate broker;

       (XII) Pest and fungus inspections;

       (XIII) The origination of a loan;

       (XIV) The taking of a loan application;

       (XV) The processing of a loan;

       (XVI) Underwriting and funding of a loan;

       (XVII) Escrow handling services;

       (XVIII) The handling of the processing; and

       (XIX) Closing of settlement.

(2)   (a)   An affiliated business arrangement is permitted where the person referring business to the affiliated business arrangement receives payment only in the form of a return on an investment and where it does not violate the provisions of section 12-10-217.

   (b)   If a licensee or the employing broker of a licensee is part of an affiliated business arrangement when an offer to purchase real property is fully executed, the licensee shall disclose to all parties to the real estate transaction the existence of the arrangement. The disclosure shall be written, shall be signed by all parties to the real estate transaction, and shall comply with the federal "Real Estate Settlement Procedures Act of 1974", as amended, 12 U.S.C. sec. 2601 et seq.

   (c)   A licensee shall not require the use of an affiliated business arrangement or a particular provider of settlement services as a condition of obtaining services from that licensee for any settlement service. For the purposes of this subsection (2)(c), "require the use" shall have the same meaning as "required use" in 24 CFR 3500.2 (b).

   (d)   No licensee shall give or accept any fee, kickback, or other thing of value pursuant to any agreement or understanding, oral or otherwise, that business incident to or part of a settlement service involving an affiliated business arrangement shall be referred to any provider of settlement services.

   (e)   Nothing in this section shall be construed to prohibit payment of a fee to:

       (I)   An attorney for services actually rendered;

      (II)   A title insurance company to its duly appointed agent for services actually performed in the issuance of a policy of title insurance;

      (III)   A lender to its duly appointed agent for services actually performed in the making of a loan.

  (f)   Nothing in this section shall be construed to prohibit payment to any person of:

      (I)   A bona fide salary or compensation or other payment for goods or facilities actually furnished or for services actually performed;

      (II)   A fee pursuant to cooperative brokerage and referral arrangements or agreements between real estate brokers.

  (g)   It shall not be a violation of this section for an affiliated business arrangement:

      (I)   To require a buyer, borrower, or seller to pay for the services of any attorney, credit reporting agency, or real estate appraiser chosen by the lender to represent the lender's interest in a real estate transaction; or

      (II)   If an attorney or law firm represents a client in a real estate transaction and issues or arranges for the issuance of a policy of title insurance in the transaction directly as agent or through a separate corporate title insurance agency that may be established by that attorney or law firm and operated as an adjunct to his or her law practice.

  (h)   No person shall be liable for a violation of this section if the person proves by a preponderance of the evidence that the violation was not intentional and resulted from a bona fide error notwithstanding maintenance of procedures that are reasonably adopted to avoid the error.

(3)   On and after July 1, 2006, a licensee shall disclose at the time the licensee enters into or changes an affiliated business arrangement, in a form and manner acceptable to the commission, the names of all affiliated business arrangements to which the licensee is a party. The disclosure shall include the physical locations of the affiliated businesses.

(4)   On and after July 1, 2006, an employing broker, in a form and manner acceptable to the commission, shall at least annually disclose the names of all affiliated business arrangements to which the employing broker is a party. The disclosure shall include the physical locations of the affiliated businesses.

(5)   The commission may promulgate rules concerning the creation and conduct of an affiliated business arrangement, including, but not limited to, rules defining what constitutes a sham affiliated business arrangement. The commission shall adopt the rules, policies, or guidelines issued by the United States department of housing and urban development concerning the federal "Real Estate Settlement Procedures Act of 1974", as amended, 12 U.S.C. sec. 2601 et seq. Rules adopted by the commission shall be at least as stringent as the federal rules and shall ensure that consumers are adequately informed about affiliated business arrangements. The commission shall consult with the insurance commissioner pursuant to section 10-11-124 (2), concerning rules, policies, or guidelines the insurance commissioner adopts concerning affiliated business arrangements. Neither the rules promulgated by the insurance commissioner nor the commission may create a conflicting regulatory burden on an affiliated business arrangement.

(6)   The division of real estate may share information gathered during an investigation of an affiliated business arrangement with the division of insurance.

* ## § 12-10-219, C.R.S. Hearing – administrative law judge – review – rules.

* *Editor's note: This section is similar to former §12-61-114 as it existed prior to 2019.*

(1) Except as otherwise provided in this section, all proceedings before the commission with respect to disciplinary actions and denial of licensure under this part 2 and part 4 of this article 10 and certifications issued under part 5 of this article 10 shall be conducted by an administrative law judge pursuant to the provisions of sections 24-4-104 and 24-4-105.

(2) The proceedings shall be held in the county where the commission has its office or in such other place as the commission may designate. If the licensee is an employed broker, the commission shall also notify the broker employing the licensee by mailing, by first-class mail, a copy of the written notice required under section 24-4-104 (3) to the employing broker's last-known business address.

(3) An administrative law judge shall conduct all hearings for denying, suspending, or revoking a license or certificate on behalf of the commission, subject to appropriations made to the department of personnel. Each administrative law judge shall be appointed pursuant to part 10 of article 30 of title 24. The administrative law judge shall conduct the hearing pursuant to the provisions of sections 24-4-104 and 24-4-105. No license shall be denied, suspended, or revoked until the commission has made its decision by a majority vote.

(4) The decision of the commission in any disciplinary action or denial of licensure under this section is subject to review by the court of appeals by appropriate proceedings under section 24-4-106 (11). In order to effectuate the purposes of parts 2, 4, and 5 of this article 10, the commission has the power to promulgate rules pursuant to article 4 of title 24. The commission may appear in court by its own attorney.

(5) Pursuant to the proceeding, the court has the right, in its discretion, to stay the execution or effect of any final order of the commission; but a hearing shall be held affording the parties an opportunity to be heard for the purpose of determining whether the public health, safety, and welfare would be endangered by staying the commission's order. If the court determines that the order should be stayed, it shall also determine at the hearing the amount of the bond and adequacy of the surety, which bond shall be conditioned upon the faithful performance by the petitioner of all obligations as a real estate broker and upon the prompt payment of all damages arising from or caused by the delay in the taking effect of or enforcement of the order complained of and for all costs that may be assessed or required to be paid in connection with the proceedings.

(6) In any hearing conducted by the commission in which there is a possibility of the denial, suspension, or revocation of a license because of the conviction of a felony or of a crime involving moral turpitude, the commission shall be governed by the provisions of section 24-5-101.

* ## § 12-10-220, C.R.S. Rules.

* *Editor's note: This section is similar to former §12-61-114.5 as it existed prior to 2019.*

All rules adopted or amended by the commission are subject to sections 24-4-103 (8)(c) and (8)(d) and 24-34-104 (6)(b).

* ## § 12-10-221, C.R.S. Broker remuneration.

* *Editor's note: This section is similar to former §12-61-117 as it existed prior to 2019.*

It is unlawful for a real estate broker registered in the commission office as in the employ of another broker to accept a commission or valuable consideration for the performance of any of the acts specified in this part 2 from any person except the broker's employer, who shall be a licensed real estate broker.

* **§ 12-10-222, C.R.S. Acts of third parties – broker's liability.**

* *Editor's note: This section is similar to former §12-61-118 as it existed prior to 2019.*

Any unlawful act or violation of any of the provisions of this part 2 upon the part of an employee, officer, or member of a licensed real estate broker shall not be cause for disciplinary action against a real estate broker, unless it appears to the satisfaction of the commission that the real estate broker had actual knowledge of the unlawful act or violation or had been negligent in the supervision of employees.

* **§ 12-10-223, C.R.S. Violations.**

* *Editor's note: This section is similar to former §12-61-119 as it existed prior to 2019.*

Any natural person, firm, partnership, limited liability company, association, or corporation violating the provisions of this part 2 by acting as real estate broker in this state without having obtained a license or by acting as real estate broker after the broker's license has been revoked or during any period for which the license may have been suspended is guilty of a misdemeanor and, upon conviction thereof, if a natural person, shall be punished by a fine of not more than five hundred dollars, or by imprisonment in the county jail for not more than six months, or by both such fine and imprisonment and, if an entity, shall be punished by a fine of not more than five thousand dollars. A second violation, if by a natural person, shall be punishable by a fine of not more than one thousand dollars, or by imprisonment in the county jail for not more than six months, or by both such fine and imprisonment.

* **§ 12-10-224, C.R.S. Subpoena compelling attendance of witnesses and production of records and documents.**

* *Editor's note: This section is similar to former §12-61-120 as it existed prior to 2019.*

The commission, the director, or the administrative law judge appointed for hearings may issue a subpoena compelling the attendance and testimony of witnesses and the production of books, papers, or records pursuant to an investigation or hearing of the commission. The subpoenas shall be served in the same manner as subpoenas issued by district courts and shall be issued without discrimination between public or private parties requiring the attendance of witnesses and the production of documents at hearings. If a person fails or refuses to obey a subpoena issued by the commission, the director, or the appointed administrative law judge, the commission may petition the district court having jurisdiction for issuance of a subpoena in the premises, and the court shall, in a proper case, issue its subpoena. Any person who refuses to obey a subpoena shall be punished as provided in section 12-10-225.

* **§ 12-10-225, C.R.S. Failure to obey subpoena – penalty.**

* *Editor's note: This section is similar to former §12-61-121 as it existed prior to 2019.*

Any person who willfully fails or neglects to appear and testify or to produce books, papers, or records required by subpoena, duly served upon him or her in any matter conducted under parts 2 and 5 of this article 10, is guilty of a misdemeanor and, upon conviction thereof, shall be punished by a fine of twenty-five dollars, or imprisonment in the county jail for not more than thirty days for each such offense, or by both such fine and imprisonment. Each day a person so refuses or neglects constitutes a separate offense.

* **§ 12-10-226, C.R.S. Powers of commission – injunctions.**

* *Editor's note: This section is similar to former §12-61-122 as it existed prior to 2019.*

The commission may apply to a court of competent jurisdiction for an order enjoining any act or practice that constitutes a violation of parts 2 and 5 of this article 10, and, upon a showing that a person is engaging or intends to engage in any such act or practice, an injunction, restraining order, or other appropriate order shall be granted by the court regardless of the existence of another remedy therefor. Any notice, hearing, or duration of any injunction or restraining order shall be made in accordance with the provisions of the Colorado rules of civil procedure.

§ 12-10-227, C.R.S. Repeal of part – subject to review.

Editor's note: This section is similar to former §12-61-123 as it existed prior to 2019.

This part 2 is repealed, effective September 1, 2026. Before the repeal, the division, including the commission, is scheduled for review in accordance with section 24-34-104.

C. Part 3 – Brokers' Commissions

§ 12-10-301, C.R.S. When entitled to commission.

Editor's note: This section is similar to former §12-61-201 as it existed prior to 2019.

No real estate agent or broker is entitled to a commission for finding a purchaser who is ready, willing, and able to complete the purchase of real estate as proposed by the owner until the same is consummated or is defeated by the refusal or neglect of the owner to consummate the same as agreed upon.

§ 12-10-302, C.R.S. Objections on account of title.

Editor's note: This section is similar to former §12-61-202 as it existed prior to 2019.

No real estate agent or broker is entitled to a commission when a proposed purchaser fails or refuses to complete his or her contract of purchase because of defects in the title of the owner, unless the owner, within a reasonable time, has the defects corrected by legal proceedings or otherwise.

§ 12-10-303, C.R.S. When owner must perfect title.

Editor's note: This section is similar to former §12-61-203 as it existed prior to 2019.

The owner shall not be required to begin legal or other proceedings for the correction of a title until the agent or broker secures from the proposed purchaser an enforceable contract in writing, binding him or her to complete the purchase whenever the defects in the title are corrected.

§ 12-10-304, C.R.S. Referral fees – conformity with federal law required – remedies for violation – definitions.

Editor's note: This section is similar to former §12-61-203.5 as it existed prior to 2019.

(1)   A person licensed under part 2, 3, or 5 of this article 10 shall not pay or receive a referral fee except in accordance with the federal "Real Estate Settlement Procedures Act of 1974", as amended, 12 U.S.C. sec. 2601 et seq., and unless reasonable cause for payment of the referral fee exists. A reasonable cause for payment means:

    (a)   An actual introduction of business has been made;

    (b)   A contractual referral fee relationship exists; or

    (c)   A contractual cooperative brokerage relationship exists.

(2)   (a)   No person shall interfere with the brokerage relationship of a licensee.

    (b)   As used in this subsection (2):

        (I)   "Brokerage relationship" means a relationship entered into between a broker and a buyer, seller, landlord, or tenant under which the broker engages in any of the acts set forth in section 12-10-201 (6). A brokerage relationship is not established until a written brokerage agreement is entered into between the parties or is otherwise established by law.

    (II) "Interfere with the brokerage relationship" means demanding a referral fee from a licensee without reasonable cause.

    (III) "Referral fee" means any fee paid by a licensee to any person or entity, other than a cooperative commission offered by a listing broker to a selling broker or vice versa.

(3) Any person aggrieved by a violation of any provision of this section may bring a civil action in a court of competent jurisdiction. The prevailing party in any such action shall be entitled to actual damages and, in addition, the court may award an amount up to three times the amount of actual damages sustained as a result of any such violation plus reasonable attorney fees.

§ 12-10-305, C.R.S. Repeal of part – subject to review.

Editor's note: This section is similar to former §12-61-204 as it existed prior to 2019.

This part 3 is repealed, effective September 1, 2026. Before the repeal, this part 3 is scheduled for review in accordance with section 24-34-104.

D. Part 4 – Brokerage Relationships

§ 12-10-401, C.R.S. Legislative declaration.

Editor's note: This section is similar to former §12-61-801 as it existed prior to 2019.

(1) The general assembly finds, determines, and declares that the public will best be served through a better understanding of the public's legal and working relationships with real estate brokers and by being able to engage any such real estate broker on terms and under conditions that the public and the real estate broker find acceptable. This includes engaging a broker as a single agent or transaction-broker. Individual members of the public should not be exposed to liability for acts or omissions of real estate brokers that have not been approved, directed, or ratified by the individuals. Further, the public should be advised of the general duties, obligations, and responsibilities of the real estate broker they engage.

(2) This part 4 is enacted to govern the relationships between real estate brokers and sellers, landlords, buyers, and tenants in real estate transactions.

§ 12-10-402, C.R.S. Definitions.

Editor's note: This section is similar to former §12-61-802 as it existed prior to 2019.

As used in this part 4, unless the context otherwise requires:

(1) "Broker" shall have the same meaning as set forth in section 12-10-201 (6), except as otherwise specified in this part 4.

(2) "Customer" means a party to a real estate transaction with whom the broker has no brokerage relationship because the party has not engaged or employed a broker.

(3) (a) "Designated broker" means an employing broker or employed broker who is designated in writing by an employing broker to serve as a single agent or transaction-broker for a seller, landlord, buyer, or tenant in a real estate transaction.

    (b) "Designated broker" does not include a real estate brokerage firm that consists of only one licensed natural person.

(4) "Dual agent" means a broker who, with the written informed consent of all parties to a contemplated real estate transaction, is engaged as a limited agent for both the seller and buyer or both the landlord and tenant.

(5)   "Limited agent" means an agent whose duties and obligations to a principal are only those set forth in section 12-10-404 or 12-10-405, with any additional duties and obligations agreed to pursuant to section 12-10-403 (5).

(6)   "Single agent" means a broker who is engaged by and represents only one party in a real estate transaction. A single agent includes the following:

   (a)   "Buyer's agent", which means a broker who is engaged by and represents the buyer in a real estate transaction;

   (b)   "Landlord's agent", which means a broker who is engaged by and represents the landlord in a leasing transaction;

   (c)   "Seller's agent", which means a broker who is engaged by and represents the seller in a real estate transaction; and

   (d)   "Tenant's agent", which means a broker who is engaged by and represents the tenant in a leasing transaction.

(7)   "Subagent" means a broker engaged to act for another broker in performing brokerage tasks for a principal. The subagent owes the same obligations and responsibilities to the principal as does the principal's broker.

(8)   "Transaction-broker" means a broker who assists one or more parties throughout a contemplated real estate transaction with communication, interposition, advisement, negotiation, contract terms, and the closing of the real estate transaction without being an agent or advocate for the interests of any party to the transaction. Upon agreement in writing pursuant to section 12-10-403 (2) or a written disclosure pursuant to section 12-10-408 (2)(c), a transaction-broker may become a single agent.

*   ### § 12-10-403, C.R.S. Relationships between brokers and the public – definition – rules.

*   *Editor's note: This section is similar to former §12-61-803 as it existed prior to 2019.*

(1)   When engaged in any of the activities enumerated in section 12-10-201 (6), a broker may act in any transaction as a single agent or transaction-broker. The broker's general duties and obligations arising from that relationship shall be disclosed to the seller and the buyer or to the landlord and the tenant pursuant to section 12-10-408.

(2)   A broker shall be considered a transaction-broker unless a single agency relationship is established through a written agreement between the broker and the party or parties to be represented by the broker.

(3)   A broker may work with a single party in separate transactions pursuant to different relationships including, but not limited to, selling one property as a seller's agent and working with that seller in buying another property as a transaction-broker or buyer's agent, but only if the broker complies with this part 4 in establishing the relationships for each transaction.

(4)   (a)   A broker licensed pursuant to part 2 of this article 10, whether acting as a single agent or transaction-broker, may complete standard forms for use in a real estate transaction, including standard forms intended to convey personal property as part of the real estate transaction, when a broker is performing the activities enumerated or referred to in section 12-10-201 (6) in the transaction.

   (b)   As used in this subsection (4), "standard form" means:

      (I)   A form promulgated by the real estate commission for current use by brokers, also referred to in this section as a "commission-approved form";

      (II)   A form drafted by a licensed Colorado attorney representing the broker, employing broker, or brokerage firm, so long as the name of the attorney or law firm and the name of the broker, employing broker, or brokerage firm for whom the form is prepared are included on the form itself;

(III)   A form provided by a party to the transaction if the broker is acting in the transaction as either a transaction-broker or as a single agent for the party providing the form to the broker, so long as the broker retains written confirmation that the form was provided by a party to the transaction;

(IV)   A form prescribed by a governmental agency, a quasi-governmental agency, or a lender regulated by state or federal law, if use of the form is mandated by the agency or lender;

(V)   A form issued with the written approval of the Colorado Bar Association or its successor organization and specifically designated for use by brokers in Colorado, so long as the form is used within any guidelines or conditions specified by the Colorado Bar Association or successor organization in connection with the use of the form;

(VI)   A form used for disclosure purposes only, if the disclosure does not purport to waive or create any legal rights or obligations affecting any party to the transaction and if the form provides only information concerning either:

(A)   The real estate involved in the transaction specifically; or

(B)   The geographic area in which the real estate is located generally;

(VII)   A form prescribed by a title company that is providing closing services in a transaction for which the broker is acting either as a transaction-broker or as a single agent for a party to the transaction; or

(VIII) A letter of intent created or prepared by a broker, employing broker, or brokerage firm, so long as the letter of intent states on its face that it is nonbinding and creates no legal rights or obligations.

(c)   A broker shall use a commission-approved form when such a form exists and is appropriate for the transaction. A broker's use of any standard form described in subsection (4)(b)(III) or (4)(b)(IV) of this section must be limited to inserting transaction-specific information within the form. In using standard forms described in subsection (4)(b)(II), (4)(b)(V), (4)(b)(VI), (4)(b)(VII), or (4)(b)(VIII) of this section, the broker may also advise the parties as to effects thereof, and the broker's use of those standard forms must be appropriate for the transaction and the circumstances in which they are used. In any transaction described in this subsection (4), the broker shall advise the parties that the forms have important legal consequences and that the parties should consult legal counsel before signing the forms.

(5)   Nothing contained in this section shall prohibit the public from entering into written contracts with any broker that contain duties, obligations, or responsibilities that are in addition to those specified in this part 4.

(6)   (a)   If a real estate brokerage firm has more than one licensed natural person, the employing broker or an individual broker employed or engaged by that employing broker shall be designated to work with the seller, landlord, buyer, or tenant as a designated broker. The employing broker may designate more than one of its individual brokers to work with a seller, landlord, buyer, or tenant.

(b)   The brokerage relationship established between the seller, landlord, buyer, or tenant and a designated broker, including the duties, obligations, and responsibilities of that relationship, shall not extend to the employing broker nor to any other broker employed or engaged by that employing broker who has not been so designated and shall not extend to the firm, partnership, limited liability company, association, corporation, or other entity that employs the broker.

(c)   A real estate broker may have designated brokers working as single agents for a seller or landlord and a buyer or tenant in the same real estate transaction without creating dual agency for the employing real estate broker, or any broker employed or engaged by that employing real estate broker.

(d)   An individual broker may be designated to work for both a seller or landlord and a buyer or tenant in the same transaction as a transaction-broker for both, as a single agent for the seller or landlord treating the buyer or tenant as a customer, or as a single agent for a buyer or tenant treating the seller or landlord as a customer, but not as a single agent for both. The applicable designated broker relationship shall be disclosed in writing to the seller or landlord and buyer or tenant in a timely manner pursuant to rules promulgated by the real estate commission.

(e)   A designated broker may work with a seller or landlord in one transaction and work with a buyer or tenant in another transaction.

(f)   When a designated broker serves as a single agent pursuant to section 12-10-404 or 12-10-405, there shall be no imputation of knowledge to the employing or employed broker who has not been so designated.

(g)   The extent and limitations of the brokerage relationship with the designated broker shall be disclosed to the seller, landlord, buyer, or tenant working with that designated broker pursuant to section 12-10-408.

(7)   No seller, buyer, landlord, or tenant shall be vicariously liable for a broker's acts or omissions that have not been approved, directed, or ratified by the seller, buyer, landlord, or tenant.

(8)   Nothing in this section shall be construed to limit the employing broker's or firm's responsibility to supervise licensees employed by the broker or firm nor to shield the broker or firm from vicarious liability.

*   ### § 12-10-404, C.R.S. Single agent engaged by seller or landlord.

*   ***Editor's note:*** *This section is similar to former §12-61-804 as it existed prior to 2019.*

(1)   A broker engaged by a seller or landlord to act as a seller's agent or a landlord's agent is a limited agent with the following duties and obligations:

(a)   To perform the terms of the written agreement made with the seller or landlord;

(b)   To exercise reasonable skill and care for the seller or landlord;

(c)   To promote the interests of the seller or landlord with the utmost good faith, loyalty, and fidelity, including, but not limited to:

(I)   Seeking a price and terms that are acceptable to the seller or landlord; except that the broker shall not be obligated to seek additional offers to purchase the property while the property is subject to a contract for sale or to seek additional offers to lease the property while the property is subject to a lease or letter of intent to lease;

(II)   Presenting all offers to and from the seller or landlord in a timely manner regardless of whether the property is subject to a contract for sale or a lease or letter of intent to lease;

(III)   Disclosing to the seller or landlord adverse material facts actually known by the broker;

(IV)   Counseling the seller or landlord as to any material benefits or risks of a transaction that are actually known by the broker;

(V)   Advising the seller or landlord to obtain expert advice as to material matters about which the broker knows but the specifics of which are beyond the expertise of the broker;

(VI)   Accounting in a timely manner for all money and property received; and

(VII) Informing the seller or landlord that the seller or landlord shall not be vicariously liable for the acts of the seller's or landlord's agent that are not approved, directed, or ratified by the seller or landlord;

(d) To comply with all requirements of this article 10 and any rules promulgated pursuant to this article 10; and

(e) To comply with any applicable federal, state, or local laws, rules, regulations, or ordinances including fair housing and civil rights statutes or regulations.

(2) The following information shall not be disclosed by a broker acting as a seller's or landlord's agent without the informed consent of the seller or landlord:

(a) That a seller or landlord is willing to accept less than the asking price or lease rate for the property;

(b) What the motivating factors are for the party selling or leasing the property;

(c) That the seller or landlord will agree to financing terms other than those offered;

(d) Any material information about the seller or landlord unless disclosure is required by law or failure to disclose the information would constitute fraud or dishonest dealing; or

(e) Any facts or suspicions regarding circumstances that may psychologically impact or stigmatize any real property pursuant to section 38-35.5-101.

(3) (a) A broker acting as a seller's or landlord's agent owes no duty or obligation to the buyer or tenant; except that a broker shall, subject to the limitations of section 38-35.5-101, concerning psychologically impacted property, disclose to any prospective buyer or tenant all adverse material facts actually known by the broker. The adverse material facts may include but shall not be limited to adverse material facts pertaining to the title and the physical condition of the property, any material defects in the property, and any environmental hazards affecting the property that are required by law to be disclosed.

(b) A seller's or landlord's agent owes no duty to conduct an independent inspection of the property for the benefit of the buyer or tenant and owes no duty to independently verify the accuracy or completeness of any statement made by the seller or landlord or any independent inspector.

(4) A seller's or landlord's agent may show alternative properties not owned by the seller or landlord to prospective buyers or tenants and may list competing properties for sale or lease and not be deemed to have breached any duty or obligation to the seller or landlord.

(5) A designated broker acting as a seller's or landlord's agent may cooperate with other brokers but may not engage or create any subagents.

* ### § 12-10-405, C.R.S. Single agent engaged by buyer or tenant.

* *Editor's note: This section is similar to former §12-61-805 as it existed prior to 2019.*

(1) A broker engaged by a buyer or tenant to act as a buyer's or tenant's agent shall be a limited agent with the following duties and obligations:

(a) To perform the terms of the written agreement made with the buyer or tenant;

(b) To exercise reasonable skill and care for the buyer or tenant;

(c) To promote the interests of the buyer or tenant with the utmost good faith, loyalty, and fidelity, including, but not limited to:

(I) Seeking a price and terms that are acceptable to the buyer or tenant; except that the broker shall not be obligated to seek other properties while the buyer is a party to a contract to purchase property or while the tenant is a party to a lease or letter of intent to lease;

        (II)   Presenting all offers to and from the buyer or tenant in a timely manner regardless of whether the buyer is already a party to a contract to purchase property or the tenant is already a party to a contract or a letter of intent to lease;

        (III)   Disclosing to the buyer or tenant adverse material facts actually known by the broker;

        (IV)   Counseling the buyer or tenant as to any material benefits or risks of a transaction that are actually known by the broker;

        (V)   Advising the buyer or tenant to obtain expert advice as to material matters about which the broker knows but the specifics of which are beyond the expertise of the broker;

        (VI)   Accounting in a timely manner for all money and property received; and

        (VII) Informing the buyer or tenant that the buyer or tenant shall not be vicariously liable for the acts of the buyer's or tenant's agent that are not approved, directed, or ratified by the buyer or tenant;

    (d)   To comply with all requirements of this article 10 and any rules promulgated pursuant to this article 10; and

    (e)   To comply with any applicable federal, state, or local laws, rules, regulations, or ordinances including fair housing and civil rights statutes or regulations.

(2)   The following information shall not be disclosed by a broker acting as a buyer's or tenant's agent without the informed consent of the buyer or tenant:

    (a)   That a buyer or tenant is willing to pay more than the purchase price or lease rate for the property;

    (b)   What the motivating factors are for the party buying or leasing the property;

    (c)   That the buyer or tenant will agree to financing terms other than those offered;

    (d)   Any material information about the buyer or tenant unless disclosure is required by law or failure to disclose the information would constitute fraud or dishonest dealing; or

    (e)   Any facts or suspicions regarding circumstances that would psychologically impact or stigmatize any real property pursuant to section 38-35.5-101.

(3)   (a)   A broker acting as a buyer's or tenant's agent owes no duty or obligation to the seller or landlord; except that the broker shall disclose to any prospective seller or landlord all adverse material facts actually known by the broker including but not limited to adverse material facts concerning the buyer's or tenant's financial ability to perform the terms of the transaction and whether the buyer intends to occupy the property to be purchased as a principal residence.

    (b)   A buyer's or tenant's agent owes no duty to conduct an independent investigation of the buyer's or tenant's financial condition for the benefit of the seller or landlord and owes no duty to independently verify the accuracy or completeness of statements made by the buyer or tenant or any independent inspector.

(4)   A buyer's or tenant's agent may show properties in which the buyer or tenant is interested to other prospective buyers or tenants without breaching any duty or obligation to the buyer or tenant. Nothing in this section shall be construed to prohibit a buyer's or tenant's agent from showing competing buyers or tenants the same property and from assisting competing buyers or tenants in attempting to purchase or lease a particular property.

(5)   A broker acting as a buyer's or tenant's agent owes no duty to conduct an independent inspection of the property for the benefit of the buyer or tenant and owes no duty to independently verify the accuracy or completeness of statements made by the seller, landlord, or independent inspectors; except that nothing in this subsection (5) shall be construed to limit the broker's duties and obligations imposed pursuant to subsection (1) of this section.

(6)   A broker acting as a buyer's or tenant's agent may cooperate with other brokers but may not engage or create any subagents.

*   ## § 12-10-406, C.R.S. Dual agent.

*   ***Editor's note:*** *This section is similar to former §12-61-806 as it existed prior to 2019.*

A broker shall not establish dual agency with any seller, landlord, buyer, or tenant.

*   ## § 12-10-407, C.R.S. Transaction-broker.

*   ***Editor's note:*** *This section is similar to former §12-61-807 as it existed prior to 2019.*

(1)   A broker engaged as a transaction-broker is not an agent for either party.

(2)   A transaction-broker shall have the following obligations and responsibilities:

(a)   To perform the terms of any written or oral agreement made with any party to the transaction;

(b)   To exercise reasonable skill and care as a transaction-broker, including, but not limited to:

(I)   Presenting all offers and counteroffers in a timely manner regardless of whether the property is subject to a contract for sale or lease or letter of intent;

(II)   Advising the parties regarding the transaction and suggesting that the parties obtain expert advice as to material matters about which the transaction-broker knows but the specifics of which are beyond the expertise of the broker;

(III)   Accounting in a timely manner for all money and property received;

(IV)   Keeping the parties fully informed regarding the transaction;

(V)   Assisting the parties in complying with the terms and conditions of any contract including closing the transaction;

(VI)   Disclosing to all prospective buyers or tenants any adverse material facts actually known by the broker including but not limited to adverse material facts pertaining to the title, the physical condition of the property, any defects in the property, and any environmental hazards affecting the property required by law to be disclosed;

(VII)   Disclosing to any prospective seller or landlord all adverse material facts actually known by the broker including but not limited to adverse material facts pertaining to the buyer's or tenant's financial ability to perform the terms of the transaction and the buyer's intent to occupy the property as a principal residence; and

(VIII)   Informing the parties that as seller and buyer or as landlord and tenant they shall not be vicariously liable for any acts of the transaction-broker;

(c)   To comply with all requirements of this article 10 and any rules promulgated pursuant to this article 10; and

(d)   To comply with any applicable federal, state, or local laws, rules, regulations, or ordinances including fair housing and civil rights statutes or regulations.

(3)   The following information shall not be disclosed by a transaction-broker without the informed consent of all parties:

(a)   That a buyer or tenant is willing to pay more than the purchase price or lease rate offered for the property;

(b)   That a seller or landlord is willing to accept less than the asking price or lease rate for the property;

(c)   What the motivating factors are for any party buying, selling, or leasing the property;

(d) That a seller, buyer, landlord, or tenant will agree to financing terms other than those offered;

(e) Any facts or suspicions regarding circumstances that may psychologically impact or stigmatize any real property pursuant to section 38-35.5-101; or

(f) Any material information about the other party unless disclosure is required by law or failure to disclose the information would constitute fraud or dishonest dealing.

(4) A transaction-broker has no duty to conduct an independent inspection of the property for the benefit of the buyer or tenant and has no duty to independently verify the accuracy or completeness of statements made by the seller, landlord, or independent inspectors.

(5) A transaction-broker has no duty to conduct an independent investigation of the buyer's or tenant's financial condition or to verify the accuracy or completeness of any statement made by the buyer or tenant.

(6) A transaction-broker may do the following without breaching any obligation or responsibility:

(a) Show alternative properties not owned by the seller or landlord to a prospective buyer or tenant;

(b) List competing properties for sale or lease;

(c) Show properties in which the buyer or tenant is interested to other prospective buyers or tenants; and

(d) Serve as a single agent or transaction-broker for the same or for different parties in other real estate transactions.

(7) There shall be no imputation of knowledge or information between any party and the transaction-broker or among persons within an entity engaged as a transaction-broker.

(8) A transaction-broker may cooperate with other brokers but shall not engage or create any subagents.

§ 12-10-408, C.R.S. Broker disclosures.

Editor's note: This section is similar to former §12-61-808 as it existed prior to 2019.

(1) (a) Any person, firm, partnership, limited liability company, association, or corporation acting as a broker shall adopt a written office policy that identifies and describes the relationships offered to the public by the broker.

(b) A broker shall not be required to offer or engage in any one or in all of the brokerage relationships enumerated in section 12-10-404, 12-10-405, or 12-10-407.

(c) Written disclosures and written agreements required by subsection (2) of this section shall contain a statement to the seller, landlord, buyer, or tenant that different brokerage relationships are available that include buyer agency, seller agency, or status as a transaction-broker. Should the seller, landlord, buyer, or tenant request information or ask questions concerning a brokerage relationship not offered by the broker pursuant to the broker's written office policy enumerated in subsection (1)(a) of this section, the broker shall provide to the party a written definition of that brokerage relationship that has been promulgated by the real estate commission.

(d) Disclosures made in accordance with this part 4 shall be sufficient to disclose brokerage relationships to the public.

(2) (a) (I) Prior to engaging in any of the activities enumerated in section 12-10-201 (6), a transaction-broker shall disclose in writing to the party to be assisted that the broker is not acting as agent for the party and that the broker is acting as a transaction-broker.

(II)   As part of each relationship entered into by a broker pursuant to subsection (2)(a)(I) of this section, written disclosure shall be made that shall contain a signature block for the buyer, seller, landlord, or tenant to acknowledge receipt of the disclosure. The disclosure and acknowledgment, by itself, shall not constitute a contract with the broker. If the buyer, seller, landlord, or tenant chooses not to sign the acknowledgment, the broker shall note that fact on a copy of the disclosure and shall retain the copy.

(III)   If the transaction-broker undertakes any obligations or responsibilities in addition to or different from those set forth in section 12-10-407, the obligations or responsibilities shall be disclosed in a writing that shall be signed by the involved parties.

(b)   Prior to engaging in any of the activities enumerated in section 12-10-201 (6), a broker intending to establish a single agency relationship with a seller, landlord, buyer, or tenant shall enter into a written agency agreement with the party to be represented. The agreement shall disclose the duties and responsibilities specified in section 12-10-404 or 12-10-405, as applicable. Notice of the single agency relationship shall be furnished to any prospective party to the proposed transaction in a timely manner.

(c)   (I)   Prior to engaging in any of the activities enumerated in section 12-10-201 (6), a broker intending to work with a buyer or tenant as an agent of the seller or landlord shall provide a written disclosure to the buyer or tenant that shall contain the following:

(A)   A statement that the broker is an agent for the seller or landlord and is not an agent for the buyer or tenant;

(B)   A list of the tasks that the agent intends to perform for the seller or landlord with the buyer or tenant; and

(C)   A statement that the buyer or tenant shall not be vicariously liable for the acts of the agent unless the buyer or tenant approves, directs, or ratifies the acts.

(II)   The written disclosure required pursuant to subsection (2)(c)(I) of this section shall contain a signature block for the buyer or tenant to acknowledge receipt of the disclosure. The disclosure and acknowledgment, by itself, shall not constitute a contract with the broker. If the buyer or tenant does not sign the disclosure, the broker shall note that fact on a copy of the disclosure and retain the copy.

(d)   A broker who has already established a relationship with one party to a proposed transaction shall advise at the earliest reasonable opportunity any other potential parties or their agents of the established relationship.

(e)   (I)   Prior to engaging in any of the activities enumerated in section 12-10-201 (6), the seller, buyer, landlord, or tenant shall be advised in any written agreement with a broker that the brokerage relationship exists only with the designated broker, does not extend to the employing broker or to any other brokers employed or engaged by the employing broker who are not so designated, and does not extend to the brokerage company.

(II)   Nothing in this subsection (2)(e) shall be construed to limit the employing broker's or firm's responsibility to supervise licensees employed by the broker or firm nor to shield the broker or firm from vicarious liability.

*   **§ 12-10-409, C.R.S. Duration of relationship.**

*   ***Editor's note:*** *This section is similar to former §12-61-809 as it existed prior to 2019.*

(1)   (a)   The relationships set forth in this part 4 shall commence at the time that the broker is engaged by a party and shall continue until performance or completion of the agreement by which the broker was engaged.

      (b)   If the agreement by which the broker was engaged is not performed or completed for any reason, the relationship shall end at the earlier of the following:

         (I)   Any date of expiration agreed upon by the parties;

         (II)   Any termination or relinquishment of the relationship by the parties; or

         (III)   One year after the date of the engagement.

(2)   (a)   Except as otherwise agreed to in writing and pursuant to subsection (2)(b) of this section, a broker engaged as a seller's agent or buyer's agent owes no further duty or obligation after termination or expiration of the contract or completion of performance.

      (b)   Notwithstanding subsection (2)(a) of this section, a broker shall be responsible after termination or expiration of the contract or completion of performance for the following:

         (I)   Accounting for all money and property related to and received during the engagement; and

         (II)   Keeping confidential all information received during the course of the engagement that was made confidential by request or instructions from the engaging party unless:

            (A)   The engaging party grants written consent to disclose the information;

            (B)   Disclosure of the information is required by law; or

            (C)   The information is made public or becomes public by the words or conduct of the engaging party or from a source other than the broker.

(3)   Except as otherwise agreed to in writing, a transaction-broker owes no further obligation or responsibility to the engaging party after termination or expiration of the contract for performance or completion of performance; except that the broker shall account for all money and property related to and received during the engagement.

*   **§ 12-10-410, C.R.S. Compensation.**

*   ***Editor's note:*** *This section is similar to former §12-61-810 as it existed prior to 2019.*

(1)   In any real estate transaction, the broker's compensation may be paid by the seller, the buyer, the landlord, the tenant, a third party, or by the sharing or splitting of a commission or compensation between brokers.

(2)   Payment of compensation shall not be construed to establish an agency relationship between the broker and the party who paid the compensation.

(3)   A seller or landlord may agree that a transaction-broker or single agent may share the commission or other compensation paid by the seller or landlord with another broker.

(4)   A buyer or tenant may agree that a single agent or transaction-broker may share the commission or other compensation paid by the buyer or tenant with another broker.

(5)   A buyer's or tenant's agent shall obtain the written approval of the buyer or tenant before the agent may propose to the seller's or landlord's agent that the buyer's or tenant's agent be compensated by sharing compensation paid by the seller or landlord.

(6)   Prior to entering into a brokerage or listing agreement or a contract to buy, sell, or lease, the identity of those parties, persons, or entities paying compensation or commissions to any broker shall be disclosed to the parties to the transaction.

(7)   A broker may be compensated by more than one party for services in a transaction if those parties have consented in writing to such multiple payments prior to entering into a contract to buy, sell, or lease.

*   ***§ 12-10-411, C.R.S. Violations.***

*   ***Editor's note:*** *This section is similar to former §12-61-811 as it existed prior to 2019.*

The violation of any provision of this part 4 by a broker constitutes an act pursuant to section 12-10-217 (1)(m) for which the real estate commission may investigate and take administrative action against any such broker pursuant to sections 12-10-217 and 12-10-219.

Chapter 2:
Rules and Regulations for Real Estate Brokers

An * in the left margin indicates a change in the statute, rule, or text since the last publication of the manual.

DEPARTMENT OF REGULATORY AGENCIES
DIVISION OF REAL ESTATE
COLORADO REAL ESTATE COMMISSION
4 CCR 725-1

RULES OF THE COLORADO REAL ESTATE COMMISSION

* **Chapter 1: Definitions**

* 1.1. Active: A current, valid License that allows a person, firm, partnership, limited liability company, association, or corporation to engage in Real Estate Brokerage Services.

* 1.2. Advertise or Advertising: The promotion, solicitation, or representation of Real Estate Brokerage Services requiring a License. Advertising may include, but is not limited to, business cards, brochures, websites, signage, property flyers, mailings (paper or electronic), social media, letterhead, email signatures, and contract documents. A uniform resource locator (URL) and an email address are not considered Advertising for purposes of Rule 6.10 so long as they are not directly used to promote or solicit Real Estate Brokerage Services.

* 1.3. Affiliated Business Arrangement: Has the same meaning pursuant to section 12-10-218(1), C.R.S.

* 1.4. Anniversary Year Cycle: The three-year licensing period commencing on a Broker's initial date of licensure (anniversary date) and expiring three (3) years later on the same date. The anniversary date may be any day of the calendar year.

* 1.5. Applicant: A person or entity seeking a License from the Commission to perform the duties pursuant to section 12-10-201(6)(a), C.R.S.

* 1.6. Associate Broker: A Broker who holds an Associate Broker level license and works under the supervision of an Employing Broker. Associate Brokers may have an Independent Broker or Employing Broker level license even if they are still acting as an Associate Broker under the supervision of an Employing Broker.

* 1.7. Broker: Any person licensed by the Commission to perform Real Estate Brokerage Services regardless if the Broker is licensed as an Associate Broker, Independent Broker, or Employing Broker.

* 1.8. Brokerage Firm: Any sole proprietor, partnership, limited liability company, corporation, or any other authorized entity licensed by the Commission to employ or engage Brokers to perform Real Estate Brokerage Services. All Brokerage Firms that employ or engage Associate Brokers must have an Active Employing Broker.

* 1.9. Brokerage Relationship: Has the same meaning pursuant to section 12-10-304(2)(b)(I), C.R.S.

* 1.10. Calendar Year Cycle: This is the three-year licensing period commencing on January 1 of year one and expiring on December 31 of year three. All Brokers will eventually be on a Calendar Year Cycle for their License renewal.

* 1.11. Commercial Real Estate: Any real property other than real property containing one to four residential units, single-family or multi-family residential units including condominiums, townhouses, or homes in a subdivision when such real estate is sold, leased, or otherwise conveyed on a unit-by-unit basis even though the units may be part of a larger building or parcel of real property containing more than four residential units as defined pursuant to section 38-22.5-102(2), C.R.S.

* 1.12. Commission: The Colorado Real Estate Commission as defined pursuant to section 12-10-201(1), C.R.S.

* 1.13. Consumer: A member of the public that has sought or is seeking to engage Real Estate Brokerage Services provided by a Broker. A Consumer is a buyer, seller, tenant, or landlord, as applicable.

* 1.14. Customer: Has the same meaning pursuant to section 12-10-402(2), C.R.S.

* 1.15. Deemed Complete: An Applicant has submitted a complete and satisfactory application in compliance with sections 12-10-202 and 12-10-203, C.R.S. that includes the Fee and the accompanying required documentation as set forth in Chapters 2 and 3 of these Rules.

* 1.16. Designated Broker: Has the same meaning pursuant to section 12-10-402(3), C.R.S.

* 1.17. Director: The Director of the Division as defined pursuant to section 12-10-101(1), C.R.S.

* 1.18. Distance Learning: Education courses offered outside the traditional classroom setting in which the instructor and learner are separated by distance and/or time.

* 1.19. Division: The Division of Real Estate as defined pursuant to section 12-10-101(2), C.R.S.

* 1.20. Duplicate: A legible photocopy, carbon copy, facsimile, or electronic copies which contain a digital or electronic signature as defined pursuant to section 24-71-101(1), C.R.S.

* 1.21. Electronic Media: The method of communicating information that are in an electronic format rather than a paper format. Electronic Media may include, but is not limited to, websites, electronic mailings, social Media such as Twitter and Facebook, banner advertisements, and YouTube.

* 1.22. Electronic Record: A record generated, communicated, received, or stored by electronic means as defined to pursuant to section 24-71.3-102(7), C.R.S.

* 1.23. Employing Broker: Has the same meaning pursuant to section 12-10-201(2), C.R.S.

* 1.24. Expired: A License that was not renewed prior to the last day of the license cycle and is no longer valid for a person or entity to perform any Real Estate Brokerage Services. Such persons cannot hold themselves out to the public as Brokers and such entities cannot Advertise as Brokerage Firms.

* 1.25. Fee: The prescribed non-refundable fee as set by the Division.

* 1.26. Initial License or Initial Licensure: The first license granted by the Commission to an Applicant pursuant to sections 12-10-202 and 12-10-203, C.R.S.

* 1.27. Inactive: A Broker who holds a valid License shown in the Commission's records as being Inactive is not permitted to engage in Real Estate Brokerage Services. To maintain licensure on Inactive status, a Broker must still continue to renew their License as set forth in Chapter 3 of these Rules.

* 1.28. Independent Broker: A Broker either holding an Independent Broker level license or Employing Broker level license acting as their own Brokerage Firm or sole proprietor and not employing or supervising any Associate Brokers.

* 1.29. Invalid Payment: If the Fees accompanying any application including Fees for the recovery fund, renewals and transfers made to the Division are paid for by check and the check is not immediately paid upon presentment to the bank upon which the check was drawn, or if payment is submitted in any other manner, and payment is denied, rescinded or returned as invalid, the application will be immediately canceled. The application will only be reinstated if the Division has received valid payment of all application Fees together with any fees incurred by the Division including the fee required by state fiscal rules for clerical services necessary for reinstatement.

* 1.30. Jurisdiction: For purposes of Chapter 2 of these Rules, all 50 states, the District of Columbia, Guam, Puerto Rico, and the U.S. Virgin Islands.

* 1.31. License: A Broker's or Brokerage Firm's license issued by the Commission pursuant to section 12-10-203, C.R.S.

* 1.32. Listing Contract: An agreement between a Brokerage Firm and a Consumer in which a Broker licensed with the Brokerage Firm is designated to provide Real Estate Brokerage Services to the Consumer. Listing Agreements include: Exclusive Tenant Contract, Exclusive Right to Sell, Exclusive Right to Lease, and Exclusive Right to Buy.

* 1.33. Management Agreement: An agreement between a Brokerage Firm and an owner of a property in which a Broker licensed with the Brokerage Firm is designated to provide Property Management Services on behalf of the owner.

* 1.34. Money Belonging to Others: Money Belonging to Others which is received by the Broker or Brokerage Firm that includes, but is not limited to, money received in connection with Management Agreements, partnerships, limited liability companies, syndications, lease agreements, advance fee contracts, guest deposits for short term rentals, earnest money deposits, or Money Belonging to Others received for any other purpose.

* 1.35. New Associate Broker: An Associate Broker with less than two (2) years of accumulative Active experience.

* 1.36. Office Policy Manual: The Manual required for all Employing Brokers or the Employing Broker's Brokerage Firm, which contains certain policies and procedures.

* 1.37. Petitioner: For the purposes of implementing the provisions of Chapter 8 of these Rules, any person who has filed with the Commission a petition or has been granted leave to intervene by the Commission for a declaratory order pursuant to section 24-4-105(11), C.R.S. and as set forth in Chapter 8 of these Rules.

* 1.38. Property Management: An on-going relationship between a Brokerage Firm and an owner of a property in which the Brokerage Firm is designated to provide Property Management Services.

* 1.39. Property Management Services: The activities performed in leasing and subsequent management of a property on behalf of an owner that are pursuant to section 12-10-201(6), C.R.S. and further described in the Management Agreement.

* 1.40. Real Estate Brokerage Services: Any of the activities pursuant to section 12-10-201(6)(a), C.R.S. when performed on behalf of a Consumer.

* 1.41. Real Estate Licensing Examination: An examination that consists of two (2) parts; a national part and a Colorado part as set forth in Rule 2.2.

* 1.42. Real Estate School: Has the same meaning pursuant to section 23-64-103(20), C.R.S.

* 1.43. RESPA – The Real Estate Settlement Procedures Act of 1974, set forth in 12 U.S.C. 2601, et. seq. (Act), effective June 1, 2018, incorporated by reference in compliance with section 24-4-103(12.5), C.R.S. and does not include any later amendments or editions to the Act. A certified copy of the Act is readily available for public inspection at the Office of the Colorado Real Estate Commission at 1560 Broadway, Suite 925, Denver, Colorado. The Act may also be examined at the internet website of the Consumer Bureau of Financial Protection (CFPB) at *www.consumerfinance.gov*. The CFPB may also be contacted at 1700 G. Street, NW, Washington, D.C. 20552 or by telephone at (202) 435-7000.

* 1.44. Recognized Depository: Any bank, savings and loan association, or credit union that accepts deposits or shares insured by the Federal Deposit Insurance Corporation (FDIC) or the National Credit Union Administration (NCUA) respectively.

* 1.45. Reinstatement or Reinstating or Reinstate: Has the same meaning pursuant to section 12-10-212(4)(a)(III), C.R.S.

* 1.46. Single Agent: Has the same meaning pursuant to section 12-10-402(6), C.R.S.

* 1.47. Standard Form: Has the meaning pursuant to section 12-10-403(4), C.R.S. and also as set forth in Rule 7.1.

* 1.48. Supervisory Broker: A Broker, such as a managing broker, team lead, office manager, etc., who has been delegated in writing by an Employing Broker to assume some of the Employing Broker's duties and responsibilities as set forth in Rule 6.3.

* 1.49. Team: Two (2) or more Brokers within a Brokerage Firm that cooperate on an on-going basis to conduct a substantial portion of their Real Estate Brokerage Services together.

* 1.50. Temporary License: Has the same meaning pursuant to section 12-10-203(6)(c), C.R.S.

* 1.51. Things of Value: Monetary considerations as well as the exchange of tangible, non-monetary assets.

* 1.52. Trademark: Any logo, service mark, or other identifying mark used in conjunction with a Brokerage Firm's legal name or Trade Name. Trademarks may be registered with the Colorado Secretary of State pursuant to section 7-70-102, C.R.S. As an example, the brokerage "A Better Choice Real Estate" uses a logo bearing the initials "ABC". The logo is used to identify the Brokerage Firm and the Real Estate Brokerage Services that it provides to Consumers; therefore, it would be the trademark for the Brokerage Firm.

* 1.53. Trade Name: The name under which a Brokerage Firm does business other than the Brokerage Firm's legal name. Any Trade Name used by a Brokerage Firm must be on file with the Commission and must be filed with the Colorado Secretary of State pursuant to section 7-71-101, C.R.S. For example, a Brokerage Firm is licensed with the Commission under its legal name of "Colorado Real Estate Group LLC". However, the Brokerage is also a franchise of "International Realty" and does business under the Trade Name "International Realty of Colorado".

* 1.54. Transaction-Broker: Has the same meaning pursuant to section 12-10-402(8), C.R.S.

* 1.55. Transition Period: The two-year licensing period plus a partial year commencing on the anniversary date when a Broker's license expires in the years of 2018, 2019, or 2020 and expiring two (2) years plus the remaining days in the third year to reach December 31. The length of the Transition Period is dependent on the anniversary date and could be as long as three (3) years or as short as two (2) years and one day.

* 1.56. Trust or Escrow Account: Any checking, demand, passbook or statement account, which has, at a minimum, the following elements:

* A. The account is separate and contains only Money Belonging to Others;

* B. The account is custodial and fiduciary;

* C. All funds are available on demand; and

* D. The account is held with a Recognized Depository.

* 1.57. Trust or Escrow Accounting Equation: The reconciled trust or escrow bank account cash balance must equal the sum total of the individual ledger balance for each owner at any given point in time.

* 1.58. Unlicensed On-Site Manager: An unlicensed person who fills in blanks, as a scrivener, on lease forms, shows prospective tenants available units, quotes rental prices established by the owner or Broker, arranges for maintenance, and collects monies, including security deposits and rents. A Brokerage Firm which employs an Unlicensed On-Site Manager must do so either as a regularly salaried employee or as an independent contractor, and pay the Unlicensed On-Site Manager through the Brokerage Firm. The salary may include rent value or other non-commission income.

* 1.59. Viewable Page: A page that may or may not scroll beyond the border of the screen and includes the use of frame pages.

* **Chapter 2: Licensure Requirements**

* 2.1. Educational Requirements

*   A.   Associate Broker Level License

*   In order to obtain an Associate Broker level license, the Applicant must successfully complete the educational requirements pursuant to section 12-10-203(4)(a), C.R.S.:

        1.   A degree from an accredited college or university with a major course of study in real estate; or

        2.   Proof of completion of one hundred sixty-eight (168) hours of classroom instruction or equivalent Distance Learning hours from any accredited college or university, or any Real Estate School for the following courses:

            a.   Real Estate Law and Real Estate Practice: 48 hours;

            b.   Colorado Real Estate Contracts: 48 hours;

            c.   Real Estate Closings: not less than 24 hours;

            d.   Trust Accounts and Record Keeping: not less than 8 hours;

            e.   Current Legal Issues: not less than 8 hours; and

            f.   Practical Application: not less than 32 hours.

*   B.   Employing Broker Level License

*   An Applicant desiring an Employing Broker level license must successfully complete the twenty-four (24) hours of classroom instruction or equivalent Distance Learning hours in Brokerage Administration pursuant to section 12-10-203(5)(c)(II), C.R.S.

*   C.   Educational Principles

*   Completion of courses of study approved by the Commission as set forth in subsections A.2. and B. of this Rule, whether through classroom or Distance Learning, must be based upon educational principles acceptable to the Commission.

*   D.   Course Audits

*   The Commission may audit courses set forth in subsection A.2. and B. of this Rule at any time and at no cost. The Commission may request all instructional materials and student attendance records from each accredited college or university, or Real Estate School for any approved course of study. The purpose of the audit is to ensure adherence to the approved course of study by verifying the course material and instruction are consistent with acceptable educational principles; and that instruction is provided in a manner that the desired learning objectives are met. Failure to comply with statutes and these Rules may result in the removal of the course provider, instructor, and/or the course from the approved provider list.

* 2.2. Examination Requirements

*   A.   Real Estate Licensing Examination

*   The Real Estate Licensing Examination is administered and developed by a third party testing service and consists of two (2) parts, which include:

        1.   a national part; and

        2.   a Colorado part.

*   B.   Test Administration Standards

*   Examinees must comply with the standards of test administration established by the Commission and the testing service provider.

* C.   Educational Requirements Completed Prior to Real Estate Licensing Examination

* Educational requirements as set forth in Rule 2.1.A. must be completed and proof filed in a manner as prescribed by the Commission prior to taking the Real Estate Licensing Examination and applying for an Associate Broker level license.

* D.   Duly Qualified Applicants

* The Real Estate Licensing Examination will be given to duly qualified Applicants; however, one (1) instructor from each accredited college or university or Real Estate School may take the examination one (1) time during any twelve (12) month period to conduct research for course content.

* E.   Retake Failed Parts of Real Estate Licensing Examination

* If an Applicant fails one or both parts of the Real Estate Licensing Examination, the Applicant may retake the failed part(s) at a subsequent time.

* F.   Valid Testing Scores

* A passing score for either part of the Real Estate Licensing Examination is valid for one (1) year. Failure to submit a complete application within one (1) year will result in the examination grade being invalid.

* G.   No Certification of Examination Results until Licensed

* The Commission will not certify to any person, state, or agency any information concerning the results of any examination as it pertains to any person who has taken the Real Estate Licensing Examination unless such person is or has been licensed as a Broker.

* 2.3.   Criminal Background Check Requirements

* Pursuant to section 12-10-203(1)(b)(I), C.R.S., an Applicant must submit a set of fingerprints to the Colorado Bureau of Investigation for the purpose of conducting a state and national criminal history record check prior to submitting an application to the Division. Fingerprints must be submitted to the Colorado Bureau of Investigation for processing in a manner acceptable to the Colorado Bureau of Investigation. Fingerprints must be readable and all personal identification data completed in a manner satisfactory to the Colorado Bureau of Investigation. The Commission may, however, acquire a name-based criminal history record check for an Applicant who has twice submitted to a fingerprint-based criminal history record check and whose fingerprints are unclassifiable.

* 2.4.   Certified License History Requirements

* An Applicant who has held a real estate license (e.g. real estate salesperson or broker) in any other Jurisdiction must file a certification of licensing history issued by each Jurisdiction where the Applicant is currently or was previously licensed to practice real estate with their application. The certificate must bear a date of not more than ninety (90) days prior to the submission date of the application.

* 2.5.   Experience Requirements

* A.   Associate Broker Level License

* Pursuant to section 12-10-203, C.R.S., there are no prescribed experience requirements to apply for a Colorado Associate Broker level license.

* B.   Independent Broker Level License

* Pursuant to section 12-10-203(5)(c)(I), C.R.S., each Applicant for a Colorado Independent Broker level license must have held an Associate Broker level license on Active status for at least two (2) years preceding the date of application.

* C.   Employing Broker Level License

* 1.   Held a Real Estate Broker License on December 31, 1996

Pursuant to section 12-10-203(5)(c), C.R.S., a Broker that held a current and valid Colorado Real Estate Broker's license on December 31, 1996 does not need to demonstrate additional experience and knowledge to act as an Employing Broker.

2. Issued an Employing Broker Level License prior to January 1, 2018 but after December 31, 1996

Pursuant to section 12-10-203(5)(c)(III), C.R.S., an Applicant that was issued an Employing Broker level license prior to January 1, 2018 but after December 31, 1996 must demonstrate additional experience and knowledge by satisfying one of the following requirements:

a. The Applicant must have held an Active Employing Broker level license for at least two (2) years within the five (5) year period immediately preceding January 1, 2019;

b. Proof of completion of classroom instruction or equivalent Distance Learning hours for the Employing Broker Refresher Course; or

c. The Applicant meets the experience requirements as set forth in subsection C.3. of this Rule.

3. Applying for an Employing Broker Level License on or after January 1, 2018

Pursuant to section 12-10-203(5)(c)(III), C.R.S., each Applicant for an Employing Broker level license who applies on or after January 1, 2018 must submit evidence satisfactory to the Commission that the Applicant has practiced as an Active Broker, as appropriate to the Broker's area of supervision, for at least two (2) years within the five (5) year period immediately preceding the date of application.

a. The evidence must qualify the Applicant for a total of at least fifty (50) points having accumulated within the five (5) year period immediately preceding the date of application, based on the following point system:

i. Each full year that the Applicant has practiced as an Employing Broker is worth ten (10) points.

ii. Each full year that the Applicant was delegated supervisory authority from an Employing Broker that included responsibility for ensuring compliance with the Commission statutes and these Rules, and that ensured responsibility for the Brokerage Firm (excluding any mentorship) is worth five (5) points. A copy of the detailed executed delegation of authority must be included.

iii. Each hour of an approved and designated continuing education course in the Broker's area of expertise completed after January 1, 2018, is worth one (1) point. This educational point category cannot exceed twenty (20) points.

iv. Each completed or closed residential sales transaction is worth three (3) points.

v. Each completed or closed commercial sales transaction is worth six (6) points.

vi. Each completed or closed vacant land sales transaction is worth six (6) points.

vii. Each administered commercial property management transaction is worth four (4) points.

viii. Each administered residential property management transaction with two (2) points.

ix. Each completed or closed commercial lease transaction is worth two (2) points.

x. Each completed or closed residential lease transaction is worth one (1) point.

xi. Each completed or closed time share sales transaction is worth two (2) points.

b. Each Applicant must complete and submit the prescribed worksheet or form developed by the Commission and supporting documents with the application for an Employing Broker level license.

2.6. Associate Broker Level License Requirements

Applicants applying for an Associate Broker level license must satisfy the licensure requirements as set forth in one of the following:

A. New License

Pursuant to section 12-10-203(4)(a), C.R.S, an Applicant who has never held a real estate license in Colorado or any other Jurisdiction must complete the following requirements:

1. Proof of completion of the educational requirements as set forth in Rule 2.1.A.;

2. Successful completion of the Real Estate Licensing Examination as set forth in Rule 2.2.A.; and

3. Submission of fingerprints as set forth in Rule 2.3.

B. Licensed Attorney

Pursuant to section 12-10-203(10), C.R.S., an Applicant who is a licensed attorney in Colorado or any other Jurisdiction must complete the following requirements:

1. Proof of completion of twelve (12) hours of classroom instruction or equivalent Distance Learning hours for the following courses:

a. Real Estate Closings as set forth in Rule 2.1.A.2.c.; and

b. Trust Accounts and Record Keeping as set forth in Rule 2.1.A.2.d.

2. Successful completion of the Real Estate Licensing Examination as set forth in Rule 2.2.A.;

3. Submission of fingerprints as set forth in Rule 2.3.; and

4. Proof of law license.

C. Expired or Less than Two Years as a Real Estate Salesperson from Another Jurisdiction

Pursuant to section 12-10-203(4)(c), C.R.S., an Applicant holding a real estate salesperson license from another Jurisdiction that is either expired or held for less than two (2) years must complete the following requirements:

1. Proof of completion of classroom instruction or equivalent Distance Learning hours for the following courses:

a. Colorado Real Estate Contracts as set forth in Rule 2.1.A.2.b.;

b. Real Estate Closings as set forth in Rule 2.1.A.2.c.;

c. Trust Accounts and Record Keeping as set forth in Rule 2.1.A.2.d.;

d. Current Legal Issues as set forth in Rule 2.1.A.2.e.; and

e. Practical Application as set forth in Rule 2.1.A.2.f.

2. Successful completion of the Real Estate Licensing Examination as set forth in Rule 2.2.A.;

3. Submission of fingerprints as required in Rule 2.3.; and

4. Submission of certified license history as set forth in Rule 2.4.

D. Expired or Less than Two Years as a Real Estate Broker from another Jurisdiction

Pursuant to section 12-10-203(4)(b), C.R.S., an Applicant holding a real estate broker license from another Jurisdiction that is either expired or held for less than two (2) years must complete the following requirements:

*   1. Proof of completion of classroom instruction or equivalent Distance Learning hours for the following courses:
*   a. Colorado Real Estate Contracts as set forth in Rule 2.1.A.2.b.; and
*   b. Real Estate Closings as set forth in Rule 2.1.A.2.c.
*   2. Successful completion of the Real Estate Licensing Examination as set forth in Rule 2.2.A.;
*   3. Submission of fingerprints as required in Rule 2.3.; and
*   4. Submission of certified license history as set forth in Rule 2.4.

*   E. Current Real Estate License from Another Jurisdiction Held for Two or More Years

*   Pursuant to section 12-10-203(5)(b), C.R.S., an Applicant holding a real estate license (e.g. real estate salesperson or broker), whether on Active or Inactive status, for two (2) or more years from another Jurisdiction must complete the following requirements:
*   1. There are no prescribed educational requirements;
*   2. Successful completion of the Real Estate Licensing Examination as set forth in Rule 2.2.A.2.;
*   3. Submission of fingerprints as set forth in Rule 2.3.; and
*   4. Submission of certified license history as set forth in Rule 2.4.

*   F. Expired Colorado Associate Broker Level License Issued After January 1, 1997

*   Pursuant to section 12-10-203, C.R.S., an Applicant who was issued a Colorado Associate Broker level license on or after January 1, 1997 that is expired beyond the three-year right to reinstate must complete the following requirements:
*   1. Verification by the Commission that the Associate Broker level license was issued by the Commission on or after January 1, 1997 to confirm prior completion of the educational requirements as set forth in Rule 2.1.A.;
*   2. Successful completion of the Real Estate Licensing Examination as set forth in Rule 2.2.A.; and
*   3. Submission of fingerprints as set forth in Rule 2.3.

*   G. Expired Colorado Salesperson License Issued on or before December 31, 1996

*   Pursuant to section 12-10-203, C.R.S., an Applicant who was issued a Colorado real estate salesperson license on or before December 31, 1996 that is expired beyond the three-year right to reinstate must complete the following requirements:
*   1. Proof of completion of classroom instruction or equivalent Distance Learning hours for the following courses:
*   a. Colorado Real Estate Contracts as set forth in Rule 2.1.A.2.b.;
*   b. Real Estate Closings as set forth in Rule 2.1.A.2.c.;
*   c. Trust Accounts and Record Keeping as set forth in Rule 2.1.A.2.d.;
*   d. Current Legal Issues as set forth in Rule 2.1.A.2.e.; and
*   e. Practical Application as set forth in Rule 2.1.A.2.f.
*   2. Successful completion of the Real Estate Licensing Examination as set forth in Rule 2.2.A.; and
*   3. Submission of fingerprints as set forth in Rule 2.3.

*   H. Expired Colorado Real Estate Broker License Issued on or before December 31, 1996

*   Pursuant to section 12-10-203, C.R.S., an Applicant who was issued a Colorado real estate broker license on or before December 31, 1996 that is expired beyond the three-year right to reinstate must complete the following requirements:

    1. Proof of completion of classroom instruction or equivalent Distance Learning hours for the following courses:

        a. Colorado Real Estate Contracts as set forth in Rule 2.1.A.2.b.; and

        b. Real Estate Closings as set forth in Rule 2.1.A.2.c.

    2. Successful completion of the Real Estate Licensing Examination as set forth in Rule 2.2.A.; and

    3. Submission of fingerprints as set forth in Rule 2.3.

2.7. Independent Broker Level License Requirements

A. Initial Licensure as an Independent Broker Level License

An Applicant with at least two (2) years of Active licensure as a Broker in either Colorado or another Jurisdiction preceding the date of application may apply for an Independent Broker level license by completing the applicable licensure requirements as set forth in Rule 2.6.

B. Upgrade to an Independent Broker Level License

Pursuant to section 12-10-203(5)(c)(I), C.R.S, an Applicant may apply to upgrade to an Independent Broker level license as set forth in Rule 2.5.B.

2.8. Employing Broker Level License Requirements on or after January 1, 2018

A. Initial Licensure as an Employing Broker Level License

An Applicant with at least two (2) years of Active licensure as a Broker in either Colorado or another Jurisdiction preceding the date of application may apply for an Employing Broker level license by completing the applicable licensure requirements as set forth in Rule 2.6. and subsection B. of this Rule.

B. Upgrade to an Employing Broker Level License

Pursuant to section 12-10-203(5)(c), C.R.S, an Applicant who applies to upgrade to an Employing Broker level license on or after January 1, 2018 must complete the following requirements:

    1. Educational Requirement

Proof of completion of classroom instruction or equivalent Distance Learning hours for Brokerage Administration as set forth in Rule 2.1.B.

    2. Experience Requirement

Submission of evidence as set forth in Rule 2.5.C. that the Applicant has practiced as an Active Broker, as appropriate to the Broker's area of supervision, for at least two (2) years within the five (5) year period immediately preceding the date of application.

    3. Criminal Background Check Requirement

Submission of fingerprints as set forth in Rule 2.3. for any Applicants who did not submit fingerprints with their Initial License.

    4. Certified License History

For Applicants licensed in another Jurisdiction, submission of certified license history as set forth in Rule 2.4.

2.9. Broker Qualifications for Sole Proprietors

A. The Broker must have either an Independent Broker or Employing Broker level license.

B. A Broker licensed as a sole proprietorship must not adopt a trade name, which includes the following words: corporation, partnership, limited liability company, limited, incorporated, or the abbreviations thereof.

C.   A Broker licensed as a sole proprietorship or as a sole proprietorship doing business under a trade name must be the sole owner of the Brokerage Firm. Otherwise, the Brokerage Firm will be considered as a partnership and the partnership must apply for a Broker's License pursuant to section 12-10-203(6), C.R.S. and as set forth in Rule 2.10.

2.10.   Broker Qualifications for Partnerships, Corporations, or Limited Liability Companies

A.   When an Independent Broker or Employing Broker submits an application to qualify a partnership, corporation, or limited liability company as a Brokerage Firm, the Applicant must certify:

1. The partnership, corporation, or limited liability company has been properly registered with the Colorado Secretary of State and is in good standing, proof of which must be included with the application;

2. If an assumed or trade name is to be used, it has been properly filed with and accepted by the Colorado Secretary of State, proof of which must be included with the application; and

3. The Independent Broker or Employing Broker has been appointed as the Independent Broker or Employing Broker by the appropriate authority of the applicable Brokerage Firm.

B.   Notice of Termination of the Employing Broker

The Employing Broker of a licensed corporation, partnership, or limited liability company must immediately notify the Commission in a manner acceptable to the Commission, of the Employing Broker's termination of employment with such licensed corporation, partnership, or limited liability company, or upon the Employing Broker's failure to continue to comply with section 12-10-203, C.R.S. and these Rules. Upon such notification, the Employing Broker and all Associate Brokers will be placed on Inactive status.

C.   Temporary Employing Broker Level License

A Temporary License may be issued to a corporation, partnership or limited liability company to prevent hardship. No application for a Temporary License will be approved unless the designated person satisfies the licensure requirements of an Employing Broker. A Temporary License is valid for up to ninety (90) days. No more than two (2) Temporary Licenses may be issued to any corporation, partnership, or limited liability company, whether consecutive or not, during any eighteen (18) month period.

Chapter 3: Licensure, Renewal, License Status, and Insurance

3.1.   Application Requirements

A.   Applying for an Initial License

1. An Applicant must successfully complete the requisite educational requirements as set forth in Chapter 2 of these Rules;

2. An Applicant must take and successfully pass the appropriate part(s) of the Real Estate Licensing Examination as set forth in Chapter 2 of these Rules;

3. An Applicant must submit a set of fingerprints to the Colorado Bureau of Investigation as set forth in Rule 2.3.;

4. An Applicant must acquire errors and omissions insurance as set forth in Rule 3.9. prior to obtaining an Active License;

5. An Applicant must complete the appropriate Commission created application and submit the required documentation, such as course completion certificates or college transcripts, certified license history, and proof of errors and omissions insurance; and

6. An Applicant must pay the Fee.

*   B.   Upgrading a License Level

*   1.   An Applicant must successfully complete the educational and experience requirements as set forth in Chapter 2 of these Rules;

*   2.   An Applicant must complete the appropriate Commission created application and submit any relevant required documentation, such as course completion certificates and experience requirements, as set forth in Chapter 2 of these Rules; and

*   3.   An Applicant must pay the Fee.

* **3.2. Invalid Payment**

*   If the Fees accompanying any application made to the Commission are paid for by check and the check is not immediately paid upon presentment to the bank upon which the check was drawn, or if payment is submitted in any other manner and payment is denied, rescinded, or returned as invalid, the application will not be deemed complete and will be canceled. The application, renewal, or transfer may be reinstated only at the discretion of the Commission and upon full payment of any Fees together with payment of the fee required by state fiscal rules for the clerical services necessary for reinstatement within thirty (30) days of the Division's notification of an incomplete application.

* **3.3. Review of Application Completeness**

*   All applications will be reviewed by the Division for completeness of all required documentation and Fee. If the application is deemed incomplete by the Division, the Applicant will be notified in writing of the deficiencies identified within the application and will have thirty (30) days to provide the documentation; otherwise, the application will be canceled and the Fee will be forfeited.

* **3.4. Applicants with Prior or Pending Criminal Record**

*   Pursuant to sections 12-10-203, and 24-5-101, C.R.S., Applicants who have at any time in the past been convicted of, entered a plea of guilty to, entered a plea of nolo contendere, received a deferred judgment and sentence to a misdemeanor (excluding misdemeanor traffic violations) or a felony or any like municipal code violation, or has such charges pending must submit with their application the required documentation as listed below. If the required documentation is no longer available, the Applicant must provide written confirmation by the appropriate authority that such documentation is no longer available. For any charges or convictions which have been dismissed, expunged, or sealed, the Applicant must include court document(s) evidencing the dismissal, expungement, or sealing of the criminal case(s). Failure to provide the required documentation within the time frame as set forth in Rule 3.3. will result in the cancellation of the application and forfeiture of the Fee. In addition to the required documentation, Applicants may submit supplemental documentation as listed below to demonstrate their rehabilitation, truthfulness, honesty, and good moral character for consideration by the Commission.

*   A.   Required Documentation includes:

*   1.   Court case disposition, registry of action, or a case action summary, which must include the following information:

*   a.   Offense(s) convicted of;

*   b.   Statute(s) or municipal code(s) violated;

*   c.   Classification(s) of offense(s) (i.e. felony or misdemeanor);

*   d.   Date of conviction;

*   e.   Date of sentencing;

*   f.   Sentencing terms; and

*   g.   Status of case.

i. If the sentencing and probation terms have been completed, the status of case should show as closed or dismissed.

ii. If the sentencing and probation terms have not been completed, documentation must be submitted that shows current compliance with the sentencing and probation terms. Proof of current compliance should include a letter from the parole or probation officer and, if applicable, a payment history from the court showing a current account balance of payment.

2. Police Officer's report(s), arrest report(s), or incident report(s);

3. A signed written explanation of the circumstances surrounding each violation and, including the statement attesting that "I have no other criminal violations either past or pending, other than those I have stated on the application";

4. If applying for an Active License, a signed written statement from the Employing Broker that indicates their understanding of the nature of the Applicant's violation(s) and willingness to supervise the Applicant if the License is granted by the Commission. The statement must also include the level of supervision, either a Reasonable or a High-Level of Supervision, that the Employing Broker feels is appropriate based upon the Applicant's violation(s). The Employing Broker may include additional comments relating to the Applicant's rehabilitation, truthfulness, honesty, and good moral character for the Commission's consideration; and

5. Any other information or documentation that the Commission deems necessary.

B. Supplemental Documentation includes:

1. Employment history for the preceding five (5) years;

2. Letter(s) of recommendation; and

3. A personal written statement that demonstrates and evidences the Applicant's rehabilitation, truthfulness, honesty, and good moral character.

3.5. Applicants with Past or Pending Professional Disciplinary Action(s)

Pursuant to sections 12-10-202 and 12-10-203(3), C.R.S., an Applicant who has any past or pending disciplinary actions of a real estate license or any other professional license from Colorado or any other jurisdiction must submit with their application any of the following information and documentation as listed below that is relevant and available to the Applicant. If the required documentation is no longer available or accessible, the Applicant must provide written confirmation by the appropriate authority that such documentation is no longer available or the reasons why the document is not accessible. Failure to provide the required documentation within the time frame as set forth in Rule 3.3. will result in the cancellation of the application and forfeiture of the Fee.

A. Any final agency order(s);

B. Any consent order(s);

C. Any stipulation(s);

D. Any investigative report(s); and

E. A signed written explanation of the circumstances surrounding each disciplinary action.

3.6. Issuance of a License

A. Submission of an application does not guarantee issuance of a License. Applicants must not represent themselves as a Broker until a License has been issued by the Commission.

B. Once an application is deemed complete and not subject to further review as set forth in Rules 3.4. and 3.5., the Commission will issue a License within ten (10) business days after review of satisfactory results from the fingerprint-based criminal history record check, if applicable.

*   C.   Each Applicant who has successfully satisfied the licensure requirements as set forth in Chapter 2 of these Rules will be issued an Initial License expiring December 31 of the year of issuance.

*   D.   A License may be issued on an Inactive status.

*   E.   The License of a Broker whose application has been approved by the Commission subject to the receipt of errors and omission insurance and/or the identification of an Employing Broker for supervision will be issued on an Inactive status if such proof is not submitted within thirty (30) days after written notification by the Commission.

*   F.   The Commission may refuse to issue a License to a partnership, limited liability company, or corporation if the name of said corporation, partnership, or limited liability company is the same as that of any person or entity whose License has been suspended or revoked or is so similar as to be easily confused with that of the suspended or revoked person or entity by members of the general public.

*   G.   An Independent Broker or Employing Broker may adopt a Trade Name according to Colorado law and such Trade Name will respectively appear in the records of the Commission relating to the Independent Broker or Employing Broker. If an Employing Broker adopts a Trade Name, both the legal name and Trade Name will appear in the records of the Commission for the Associate Brokers.

*   H.   No License will be issued to an Independent or Employing Broker under a Trade Name, corporate name, partnership name, or limited liability company name which is identical to another licensed Independent Broker's or Employing Broker's Trade Name, corporate, partnership, or limited liability company name.

*   3.7.   Denial of a License

*   A.   The Commission may deny an application for licensure pursuant to section 12-10-203(3), C.R.S.

*   B.   If an Applicant for licensure is denied by the Commission for any reason, the Applicant will be informed of the denial and the reasons for the denial in writing.

*   3.8.   Preliminary Advisory Opinions

*   Prior to an application for licensure, a person may request that the Commission issue a preliminary advisory opinion regarding the potential effect that previous professional conduct, criminal conviction(s), plea(s) of guilt or nolo contendere, deferred judgment(s) and sentence for criminal offense(s), or violation(s) of the real estate license law may have on a future formal application for licensure. A person requesting such an opinion is not an Applicant for licensure. The Commission may, at its sole discretion, issue an opinion which will not be binding on the Commission; is not appealable; and will not limit the authority of the Commission to investigate a future application for licensure. However, if the Commission issues a favorable advisory opinion, the Commission may elect to adopt such advisory opinion as the final decision of the Commission without further investigation or hearing. The issuance of a negative or unfavorable opinion will not prohibit a person from submitting an application for licensure. A person requesting an opinion must do so in a form prescribed by the Commission. Such form must be supported and documented by, without limitation, the following:

*   A.   Pending or Past Criminal Record

*   The required and supplemental documentation as set forth in Rule 3.4. for any pending or past criminal record.

*   B.   Pending or Past Professional Disciplinary Action(s)

*   The documentation as set forth in Rule 3.5. for any pending or past professional conduct.

* 3.9. Errors and Omissions Insurance

* Pursuant to section 12-10-204, C.R.S., every Active Broker, including Brokerage Firms with more than one (1) Broker, must have in effect a policy of errors and omissions insurance to cover all acts requiring a License.

* A. The Division must enter into a contract with a qualified insurance carrier to make available a group policy of insurance ("Commission Insurance Policy") under the following terms and conditions:

* 1. The insurance carrier is licensed or authorized by the Colorado Division of Insurance to write policies of errors and omissions insurance in this State.

* 2. The insurance carrier maintains an A.M. Best rating of "A-" or better.

* 3. The insurance carrier will collect premiums, maintain records and report names of those insured and a record of claims to the Commission on a timely basis and at no expense to the Division.

* 4. The insurance carrier has been selected through a competitive bidding process.

* 5. The contract and policy are in conformance with this Rule and all relevant Colorado statutory requirements.

* B. The Commission Insurance Policy must provide, at a minimum, the following terms of coverage:

* 1. Coverage for all acts for which a License is required, except those illegal, fraudulent, or other acts which are normally excluded from such coverage.

* 2. That the coverage cannot be canceled by the insurance carrier except for nonpayment of the premium or in the event a Broker or Brokerage Firm becomes Inactive or is revoked or an Applicant is denied a License.

* 3. Pro-ration of premiums for coverage which is purchased during the course of a calendar year but with no provision for refunds of unused premiums.

* 4. Not less than one hundred thousand dollars ($100,000) coverage for each licensed person and entity per covered claim regardless of the number of Brokers or Brokerage Firms to which a settlement or claim may apply, not including costs of investigation and defense.

* 5. An annual aggregate limit of not less than three hundred thousand dollars ($300,000) per licensed Broker or Brokerage Firm, not including costs of investigation and defense.

* 6. Coverage for investigation and defense must be provided in addition to policy coverage limits.

* 7. A deductible amount for each occurrence of not more than one thousand dollars ($1,000) for claims and no deductible for legal expenses and defense.

* 8. The obligation of the insurance carrier to defend all covered claims and the ability of the insured Broker or Brokerage Firm to select counsel of choice subject to the written permission of the carrier, which must not be unreasonably withheld.

* 9. Coverage of a Broker's use of lock boxes, which coverage must not be less than twenty-five thousand dollars ($25,000) per occurrence.

* 10. The ability of a Broker or Brokerage Firm, upon payment of an additional premium, to obtain higher or excess coverage or to purchase additional coverage from the state carrier as may be determined by the carrier.

* 11. That coverage is individual and license specific and will cover the Broker or Brokerage Firm regardless of changes in Employing Broker.

12. The ability of a Broker or Brokerage Firm, upon payment of an additional premium to obtain an extended reporting period of not less than three hundred sixty-five (365) days.

13. A conformity endorsement allowing a Colorado resident Broker to meet the errors and omissions insurance requirement for a real estate license in another group mandated jurisdiction without the need to purchase separate coverage in that jurisdiction.

14. Prior acts coverage will be offered to Brokers or Brokerage Firms with continuous past coverage.

C.   Brokers, Brokerage Firms, or Applicants may obtain errors and omissions coverage independent of the Commission Insurance Policy from any insurance carrier subject to the following terms and conditions:

1. For both individual and entity/group policies, the insurance carrier is in compliance with all applicable statutes and rules set forth by the Colorado Division of Insurance and is licensed or authorized to write policies of errors and omissions insurance in this State.

2. The insurance provider maintains an A.M. Best rating of "A-" or better.

3. Individual policies must, at a minimum, comply with the following conditions and the insurance carrier must certify compliance in an affidavit issued to the insured Broker, Brokerage Firm, or Applicant in a form specified by the Commission. Insurance carrier agrees to immediately notify the Commission of any cancellation or lapse in coverage. Independent individual coverage must provide, at a minimum, the following:

    a. The contract and policy are in conformance with all relevant Colorado statutory requirements.

    b. Coverage includes all acts for which a License is required, except those illegal, fraudulent, or other acts that are normally excluded from such coverage.

    c. Coverage cannot be canceled by the insurance carrier except for nonpayment of the premium or in the event a Broker or Brokerage Firm becomes Inactive or is revoked or an Applicant is denied a License. Cancellation notice must be provided in a manner that complies with section 10-4-109.7(1), C.R.S.

    d. Coverage is for not less than one hundred thousand dollars ($100,000) for each licensed Broker and Brokerage Firm per covered claim, with an annual aggregate limit of not less than three hundred thousand dollars ($300,000) per licensed person and entity, not including costs of investigation and defense. Coverage for investigation and defense must be provided in addition to policy coverage limits.

    e. A deductible amount for each occurrence of not more than one thousand dollars ($1,000) for claims and the insurance carrier must look to the insured for payment of any deductible.

    f. Payment of defense costs by the insurance carrier must be on a first dollar basis. That is, the insured is not required to pay anything towards the cost of defense of any claim or complaint.

    g. The ability of a Broker or Brokerage Firm, upon payment of an additional premium, to obtain an extended reporting period of not less than three hundred sixty-five (365) days within sixty (60) days of the initial coverage ending.

    h. Coverage of a Broker's use of lock boxes, which coverage must not be less than twenty-five thousand dollars ($25,000) per occurrence.

i. The obligation of the insurance carrier to defend all covered claims and the ability of the insured Broker or Brokerage Firm to select counsel of choice subject to the written permission of the carrier, which must not be unreasonably withheld.

j. Prior acts coverage must be offered to Brokers or Brokerage Firms with continuous past coverage.

k. Upon request, insurance carrier will execute an affidavit in a form and manner specified by the Commission attesting that the independent policy is in force and, at a minimum, complies with all relevant conditions set forth in this Rule and that the insurance carrier will immediately notify the Commission in writing of any cancellation or lapse in coverage of any independent policy.

4. For Brokerage Firms with independently carried firm coverage, all the requirements as set forth in subsection C.3. of this Rule will apply except subsections C.3.d. through e. and j. of this Rule, will be replaced with the following:

a. The per claim limit must be not less than a million dollars ($1,000,000).

b. The aggregate limit must be not less than a million dollars ($1,000,000).

c. The maximum deductible amount for each occurrence must not exceed ten thousand dollars ($10,000) and the insurance carrier must look to the insured for payment of any deductible.

D. Applicants for licensure, activation, renewal, and Reinstatement must certify compliance with this Rule and section 12-10-204, C.R.S. in a manner prescribed by the Commission. Any Active Broker or Brokerage Firm who so certifies and fails to obtain errors and omissions coverage or to provide proof of continuous coverage, either through the state carrier or directly to the Commission, will be placed on Inactive status:

1. Immediately, if certification of current insurance coverage is not provided to the Commission; or

2. Immediately upon the expiration of any current insurance when certification of continued coverage is not provided.

3.10. Office

Every Independent Broker or Employing Broker residing in Colorado must maintain a place of business in this State, except for Associate Brokers or Brokers registered as Inactive.

3.11. Renewal

A. No Renewal Requirement for Brokerage Firms

Brokerage Firms are not required to renew their License; however, the Independent Broker or Employing Broker associated with the Brokerage Firm must renew as set forth in Rule 3.11.B.

B. Renewal Requirements for Brokers

1. Licensing Cycle for Renewal (Renewal Periods)

a. Initial Licenses Issued on or after January 1, 2018

Brokers who were issued an Initial License on or after January 1, 2018 will renew a License on a Calendar Year Cycle commencing on January 1 of year one and expiring on December 31 of year three.

b. Initial Licenses Issued Prior to January 1, 2018

For Brokers who were issued an Initial License prior to January 1, 2018, the Commission will renew a License expiring on the anniversary date in the years of 2018, 2019, or 2020, for a period of time equal to two years plus the remaining days in the third year to reach December 31. Thereafter, Brokers will renew a

License on a Calendar Year Cycle commencing on January 1 of year one and expiring on December 31 of year three.

2. Notification of Renewal

   Notification that a License will expire, unless renewed, will be sent to the electronic mail address on file with the Commission.

3. Renewal Application

   a. All Brokers, whether on Active or Inactive status, may renew their License beginning forty-five (45) days prior to the expiration date of their License by use of the renewal application form provided by the Commission.

   b. Pay the renewal Fee.

   c. Any Broker who has not submitted fingerprints to the Colorado Bureau of Investigation to be used to complete a one-time only criminal history record check must do so prior to renewal of an Active License. Fingerprints must be submitted to the Colorado Bureau of Investigation for processing in a manner acceptable to the Colorado Bureau of Investigation. Fingerprints must be readable and all personal identification data completed in a manner satisfactory to the Colorado Bureau of Investigation. The Commission may, however, acquire a name-based criminal history record check for an Applicant who has twice submitted to a fingerprint-based criminal history record check and whose fingerprints are unclassifiable. The renewed License will remain on Inactive status until the Commission has received and reviewed the results of a criminal record check.

3.12. Inactivation of License

A. A Broker may request that the Commission records show their License as Inactive until proper request for reactivation has been made.

B. It is the joint duty of both the Employing Broker and the Associate Broker to immediately notify the Commission when the employment of the Associate Broker terminates with the Brokerage Firm. Either party may give notice in a manner acceptable to the Commission. The party giving notice must notify the other party in person or in writing of the termination of employment.

C. A Broker whose License is on Inactive status must apply for renewal of such Inactive License and pay the renewal Fee.

D. A Broker whose License is on Inactive status may be compensated directly by a former Employing Broker for commissions earned during the term of employment when the Broker's License was on Active status.

3.13. Change in License Status

No changes in License status, whether Active or Inactive, will be made except in the manner acceptable to the Commission to affect such change and upon payment of the Fee for such change request.

3.14. Transfers

A. When an Associate Broker transfers to a different Brokerage Firm, the License must be transferred to the subsequent Employing Broker in the manner acceptable to the Commission to affect such transfer and upon payment of the Fee for such transfer request.

B. When a License has been transferred to a subsequent Employing Broker, an Associate Broker may be compensated directly by the former Employing Broker for commissions earned during that term of employment.

* 3.15. Transition Period License Reinstatement

* For Brokers who failed to renew a License that was initially issued prior to January 1, 2018 may Reinstate the Expired License as follows:

* A. If a proper application is made within thirty-one (31) days after the date of expiration of a License, by payment of the renewal Fee, the License will be issued as set forth in Rule 3.11.B.3.

* B. If a proper application is made more than thirty-one (31) days but within one (1) year after the date of expiration of a License, by payment of the renewal Fee and payment of a reinstatement Fee equal to one-half (1/2) the renewal Fee, the License will be issued with an expiration date of December 31 of the year of issuance. Thereafter, a Broker will renew a License on a Calendar Year Cycle commencing on January 1 of year one and expiring on December 31 of year three.

* C. If a proper application is made more than one (1) year but within three (3) years after the date of expiration of a License, by payment of the renewal Fee and payment of a reinstatement Fee equal to the renewal Fee, the License will be issued with an expiration date of December 31 of the year of issuance. Thereafter, a Broker will renew a License on a Calendar Year Cycle commencing on January 1 of year one and expiring on December 31 of year three.

* **Chapter 4: Continuing Education Requirement**

* 4.1. Continuing Education Requirement

* A. Brokers must satisfy the continuing education requirement for a licensing cycle prior to applying to renew an Active License, to activate an Inactive License, or to Reinstate an Expired License to Active status. The licensing cycles include: Anniversary Year, Calendar Year, and Transition Period.

* B. Pursuant to section 12-10-213(4), C.R.S., Brokers applying for renewal of a License which expires on December 31 of the year in which it was first issued are not subject to the continuing education requirement pursuant to section 12-10-213(1)(a), C.R.S.

* 4.2. Methods for Satisfying Continuing Education

* A. Brokers must satisfy the continuing education requirement for a licensing cycle through one (1) of the following options:

* 1. Brokers may complete the twelve (12) credit hours of continuing education pursuant to section 12-10-213(1)(a), C.R.S. and as set forth in subsection A.1. of this Rule in annual 4-hour increments developed by the Commission, the "Annual Commission Update". Brokers must also complete an additional twelve (12) credit hours of electives to meet the total 24-hour continuing education requirement during the licensing cycle in subject areas pursuant to section 12-10-213(3), C.R.S. and as set forth in Rule 4.4.B.1. A Broker may not take the same version of the Annual Commission Update more than once.

* 2. During the Transition Period licensing cycle, Brokers may complete two (2) different versions of the Annual Commission Update for eight (8) credit hours of continuing education pursuant to section 12-10-213(1)(b), C.R.S. Brokers must also complete an additional sixteen (16) credit hours of electives to meet the total 24-hour continuing education requirement during the Transition Period in subject areas pursuant to section 12-10-213(3), C.R.S. and as set forth in Rule 4.4.B.1.

* 3. Brokers may complete the Commission approved 24-hour "Broker Reactivation Course". This option is only available to Brokers under one (1) of the following conditions:

a. The Broker is currently Active and did not use the Broker Reactivation Course to satisfy the continuing education requirement in the previous licensing cycle; or

b. The Broker is Inactive or Expired for an accumulative time period of up to thirty-six (36) months prior to activating an Inactive License or Reinstating an Expired License to Active status and unable to comply with the continuing education requirement as set forth in subsections A.1. or A.2. of this Rule.

4. Pass the Colorado portion of the Real Estate Licensing Examination as set forth in Rule 2.2.A.2.

5. Complete seventy-two (72) total hours of the educational requirements as set forth in Rules 2.1.A.2.b. and 2.1.A.2.c.

B. If a Broker cannot satisfy the continuing education requirement as set forth in subsections A.1. through A.3. of this Rule, the Broker must comply with the continuing education requirement as set forth in subsections A.4. or A.5. of this Rule prior to activating an Inactive License or Reinstating an Expired License to Active status.

4.3. Annual Commission Update Course Standards

A. Pursuant to section 12-10-213(2), C.R.S. and as set forth in Rule 4.2.A., the Annual Commission Update will be developed, presented by the Division, and furnished only to approved course providers. The course will be presented without any additional content by the course provider and/or instructor.

B. All course providers must apply annually for approval to offer the Annual Commission Update as set forth in Rule 4.6.B., except that the course outline as set forth in Rule 4.6.B.1. and course exam as set forth in Rule 4.6.B.2. will be furnished by the Commission.

C. Each Broker must complete the Annual Commission Update by achieving a passing score of seventy percent (70%) on a written or on-line course examination developed by the Commission. The Commission will provide an alternate examination for successive use by Brokers failing the end-of-course examination.

4.4. Standards for Continuing Education Courses

Courses approved for continuing education must meet the following standards:

A. Course Content

1. The course content must have been developed by persons qualified in the subject matter;

2. The content of the course must be current;

3. The course must maintain and improve a Broker's skill, knowledge, and competency in the real estate practice; and

4. The course must be at least one (1) hour increment in length, containing at least fifty (50) instructional minutes per one (1) hour increment.

B. Topics for Continuing Education Courses

1. Eligible Topics for Continuing Education Courses

Pursuant to section 12-10-213(3), C.R.S., courses approved for continuing education must include one (1) or more of the following topics:

a. Real Estate Law;

b. Property Exchanges;

c. Real Estate Contracts;

d. Real Estate Finance;

e. Real Estate Appraisal;

          f.   Real Estate Closing;

          g.   Real Estate Ethics;

          h.   Condominiums and Cooperatives;

          i.   Real Estate Time-Sharing;

          j.   Real Estate Marketing Principles;

          k.   Real Estate Construction;

          l.   Land Development;

          m. Real Estate Energy Concerns;

          n.   Real Estate Geology;

          o.   Water and Waste Management;

          p.   Commercial Real Estate;

          q.   Real Estate Securities and Syndications;

          r.   Property Management;

          s.   Real Estate Computer Principles;

          t.   Brokerage Administration and Management;

          u.   Agency; and

          v.   Any other subject matter as approved by the Commission.

    2. Ineligible Topics for Continuing Education Courses

        The following types of courses will not qualify and be approved for continuing education:

        a.   Sales or marketing meetings conducted in the general course of a real estate brokerage practice;

        b.   Orientation, personal growth, self-improvement, self-promotion, or marketing sessions;

        c.   Motivational meetings or seminars; or

        d.   Examination preparation or exam technique courses.

 C.   Course Format

     All continuing education courses may be offered and completed by classroom or Distance Learning.

4.5. Continuing Education Credit Requirements

 A.   A maximum of eight (8) hours of credit may be earned per day.

 B.   No course may be repeated for credit in the same calendar year.

 C.   Hours in excess of twenty-four (24) may not be carried forward to satisfy a subsequent licensing cycle.

 D.   Education stipulated to between a Broker and the Commission as part of a disciplinary action or alternative to disciplinary action will not be accepted to fulfill a Broker's continuing education requirement.

 E.   All continuing education must be taken from course providers either approved by the Commission or exempt as set forth in Rule 4.6.A.2.

 F.   Brokers must complete an entire course to receive any continuing education credit. Brokers will not be awarded partial credit for partial or incomplete attendance.

 G.   Instructors may receive continuing education credit for teaching an approved course; however, credit will be awarded for only one (1) course taught per calendar year.

*   H.   The Commission will award two (2) hours of continuing education credit for Brokers who attend a Commission's public meeting in person under the following conditions:

1. The meeting must be open to the public and must be a minimum of two (2) hours in length;

*   2. The Broker must be present for at least a two (2) hour segment of the meeting to be eligible for elective credit; and

*   3. Elective credit will be awarded for a single Commission meeting per calendar year.

*   I.   Each Broker is responsible for securing from the course provider proof of course completion in the form of an affidavit, certificate, or official transcript of the course as set forth in Rule 4.7.A.

*   J.   Brokers must retain proof of continuing education completion certificates for four (4) years from the date of the Broker's most current renewal or, if newly licensed, from Initial Licensure.

*   K.   The act of submitting an application for renewal, activation, or Reinstatement of a License means that the Broker attests to compliance with the continuing education requirement pursuant to section 12-10-213, C.R.S. However, if a Broker did not comply with the continuing education requirement, the Broker must provide written notification to the Division prior to submitting an application for renewal, activation, or Reinstatement of a License.

*   L.   Upon written notification from the Commission, Brokers must provide proof of completion of the continuing education requirement in a manner that is acceptable to the Commission. Failure to provide said proof within the prescribed time set by the Commission in its notification will be grounds for disciplinary action unless the Commission has granted an extension.

*   4.6.   Process for Course Approval

*   A.   Course Providers

*   Continuing education must be taken from course providers either approved by the Commission or exempt as set forth in subsection A.2. of this Rule.

*   1. Approval of Course Providers

*   All course providers must receive approval from the Commission prior to any course offering except for the course providers specifically exempted as set forth in subsection A.2. of this Rule.

*   2. Course Providers Exempt from Commission Approval

*   The following course providers may provide course offerings for elective continuing education credit without Commission pre-approval only if the courses are within the topic areas pursuant to section 12-10-213(3), C.R.S. and as set forth in Rule 4.4.B.1. and comply with all other provisions of Chapter 4 of these Rules.

*   a.   Courses offered by accredited colleges, universities, community or junior colleges, public or parochial schools, or government agencies.

*   b.   Courses developed and offered by quasi-governmental agencies.

*   c.   Courses approved by and taken in satisfaction of another occupational licensing authority's education requirements.

*   d.   Courses in real property law by a provider approved by the Colorado Board of Continuing Legal and Judicial Education.

*   B.   Course providers must, as set forth in Chapter 4 of these Rules, submit an application form prescribed by the Commission, along with the following information at least thirty (30) days prior to the initial proposed course date(s):

1. Detailed course outline or syllabus, including the intended learning outcomes, the course objectives, and the approximate time allocated for each topic.

2. A copy of the course exam(s) and instructor answer sheet, if applicable.

3. Copy of the instructor's teaching credential; if none, a resume showing education and experience which evidence a mastery of the material to be presented.

4. Upon Commission request, a copy of any advertising or promotional material used to announce the offering.

5. Upon Commission request, a copy of any textbook, manual, audio or videotapes, or other instructional material.

6. Course providers of continuing education offered through Distance Learning must submit evidence in a form prescribed by the Commission that the method of delivery and course structure is consistent with acceptable educational principles assuring that the desired learning objectives are met. The Commission will approve methods of delivery certified by the Association of Real Estate License Law Officials (ARELLO), or by a substantially equivalent authority and method.

7. Course approval certification will be for a period of three (3) years, except that an annual or one-time seminar or conference offering may be approved for a specific date or dates.

4.7. Course Provider Requirements

    A. Course providers must provide to each student who successfully completes an approved course for continuing education credit with an affidavit, certificate, or official transcript, which must include the following information:

        1. Name of the course provider;

        2. Course title, which must describe the topical content;

        3. Course number;

        4. Number of continuing education hours/credits;

        5. Course date(s);

        6. Name of the student;

        7. Authentication by the course provider; and

        8. Course approval number as issued by the Division, if applicable.

    B. A course provider may not waive, excuse completion of, or award partial credit for the full number of course hours.

    C. Each course provider must retain copies of course outlines or syllabi and complete records of attendance for a period of four (4) years from the date of the course and provide the records to the Commission upon request.

    D. By offering continuing education, each course provider agrees to comply with relevant Commission statutes and these Rules and to permit Commission audit of said courses at any time and at no cost. Failure to comply with the standards and requirements as set forth in Chapter 4 of these Rules may result in the invalidation of the course provider, instructor, and/or the course.

Chapter 5: Separate Accounts and Accounting

5.1. Establishment of Internal Accounting Controls

Any Brokerage Firm or Broker who receives Money Belonging to Others must establish written accounting control policies and procedures, which must include adequate checks and balances over the financial activities of the Broker, Brokerage Firm, and unlicensed persons, as well as manage the risk of fraud or illegal acts.

*   5.2.   Trust or Escrow Accounts

*   All Money Belonging to Others accepted by a Brokerage Firm must be deposited in one or more accounts separate from other money belonging to the Broker or Brokerage Firm. The Brokerage Firm must identify the fiduciary nature of each separate account in deposit agreements with a Recognized Depository by the use of the word "trust" or "escrow" and a label identifying the purpose of such account, such as "sales escrow", "rental escrow", "security deposit escrow", or other abbreviated form defined in the deposit agreement. The Brokerage Firm must retain a copy of each executed account deposit agreement for inspection by the Commission.

*   5.3.   Accounts in the Name of the Brokerage Firm or Broker

*   A.   Brokerage Firms acting in the name of the Employing Broker or Independent Broker as a sole- proprietor must maintain separate Trust or Escrow Accounts in the name of the Employing Broker or Independent Broker.

*   B.   Brokerage Firms licensed as a partnership, corporation, or limited liability company must maintain separate Trust or Escrow Accounts in the name of the licensed partnership, corporation, or limited liability company.

*   C.   The Employing Broker or Independent Broker are responsible for, must maintain and be able to withdraw money from each separate account, but may authorize other licensed or unlicensed cosigners. However, such authorization will not relieve the Employing Broker or Independent Broker of any responsibility under the Commission statutes and these Rules.

*   5.4.   Number of Separate Trust or Escrow Accounts may vary from Zero to Unlimited

*   A Brokerage Firm is not limited as to the number of separate accounts, which may be maintained for Money Belonging to Others. If the Brokerage Firm is not in possession of Money Belonging to Others, there is no obligation to maintain a separate Trust or Escrow Account.

*   5.5.   Separate Trust or Escrow Accounts Required for Rental Receipts and Security Deposits

*   A Brokerage Firm who engages in Property Management must deposit rental receipts and security deposits and disburse money collected for such purposes in separate Trust or Escrow Accounts, a minimum of one for rental receipts and a minimum of one for security deposits.

*   5.6.   Trust or Escrow Funds must be Available Immediately without Penalty

*   Unless otherwise agreed to in writing by the parties, Money Belonging to Others must not be invested in any type of account, security, or certificate of deposit that has a fixed term for maturity or imposes any fee or penalty for withdrawal prior to maturity.

*   5.7.   Time Limits for Deposit of Money Belonging to Others

*   A.   All Money Belonging to Others received by a Brokerage Firm for Property Management must be deposited in the Brokerage Firm's appropriate Trust or Escrow Account no later than five (5) business days following receipt of funds or mutual execution of a lease, whichever is later.

*   B.   All other Money Belonging to Others which is received by a Brokerage Firm must be deposited in the Brokerage Firm's Trust or Escrow Account no later than three (3) business days following receipt of funds or mutual execution of contract, whichever is later.

*   5.8.   Transfer of Security Deposits

*   A.   Owner-Held

*   A Brokerage Firm receipting for security deposits will not deliver such security deposits to an owner without the tenant's written authorization in a lease or unless written notice has been given to the tenant. Such notice must be given in a manner so the tenant will know who is holding the security deposit and the specific requirements for the procedure in which the tenant may request return of the security deposit. If a security deposit is delivered to the owner, the Management Agreement should place financial responsibility on the owner for its return, and in the event of a dispute over ownership of the security deposit, must authorize disclosure to the tenant of the owner's true name and current mailing address.

B. New Property Management Company

A Brokerage Firm which begins management of a property most recently managed by another Brokerage Firm must disclose to the owner and the current tenant, in writing, and within thirty (30) days after execution of a Management Agreement, the status of any security deposit held by the previous Brokerage Firm, including the amount of the security deposit and confirmation of receipt of the funds. The Brokerage Firm must verify that each security deposit transferred to them matches the amount listed in the current lease and disclose any discrepancy to the owner and current tenant. The Brokerage Firm must inform the tenant, in writing, if the owner is holding the security deposit.

5.9. Diversion and Conversion Prohibited

Money Belonging to Others belonging to one beneficiary must not be used for the benefit of another beneficiary. Money Belonging to Others must not be used for the benefit of the Brokerage Firm or Broker.

5.10. Commingling Prohibited

A Broker's or Brokerage Firm's personal or business operating funds must not be commingled with Money Belonging to Others. One or more separate Trust or Escrow Accounts may be maintained by a Brokerage Firm pursuant to the following duties and limitations:

A. Money held in a Trust or Escrow Account which becomes due and payable to the Brokerage Firm must be withdrawn monthly.

B. Money advanced by a Brokerage Firm for the benefit of another may be placed in the Trust or Escrow Account and identified as an advance but may be withdrawn by the Brokerage Firm only on behalf of such person. Any amount advanced to a Trust or Escrow Account must be identified and recorded in the journal and the ledger and disclosed in accounting to the beneficiary as set forth in Rule 5.15.

C. In the absence of a specific written agreement to the contrary, commissions, fees, and other charges collected by a Brokerage Firm for performing any service on behalf of another are considered "earned" and available for use by the Brokerage Firm only after all contracted services have been performed and there is no remaining right of recall by others for such money. The Brokerage Firm must identify and record all commissions, fees, or other charges withdrawn from a Trust or Escrow Account on the account journal and individual ledgers of those against whom the fees or commissions are charged. If a single disbursement of fees or commissions includes more than one (1) transaction, rental period or occupancy or includes withdrawals from the account of more than one (1) Trust or Escrow Account beneficiary, the Brokerage Firm, upon request, must produce for inspection by the Commission a schedule which details:

1. The individual components of all amounts included in the sum of such disbursement; and

2. Specifically identifies the affected beneficiary or property ledgers as set forth in Rule 5.14.B.

D. Funds received by a Broker for managing Broker's own properties through the Broker's Brokerage Firm, including any Broker's properties held in partnership with others, joint ventures, or syndications subject to the Broker meeting the ownership threshold pursuant to section 12-10-201(6)(b), C.R.S. must be deposited in an account separate from any other Trust or Escrow Accounts maintained for Money Belonging to Others. Such funds are not subject to Trust or Escrow Accounts and record keeping requirements as set forth in Rules 5.2. and 5.14.

5.11. Earnest Money on New Construction

If a Broker is acting as a builder in a transaction, all deposit money received from a buyer must be placed in a Trust or Escrow Account and not used by the Broker for any purpose, including construction, unless the Broker receives written consent from the buyer.

5.12. Earnest Money

A. Any Broker receiving earnest money must deliver such earnest money to the earnest money holder to be deposited in accordance with the contract. The Broker must obtain a dated and signed receipt from the person or entity to whom the Broker has been instructed to deliver the deposit.

B. If the Brokerage Firm will be holding the earnest money in a transaction, the earnest money must be deposited as set forth in Rule 5.7.B. The Brokerage Firm may transfer the earnest money from the Brokerage Firm's Trust or Escrow Account to a lawyer or a closing entity closing the transaction. The Brokerage Firm delivering the earnest money deposit to a lawyer or a closing entity providing settlement services must obtain a dated and signed receipt from the person or entity providing settlement services.

5.13. Promissory Note for Earnest Money

If a promissory note is received as earnest money pursuant to an executed contract, the seller must be informed of the date such promissory note becomes due. If payment is not made by the due date of the promissory note, the Broker must promptly notify the seller and deliver the original promissory note.

5.14. Recordkeeping Requirements

An Employing Broker or Independent Broker must maintain, at the Brokerage Firm's licensed place of business, a record keeping system as set forth in Rule 5.16., consisting of at least the following elements for each required Trust or Escrow Account:

A. A "journal" or an equivalent accounting system which records, in chronological order, all Money Belonging to Others which is received or disbursed by the Brokerage Firm.

   1. For funds received, each journal record must include:

      a. The date of receipt and deposit;

      b. The name of the person who is giving the money;

      c. The name of the person and property for which the money was received;

      d. The purpose of the receipt;

      e. The amount; and

      f. A resulting cash balance for the account.

   2. For funds disbursed, each journal record must include:

      a. The date of payment;

      b. The check number or electronic transfer record;

      c. The name of the payee;

      d. A reference to vendor documentation or other physical records verifying purpose for payment;

      e. The amount paid; and

      f. Resulting cash balance for the account.

B. A "ledger" or an equivalent component of an accounting system which records, in chronological order, all money which is received or disbursed by the Broker on behalf of each particular beneficiary of a Trust or Escrow Account. The ledger record must show the monetary transactions affecting each individual beneficiary and must segregate such transactions from those pertaining to other beneficiaries of the Trust or Escrow Account. The ledger record for each beneficiary must contain the same transactional information as set forth in subsection A of this Rule. No ledger may ever be allowed to have a negative cash balance. The sum of all ledger balances must agree at all times with the corresponding journal after each transaction has been posted.

*   C.   Three-way reconciliation must be performed monthly to show that on the same date the cash balance shown in the journal, the sum of the cash balances for all ledgers, and the reconciled bank balance are the same. A three-way reconciliation report must be completed and maintained monthly to show such three-way reconciliation. The Broker is not required to maintain records or reconcile any Trust or Escrow Account when such account does not contain Money Belonging to Others.

*   D.   A Brokerage Firm may deposit personal funds as may be required to pay any bank charges incurred in connection with maintaining a Trust or Escrow Account without violating Rule 5.10. An entry showing such money must be made in the journal and on the ledger as set forth in subsections A and B of this Rule.

*   E.   The three-way reconciliation reports, ledgers, journals, and bank account statements may be kept electronically.

*   5.15.   Maintenance and Production of Reports to Beneficiaries

*   A.   Brokerage Firms holding Money Belonging to Others must provide detailed reports to each beneficiary. Any accounting report furnished to beneficiaries must be prepared and delivered according to the terms of the Management Agreement. In the absence of a provision in the Management Agreement to the contrary, Brokerage Firms must deliver these reports within thirty (30) days after the end of the month in which funds were either received or disbursed.

*   B.   The Brokerage Firm must maintain supporting records, which accurately detail all cash received and disbursed under the terms of any Management Agreement.

*   1.   All deposits of funds into a Trust or Escrow Account must identify each person tendering funds, the amount of funds tendered, types of funds received from each person, and the property address affected.

*   2.   All disbursements of funds from a Trust or Escrow Account must be supported by documents such as bids, invoices, contracts, etc. Ledger and journal records must identify the payees, property addresses affected and amount of funds transferred for each property.

*   5.16.   Method of Accounting

*   In the absence of a written agreement to the contrary, the "cash basis" of accounting must be used for maintaining all required Trust or Escrow Accounts and corresponding records. A Brokerage Firm may use another method of accounting if it is agreed upon in writing by the Brokerage Firm and the beneficiary. The Brokerage Firm must maintain separate Trust and Escrow Accounts and corresponding records for each beneficiary using a different accounting method.

*   5.17.   Mark-Ups

*   Pursuant to sections 12-10-217(1)(d) and (t) and 6-1-105, C.R.S., the Broker and Brokerage Firm must obtain prior written consent from the owner to assess and receive mark-ups and/or other compensation for services performed, regardless if for the benefit of the Broker or another third party. The Broker and Brokerage Firm must retain accurate on-going records, which verify disclosure and consent and which fully account for the amounts or percentages of compensation assessed or received.

* 5.18. Items in Lieu of Cash

* Any instrument, equity, or Thing of Value taken in lieu of cash must be held by the Brokerage Firm, except as otherwise agreed.

* 5.19. Branch Office Trust or Escrow Accounts Require Branch Office Recordkeeping

* In the event a branch office of a Brokerage Firm maintains a Trust or Escrow Account separate from the Trust or Escrow Account(s) maintained by the Brokerage Firm's main office, a separate record keeping system must be maintained in the branch office. The responsibility of maintaining separate record keeping systems will be the responsibility of the Employing Broker.

* 5.20. Money Collected by Brokerage Firm

* A. When money is collected by a Brokerage Firm for the performance of specific services or for the expenses of performing such services, or for any other expense, and such money is collected before the services have been performed, the Brokerage Firm must deposit such money in a Trust or Escrow Account pursuant to section 12-10-217(1)(i), C.R.S. No money may be withdrawn from the Trust or Escrow Account, except for authorized expenses for performing such services. A full and itemized accounting must be furnished as set forth in Rule 5.15.

* B. Nothing in this Rule will prohibit a Brokerage Firm from taking a non-refundable retainer that need not be deposited into a Trust or Escrow Account provided this be specifically agreed to in writing between the Brokerage Firm and the person paying the retainer.

* 5.21. Production of Documents and Records

* A Broker and Brokerage Firm must produce for inspection by the Commission any document or record as may be reasonably necessary for investigation or audit in the enforcement of the Commission statutes and these Rules. Failure to submit such documents or records within the time set by the Commission in its notification will be grounds for disciplinary action unless the Commission has granted an extension of time for such production.

* 5.22. Responsibility of the Employing Broker or Independent Broker for Brokerage Firm's Compliance

* The Employing Broker or Independent Broker are held jointly responsible with the Brokerage Firm in complying with Chapter 5 of these Rules.

* **Chapter 6: Practice Standards**

* 6.1. Real Estate License

* A. A License is nontransferable.

* B. Neither a Broker nor Brokerage Firm may lend their name or License for the benefit of another person, partnership, limited liability company, or corporation.

* C. Associate Brokers must not present or hold themselves out to the public as an Employing Broker or Independent Broker.

* D. An Employing Broker must not knowingly permit Associate Brokers to present or hold themselves out to the public as an Employing Broker or Independent Broker.

* E. A Broker must not procure or attempt to procure a License by fraud, misrepresentation, deceit, or by making a material misstatement of fact in an application for such License pursuant to section 12-10-217(1)(s), C.R.S.

* 6.2. Competency

* A. In order to conduct Real Estate Brokerage Services, a Broker must possess the necessary experience, training, and knowledge to provide Real Estate Brokerage Services and

maintain compliance with the applicable federal, state and local laws, rules, regulations and ordinances.

*   B.   If a Broker does not have the necessary experience, training, and knowledge, the Broker must:

*   1.   Decline to provide Real Estate Brokerage Services;

*   2.   Obtain the necessary experience, training, and knowledge;

*   3.   Obtain the assistance of their Employing Broker, Supervisory Broker, a Broker who meets the requirements as set forth in subsection A. of this Rule, or legal counsel that is competent in the matter; or

*   4.   Co-list with another Broker who meets the requirements as set forth in subsection A. of this Rule.

*   6.3.   Employing Broker's Responsibilities and Supervision

*   A.   Employing Broker Exercises Authority, Direction, and Supervision

*   1.   Employing Brokers must exercise authority, direction, and supervision over any Associate Brokers shown in the records of the Commission as supervised by the Employing Broker to ensure conformance to the Commission statutes and these Rules in the performance of the Associate Broker's activities pursuant to sections 12-10-203(5)(c)(I), 12-10-217(1)(r), and 12-10-222, C.R.S., and these Rules. Whenever a complaint is filed with the Commission against an Associate Broker, the Commission may investigate whether there have been violations of section 12- 10-217(1)(r), C.R.S. by the Employing Broker.

*   2.   Employing Brokers must also supervise, pursuant to section 12-10-222, C.R.S., all unlicensed employees, including, but not limited to, Unlicensed On-Site Managers, secretaries, bookkeepers, and personal assistants of Associate Brokers.

*   B.   Employing Broker's Responsibilities Employing Brokers must:

*   1.   Maintain all Trust and Escrow Accounts and records as set forth in Chapter 5 of these Rules;

*   2.   Maintain all transaction records as set forth in Rule 6.20.;

*   3.   Develop the Brokerage Firm's written policies as set forth in Rule 6.4.;

*   4.   Provide for a "Reasonable-Level of Supervision" for all Associate Brokers as set forth in subsection C. of this Rule;

*   5.   Provide for a "High-Level of Supervision" for New Associate Brokers as set forth in subsection D. of this Rule;

*   6.   Take reasonable steps to ensure that violations of statutes, rules, and office policies do not occur or reoccur; and

*   7.   Provide for adequate supervision of all branches or offices operated by the Employing Broker.

*   C.   "Reasonable-Level of Supervision" by Employing Brokers

*   Pursuant to section 12-10-217(1)(r), C.R.S., Employing Brokers are required to provide all Associate Brokers with a "Reasonable-Level of Supervision," which includes:

*   1.   Maintaining a written Office Policy Manual as set forth in Rule 6.4.B., which must:

*   a.   Be given to and signed by each Associate Broker; and

*   b.   Be available for inspection, upon request, by any authorized representative of the Commission.

2. Ensuring all executed contracts are reviewed to maintain assurance of competent preparation. If the Employing Broker has concerns about the preparation of a contract, Employing Broker should contact the Associate Broker.

3. Ensuring all transaction files are reviewed for the required documents. If required documents are not present, the Employing Broker should contact the Associate Broker.

D. "High-Level of Supervision" by Employing Brokers

In addition to the requirements of subsection C. of this Rule and pursuant to section 12-10- 203(5)(c)(I), C.R.S., an Employing Broker must provide a "High-Level of Supervision" for New Associate Brokers. "High-Level of Supervision" includes:

1. Providing specific training in office policies and procedures;

2. Being reasonably available for consultation;

3. Providing assistance in preparing contracts;

4. Monitoring transactions from contracting to closing;

5. Reviewing documents in preparation for closing; and

6. Ensuring that the Employing Broker or an experienced Associate Broker with more than two (2) years' Active licensure attends closings with a New Associate Broker or is available for assistance.

E. Supervision of Unlicensed On-Site Manager Employing Brokers must:

1. Actively and diligently supervise all activities of any Unlicensed On-Site Manager or delegate supervisory authority as set forth in subsection F. of this Rule;

2. Require the Unlicensed On-Site Manager to report directly to either the Employing Broker or a Supervisory Broker;

3. Require the Unlicensed On-Site Manager to account for and remit all monies, including rents and security deposits, collected on behalf of the Employing Broker or owner to the Employing Broker or Supervisory Broker;

4. Ensure that property maintenance scheduled by the Unlicensed On-Site Manager is performed in accordance with the Property Management Agreement; and

5. Instruct the Unlicensed On-Site Manager not to negotiate any of the material terms of a lease or rental agreement with a Consumer.

F. Delegation of Supervision

Employing Brokers may delegate supervisory authority to other experienced Associate Brokers for both "Reasonable-Level of Supervision" and "High-Level of Supervision" as follows:

1. Supervisory Brokers must bear responsibility along with the Employing Broker for ensuring compliance with the Commission statutes and these Rules for those persons the delegated Associate Broker is supervising.

2. Any delegation of authority must be in writing and signed by the Supervisory Broker. A copy of such delegation must be maintained by the Employing Broker for inspection, upon request, by any authorized Commission representative.

3. The Supervisory Broker must have competency as set forth in Rule 6.2. in the area of practice in which the Supervisory Broker is supervising.

4. An Employing Broker must not contract with any Associate Broker so as to circumvent the requirement that the Employing Broker supervise Associate Brokers. While an Employing Broker may delegate supervision duties, the Employing Broker is still ultimately responsible for the supervision provided.

*   G.   Confidential Information Revealed to Employing Broker or Supervisory Broker

*   Associate Brokers may reveal to an Employing Broker or a Supervisory Broker confidential information about the Associate Broker's client. Associate Brokers' disclosure of such confidential information does not change or extend the Brokerage Relationship beyond the Associate Broker. Confidential information includes the information pursuant to sections 12-10-404(2), 12-10-405(2) and 12-10-407(3), C.R.S.

*   6.4.   Brokerage Firm's Policies

*   A.   Brokerage Firm's Brokerage Relationship Policy

*   1.   An Employing Broker or Independent Broker must adopt a written office policy which identifies and describes the relationships in which such Employing Broker, Independent Broker, and any Associate Brokers may engage with any Consumers prior to providing any Real Estate Brokerage Services pursuant to sections 12-10-403 and 12-10-408, C.R.S.

*   2.   An Employing Broker or Associate Broker must be designated in writing by the Employing Broker to serve as a Single Agent or Transaction-Broker for a Consumer pursuant to section 12-10-402(3), C.R.S. and as set forth in Rule 6.6.

*   B.   Office Policy Manual

*   Employing Brokers must also adopt any written policies suitable to the Brokerage Firm's business, subject to the following as applicable:

*   1.   Applies to all Associate Brokers in the Brokerage Firm.

*   2.   Be given to and signed by each Associate Broker.

*   3.   Identifies the procedures for the designation of Brokers who are to work with Consumers pursuant to section 12-10-403(6), C.R.S. and as set forth in subsection A. of this Rule.

*   4.   Identifies and provides adequate means and procedures for the maintenance and protection of confidential information that:

*   a.   The seller or landlord is willing to accept less;

*   b.   The buyer or tenant is willing to pay more;

*   c.   Information regarding motivating factors for the parties;

*   d.   Information that a party will agree to other financing terms;

*   e.   Material information about a party not required by law to be disclosed;

*   f.   Facts or suspicions which may psychologically impact or stigmatize a property; and

*   g.   All information required to be kept confidential pursuant to sections 12-10-404(2), 12-10-405(2) and 12-10-407(3), C.R.S.

*   5.   Permits an Employing Broker to supervise a transaction and to participate in the same transaction as a Designated Broker.

*   6.5.   Brokerage Relationships Disclosures in Writing

*   A.   Written disclosures pursuant to section 12-10-408, C.R.S. must be made to a Consumer prior to eliciting or discussing confidential information from a Consumer for Real Estate Brokerage Services.

*   B.   Such activities do not include preliminary conversations or "small talk" concerning price range, location and property styles, or responding to general factual questions from a potential Consumer concerning properties which have been Advertised for sale or lease.

* 6.6. Brokerage Relationships

*   A.   Listing Contract by Individual Associate Broker: An Associate Broker may enter into a Listing Contract as the Designated Broker for a particular Consumer in a particular transaction as either a Single Agent or Transaction-Broker.

*   B.   Listing Contract by Members of a Team: The individual team member(s) must all be the Designated Broker for a particular Consumer in a particular transaction as either Single Agents or Transaction-Brokers. The names of all the members of the Team must be disclosed in the Listing Contract.

*   C.   Transaction-Broker: A written disclosure that a Broker working with a Consumer as a Transaction-Broker is the Designated Broker for that Consumer.

*   D.   Substitute or Additional Designated Brokers: The Employing Broker may substitute or add other Designated Brokers, as appropriate, which must be disclosed to the Consumer.

* 6.7. Brokers or Teams working with Consumers on Both Sides of the Same Transaction

* Neither Brokers nor Teams may enter into a Brokerage Relationship with one Consumer as a Single Agent and the other Consumer as a Single Agent or Transaction-Broker in the same transaction. If properly disclosed, in writing (e.g. Listing Contracts), the Broker or Team that works with both Consumers in the same real estate transaction may do so as:

*   A.   A Transaction-Broker for both Consumers to the transaction;

*   B.   A Transaction-Broker for one Consumer in the transaction and treating the other Consumer as a Customer; or

*   C.   A Single Agent for one Consumer and treating the other Consumer as a Customer.

* 6.8. Ministerial Tasks

* When a Broker is engaged as a Single Agent or a Transaction-Broker for one party and treating the other party as a Customer, the Broker may assist the Customer by performing ministerial tasks following proper disclosure. Ministerial tasks include: showing a property, preparing as a scrivener, and conveying written offers and counteroffers, making known the different types of financing alternatives, and providing information related to professional, governmental, and community services which will contribute to completion of the transaction. Performing ministerial tasks will not of themselves violate the terms of any relationship between the Broker and the Consumer with which the Broker has a Brokerage Relationship and will not create an agency or Transaction-Broker relationship with the Customer being assisted.

* 6.9. Change of Status Disclosure in Writing

* A Broker or Team who changes their Brokerage Relationship from a Single Agent for one Consumer to assisting both Consumers in the same real estate transaction as a Transaction-Broker must provide the written Commission-Approved "Change of Status" Form to the Consumer that has the changed relationship with the Broker, at the time the Broker begins to assist both Consumers as a Transaction-Broker, but not later than at the time the Consumer signs the contract.

* 6.10. Advertising

*   A.   Names

*   1.   Pursuant to section 12-10-203(9), C.R.S., no Broker will be licensed to conduct Real Estate Brokerage Services under more than one (1) Brokerage Firm.

*   2.   Pursuant to section 12-10-203(9), C.R.S., no Broker or Brokerage Firm will conduct or promote Real Estate Brokerage Services except in the name under which that Broker or Brokerage Firm appears in the records of the Commission.

*   3.   Brokers will not Advertise so as to mislead the public concerning the identity of the Broker or the Broker's Brokerage Firm.

4. All Advertising must be done clearly and conspicuously in the name of the Broker's Brokerage Firm. However, a Broker who Advertises real property owned by the Broker which is not listed for sale or lease with the Broker's Brokerage Firm is exempt from Advertising the Broker's own property in the Broker's Brokerage Firm's name.

5. A Brokerage Firm may use a Trade Name in addition to or instead of the Brokerage Firm's legal name. The Trade Name must be filed with the Commission.

6. A Brokerage Firm may use a Trademark in conjunction with the Brokerage Firm's legal name or Trade Name with permission of the owner of such Trademark.

   a. A Brokerage Firm that uses a Trade Name or Trademark owned by a third party is required to use one (1) of the following statements, which must appear in a clear and conspicuous manner so as to attract the attention of the public:

      i. "Each (insert general Trade Name) brokerage business is independently owned and operated." or

      ii. "Each office independently owned and operated."

   b. Upon written request, the above statements may be modified with consent of the Commission.

7. No Brokerage Firm will use more than one (1) Trade Name; however, upon written request and with the consent of a representative of the Commission, a Brokerage Firm may use more than one (1) Trademark. Use of the Trademark(s) is only acceptable if the Brokerage Firm has obtained permission of the registrant of such Trademark.

8. No Broker may use a professional designation in Advertising unless the Broker is in good standing and the designation is easily verifiable by the public and the Commission. A Broker that Advertises an award, membership, or achievement must be able to provide verification of the validity of such claims upon request from any member of the public or Commission.

B. Teams

1. Brokers who form a Team must not Advertise in a manner that misleads the public as to the identity of the Team's Brokerage Firm. Teams are prohibited from using the following terms in the Team's name:

   a. Realty,

   b. Real estate,

   c. Realtors,

   d. Company,

   e. Corporation,

   f. Corp.,

   g. Inc.,

   h. LLC,

   i. LP or LLP, or

   j. Any other term that would imply a separate entity from the Brokerage Firm with which the Team Brokers are licensed.

2. All Team Advertising must clearly and conspicuously include and be in conjunction with the legal name or Trade Name of the Brokerage Firm.

3. If requested by a Consumer, the Commission, another Brokerage Firm or Broker, the Brokerage Firm will provide the names of the Brokers that belong to any Team licensed with the Brokerage Firm.

*   4.   Brokers may not allow the use of the Team's name by other Brokers outside the Team's Brokerage Firm.

*   C.   Brokerage Firms and Brokers are responsible for ensuring that all Advertising is accurate and complies with copyright laws and other applicable laws and regulations.

*   D.   Electronic Media

*   1.   When a Broker owns or controls Electronic Media, each Viewable Page must include: the Broker's name or Broker's Team name and the Broker's Brokerage Firm's name. Any expired listings must be removed from the Broker's Electronic Media within three (3) days of a Listing Contract expiring.

*   2.   If a Broker authorizes a third party for the Broker's Electronic Media Advertising, the Broker is responsible for ensuring that the information provided to such third party is accurate. The Broker must submit a written request to any third party syndicators to have all expired listings removed from Electronic Media within three (3) days of a Listing Contract expiring.

*   3.   A Broker who communicates through email, chat, instant messages, newsgroups, discussion lists, bulletin boards, blogs, or other similar means for purposes of Advertising the Broker's Real Estate Brokerage Services must use the Broker's name or Team's name and the name of the Broker's Brokerage Firm. However, once a Broker has disclosed the Broker's name or Team's name and the Broker's Brokerage Firm to a specific Consumer, the Broker is not required to continue to make the same disclosure to the specific Consumer.

*   4.   When it is not reasonable for a Broker to disclose the Broker's name or Team's name and the Brokerage Firm's name in an Electronic Media because space is limited, the Broker will disclose the Broker's name or Team's name and the Brokerage Firm's name clearly and conspicuously within the first click of the mouse.

*   E.   Sales Data

*   General sales data Advertising, regardless of the medium, which recaps sales activity over a period of time in a given subdivision or geographical area must include all of the following:

*   1.   Cite the source of the data; and

*   2.   Include a disclaimer, if accurate, that all reported sales:

*   a.   Were not necessarily listed or sold by the Broker; and

*   b.   Are intended only to show trends in the area or will separately identify the Broker's own sales activity.

*   F.   Authority to Advertise

*   Brokers may not Advertise the availability or price of a property whether for sale or lease without authority from the owner or the owner's Broker and disclosure of the owner's Brokerage Firm.

*   G.   Price Set by Owner

*   The price quoted in any Advertising will not be anything other than the price agreed upon between the Broker and the owner.

* 6.11. Square Footage Disclosure

*   When a Broker Advertises the square footage of a residential property, including for submission to a multiple listing service, the Broker must disclose the source of the square footage of the floor space of the living area of the residence to Consumers on the Commission-Approved Form.

    A.   Broker Measurement

    A Broker is not required to measure the square footage of a property. If the Broker takes an actual measurement, it does not have to be exact; however, the Broker's objective must be to measure accurately and calculate competently in a manner that is not misleading and must:

    1.   Disclose to the Consumer the standard, methodology, or manner in which the measurement was taken;

    2.   Advise that the measurement is for purposes of marketing and is not a measurement for loan, valuation, or any other purpose; and

    3.   Advise that if exact square footage is a concern, then the property should be independently measured.

    B.   Other Sources of Square Footage

    If a Consumer is provided information from a source other than the Broker's own measurement for square footage, that source (whether an actual measurement, building plans, prior appraisals, assessor's office, etc.) must include the date of issuance, if any, and must be disclosed to the Consumers in writing by the Broker in a timely manner. Such disclosure must be on the Commission-Approved Form. A Broker may not provide information to a person from a source known to be unreliable and is responsible for indicating obvious mismeasurement by others.

6.12. Notice Required on Competitive Market Analysis (CMA) or Broker's Price Opinion (BPO) for Purposes Other Than Marketing

    When a Broker prepares a CMA or BPO for any reason other than the anticipated sale or purchase of the property, the Broker must include a notice stating: "This evaluation was prepared by a licensed real estate broker and is not an appraisal. This evaluation cannot be used for the purposes of obtaining financing." Pursuant to section 12-10-602(9)(b)(II), C.R.S, Brokers are prohibited from completing CMAs or BPOs that are used for the purpose of obtaining financing. Preparation of CMAs or BPOs for reasons other than anticipated sale, purchase, or lease is not considered Real Estate Brokerage Services. As such, any compensation received for such preparation is not required to be paid to the Broker's Brokerage Firm unless stated otherwise in Brokerage Firm's Office Policy Manual.

6.13. Offers must be Presented to Other Broker

    A Broker must present all offers to the other Consumer's Broker if such other Consumer has an unexpired Listing Contract. If the Broker has made reasonable, but unsuccessful, attempts to present an offer to the other Consumer's Broker, the Broker must present the offer to the other Consumer's Broker's Employing Broker. If no Employing Broker exists, or if reasonable attempts to present the offer to the Employing Broker have failed, the Broker may present the offer directly to the other Consumer.

6.14. Contracts

    A.   Document Preparation and Duplicates

    1.   Contracting instruments prepared by a Broker performing Real Estate Brokerage Services for all real estate or business opportunity transactions must accurately reflect the financial terms of the transaction by itemizing Things of Value paid or received and identifying the party or parties conveying, receiving and/or ultimately benefitting from such Things of Value. All such terms made subsequent to the original contract must be disclosed in an amendment to the contract.

    2.   A Broker must deliver Duplicates of all documents prepared by the Broker to all Consumers or their representatives at the time such document was prepared by the Broker as set forth in Rule 6.19.

*   **B.** No Fees to Brokers for Legal Document Preparation

*   Brokers are not obligated to prepare any legal documents as part of a real estate transaction. If the Broker or the Broker's designee prepares any legal document, the Broker or the Broker's designee may not charge a separate fee for preparation of such legal documents. The Broker is not responsible for fees charged for the preparation of legal documents where they are prepared by an attorney representing the Consumer. Costs of closing not related to preparation of legal documents may be paid by the Broker or by any other person. A Broker who closes transactions and charges separately for costs of closing not related to the preparation of legal documents must specify the costs and obtain the written consent of the parties to be charged.

*   **C.** Listing must be in Writing

*   Regardless of the Brokerage Relationship, all Listing Contracts for the sale, lease or exchange of real property must be in writing prior to performing any Real Estate Brokerage Services.

*   **D.** Listings must have Termination Date

*   All Listing Contracts or other written agreements between a Consumer and a Brokerage Firm or Broker to perform Real Estate Brokerage Services must have a definite date for termination pursuant to section 12-10-409(1)(b), C.R.S.

*   **E.** Holdover Agreement

*   When a Listing Contract or other written agreement contains a provision entitling a Brokerage Firm to a commission made after the expiration of the agreement, such provision must refer only to those persons or properties with whom or on which the Broker negotiated during the term of the agreement, and whose names or addresses were submitted in writing to the Consumer during the term of the agreement, including any extension thereof.

*   **F.** Brokers must recommend title exam and legal counsel

*   Brokers are not permitted to give advice on exceptions to title as such conduct would constitute the unauthorized practice of law. Brokers must recommend, before the applicable deadlines, that Consumers should examine all title exceptions and encourage Consumers to seek guidance from a licensed attorney.

*   **G.** Review of Deeds

*   Brokers should not give advice based on their review of deeds for conveyance of real property unless such deeds are drafted by the Broker.

* **6.15.** Sign Crossing

*   **A.** Brokers will not negotiate a Listing Contract directly with a Consumer for compensation from said Consumer if such Broker knows the Consumer has an unexpired Listing Contract with another Brokerage Firm granting said Brokerage Firm an exclusive contract.

*   **B.** However, if a Broker is contacted by a Consumer who is currently subject to an exclusive Listing Contract, and the Broker has not initiated the discussion, the Broker may negotiate the terms upon which to take a future Listing Contract or, alternatively, may take a Listing Contract to become effective upon expiration or termination of any existing Exclusive Listing.

*   **C.** The burden of inquiry is on the Broker to determine the existence of the Listing Contract and to advise the Consumer to seek guidance from a licensed attorney.

* 6.16. Access Information for a Property

* A Broker who is not the owner's Broker is prohibited from sharing access information to a property with any third party, such as an assistant, home inspector, contractor, or a Consumer without prior authorization from the owner's Broker.

* 6.17. Duty to Disclose Conflict of Interest and License Status

* A. Brokerage Firms and Brokers have a continuing duty to disclose, in writing, any known conflict of interest that may arise in the course of any real estate transaction.

* B. If a Broker sells, buys, or leases real property on the Broker's own account, such Broker must disclose in the contracting instrument, or in a separate concurrent writing, that they are a licensed Broker.

* C. A Brokerage Firm or Broker engaged in Property Management Services has a duty to disclose, in writing, any known conflict of interest that may arise in the selection or use of a business or vendor that provides services applicable to lease transactions, including property maintenance. The Brokerage Firm or Broker is required to disclose any ownership, financial, or familial interest associated with the selection or use of a particular business or vendor.

* 6.18. Affiliated Business Arrangement Disclosures

* Pursuant to section 12-10-218(2)(b), C.R.S., an Employing Broker and/or a Broker must make the following disclosures in writing:

* A. The existence of an Affiliated Business Arrangement to the Consumer they are referring at or prior to the time the referral is made. The disclosure must comply with RESPA.

* B. Prior to or at the time the Contract to Buy and Sell is executed by the Consumers, the existence of an Affiliated Business Arrangement with the Brokerage Firm or Broker must be disclosed in writing to all parties to the transaction.

* C. A Broker is required to make the following disclosures to the Commission.

* 1. At the time a Broker enters into or changes an Affiliated Business Arrangement, the Broker must disclose the names of all Affiliated Business Arrangements to which the Broker is a party. The written disclosure must include the physical location of the affiliated businesses.

* 2. On an annual basis, each Employing Broker must disclose the names of all Affiliated Business Arrangements to which the Employing Broker or Brokerage Firm is a party. The written disclosure must include the physical location of the affiliated businesses.

* D. Written disclosures to the Commission must be made through the Colorado Affiliated Business Online Services database, which is accessible through the Division's website.

* 6.19. Closing Responsibility

* A. Pursuant to section 12-10-217(1)(j), C.R.S, at the time of closing, the Broker who has established a Brokerage Relationship with one or multiple Consumers in a transaction will be responsible for the proper closing of the transaction. The Broker must ensure such Consumer receives an accurate, complete and detailed closing statement that is signed by the Broker. If Broker is licensed with a Brokerage Firm, Broker must deliver closing statements to the Brokerage Firm along with any other closing documents, immediately following closing. Nothing in this Rule relieves an Employing Broker of the responsibility for fulfilling supervisory responsibilities pursuant to sections 12-10-203(5)(c)(I), 12-10- 217(1)(r), and 12-10-222, C.R.S and as set forth in subsections C. and D. of this Rule.

* B. If closing documents and closing statements are prepared and closed by a Broker, the Broker is responsible for the accuracy and completeness of the closing statements and closing documents.

*   C.   If a Broker has a Brokerage Relationship with a Consumer in a transaction, the Broker must review closing documents and attend closing or be reasonably available. If a Broker will not be available to attend closing and review closing documents, another Broker designated by the Brokerage Firm may review and attend closing on the Broker's behalf and will assume joint responsibility with the absent Broker for its accuracy, completeness, and delivery of the signed closing statement as set forth in subsection A. of this Rule.

*   D.   Any Broker receiving earnest money must deliver earnest money as set forth in Rule 5.12.A.

*   E.   Pursuant to section 38-35-125, C.R.S, a Broker or a Brokerage Firm must not disburse or authorize disbursement of funds until those funds have been received and are either:

*   1.   Available for immediate withdrawal as a matter of right from the financial institution in which the funds have been deposited; or

*   2.   Available for immediate withdrawal as a consequence of an agreement with a financial institution in which the funds are to be deposited or a financial institution upon which the funds are to be drawn. The agreement with a financial institution must be for the benefit of the Broker and Brokerage Firm providing the closing service. If the agreement contains contingencies or reservations, no disbursements can be made until these are satisfied.

*   **6.20. Transaction File Requirements**

*   Both a Broker and a Brokerage Firm must retain transactions files for all transactions for a period of four (4) years beginning from the consummation date of the transaction or the expiration date of any Listing Contracts that do not consummate. Required documents in a transaction file are designated in the Commission's Transaction File Checklist and may be found on the Division's website. A Broker is not required to obtain and retain copies of existing public records, title commitments, loan applications, lender required disclosures, or related affirmations from independent third party closing entities after the closing date.

*   **6.21. Referral Fees and RESPA**

*   A.   Brokers and Brokerage Firms will not pay or receive a referral fee except in accordance with RESPA and unless a reasonable cause for payment of the referral fee exists pursuant to section 12-10-304(1), C.R.S.

*   B.   RESPA prohibits settlement service providers from giving or receiving any Thing of Value to another settlement service provider for the referral of business when the transaction involves a federally related residential mortgage.

*   1.   Transactions Involving a Federally related Residential Mortgage

*   A Broker or Brokerage Firm, whether engaged in an Affiliated Business Arrangement pursuant to section 12-10-218, C.R.S. or not, will not accept or give any incentive, disincentive, remuneration, commission, fee, or other Thing of Value to or from a settlement service provider for the referral of business in a real estate transaction involving a federally related residential mortgage transaction. Nothing in subsection B. of this Rule prohibits a person or entity from receiving a bona fide salary, commission, or other compensation for services rendered or as a return on their ownership interest in an Affiliated Business Arrangement.

*   2.   Transaction Not Involving a Federally related Residential Mortgage

*   A Broker or Brokerage Firm will not accept, directly or indirectly, a placement fee, commission or other Thing of Value for referring a settlement service provider in any real estate transaction unless the Broker or Brokerage Firm first discloses in writing such compensation to whomever the Broker or Brokerage Firm is referring at the time of making such referral.

*   C.   Only Brokerage Firms licensed in Colorado are permitted to receive a commission on transactions for real estate located in Colorado. Pursuant to section 12-10-217(1)(l), C.R.S., a Colorado Brokerage Firm may pay a brokerage firm or broker licensed in another Jurisdiction or country a referral fee under the following circumstances:

*   1.   The brokerage firm or broker licensed in another Jurisdiction or country actually referred a client to the Broker or Brokerage Firm.

*   2.   The brokerage firm or broker licensed in the other Jurisdiction or country must reside and maintain an office in the other Jurisdiction or country. Subsection C. of this Rule applies to payment made to citizens or residents of a country which does not license real estate brokers if the payee represents that they are in the business of selling real estate in that country.

*   3.   All Advertising, negotiations, contracting, and conveyancing regarding the Colorado property must be performed by a Broker licensed in Colorado.

*   4.   All money collected from the parties to the transaction prior to closing must be deposited in the name of the Brokerage Firm licensed in Colorado as set forth in Chapter 5 of these Rules.

* 6.22. Prohibited Remedies for Compensation

*   A.   If for any reason the seller fails, refuses, neglects, or is unable to consummate the transaction as provided for in the contract, and through no fault or neglect of the buyer the real estate transaction cannot be completed, the Brokerage Firm has no right to any portion of the earnest money deposit which was deposited by the buyer.

*   B.   In a residential transaction, unless Broker has adjudicated a claim and a judgment is entered, no Broker will file or threaten to file a lien, a lis pendens, record a Listing Contract to secure the payment of a commission or other fee associated with Real Estate Brokerage Services, cause the title to a property to become clouded or interfere with the transfer of title when the Broker is not a principal in the transaction.

*   C.   A Brokerage Firm and Broker who has Commercial Real Estate listed for lease and has provided Real Estate Brokerage Services that resulted in procuring a tenant who has leased any interest in the Commercial Real Estate in accordance with the written agreement between the Brokerage Firm and the owner may file a lien pursuant to section 38-22.5-103, C.R.S. against the Commercial Real Estate in the amount of the compensation set forth in the written agreement. If the Commercial Real Estate has been conveyed to a bona fide buyer prior to the recording of the notice to lien pursuant to section 38-22.5-104, C.R.S., a Brokerage Firm or Broker may not file a lien for a commission that is due as the result of a lease renewal.

* 6.23. Immediate Notification of Conviction, Plea or Violation Required

*   A Broker must provide written notification to the Commission within thirty (30) calendar days for any of the following:

*   A.   A plea of guilty, a plea of nolo contendere, or a conviction of any crime as pursuant to section 12-10-217(1)(n), C.R.S.;

*   B.   A violation or aiding and abetting in the violation of the Colorado or federal fair housing laws;

*   C.   Any disciplinary action taken against a Broker in any other Jurisdiction, if the Broker's action(s) would constitute a violation of Commission statutes and these Rules; and

*   D.   A suspension or revocation of a license, registration, or certification by Colorado or another Jurisdiction, within the last five (5) years, for fraud, deceit, material misrepresentation, theft, or the breach of a fiduciary duty that denied the Broker the authorization to practice as a mortgage loan originator, a real estate broker or salesperson, a real estate appraiser, an insurance producer, an attorney, a securities broker-dealer, a securities sales representative, an investment advisor, or an investment advisor representative.

* 6.24. Electronic Records and Production of Records

* All records required to be maintained by Brokers or Brokerage Firms may be maintained as Electronic Records. Electronic Records or printed records must be produced upon request by the Commission or any principal party to a transaction and must be in a format that has the continued capability to be retrieved and legibly printed.

* 6.25. Investigations or Audits by Commission

* A. Notification of a Complaint that has been Assigned for Investigations or an Audit

* 1. A Broker or Brokerage Firm will receive written notification from the Commission regarding the following:

* a. A complaint has been filed and an investigation has been initiated. A copy of the complaint that has been filed against the Broker or Brokerage Firm will be provided; or

* b. The Broker or Brokerage Firm has been selected for an audit.

* 2. Upon receipt of the Commission's notification, a Broker or Brokerage Firm must submit a written response to the Commission. Failure to submit a written response within the time set by the Commission in its notification will be grounds for disciplinary action regardless of the question of whether the underlying complaint or audit warrants further investigation or subsequent action by the Commission. The written response must contain the following:

* a. A complete and specific answer to the factual recitations, allegations, or averments made in the complaint filed against the Broker or Brokerage Firm, whether made by a member of the public, on the Commission's own motion, or by an authorized representative of the Commission.

* b. A complete and specific response to any additional questions, allegations, or averments presented in the notification letter.

* c. A complete transaction file and any documents or records requested in the notification letter.

* d. Any further information relative to the complaint or audit that the Broker or Brokerage Firm believes to be relevant or material to the matters addressed in the notification letter.

* B. Extension to Respond

* Upon request, the Commission will grant extensions of time for Brokers or Brokerage Firms to respond to any complaint or audit provided such request is reasonable.

* C. Produce Records for Investigation or Audit

* Brokers and Brokerage Firms must retain and produce for inspection by the Commission any document or record as may be reasonably necessary for investigation or audit in the enforcement of Commission statutes and these Rules. Failure to submit such documents or records within the time set by the Commission in its notification will be grounds for disciplinary action unless the Commission has granted an extension of time for such production.

* 6.26. Actions when License is Suspended, Revoked, Expired or Inactive

* Upon suspension, revocation, expiration, or transfer to Inactive Status of a License, the Broker or Brokerage Firm is responsible for immediate compliance with the following:

* A. If an Associate Broker:

* 1. Cease any activities requiring a License.

2. Inform the Employing Broker of the change in license status.

3. Cease all Advertising, including, but not limited to, use of office signs, yard signs, billboards, newspapers, magazines, the internet, direct mailings, and multiple listing services.

4. Inform all impacted Consumers within seven (7) days of the action taken and the impact that the change in license status will have on any pending transaction. It is the responsibility of the Employing Broker to ensure that another Associate Broker is designated to perform the duties requiring a License in all pending transactions, or to release the affected parties from any Listing Contract(s) with the Brokerage Firm.

B. If an Independent Broker:

1. Cease any activities requiring a License.

2. Cease all Advertising, including, but not limited to, use of office signs, yard signs, billboards, newspapers, magazines, the internet, direct mailings, and multiple listing services.

3. Notify all impacted Consumers within seven (7) days of the action taken and the impact that the change in license status will have on any pending transaction.

4. Release the affected parties from any active Listing Contract(s) with the Independent Broker.

5. Instruct the affected parties to seek guidance from a licensed attorney or retain a new Brokerage Firm regarding any pending transactions.

6. The Independent Broker is responsible for accounting for all funds, returning all Trust and Escrow Account records and making all final disbursements to the rightful beneficiaries within thirty (30) days of the change in license status. The Independent Broker is also responsible for providing the Commission with a full list of all impacted Consumers' contact information within seven (7) days and for maintaining all records for four (4) years.

C. If an Employing Broker:

1. Cease any activities requiring a License.

2. Cease all Advertising, including, but not limited to, use of office signs, yard signs, billboards, newspapers, magazines, the internet, direct mailings, and multiple listing services.

3. The Employing Broker is personally responsible for the handling of any and all earnest money deposits, Trust or Escrow Account funds received or disbursed by the Brokerage Firm. The Employing Broker is responsible for returning all Trust and Escrow Account records to the Brokerage Firm.

4. The Brokerage Firm must designate a new Employing Broker to be responsible for the management and supervision of the licensed actions of the Brokerage Firm and all Associate Brokers shown in the Commission's records as being in the employ of the Brokerage Firm. Pursuant to section 12-10-203(6)(c), C.R.S., the Brokerage Firm may also seek a Temporary License to prevent hardship if none of the Brokerage Firm's Associate Brokers hold an Employing Broker level license.

5. If the Brokerage Firm is unable to designate a new Employing Broker or is not granted a Temporary License, the Licenses of the Brokerage Firm and any Associate Brokers will be placed on Inactive status. The Employing Broker must also perform all duties as set forth in subsection C.6. of this Rule.

6. If a Brokerage Firm's License becomes Inactive, Expired or revoked, the Employing Broker will have seven (7) days to notify all Consumers impacted as to the effect of such license status change will have on the Associate Brokers and all pending

transactions. The Employing Broker is responsible for accounting for all funds, returning all Trust and Escrow Account records and making all final disbursements to the rightful beneficiaries within thirty (30) days of the change in license status. The Employing Broker is also responsible for providing the Commission with a full list of all impacted Consumers' contact information within seven (7) days and for maintaining all records for four (4) years.

*   D.   Commissions or fees may be received by a Broker or Brokerage Firm only for transactions where the commission or fee was earned prior to that Broker's or Brokerage Firm's suspension, revocation, expiration, or transfer to Inactive status.

Commission Approved Forms

*   Through the adoption and promulgation of the Chapter 7 Rules: Use of Standard Forms, it became compulsory for all real estate brokers licensed by the State of Colorado to use Commission approved forms in most of their contracting. §12-10-403(4), C.R.S., grants the Colorado Real Estate Commission statutory authority to promulgate standard forms for use by licensees.

*   One of the major purposes of the rule is to help to insure broker compliance with the Colorado Supreme Court Conway-Bogue decision. (See case summary in Chapter 10 – Landmark Case Law) A second purpose is to help promote uniformity in contracting to the end that the public is better protected. The privileges granted should not be abused by the real estate broker.

*   **Chapter 7: Use of Standard Forms**

*   7.1.   Standard Forms

*   Pursuant to section 12-10-403(4), C.R.S., a Broker is authorized to complete Standard Forms for use in a real estate transaction, including Standard Forms intended to convey personal property as part of the real estate transaction, when a Broker is performing the activities for which a License is required and the Broker is acting as either a Single Agent or Transaction-Broker. The Broker's use of Standard Forms must be appropriate for the transaction and the circumstances in which they are used. The Broker must advise the parties that Standard Forms have important legal consequences and that the parties should consult legal counsel before signing such forms. A Standard Form is:

*   A.   Commission-Approved Form

*   A "Commission-Approved Form" is a form promulgated by the Commission for current use by Brokers. A Broker must use a Commission-Approved Form when such form exists and is appropriate for the transaction. The Broker may advise the parties as to the effects thereof. To obtain the forms promulgated by the Commission, visit the Division's website.

*   B.   Attorney Form

*   An "Attorney Form" is a form drafted by a licensed Colorado attorney representing the Broker, the Employing Broker, or the Brokerage Firm. A Broker may only use an Attorney Form if a Commission-Approved Form does not exist or is not appropriate for the transaction. The form must contain the language that says: "This form has not been approved by the Colorado Real Estate Commission". The form must also include: the name of the attorney or law firm that prepared the Attorney Form and the name of the Broker, Employing Broker, or the Brokerage Firm for whom the form was prepared. The form may not be altered by the Broker other than by completing any blank spaces in the form. The Broker may advise the parties as to the effects thereof.

C. Client Form

A "Client Form" is a form provided by a party to the transaction if the Broker is acting in the transaction as either a Single Agent or Transaction-Broker for the party providing the form. The Broker must retain written confirmation that the form was provided by said party to the transaction. A Broker's use of such form is limited to inserting transaction-specific information within the form.

D. Government/ Lender Form

A "Government/Lender Form" is a form prescribed by a governmental agency, a quasi-government agency, or a lender regulated by state or federal law and the use of the form is mandated by such agency or lender. A Broker's use of such form is limited to inserting transaction-specific information within the form.

E. Colorado Bar Association Form

A "Colorado Bar Association Form" is a form used with the written approval of the Colorado Bar Association, or its successor organization, and specifically designated for use by Brokers in Colorado. Brokers may only use the form when a Commission-Approved Form does not exist or is not appropriate for the transaction. A Broker must use the form within any guidelines or conditions specified by the Colorado Bar Association or its successor organization. The form may not be altered by the Broker other than by completing any blank spaces in the form. A Broker may not use any forms published or distributed by the Colorado Bar Association unless such form contains the following language that says: "This form has been approved by the Colorado Bar Association for use by Real Estate Brokers in Colorado in accordance with the guidelines provided with this form". The Broker may advise the parties as to the effects thereof.

F. Disclosure Form

A "Disclosure Form" is a form used for disclosure purposes only and the disclosure does not claim to waive or create any legal rights or obligations affecting any party to the transaction. The form must contain the language that says: "This form has not been approved by the Colorado Real Estate Commission". The Broker may advise the parties as to the effects thereof. The form may only provide information concerning:

1. The real estate involved in the transaction specifically; or

2. The geographic area in which the real estate is located generally.

G. Title Company Form

A "Title Company Form" is a form prescribed and completed by a title company that is providing closing services in a transaction. The Broker may advise the parties as to the effects thereof.

H. Letter of Intent

A "Letter of Intent" is created or prepared by a Broker, Employing Broker, or Brokerage Firm. The Letter of Intent must state on its face that it is nonbinding and creates no legal rights or obligations. The form must contain the language that says: "This form has not been approved by the Colorado Real Estate Commission". The Broker may advise the parties as to the effects thereof.

7.2. Permitted and Prohibited Modifications and Form Reproduction of Commission-Approved Forms as set forth in Rule 7.1.A.

A. A Broker or Brokerage Firm may add the Brokerage Firm's name, Trade Name, address, telephone, e-mail, Trademark or other identifying information on a Commission-Approved Form.

B. A Broker or Brokerage Firm may add initial lines at the bottom of a page of any Commission-Approved Form.

C. Any deletion or modification to the printed body of a Commission-Approved Form must result from negotiations or the instruction(s) of a party to the transaction. Any deletion must be made directly on the printed body of the form by striking through the deleted portion in a legible manner that does not obscure the deletion that has been made.

D. Blank spaces on a Commission-Approved Form may be lengthened or shortened to accommodate the relevant data or information.

E. Provisions that are inserted into blank spaces must be printed in a font style or type that clearly differentiates such insertions from the font style or type used for the Commission-Approved Form language.

F. A Broker may delete part or all of the following provisions of the Commission-Approved "Contract to Buy and Sell Real Estate" Forms (even if the provision has since been changed to a different section number) or corresponding provisions in other Commission-Approved Forms, if such provisions do not apply to the transaction. In the event any provision is deleted, the provision's caption or heading must remain unaltered on the form followed by the words "omitted-not applicable".

1. Section 2.5. Inclusions

2. Section 2.6. Exclusions

3. Section 2.7. Water Rights/Well Rights

4. Section 4.2. Seller Concession

5. Section 4.5. New Loan

6. Section 4.6. Assumption

7. Section 4.7. Seller or Private Financing

8. Section 5. Financing Conditions and Obligations

9. Section 6. Appraisal Provisions

10. Section 7. Owners' Association

11. Section 8.6. Right of First Refusal or Contract Approval

12. Section 9. New ILC; New Survey

13. Section 10.6. Due Diligence

14. Section 10.8. Source of Potable Water (CBS1, CBS2, CBS4, CBSF1)

15. Section 10.9. Existing Leases; Modification of Existing Leases; New Leases (CBS2, CBS3, CBS4)

16. Section 11. Estoppel Statements (CBS2, CBS3, CBS4)

17. Section 15.3. Status Letter and Record Change Fees

18. Section 15.4. Local Transfer Tax

19. Section 15.5. Private Transfer Fee

20. Section 15.7. Sales and Use Tax

21. Section 16.2. Rents

22. Section 16.3. Association Assessments

G. A Broker may delete part or all of the following provisions of the "Counterproposal" and the "Agreement to Amend/Extend Contract" if such provisions do not apply to the transaction. In the event any provision is deleted, the provision's caption or heading must remain unaltered on the form followed by the words "omitted-not applicable".

1. Section 3. Dates and Deadlines Table

2. Section 4. Purchase Price and Terms [in the Counterproposal only]

*   H.   A Broker or Brokerage Firm may add signature lines and identifying labels for the parties' signatures on a Commission-Approved Form.

*   I.   A Broker or Brokerage Firm may modify, strike, or delete such language on a Commission-Approved Form as the Commission may from time to time authorize the language to be modified, stricken, or deleted.

*   J.   A Broker must explain all permitted modifications, deletions, omissions, insertions, additional provisions, and addenda to the principal party and must recommend that the parties obtain expert advice as to the material matters that are beyond the expertise of the Broker.

*   K.   Commission-Approved Forms used by a Broker, including permitted modifications made by a Broker, must be legible.

*   L.   Brokers or Brokerage Firms generating Commission-Approved Forms in an electronic format must ensure that the forms are protected so as to prevent inadvertent changes or prohibited modifications of Commission-Approved Forms by the Broker or recipient.

*   7.3.   Additional Provisions

*   A.   Any "Additional Provision" which by its terms serves to delete or modify portions of a Standard Form as set forth in Rule 7.1. must result from negotiations or the instruction(s) of a party to the transaction.

*   B.   A Broker who uses a transaction-specific clause or clauses drafted by the Broker's, Employing Broker's, or Brokerage Firm's licensed Colorado attorney must ensure that the Broker understands the clause, and the clause is used and completed appropriately. The Broker must retain the clause(s) prepared by the Broker's, Employing Broker's, or Brokerage Firm's licensed Colorado attorney for four (4) years from the date that the clause was last used by the Broker. The Broker must provide those clause(s) and the name of the licensed Colorado attorney or law firm that prepared the clause(s) upon request by the Commission.

*   7.4.   Prohibited Provisions

*   A.   No contract provision, including modifications or additional provisions permitted as set forth in Rules 7.2. and 7.3., will relieve a Broker, Employing Broker, or Brokerage Firm from compliance with section 12-10-201, C.R.S., et seq., or these Rules.

*   B.   A Broker who is not a principal party to the contract may not have personal provisions, personal disclaimers, or exculpatory language in favor of the Broker, Employing Broker, or Brokerage Firm inserted into a Standard Form. A Broker may, at the direction of a principal party, include language regarding the payment of the Broker's or Brokerage Firm's commission if this is a negotiated term between the principal parties of the Commission-Approved "Contract to Buy and Sell Real Estate" Form.

> Ed. Note: The most current version of approved forms can be found on the Division of Real Estate website at: **www.dora.state.co.us/dre.**

*   Real estate brokers are required to use Commission-approved forms as appropriate to a transaction or circumstance to which a relevant form is applicable. Commission-approved forms are posted on the Division of Real Estate's website. Effective June 2009, the Commission will no longer post forms in the Code of Colorado Regulations. The Commission hereby withdraws all forms from the Code of Colorado Regulations. In instances when the Commission has not developed an approved form within the purview of this rule, and other forms are used, they are not governed by Chapter 7 of the Rules. Other forms used by a broker shall not be prepared by a broker, unless otherwise permitted by law.

* To obtain the forms promulgated by the real estate commission that are within the purview of Chapter 7, visit the Division of Real Estate website at: *http://www.dora.state.co.us/dre* or the Division of Real Estate's offices at 1560 Broadway, Suite 925, Denver, Colorado 80202.

* **Chapter 8: Declaratory Orders**

* 8.1.   Petition for a Declaratory Order

* Pursuant to section 24-4-105(11), C.R.S., a Petitioner may petition the Commission for a declaratory order to terminate controversies or to remove uncertainties as to the applicability of any statutory provision, rule, or order of the Commission as it would apply to the Petitioner.

* 8.2.   Parties to the Proceedings

* The parties to any proceeding as set forth in Chapter 8 of these Rules will be the Commission and the Petitioner. Any other person may seek leave of the Commission to intervene in such a proceeding. Permission to intervene will be granted at the sole discretion of the Commission. A petition to intervene will set forth the same matters as set forth in Rule 8.3.

* 8.3.   Petition Contents

* Any petition filed as set forth in Chapter 8 of these Rules will state the following:

* A.   The name and address of the Petitioner;

* B.   The statute, rule, or order to which the petition relates;

* C.   A concise statement of all the facts and law necessary to show the nature of the controversy or uncertainty and the manner in which the statute, rule, or order in question applies or potentially applies to the Petitioner; and

* D.   The Petitioner may submit a concise statement of the declaratory order sought.

* 8.4.   Commission's Considerations Whether or Not to Rule

* The Commission may determine, in its sole discretion and without prior notice to the Petitioner, whether or not to rule upon a petition. In determining whether or not to rule upon a petition filed as set forth in Chapter 8 of these Rules, the Commission may consider the following matters, among others:

* A.   Whether a ruling on the petition will terminate a controversy or remove uncertainties as to the applicability to the Petitioner of any statutory provision, rule, or order of the Commission.

* B.   Whether the petition involves any subject, question, or issue which is the subject of a formal or informal matter or investigation currently pending before the Commission or a court involving one or more of the Petitioners.

* C.   Whether the petition involves any subject, question, or issue which is the subject of a formal or informal matter or investigation currently pending before the Commission or a court not involving the Petitioner.

* D.   Whether the petition seeks a ruling on a hypothetical question.

* E.   Whether the Petitioner has some other adequate legal remedy, other than an action for declaratory order which will terminate the controversy or remove any uncertainty as to the applicability to the Petitioner of the statute, rule, or order in question.

* 8.5.   Commission Determines Not to Rule

* If the Commission determines it will not rule on a petition, the Commission will issue its written decision disposing of the petition, stating the reasons for declining to rule upon the petition. A copy of the decision will be provided to the Petitioner. A decision not to rule on a petition for a declaratory order is not final agency action subject to judicial review.

* 8.6. Commission Determines to Rule

* If the Commission determines that it will rule on the petition:

    A.   The Commission may order the Petitioner to file an additional written brief, memorandum, statement of position, or request the Petitioner to submit additional facts or arguments in writing.

    B.   The Commission may take administrative notice of facts pursuant to the Administrative Procedure Act, section 24-4-105(8), C.R.S., and may utilize its experience, technical competence, and specialized knowledge when ruling on the petition.

    C.   The Commission may set the petition, upon due notice to the Petitioner, for a non-evidentiary hearing.

    D.   The Commission may, upon due notice to the Petitioner, set the petition for hearing for the purpose of obtaining additional facts or information, or to determine the truth of any facts set forth in the petition, or to hear oral arguments on the petition. Notice to the Petitioner setting such formal hearing will set forth, to the extent known, the factual or other matters into which the Commission intends to inquire. The Petitioner will have the burden of proving all of the facts stated in the petition, all of the facts necessary to show the nature of the controversy or uncertainty and the manner in which the statute, rule, or order in question applies or potentially applies to the Petitioner and any other facts the Petitioner desires the Commission to consider.

    E.   Any ruling by the Commission may be based solely on the matters set forth in the petition or may be based on any amendments to the petition, any information gathered by the Commission through a non-evidentiary hearing, formal hearing or otherwise, or any facts the Commission may take administrative notice of. Upon ruling on a petition, the Commission will issue its written order stating its basis for the order. A copy of the order will be provided to the Petitioner.

* 8.7. Declaratory Orders Subject to Judicial Review

* Any declaratory order of a petition as set forth in Chapter 8 of these Rules will constitute agency action subject to judicial review pursuant to section 24-4-106, C.R.S.

* **Chapter 9: Commission Review of Initial Decisions and Exceptions**

* 9.1. Written Form, Filing Requirements, and Service

    A.   All pleadings must be in written form, mailed with a certificate of service to the Commission.

    B.   All pleadings must be filed with the Commission on the date the filing is due. A pleading is considered filed upon receipt by the Commission. Chapter 9 of these Rules does not provide for any additional time for service by mail.

    C.   All pleadings must be filed with the Commission and not with the Office of Administrative Courts. Any pleadings filed in error with the Office of Administrative Courts will not be considered. The Commission's address is:

         Colorado Real Estate Commission
         1560 Broadway, Suite 925
         Denver, CO 80202

    D.   All pleadings must be served on the opposing party on the date which the pleading is filed with the Commission. Electronic service between the parties is encouraged. The date and manner must be noted on the certificate of service.

* 9.2. Initial Decision

*   Upon receipt of the initial decision prepared and filed by the Administrative Law Judge from the Office of Administrative Courts, the Division will timely mail a copy of the initial decision to the parties at their respective addresses of record with the Commission pursuant to section 24-4-105(16)(a), C.R.S.

* 9.3. Commission's Authority to Review the Initial Decision

*   Pursuant to section 24-4-105(14)(a)(II), C.R.S., the Commission may initiate a review of an initial decision on its own motion within thirty (30) days of the date on which the Division mails the initial decision to the parties. A letter from the Division initiating the review of the initial decision constitutes a motion within the meaning of section 24-4-105(14)(a)(II), C.R.S.

* 9.4. Appeal of the Initial Decision by the Parties

*   A.   Any party wishing to reverse or modify an initial decision of an Administrative Law Judge must file written exceptions with the Commission in accordance with the procedures and time frames as set forth in Rule 9.5.

*   B.   If neither party appeals the initial decision by filing exceptions, the initial decision will become the final order of the Commission after thirty (30) days from the date on which the Division mails the initial decision pursuant to section 24-4-105(14)(b)(III), C.R.S. Failure to file exceptions will result in a waiver of the right to judicial review of the final order of the Commission unless the portion of the final order subject to review differs from the contents of the initial decision pursuant to section 24-4-105(14)(c), C.R.S.

* 9.5. Filing of Exceptions

*   A.   Pursuant to section 24-4-105(15)(a), C.R.S., any party seeking to file exceptions must initially file with the Commission a designation of the relevant parts of the record and of parts of the transcript of the hearing within twenty (20) days of the date on which the Division mails the initial decision to the parties.

*   B.   Transcripts:

*   Any party may designate the entire transcript, or may identify witness(es) whose testimony is to be transcribed, the legal ruling or argument to be transcribed, or other information necessary to identify a portion of the transcript. However, no transcript is required if the Commission's review is limited to pure questions of law. The deadline for filing exceptions depends on whether either of the parties designates a portion of the transcript.

*   1.   If the parties do not designate parts of the transcript, exceptions are due within thirty (30) days from the date on which the Division mails the initial decision to the parties. Both parties' exceptions are due on the same day.

*   2.   Any party wishing to designate all, or any part, of the transcript must adhere to the following procedures:

*   a.   Transcripts will not be deemed part of a designation unless specifically identified and ordered.

*   b.   If one party designates a portion of the transcript, the other party may file a supplemental designation in which that party may designate additional portions of the transcript. The supplemental designation must be filed with the Commission and served on the other party within ten (10) days after the date on which the original designation was filed.

*   c.   Any party who designates a transcript must order the transcript by the date on which they file their designation with the Commission whether they are filing an original or supplemental designation.

d. The party ordering a transcript must direct the court reporter or transcribing service to complete and file with the Commission the original transcript and one (1) copy within thirty (30) days of their order.

e. The party that designates a transcript must pay for such transcripts.

f. Transcripts that are ordered and not filed with the Commission in a timely manner due to non-payment, insufficient payment, or failure to direct as set forth above may not be considered by the Commission.

g. Upon receipt of transcripts identified in all designations and supplemental designations, the Commission will mail a notification to the parties stating that the transcripts have been received by the Commission.

h. Exceptions are due within thirty (30) days from the date on which such notification is mailed. Both parties' exceptions are due on the same date.

C. A party's exceptions must include specific objections to the initial decision.

D. Either party may file a response to the other party's exceptions. All responses must be filed within ten (10) days of the date on which the exceptions were filed with the Commission. Subsequent replies will not be considered except for good cause shown.

E. The Commission may in its sole discretion grant an extension of time to file exceptions or responses, or may delegate the discretion to grant such an extension of time to the Commission's designee.

9.6. Request for Oral Arguments

A. All requests for oral argument must be in writing and included with a party's exceptions or response.

B. It is within the sole discretion of the Commission to grant or deny a request for oral argument. The Commission generally does not grant requests for oral argument. If an oral argument is granted, each party will have ten (10) minutes to present their argument. Questioning by members of the Commission will not count against the allocated ten (10) minutes.

C. The Commission or its designee may extend the time for oral arguments upon good cause shown.

9.7. Final Orders

A. The Commission may deliberate and vote on exceptions immediately following oral arguments or the Commission may take the matter under advisement.

B. When the Commission votes on exceptions, whether after oral arguments or at a subsequent Commission meeting, the ruling of the Commission will not be considered final until a written order is issued.

C. The date of the Commission's final order is the date on which the written order is signed, irrespective of any motions for reconsideration that are filed.

Chapter 3:
Commission Position Statements

An * in the left margin indicates a change in the statute, rule or text since the last publication of the manual.

3. Position Statements

CP-1 Commission Policy on Homebuilder's Exemption from Licensing

Corporations that build structures on land they own may sell the land and building together without licensing, provided that the sales are made by corporate officers or regularly salaried employees. The land and building must be sold as a unit and the building must not have been previously occupied. This exemption is usually referred to as the homebuilder's exemption. Since employees who sell must be regularly salaried employees, the question often arises as to what a regular salary is. This is the position of the Commission: 12-10-201(6)(b)(X), C.R.S., among other requirements, requires that a corporation use "regular salaried employees" to sell or negotiate the sale of real property.

It is the position of the Commission that the phrase, "regular salaried employees" means that:

1. The salary must be an actual and stated amount and must not be a draw or advance against future commissions.

2. The salary must be regularly paid (*i.e.*, weekly, monthly, etc.).

3. Although the amount of salary may vary, an employee must be paid at least the prevailing federal minimum wage.

4. The corporation should deduct amounts for state and federal withholding taxes, FICA taxes, and other commonly deductible expenses, which the corporation would employ with respect to other employees.

Payment of a commission, in addition to a regular salary, will not invalidate the exemption if the above guidelines are met.

CP-2 Commission Position on Earned Fees

(revised 10/03/2017)

Commissions:

Section 12-10-217(1)(l), C.R.S., of the license law forbids a broker from paying a commission or valuable consideration, for performing brokerage functions, to any person who is not licensed as a real estate broker. Brokerage functions include negotiating the purchase, sale or exchange of real estate. *See* section 12-10-201(6)(a), C.R.S. Pursuant to Colorado case law, "negotiating" means "the act of bringing two parties together for the purpose of consummating a real estate transaction." *Brakhage vs. Georgetown Associates, Inc.*, 523 P. 2d 145, 147 (1974). Therefore, any unlicensed person who directly or indirectly brings a buyer and seller together, is negotiating and would need a broker's license in order to be compensated. This includes, but is not limited to, such activities as referring potential time-share purchasers to a developer or referring potential purchasers to a homebuilder.

Referral Fees:

Section 12-10-304(1), C.R.S., permits a real estate broker to pay a referral fee if it is not prohibited by the federal "Real Estate Settlement and Procedures Act of 1974" ("RESPA") and reasonable cause for payment exists. Reasonable cause exists when:

1) An actual introduction of business has been made;

2) A contractual referral fee relationship exists; or

3) A contractual cooperative brokerage relationship exists.

Section 12-10-304(2)(b)(III), C.R.S., defines a referral fee as "any fee paid by a licensee to any person or entity, other than a cooperative commission offered by a listing broker to a selling broker or vice versa." Payment for providing a name to a licensed broker is not specifically addressed in Colorado statute. However, it would be illegal to pay such a fee to anyone performing acts that require a license (*e.g..*, negotiating, listing, and contracting). Care should be taken. At best, the unlicensed referrer can have no active involvement in the transaction beyond merely giving to a licensee the name of a prospective buyer, seller or tenant. If the payment is simply for the referral of a name to a licensee, with no further activity on the part of the referrer, and the referrer is not a provider of a settlement service, the Commission will not consider it to be a violation of the license law. Complaints and inquiries are dealt with on a case-by-case basis.

In real estate transactions involving federally related mortgage loans, Section 8 of RESPA, 12 U.S.C. §§ 2601 et seq., governs the payment of referral fees. Pursuant to 12 U.S.C. § 2602(1) of RESPA, the term "federally related mortgage loan" is defined to include:

(1) any loan (other than temporary financing such as a construction loan) which—

(A) is secured by a first or subordinate lien on residential real property (including individual units of condominiums and cooperatives) designed principally for the occupancy of from one to four families, including any such secured loan, the proceeds of which are used to prepay or pay off an existing loan secured by the same property; and

(B) (i) is made in whole or in part by any lender the deposits or accounts of which are insured by any agency of the Federal Government, or is made in whole or in part by any lender which is regulated by any agency of the Federal Government; or

(ii) is made in whole or in part, or insured, guaranteed, supplemented, or assisted in any way, by the Secretary or any other officer or agency of the Federal Government or under or in connection with a housing or urban development program administered by the Secretary or a housing or related program administered by any other such officer or agency; or

(iii) is intended to be sold by the originating lender to the Federal National Mortgage Association, the Government National Mortgage Association, the Federal Home Loan Mortgage Corporation, or a financial institution from which it is to be purchased by the Federal Home Loan Mortgage Corporation; or

(iv) is made in whole or in part by any "creditor", as defined in section 103(f) of the Consumer Credit Protection Act (15 U.S.C. § 1602(f)), who makes or invests in residential real estate loans aggregating more than $ 1,000,000 per year, except that for the purpose of this Act, the term "creditor" does not include any agency or instrumentality of any State.

* RESPA and Commission Rule 6.21 prohibit the payment or receipt of referral fees and kickbacks which tend to increase unnecessarily the costs of settlement services. As part of this prohibition, any referral of a settlement service, including real estate brokerage services, is not compensable. Thus, an individual or company is not allowed to pay another individual or company for the referral of settlement business. Moreover, it is not appropriate for a settlement service provider to pay a broker, or offset a broker's expenses, for lead generation. The Commission views this as payment for the referral of business, which would be a violation of Rule 6.21. Additionally, Section 12-10-217(10), C.R.S., requires the Commission to refer such issues to the Consumer Financial Protection Bureau for investigation as a potential violation of RESPA.

RESPA, however, does permit:

1) A payment to an attorney at law for services actually rendered:

2) A payment by a title company to its duly appointed agent for services actually performed in the issuance of a policy of title insurance;

3) A payment by a lender to its duly appointed agent or contractor for services actually performed in the origination, processing, or funding of a loan;

4) A payment to any person of a bona fide salary or compensation for goods or facilities actually furnished or for services actually performed;

5) A payment pursuant to cooperative brokerage and referral arrangements or agreements between real estate brokers (all parties must be acting in a real estate brokerage capacity);

6) Normal promotional and educational activities that are not conditioned on the referral of business and that do not involve the defraying of expenses that otherwise would be incurred by persons in a position to refer settlement services or business incident thereto; or

7) An employer's payment to its own employees for any referral activities.

Administrative Fees:

As a result of the United States Supreme Court's decision in *Freeman v. Quicken Loans, Inc.*, 132 S. Ct. 2034, 2012 U.S. Lexis 3940 (2012), real estate brokers may charge administrative fees, either for services performed by the broker or the real estate brokerage, in addition to the broker's commission. In *Quicken* Loans, the Supreme Court held that while RESPA prohibits the splitting of fees if the charges are divided between two or more persons (i.e. settlement service providers) and the fee was paid for services not actually performed, dividing or splitting fees amongst a single settlement service provider is not prohibited. The Commission considers a real estate broker and his or her licensed broker-employer (or brokerage) to be a single provider of settlement services and fees may be split amongst them.

CP-3 Position Statement Concerning Commission Rule 6.15.

Commission Rule 6.15, commonly referred to as the "sign-crossing" rule, states as follows:

6.15.A. "Brokers will not negotiate a Listing Contract directly with a Consumer for compensation from said Consumer if such Broker knows the Consumer has an unexpired Listing Contract with another Brokerage Firm granting said Brokerage Firm an exclusive contract."

6,15.B. "However, if a Broker is contacted by a Consumer who is currently subject to an exclusive Listing Contract, and the Broker has not initiated the discussion, the Broker may negotiate the terms upon which to take a future Listing Contract or, alternatively, may take a Listing Contract to become effective upon expiration or termination of any existing Exclusive Listing."

6.15.C. "The burden of inquiry is on the Broker to determine the existence of the Listing Contract and to advise the Consumer to seek guidance from a licensed attorney."

The Commission's intent in promulgating Rule 6.15 was (1) to prevent brokers from interfering with existing listing contracts to the detriment of the owner and (2) to protect the owner from possible claims that two commissions are owed.

Many owners are extremely dependent on the expertise of the licensee. They may sincerely believe an existing listing contract is not in effect when, in fact, it is. The burden of inquiry is on the licensee.

Earlier versions of 6.15 had been criticized for being too restrictive. The current rule still provides that licensees shall not negotiate directly with an owner if they know that the owner has a written unexpired Exclusive Right to Sell or Lease. However, the licensee is now allowed to negotiate the terms for a future listing or take a listing effective upon expiration of a current listing so long as the licensee is first contacted by the owner.

This recognizes the fact that an owner with property currently listed may initiate the negotiations concerning a future listing. In addition, the current rule recognizes that in some instances owners become dissatisfied with the services of the broker with whom they have a listing and wish to cancel the listing. If a knowledgeable and informed seller wishes to cancel a listing and list with another company, this cannot be prevented. Of course, the seller runs the risk that improper cancellation of a listing contract can result in legal consequences. Brokers should never independently advise a seller in this area. Instead, an inquiring seller should be advised to seek legal counsel to explain the consequences of canceling an unexpired listing.

If the rule is followed closely it will provide greater opportunities for licensees to negotiate listings where a seller does not wish to re-list with the same broker while maintaining the integrity of the principal/agent brokerage relationship.

CP-4 Commission Position on Interest Bearing Trust Accounts

(Revised Position 8-04)

* Section 12-10-217(1)(i), C.R.S., permits brokers to place entrusted money in an interest bearing account.

* The Commission has taken the position that in the absence of a contract signed by the proper parties to the contrary, any interest accumulating on a trust account does not belong to the broker who is acting as escrow agent. (This position is based upon 12-10-217(1)(t) and upon the well-established tenet of agency that the agent may not profit personally from the agency relationship except for agreed upon compensation.)

Contracts calling for large earnest money deposits or other payments should contain a provision specifying which party is entitled to interest earned and under what conditions. In the absence of such a provision, accrued interest normally belongs to the seller if the contract is consummated or if the seller is successful in declaring a forfeiture. The entrusted money normally belongs to the purchaser if the contract fails.

In a property management trust account, the accrued interest on that portion of rental money received that belongs to the lessor beneficiary (landlord), would belong to the lessor beneficiary. The accrued interest on security deposits would belong to the respective tenants unless the lessor can establish a right to the security deposit (in the absence of a contract to the contrary).

However, in the case of the property management of mobile homes, by Colorado statute, the interest earned on security deposits may be retained by the landlord of a mobile home park as compensation for administering the trust account. (38-12-209(2)(b) C.R.S.)

Nothing in this position statement precludes a real estate broker from voluntarily transferring interest earned on a trust account to a fund established for the purpose of providing affordable housing to Colorado residents if such a fund is established.

CP-5 Commission Position on Advance Rentals and Security Deposits

* Pursuant to C.R.S. 12-10-217(1)(i) and Commission Rules 5.2 and 5.8.A., all money belonging to others which is received by a broker must be placed in an escrow or trust account. This applies to tenant security deposits and advance rental deposits, including credit card receipts, held by a broker.

A broker may not deliver a security deposit to an owner unless notice is given to the tenant in the lease, rental agreement, or in a separate written notice that the security deposit will be held by the owner. Such notice must be given in a manner so that the tenant will know who is holding the security deposit, and shall include either the true' name and current mailing address of the owner or the true name and current mailing address of a person authorized to receive legal notices on behalf of such owner, along with specific requirements for how the tenant is to request return of the deposit.

If, after receipt by the broker, the security deposit is to be transferred to the owner or used for the owner's benefit, the broker, in addition to properly notifying the tenant, must secure the consent of the owner to assume full financial responsibility for the return of any deposit which may be refundable to the tenant. The broker shall not withhold the identity of the owner from the tenant if demand for the return of the deposit is properly made according to the lease, rental agreement, or separate notice, and the owner has refused to return the security deposit. The lease, rental agreement, or separate notice may also give notice that the security deposit will be transferred upon the happening of certain events, *e.g.*, sale of the property or the naming of a new property manager.

Delivery of the security deposit to the owner or to anyone (including a succeeding broker/manager of the property) without proper notice to the tenant, in addition to subjecting the broker to possible civil liability, will constitute a violation of the license law escrow statute cited above. The licensee must retain copies of such notices for inspection by the Commission.

*   Under a property management contract, the broker must transfer all escrowed money belonging to the owner of the property at reasonable and agreed upon intervals and with proper accounting pursuant to statutory requirements and Commission Rules in Chapter 5. If advance rental money is held by a broker but is subject to recall by the tenant or occupant, it must be escrowed until such time as it is earned and rightfully transferred or credited to the owner. A broker has no claim on or right to use advance deposits which are subject to recall by a tenant or prospective occupant. Deposits which are not subject to recall are the property of the owner and may not be transferred to the broker's account or used for the broker's benefit unless specifically authorized and agreed to by the owner in the management agreement.

If litigation concerning escrow money commences, the money may be placed with the court. The jurisdiction of the court will, of course, supersede the statutory requirement for escrowing money belonging to others.

CP-6 Commission Position on Release of Earnest Money Deposits

(Revised Position 8-6-2008)

*   Rule 6.22.A. states that: "If for any reason the seller fails, refuses, neglects or is unable to consummate the transaction as provided for in the contract, and through no fault or neglect of the buyer the real estate transaction cannot be completed, the Brokerage Firm has no right to any portion of the earnest money deposit which was deposited by the buyer."

The Commission will not pursue disciplinary action against a broker for refusal to disburse disputed funds when the broker is acting in accordance with the language of the appropriate Commission-approved contract to buy and sell. It is clear in the contract to buy and sell real estate that the broker holds the earnest money on behalf of both buyer and seller. If there is no dispute, the broker should disburse to the appropriate party immediately.

Some brokers unnecessarily require a signed release by both parties even when there is no disagreement. Audits have disclosed many instances where brokers have held deposits for extended periods just because one or both parties will not sign a release. While good judgment is always urged, releases are not a requirement of the Real Estate Commission. In addition, where one party has given written authorization for the release of a deposit to another, a written release by the other party is not required.

Exculpatory provisions holding the broker harmless do not belong in an agreement for the release of earnest money and should not be used to relieve the broker from liability unrelated to earnest money.

In the case of a dispute between the parties, the broker is authorized by the contract to buy and sell to obtain mutual written instructions (such as a release) before turning a deposit over to a party. The Commission has approved an optional use "Earnest Money Release" form when such a written release might help facilitate expeditious disbursement.

Unless otherwise indicated in the Commission-approved contract to buy and sell, a broker is not required to take any action regarding the release of the earnest money deposit when there is a controversy. If the following provisions are included in the contract, the broker may exercise three options in the event of an earnest money dispute, if the broker is the holder of the earnest money deposit. One option is that the broker may await any proceeding between the parties. Another option for the broker is to interplead all parties and deposit the earnest money into a court of competent jurisdiction. If included in the contract to buy and sell, the broker is entitled to recover court costs and reasonable attorney and legal fees. However, if this provision is struck from the contract to buy and sell, the broker may not be entitled to recover those costs. A third option available to the broker is to provide notice to the buyer and seller that unless the broker receives a copy of the Summons and Complaint or Claim (between the buyer and seller) containing a case number of the lawsuit within one hundred twenty (120) days of the broker's notice to the parties, the broker will be authorized to return the earnest money to the buyer.

If the broker is unable to locate the party due the refund, the broker may be required to transfer the deposit to the Colorado State Treasurer under the provisions of the Colorado "Unclaimed Property Act" C.R.S. 38-13-101. Notice of funds held is published in local newspapers under the "Great Colorado Payback Program" each year. Further information and reporting forms may be obtained from that office.

CP-7 Commission Position on Closing Costs

*   In the past, the Commission's position had been that real estate licensees were responsible for all costs of closing. This position has been modified after a re-examination of the Colorado Supreme Court case of Conway-Bogue vs. The Denver Bar Association and after the adoption of Rule 6.14.B.

*   Commission Rule 6.14.B. states:

*   "Brokers are not obligated to prepare any legal documents as part of a real estate transaction. If the Broker or the Broker's designee prepares any legal document, the Broker or the Broker's designee may not charge a separate fee for preparation of such legal documents. The Broker is not responsible for fees charged for the preparation of legal documents where they are prepared by an attorney representing the Consumer. Costs of closing not related to preparation of legal documents may be paid by the Broker or by any other person. A Broker who closes transactions and charges separately for costs of closing not related to the preparation of legal documents must specify the costs and obtain the written consent of the parties to be charged."

Based on the new rule the position is as follows:

1. Licensees are still responsible for paying the costs of legal document preparation when they are preparing such documents for their clients. If the broker delegates this function to an agent (title company or closing service) the broker is still responsible for bearing the cost.

2. Other costs associated with closings can be paid for by the licensee or any other party. The Commission will no longer require that licensees bear these costs. Licensees are urged to use the Closing Instructions and Earnest Money Receipt form developed by the Commission.

3. It is now permissible for brokers to close their own transactions and make additional charges for providing closing services so long as the charges are not tied to legal document preparation. If a licensee does this it must be with the consent of the parties and all charges must be specified. This consent may be obtained through the Listing Contract, the Contract to Buy and Sell, the Closing Instructions and Earnest Money Receipt form, or otherwise.

4. Licensees are not responsible for bearing the cost of legal document preparation where the documents are prepared by an attorney representing the parties to the transaction. However, the broker should not designate the broker's own attorney to prepare legal documents for the parties and then charge as if the attorney had prepared the documents on behalf of a client.

5. The broker must still provide accurate closing statements.

Particular note should be paid to the first sentence of the rule. While there is no legal obligation for a broker to prepare the legal documents in a transaction the Commission strongly advises that licensees make this clear in the Listing Contract. Many persons, purchasers and sellers alike, normally look to the broker for the preparation of these documents. If the broker has not made it clear that the broker's company will not undertake the preparation of legal documents, the parties might well assume that the broker will do so at the broker's cost.

CP-8 Commission Position on Assignment of Contracts and Escrowed Funds

Assignments of contracts and escrowed funds usually occur when one real estate company is purchased or taken over by another real estate company.

The following reflects the general position of the Commission concerning the assignment of contracts and escrowed funds as it concerns the brokers.

1. All parties to a contract must be informed of assignments and all beneficiaries of escrowed funds must be informed of any transfer of escrowed funds.

2. Listing contracts may not be assigned by the listing broker to another broker (without the consent of the owner), because the listing contract is a personal contract of a type which would not be entered into except when the owner relies on the personal skills and expertise of the broker.

3. The broker concerned with an executory contract is not a party principal to the contract itself and, therefore, has no voice in its assignment. The broker signs the sales contract only as the receipting agent.

4. The right of entitlement of a broker to a commission, pursuant to a contract between the broker and a seller, is assignable. In the Commission approved form of executory contract, the agreement of the seller in regard to a commission is placed outside the body of the contract between the purchaser and seller.

5. The contract between the seller and the broker concerning commissions does not affect the contract between the principal parties in the sale.

* 6. Earnest money taken pursuant to an executory contract is money belonging to others and falls within the purview of 12-10-217(1)(h) and (i), C.R.S. Earnest money being held by the broker is not transferable to any party except to a closing agent as immediately prior to closing as is practicable.

* 7. The maintenance of earnest money held in escrow must be pursuant to the rules of the Commission. The broker may, for convenience, authorize other persons to withdraw money from this escrow account (see Commission Rule 5.3.C.), but the withdrawal must be pursuant to law and Commission rules.

8. Unless contracted to the contrary, the mechanical act of closing the transaction may be performed by any qualified person or persons with the agreement of the principal parties to the contract.

* 9. The absence of the closing broker or the Broker's agent will not relieve such broker from the broker's responsibilities of approving the Statement of Settlement. (See Commission Rule 6.19.). However, the absence of the broker cannot impede the closing of the transaction pursuant to the executory contract.

10. If a licensed broker receipts for earnest money pursuant to an executory contract and then transfers such earnest money to an unauthorized person, who is also a licensed broker, the licensed transferee, (as well as the transferor), is also subject to the law and rules of the Commission in regard to money belonging to others. Such licensed transferee is obligated to retain such money in a trust account until the transaction is consummated, defeated, or settlement has occurred, or unless directed otherwise by a court of law. If litigation concerning escrowed money commences, the money may be placed with the court. The jurisdiction of the court will supersede the statutory requirements and the Commission Rules.

11. If the seller and the buyer, who are the sole beneficiaries of the escrowed money, both agree that such escrowed money be transferred, then settlement has occurred and the broker must transfer the money according to the wishes of the beneficiaries. This does not defeat the broker's right to a commission whether by original contract with the seller or by assignment of such contract right.

CP-9 Commission Position on Record Keeping by Brokers

The Commission is often asked what documents must be kept in the broker's files which concern a particular transaction.

* A duplicate means photocopy, carbon copy, or facsimile, or electronic copies which contain a digital or electronic signature as defined in 24-71-101(1) C.R.S. Pursuant to Rule 6.14.A. and 6.19.A., a broker shall maintain a duplicate of the original of any document (except deeds, notes and trust deeds or mortgages prepared for the benefit of third party lenders) which was prepared by or on behalf of the licensee and pertains to the consummation of the leasing, purchase, sale or exchange of real property in which the broker participates as a broker. The payoff statement and new loan statement monetarily affect the settlement statements and should be retained by the respective broker concerned. Cooperating brokers, including brokers acting as agents for buyers in a specific real estate transaction, shall have the same requirements for retention of duplicate records as is stated above, except that a cooperating broker who is not a party to the listing contract need not retain a copy of the listing contract or the seller's settlement statement. A broker is not required to obtain and retain copies of existing public records, title commitments, loan applications, lender required disclosures or related affirmations from independent third party closing entities after the settlement date. The broker shall retain documents bearing a duplicate signature for the disclosures required by Commission Rule 7.1. The broker engaged by a party shall insure that the final sales agreement, settlement statement, or amendment of the settlement, delivered at closing for that party's tax reporting or future use, shall bear duplicate signatures as authorized by the parties concerned.

A complete listing of the documents normally required by the Commission for sales transactions and management activities can be found in the current edition of the Colorado Real Estate Manual, Chapter 20, and at the website address: http://www.dora.state.co.us/real-estate.

CP-10 Commission Position on Compensation Agreements Between Employing and Employed Brokers

In regard to an employed broker's claim for compensation from an employing broker, the Real Estate Commission has no legal authority to render a monetary judgment in a money dispute nor will it arbitrate such a matter. A broker's failure to pay an employee does not warrant disciplinary action.

The Commission's position is:

1. An employed broker is an employee of the employing broker.

* 2. That an employed broker may not accept a commission or valuable consideration for the sale of real property except from his or her employing broker. (12-10-221, C.R.S.)

* 3. That a commission or compensation paid to the employing or independent broker for real estate services is money belonging to such broker and is not money belonging to others as defined in 12-10-217(1)(h) and (i), C.R.S.

4. That a claim by an employed licensee for money allegedly owed by an employing broker must be decided by the civil courts on the basis of contract or "quantum merit."

5. That an employing broker pays their licensed or unlicensed employees pursuant to an oral or written employment contract.

Therefore, the contractual relationship between employing and employed brokers, as well as the office policy manual, should adequately cover the compensation of employed brokers.

CP-11 Commission Position on Assignments of Broker's Rights to a Commission

* The Real Estate Commission recognizes and will enforce the statutory obligation of employed licensees as described in (12-10-217(1), C.R.S.), and more particularly:

* "12-10-217(1)(g), C.R.S. In the case of a broker registered as in the employ of another broker, failing to place, as soon after receipt as is practicably possible, in the custody of that licensed broker-employer any deposit money or other money or fund entrusted to the employee by any person dealing with the employee as the representative of that licensed broker-employer."

*   The Commission recognizes and will enforce the prohibition described in 12-10-221, C.R.S.:

*   "12-10-221, C.R.S. It is unlawful for a real estate broker registered in the commission office as in the employ of another broker to accept a commission or valuable consideration for the performance of any of the acts specified in this part 2 from any person except the broker's employer, who shall be a licensed real estate broker."

*   However: If a broker is entitled to a commission pursuant to 12-10, Part 3, C.R.S., or, a broker is entitled to a commission in a transaction and title has passed from a seller to a buyer, the broker may assign any or all legal rights to such commission to any person including employed licensees and no disciplinary action will be invoked against such broker for having made such an assignment.

CP-12 Commission Position on the Broker's Payment or Rebating a Portion of an Earned Commission

The License Law forbids a broker from paying a commission or valuable consideration for performing brokerage functions to any person who is not licensed as a real estate broker. Thus, "referral fees" or "finder's fees" paid as the result of performing brokerage activities are prohibited.

The question of whether or not a broker may make payments from their earned commission to a buyer or a seller in a particular transaction will arise because usually neither the buyer nor the seller is licensed.

However, the License Law also permits any person to sell or acquire real property on such person's own account.

In a listing contract, the broker is principal party to the contract and the consideration offered is the brokerage services. The broker may add to this consideration the payment of money to the property owner in order to secure the listing. This is not a violation of the License Law.

Also, in a particular real estate transaction, the broker may pay a portion of commission to the unlicensed seller. This is merely a reduction in the amount of the earned commission and does not violate the License Law.

Payment to the unlicensed purchaser is often referred to as "rebating" and the intention to pay money to the purchaser is sometimes advertised and promoted as a sales inducement. The payment to the purchaser in itself is not a violation of the License Law because the broker is licensed to negotiate and the purchaser may negotiate on their own account. However, a broker representing the seller in a transaction should take care to insure that such payments do not conflict with fiduciary duties. For example, the "rebate" of a portion of a commission to a purchaser to be used by the purchaser as a down payment could distort the purchaser's financial qualifications and ultimately harm the seller. Additionally, a purchaser who does not receive a promised rebate of a partial commission may try to hold the seller liable for the wrongdoing of the broker on the theory of respondent superior. The Commission recommends that brokers disclose such payments to the seller and obtain the seller's consent prior to acceptance of any offer to purchase.

Gratuitous gifts to a purchaser subsequent to closing and not promised or offered as an inducement to buy would also be allowed (*i.e.*, a door knocker or dinner). Such gifts would not require disclosure and consent inasmuch as fiduciary duties would not be involved.

CP-13 Commission Policy on Single-Party Listings

Brokers often secure single-party listings because they have what they believe to be a good prospect for purchase. These listings are usually only for a few days, but occasionally the broker wishes to be protected for a longer period while the broker is negotiating with a particular prospective purchaser.

A single-party listing, when placed on a Commission approved form for an Exclusive Right to Sell or Exclusive Agency, results in greater protection to the broker than the broker needs to have and the owner is placed in a position which is unfair. The owner may not realize that if the owner signs a listing contract with another broker, the owner may become liable for the payment of two commissions even though the owner has excepted a sale to the person mentioned in a single-party listing contract.

In any and all contracting, the intent of the parties is paramount in its importance, in a listing contract, a broker is dealing with those less informed than the broker, and the broker has a duty to disclose the true meaning of the listing contract.

The Commission does not wish to limit any owner of the freedom to contract. However, the broker should fully disclose to the owner the effect of the exclusive right to sell listing contract or the exclusive agency contract.

Usually, when an owner signs an exclusive right to sell or exclusive agency agreement concerning a single party, the owner wishes to limit the rights of the broker under the listing contract. Therefore, in the space provided for additional provisions, one, two, or all of the following limitations should be inserted in this space:

1. The provisions of this listing contract shall apply only in the event a sale is made to

   _____.

2. The termination date shall not be extended by the "Holdover Period" of this listing contract.

3. In the event a sale is made by the owner or their broker to any other party than the above names, this listing contract is void.

If an owner is misled to their disadvantage, the broker may be found guilty of endangering the public.

CP-14 Commission Position on Sale of Modular Homes by Licensees

The Commission is aware that many services rendered by licensees may or may not, in themselves, require licensing. Such services as collection of rents on real property, subdivision development services other than sales, or the general management of real property not involving renting or leasing may all be performed independently by an unlicensed person. When performed by a licensee, these services are all so integrated with real estate brokerage that all money received in connection therewith must be held or disbursed according to the law and rules of the Real Estate Commission.

* Therefore, it is the position of the Commission that a licensee who sells land and a modular home to be affixed to the land, to the purchaser in concurrent or an arranged or pre-arranged or packaged transaction, is subject to the laws and rules of the Commission. Consequently, all money received concerning the integrated transaction, including the modular home, should be processed through the broker or the employing broker pursuant to 12-10-221, C.R.S., and 12-10-217(1)(g), C.R.S. and Commission Rules in Chapter 5 and Rule 6.19.

* It is also the position of the Commission that if a licensee sells to an owner of land, a modular home to be affixed to the land, and there has been no brokerage relationship between the owners of the land and the licensee, such licensee in such a sale will not be required to comply with the requirements of 12-10-221, C.R.S., or 12-10-217(1)(g), C.R.S., or Commission Rules in Chapter 5 and 6.19.

CP-15 Commission Position on Sale of Items Other Than Real Estate

Inquiries have been made to the Commission as to the proper handling of sales, made by licensees, of items or services other than real estate. The following is the position of the Commission:

If the item, appliance, repair, remodeling or installation is performed in conjunction with a management contract or lease for a particular party or pursuant to an oral or written contingency in a specific executed contract of sale of the property, the employed licensee must process any fees or commissions received from the vendor or contractor through the employing broker. Also, disclosure must be made by the licensee to both the buyer and the seller of the property that the licensee is compensated by the vendor or contractor.

It is also the position of the Commission that if the sale of the item, appliance, repair, remodeling or installation is performed pursuant to a separate contract, and without reference to a specific contract of sale of the property, then the employed licensee may receive compensation directly from the vendor, or contractor and payment need not be made through the employing broker. However, if the sale of items or services is made to a buyer of real property during the term of the brokerage agreement with the seller of such property, then disclosure must be made by the licensee to both the buyer and the seller of the property that the licensee is compensated by the vendor or contractor.

The Commission takes no position when the licensee engages in selling items or services unconnected with real estate sales.

In any of the above situations the employed licensee may be subject to any requirements or prohibitions imposed by the employment agreement with the employing broker.

CP-16 Commission Position on Access to Properties Offered for Sale

(Revised November 1, 2005)

The Commission approved listing agreements (LC series) include a section titled OTHER BROKERAGE FIRMS ASSISTANCE – MULTIPLE LISTING SERVICE – MARKETING.

Provisions of this section allow the seller and listing broker to agree on whether or not to submit the property to a multiple listing service, information exchange, and whether there are limitations on the methods of marketing the property.

The provisions of the section also allow for discussion and the establishment of "Other Instructions" regarding access to the property by other brokerage firms such as through a lock box, for example.

It is the position of the Commission that the access information, and adherence to the Other Instructions, whether through lock box code or other means, is the responsibility of the listing broker. Listing brokers should take every effort to safeguard the access information on behalf of the seller. The listing agreements also include a section titled MAINTENANCE OF THE PROPERTY, which addresses the broker's liability for damage of any kind occurring to the property caused by the broker's negligence. Brokers are advised that failure to safeguard the access information and adhere to the instructions of the Seller related to access by other brokerage firms could result in a claim of negligence brought against the listing broker.

Selling brokers who obtain access information should safeguard that information at all times. At no time should a selling broker share the access information with a third party (inspector, appraiser, buyer, etc.) without the listing broker's authorization. Selling brokers are reminded that pursuant to the Contract to Buy and Sell, the Buyers indemnify the Seller against damage to the property in connection with the property inspection provision.

CP-18 Commission Position on Payments to a Wholly Owned Employee's Corporation

The Commission has received several inquiries concerning the payment of commissions or fees by an employing broker to a corporation that is wholly owned by an employed licensee.

* C.R.S. 12-10-203(8), which prohibits the licensing of an employed broker as a corporation, partnership or limited liability company and the limitations on the payment or receipt of real estate fees, as described in 12-10-217(1)(i) and 12-10-221, are recognized by the Commission; however, it is the position of the Commission that:

* An employing broker's payment of earned real estate fees to a corporation which is solely owned by an employed licensee of such employing broker shall not be considered by the Commission as a violation of 12-10-217(1)(i) or 12-10-221; however, a contract between the employing broker and such corporation or employed licensee shall not relieve the broker of any obligation to supervise such employed licensee or any other requirement of the licensing statute and Commission rules. It is not the intent of this position statement that the employed licensee be relieved from personal civil responsibility for any licensed activities by interposing the corporate form.

It must be stressed that the above position statement does not allow such corporations to be licensed under a broker and specifically refers only to corporations which are owned solely by the employed licensee.

CP-19 Commission Position on Short Term Occupancy Agreements

The Commission has been asked for its position concerning the need for a real estate broker to escrow funds coming into their possession involving short-term occupancies.

A short-term occupancy can be distinguished from a lease in that it is in the nature of a hotel reservation and a license to use. Short-term occupancy agreements, if properly treated, are not considered lease agreements. Activities relating to these agreements are exempt from the definition of real estate brokerage. Concerns arise when a licensed real estate broker wants to engage in short term occupancy activities either exclusively or as part of their separate brokerage practice. In some instances brokers have objected to holding money belonging to others in their trust accounts or accounting for these funds if the activity itself is exempt.

*   C.R.S. 12-10-217(1)(h) subjects a licensee to disciplinary action for "Failing to account for or to remit, within a reasonable time, any moneys coming into the licensee's possession that belong to others, whether acting as real estate brokers or otherwise, and failing to keep records relative to said moneys...." In addition, the case of Seibel vs. Colorado Real Estate Commission, 533 P.2nd 1290, gives the Commission jurisdiction over the acts of a licensed broker even where those acts would otherwise exempt the person from original licensure.

Based on the above, it is the position of the Commission that a licensed real estate broker engaging in short term occupancy agreements must escrow and account for funds coming into their possession which belong to others. To hold otherwise, would be to invite further confusion and mistrust on the part of the public in an already confusing real estate related practice. It has been the Commission's experience that most brokerage companies engaging in short term occupancy activities combine those activities with those requiring a license (*i.e.*, long term rental and lease agreements, sales). In addition, brokers continually hold themselves out to the public as being both licensed and professional. The public does not distinguish between an activity technically exempt from licensure and the overall business practices of a licensed real estate broker.

CP-20 Commission Position Statement on Personal Assistants

(Revised October 2, 2012)

Personal assistants ("assistants") are generally thought of as employees or independent contractors ("employees") that perform various functions, including clerical duties, on behalf of a licensed real estate broker ("broker"). Assistants can be grouped into two separate categories: unlicensed assistants and licensed assistants. An unlicensed assistant cannot perform the same duties that a licensed assistant can perform. A broker needs to be cognizant of these differences, along with the broker's individual supervision responsibilities to the assistant. If a "licensed" assistant's broker's license is currently on inactive or expired status, the assistant is limited to performing only those tasks that may be completed by an unlicensed assistant.

*   §12-10-222, C.R.S., mandates that a broker can be held liable for any unlawful act or violations of the license law committed by an employee of a broker, if the broker had actual knowledge of the unlawful act or violation or had been negligent in the supervision of such employees. Commission Rule 6.3.A.2. clarifies that employees include but not limited to, "Unlicensed On-Site Managers, secretaries, bookkeepers and personal assistants..." Employing brokers that employ assistants, or allow their employed brokers to employ assistants, need to include procedures on the use of licensed and/or unlicensed assistants in the office policy manual.

The license law prohibits unlicensed persons, including unlicensed assistants, from practicing real estate brokerage, which includes negotiating the sale, exchange or lease of real property on behalf of another person. An unlicensed assistant should promptly disclose to brokers, other industry professionals (i.e. loan originators, lenders, appraisers, property inspectors, etc.) and consumers that he or she is not a broker, and disclose the name of the broker for whom the assistant works. An unlicensed assistant may complete the following tasks:

1. Complete forms prepared for, and as directed by a broker. Unlicensed assistants cannot independently draft legal documents such as listing or sales contracts, and they cannot offer opinions, advice or interpretations of these documents.

2. Distribute preprinted, objective information prepared by the broker about a property listed for sale.

3. Perform clerical duties, including gathering information for a listing.

4. If authorized by the seller, provide access to property, conduct showings or open houses.

5. Deliver paperwork to other brokers, buyers or sellers.

6. Deliver paperwork that requires signatures in regard to financing documents that are prepared by lending institutions.

7. Prepare market analyses on behalf of the broker, if the analyses are approved and submitted by the broker to the client with a disclosure that the market analyses were prepared by the unlicensed assistant. The broker must ensure that market analyses comply with Commission Rule 6.12.

8. Collect and receipt for earnest money deposits, security deposits or rents.

9. Schedule property repairs on behalf of the broker, if there is an existing agreement that authorizes the broker to make repairs to the property.

The broker should inquire as to whether any of the unlicensed assistant's activities are covered by the broker's errors and omissions insurance policy. Furthermore, licensed assistants may need their own separate errors and omissions insurance policy to cover the acts they perform on behalf of the broker.

CP-21 Commission Position on Office Policy Manuals

(Revised and Adopted December 4, 2018)

12-10-Part 4 C.R.S., and Commission Rules 6.3. and 6.4. set out a broker's supervising responsibilities. In order to help brokers comply with the rules it is suggested that a policy manual contain procedures for at least the following:

1) typical real estate transactions

   a) review of contracts

   b) handling of earnest money deposits, including the release thereof

   c) back-up contracts

   d) closings

2) non-qualifying assumptions and owner financing

3) guaranteed buyouts

4) investor purchases

5) identifying brokerage relationships offered to public (required by 12-10-408, C.R.S.)

* 6) procedures for designation of brokers who are to work with a seller, landlord, buyer or tenant, individually or in teams (required by Rule 6.4.) (Does not apply to brokerage firms that consist of only one licensed natural person.)

* 7) identify and provide adequate means and procedures for the maintenance and protection of confidential information (required by Rule 6.4.B.4.)

8) procedures and practices for the reasonably secure maintenance and protection of personal identifying information (required by 6-1-713.5, C.R.S.)

9) procedures for the destruction or proper disposal of paper or electronic records by shredding, erasing, or otherwise modifying the following information to make it unreadable or indecipherable through any means:

   a) a social security number;

   b) a personal identification number;

   c) a password;

   d) a pass code;

   e) an official state or government-issued driver's license or identification card;

   f) a government passport number;

   g) biometric data, as defined in 6-1-716(1)(a), C.R.S.;

   h) an employer, student or military identification number; or

   i) a financial transaction device, as defined in 18-5-701, C.R.S.

10) procedures and practices for the identification and notification of a security breach of personal identifying information (required by 6-1-716, C.R.S.)

11) licensee's purchase and sale of property

12) monitoring of license renewals and transfers

13) delegation of authority

14) property management

15) property listing procedures, including release of listings

16) training

   a) dissemination of information

   b) staff meetings

17) use of personal assistants

18) fair housing/affirmative action marketing

19) listing syndication

   a) brokerage participation

   b) entry and maintenance of information

20) performance of and compensation for real estate related activities (i.e. broker price opinions, etc.)

Brokers are encouraged to add other policies as appropriate to their practice.

In the event that one or several of these suggested topics (e.g., guaranteed buyouts) are not applicable in a particular office, they should be addressed by stating that the office does not participate in that activity.

The Commission does not become involved in matters relating to independent contractor agreements, and disputes over earned commissions. Office policies in these areas do not fall within the purview of Commission rules.

CP-22 Commission Position Statement on Handling of Confidential Information in Real Estate Brokerage

(Adopted October 1, 2003)

* Prior to designated brokerage, it was common for brokers to share the motivations of a buyer or seller during office sales meetings, for example. Under designated brokerage, the law specifically prohibits sharing of such information. Confidential information, and the broker responsibility thereto, are defined in C.R.S. 12-10-404(2), 12-10-405(2), 12-10-407(3), and Rules 6.3.D. and 6.4.B. Confidential information can include, but is not limited to, motivation of the parties.

Brokers are required to have a written office policy that identifies and provides adequate means and procedures for the maintenance and protection of confidential information. Situations where inadvertent disclosure of confidential information may occur, include, but are not limited to:

- sales meetings or marketing sessions,
- shared fax or copy machines,
- shared computer networks, printers and file directories,
- in-office mail boxes,
- hand written telephone messages,
- phone conversations or meetings with clients,
- relocation, divorce, pending foreclosure and other sensitive documents,
- conversations with affiliated business providers,
- production boards,
- social functions

Brokers must develop office policies and procedures to address the handling of confidential information. For example, some offices may have "locked" transaction files that include confidential information and other offices may elect not to include confidential information in transaction files.

A designated broker is permitted to share confidential information with a supervising broker without changing or extending the brokerage relationship beyond the designated broker. Brokers may want to consult legal counsel regarding the necessity of securing the authorization of the party to whom the information is confidential before the designated broker shares that confidential information with the supervising broker. Such advice could include modifications to the listing agreement or buyer agreement that create such authorization.

CP-23 Commission Position on Use of "Licensee Buyout Addendum"

(Revised January 17, 2006)

* Rule 7.1.A. requires real estate licensees to use the Commission approved "Licensee Buyout Addendum to Contract to Buy and Sell Real Estate", when purchasing certain listed properties.

* It is the Commission's position that Rule 7.1.A. requires use of the Buyout Addendum under the following circumstances:

1. When a licensee enters into a contract to purchase a property concurrent with the listing of such property.

2. When a licensee enters into a contract to purchase a property as an inducement or to facilitate the property owner's purchase of another property, the purchase or sale of which will generate a commission or fee to the licensee.

3. When a licensee enters into a contract to purchase a property from an owner but continues to market that property on behalf of the owner under an existing listing contract.

Unless one of the above situations exists, licensees are not required to use the Buyout Addendum.

The term "licensee", as used above, refers to the individual licensee who has personally taken a listing or to the listing broker or brokerage entity if the buyout is to be accomplished by that broker or brokerage entity. If the listing licensee or broker desires to acquire a listed property solely for personal use or future resale and not as an inducement to the owner, the licensee or broker is advised to (1) clearly sever their agency or listing relationship in writing; (2) renounce the right to any commission, fee or compensation in conjunction with acquisition of the listed property; and, (3) advise the owner to seek other assistance, representation or legal advice.

* Future resale of a purchased property, as referred to above, means resale to a third party purchaser with whom the licensee has not negotiated during the listing period. Resale to a person with whom a licensee has conducted previous negotiations concerning the subject property during the listing period (often referred to as a "pocket buyer"), would constitute a violation of 12-10-217(1)(q) in the absence of full written disclosure and acknowledgment by the owner.

CP-24 Commission Position on Preparation of Market Analyses and Real Estate Evaluations Used for Loan Purposes

* The Colorado Real Estate Appraiser Licensing Act contains special provisions which allow licensed real estate brokers to perform certain real estate valuation related activities without being registered, licensed or certified as real estate appraisers. These provisions are found in Sections 12-10-602 and 12-10-618, C.R.S.

The first of these allows a broker to prepare an "estimate of value" which is not represented as an appraisal and is not used to obtain financing. The position of the Commission is that this provision allows a broker to prepare a market analysis for use in the real estate brokerage process and to offer their estimate as to the value or market price of real estate for court testimony or tax purposes.

The second provision allows a broker to prepare what are termed "evaluations" in federal banking regulations. These evaluations may be used for lending purposes. This provision is very narrow in scope—a broker may prepare such an evaluation only for a federally regulated bank, savings and loan or credit union with whom they have a contract. The loan amount must be below the threshold which invokes the requirement for a true appraisal.

* As the authority to prepare such estimates of value and evaluations is tied to the holding of a Colorado real estate broker license, the Colorado Real Estate Commission has jurisdiction over the activities of brokers engaged in such activities. The Commission will consider the conduct of licensees who prepare estimates of value and evaluations in light of Sections 12-10-217(1)(q) and (w), which speak to unworthiness, incompetency and dishonest dealing.

It is the position of the Commission that the mere holding of a broker license does not in itself assure the competency necessary to prepare more complex estimates of value or evaluations. Licensees preparing estimates of value and evaluations have a responsibility to possess training and experience commensurate with the complexity of the assignment undertaken.

Investigations undertaken by the Commission relating to unworthiness, incompetency and dishonest dealing will take into account the following:

- Brokers preparing estimates of value and evaluations must act independently at all times. The estimate or evaluation must be unbiased.

- The broker preparing an estimate or evaluation must not represent themselves as an appraiser, nor represent the work product as being an appraisal.

* - The broker preparing an estimate or evaluation must at all times comply with the statutory requirement in Sections 12-10-602 and 12-10-618, Colorado Revised Statutes, for a written notice that they are not an appraiser. The wording and use of the written notice are specified in the Rules of the Board of Real Estate Appraisers. The required wording is:

> "NOTICE: The preparer of this appraisal is not registered, licensed or certified as a real estate appraiser by the State of Colorado".

- The broker must not prepare an estimate of value or evaluation of real property which requires a level of competency beyond the level of training and experience possessed by the licensee.

CP-25 Commission Position on Recording Contracts

Over the years the Commission has received many inquiries and complaints concerning the recording of listing contracts to protect claims for commissions. In addition, some licensees have attempted more "creative" ways of holding up a closing, such as filing mechanics liens or notices of lis pendens, as well as recording demand letters or purchase contracts. The end result is usually a cloud on the title and sometimes a slander of title action.

Some states have passed statutes authorizing the filing of such liens. Colorado has not. Filings and recordings such as these are inappropriate and will result in Commission action.

Here is a typical scenario: Broker lists a property at $125,000 for 120 days and actively markets it. No offers come in during the first 30 days. Broker advises her seller to lower the price by $5,000 to encourage some activity. The seller is adamant that the property is worth the list price and refuses. After another 15 days with no offers, the seller reluctantly lowers the price. He also tells the broker that he doesn't feel she is trying hard enough to sell the property and he's going to take it off the market if nothing happens.

A week later an offer for $100,000 comes in from another company, which is presented and rejected. The seller is quite upset at the low offer and demands to be released from the listing. There is no further communication between the parties, but the listing is never formally terminated. Three weeks later the broker learns that the seller has entered into a contract with the same buyer for $110,000 and closing is set. The broker is very upset and wants to protect her commission. What can she do?

1. File a mechanics lien?

   ANS: No. Real estate licensees are not a protected class of lien claimant under the statute except as provided in C.R.S. 38-22.5 (Commercial Real Estate Brokers Commission Security Act).

2. File a lis pendens (notice of pending lawsuit)?

   ANS: No. A lis pendens relates to a title or ownership dispute involving the land itself. The broker has no legal interest in the real estate.

3. Record the listing contract?

   ANS: No. This will usually have the effect of clouding title to the property, which in turn affects the closing between buyer and seller. The broker should not interfere in the process of transferring title to property.

4. Escrow the disputed commission?

   ANS: Maybe. This is a touchy area. If the broker makes demand on the seller for the commission prior to closing and states her possible rights (mediation; arbitration; civil action) the parties may agree to an escrow pending settlement of the dispute. However, there is no legal requirement that the closing entity escrow funds absent an agreement.

5. Commence mediation, arbitration or civil action (as appropriate).

   ANS: Yes. Nothing prevents a licensee from asserting any legal claim against a principal.

A commission dispute is an emotional issue. Sometimes a licensee has put in considerable time on a listing only to be faced with a seller who refuses to pay, attempts to renegotiate or is outright deceitful. On the other side, the Commission has witnessed instances in which the licensee had no legitimate right to a commission and was using superior knowledge and scare tactics to force payment. Clearly this is a time to consult a good real estate attorney and avoid the risk of a complaint based on a hasty decision.

CP-26 Commission Position on Auctioning

(Adopted 5-1-97)

Real estate experts predict that the next decade will see a significant increase in the sale of real estate through auctions. For many years auctioning was associated with rural or distressed properties. However, forecasts are for a proliferation of sales activity in both residential and commercial real estate. Sales by auction are already occurring in the residential market in Colorado and other parts of the country.

*   The brokers act requires that real estate auctions be conducted by a licensed broker and defines the activity as ". . .offering, attempting or agreeing to auction real estate, or interest therein, or improvements affixed thereon. . ." (C.R.S. 12-10-201(6)(a)(VI)).

A long-standing Attorney General's opinion allows an unlicensed auctioneer to "cry" the bid at a real estate auction in the presence of a broker or seller. However, the control of the sale, including listing, advertising, showing the property and writing contracts must remain with the broker or the auctioneer will be violating the law.

Based on the statute and Attorney General's opinion, the following guidelines are established for unlicensed persons involved in the auction process:

1. Auctioneers should never hold themselves out as providing real estate brokerage services to the public (*e.g.*, listing, advertising, negotiating, contracting, legal document preparation);

2. Inquiries from sellers should be referred to a licensed broker or attorney;

3. Inquiries from buyers should be referred to the seller, listing broker or sellers attorney;

4. Only auctioning services should be advertised to buyers and sellers;

5. A potential buyer may be chauffeured to a property, so long as the property is shown by the seller or a licensed broker;

6. Information on listed properties may be distributed when such information has been prepared by a broker;

7. Auctioneers may "cry" the sale, but may not engage in subsequent negotiations, document drafting and the handling of earnest money;

8. Payment should be based on auctioning services performed regardless of the success of a sale.

CP-27 Commission Position on the Performance of Residential Leasing and Property Management Functions

(Adopted August 1998 – Revised August 2013)

Property management is one of the leading sources of complaints received by the Commission. This position statement is designed to identify common issues found during the course of a complaint investigation or an audit; however it does not encompass all of the potential issues associated with property management. Any licensed real estate broker ("Broker") interested in performing property management duties are strongly encouraged to complete educational offerings specific to property management, train with a Broker experienced in property management, and develop a strong familiarity with the Colorado Real Estate Manual chapters titled Escrow Records, and Property Management and Leases.

License Requirements

*   Pursuant to C.R.S. §12-10-201(6), the leasing and subsequent management of real estate for a fee or compensation, is included among the activities for which a license is required. As a result of the complaints received and issues identified in Commission investigations and audits, the Commission considers property management to be a complex area of practice. C.R.S. §12-10-217(1)(q) requires that a Broker be competent and worthy in the performance of their duties so as to not endanger the interest of the public. Furthermore, it is the Commission's position that prior to performing any acts that require a Broker's license, a Broker should determine whether he or she possesses the knowledge, experience and/or training necessary to perform the terms of the transaction and to maintain compliance with the applicable federal, state or local laws, rules, regulations, or ordinances. If the Broker does not have the requisite knowledge, experience and/or training necessary to fulfill the terms of the agreement, the Broker should either decline to provide brokerage services or seek the assistance of another Broker who does have the necessary experience, training and/or knowledge. A Broker who agrees to lease property, or perform ongoing property management duties, needs to ensure that he or she is competent to perform the duties he or she agrees to undertake and must have permission from the Broker's employing broker. Similarly, the employing broker has the responsibility to ensure that he or she is competent to supervise a broker that performs leasing or property management duties.

Leasing v. Property Management

While leasing and property management are similar, they are two distinctively different services. Leasing is a onetime activity in which the broker acts as a special agent, while property management is an ongoing relationship in which the broker is a general agent. If a Broker is performing leasing, the Broker may list a property for lease, advertise the property, help screen tenants and/or help negotiate a lease. Once the lease is signed by the landlord and tenant, the Broker's duty to the landlord or tenant is complete. With property management, a broker's obligations continue beyond the formation of the lease. A Broker performing property management duties may also perform leasing duties; where a Broker only performing leasing duties is not performing property management duties.

Generally, a Broker will function in one of three capacities with regards to rental properties. The Broker may provide leasing services only for a landlord, where the broker is involved in procuring a tenant and negotiating the lease terms. Alternatively, the broker may provide leasing services on behalf of the tenant in locating a suitable rental property and negotiating a lease. In the first two scenarios, the Broker's duties are fulfilled once the lease is executed and the broker is not involved in the transaction any further. In the third scenario, the Broker agrees not only to provide leasing services, but is also responsible for one or more of the following: maintaining the property's physical condition, communicating with tenants, collecting rent and/or collecting security deposits. In this scenario, the Broker's duties are ongoing; therefore the Broker is conducting property management services. Regardless of whether the Broker is working with the landlord or the tenant, the Broker must establish clear expectations regarding the services the Broker agrees to provide and communicate these expectations to the consumer.

Supervision

* Before engaging in property management or leasing, the Broker should discuss with the employing broker whether the Broker is capable of and allowed to perform property management or leasing duties. The employing broker is responsible for maintaining all trust accounts and all transaction records, and the employing broker is responsible for exercising authority, direction and control over the Broker's conformance to statutes and Commission rules (Rules 6.3.A. and 6.3.B.). This includes reviewing all contracts to ensure competent preparation and reviewing all transaction files to ensure that required documents exist (Rule 6.3.C.). If the employing broker does not allow Brokers to perform leasing and/or property management duties, the Broker needs to refrain from leasing and/or property management activities or seek employment elsewhere. If the real estate brokerage firm does allow leasing and/or property management, regardless of how minor, the employing broker must ensure that the office policy manual addresses these activities, including management of the Broker's own property. Both the Broker and the employing broker need to be aware of state and local laws that impact the performance of property management duties, which include, but are not limited to, laws pertaining to security deposits, habitability, carbon monoxide alarms, asbestos, lead-based paint, handling of confidential information, zoning and agency.

Forms

* C.R.S. §12-10-403(4)(a) indicates that a Broker may complete standard forms including those promulgated by the Commission. Forms that are not promulgated by the Commission must be drafted by an attorney. When the Broker provides leasing services for a tenant, the Broker should complete the Exclusive Tenant Listing Contract. When the Broker provides ONLY leasing services for the landlord, the Broker should complete the Commission-approved Exclusive Right to Lease Listing Contract. If the Broker also will be providing property management services in addition to leasing services for the landlord, a Broker should use the Brokerage Duties Addendum to Property Management Agreement with a property management agreement drafted by an attorney. Under Rule 6.14.A.2., the Broker must provide a copy of any executed contracts to the consumer. While not all property managers provide a physical copy of the lease to the landlord, because sometimes it is executed by the Broker on behalf of the landlord, the Broker should make the document available to the landlord upon request.

If the Broker is going to provide property management services, the Broker needs to provide a property management agreement. The property management agreement must be drafted by an attorney. The property management agreement should outline the duties and responsibilities of both parties. The property management agreement should, at the very minimum, address:

- Duration of the relationship;
- The parties;
- Identify the property to be managed;
- General duties performed by the Broker, including the signing of leases.

*
- Fees for the manager's services, including disclosure of any mark-ups (Commission Rule 5.17.). Before a mark-up can be charged, the Broker must obtain prior written consent to assess and receive mark-ups and/or other compensation for services performed by any third party or affiliated business entity;

- Tenant selection criteria. If the decision to lease will be based on criminal history or financial worthiness, the property management agreement should indicate who is responsible for collecting this data and what sources will be used. Additionally, the Broker must ensure compliance with the Fair Housing and Fair Credit Acts.

- Posting of eviction notices. If a Forcible Entry and Detainer (a/k/a eviction) is necessary, an attorney should represent the landlord in the filing of the Forcible Entry and Detainer. A Broker that files a Forcible Entry and Detainer without the assistance of an attorney may be practicing law without a license;

*
- Ownership Interest. The Broker must disclose a Broker's direct or indirect ownership interest in any company which will be providing maintenance or other services to the landlord, and any other conflicts of interest (Rule 6.17.);

- Identity of the entity responsible for holding the security deposit, and if interest is earned on security deposit escrow accounts, who benefits from such interest and consent to transfer the interest to the beneficiary;

*
- Process to be followed for any subsequent transfer of the landlord's monies, security deposits, keys and documents (Rule 5.8.A.); and,

- Requirement that the landlord receive regular monthly accounting of all funds received and disbursed.

* While these general duties should be addressed in the property management agreement, it is not an all-inclusive list of all the duties that may be performed by a property manager or that should be addressed within the property management agreement. Brokers are encouraged to pay close attention not only to Commission rules and regulations, but also the "Property Management and Leases" chapter in the Colorado Real Estate Manual.

* Regardless of whether the Broker is acting as a leasing agent or a property manager, prior to engaging in any of the activities that require a real estate broker's license, the Broker is required to disclose in writing the different brokerage relationships that are available to the tenant (Rule 6.5.). The Commission-approved Brokerage Disclosure to Tenant form should be used to disclose the brokerage relationships available.

In Colorado there is not an approved lease form. Therefore, prior to a tenant being procured, the Broker must: 1) hire an attorney to draft a lease form for the Broker to use; or 2) the landlord will need to designate a lease. The terms of the lease need to be clear and in writing. A Broker may choose to limit which lease is used to only the lease form provided by their attorney so long as the landlord authorizes the Broker to use their attorney prepared lease form in the property management agreement.

Trust Accounts and Record Keeping

* Any Broker performing property management duties in which the Broker is responsible for the collection and distribution of rent or security deposits needs to be especially cognizant of the Commission rules and regulations pertaining to the management of funds of others and records retention. Brokers should pay close attention to the chapters titled "Escrow Records" and "Property Management and Leases" in the Colorado Real Estate Manual. C.R.S §12-10-217(1)(h) requires that a Broker account for and remit, within a reasonable time, any moneys coming into the Broker's possession that belong to others. Rule 1.34. defines money belonging to others as including, but not limited to, funds received by a Broker in connection with property management agreements, rent or lease contracts, and money belonging to others that is collected for future investment or other purposes. All money belonging to others which is received by a Broker acting as a property manager must be deposited in the Broker's escrow or trust account within five (5) business days of receipt (Rule 5.7.A.).

* If a Broker is going to deposit rent or security deposits into the employing broker's trust account(s), the Broker is required to keep records relative to these monies. Rule 5.10.requires that all money belonging to others that is accepted by the Broker be deposited in one or more accounts separate from money belonging to the Broker, employing broker or brokerage entity. Separate trust accounts must be maintained in the name of the employing broker, or the employing broker and the licensed business entity, and the maintenance of the separate accounts is the responsibility of the employing broker (Rule 5.3. and 5.6.). This includes rent checks. Rule 5.5. requires that "A Brokerage Firm who engages in Property Management must deposit rental receipts and security deposits and disburse money collected for such purposes in separate Trust or Escrow Accounts, a minimum of one for rental receipts and a minimum of one for security deposits." As an alternative to trust accounts, a Broker may deposit rent monies or security deposits directly into an account owned and controlled by the landlord.

* Rule 5.8.A. prohibits a Broker who receipts for security deposits from delivering such deposits to a landlord, unless the tenant's written authorization is given in the lease or written notice is given to the tenant by first-class mail. The notice must identify who is holding the security deposit and the procedure the tenant must follow to request the return of the deposit. If the security deposit is held by or transferred to the landlord, the property management agreement must specify that the landlord is responsible for the security deposit's return and that, in the event of a dispute, the Broker is authorized to reveal the true name and current mailing address of the landlord. The Broker may not use any portion of the security deposit for the Broker's benefit.

* Pursuant to Rule 5.14., a Broker is required to supervise and maintain a record keeping system, at the Broker's licensed place of business that consists of an "escrow or trust account journal", a "ledger" and a "bank reconciliation worksheet". The Broker must also maintain supporting records

that detail all cash received and disbursed under the terms of the management and rental agreements. If a Broker has deposited personal funds into the trust account to open and maintain the trust account, the journal and "broker's ledger record" must contain entries documenting this money. The Broker's personal funds must also be included in the bank reconciliation worksheet. All deposits of funds into an escrow or trust account must be documented, as must all disbursements of funds from an escrow or trust account.

Absent a written agreement that indicates otherwise, the "cash basis" of accounting is required for maintaining all required escrow or trust accounts and records. Funds from one owner cannot be used to supplement operating capital, or to finance expenditures of other owners or the Broker (C.R.S. §§12-10-217(1)(h) and (i) and Rules 1.34. 5.9., 5.11., 5.18., 6.3.A. and 6.3.B.). The Broker is required to retain accurate, on-going records which verify disclosure of and consent to any mark-ups assessed or received, and fully account for the amounts or percentage of compensation assessed or received (Rule 5.17.). For Commission purposes, brokers may maintain their records in electronic format as long as the records are stored in a format that can be continually retrieved and legibly printed (Rule 6.24.). C.R.S. §12-10-217(1)(k) requires Brokers to maintain possession of their records for four (4) years.

Security Deposits

Brokers have to be very careful how they handle security deposits. The security deposit law is complicated and legal assistance is advisable. Wrongful withholding of a security deposit may result in the landlord, and the Broker as the landlord's agent, being liable for treble the amount wrongfully withheld, plus reasonable attorneys' fees and court costs. C.R.S. §38-12-103 requires that the security deposit be returned to the tenant within one month after a lease is terminated or the premises have been vacated and accepted, whichever occurs last. The lease may indicate a longer period of time to return the security deposit to the tenant; however state law does not allow this extension of time to exceed sixty days. Security deposits cannot be retained to cover normal wear and tear. C.R.S. §38-12-102 defines normal wear and tear as:

> "deterioration which occurs, based upon the use for which the rental unit is intended, without negligence, carelessness, accident, or abuse of the premises or equipment or chattels by the tenant or members of his household, or their invitees or guests."

Normal wear and tear is at the core of most security deposits lawsuits. Security deposits may be retained for nonpayment of rent, abandonment of the premises, or nonpayment of utility charges, repairs or cleaning contracted for by the tenant in the lease. If there is cause to retain any portion of the security deposit, the tenant must be provided with a written statement listing the exact reasons why all or a portion of the security deposit is being retained. The statement must be delivered with the difference between the amount of the security deposit and the amount retained. The Broker or the landlord is deemed to have complied with this requirement by mailing the statement and payment to the tenant's last known address. If the Broker or the landlord fails to provide the statement to the tenant within 30 days (or the alternative deadline specified in the lease) of the lease terminating or the surrender and acceptance of the premises, whichever occurs last, the landlord or the Broker may forfeit his right to retain any portion of the security deposit to offset amounts owed. The landlord does not lose the right to pursue amounts due, they just lose the right to utilize the security deposit to offset amounts owed. Furthermore, if the tenant pursues court action regarding any portion of the security deposit being retained, the landlord or the Broker bears the burden to prove that retention of any portion of the security deposit was not wrongful.

In the rare event that a lease is nullified and voided due to the landlord's failure to repair a hazardous condition attributed to a gas appliance, piping, or other gas equipment, the landlord or the Broker must deliver all, or the appropriate portion of, the security deposit plus any rent rebate owed to the tenant for the time period that the tenant vacated the premises. Payment must be made to the tenant within 72 hours of the tenant vacating the premises. If the 72nd hour falls on a Saturday, Sunday, or legal holiday, the security deposit, and any rent rebate due, must be delivered to the tenant by noon on the next day that is not a Saturday, Sunday, or legal holiday. If a portion of the security deposit is retained, the tenant must be provided with a written statement listing the exact reasons why all or a portion of the security deposit is being retained and payment of the remaining balance of the security deposit. If the tenant does not receive all or a portion of the security deposit with the statement within the required deadlines, the tenant may be entitled to three times the amount of the security deposit and reasonable attorney fees (C.R.S. §38-12-104).

Transfer of Services

If a Broker no longer will be managing a property, the Broker must transfer a copy of the entire file to the landlord or, upon written authorization from the landlord, to the new Broker engaged to perform the property management. At a minimum, the entire file should include:

(a)	Copy of existing lease	(d)	Outstanding tenant balances
(b)	Copy of check-in condition report	(e)	Tenant(s) security deposit(s)
(c)	Keys	(f)	Owner's funds (subject to outstanding obligations)

* Although the Commission rules do not specifically address the transfer of management duties, there should be no delay in transferring the tenant's security deposit to either the landlord or the new Broker. The Broker must give written notice by first class mail to the tenant that the security deposit has been transferred to the landlord or new Broker along with the landlord's or new Broker's contact information. The notice must indicate who is holding the security deposit and the specific requirements for the procedure in which the tenant may request return of the deposit [reference Rule 5.8.A. and C.R.S. §38-12-103(4)]. Timely transfer of the deposit protects the Broker from getting caught between the landlord and the tenant regarding the accounting of the deposit. The Broker must also provide the landlord with a final accounting of all trust funds held by the Broker. Although the Broker may delay the transfer of the landlord's funds until all outstanding invoices or debts have been resolved, the transfer of the landlord's funds needs to occur within a reasonable amount of time. A Broker that fails to transfer funds in a reasonable amount of time may be subject to discipline by the Commission for unworthiness or incompetency, C.R.S. §12-10-217(1)(q).

Managing Broker's Own Property

* Brokers are subject to the license law and Commission rules when they participate in real estate matters as principals, including managing the Broker's own property. See Seibel v. Colorado Real Estate Commission, 34 Colo. App. 415, 530 P.2d 1290 (1974). A Broker who manages his or her own rental property needs to disclose known conflicts of interest and that the Broker possesses a Colorado real estate broker's license (Rule 6.17.). The Broker also needs to use a lease drafted by an attorney for the transaction, along with disclosing in writing to the tenant the brokerage relationships under Colorado law (Rule 6.5.).

* If the Broker has an employing broker, it is important for the Broker to consult with the employing broker regarding the brokerage firm's requirements or limitations regarding managing a Broker's own property. When a Broker personally receipts for a security deposit on his or her own property, the license law does not require that the security deposit be placed in an escrow account. Additionally, a Broker cannot deposit rental proceeds into the brokerage firm's escrow account(s) for properties owned by the Broker [Rule 1.34.].

CP-28 Commission Position on Showing Properties

(Adopted March 4th 1999)

The Real Estate Commission reminds licensees that the Brokerage Relationships Act imposes duties on agents to promote the interests of their buyers or sellers with the utmost good faith as well as to counsel their principals on material benefits or risks of a transaction. A transaction-broker must exercise reasonable skill and care, advise the parties and keep the parties fully informed regarding the transaction. Whether working as an agent or a transaction-broker, these duties include disclosing the accessibility of and actual access to a property or properties.

Working With a Seller: Pursuant to the section in the various listing contracts entitled, "OTHER BROKERS, ASSISTANCE", the licensee should advise the seller of the advantages and disadvantages of using multiple listing services and other methods of making the property accessible by other brokers (*e.g.*, using lock boxes, by appointment only showings, etc.). If applicable, it should be explained that some methods may limit the ability of a selling broker to access and show a particular property. The chosen methods of cooperating with other brokers should be included in the listing agreement.

Working With a Buyer: A licensee working with a buyer has an obligation to explain the possible methods used by a listing broker and seller to show a particular property. These methods may include limitations on the buyer and selling broker being able to access a property due to the type of lock box placed on the property, the seller's choice to have the property shown by appointment only, etc. The selling broker should include such showing limitations in the Exclusive Right to Buy Contract (agency or transaction-broker).

There should be no instances of a listing broker refusing to allow a property to be shown, unless the seller has given prior explicit, written authorization to do so.

CP-29 Commission Position on "Megan's Law"

(Adopted July 1, 1999)

The Commission has been asked for its position as to the disclosure requirements for real estate licensees with regard to "Megan's Law." In 1994, and primarily as a response to the murders of two young girls, a federal law was passed creating a registration and notification procedure to alert the public as to the presence of certain types of convicted sex offenders living in a neighborhood. This is commonly referred to as "Megan's Law." Identified sex offenders are required to register with local law enforcement officials. The federal law also required states to establish registries of convicted sex offenders. It contains no disclosure requirements for real estate licensees when working with the public.

In compliance with federal law, Colorado enacted legislation that sets procedures and timeframes for local registration. The office of chief of police is the designated place of registration for those offenders residing within any city, town or city and county. The office of the county sheriff is the designated place of registration for those living outside any city, town or city and county, in addition, the law enforcement agency is required to release information regarding registered persons. However, the duty to release information may differ depending on whether the inquiring party does or does not live within that jurisdiction.

While legislation in a few states has specifically imposed disclosure requirements on real estate licensees working with buyers and sellers, Colorado's legislation imposes no such requirements. Colorado's legislation clearly places the duty to release information on the local law enforcement agency, after considering a request.

It is the position of the Real Estate Commission that all real estate licensees should inform a potential buyer to contact local law enforcement officials for further information if the presence of a registered sex offender is a matter of concern to the buyer.

Editor's Note:

C.R.S. 18-3-412.5 requires the Colorado Bureau of Investigation to post on the Internet identifying information, including a picture, of each sex offender:

- *Sentenced as a sexually violent predator; or*
- *Convicted of a sexual offense involving children*

CP-30 State of Colorado Real Estate Commission and Board of Real Estate Appraisers Joint Position Statement

(Revised January 8, 2009)

The Colorado Real Estate Commission and the Colorado Board of Real Estate Appraisers have issued this Joint Position Statement to address mutual concerns pertaining to practices of real estate brokers and real estate appraisers with regard to residential sales transactions involving seller assisted down payments, seller concessions, personal property transferred with real property and other items of value included in the sale of residential real property.

A residential real estate transaction has a life well beyond closing and possession of the property. Accurate sales data is crucial for appraisals and comparative market analysis (CMA) work products. Both appraisers and real estate brokers can effectively work together to maintain the safeguards that accurate sold data affords.

A **real estate broker** can facilitate these safeguards by adherence to the following:

- Note the amount of any seller paid costs (including a seller assisted down payment or fee paid to a charitable organization on behalf of the buyer) or other seller concession in the proper transaction documents, including the Buy/Sell Contract, Closing Statements, and Real Property Transfer Declaration.
- Utilize all available fields in the multiple listing service to report sold information including all transaction terms and seller concessions. Sold information should be entered promptly following closing and be specific and detailed particularly when the sold price includes a seller assisted down payment or concessions.
- Advise buyers and sellers to consult legal and tax counsel for advice on tax consequences of seller contributions and inducements to purchase.
- Cooperate with appraisers as they perform their due diligence in asking questions about sales.

An **appraiser** can facilitate these safeguards by adherence to the following:

- Research and confirm subject property and comparable sales, including obtaining details of the contract and financing terms.
- Research and confirm all relevant information about a transaction, including determination of seller paid costs.
- Utilize all available data search tools, including the listing history and seller contributions features of multiple listing services.
- Make appropriate adjustments to comparables with seller contributions and inducements to purchase when developing work products.
- Comply with the applicable provisions of the Ethics Rule and Standards 1 & 2 of the Uniform Standards of Professional Appraisal Practice.
- Comply with any scope of work requirements required by agencies such as the Federal Housing Administration.

CP-31 Commission Position on Acting as a Transaction Broker or Agent in Particular Types of Transactions

(Adopted 9-8-04)

The public may enter into either a Transaction-Broker relationship or an Agency relationship with a Broker. Fundamental among the differences between Agency and Transaction-Brokerage is that an Agent is an advocate with fiduciary duties, while a Transaction-Broker should remain neutral, not advocate. However, in some situations the relationship of the Broker with a particular party or property may make a particular relationship inappropriate or problematic.

Before acting as a Transaction-Broker in transactions where neutrality is difficult, the Broker should consider whether the Transaction-Brokerage arrangement is suitable, consult with the Broker's supervising Broker and then make the necessary disclosures. Some examples of these situations include:

1. Selling or purchasing for one's own account (whether the property is solely or partially owned or to be acquired by the Broker), (See Rule 6.17. regarding proper disclosures);

2. Selling or purchasing for the account of a spouse or family member of the Broker;

3. Selling or purchasing for the account of a close personal friend, business associate, or other person where it would be difficult for the Broker to remain neutral; or

4. Selling or purchasing for the account of a repeat or regular client/party where it would be difficult for the Broker to remain neutral (*i.e.*, undertaking as a Transaction-Broker the listing of multiple units, lots or properties such as listing a real estate development or condominium complex for a single developer, listing multiple residential or commercial properties for the same seller that will be sold to different buyers, or listing for lease a multiple unit residential or commercial property that will be leased to different tenants).

An agency relationship between a Broker and a seller or landlord, buyer or tenant, requires a written agency agreement. The duties of an agent go beyond facilitation of the transaction as a neutral party and require representing the interests of the Broker's principal over the interests of the other party. In certain circumstances, fulfilling the duties of an Agent including acting as an advocate may be difficult. A Broker who enters into an agency relationship must fulfill the duties of advocacy, fidelity, loyalty and other fiduciary duties associated with a single agency relationship. In circumstances where the Broker may not be able to fulfill the duties imposed on an agent the Broker should consider whether the agency arrangement is appropriate, consult with the Broker's supervising Broker and act accordingly.

This Position Statement applies to relationships where Brokers are working with landlords or tenants, as well as sellers and buyers. It applies equally to residential and commercial transactions.

CP-32 Commission Position on Brokerage Disclosures

(Adopted 9-8-04)

The Commission believes that a broker who intends to act as a buyer's or tenant's agent in a transaction should attempt to secure a written agency agreement as early in the brokerage relationship as possible. However, the Commission also recognizes that in some instances, the buyer or tenant will not immediately execute such a written agency agreement.

In these situations, the broker should initially function as a transaction-broker by either entering into:

BC 60: Exclusive Right-to-Buy Contract (All Types of Properties); or
LC 57: Exclusive Right-to-Lease Listing Contract (All Types of Properties; or
ETC 59: Exclusive Tenant Contract (All Types of Properties)

With any of the three forms the broker should check the box "Transaction-Brokerage" whereby only the brokerage services and duties contained in Section 4 of the agreement would apply; or present a buyer or tenant with BD24 Brokerage Disclosure to Buyer.

The broker may then engage as a transaction-broker and may perform any of the activities enumerated in section 12-10-201(6), C.R.S., which are the acts of real estate brokerage.

However, **before** the broker begins to work as the buyer's or tenant's **agent** and advocate to secure the best possible price or lease rate and terms for the buyer or tenant, the parties must execute one of the above listed agreements with the "Agency" box checked. In an agency relationship the broker has the duties and responsibilities contained in Section 4 of the agreement, and the additional duties of an agent contained in Section 5 of the agreement.

CP-33 Joint Position Statement from the Division of Real Estate and Division of Insurance Concerning Application of the Good Funds Laws (Repealed)

CP-34 Commission Position on Settlement Service Provider Selection, Closing Instructions and Earnest Money Deposits (revised 08/07/2012)

The Commission issues this position statement to clarify how settlement service providers are selected, when closing instructions must be completed by a real estate broker ("broker") and how earnest money is to be handled.

Selection of settlement service providers

*   Regardless of whether a broker is acting as a single agent or transaction broker, all brokers acting in their licensed capacities are required to advise their clients to obtain expert advice as to material matters about which the broker knows but the specifics of which are beyond the expertise of the broker. See C.R.S. 12-10-404(1)(c)(V), 12-10-405(1)(c)(V), and 12-10-407(2)(b)(II). Expert advice includes, but is not limited to, the brokering of a mortgage, performing title searches and issuing insurance, appraising real property, surveying and issuing improvement location certificates, performing property inspections and other due diligence (including environmental) and practicing law (which also includes analyzing the legal implications of the foregoing). Brokers need to ensure that they perform the acts required by the real estate brokerage practice act, based on the capacity in which they have agreed to practice, i.e. as a single agent or transaction broker. A common standard of practice amongst brokers is to provide the names of three settlement services providers in a specific area of practice and allow the consumer to choose. The Commission understands that there are occasions when a broker cannot provide the names of three separate settlement service providers that practice in one specific area, but regardless of how many names may be provided, it is imperative that final selection of the settlement service provider be left to the consumer, not the broker.

Closing Instructions

*   The purpose of closing instructions is for the consumer to engage the company that will be responsible for ultimately closing the sales transaction. In most transactions, the company responsible for closing the transaction is a title company, although there are brokers that provide these services. As stated above, the consumer is responsible for the selection of settlement service providers, including the individual or company that performs the closing services. If the broker is performing the closing services, including the preparation, delivery and recording of closing documents and the disbursement of funds, the broker is the "Closing Company" and thereby is responsible for completing the Commission-approved Closing Instructions at the time that the Contract to Buy and Sell Real Estate is executed by the buyer and seller. As required by Commission Rule 5.21. and C.R.S. 12-10-217(1)(k), the broker shall retain a copy of the Closing Instructions for future use or inspection by an authorized representative of the Real Estate Commission.

*   If a title company is engaged to perform the closing services, the Division of Insurance requires that a title entity provide closing and settlement services only when there are written instructions from all necessary parties. See Division of Insurance Rule 3-5-1. All amendments to existing written instructions with a title entity must also be in writing. If a title company is engaged to provide the closing services, it is the "Closing Company" and it is the responsibility of the title company to complete the closing instructions as required by the Division of Insurance. The broker should make a reasonable effort to obtain a copy of the closing instructions from the title entity for the broker's transaction file, to ensure compliance with Commission Rule 5.21. and C.R.S. 12-10-217(1)(k) as stated above.

Earnest Money Deposits

*   A listing broker who receives earnest money is required to deposit the money in the broker's escrow or trust account in a recognized depository no later than the third business day following the day on which the broker receives notice of contract acceptance. If the selling broker receipts for a promissory note, or thing of value, such note or thing of value must be delivered with the contract to the listing broker to be held by the listing broker. Any check or note must be payable, or assigned, to the listing broker. Upon receipt of the earnest money, the listing broker must complete the Earnest Money Receipt as the Earnest Money Holder. A copy of the receipt must be retained by the broker to ensure compliance with Commission Rule 5.21. and C.R.S. 12-10-217(1)(k).

*   If the buyer and seller have agreed in writing that a third party or entity will hold the earnest money, the listing broker must deliver the earnest money to the third party or entity. The listing broker must obtain a dated and signed Earnest Money Receipt from the third party or entity upon delivery of the earnest money. For record keeping purposes, the broker must retain a copy of the Earnest Money Receipt and a copy of the earnest money check, note or other thing of value as required by Commission Rule 5.21, and C.R.S. 12-10-217(1)(k).

CP-35 Commission Position on Brokers as Principals

*   The Commission regularly receives public complaints regarding real estate transactions involving a licensed real estate broker acting as a principal. Predominantly these complaints allege that the broker, who is a principal to the transaction, and may or may not also be serving as a broker in the transaction, has failed to disclose an adverse material fact; has failed to disclose brokerage relationships (when acting as more than a principal); has failed to ensure that the contract documents and/or settlement statements accurately reflect the terms of the transaction; has filed a document that unlawfully clouds the title to the property; has failed to disclose the broker's licensed status; has mismanaged funds belonging to others; and/or has falsified information used for the purpose of obtaining financing.

The Commission reminds licensees that the Commission may investigate and discipline a license if a licensee is acting in the capacity of a principal in a real estate transaction and violations of the license law occur. The Commission's authority to investigate and impose discipline in these transactions was determined by the Colorado Court of Appeals. See *Seibel v. Colorado Real Estate Commission*, 34 Colo.App. 415, 530 P.2d 1290 (1974). The court's decision affirmed that licensed real estate brokers are subject to the real estate brokers licensing act and rules adopted by the Commission when they participate in real estate matters as principals. In such cases, licensees need to be mindful of Rule 6.17. (regarding conflict of interest and license status disclosures) and position statement CP-31 (regarding acting as a transaction broker).

CP-36 Commission Position on Minimum Service Requirements

*   The Commission has received numerous inquiries regarding the minimum services that brokers must provide to buyers or sellers of real property. §12-10-403, C.R.S. requires that any broker performing the activities requiring a real estate broker's license as set forth in §12-10-201(6), C.R.S., act in the capacity of either a transaction broker or a single agent in the transaction. The minimum duties required to be performed by a real estate broker acting in the capacity of a single agent are set forth in §§12-10-404 and 12-10-405, C.R.S. §12-10-404, C.R.S. Single agent engaged by seller or landlord states, in part:

(1) A broker engaged by a seller or landlord to act as a seller's agent or a landlord's agent is a limited agent with the following duties and obligations:

    (a) To perform the terms of the written agreement made with the seller or landlord;

    (b) To exercise reasonable skill and care for the seller or landlord;

    (c) To promote the interests of the seller or landlord with the utmost good faith, loyalty, and fidelity, including, but not limited to:

        (I) Seeking a price and terms which are acceptable to the seller or landlord; except that the broker shall not be obligated to seek additional offers to purchase the property while the property is subject to a contract for sale or to seek additional offers to lease the property while the property is subject to a lease or letter of intent to lease;

(II) *Presenting all offers to and from the seller or landlord in a timely manner regardless of whether the property is subject to a contract for sale or a lease or letter of intent to lease;*

(III) *Disclosing to the seller or landlord adverse material facts actually known by the broker;*

(IV) *Counseling the seller or landlord as to any material benefits or risks of a transaction which are actually known by the broker;*

(V) *Advising the seller or landlord to obtain expert advice as to material matters about which the broker knows but the specifics of which are beyond the expertise of such broker;*

(VI) *Accounting in a timely manner for all money and property received; and*

(VII) *Informing the seller or landlord that such seller or landlord shall not be vicariously liable for the acts of such seller's or landlord's agent that are not approved, directed or ratified by such seller or landlord.*

(d) *To comply with all requirements of this article and any rules promulgated pursuant to this article; and*

(e) *To comply with any applicable federal, state, or local laws, rules, regulations, or ordinances including fair housing and civil rights statutes or regulations.*

* §12-10-405, C.R.S. Single agent engaged by buyer or tenant states, in part:

(1) *A broker engaged by a buyer or tenant to act as a buyer's or tenant's agent shall be a limited agent with the following duties and obligations:*

(a) *To perform the terms of the written agreement made with the buyer or tenant;*

(b) *To exercise reasonable skill and care for the buyer or tenant;*

(c) *To promote the interests of the buyer or tenant with the utmost good faith, loyalty, and fidelity, including but not limited to:*

(I) *Seeking a price and terms which are acceptable to the buyer or tenant; except that the broker shall not be obligated to seek other properties while the buyer is a party to a contract to purchase property or while the tenant is a party to a lease or letter of intent to lease;*

(II) *Presenting all offers to and from the buyer or tenant in a timely manner regardless of whether the buyer is already a party to a contract to purchase property or the tenant is already a party to a contract or a letter of intent to lease;*

(III) *Disclosing to the buyer or tenant adverse material facts actually known by the broker;*

(IV) *Counseling the buyer or tenant as to any material benefits or risks of a transaction which are actually known by the broker;*

(V) *Advising the buyer or tenant to obtain expert advice as to material matters about which the broker knows but the specifics of which are beyond the expertise of such broker;*

(VI) *Accounting in a timely manner for all money and property received; and*

(VII) *Informing the buyer or tenant that such buyer or tenant shall not be vicariously liable for the acts of such buyer's or tenant's agent that are not approved, directed, or ratified by such buyer or tenant;*

(d) *To comply with all requirements of this article and any rules promulgated pursuant to this article; and*

(e) *To comply with any applicable federal, state, or local laws, rules, regulations, or ordinances including fair housing and civil rights statutes or regulations.*

* The minimum duties required to be performed by a real estate broker acting in the capacity of a transaction broker are set forth in §12-10-407, C.R.S., which states, in part:

(1) *A broker engaged as a transaction-broker is not an agent for either party;*

(2) *A transaction-broker shall have the following obligations and responsibilities:*

(a) *To perform the terms of any written or oral agreement made with any party to the transaction;*

(b) *To exercise reasonable skill and care as a transaction-broker, including, but not limited to:*

(I) *Presenting all offers and counteroffers in a timely manner regardless of whether the property is subject to a contract for sale or lease or letter of intent;*

(II) *Advising the parties regarding the transaction and suggesting that such parties obtain expert advice as to material matters about which the transaction-broker knows but the specifics of which are beyond the expertise of such broker;*

(III) *Accounting in a timely manner for all money and property received;*

(IV) *Keeping parties fully informed regarding the transaction;*

(V) *Assisting the parties in complying with the terms and conditions of any contract including closing the transaction;*

(VI) *Disclosing to prospective buyers or tenants any adverse material facts actually known by the broker including but not limited to adverse material facts pertaining to the title, the physical condition of the property, any defects in the property, and any environmental hazards affecting the property required by law to be disclosed;*

(VII) *Disclosing to any prospective seller or landlord all adverse material facts actually known by the broker including but not limited to adverse material facts pertaining to the buyer's or tenant's financial ability to perform the terms of the transaction and the buyer's intent to occupy the property as a principal residence; and*

(VIII) *Informing the parties that as a seller and buyer or as landlord and tenant they shall not be vicariously liable for any acts of the transaction-broker;*

(c) *To comply with all requirements of this article and any rules promulgated pursuant to this article; and*

(d) *To comply with any applicable federal, state, or local laws, rules, regulations, or ordinances including fair housing and civil rights statutes or regulations.*

* §12-10-403, C.R.S. allows real estate brokers to perform duties in addition to those established in §§12-10-404, 12-10-405 and 12-10-407, C.R.S. The additional duties may include, but are not limited to, holding open houses, property showings, providing a lockbox, use of multiple listing services or other information exchanges, etc. Additional services that brokers agree to provide their clients must be documented in writing. A broker is not allowed to solely perform "additional" services which require a real estate broker's license, i.e. offering the real property of another for sale through advertisements, without providing the minimum duties required by single agency or transaction brokerage. The Commission does not regulate the fees or commissions charged by brokers for minimum or additional services provided. Fees and commissions are negotiable between the broker and the principal.

CP-37 Commission Position on Survey and Lease Objections to the Contract to Buy and Sell Real Estate

The intention of the Commission in adopting the Contract to Buy and Sell Real Estate (CBS1-8-10 and the other versions of the Contract) is set forth below.

1. As background, under Section 8.1, Buyer has the right to object to title matters up to the **Title Objection Deadline**. Under Section 8.5, Seller has the obligation and right to use reasonable efforts to correct such objections and bear nominal expense prior to Closing. If any unsatisfactory title condition is not corrected prior to Closing, Buyer may either terminate the Contract or waive objection to any unsatisfactory title condition prior to Closing.

2. Under Section 8.2, if Buyer objects to any off-record matter on or before the **Off-Record Matters Objection Deadline**, the Contract will terminate. Seller has no right to cure such off-record matters. Seller does not have a right to cure any objection to existing surveys or leases under Section 8.2. Section 8.5 does not apply to objections under Section 8.2.

3. Under Section 7.3, Buyer may obtain a new, updated or recertified Survey (Current Survey) on or before the **Survey Deadline**. Current Surveys are different than existing surveys, surveys which are <u>not</u> current and which may be delivered to Buyer under Section 8.2 as an off-record matter; objections to existing surveys must be made on or before the **Off-Record Matters Objection Deadline**. Buyer may object to the Current Survey on or before the **Survey Objection Deadline**. If Buyer timely objects to the Current Survey, the Contract will terminate. Buyer's objection to the Current Survey is governed by Section 8.3.2, and Seller has no right to cure any objection to the Survey. Section 8.5 does not apply to objections under Section 8.3.2.

4. Under Sections 10.8.2 (Survey) and 10.8.3 (Leases) Buyer has a right to "terminate" the Contract. Seller has no right to cure any such objection. Section 8.5 does not apply to objections under Sections 10.8.2 and 10.8.3.

Conclusion: Buyer has a right terminate the Contract due to objections with any Survey (Existing or Current) or to any Lease. Seller has no right to cure any objection to the Survey or Lease (whether such objection is based on Section 7, 8 or 10 as Section 8.5 does not apply to Survey or Lease objections).

CP-38 Commission Position on Disclosure of Affiliated Business Arrangements and Conflicts of Interest (4-5-2011)

*   This statement supplements Rule 6.18. Affiliated Business Arrangements. §12-10-218, C.R.S. *Affiliated Business Arrangements* was enacted in Colorado to provide transparency, accountability, and consumer protection through disclosure and consistency concerning affiliated business arrangements. Affiliated business arrangements have also been regulated for many years by the Real Estate Settlement Procedures Act (RESPA). RESPA was precipitated by significant reforms identified by Congress as necessary to ensure that consumers did not pay disproportionately high settlement costs as the result of certain deleterious business practices by settlement service providers. RESPA is applicable to any residential mortgage transaction involving a federally related mortgage loan. However, Colorado law requires disclosure of affiliated business arrangements to consumers even if the transaction does not involve a federally related residential mortgage loan.

*   Colorado law C.R.S. 12-10-218(1)(a) defines an "affiliated business arrangement" as an arrangement in which:

> *"A provider of settlement services or an associate of a provider of settlement services has either an affiliate relationship with or a direct beneficial ownership interest of more than one percent in another provider of settlement services;"*

and the provider directly or indirectly refers business to the other provider or affirmatively influences the selection of another provider of settlement services.

It is the Commission's position that real estate brokers must disclose affiliated business arrangements to consumers in all transactions intended to result in the transfer of title from one party to another. RESPA requires that affiliated business arrangements be disclosed before or at the time a referral is made to a provider of settlement services. Colorado law requires a licensee to disclose any affiliated business arrangement when an offer to purchase real property is fully executed. In Colorado, the disclosure is required to be in writing, must be given to both agents and transaction brokers, must comply with RESPA and Colorado law, and must be made using the Federal RESPA disclosure form. Colorado law requires real estate brokers to disclose their affiliated business arrangements to all parties to the real estate transaction and all parties are expected to sign the disclosure form. The Commission recommends that real estate brokers disclose their affiliated business arrangements to the party with whom they are working early in their relationship, i.e. at the time brokerage relationships are disclosed or when the listing contract or buyer broker agreement is negotiated. In those transactions where the broker does not deal with another party until the time of contracting written disclosure should be made to all parties at the time the purchase contract is fully executed.

Additionally, real estate brokers are required to make certain disclosures to the Division of Real Estate regarding their affiliated business arrangements. Colorado law requires every licensee to disclose to the Commission when they enter into or change an affiliated business arrangement. All affiliated business arrangements to which the licensee is a party must be disclosed. Disclosure is required at the time of a new application for licensure or at the time of activation of an inactive license. The disclosure must include the physical location of the affiliated business. Employing brokers are required to disclose the names of all affiliated business arrangements to which the employing broker is a party on an annual basis, at the least. The disclosure must include the physical location of the affiliated businesses. The Commission has determined that these disclosures shall be made electronically through the Division of Real Estate's website at www.dora.state.co.us/pls/real/AFB_Web.Logon?p_div=REC.

* It is the Commission's position that Rule 6.17. *Continuing duty to disclose conflict of interest and license status*, applies to all licensees including real estate brokers who perform licensed property management services and are affiliated with businesses or vendors that provide services applicable to lease transactions. For example, a real estate broker acting on behalf of a landlord is required to disclose to the landlord that the real estate broker has partial ownership of the maintenance company that the real estate broker utilizes for the landlord's property repairs. The Commission strongly recommends that this type of information be disclosed to the principal early in the business relationship, i.e. at the time brokerage relationships are disclosed or when the listing contract is negotiated. Additionally, this disclosure should be made in writing.

CP-39 Commission Position on Lease Options, Lease Purchase Agreements and Installment Land Contracts (4-5-2011)

* The Commission recognizes that in order to maintain the resilience of the real estate market during times when conventional lending requirements are rigorous, alternative funding practices are utilized to sustain the market conditions of supply and demand. The Commission has received and investigated numerous complaints pertaining to lease options, lease purchase agreements and installment land contracts. Although the Commission does not have the authority to prohibit the types of real estate transactions that real estate brokers participate in, the Commission strongly cautions real estate brokers to utilize the services of an attorney licensed to practice law within the State of Colorado. It has been the Commission's observation, based on complaints received, that lease option and lease purchase transactions are complex and generally contain provisions with significant financial risk posed to the prospective buyer and seller. Installment land contracts and the other transactions mentioned in this position statement afford buyers the opportunity to take possession of the real property and make installment payments to the seller. There is a significant potential for harm to the seller, buyer or assignee if the installment land contract is not properly drafted. In all of the above transactions, the seller retains legal title to the property while the buyer may acquire equitable title. The Commission does not have an approved contract form necessary to memorialize the terms and nuances related to these complex transactions, or any jurisdictional regulations that may be germane. Pursuant to Rule 7.1., et seq., the appropriate provisions of the license law and the brokerage relationship act (§§12-10-217, 12-10-404, 405 and 407, C.R.S.), real estate brokers are prohibited from drafting a contract document that would reflect the terms of such a transaction as it would exceed their level of competency and is a matter requiring the expertise and advice of an attorney. Additionally, such behavior may be construed as the unauthorized practice of law by the real estate broker and subject to civil penalties. The contracts for these transactions should not be prepared by a real estate broker; rather, the documents should be drafted by a licensed Colorado attorney-at-law engaged for each particular transaction.

CP-40 Commission Position on Teams (4-5-2011)

The Commission recognizes that there are benefits to both real estate brokers and consumers in the usage of real estate broker teams. Teams may be formed within a licensed brokerage firm with the approval of the employing broker. Real estate brokers operating as teams need to ensure that they are compliant with Commission rules regarding advertising, name usage and supervision.

Advertising and name usage:

* While there is no prohibition of teams, real estate brokers need to ensure that they do not advertise in a manner that misleads the public as to the identity of the brokers' licensed brokerage. Real estate brokers that function as teams should not advertise teams using the terms "realty", "real estate", "company", "corporation", "corp.", "inc.", "LLC" or other similar language that would indicate a company other than the employing brokerage firm. Advertising includes, but is not limited to, websites, signage, property flyers, mailings, business cards, letterhead and contracts. The advertising of team names should never give the impression that the team is an entity separate from the licensed real estate brokerage. If the identity of the employing broker or the brokerage firm is difficult for the public or the Commission to ascertain, the team may be in violation of Rule 6.10. Advertising.

Supervision:

* In addition to the supervision requirements set forth in Rules 6.3.C. and 6.3.D., Rule 6.3.B. Employing broker responsibilities requires that the broker designated to act as the broker for any partnership, limited liability company or corporation, i.e. the employing broker, fulfill the following duties:

1) Maintain all trust accounts and trust account records;

2) Maintain all transaction records;

3) Develop an office policy manual and periodically review office policies with all employees;

* 4) Provide for a high level of supervision for newly licensed persons pursuant to Rule- 6.3.D.;

* 5) Provide for a reasonable level of supervision for experienced licensees pursuant to Rule 6.3.C.;

6) Take reasonable steps to ensure that violations of statutes, rules and office policies do not occur or reoccur;

7) Provide for adequate supervision of all offices operated by the broker, whether managed by licensed or unlicensed persons.

* Pursuant to §12-10-222, C.R.S., and Rule 6.3.A., employing brokers are also responsible for providing supervision over such activities with reference to the licensing statutes and Commission rules for all brokerage employees, including but not limited to administrative assistants, bookkeepers and personal assistants of licensed employees. Thus, employing brokers are responsible for the actions of unlicensed persons who perform functions within the real estate broker team. Employing brokers need to ensure that any unlicensed person acting within the team is not engaged in practices that require a real estate broker's license. Employing brokers also need to establish that the compensation paid to an unlicensed person for services provided is not in the form of a commission. Compensation paid to an unlicensed person is not required to be paid solely by the employing broker. However, §12-10-221, C.R.S., requires that all licensee compensation or valuable consideration for the performance of any acts requiring a broker's license is paid solely by the employing broker.

CP-41 Commission Position on Competency (December 6, 2011)

* Pursuant to sections 12-10-404, 12-10-405 and 12-10-407, C.R.S., which are the laws that govern the duties of a real estate broker acting in the capacity of a single agent or transaction broker, real estate brokers are required to perform the terms of written or oral agreements they make with certain parties to a real estate transaction. Pursuant to sections 12-10-404 and 12-10-405, C.R.S., real estate brokers acting in the capacity of a single agent have a duty to promote the interests of their clients with the utmost good faith, loyalty, and fidelity. Pursuant to section 12-10-217(1)(q), C.R.S., it is a violation of the license law if a licensee demonstrates unworthiness or incompetency to act as a real estate broker by conducting business in such a manner as to endanger the interest of the public.

Prior to performing any acts that require a real estate broker's license, a broker should determine whether he or she possesses the knowledge, experience, and/or training necessary to perform the terms of the transaction and maintain compliance with the applicable federal, state or local laws, rules, regulations, or ordinances. If the broker does not have the requisite knowledge, experience and/or training necessary to consummate the terms of the agreement, the broker should either decline to provide brokerage services or seek the assistance of another real estate broker who does have the necessary experience, training, and/or knowledge. The Commission will have grounds to discipline a broker's license if a broker fails to take the measures necessary to gain competence and violations of the license law are substantiated.

CP-42 Commission Position on Apartment Building or Complex Management

The Commission recognizes that owners of apartment buildings or complexes will engage the services of real estate brokerages or unlicensed, on-site managers, or both. An "owner" includes either a person or an entity recognized under Colorado law. The owner must have a controlling interest in the entity formed by the owner to manage the apartment building or complex. In the instance of an entity, the "owner" may form a separate entity to manage the apartment building or complex. The ownership entity and the entity formed by the owner to manage the apartment building or complex must be under the control of the same person or persons.

* Pursuant to §12-10-201(6)(b)(XII), C.R.S., a regularly salaried employee of the owner of an apartment building or complex is permitted to perform customary duties for his or her employer without a real estate broker's license. The unlicensed, on-site manager must either report directly to the owner or to the real estate broker, if a real estate broker is engaged to manage the property. The Commission views the following to be customary duties of an unlicensed, on-site manager:

1. Performance of clerical duties, including gathering information about competing projects.
2. Obtain information necessary to qualify perspective tenants for a lease. This includes obtaining and verifying information regarding employment history, credit information, references and personal information as necessary.
3. Provide access to a property available for lease and distribute preprinted, objective information prepared by a broker as long as no negotiating, offering or contracting is involved.
4. Distribute preprinted, objective information at an on-site leasing office that is prepared by an owner or broker, as long as no negotiating, offering or contracting is involved.
5. Quote the rental price established by the owner or the owner's licensed broker.

6. Act as a scrivener to the owner or the broker for purposes of completing predetermined lease terms on preprinted forms as negotiated by the owner or broker.

7. Deliver paperwork to other brokers.

8. Deliver paperwork to landlords and tenants, if such paperwork has already been reviewed by the owner, or a broker or has been prepared in accordance with the supervising broker's instructions.

9. Collect and deposit rents and security deposits in accordance with the owner's lease agreement or the brokerage firm's written office policy.

10. Schedule property maintenance in accordance with the brokerage firm's management agreement or the owner's lease agreement.

If the owner has executed a Power of Attorney form or a written delegation of authority that authorizes the unlicensed, on-site manager to sign and execute leases on behalf of the owner, the unlicensed, on-site manager may execute those without possessing a real estate broker's license. Brokers supervising unlicensed, on-site managers with this authority are expected to review the executed documents to ensure compliance with lease terms, management agreements, local, state and federal laws, including the real estate brokerage practice act and Commission rules.

Employing brokers need to be especially aware of their supervisory duties under the license law. Supervisory duties apply whether the on-site manager is an employee or independent contractor of the broker or brokerage firm, or if the on-site manager is a regularly salaried employee of the apartment building or complex owner. The employing broker should have a written office policy explaining the duties, responsibilities and limitation on the use of on-site managers. This policy should be periodically reviewed with all employees.

CP-43 Commission Position on Property Inspection Resolutions

The Commission has received inquiries and complaints claiming that real estate brokers ("Brokers") misrepresent property conditions and negotiate repairs in a manner that conceals issues from the buyer's lender, particularly when the property's condition would affect a lending decision. The Commission issues this position statement to clarify how Brokers can advise buyers regarding inspection objection issues and maintain compliance with Commission rules and regulations. Brokers must understand that in working with their clients to resolve inspection issues, Colorado law imposes upon Brokers the duty to avoid misrepresentations [C.R.S.§ 12-10-217(1)(a)] and dual contracts [C.R.S. § 18-5-208].

Other than terminating the contract based on inspection, there are generally five alternatives available to address property condition issues in a sales transaction: 1) the seller can repair the property prior to closing; 2) the seller can agree to pay a concession or contribution, for example, a portion of the buyer's closing costs; 3) after closing, the buyer can make the repair without assistance from the seller; 4) the buyer and the seller can negotiate a modification to the sales price; or 5) at closing, the seller can escrow funds or pay a contractor (if allowed by the lender).

If the buyer is obtaining a loan to fund the purchase of the property, any of these options can affect the mortgage financing. Prior to negotiating any of these alternatives, the broker should advise the buyer to ask their mortgage loan originator or lender whether the resolution may (1) have a detrimental impact on the Buyer's ability to get the loan; (2) cause delays in the lender's processing and funding of the loan by Closing; and (3) require further inspections and repairs.

Once items to negotiate have been identified, the buyer broker should use the Commission-approved Inspection Objection form to identify the inspection issues that the buyer seeks to have resolved (Note: the Inspection Objection form is a notice form and is not part of the contract). Then, once the buyer and seller have reached a resolution, the Brokers can memorialize the terms on the Commission-approved Inspection Resolution form or the Agreement to Amend/Extend the Contract.

CP-44 Commission Position on Coming Soon Listings

The Commission has received inquiries and complaints regarding real estate brokers ("brokers") who advertise properties as "coming soon" to the market. The common complaint the Commission receives about "coming soon" listings is that the listing broker provides limited exposure of the property on the open market in an effort to broker both sides of the transaction, or "double end the deal". Many of the complaints that the Commission receives indicate that once the property is entered into a multiple listing service, becomes available for showings or is otherwise given full market exposure, the listing broker notifies any parties interested that the property is already under contract. While the Commission cannot impose limitations on how a property is marketed for sale or lease, a broker must comply with the license law.

*   Among other duties, §12-10-404(1), C.R.S., requires a broker acting as a single agent engaged by a seller or a landlord, to " exercise reasonable skill and care for the seller or landlord" and "promote the interests of the seller or landlord with the utmost good faith, loyalty, and fidelity". A broker who acts as a transaction broker for the seller or landlord is also required to "exercise reasonable skill and care", among the other responsibilities and obligations enumerated in §12-10-407, C.R.S.

During the negotiation of the listing contract, and as part of the broker's obligation to exercise reasonable skill and care, a broker is responsible for advising the seller or landlord "of any material benefits or risks of a transaction which are actually known by the broker". This includes limiting a property's market exposure by delaying access for showings or open houses, or limiting the amount of time that the seller or landlord will consider offers. Motivation for limiting exposure of the property should be carefully considered. Is the property being marketed as "coming soon" because the seller is preparing it for sale or lease? This would be a legitimate use of that particular marketing method. However, if the property is being marketed as "coming soon" in an effort for the listing broker to acquire a buyer and "double end" the transaction, this would be a violation of the license law because the broker is not exercising reasonable skill and care. If the broker is a single agent for the seller or landlord, the broker may be viewed by the Commission as also failing to promote the interests of the seller or landlord with the utmost good faith, loyalty and fidelity. Finally, a broker who places the importance of his commission above his duties, responsibilities or obligations to the consumer who has engaged him is practicing business in a manner that endangers the interest of the public.

Ultimately, it is the seller or landlord's decision how, when and where the property will be marketed. A broker who fails to advise a seller or landlord of the material benefits or risks, or does not allow the seller or landlord to decide how the property will be marketed, may be subject to license discipline by the Commission. The manner in which the broker and seller or landlord agree to market the property must be memorialized in writing in the listing contract prior to any marketing being performed.

CP-45 Commission Position on Defined Terms

The purpose of this position statement is to provide definitions of the terms that regularly appear in the regulations promulgated by the Commission through the rule-making process.

Advertise or Advertising: The promotion, solicitation or representation of real estate brokerage services requiring a real estate broker's license. Advertising may include, but is not limited to, business cards, brochures, websites, signage, property flyers, mailings (paper or electronic), social media, letter head, email signatures and contract documents.

*   Applicant: An individual or entity seeking a license from the Commission to perform the duties enumerated in C.R.S. §12-10-201(6)(a).

*   Broker: Any individual licensed by the Colorado Real Estate Commission to perform the acts enumerated in C.R.S. §12-10-201(6)(a) regardless if such broker is licensed as an associate broker, independent broker or employing broker.

*   <u>Brokerage or Brokerage Firm:</u> Any sole proprietor, partnership, limited liability company, corporation or any other authorized entity licensed by the Commission to perform the acts enumerated in C.R.S. §12-10-201(6)(a).

*   <u>Commission:</u> The Colorado Real Estate Commission, created pursuant to C.R.S. §12-10-206.

<u>Division:</u> The Division of Real Estate.

<u>Licensee:</u> A broker or brokerage firm licensed by the Commission.

<u>Team:</u> Two (2) or more brokers within a brokerage firm that conduct their real estate brokerage business together.

<u>Trademark:</u> Any logo, service mark or other identifying mark used in conjunction with a brokerage firm's legal name or trade name. Trademarks may be registered with the Colorado Secretary of State pursuant to C.R.S. §7-70-102, C.R.S. As an example, the brokerage "A Better Choice Real Estate" uses a logo bearing the initials "ABC". The logo is used to identify the brokerage and the real estate services that it provides, therefore it would be the trademark for the brokerage.

<u>Trade Name:</u> The name under which a brokerage firm does business other than the brokerage firm's legal name. Any trade name used by a brokerage firm must be on file with the Commission and must be filed with the Colorado Secretary of State pursuant to C.R.S. §7-71-101. For example, a brokerage is licensed with the Commission under its legal name of "Colorado Real Estate Group LLC". However, the brokerage is also a franchise of "International Realty" and does business under the trade name "International Realty of Colorado".

<u>Viewable Page:</u> A page that may or may not scroll beyond the border of the screen and includes the use of frame pages.

CP-46 Commission Position on Broker Disclosure of Adverse Material Facts

(revised 08/01/2017)

Brokers must disclose known adverse material facts.

*   In all real estate transactions, brokers are obligated to disclose known adverse material facts to all of the parties involved in the transaction. C.R.S. §§ 12-10-404(1)(c)(III), -404(3)(a), - 405(1)(c)(III), -405(3)(a), -407(2)(b)(VI), and -407(2)(b)(VII). While clients have certain disclosure obligations, they are not addressed in this Position Statement. Brokers should refrain from advising clients about clients' disclosure duties, which may be different.

What is an adverse material fact?

During the course of a real estate transaction, a broker for either side of the transaction may become aware of certain information pertaining to the property. For example, a broker may become aware that the roof of the property was recently repaired, or that the property was hit by lightning several times, or that one of the owners of the home for sale is a smoker. Brokers may have difficulty in ascertaining whether to disclose such facts.

In order to answer these types of questions, brokers first should consider whether the information is material. Factual information is material when a reasonable person would have ascribed actual significance to the information. *Moye White LLP v. Beren*, 320 P.3d 373, 378 (Colo. App. 2013). Examples of material facts include facts affecting title, facts affecting the physical condition of the property and environmental hazards affecting the property. "Undisclosed facts are 'material' if the consumer's decision might have been different had the truth been disclosed." *In re Gattis*, 318 P.3d 549, 554 (Colo. App. 2013) (quoting *Briggs v. Am. Nat'l Prop. & Cas. Co.*, 209 P.3d 1181, 1186 (Colo. App. 2009)).

Next, brokers should consider whether that material information is adverse to a party's interest in the transaction. *See In re Fisher*, 202 P.3d 1186, 1196 (Colo. 2009); *Black's Law Dictionary* 62 (9th ed. 2009) (defining "adverse"). A broker must consider how that material information affects each of the parties in the transaction, not just the individual party they are representing. If that material information is contrary (i.e. "adverse") to the interest of one of the parties, then the broker must disclose it to all the parties.

An "adverse material fact" includes but is not limited to a fact that affects the structural integrity of the real property, presents a documented health risk to occupants of the property including environmental hazards and facts that have a material effect on title or occupancy of the property. Examples of adverse material facts include building or zoning violations, water damage to the flooring of property caused by marijuana plants, structural damage to a home caused by insect infestations or expansive soils or any type of lien filed against the property.

Brokers need only disclose known adverse material facts.

A broker need only disclose facts of which the broker has actual knowledge. *See Baumgarten v. Coppage*, 15 P.3d 304, 307 (Colo. App. 2000). For example, if a property owner knows that the foundation is crumbling but never tells his broker, the broker has no duty to disclose that fact because the broker has no knowledge. Because a broker must actually know the adverse material fact, a broker does not violate Commission rules if he or she did not know the adverse material fact but only should have known the fact.

The Commission believes that disclosure of known adverse material facts is an important requirement that brokers must undertake in order to protect Colorado buyers and sellers. Accordingly, real estate brokers must disclose those facts they actually know, that a reasonable person would ascribe actual significance to and are contrary to the interests of a party in a real estate transaction. To the extent a broker is unclear about whether a known fact that affects the physical property is adverse or material, the broker should err on the side of disclosing the fact.

Brokers must not disclose circumstances that may psychologically impact or stigmatize real property.

Understanding a broker's obligation to disclose known adverse material facts is as important as a broker's duty not to disclose information that may psychologically impact or stigmatize real property. Without the informed consent of the client, brokers must not disclose facts or suspicions regarding circumstances which may psychologically impact or stigmatize real property. C.R.S. §§ 12-10-404(2)(e), - 405(2)(e), - 407(3)(e). The law states that:

> [f]acts or suspicions regarding circumstances occurring on a parcel of property which could psychologically impact or stigmatize such property are not material facts subject to a disclosure requirement in a real estate transaction.

C.R.S. § 38-35.5-101(1) (2016).

There is minimal guidance in Colorado as to what equates to a psychological impact or stigmatization of a property. However, Colorado law identifies two specific circumstances that brokers are prohibited from disclosing due to the potential stigmatization of that property to potential buyers.

The first circumstance that cannot be disclosed is when an occupant of real property was suspected to be or was infected with the human immunodeficiency virus (HIV) or diagnosed with acquired immune deficiency syndrome, or any other disease which has been determined by medical evidence to be highly unlikely to be transmitted through the occupancy of a dwelling place. C.R.S. § 38-35.5-101(1)(a).

The second circumstance that a broker cannot disclose is when "the property was the site of a homicide or other felony or of a suicide." C.R.S. § 38-35.5-101(1)(b). Colorado courts have not provided any greater guidance concerning the types of felony crimes that fall under its definition.

A broker's obligation to avoid disclosure of circumstances which may psychologically impact or stigmatize real property should not impede a party's right to be informed about all known adverse material facts. The Commission concludes that the only circumstances in which a broker is not obligated to disclose facts or suspicions regarding circumstances that may psychologically impact or stigmatize real property are those two set forth immediately above in section 38-35.5-101(1)(a) and (b).

Brokers must disclose all known adverse material facts, unless it is one of the circumstances set forth in section 38-35.5-101(1).

The Commission's primary purpose is to protect the public. *Albright v. McDermond*, 14 P.3d 318, 322 (Colo. 2000). The Commission believes it is in the public's best interest for brokers to disclose all known adverse material facts to the parties to a real estate transaction because this disclosure increases each party's awareness of those facts prior to completion of the transaction, it reduces the potential for creating an unfair transaction, and it otherwise protects the overall integrity of the transaction.

The Commission suggests that brokers have robust conversations with their clients about broker disclosures, with an eye towards full and complete disclosure. Brokers who are aware of either of the two factual scenarios set forth in C.R.S. § 38-35.5-101 are encouraged to obtain their clients' consent to permit disclosure of these facts.

Chapter 4:
Subdivision Laws

An * in the left margin indicates a change in the statute, rule, or text since the last publication of the manual.

I. Jurisdiction of Commission

A. Introduction

The Subdivision Developer's Act ("Act") affects the types of subdivisions that must be registered with the Real Estate Commission. The following types of subdivisions within the State of Colorado, and subdivisions located outside the state being offered for sale in Colorado, must be registered before offering, negotiating, or agreeing to sell, lease, or transfer any portion of the subdivision:

1. Any division of real property into twenty (20) or more interests intended solely for residential use, with each interest comprising thirty-five (35) or more acres of land offered for sale, lease or transfer;

2. Subdivisions consisting of twenty (20) or more timeshare interests (a timeshare interest includes a deeded or non-deeded interest, including but not limited to a fee simple interest, a leasehold, a contract to use, a membership or club agreement, or an interest in common);

3. Subdivisions consisting of twenty (20) or more residential units created by converting an existing structure (e.g., condominium conversions); and

4. Subdivisions created by cooperative housing corporations with twenty (20) or more shareholders with proprietary leases, whether the project is completed or not.

B. Exemption from Registration under the Act

1. The selling of memberships in campgrounds;

2. Bulk sales and transfers between developers;

3. Property upon which there has been or upon which there will be erected residential buildings that have not been previously occupied and where the consideration paid by the purchaser for such property includes the cost of such buildings (this does not apply to conversions of an existing structure, timeshare, or cooperative housing projects);

4. Lots that, at the time of closing of a sale or occupancy under a lease, are situated on a street or road and the street or road system is improved to standards at least equal to streets and roads maintained by the county, city, or town in which the lots are located; have a feasible plan to provide potable water and sewage disposal; and have telephone and electricity facilities and systems adequate to serve the lots, which facilities and systems are installed and in place on the lots or in a street, road, or easement adjacent to the lots and which facilities and systems comply with applicable state, county, municipal, or other local laws, rules, and regulations; or any subdivision

that has been or is required to be approved after September 1, 1972 by a regional, county, or municipal planning authority pursuant to Article 28 of Title 30 or Article 23 of Title 31, C.R.S.; and

5. Sales by public officials in the official conduct of their duties.

C. Additional Provisions of the Act

1. A "Developer" means any person, firm, partnership, joint venture, association, or corporation participating as owner, promoter, developer, or sales agent in the planning, platting, development, promotion, sale, or lease of a subdivision.

2. A registration expires on December 31st of each year unless it is renewed. A registration that has expired may be reinstated within two (2) years after such expiration upon submission of a renewal application and payment of the appropriate renewal fee, as well as meeting all other requirements of the Act. A Developer is not authorized to transact business during the period of time between expiration of the subdivision registration and reinstatement.

3. The Act requires a five (5) day cancellation period after the execution of a contract, which right cannot be waived, and applies to any subdivision regulated pursuant to the Act. This cancellation period runs until midnight on the fifth (5th) day following the execution of the contract.

4. Any agreement or contract for the sale or lease of a subdivision or part thereof shall be voidable by the purchaser and unenforceable by the Developer unless such Developer was duly registered under the provisions of the Act when such agreement or contract was made.

II. Subdivision Statutes

§ 12-10-501, C.R.S. Definitions.

Editor's note: *This section is similar to former §12-61-401 as it existed prior to 2019.*

As used in this part 5, unless the context otherwise requires:

(1) "Commission" means the real estate commission established under section 12-10-206.

(2) "Developer" means any person, as defined in section 2-4-401 (8), that participates as owner, promoter, or sales agent in the promotion, sale, or lease of a subdivision or any part thereof.

(3) (a) "Subdivision" means any real property divided into twenty or more interests intended solely for residential use and offered for sale, lease, or transfer.

  (b) (I) The term "subdivision" also includes:

   (A) The conversion of an existing structure into a common interest community, as defined in article 33.3 of title 38, of twenty or more residential units;

   (B) A group of twenty or more time shares intended for residential use; and

   (C) A group of twenty or more proprietary leases in a cooperative housing corporation, as described in article 33.5 of title 38.

  (II) The term "subdivision" does not include:

   (A) The selling of memberships in campgrounds;

   (B) Bulk sales and transfers between developers;

(C)   Property upon which there has been or upon which there will be erected residential buildings that have not been previously occupied and where the consideration paid for the property includes the cost of the buildings;

(D)   Lots that, at the time of closing of a sale or occupancy under a lease, are situated on a street or road and street or road system improved to standards at least equal to streets and roads maintained by the county, city, or town in which the lots are located; have a feasible plan to provide potable water and sewage disposal; and have telephone and electricity facilities and systems adequate to serve the lots, which facilities and systems are installed and in place on the lots or in a street, road, or easement adjacent to the lots and which facilities and systems comply with applicable state, county, municipal, or other local laws, rules, and regulations; or any subdivision that has been or is required to be approved after September 1, 1972, by a regional, county, or municipal planning authority pursuant to article 28 of title 30 or article 23 of title 31;

(E)   Sales by public officials in the official conduct of their duties.

(4)   "Time share" means a time share estate, as defined in section 38-33-110 (5), or a time share use, but the term does not include group reservations made for convention purposes as a single transaction with a hotel, motel, or condominium owner or association. For the purposes of this subsection (4), "time share use" means a contractual or membership right of occupancy, that cannot be terminated at the will of the owner, for life or for a term of years, to the recurrent, exclusive use or occupancy of a lot, parcel, unit, or specific or nonspecific segment of real property, annually or on some other periodic basis, for a period of time that has been or will be allotted from the use or occupancy periods into which the property has been divided.

§ 12-10-502, C.R.S. Registration required.

* *Editor's note: This section is similar to former §12-61-402 as it existed prior to 2019.*

(1)   Unless exempt under the provisions of section 12-10-501 (3), a developer, before selling, leasing, or transferring or agreeing or negotiating to sell, lease, or transfer, directly or indirectly, any subdivision or any part thereof, shall register pursuant to this part 5.

(2)   Upon approval by the commission, a developer who has applied for registration pursuant to section 12-10-503 may offer reservations in a subdivision during the pendency of the application and until the application is granted or denied if the fees for the reservations are held in trust by an independent third party and are fully refundable.

§ 12-10-503, C.R.S. Application for registration.

* *Editor's note: This section is similar to former §12-61-403 as it existed prior to 2019.*

(1)   Every person who is required to register as a developer under this part 5 shall submit to the commission an application that contains the information described in subsections (2) and (3) of this section. If the information is not submitted, the commission may deny the Application for registration.

If a developer is currently regulated in another state that has registration requirements substantially equivalent to the requirements of this part 5 or that provide substantially comparable protection to a purchaser, the commission may accept proof of the registration along with the developer's disclosure or equivalent statement from the other state in full or partial satisfaction of the information required by this section. In addition, the applicant shall be under a continuing obligation to notify the commission within ten days of any change in the information so submitted, and a failure to do so shall be a cause for disciplinary action.

(2) (a) Registration information concerning the developer shall include:

    (I) The principal office of the applicant wherever situate;

    (II) The location of the principal office and the branch offices of the applicant in this state;

    (III) The names and residence and business addresses of all natural persons who have a twenty-four percent or greater financial or ultimate beneficial interest in the business of the developer, either directly or indirectly, as principal, manager, member, partner, officer, director, or stockholder, specifying each such person's capacity, title, and percentage of ownership. If no natural person has a twenty-four percent or greater financial or beneficial interest in the business of the developer, the information required in this subsection (2)(a)(III) shall be submitted regarding the natural person having the largest single financial or beneficial interest.

    (IV) The length of time and the locations where the applicant has been engaged in the business of real estate sales or development;

    (V) Any felony of which the applicant has been convicted within the preceding ten years. In determining whether a certificate of registration shall be issued to an applicant who has been convicted of a felony within such period of time, the commission shall be governed by the provisions of section 24-5-101.

    (VI) The states in which the applicant has had a license or registration similar to the developer's registration in this state granted, refused, suspended, or revoked or is currently the subject of an investigation or charges that could result in refusal, suspension, or revocation;

    (VII) Whether the developer or any other person financially interested in the business of the developer as principal, partner, officer, director, or stockholder has engaged in any activity that would constitute a violation of this part 5.

(b) If the applicant is a corporate developer, a copy of the certificate of authority to do business in this state or a certificate of incorporation issued by the secretary of state shall accompany the application.

(3) Registration information concerning the subdivision shall include:

(a) The location of each subdivision from which sales are intended to be made;

(b) The name of each subdivision and the trade, corporate, or partnership name used by the developer;

(c) Evidence or certification that each subdivision offered for sale or lease is registered or will be registered in accordance with state or local requirements of the state in which each subdivision is located;

(d) Copies of documents evidencing the title or other interest in the subdivision;

(e) If there is a blanket encumbrance upon the title of the subdivision or any other ownership, leasehold, or contractual interest that could defeat all possessory or ownership rights of a purchaser, a copy of the instruments creating the liens, encumbrances, or interests, with dates as to the recording, along with documentary evidence that any beneficiary, mortgagee, or trustee of a deed of trust or any other holder of the ownership, leasehold, or contractual interest will release any lot or time share from the blanket encumbrance or has subordinated its interest in the subdivision to the interest of any purchaser or has established any other arrangement acceptable to the commission that protects the rights of the purchaser;

(f) A statement that standard commission-approved forms will be used for contracts of sale, notes, deeds, and other legal documents used to effectuate the sale or lease of the subdivision or any part thereof, unless the forms to be used were prepared by an attorney representing the developer;

(g) A true statement by the developer that, in any conveyance by means of an installment contract, the purchaser shall be advised to record the contract with the proper authorities in the jurisdiction in which the subdivision is located. In no event shall any developer specifically prohibit the recording of the installment contract.

(h) A true statement by the developer of the provisions for and availability of legal access, sewage disposal, and public utilities, including water, electricity, gas, and telephone facilities, in the subdivision offered for sale or lease, including whether such are to be a developer or purchaser expense;

(i) A true statement as to whether or not a survey of each lot, site, or tract offered for sale or lease from the subdivision has been made and whether survey monuments are in place;

(j) A true statement by the developer as to whether or not a common interest community is to be or has been created within the subdivision and whether or not the common interest community is or will be a small cooperative or small and limited expense planned community created pursuant to section 38-33.3-116;

(k) A true statement by the developer concerning the existence of any common interest community association, including whether the developer controls funds in the association.

(4) The commission may disapprove the form of the documents submitted pursuant to subsection (3)(f) of this section and may deny an application for registration until such time as the applicant submits the documents in a form that is satisfactory to the commission.

(5) Each registration shall be accompanied by fees established pursuant to section 12-10-215.

* ## § 12-10-504, C.R.S. Registration of developers.

* *Editor's note: This section is similar to former §12-61-404 as it existed prior to 2019.*

(1) The commission shall register all applicants who meet the requirements of this part 5 and provide each applicant so registered with a certificate indicating that the developer named therein is registered in the state of Colorado as a subdivision developer. The developer that will sign as seller or lessor in any contract of sale, lease, or deed purporting to convey any site, tract, lot, or divided or undivided interest from a subdivision shall secure a certificate before offering, negotiating, or agreeing to sell, lease, or transfer before the sale, lease, or transfer is made. If such person or entity is acting only as a trustee, the beneficial owner of the subdivision shall secure a certificate. A certificate issued to a developer shall entitle all sales agents and employees of the developer to act in the capacity of a developer as agent for the developer. The developer shall be responsible for all actions of the sales agents and employees.

(2) All certificates issued under this section shall expire on December 31 following the date of issuance. In the absence of any reason or condition under this part 5 that might warrant the denial or revocation of a registration, a certificate shall be renewed by payment of a renewal fee established pursuant to section 12-10-215. A registration that has expired may be reinstated within two years after the expiration upon payment of the appropriate renewal fee if the applicant meets all other requirements of this part 5.

(3) All fees collected under this part 5 shall be deposited in accordance with section 12-10-214.

(4) With regard to any subdivision for which the information required by section 12-10-503 (3) has not been previously submitted to the commission, each registered developer shall register the subdivision by providing the commission with the information before sale, lease, or transfer, or negotiating or agreeing to sell, lease, or transfer, any such subdivision or any part thereof.

*   **§ 12-10-505, C.R.S. Refusal, revocation, or suspension of registration – letter of admonition – probation.**

*   ***Editor's note:*** *This section is similar to former §12-61-405 as it existed prior to 2019.*

(1)   The commission may impose an administrative fine not to exceed two thousand five hundred dollars for each separate offense; may issue a letter of admonition; may place a registrant on probation under its close supervision on such terms and for such time as it deems appropriate; and may refuse, revoke, or suspend the registration of any developer or registrant if, after an investigation and after notice and a hearing pursuant to the provisions of section 24-4-104, the commission determines that the developer or any director, officer, or stockholder with controlling interest in the corporation:

(a)   Has used false or misleading advertising or has made a false or misleading statement or a concealment in his or her application for registration;

(b)   Has misrepresented or concealed any material fact from a purchaser of any interest in a subdivision;

(c)   Has employed any device, scheme, or artifice with intent to defraud a purchaser of any interest in a subdivision;

(d)   Has been convicted of or pled guilty or nolo contendere to a crime involving fraud, deception, false pretense, theft, misrepresentation, false advertising, or dishonest dealing in any court;

(e)   Has disposed of, concealed, diverted, converted, or otherwise failed to account for any funds or assets of any purchaser of any interest in a subdivision or any homeowners' association under the control of the developer or director, officer, or stockholder;

(f)   Has failed to comply with any stipulation or agreement made with the commission;

(g)   Has failed to comply with or has violated any provision of this article 10, including any failure to comply with the registration requirements of section 12-10-503, or any lawful rule promulgated by the commission under this article 10;

(h)   Has refused to honor a buyer's request to cancel a contract for the purchase of a time share or subdivision or part thereof if the request was made within five calendar days after execution of the contract and was made either by telegram, mail, or hand delivery. A request is considered made if by electronic mail when sent, if by mail when postmarked, or if by hand delivery when delivered to the seller's place of business. No developer shall employ a contract that contains any provision waiving a buyer's right to such a cancellation period.

(i)   Has committed any act that constitutes a violation of the "Colorado Consumer Protection Act", article 1 of title 6;

(j)   Has employed any sales agent or employee who violates the provisions of this part 5;

(k)   Has used documents for sales or lease transactions other than those described in section 12-10-503 (3)(f);

(*l*)   Has failed to disclose encumbrances to prospective purchasers or has failed to transfer clear title at the time of sale, if the parties agreed that the transfer would be made at that time.

(2)   A disciplinary action relating to the business of subdivision development taken by any other state or local jurisdiction or the federal government shall be deemed to be prima facie evidence of grounds for disciplinary action, including denial of registration, under this part 5. This subsection (2) shall apply only to such disciplinary actions as are substantially similar to those set out as grounds for disciplinary action or denial of registration under this part 5.

(3)   Any hearing held under this section shall be in accordance with the procedures established in sections 24-4-105 and 24-4-106.

(4)   When a complaint or investigation discloses an instance of misconduct that, in the opinion of the commission, does not initially warrant formal action by the commission but that should not be dismissed as being without merit, the commission may send a letter of admonition by certified mail, return receipt requested, to the registrant who is the subject of the complaint or investigation and a copy thereof to any person making the complaint. The letter shall advise the registrant that he or she has the right to request in writing, within twenty days after proven receipt, that formal disciplinary proceedings be initiated against him or her to adjudicate the propriety of the conduct upon which the letter of admonition is based. If the request is timely made, the letter of admonition shall be deemed vacated, and the matter shall be processed by means of formal disciplinary proceedings.

(5)   All administrative fines collected pursuant to this section shall be transmitted to the state treasurer, who shall credit the same to the division of real estate cash fund.

*   ### § 12-10-506, C.R.S. Powers of commission – injunction – rules.

*   *Editor's note: This section is similar to former §12-61-406 as it existed prior to 2019.*

(1)   The commission may apply to a court of competent jurisdiction for an order enjoining any act or practice that constitutes a violation of this part 5, and, upon a showing that a person is engaging or intends to engage in any such act or practice, an injunction, restraining order, or other appropriate order shall be granted by the court, regardless of the existence of another remedy therefor. Any notice, hearing, or duration of any injunction or restraining order shall be made in accordance with the provisions of the Colorado rules of civil procedure.

(2)   The commission may apply to a court of competent jurisdiction for the appointment of a receiver if it determines that the appointment is necessary to protect the property or interests of purchasers of a subdivision or part thereof.

(3)   The commission shall issue or deny a certificate or additional registration within sixty days from the date of receipt of the application by the commission. The commission may make necessary investigations and inspections to determine whether any developer has violated this part 5 or any lawful rule promulgated by the commission. If, after an application by a developer has been submitted pursuant to section 12-10-503 or information has been submitted pursuant to section 12-10-504, the commission determines that an inspection of a subdivision is necessary, it shall complete the inspection within sixty days from the date of filing of the application or information, or the right of inspection is waived and the lack thereof shall not be grounds for denial of a registration.

(4)   The commission, the director, or the administrative law judge appointed for a hearing may issue a subpoena compelling the attendance and testimony of witnesses and the production of books, papers, or records pursuant to an investigation or hearing of the commission. Any such subpoena shall be served in the same manner as for subpoenas issued by district courts.

(5)   The commission has the power to make any rules necessary for the enforcement or administration of this part 5.

(6)   The commission shall adopt, promulgate, amend, or repeal such rules as are necessary to:

    (a)   Require written disclosures to any purchasers as provided in subsection (7) of this section and to prescribe and require that standardized forms be used by subdivision developers in connection with the sale or lease of a subdivision or any part thereof, except as otherwise provided in section 12-10-503 (3)(f); and

    (b)   Require that developers maintain certain business records for a period of at least seven years.

(7)   The commission may require any developer to make written disclosures to purchasers in their contracts of sale or by separate written documents if the commission finds that the disclosures are necessary for the protection of the purchasers.

(8)   The commission or its designated representative may audit the accounts of any homeowners' association, the funds of which are controlled by a developer.

*   ## § 12-10-507, C.R.S. Violation – penalty.

*   ***Editor's note:*** *This section is similar to former §12-61-407 as it existed prior to 2019.*

Any person who fails to register as a developer in violation of this part 5 commits a class 6 felony and shall be punished as provided in section 18-1.3-401. Any agreement or contract for the sale or lease of a subdivision or part thereof shall be voidable by the purchaser and unenforceable by the developer unless the developer was duly registered under the provisions of this part 5 when the agreement or contract was made.

*   ## § 12-10-508, C.R.S. Repeal of part – subject to review.

*   ***Editor's note:*** *This section is similar to former §12-61-408 as it existed prior to 2019.*

This part 5 is repealed, effective September 1, 2026. Before the repeal, this part 5 is scheduled for review in accordance with section 24-34-104.

III. Rules and Regulations for Subdivision Developers

Adopted, and Published by the

COLORADO REAL ESTATE COMMISSION

Approved by the Attorney General and the Executive Director of the Department of Regulatory Agencies.

*   In pursuance of and in compliance with Title 12, Article 10, C.R.S. 1973, as amended, and in pursuance of and in compliance with Title 24, Article 4, C.R.S. 1973. as amended. With respect to certain statutory definitions used herein, see § 12-10-201, C.R.S., and § 12-10-501, C.R.S.

CHAPTER 1: REGISTRATION, CERTIFICATION AND APPLICATION

*   1.1   The Registration and Certification of a Subdivision Developer (Developer) under Title 12, Article 1010, Part 5, C.R.S., does not exempt the developer from the requirements for the licensing of real estate brokers under Title 12, Article 1010, Part 1, C.R.S. Exemptions from the licensing of real estate brokers are made pursuant to §12-10-201(6)(b), C.R.S.

*   1.2   The person, firm, partnership, joint venture, limited liability company, association, corporation or other legal entity, or combination thereof, who will sign as seller or lessor in any contract of sale, lease, deed or any other instrument purporting to convey any site, tract, lot, divided or undivided interest from a subdivision, must secure a registration under §12-10-503, C.R.S., (Developer Certificate) before negotiating or agreeing to sell, lease or transfer and before any sale, lease or transfer is made. If such person is acting only as a trustee, the beneficial owner of the subdivision must secure a Developer Certificate.

1.3   If an applicant is:

a.   A corporation, a director or an authorized officer must apply on behalf of said corporation.

b.   A partnership or limited partnership, one of the general partners must apply on behalf of the partnership or limited partnership.

  c. A joint owner of the subdivision, such owner may apply on behalf of all joint owners of such subdivision.

  d. A limited liability company, one of the managers or member-managers must apply on behalf of the company.

  e. With respect to any other type of developer that is other than a natural person, a person authorized to act on behalf of such entity, as demonstrated by such documents in a form satisfactory to the Commission, will apply on behalf of that entity.

1.4 The Real Estate Commission (Commission) will issue a developer certificate, deny registration or demand further information within sixty (60) calendar days from the date of receipt of the application by the Commission.

1.5 If the Commission requires additional information, the Commission will give written notice in detail of the information so required and will allow an additional sixty (60) calendar days to present such material before denial of the application, which period may be extended only upon showing of good cause.

* 1.6 Notification in writing must be made to the Commission within ten (10) calendar days of any change in the principal office address of the developer or the natural person, or any other change in the information submitted pursuant to §12-10-503, C.R.S.

* 1.7 Pursuant to §12-10-505, C.R.S., any developer who has received written notification from the Commission that a complaint has been filed against the developer, must submit a written answer to the Commission within a reasonable time as set by the Commission.

1.8 Failure to submit any written response required by Rule 1.7 will be grounds for disciplinary action unless the Commission has granted an extension of time, or unless such answer would subject such person to a criminal penalty.

CHAPTER 2: RECORDS, REQUIRED INFORMATION

* 2.1 Records as required by Title 12, Article 10, C.R.S., and rules promulgated by the Commission, may be maintained in electronic format as permitted by Title 24, Article 71.3, C.R.S. such electronic records must be in a format that has the continued capability to be retrieved and legibly printed. The developer must produce printed records upon request of the Commission, or by any principal party to a transaction.

* 2.2 In addition to §12-10-503, C.R.S., the applicant for a developer certificate must provide the Commission with the following information concerning the subdivision(s) to be registered:

  a. The address or actual physical location of each subdivision from which sales are intended to be made.

  b. Copies of a recorded deed or other documents evidencing the developer's title or other interest in the subdivision(s) and a title commitment, policy or report, abstract and opinion, or other evidence acceptable to the Commission documenting the condition of such title or interest.

  c. Sample copies of contracts of sale, notes, deeds, leases and other legal documents prepared by the developer or an attorney representing the developer which are to be used to effectuate the sale or lease of the subdivision or any part thereof. The Commission may disapprove the form of the documents submitted and may deny an application for registration until such time as the applicant submits such documents in forms that are satisfactory to the Commission.

* d. In compliance with §12-10-503(3)(e), C.R.S., a developer registering a subdivision that incorporates time share use and is subject to one or more blanket encumbrances must submit to the Commission a " Nondisturbance Agreement" by which the holder of each blanket encumbrance against the subdivision agrees that its rights in the subdivision will be subordinate to the rights of the time share use purchasers. From and after the recording of a nondisturbance agreement, the holder of the blanket encumbrance executing the same, such holder's successors and assigns, and any person who acquires all or part of the subdivision through the subject blanket encumbrance, will take the property subject to the rights of the time share use purchasers. Every nondisturbance agreement must contain the covenant of the holder of the blanket encumbrance that such person or any other person acquiring all or part of the subdivision through such blanket encumbrance will not use or cause the subdivision to be used in a manner which would prevent the time share use purchasers from using and occupying the subdivision in a manner contemplated by the time share use plan. any other "trust" or "escrow" arrangement which fully protects the time share use purchasers' interest in the subdivision as contemplated by §12-10-503(3)(e), C.R.S., may be approved by the Commission.

    e. If the developer is other than a natural person, proof of formation and registration in accordance with state and local requirements must accompany the application.

    f. Copies of the recorded declaration, covenants, filed articles of incorporation/organization and bylaws/operating agreement of any homeowners' association.

* 2.3 Pursuant to §12-10-502(2), C.R.S., where a developer receives cash or receivables from a purchaser for an uncompleted subdivision, the Commission will register such developer only after:

    a. The developer deposits in an escrow account, with an independent escrow agent, all funds and receivables received from purchasers, or

    b. The developer obtains a letter of credit or bond payable to an independent escrow agent or establishes any other financial arrangement acceptable to the Commission, the purpose of which is to ensure completion of subdivision accommodations and facilities and to protect the purchaser's interest in the subdivision accommodations and facilities.

* 2.4 A developer must furnish to the Commission such additional information as the Commission deems necessary both during the application process and during the active registration period of the subdivision for the enforcement of §12-10-501, *et seq.*, C.R.S.

2.5 Developer must maintain all business records related to the subdivision development in a safe and secure manner for a period of at least seven (7) years from the effective date of each such business record.

2.6 Renewal of the registration and certification as a developer can be executed only on the renewal application provided by the Commission, and must be delivered to the Commission, accompanied by the proper fees, on or before December 31st of each year.

* 2.7 Pursuant to §12-10-506(6)(a), C.R.S., and §12-10-506(7), C.R.S., developer must supply the following information to the Commission in addition to the requirements of §12-10-503, C.R.S., and §12-10-504(4), C.R.S., and prior to contracting with the public must disclose to prospective purchasers in the sales contract or in a separate written disclosure document, the following:

    a. The name and address of the developer and of the subdivision lots or units.

    b. An explanation of the type of ownership or occupancy rights being offered.

    c. A general description of all facilities, amenities and accommodations, together with provisions for and the availability of legal access, roads, sewage disposal, public utilities (including water, electricity, gas, internet and telephone) and other promised facilities in the subdivision. The disclosure must identify and describe the specific amenities promised, the ownership of such amenities, the projected completion date of any amenities not completed, a statement setting forth the type of financial arrangements established in compliance with rule 2.3, and the allocation of the amenity expense among the developer, the purchaser and any third party.

*   d.   In compliance with §12-10-505(1)(h), C.R.S., a statement in bold print immediately prior to the purchaser's signature line on the sales contract disclosing the rescission right available to purchasers and that the rescission right cannot be waived; the minimum allowable rescission period in Colorado is five (5) calendar days after execution of the sales contract.

     e.   A general description of all judgments and administrative orders issued against the seller, developer, homeowners' association or managing entity which are material to the subdivision development and operational plan.

     f.   Any taxes or assessments, existing or proposed, to which the purchaser may be subject or which are unpaid at the time of contracting, including obligations to special taxing authorities or districts.

*   G.   A statement that sales must be made by brokers licensed by the State of Colorado unless specifically exempted pursuant to §12-10-201(6)(b), C.R.S.; the sales contract must disclose the name of the real estate brokerage firm and the name of the broker establishing a brokerage relationship with the developer.

     h.   When a separate document is used to make any of the disclosures required in rule 2.7 herein, this statement must appear in bold print on the first page of the document and preceding the disclosure: **"the State of Colorado has not prepared or issued this document nor has it passed on the merits of the subdivision described herein."**.

     i.   A statement that all funds paid by the purchaser prior to delivery of the lease, deed or other instrument purporting to convey any interest in the site, tract, lot, divided or undivided interest from a subdivision will be held in trust by the licensed real estate broker named in the contract or a clear statement specifically setting forth who such funds will be delivered to, when such delivery will occur, the use of said funds, and whether or not there is any restriction on the use of such funds. (This must be disclosed in the contract.)

     j.   Where a deed is issued, a statement that, immediately following the date of closing, the purchaser's deed will be delivered to the appropriate county clerk and recorder's office for recording, or a clear statement specifically setting forth when such delivery and recording of the deed will occur; for the purposes of this rule, the date of closing is defined as the date the purchaser has either paid the full cash purchase price or has made partial cash payment and executed a promissory note or other evidence of indebtedness for the balance of the purchase price. (See rule 4.7) (This must be disclosed in the contract.)

     k.   A statement that a title insurance policy will be delivered at no expense to the purchaser within sixty (60) calendar days following recording of the deed or the closing, whichever is earlier, unless specifically agreed to the contrary by the parties in the contracting instrument. (See Rule 4.8) (This must be disclosed in the contract.)

*   *l.*   A contract which requires the execution of a promissory note or other evidence of indebtedness that accrues interest or requires payments prior to the recording of a deed, will be deemed to be an installment contract pursuant to §12-10-503(3)(g), C.R.S. where an installment contract is used:

         1.   Whether or not the purchaser's deed is escrowed with an independent escrow agent and if so, the name and address of the escrow agent. (this must be disclosed in the contract.);

         2.   The amount of any existing encumbrance(s), the name and address of the encumbrancer, and the conditions, if any, under which a purchaser may cure a default caused by non-payment;

3. A clear statement that a default on any underlying encumbrance(s) could result in the loss of the purchaser's entire interest in the property;

4. A clear statement advising the purchaser to record the installment contract; and

5. Pursuant to §12-10-503(3)(e), C.R.S., an agreement by which the holder of any blanket encumbrance against the subdivision agrees that its rights and the rights of its successors or assigns in the subdivision will be subordinate to the rights of purchasers, or any other "trust", "escrow" or release arrangement which fully protects the purchasers' interest in the subdivision.

m. If the subdivision has a homeowners' or similar association:

1. Whether membership in such association is mandatory;

2. An estimate of association dues and fees which are the responsibility of the purchaser and the developer, respectively;

3. A description of the services and amenities provided by the association;

4. Whether the developer has voting control of the association and the manner in which such control can or will be transferred; and

5. Whether the developer has any financial interest in or will potentially derive any income or profit from such association, including the developer's right to borrow or authorize borrowing from the association.

n. In addition to the disclosures in (A) through (M) above, if time share sales are to be made from a subdivision:

1. A description of the time share units including the number of time share units, the length, type and number of time share interests in each unit, and the time share periods constituting the time share plan;

2. The name and business address of the managing entity appointed by the developer or homeowners' association, a description of the services that the managing entity will provide, a statement as to whether the developer has any financial interest in or will potentially derive any income or profit from such managing entity, and the manner, if any, by which the purchaser or developer may change the managing entity or transfer the control of the managing entity;

3. An estimate of the dues, maintenance fees, real property taxes and similar periodic expenses which are the responsibility of the purchaser and the developer, respectively, and a general statement of the conditions under which future charges, changes or additions may be imposed. Such estimate must include a statement as to whether a maintenance reserve fund has been or will be established; the manner in which such reserve fund is financed; an accounting of any outstanding obligations either in favor of or against the fund; the developer's right to borrow or authorize borrowing from the fund; and the method of periodic accounting which will be provided to the purchaser;

4. A description of any insurance coverage(s) provided for the benefit of purchasers; and

5. That mechanic's liens law may authorize enforcement of the lien by selling the entire time share unit.

o. In addition to the disclosures in (A) through (N) above, if time share sales are to be made from a subdivision:

1. The specific term of the contract to use and what will happen to a purchaser's interest upon termination of said contract;

2. A statement as to the effect a voluntary sale, by the developer to a third party, will have on the contractual rights of time share owners;

3. A statement that an involuntary transfer by bankruptcy of the developer may have a negative effect on the rights of the time share owners; and

4. A statement that a federal or state tax lien could be enforced against the developer by compelling the sale of the entire subdivision.

p. If time shares are to be sold from a subdivision which: (1) contains two or more component sites situated at different geographic locations or governed by separate sets of declarations, by-laws or equivalent documents; and (2) does not include a guaranteed, recurring right of use or occupancy at a single component site:

1. For each component site, the information and disclosures required by Rule 2.7 (A) through (O);

2. A general description of the subdivision;

3. For each term of usage or interest offered for sale, the total annual number of available daily use periods within the entire subdivision and within each component site for that term, regardless of whether such use periods are offered to a purchaser by days, weeks, points or otherwise, and a calculation represented on a chart or grid showing each component site's annual daily use periods as a percentage of the entire subdivision's annual daily use periods;

4. A clear description in the sales contract of the interest and term of usage being purchased and a definite date of termination of the purchaser's interest in the subdivision, which date will be not later than the termination date of the subdivision's interest in a specifically identified component site;

5. A clear disclosure and description of any component site which is not legally guaranteed to be available for the purchaser's use for the full term of the purchaser's usage interest;

6. The system and method in place to assure maintenance of no more than a one-to-one ratio of purchasers' use rights to the number of total use rights in the subdivision for each term of usage being offered for sale, including provisions for compensation to purchasers resulting from destruction of a component site or loss of use rights to any component site;

7. Whether the developer maintains any type of casualty insurance for the component sites in addition to that maintained by the site's homeowners' association or other interested parties, including the manner of disposition of any proceeds of such insurance resulting from the destruction or loss of use rights to any component site;

8. A description of the system or program by which a purchaser obtains a recurring right to use and occupy accommodations and facilities in any component site through use of a reservation system or otherwise, including any restrictions on such rights or any method by which a purchaser is denied an equal right with all other users to obtain the use of any accommodation in the subdivision;

9. A description of the management and ownership of such reservation system or program, whether through the developer, a homeowners' association, a club or otherwise, including the purchaser's direct or indirect ownership interest or rights of control in such reservation system;

10. Whether the developer, club or association which controls the reservation system or any other person has or is granted any interest in unsold, non-reserved or unused use rights and whether the developer, club, association or other person may employ such rights to compete with purchasers for use of accommodations in the subdivision or any component site and, if so, the nature and specifics of those rights, including the circumstances under which they may be employed;

11. The method and frequency of accounting for any income derived from unsold, non-reserved or unused use rights in which the purchaser, either directly or indirectly, has an interest;

12. The system and method in place, including business interruption insurance or bonding, to provide secure back-up or replacement of the reservation system in the event of interruption, discontinuance or failure;

13. The amount and details of any component site, reservation system or other periodic expense required to be paid by a purchaser, the name of the person or entity to which such payments will be made, and the method by which the purchaser will receive a regular periodic accounting for such payments;

14. If component site expenses are included in those periodic payments made by a purchaser, a statement for each component site from the homeowners' association or other responsible entity acknowledging that payment of such expenses as taxes, insurance, dues and assessments are current and are being made in the name of the subdivision;

15. Evidence that an escrow system with an independent escrow agent is in place for receipt and disbursement of all moneys collected from purchasers that are necessary to pay such expenses as taxes, insurance and common expenses and assessments owing to component site homeowners' associations or others, or a clear description of the method by which such funds will be paid, collected, held, disbursed and accounted for;

16. A clear statement in the sales contract as to whether a purchaser's rights, interests or terms of usage for any component site within the subdivision can subsequently be modified from those terms originally represented and a description of the method by which such modification may occur;

17. If the subdivision documents allow additions or substitutions of accommodations or component sites, a clear description of the purchaser's rights and obligations concerning such additions or substitutions and the method by which such additions or substitutions will comply with the provisions of this rule; and

18. A clear description of any existing incidental benefits or amenities which are available to the purchaser at the time of sale but to which the purchaser has no guaranteed right of recurring use or enjoyment during the purchaser's full term of interest in the subdivision.

CHAPTER 3: TIMESHARE – ADDITIONAL INFORMATION AND DISCLOSURES

3.1 A developer of time share must disclose to the public whether or not a time share plan involves an exchange program and, if so, will disclose and deliver to prospective purchasers, a separate written document, which may be provided by an exchange company if the document discloses the following information:

a. The name and the business address of the exchange company;

b. Whether the purchaser's contract with the exchange program is separate and distinct from the purchaser's contract with the developer;

c. Whether the purchaser's participation in the exchange program is dependent upon the developer's continued affiliation with the exchange program;

d. Whether or not the purchaser's participation in the exchange program is voluntary;

e. The specific terms and conditions of the purchaser's contractual relationship with the exchange program and the procedure by which changes, if any, may be made in the terms and conditions of such contractual relationship;

f. The procedure of applying for and effecting any changes;

g. A complete description of all limitations, restrictions, accrual rights, or priorities employed in the operation of the exchange program, including but not limited to limitations on exchanges based on seasonality, unit size, or levels of occupancy; and if the limitations, restrictions or priorities are not applied uniformly by the exchange program, a complete description of the manner of their application;

h. Whether exchanges are arranged on a space-available basis or whether guarantees of fulfillment of specific requests for exchanges are made by the exchange company;

i. Whether and under what conditions a purchaser may, in dealing with the exchange program, lose the use and occupancy of the time share period in any properly applied for exchange without being offered substitute accommodations by the exchange program;

j. The fees for participation in the exchange program, and whether the fees may be altered and the method of any altering; and

k. The name and location of each accommodation or facility, including the time sharing plans participating in the exchange program.

CHAPTER 4: MISCELLANEOUS PROVISIONS, ADDITIONAL INFORMATION

* 4.1 All approvals for the use of reservation agreements issued pursuant to §12-10-502(2), C.R.S., will expire on December 31st following the date of issuance. Approval will be renewed, except as provided in section §12-10-505, C.R.S., by payment of a renewal fee established pursuant to section §12-10-215, C.R.S., and upon submission and acceptance of a renewal application.

4.2 upon request of the Commission pursuant to an investigation, a developer will file with the Commission an audited financial statement in conformity with accepted accounting principles, and sworn to by the developer as an accurate reflection of the financial condition of the developer and/or the homeowners' association controlled by the developer.

4.3 any adverse order, judgment, or decree entered in connection with the subdivided lands by any regulatory authority or by any court of appropriate jurisdiction must be filed with the Commission by the developer within thirty (30) calendar days of such order, judgment or decree being final.

* 4.4 A developer is not required to file amendments to its registration filed with the Commission when revisions are made to documents previously submitted to the Commission, so long as the revised documents continue to: (a) comply with Title 12, Article 10, Part 5, C.R.S., and the rules and regulations promulgated thereunder; and (b) accurately reflect the subdivision offering.

4.5 Notice of events:

a. Notwithstanding Rules 4.3 and 4.4 above, and in addition to the notice requirements under rule 1.6, developer must provide the Commission with notice of the following events within ten (10) calendar days after such event, unless otherwise provided below:

*   1. Any change in the information provided in the registration pursuant to Sections §12-10-503 (2)(a)(III), (V), (VI) or (VII), C.R.S.;

*   2. Any change in the terms of any non-disturbance agreement(s) or partial release provisions in connection with any documents previously submitted to the Commission pursuant to section §12-10-503(3)(e), C.R.S., and Rule 2.2(d);

3. Any new lien encumbering the subdivision or any part thereof other than encumbrances created or permitted by purchasers;

4. The termination or transfer of any escrow account, letter of credit, bond, or other financial assurance approved by the Commission pursuant to Rule 2.3; notice of

which must be filed with the Commission prior to the effective date of such termination or transfer;

5. Cancellation, revocation, suspension, or termination of the developer's activity or authority to do business in the state of Colorado; and

6. Any lis pendens, lawsuit or other proceeding filed against the subdivision or developer affecting the developer's ability: (a) to convey marketable title of the registered subdivision or any interest therein, or (b) to perform the developer's obligations in connection with the registered subdivision.

b. Notification under this rule must be provided on a form approved by the Commission. The developer will have a period of ten (10) calendar days after receipt of notice to take such action as may be required by the Commission in connection with any filings made under this rule.

c. Within ten (10) calendar days after receipt of a written request from the Commission, a developer will have the duty to provide to the Commission copies of all documents then in use with regard to the subdivision.

4.6 No developer will make misrepresentations regarding the future availability or costs of services, utilities, character, or use of real property for sale or lease of the surrounding area of the subdivision.

4.7 delivery of deed:

a. Unless a sale is by means of an installment contract, the delivery of a deed must be made within sixty (60) calendar days after closing. For the purposes of this rule, the date of closing is defined as the date the purchaser has either paid the full cash purchase price or has made partial cash payment and executed a promissory note or other evidence of indebtedness for the balance of the purchase price. (This must be disclosed in the contract.)

b. If a sale is by means of an installment contract, the delivery of a deed must be made within sixty (60) calendar days after the completion of payments.

4.8 Where the sales contract contemplates the delivery of a deed, an abstract of title or title insurance policy must be delivered within a reasonable time after the completion of payments by a purchaser. Any period of time exceeding sixty (60) calendar days will be deemed unreasonable for the purposes of this rule. The parties may contract to eliminate this requirement, but any such mutually acceptable waiver must be in writing and in a conspicuous manner or print. The presence of waiver on the back of a contract will not be deemed conspicuous for the purposes of this rule.

4.9 Developer must provide a title insurance commitment or other evidence of title approved by the Commission within a reasonable time after execution of any lease, sales contract or other instrument purporting to convey any interest in the site, tract, lot, divided or undivided interest from a subdivision. Any period of time in excess of sixty (60) calendar days will be deemed unreasonable for the purposes of this rule. The parties may contract to eliminate this requirement, but any such mutually acceptable waiver must be in writing and in a conspicuous manner or print. The presence of waiver on the back of a contract will not be deemed conspicuous for the purposes of this rule.

* 4.10 Failure to disclose to the purchaser the availability of legal access, sewage disposal, public utilities, including water, electricity, gas and telephone facilities, in the subdivision offered for sale or lease, including whether such are to be a developer or purchaser expense, when proven, is a violation of §12-10-505(1)(b), C.R.S.

* 4.11 Pursuant to §12-10-505(1)(e), C.R.S., §12-10-506(6)(b), C.R.S., and §12-10-506(8), C.R.S., a developer must maintain in a Colorado place of business, and produce for inspection upon reasonable request by an authorized representative of the Commission copies of the following documents and business records:

    a.   The sales contract, transfer or lease agreement, installment sale agreement, financing agreement, buyer and seller settlement statement, title policy or commitment, trust deed, escrow agreement, and any other documents executed by the parties or on behalf of the developer in the sale, lease or transfer of any interest in a subdivision.

    b.   Records showing the receipt and disbursement of any money or assets received or paid on behalf of any homeowners' or similar association managed or controlled by a developer.

CHAPTER 5: DECLARATORY ORDERS PURSUANT TO § 24-4-105(11), C.R.S.

5.1   Any person may petition the Commission for a declaratory order to terminate controversies or to remove uncertainties as to the applicability to the petitioner of any statutory provisions or of any rule or order of the Commission.

5.2   The Commission will determine, in its discretion and without prior notice to petitioner, whether to entertain any such petition. If the Commission decides that it will not entertain such a petition, the Commission will promptly notify the petitioner in writing of its decision and the reasons for that decision. A copy of the order will be provided to the petitioner.

5.3   In determining whether to entertain a petition filed pursuant to this rule, the Commission may consider the following matters, among others:

    a.   Whether a ruling on the petition will terminate a controversy or remove uncertainties as to the applicability to petitioner of any statutory provision or rule or order of the Commission.

    b.   Whether the petition involves any subject, question or issue which is the subject of a formal or informal matter or investigation currently pending before the Commission or a court involving any petitioner.

    c.   Whether the petition involves any subject, question or issue which is the subject of a formal or informal matter or investigation currently pending before the Commission or a court but not involving any petitioner.

    d.   Whether the petition seeks a ruling on a moot or hypothetical question or will result in an advisory ruling or opinion.

    e.   Whether the petitioner has some other adequate legal remedy, other than an action for declaratory relief pursuant to rule 57, C.R.C.P., which will terminate the controversy or remove any uncertainty as to the applicability to the petitioner of the statute, rule or order in question.

5.4   Any petition filed pursuant to this rule must set forth the following:

    a.   The name and address of the petitioner and whether the petitioner holds a license or registration issued pursuant to section §12-10-501, *et seq.*, C.R.S. (as amended).

    b.   The statute, rule or order to which the petition relates.

    c.   A concise statement of all of the facts necessary to show the nature of the controversy or uncertainty and the manner in which the statute, rule or order in question applies or potentially applies to the petitioner.

    d.   A concise statement of the legal authorities if any, and such other reasons upon which the petitioner relies.

    e.   A concise statement of the declaratory order sought by the petitioner.

5.5   If the Commission determines that it will rule on the petition, the following procedures will apply:

    a.   The Commission may rule upon the petition without a hearing. In such case:

1. The Commission may dispose of the petition on the sole basis of the matters set forth in the petition.

2. The Commission may request the petitioner to submit additional facts in writing. In such event, such additional facts will be considered as an amendment to the petition.

3. Any ruling of the Commission will apply only to the extent of the facts presented in the petition and any amendment to the petition.

4. The Commission may order the petitioner to file a written brief, memorandum or statement of position based on the facts set forth in the petition and any amendment to the petition.

5. The Commission may take administrative notice of facts pursuant to the administrative procedures act, (§ 24-4-105(8), C.R.S., (as amended)), and may utilize its experience, technical competence and specialized knowledge in the disposition of the petition.

6. If the Commission rules upon the petition without hearing, it will promptly notify the petitioner in writing of its decision.

b.   The Commission may, in its discretion, set the petition for hearing, upon due notice to petitioner, for the purpose of obtaining additional facts or information or to determine the truth of any facts set forth in the petition or to hear oral argument on the petition. The notice to the petitioner setting such hearing will set forth, to the extent known, the factual or other matters into which the Commission intends to inquire and whether the hearing will be evidentiary or non-evidentiary in nature. For the purpose of such a hearing, to the extent necessary, the petitioner will have the burden of proving all of the facts stated in the petition, all of the facts necessary to show the nature of the controversy or uncertainty and the manner in which the statute, rule or order in question applies or potentially applies to the petitioner and any other facts the petitioner desires the Commission to consider.

5.6   The parties to any proceeding pursuant to this rule will be the Commission and the petitioner. Any other person may seek leave of the Commission to intervene in such a proceeding, and leave to intervene will be granted at the sole discretion of the Commission. A petition to intervene must set forth the same matters as required by rule 5.4. Any reference to a "petitioner" in this rule also refers to any person who has been granted leave to intervene by the Commission.

5.7   Any declaratory order or other order disposing of a petition pursuant to this rule will constitute agency action subject to judicial review pursuant to § 24-4-106, C.R.S., (as amended).

CHAPTER 6: EXCEPTIONS AND COMMISSION REVIEW OF INITIAL DECISIONS

6.1   Written form, service, and filing requirements:

a.   All designations of record, requests, exceptions and responsive pleadings ("pleadings") must be in written form, mailed with a certificate of mailing to the Commission.

b.   All pleadings must be received by the Commission by 5:00 p.m. (MST), on the date the filing is due. Pleadings are considered filed upon receipt by the Commission. These rules do not provide for any additional time for service by mail.

c.   All pleadings must be served on the opposing party by mail or by hand delivery on the date which the pleadings are filed with the Commission.

d.   All pleadings must be filed with the Commission and not with the office of administrative courts. Any designations of record, requests, exceptions or responsive pleadings filed in error with the office of administrative courts will not be considered. The Commission's address is:

Colorado Real Estate Commission
1560 Broadway, Suite 925
Denver, Colorado 80202

6.2 Authority to review:

    a. The Commission hereby preserves the Commission's option to initiate a review of an initial decision on its own motion pursuant to § 24-4-105(14) (a) (ii) and (b) (iii), C.R.S., outside of the thirty (30) day period after service of the initial decision upon the parties without requiring a vote for each case.

    b. This option to review will apply regardless of whether a party files exceptions to the initial decision.

6.3 Designation of record and transcripts:

    a. Any party seeking to reverse or modify the initial decision of the administrative law judge must file with the Commission a designation of the relevant parts of the record for review ("designation of record"). Designations of record must be filed with the Commission within twenty (20) days of the date on which the Commission mails the initial decision to the parties' address of record with the Commission.

    b. Within ten (10) days after a party's designation of record is due, any other party may file a supplemental designation of record requesting inclusion of additional parts of the record.

    c. Even if no party files a designation of record, the record will include the following:

       1. All pleadings;

       2. All applications presented or considered during the hearing;

       3. All documentary or other exhibits admitted into evidence;

       4. All documentary or other exhibits presented or considered during the hearing;

       5. All matters officially noticed;

       6. Any findings of fact and conclusions of law proposed by any party; and

       7. Any written brief filed.

    d. Transcripts will not be deemed part of a designation of record unless specifically identified and ordered. Should a party wish to designate a transcript or portion thereof, the following procedures will apply:

       1. The designation of record must identify with specificity the transcript or portion thereof to be transcribed. For example, a party may designate the entire transcript, or may identify any witness whose testimony is to be transcribed, the legal ruling or argument to be transcribed, or other information necessary to identify a portion of the transcript.

       2. Any party who includes a transcript or a portion thereof as part of the designation of record must order the transcript or relevant portions by the date on which the designation of record must be filed (within twenty (20) days of the date on which the Commission mails the initial decision to the parties).

       3. When ordering the transcript, the party must request a court reporter or transcribing service to prepare the transcript within thirty (30) days. The party must timely pay the necessary fees to obtain and file with the Commission an original transcription and one copy within thirty (30) days.

       4. The party ordering the transcript will direct the court report or transcribing service to complete and file with the Commission the transcript and one copy of the transcript within thirty (30) days.

5. If a party designates a portion of the transcript, the opposing party may also file a supplemental designation of record, in which the opposing party may designate additional portions of the transcript.

6. An opposing party filing a supplemental designation of record designating additional portions of the transcript must order and pay for such transcripts or portions thereof within the deadlines set forth above. An opposing party must also cause the court reporter to complete and file with the Commission the transcript and one copy of the transcript within thirty (30) days.

7. Transcripts that are ordered and not filed with the Commission in a timely manner by the reporter or the transcription service due to non-payment, insufficient payment or failure to direct as set forth above will not be considered by the Commission.

6.4 Filing of exceptions and responsive pleadings:

a. Any party wishing to file exceptions must adhere to the following timelines:

1. If no transcripts are ordered, exceptions are due within thirty (30) days from the date on which the Commission mails the initial decision to the parties. Both parties' exceptions are due on the same date.

2. If transcripts are ordered by either party, the following procedure will apply. Upon receipt of all transcripts identified in all designations of record and supplemental designations of record, the Commission will mail notification to the parties stating that the transcripts have been received by the Commission. Exceptions are due within thirty (30) days from the date on which such notification is mailed. Both parties' exceptions are due on the same date.

b. Either party may file a responsive pleading to the other party's exceptions. All responsive pleadings must be filed within ten (10) days of the date on which the exceptions were filed with the Commission. No other pleadings will be considered except for good cause shown.

c. The Commission may in its sole discretion grant an extension of time to file exceptions or responsive pleadings, or may delegate the discretion to grant such an extension of time to the Commission's designee.

6.5 Request for oral argument:

a. All requests for oral argument must be in writing and filed by the deadline for responsive pleadings.

b. It is within the sole discretion of the Commission to grant or deny a request for oral argument. If oral argument is granted, both parties will have the opportunity to participate.

c. If a request for oral argument is granted, each side will be permitted ten (10) minutes of oral argument unless such time is extended by the Commission or its designee.

IV. Licensee's Responsibilities

A real estate licensee cannot be expected to be completely familiar with all county and municipal planning laws, regulations, ordinances, and zoning requirements. However, the licensee in negotiations should be very much aware of the existence of these laws, ordinances, zoning requirements, etc. It is very easy to misrepresent property through ignorance. If uninformed, the licensee should seek the information from the proper source before making a representation, or refer prospective clients to the proper source of the information.

Some facts should be known to the licensee through reading or logic, such as:

1. The sale of a portion of a seller's land divides the land into two parcels and a subdivision is created that must be approved by the proper authorities.

2. If a structure is suitable for conversion into a duplex and/or a four-plex, it does not in itself mean that such a conversion does not violate the law.

3. If an area is zoned for keeping horses, it does not necessarily follow that the acreage of the property is great enough for this purpose.

4. Even if an area is zoned for a home business, there may be a prohibition against having employees. Other complexities may also arise through various branches of local government involving utilities existent and future utilities. Representations concerning future services, zoning variances, etc. may endanger both the public and the licensee.

* The following may also be subdivisions under county planning laws: the conversion of an existing building into a common interest community complex or the division of a single condominium unit into "time shares" or "interval estates." These are subdivisions as defined in § 12-10-501(3), C.R.S., and are subject to the registration requirements of §§ 12-10-501, *et seq.*, C.R.S.

A stock cooperative or cooperative housing corporation is defined in this chapter, and in Colorado is considered a subdivision of real estate. The sale of these "apartments" is accomplished by transfer of a stock certificate, together with a proprietary lease. In most states, the sale of the stock, together with the lease, would be considered the sale of a security and would fall under the jurisdiction of the division of securities. In Colorado, such sales are exempt from the Securities Act and are declared real estate (see §§ 38-33.5-101, *et seq.*, C.R.S., printed in this chapter). Therefore, such cooperatives must be registered as subdivisions, and the sale of the stock and proprietary leases must be performed by licensed real estate brokers. The act also provides that commercial banks and savings and loan associations may make a first mortgage loan on the stock and proprietary lease of each "apartment" owner.

V. Municipal Planning and Zoning Laws

Sections 31-23-101 through -313, C.R.S., address municipal planning and zoning in incorporated areas of the state. A "subdivision" also is defined as a division of a parcel of land into two or more parcels. The definition includes condominiums, apartments, and multiple-dwelling units.

Sections 31-23-201, *et seq.*, C.R.S., authorize the creation of a municipal planning commission, which must make or adopt a master plan that, among other things, includes a zoning plan. This planning commission has all the powers of a zoning commission.

* The zoning commission must approve subdivisions. Developers who sell land from an unapproved subdivision are subject to a financial penalty, and the zoning commission may also enjoin any such sale. Note that even though the Subdivision Act, in § 12-10-502(2), C.R.S., allows for the use of a reservation agreement prior to final approval by the Real Estate Commission, the developer should check with the municipality regarding the use of reservation agreements. The governing body of a municipality provides for the appointment of a board of adjustment that hears appeals made from any ordinance or order of any administrative official. This board may grant variances from an ordinance or reverse an order.

VI. County Planning Laws

In addition to the provisions of the Subdivision Act, jurisdiction concerning the use of land within Colorado also falls within the powers of the county commissioners of each county. The county commissioners have the authority to enact zoning law for un-incorporated areas, and many counties have done so. Prior to surveying and offering subdivided property, a developer or real estate licensee should contact the county planning and zoning department regarding compliance with the county's requirements.

In regard to a county commissioner's jurisdiction, §§ 30-28-101 through -209, C.R.S., define a subdivision as any parcel of land that is divided into two or more parcels, separate interests, or interests in common. "Interests" means interests in surface land or in the air above the surface of the land, but excludes sub-surface interests. Divisions of land that create parcels of 35 acres or more and of which none is intended for use by multiple owners are exempt.

Condominiums, apartments, and multiple dwellings are included in the definition, unless they had been previously included in a filing with substantially the same density.

Subdivisions must submit the following information to the county authorities before sales within the subdivision are made:

1. Survey and ownership;

2. Site characteristics, such as topography;

3. A plat showing the plan of development and plan of the completed development;

4. Estimates of the water and sewage requirements, streets, utilities, and related facilities and estimated construction cost;

5. Evidence to ensure an adequate supply of potable water; and

6. Dedication of areas for public facilities.

Upon request of a complete preliminary plan, copies will be distributed to 10 interested public agencies for recommendations. An approved plat must be recorded before any lots are sold.

No plat will be approved until the subdivision has submitted a subdivision improvement contract agreeing to construct the required improvements, accompanied by collateral sufficient to ensure completion of the improvements.

The county commissioners must approve a final plat of the subdivision before it can be filed and recorded. Violations by a subdivider or agent of a subdivider are punishable by a fine of up to $1,000 for each parcel sold or offered for sale by a subdivider or agent of a subdivider. A sale made before a final plat is approved is considered prima facie evidence of a fraudulent sale and is grounds for the purchaser voiding the sale. The county commissioners also have the power to bring an action to enjoin any subdivider from offering to sell undivided land before a final plat has been approved.

VII. Special Types of Subdivisions

A. Condominiums as Subdivisions

"Estates above the surface" may be created in areas above the surface of the ground, and title to such "air rights" may be conveyed separate from title to the surface of the ground.

It follows that a division of air rights is a subdivision under county planning laws. A declaration must be recorded with the county and must be approved by county authorities. The declaration must provide for the recording of a map properly locating the condominium units. It is similar to the filing of a plat of surface land insofar as it describes each unit. The division however, is a division of the air space.

* The conversion of an existing building into a condominium complex or the division of a single condominium unit into "time shares" or "interval estates" also may be a subdivision under county planning laws, and are considered a subdivision as defined in § 12-10-501(3), C.R.S., and subject to the registration requirements of §§ 12-10-501, *et seq.*, C.R.S.

VIII. Condominium Ownership Act – Referenced in Chapter 5, Condominium Ownership Act, pages 5-5 to 5-12

IX. Colorado Common Interest Ownership Act – Referenced in Chapter 5, Colorado Common Interest Ownership Act, pages 5-12 to 5-80

X. Cooperative Housing Corporations

§ 38-33.5-101, C.R.S. Method of formation – purpose.

Cooperative housing corporations may be formed by any three or more adult residents of this state associating themselves to form a cooperative or nonprofit corporation, pursuant to article 55, 56, or 58 of title 7, C.R.S., or the "Colorado Revised Nonprofit Corporation Act", articles 121 to 137 of title 7, C.R.S. The specified purpose of the entity must be to provide each stockholder in or member of the entity with the right to occupy, for dwelling purposes, a house or an apartment in a building owned or leased by the entity.

§ 38-33.5-102, C.R.S. Requirements for articles of incorporation of cooperative housing corporations.

(1) In addition to any other requirements for articles of incorporation imposed by the "Colorado Revised Nonprofit Corporation Act", articles 121 to 137 of title 7, C.R.S., such articles of incorporation shall, in the case of cooperative housing corporations, include the following provisions:

    (a) That the corporation shall have only one class of stock outstanding;

    (b) That each stockholder is entitled, solely by reason of his ownership of stock in the corporation, to occupy, for dwelling purposes, a house or an apartment in a building owned or leased by the corporation;

    (c) That the interest of each stockholder in the corporation shall be inseparable from and appurtenant to the right of occupancy, and shall be deemed an estate in real property for all purposes, and shall not be deemed personal property;

(d)   That no stockholder is entitled to receive any distribution not out of earnings and profits of the corporation except on a complete or partial liquidation of the corporation.

§ 38-33.5-103, C.R.S. Provisions relating to taxes, interest, and depreciation on corporate property.

(1)   The bylaws of a cooperative housing corporation shall provide that no less than eighty percent of the gross income of the corporation in any taxable year shall be derived from payments from tenant-stockholders. For the purposes of this article, "tenant-stockholder" means an individual who is a stockholder in the corporation and whose stock is fully paid when measured by his proportionate share of the value of the corporation's equity in the property.

(2)   The bylaws shall further provide that each tenant-stockholder shall be credited with his proportionate payment of real estate taxes paid or incurred in any year on the buildings and other improvements owned or leased by the corporation in which the tenant-stockholder's living quarters are located, together with the land to which such improvements are appurtenant, and likewise with respect to interest paid or incurred by the corporation as well as depreciation on real and personal property which are proper deductions related to the said lands and improvements thereon for purposes of state and federal income taxation.

§ 38-33.5-104, C.R.S. Financing of cooperative housing – stock certificates held by tenant stockholders.

Stock certificates or membership certificates issued by cooperative housing corporations to tenant-stockholders shall be valid securities for investment by savings and loan associations, when the conditions imposed by section 11-41-119 (13), C.R.S., are met.

§ 38-33.5-105, C.R.S. Provisions to be included in proprietary lease or right of tenancy issued by corporation.

(1)   Every stockholder of a cooperative housing corporation shall be entitled to receive from the corporation a proprietary lease or right of tenancy document which shall include the following provisions:

(a)   That no sublease in excess of one year, amendment, or modification to such proprietary lease or right of tenancy in the property shall be permitted or created without the lender's prior written consent; and

(b)   That the security for a loan against the tenant-stockholder's interest shall be in the nature of a real property security interest, and any default of such loan shall entitle the lender to treat such default in the same manner as a default of a loan secured by real property.

§ 38-33.5-106, C.R.S. Exemption from securities laws.

Any stock certificate or other evidence of membership issued by a cooperative housing corporation as an investment in its stock or capital to tenant-stockholders of such corporation is exempt from securities laws contained in article 51 of title 11, C.R.S.

Chapter 5:
Common Interest Communities

An * in the left margin indicates a change in the statute, rule, or text since the last publication of the manual.

I. HOA Information and Resource Center

* The HOA Information and Resource Center ("Center"), as promulgated by the Colorado Legislature in HB10-1278, and codified in § 12-10-801(1), C.R.S., became operational on January 1, 2011. The Center is organized within the Division of Real Estate under the Department of Regulatory Agencies ("DORA").

The Center collects information via registrations directly from unit owners' associations ("HOAs") and from inquiries and complaints filed by unit owners. The Center provides education, assistance and information to unit owners, HOA boards, declarants and other interested parties concerning their rights and responsibilities as enumerated in the Colorado Common Interest Ownership Act ("CCIOA"), § 38-33.3-101, C.R.S., *et seq*.

* The HOA Information Officer oversees the Center, and reviews, analyzes, and reports the data and information compiled in an Annual Report to the Director of the Division of Real Estate, pursuant to § 12-10-801(3)(c), C.R.S.

II. HOA Registration

Every unit owners' association shall register annually with the Director of the Division of Real Estate and shall submit with its annual registration and basic association information, a fee in the amount set by the Director of the Division of Real Estate. The association must complete an initial registration and renew its registration on an annual basis, as well as updating any relevant information within ninety (90) days of any change, as per § 38-33.3-401, C.R.S.

As part of the registration process, associations indicate whether they collect over $5,000. Associations that collect greater than $5,000 in annual revenue are required to pay the annual registration fee. Associations that are not authorized to make assessments and do not have any revenue, or that collect $5,000 or less in annual revenue are not required under the statute to pay the registration fee, however, this provision does not absolve associations from registering.

If an association fails to register, or if its annual registration has expired, its right to impose or enforce a lien for assessments under § 38-33.3-316, C.R.S., or to pursue an action or employ an enforcement mechanism otherwise available to it under § 38-33.3-123, C.R.S., is suspended until the association is validly registered. A lien for assessments that was previously recorded during a period in which the association was validly registered or before registration was required is not extinguished by the expiration of the association's registration; however, any pending enforcement proceedings related to the lien is suspended, and any applicable time limits are delayed, until the association is validly registered. An association's previously suspended right will be revived without penalty, once the association is validly registered.

* III. Community Association Manager Licensing

*   (NOTE: The Community Association Manager (CAM) licensing program ended at the Division of Real Estate on June 30, 2019, and the Division no longer has any jurisdiction over community association managers. The Division has ceased to enforce any licensing, investigations, insurance, and continuing education requirements in this regard.)

IV. HOA Statutes

> *§ 12-10-501, C.R.S. Definitions. – Referenced in Chapter 4 Subdivision Laws, pages 4-2 to 4-3.*

> *   *§ 12-10-801, C.R.S. HOA information and resource center – creation – duties – rules – subject to review – repeal.*

*   *Editor's note: This section is similar to former §12-61-406.5 as it existed prior to 2019.*

(1)   There is hereby created, within the division, the HOA information and resource center, the head of which shall be the HOA information officer. The HOA information officer shall be appointed by the executive director pursuant to section 13 of article XII of the state constitution.

(2)   The HOA information officer shall be familiar with the "Colorado Common Interest Ownership Act", article 33.3 of title 38, also referred to in this section as the "act". No person who is or, within the immediately preceding ten years, has been licensed by or registered with the division or who owns stocks, bonds, or any pecuniary interest in a corporation subject in whole or in part to regulation by the division shall be appointed as HOA information officer. In addition, in conducting the search for an appointee, the executive director shall place a high premium on candidates who are balanced, independent, unbiased, and without any current financial ties to an HOA board or board member or to any person or entity that provides HOA management services. After being appointed, the HOA information officer shall refrain from engaging in any conduct or relationship that would create a conflict of interest or the appearance of a conflict of interest.

(3)   (a)   The HOA information officer shall act as a clearing house for information concerning the basic rights and duties of unit owners, declarants, and unit owners' associations under the act by:

      (I)   Compiling a database about registered associations, including the name; address; e-mail address, if any; website, if any; and telephone number of each;

      (II)   Coordinating and assisting in the preparation of educational and reference materials, including materials to assist unit owners, executive boards, board members, and association managers in understanding their rights and responsibilities with respect to:

          (A)   Open meetings;

          (B)   Proper use of executive sessions;

          (C)   Removal of executive board members;

          (D)   Unit owners' right to speak at meetings of the executive board;

          (E)   Unit owners' obligation to pay assessments and the association's rights and responsibilities in pursuing collection of past-due amounts; and

        (F)   Other educational or reference materials that the HOA information officer deems necessary or appropriate;

    (III)   Monitoring changes in federal and state laws relating to common interest communities and providing information about the changes on the division's website; and

    (IV)   Providing information, including a "frequently asked questions" resource, on the division's website.

(b)   The HOA information officer may:

    (I)   Employ one or more assistants as may be necessary to carry out his or her duties; and

    (II)   Request certain records from associations as necessary to carry out the HOA information officer's duties as set forth in this section.

(c)   The HOA information officer shall track inquiries and complaints and report annually to the director regarding the number and types of inquiries and complaints received.

(4)   The operating expenses of the HOA information and resource center shall be paid from the division of real estate cash fund, created in section 12-10-215, subject to annual appropriation.

(5)   The director may adopt rules as necessary to implement this section and section 38-33.3-401. This subsection (5) shall not be construed to confer additional rule-making authority upon the director for any other purpose.

(6)   This section is repealed, effective September 1, 2020. Before the repeal, the HOA information and resource center and the HOA information officer's powers and duties under this section are scheduled for review in accordance with section 24-34-104.

§ 38-12-601, C.R.S. Unreasonable restrictions on electric vehicle charging systems – definitions.

(1)   Notwithstanding any provision in the lease to the contrary, and subject to subsection (2) of this section:

(a)   A tenant may install, at the tenant's expense for the tenant's own use, a level 1 or level 2 electric vehicle charging system on or in the leased premises; and

(b)   A landlord shall not assess or charge a tenant any fee for the placement or use of an electric vehicle charging system; except that:

    (I)   The landlord may require reimbursement for the actual cost of electricity provided by the landlord that was used by the charging system or, alternatively, may charge a reasonable fee for access. If the charging system is part of a network for which a network fee is charged, the landlord's reimbursement may include the amount of the network fee. Nothing in this section requires a landlord to impose upon a tenant any fee or charge other than the rental payments specified in the lease.

    (II)   The landlord may require reimbursement for the cost of the installation of the charging system, including any additions or upgrades to existing wiring directly attributable to the requirements of the charging system, if the landlord places or causes the electric vehicle charging system to be placed at the request of the tenant; and

    (III)   If the tenant desires to place an electric vehicle charging system in an area accessible to other tenants, the landlord may assess or charge the tenant a reasonable fee to reserve a specific parking spot in which to install the charging system.

(2)   A landlord may require a tenant to comply with:

(a)   Bona fide safety requirements, consistent with an applicable building code or recognized safety standard, for the protection of persons and property;

(b)   A requirement that the charging system be registered with the landlord within thirty days after installation; or

(c)   Reasonable aesthetic provisions that govern the dimensions, placement, or external appearance of an electric vehicle charging system.

(3)   A tenant may place an electric vehicle charging system in an area accessible to other tenants if:

(a)   The charging system is in compliance with all applicable requirements adopted pursuant to subsection (2) of this section; and

(b)   The tenant agrees in writing to:

(I)   Comply with the landlord's design specifications for the installation of the charging system;

(II)   Engage the services of a duly licensed and registered electrical contractor familiar with the installation and code requirements of an electric vehicle charging system; and

(III) (A)   Provide, within fourteen days after receiving the landlord's consent for the installation, a certificate of insurance naming the landlord as an additional insured on the tenant's renters' insurance policy for any claim related to the installation, maintenance, or use of the system or, at the landlord's option, reimbursement to the landlord for the actual cost of any increased insurance premium amount attributable to the system, notwithstanding any provision to the contrary in the lease.

(B)   A certificate of insurance under sub-subparagraph (A) of this subparagraph (III) must be provided within fourteen days after the tenant receives the landlord's consent for the installation. Reimbursement for an increased insurance premium amount under sub-subparagraph (A) of this subparagraph (III) must be provided within fourteen days after the tenant receives the landlord's invoice for the amount attributable to the system.

(4)   If the landlord consents to a tenant's installation of an electric vehicle charging system on property accessible to other tenants, including a parking space, carport, or garage stall, then, unless otherwise specified in a written agreement with the landlord:

(a)   The tenant, and each successive tenant with exclusive rights to the area where the charging system is installed, is responsible for any costs for damages to the charging system and to any other property of the landlord or of another tenant that arise or result from the installation, maintenance, repair, removal, or replacement of the charging system;

(b)   Each successive tenant with exclusive rights to the area where the charging system is installed shall assume responsibility for the repair, maintenance, removal, and replacement of the charging system until the system has been removed;

(c)   The tenant and each successive tenant with exclusive rights to the area where the system is installed shall at all times have and maintain an insurance policy covering the obligations of the tenant under this subsection (4) and shall name the landlord as an additional insured under the policy; and

(d)   The tenant and each successive tenant with exclusive rights to the area where the system is installed is responsible for removing the system if reasonably necessary or convenient for the repair, maintenance, or replacement of any property of the landlord, whether or not leased to another tenant.

(5) A charging system installed at the tenant's cost is property of the tenant. Upon termination of the lease, if the charging system is removable, the tenant may either remove it or sell it to the landlord or another tenant for an agreed price. Nothing in this subsection (5) requires the landlord or another tenant to purchase the charging system.

(6) As used in this section:

(a) "Electric vehicle charging system" or "charging system" means a device that is used to provide electricity to a plug-in electric vehicle or plug-in hybrid vehicle, is designed to ensure that a safe connection has been made between the electric grid and the vehicle, and is able to communicate with the vehicle's control system so that electricity flows at an appropriate voltage and current level. An electric vehicle charging system may be wall-mounted or pedestal style and may provide multiple cords to connect with electric vehicles. An electric vehicle charging system must be certified by underwriters laboratories or an equivalent certification and must comply with the current version of article 625 of the national electrical code.

(b) "Level 1" means a charging system that provides charging through a one-hundred-twenty volt AC plug with a cord connector that meets the SAE international J1772 standard or a successor standard.

(c) "Level 2" means a charging system that provides charging through a two-hundred-eight to two-hundred-forty volt AC plug with a cord connector that meets the SAE international J1772 standard or a successor standard.

(7) This section applies only to residential rental properties.

* V. Condominium Ownership Act

Title 38, Article 33, C.R.S. – Condominium Ownership Act

Also see Colorado Common Interest Ownership Act in Part VI of this chapter

Note: The portions printed below are only those portions of the old condominium act that pertain to timeshare and conversion projects and that are still in place. This Condominium Act was *superseded* by the Colorado Common Interest Ownership Act July 1, 1992.

§ 38-33-101, C.R.S. Short title.

This article shall be known and may be cited as the "Condominium Ownership Act".

§ 38-33-102, C.R.S. Condominium ownership recognized.

Condominium ownership of real property is recognized in this state. Whether created before or after April 30, 1963, such ownership shall be deemed to consist of a separate estate in an individual air space unit of a multi-unit property together with an undivided interest in common elements. The separate estate of any condominium owner of an individual air space unit and his common ownership of such common elements as are appurtenant to his individual air space unit by the terms of the recorded declaration are inseparable for any period of condominium ownership that is prescribed by the recorded declaration. Condominium ownership may exist on land owned in fee simple or held under an estate for years.

§ 38-33-103, C.R.S. Definitions.

As used in this article, unless the context otherwise requires:

(1) "Condominium unit" means an individual air space unit together with the interest in the common elements appurtenant to such unit.

(2) "Declaration" is an instrument recorded pursuant to section 38-33-105 and which defines the character, duration, rights, obligations, and limitations of condominium ownership.

(3) Unless otherwise provided in the declaration or by written consent of all the condominium owners, "general common elements" means: The land or the interest therein on which a building or buildings are located; the foundations, columns, girders, beams, supports, main walls, roofs, halls, corridors, lobbies, stairs, stairways, fire escapes, entrances, and exits of such building or buildings; the basements, yards, gardens, parking areas, and storage spaces; the premises for the lodging of custodians or persons in charge of the property; installations of central services such as power, light, gas, hot and cold water, heating, refrigeration, central air conditioning, and incinerating; the elevators, tanks, pumps, motors, fans, compressors, ducts, and in general all apparatus and installations existing for common use; such community and commercial facilities as may be provided for in the declaration; and all other parts of the property necessary or convenient to its existence, maintenance, and safety, or normally in common use.

(4) "Individual air space unit" consists of any enclosed room or rooms occupying all or part of a floor or floors in a building of one or more floors to be used for residential, professional, commercial, or industrial purposes which has access to a public street.

(5) "Limited common elements" means those common elements designated in the declaration as reserved for use by fewer than all the owners of the individual air space units.

§ 38-33-104, C.R.S. Assessment of condominium ownership.

Whenever condominium ownership of real property is created or separate assessment of condominium units is desired, a written notice thereof shall be delivered to the assessor of the county in which said real property is situated, which notice shall set forth descriptions of the condominium units. Thereafter all taxes, assessments, and other charges of this state or of any political subdivision, or of any special improvement district, or of any other taxing or assessing authority shall be assessed against and collected on each condominium unit, each of which shall be carried on the tax books as a separate and distinct parcel for that purpose and not on the building or property as a whole. The valuation of the general and limited common elements shall be assessed proportionately upon the individual air space unit in the manner provided in the declaration. The lien for taxes assessed to any individual condominium owner shall be confined to his condominium unit and to his undivided interest in the general and limited common elements. No forfeiture or sale of any condominium unit for delinquent taxes, assessments, or charges shall divest or in any way affect the title of other condominium units.

§ 38-33-105, C.R.S. Recording of declaration – certain rules and laws to apply.

(1) The declaration shall be recorded in the county where the condominium property is located. Such declaration shall provide for the filing for record of a map properly locating condominium units. Any instrument affecting the condominium unit may legally describe it by the identifying condominium unit number or symbol as shown on such map. If such declaration provides for the disposition of condominium units in the event of the destruction or obsolescence of buildings in which such units are situate and restricts partition of the common elements, the rules or laws known as the rule against perpetuities and the rule prohibiting unlawful restraints on alienation shall not be applied to defeat or limit any such provisions.

(2) To the extent that any such declaration contains a mandatory requirement that all condominium unit owners be members of an association or corporation or provides for the payment of charges assessed by the association upon condominium units or the appointment of an attorney-in-fact to deal with the property upon its destruction or obsolescence, any rule of law to the contrary notwithstanding, the same shall be considered as covenants running with the land binding upon all condominium owners and their successors in interest. Any common law rule

terminating agency upon death or disability of a principal shall not be applied to defeat or limit any such provisions.

§ 38-33-105.5, C.R.S. *Contents of declaration.*

(1) The declaration shall contain:

(a) The name of the condominium property, which shall include the word "condominium" or be followed by the words "a condominium";

(b) The name of every county in which any part of the condominium property is situated;

(c) A legally sufficient description of the real estate included in the condominium property;

(d) A description or delineation of the boundaries of each condominium unit, including its identifying number;

(e) A statement of the maximum number of condominium units that may be created by the subdivision or conversion of units in a multiple-unit dwelling owned by the declarant;

(f) A description of any limited common elements;

(g) A description of all general common elements;

(h) A description of all general common elements which may be conveyed to any person or entity other than the condominium unit owners;

(i) A description of all general common elements which may be allocated subsequently as limited common elements, together with a statement that they may be so allocated, and a description of the method by which the allocations are to be made;

(j) An allocation to each condominium unit of an undivided interest in the general common elements, a portion of the votes in the association, and a percentage or fraction of the common expenses of the association;

(k) Any restrictions on the use, occupancy, or alienation of the condominium units;

(*l*) The recording data for recorded easements and licenses appurtenant to, or included in, the condominium property or to which any portion of the condominium property is or may become subject;

(m) Reasonable provisions concerning the manner in which notice of matters affecting the condominium property may be given to condominium unit owners by the association or other condominium unit owners; and

(n) Any other matters the declarant deems appropriate.

(2) This section shall apply to any condominium ownership of property created on or after July 1, 1983.

§ 38-33-106, C.R.S. *Condominium bylaws – contents – exemptions.*

(1) Unless exempted, the administration and operation of multi-unit condominiums shall be governed by the declaration.

(2) At or before the execution of a contract for sale and, if none, before closing, every initial bona fide condominium unit buyer shall be provided by the seller with a copy of the bylaws, with amendments, if any, of the unit owners' association or corporation, and such bylaws and amendments shall be of a size print or type to be clearly legible.

(3) The bylaws shall contain or provide for at least the following:

(a) The election from among the unit owners of a board of managers, the number of persons constituting such board, and that the terms of at least one-third of the members of the board shall expire annually; the powers and duties of the board; the compensation, if any, of the members of the board; the method of removal from office of members of the board; and whether or not the board may engage the services of a manager or managing agent, or both, and specifying which of the powers and duties granted to the board may be delegated by the board to either or both of them; however, the board when so delegating shall not be relieved of its responsibility under the declaration;

(b) The method of calling meetings of the unit owners; the method of allocating votes to unit owners; what percentage of the unit owners, if other than a majority, constitutes a quorum; and what percentage is necessary to adopt decisions binding on all unit owners;

(c) The election of a president from among the board of managers, who shall preside over the meetings of the board of managers and of the unit owners;

(d) The election of a secretary, who shall keep the minutes of all meetings of the board of managers and of the unit owners and who, in general, shall perform all the duties incident to the office of secretary;

(e) The election of a treasurer, who shall keep the financial records and books of account. The treasurer may also serve as the secretary.

(f) The authorization to the board of managers to designate and remove personnel necessary for the operation, maintenance, repair, and replacement of the common elements;

(g) A statement that the unit owners and their mortgagees, if applicable, may inspect the records of receipts and expenditures of the board of managers pursuant to section 38-33-107 at convenient weekday business hours, and that, upon ten days' notice to the manager or board of managers and payment of a reasonable fee, any unit owner shall be furnished a statement of his account setting forth the amount of any unpaid assessments or other charges due and owing from such owner;

(h) A statement as to whether or not the condominium association is a not for profit corporation, an unincorporated association, or a corporation;

(i) The method of adopting and of amending administrative rules and regulations governing the operation and use of the common elements;

(j) The percentage of votes required to modify or amend the bylaws, but each one of the particulars set forth in this section shall always be embodied in the bylaws;

(k) The maintenance, repair, replacement, and improvement of the general and limited common elements and payments therefor, including a statement of whether or not such work requires prior approval of the unit owners' association or corporation when it would involve a large expense or exceed a certain amount;

(*l*) The method of estimating the amount of the budget; the manner of assessing and collecting from the unit owners their respective shares of such estimated expenses and of any other expenses lawfully agreed upon; and a statement concerning the division, if any, of the assessment charge between general and limited common elements and the amount or percent of such division;

(m) A list of the services provided by the unit owners' association or corporation which are paid for out of the regular assessment;

(n) A statement clearly and separately indicating what assessments, debts, or other obligations are assumed by the unit owner on his condominium unit;

(o) A statement as to whether or not additional liens, other than mechanics' liens, assessment liens, or tax liens, may be obtained against the general or limited common elements then existing in which the unit owner has a percentage ownership;

(p) Such restrictions on and requirements respecting the use and maintenance of the units and the use of the general and limited common elements as are designed to prevent unreasonable interference with the use of their respective units and said common elements by the several unit owners;

(q)   Such restrictions on and requirements concerning the sale or lease of a unit including rights of first refusal on sale and any other restraints on the free alienability of the unit;

(r)   A statement listing all major recreational facilities and to whom they are available and clearly indicating whether or not fees or charges, if any, in conjunction therewith, are in addition to the regular assessment;

(s)   A statement relating to new additions of general and limited common elements to be constructed, including but not limited to:

    (I)   The effect on a unit owner in reference to his obligation for payment of the common expenses, including new recreational facilities, costs, and fees, if any;

    (II)   The effect on a unit owner in reference to his ownership interest in the existing general and limited common elements and new general and limited common elements;

    (III)   The effect on a unit owner in reference to his voting power in the association.

(4)   Any declaration recorded on or after January 1, 1976, shall not conflict with the provisions of this section or bylaws made in accordance with this section. The requirements contained in paragraphs (k) to (s) of subsection (3) of this section need not be included in the bylaws if they are set forth in the declaration.

(5)   This section shall not apply to:

(a)   Commercial or industrial condominiums or any other condominiums not used for residential use;

(b)   Condominiums of ten units or less;

(c)   Condominiums established by a declaration recorded prior to January 1, 1976.

§ 38-33-107, C.R.S. Records of receipts and expenditures – availability for examination.

The manager or board of managers, as the case may be, shall keep detailed, accurate records of the receipts and expenditures affecting the general and limited common elements. Such records authorizing the payments shall be available for examination by the unit owners at convenient weekday business hours.

§ 38-33-108, C.R.S. Violations – penalty.

Any person who knowingly and willfully violates the provisions of section 38-33-106 or 38-33-107 is guilty of a misdemeanor and, upon conviction thereof, shall be punished by a fine of not more than five hundred dollars.

§ 38-33-109, C.R.S. Unit owners' liability.

In any suit or arbitration against a condominium unit owners' association wherein damages are awarded or settlement is made, the individual unit owner's liability in his capacity as a percentage owner of the general or limited common elements or as a member of the condominium association shall not exceed the amount of damages or settlement multiplied by his percentage ownership in the general or limited common elements, as the case may be. In the case of incorporation by unit owners, their liability as stockholders shall be determined as any other corporate stockholder.

§ 38-33-110, C.R.S. Time-sharing – definitions.

As used in this section and section 38-33-111, unless the context otherwise requires:

(1)   (a)   "Interval estate" means a combination of:

    (I)   An estate for years terminating on a date certain, during which years title to a time share unit circulates among the interval owners in accordance with a fixed schedule, vesting in each such interval owner in turn for a period of time established by the said schedule, with the series thus established recurring annually until the arrival of the date certain; and

(II) A vested future interest in the same unit, consisting of an undivided interest in the remainder in fee simple, the magnitude of the future interest having been established by the time of the creation of the interval estate either by the project instruments or by the deed conveying the interval estate. The estate for years shall not be deemed to merge with the future interest, but neither the estate for years nor the future interest shall be conveyed or encumbered separately from the other.

(b) "Interval estate" also means an estate for years as described in subparagraph (I) of paragraph (a) of this subsection (1) where the remainder estate, as defined either by the project instruments or by the deed conveying the interval estate, is retained by the developer or his successors in interest.

(2) "Interval owner" means a person vested with legal title to an interval estate.

(3) "Interval unit" means a unit the title to which is or is to be divided into interval estates.

(4) "Project instruments" means the declaration, the bylaws, and any other set of restrictions or restrictive covenants, by whatever name denominated, which limit or restrict the use or occupancy of condominium units. "Project instruments" includes any lawful amendments to such instruments. "Project instruments" does not include any ordinance or other public regulation governing subdivisions, zoning, or other land use matters.

(5) "Time share estate" means either an interval estate or a time-span estate.

(6) "Time share owner" means a person vested with legal title to a time share estate.

(7) "Time share unit" means a unit the title to which is or is to be divided either into interval estates or time-span estates.

(8) "Time-span estate" means a combination of:

(a) An undivided interest in a present estate in fee simple in a unit, the magnitude of the interest having been established by the time of the creation of the time-span estate either by the project instruments or by the deed conveying the time-span estate; and

(b) An exclusive right to possession and occupancy of the unit during an annually recurring period of time defined and established by a recorded schedule set forth or referred to in the deed conveying the time-span estate.

(9) "Time-span owner" means a person vested with legal title to a time-span estate.

(10) "Time-span unit" means a unit the title to which is or is to be divided into time-span estates.

(11) "Unit owner" means a person vested with legal title to a unit, and, in the case of a time share unit, "unit owner" means all of the time share owners of that unit. When an estate is subject to a deed of trust or a trust deed, "unit owner" means the person entitled to beneficial enjoyment of the estate and not to any trustee or trustees holding title merely as security for an obligation.

§ 38-33-111, C.R.S. Special provisions applicable to time share ownership.

(1) No time share estates shall be created with respect to any condominium unit except pursuant to provisions in the project instruments expressly permitting the creation of such estates. Each time share estate shall constitute for all purposes an estate or interest in real property, separate and distinct from all other time share estates in the same unit or any other unit, and such estates may be separately conveyed and encumbered.

(2) Repealed.

(3) With respect to each time share unit, each owner of a time share estate therein shall be individually liable to the unit owners' association or corporation for all assessments, property taxes both real and personal, and charges levied pursuant to the project instruments against or

with respect to that unit, and such association or corporation shall be liable for the payment thereof, except to the extent that such instruments provide to the contrary. However, with respect to each other, each time share owner shall be responsible only for a fraction of such assessments, property taxes both real and personal, and charges proportionate to the magnitude of his undivided interest in the fee to the unit.

(4)   No person shall have standing to bring suit for partition of any time share unit except in accordance with such procedures, conditions, restrictions, and limitations as the project instruments and the deeds to the time share estates may specify. Upon the entry of a final order in such a suit, it shall be conclusively presumed that all such procedures, conditions, restrictions, and limitations were adhered to.

(5)   In the event that any condemnation award, any insurance proceeds, the proceeds of any sale, or any other sums shall become payable to all of the time share owners of a unit, the portion payable to each time share owner shall be proportionate to the magnitude of his undivided interest in the fee to the unit.

§ 38-33-112, C.R.S. Notification to residential tenants.

(1)   A developer who converts an existing multiple-unit dwelling into condominium units, upon recording of the declaration as required by section 38-33-105, shall notify each residential tenant of the dwelling of such conversion.

(2)   Such notice shall be in writing and shall be sent by certified or registered mail, postage prepaid, and return receipt provided. Notice is complete upon mailing to the tenant at the tenant's last known address. Notice may also be made by delivery in person to the tenant of a copy of such written notice, in which event notice is complete upon such delivery.

(3)   Said notice constitutes the notice to terminate the tenancy as provided by section 13-40-107, C.R.S.; except that no residential tenancy shall be terminated prior to the expiration date of the existing lease agreement, if any, unless consented to by both the tenant and the developer. If the term of the lease has less than ninety days remaining when notification is mailed or delivered, as the case may be, or if there is no written lease agreement, residential tenancy may not be terminated by the developer less than ninety days after the date the notice is mailed or delivered, as the case may be, to the tenant, unless consented to by both the tenant and the developer. The return receipt shall be prima facie evidence of receipt of notice. If the term of the lease has less than ninety days remaining when notification is mailed or delivered, as the case may be, the tenant may hold over for the remainder of said ninety-day period under the same terms and conditions of the lease agreement if the tenant makes timely rental payments and performs other conditions of the lease agreement.

(4)   The tenancy may be terminated within the ninety days prescribed in subsection (3) of this section upon agreement by the tenant in consideration of the payment of all moving expenses by the developer or for such other consideration as mutually agreed upon. Such tenancy may also be terminated within the ninety days prescribed in subsection (3) of this section upon failure by the tenant to make timely rental or lease payments.

(5)   Any person who applies for a residential tenancy after the recording of the declaration shall be informed of this recording at the time of application, and any leases executed after such recording may provide for termination within less than ninety days provided that the terms of the lease conspicuously disclose the intention to convert the property containing the leased premises to condominium ownership.

(6)   The general assembly hereby finds and declares that the notification procedure set forth in this section is a matter of statewide concern. No county, municipality, or other political subdivision whether or not vested with home rule powers under article XX of the Colorado constitution, shall adopt or enforce any ordinance, rule, regulation, or policy which conflicts with the provisions of this section.

§ 38-33-113, C.R.S. License to sell condominiums and time-shares.

The general assembly hereby finds and declares that the licensing of persons to sell condominiums and time shares is a matter of statewide concern.

* VI. Colorado Common Interest Ownership Act

§ 38-33.3-101, C.R.S. Short title.

This article shall be known and may be cited as the "Colorado Common Interest Ownership Act".

§ 38-33.3-102, C.R.S. Legislative declaration.

(1)   The general assembly hereby finds, determines, and declares, as follows:

(a)   That it is in the best interests of the state and its citizens to establish a clear, comprehensive, and uniform framework for the creation and operation of common interest communities;

(b)   That the continuation of the economic prosperity of Colorado is dependent upon the strengthening of homeowner associations in common interest communities financially through the setting of budget guidelines, the creation of statutory assessment liens, the granting of six months' lien priority, the facilitation of borrowing, and more certain powers in the association to sue on behalf of the owners and through enhancing the financial stability of associations by increasing the association's powers to collect delinquent assessments, late charges, fines, and enforcement costs;

(c)   That it is the policy of this state to give developers flexible development rights with specific obligations within a uniform structure of development of a common interest community that extends through the transition to owner control;

(d)   That it is the policy of this state to promote effective and efficient property management through defined operational requirements that preserve flexibility for such homeowner associations;

(e)   That it is the policy of this state to promote the availability of funds for financing the development of such homeowner associations by enabling lenders to extend the financial services to a greater market on a safer, more predictable basis because of standardized practices and prudent insurance and risk management obligations.

§ 38-33.3-103, C.R.S. Definitions.

As used in the declaration and bylaws of an association, unless specifically provided otherwise or unless the context otherwise requires, and in this article:

(1)   "Affiliate of a declarant" means any person who controls, is controlled by, or is under common control with a declarant. A person controls a declarant if the person: Is a general partner, officer, director, or employee of the declarant; directly or indirectly, or acting in concert with one or more other persons or through one or more subsidiaries, owns, controls, holds with power to vote, or holds proxies representing more than twenty percent of the voting interests of the declarant; controls in any manner the election of a majority of the directors of the declarant; or has contributed more than twenty percent of the capital of the declarant. A person is controlled by a declarant if the declarant: Is a general partner, officer, director, or employee of the person; directly or indirectly, or acting in concert with one or more other persons or through one or more subsidiaries, owns, controls, holds with power to vote, or holds proxies representing more than twenty percent of the voting interests of the person; controls in any manner the election of a majority of the directors of the person; or has contributed more than

twenty percent of the capital of the person. Control does not exist if the powers described in this subsection (1) are held solely as security for an obligation and are not exercised.

(2) "Allocated interests" means the following interests allocated to each unit:

    (a) In a condominium, the undivided interest in the common elements, the common expense liability, and votes in the association;

    (b) In a cooperative, the common expense liability and the ownership interest and votes in the association; and

    (c) In a planned community, the common expense liability and votes in the association.

(2.5) "Approved for development" means that all or some portion of a particular parcel of real property is zoned or otherwise approved for construction of residential and other improvements and authorized for specified densities by the local land use authority having jurisdiction over such real property and includes any conceptual or final planned unit development approval.

(3) "Association" or "unit owners' association" means a unit owners' association organized under section 38-33.3-301.

(4) "Bylaws" means any instruments, however denominated, which are adopted by the association for the regulation and management of the association, including any amendments to those instruments.

(5) "Common elements" means:

    (a) In a condominium or cooperative, all portions of the condominium or cooperative other than the units; and

    (b) In a planned community, any real estate within a planned community owned or leased by the association, other than a unit.

(6) "Common expense liability" means the liability for common expenses allocated to each unit pursuant to section 38-33.3-207.

(7) "Common expenses" means expenditures made or liabilities incurred by or on behalf of the association, together with any allocations to reserves.

(8) "Common interest community" means real estate described in a declaration with respect to which a person, by virtue of such person's ownership of a unit, is obligated to pay for real estate taxes, insurance premiums, maintenance, or improvement of other real estate described in a declaration. Ownership of a unit does not include holding a leasehold interest in a unit of less than forty years, including renewal options. The period of the leasehold interest, including renewal options, is measured from the date the initial term commences.

(9) "Condominium" means a common interest community in which portions of the real estate are designated for separate ownership and the remainder of which is designated for common ownership solely by the owners of the separate ownership portions. A common interest community is not a condominium unless the undivided interests in the common elements are vested in the unit owners.

(10) "Cooperative" means a common interest community in which the real property is owned by an association, each member of which is entitled by virtue of such member's ownership interest in the association to exclusive possession of a unit.

(11) "Dealer" means a person in the business of selling units for such person's own account.

(12) "Declarant" means any person or group of persons acting in concert who:

    (a) As part of a common promotional plan, offers to dispose of to a purchaser such declarant's interest in a unit not previously disposed of to a purchaser; or

    (b) Reserves or succeeds to any special declarant right.

(13) "Declaration" means any recorded instruments however denominated, that create a common interest community, including any amendments to those instruments and also including, but not limited to, plats and maps.

(14) "Development rights" means any right or combination of rights reserved by a declarant in the declaration to:

    (a)   Add real estate to a common interest community;

    (b)   Create units, common elements, or limited common elements within a common interest community;

    (c)   Subdivide units or convert units into common elements; or

    (d)   Withdraw real estate from a common interest community.

(15) "Dispose" or "disposition" means a voluntary transfer of any legal or equitable interest in a unit, but the term does not include the transfer or release of a security interest.

(16) "Executive board" means the body, regardless of name, designated in the declaration to act on behalf of the association.

(16.5) "Horizontal boundary" means a plane of elevation relative to a described bench mark that defines either a lower or an upper dimension of a unit such that the real estate respectively below or above the defined plane is not a part of the unit.

(17) "Identifying number" means a symbol or address that identifies only one unit in a common interest community.

(17.5) "Large planned community" means a planned community that meets the criteria set forth in section 38-33.3-116.3 (1).

(18) "Leasehold common interest community" means a common interest community in which all or a portion of the real estate is subject to a lease, the expiration or termination of which will terminate the common interest community or reduce its size.

(19) "Limited common element" means a portion of the common elements allocated by the declaration or by operation of section 38-33.3-202 (1) (b) or (1) (d) for the exclusive use of one or more units but fewer than all of the units.

(19.5) "Map" means that part of a declaration that depicts all or any portion of a common interest community in three dimensions, is executed by a person that is authorized by this title to execute a declaration relating to the common interest community, and is recorded in the real estate records in every county in which any portion of the common interest community is located. A map is required for a common interest community with units having a horizontal boundary. A map and a plat may be combined in one instrument.

(20) "Master association" means an organization that is authorized to exercise some or all of the powers of one or more associations on behalf of one or more common interest communities or for the benefit of the unit owners of one or more common interest communities.

(21) "Person" means a natural person, a corporation, a partnership, an association, a trust, or any other entity or any combination thereof.

(21.5) "Phased community" means a common interest community in which the declarant retains development rights.

(22) "Planned community" means a common interest community that is not a condominium or cooperative. A condominium or cooperative may be part of a planned community.

(22.5) "Plat" means that part of a declaration that is a land survey plat as set forth in section 38-51-106, depicts all or any portion of a common interest community in two dimensions, is executed by a person that is authorized by this title to execute a declaration relating to the common interest community, and is recorded in the real estate records in every county in which any portion of the common interest community is located. A plat and a map may be combined in one instrument.

(23) "Proprietary lease" means an agreement with the association pursuant to which a member is entitled to exclusive possession of a unit in a cooperative.

(24) "Purchaser" means a person, other than a declarant or a dealer, who by means of a transfer acquires a legal or equitable interest in a unit, other than:

    (a)   A leasehold interest in a unit of less than forty years, including renewal options, with the period of the leasehold interest, including renewal options, being measured from the date the initial term commences; or

    (b)   A security interest.

(25) "Real estate" means any leasehold or other estate or interest in, over, or under land, including structures, fixtures, and other improvements and interests that, by custom, usage, or law, pass with a conveyance of land though not described in the contract of sale or instrument of conveyance. "Real estate" includes parcels with or without horizontal boundaries and spaces that may be filled with air or water.

(26) "Residential use" means use for dwelling or recreational purposes but does not include spaces or units primarily used for commercial income from, or service to, the public.

(27) "Rules and regulations" means any instruments, however denominated, which are adopted by the association for the regulation and management of the common interest community, including any amendment to those instruments.

(28) "Security interest" means an interest in real estate or personal property created by contract or conveyance which secures payment or performance of an obligation. The term includes a lien created by a mortgage, deed of trust, trust deed, security deed, contract for deed, land sales contract, lease intended as security, assignment of lease or rents intended as security, pledge of an ownership interest in an association, and any other consensual lien or title retention contract intended as security for an obligation.

(29) "Special declarant rights" means rights reserved for the benefit of a declarant to perform the following acts as specified in parts 2 and 3 of this article: To complete improvements indicated on plats and maps filed with the declaration; to exercise any development right; to maintain sales offices, management offices, signs advertising the common interest community, and models; to use easements through the common elements for the purpose of making improvements within the common interest community or within real estate which may be added to the common interest community; to make the common interest community subject to a master association; to merge or consolidate a common interest community of the same form of ownership; or to appoint or remove any officer of the association or any executive board member during any period of declarant control.

(30) "Unit" means a physical portion of the common interest community which is designated for separate ownership or occupancy and the boundaries of which are described in or determined from the declaration. If a unit in a cooperative is owned by a unit owner or is sold, conveyed, voluntarily or involuntarily encumbered, or otherwise transferred by a unit owner, the interest in that unit which is owned, sold, conveyed, encumbered, or otherwise transferred is the right to possession of that unit under a proprietary lease, coupled with the allocated interests of that unit, and the association's interest in that unit is not thereby affected.

(31) "Unit owner" means the declarant or other person who owns a unit, or a lessee of a unit in a leasehold common interest community whose lease expires simultaneously with any lease, the expiration or termination of which will remove the unit from the common interest community but does not include a person having an interest in a unit solely as security for an obligation. In a condominium or planned community, the declarant is the owner of any unit created by the declaration until that unit is conveyed to another person; in a cooperative, the declarant is treated as the owner of any unit to which allocated interests have been allocated pursuant to

section 38-33.3-207 until that unit has been conveyed to another person, who may or may not be a declarant under this article.

(32) "Vertical boundary" means the defined limit of a unit that is not a horizontal boundary of that unit.

(33) "Xeriscape" means the combined application of the seven principles of landscape planning and design, soil analysis and improvement, hydro zoning of plants, use of practical turf areas, uses of mulches, irrigation efficiency, and appropriate maintenance under section 38-35.7-107 (1) (a) (III) (A).

§ 38-33.3-104, C.R.S. Variation by agreement.

Except as expressly provided in this article, provisions of this article may not be varied by agreement, and rights conferred by this article may not be waived. A declarant may not act under a power of attorney or use any other device to evade the limitations or prohibitions of this article or the declaration.

§ 38-33.3-105, C.R.S. Separate titles and taxation.

(1) In a cooperative, unless the declaration provides that a unit owner's interest in a unit and its allocated interests is personal property, that interest is real estate for all purposes.

(2) In a condominium or planned community with common elements, each unit that has been created, together with its interest in the common elements, constitutes for all purposes a separate parcel of real estate and must be separately assessed and taxed. The valuation of the common elements shall be assessed proportionately to each unit, in the case of a condominium in accordance with such unit's allocated interests in the common elements, and in the case of a planned community in accordance with such unit's allocated common expense liability, set forth in the declaration, and the common elements shall not be separately taxed or assessed. Upon the filing for recording of a declaration for a condominium or planned community with common elements, the declarant shall deliver a copy of such filing to the assessor of each county in which such declaration was filed.

(3) In a planned community without common elements, the real estate comprising such planned community may be taxed and assessed in any manner provided by law.

§ 38-33.3-106, C.R.S. Applicability of local ordinances, regulations, and building codes.

(1) A building code may not impose any requirement upon any structure in a common interest community which it would not impose upon a physically identical development under a different form of ownership; except that a minimum one hour fire wall may be required between units.

(2) In condominiums and cooperatives, no zoning, subdivision, or other real estate use law, ordinance, or regulation may prohibit the condominium or cooperative form of ownership or impose any requirement upon a condominium or cooperative which it would not impose upon a physically identical development under a different form of ownership.

§ 38-33.3-106.5, C.R.S. Prohibitions contrary to public policy – patriotic and political expression – emergency vehicles – fire prevention – renewable energy generation devices – affordable housing – drought prevention measures – definitions.

(1) Notwithstanding any provision in the declaration, bylaws, or rules and regulations of the association to the contrary, an association shall not prohibit any of the following:

(a) The display of the American flag on a unit owner's property, in a window of the unit, or on a balcony adjoining the unit if the American flag is displayed in a manner consistent with the federal flag code, Pub.L. 94-344; 90 Stat. 810; 4 U.S.C. secs. 4 to 10. The association may adopt reasonable rules regarding the placement and manner of display of the American flag. The association rules may regulate the location and size of flags and flagpoles, but shall not prohibit the installation of a flag or flagpole.

(b) The display of a service flag bearing a star denoting the service of the owner or occupant of the unit, or of a member of the owner's or occupant's immediate family, in the active or reserve military service of the United States during a time of war or armed conflict, on the inside of a window or door of the unit. The association may adopt reasonable rules regarding the size and manner of display of service flags; except that the maximum dimensions allowed shall be not less than nine inches by sixteen inches.

(c) (I) The display of a political sign by the owner or occupant of a unit on property within the boundaries of the unit or in a window of the unit; except that:

    (A) An association may prohibit the display of political signs earlier than forty-five days before the day of an election and later than seven days after an election day; and

    (B) An association may regulate the size and number of political signs in accordance with subparagraph (II) of this paragraph (c).

(II) The association shall permit at least one political sign per political office or ballot issue that is contested in a pending election. The maximum dimensions of each sign may be limited to the lesser of the following:

    (A) The maximum size allowed by any applicable city, town, or county ordinance that regulates the size of political signs on residential property; or

    (B) Thirty-six inches by forty-eight inches.

(III) As used in this paragraph (c), "political sign" means a sign that carries a message intended to influence the outcome of an election, including supporting or opposing the election of a candidate, the recall of a public official, or the passage of a ballot issue.

(d) The parking of a motor vehicle by the occupant of a unit on a street, driveway, or guest parking area in the common interest community if the vehicle is required to be available at designated periods at such occupant's residence as a condition of the occupant's employment and all of the following criteria are met:

(I) The vehicle has a gross vehicle weight rating of ten thousand pounds or less;

(II) The occupant is a bona fide member of a volunteer fire department or is employed by a primary provider of emergency fire fighting, law enforcement, ambulance, or emergency medical services;

(III) The vehicle bears an official emblem or other visible designation of the emergency service provider; and

(IV) Parking of the vehicle can be accomplished without obstructing emergency access or interfering with the reasonable needs of other unit owners or occupants to use streets, driveways, and guest parking spaces within the common interest community.

(e) The removal by a unit owner of trees, shrubs, or other vegetation to create defensible space around a dwelling for fire mitigation purposes, so long as such removal complies with a written defensible space plan created for the property by the Colorado state forest service, an individual or company certified by a local governmental entity to create such a plan, or the fire chief, fire marshal, or fire protection district within whose jurisdiction the unit is located, and is no more extensive than necessary to comply with such plan.

The plan shall be registered with the association before the commencement of work. The association may require changes to the plan if the association obtains the consent of the person, official, or agency that originally created the plan. The work shall comply with applicable association standards regarding slash removal, stump height, revegetation, and contractor regulations.

(f) (Deleted by amendment, L. 2006, p. 1215, §2, effective May 26, 2006.)

(g) Reasonable modifications to a unit or to common elements as necessary to afford a person with disabilities full use and enjoyment of the unit in accordance with the federal "Fair Housing Act of 1968", 42 U.S.C. sec. 3604 (f)(3)(A);

(h) (I) The right of a unit owner, public or private, to restrict or specify by deed, covenant, or other document:

    (A) The permissible sale price, rental rate, or lease rate of the unit; or

    (B) Occupancy or other requirements designed to promote affordable or workforce housing as such terms may be defined by the local housing authority.

    (II) (A) Notwithstanding any other provision of law, the provisions of this subsection (1)(h) shall only apply to a county the population of which is less than one hundred thousand persons and that contains a ski lift licensed by the passenger tramway safety board created in section 12-150-104 (1).

    (B) The provisions of this paragraph (h) shall not apply to a declarant-controlled community.

    (III) Nothing in subparagraph (I) of this paragraph (h) shall be construed to prohibit the future owner of a unit against which a restriction or specification described in such subparagraph has been placed from lifting such restriction or specification on such unit as long as any unit so released is replaced by another unit in the same common interest community on which the restriction or specification applies and the unit subject to the restriction or specification is reasonably equivalent to the unit being released in the determination of the beneficiary of the restriction or specification.

    (IV) Except as otherwise provided in the declaration of the common interest community, any unit subject to the provisions of this paragraph (h) shall only be occupied by the owner of the unit.

(i) (I) The use of xeriscape or drought-tolerant vegetative landscapes to provide ground covering to property for which a unit owner is responsible, including a limited common element or property owned by the unit owner. Associations may adopt and enforce design or aesthetic guidelines or rules that require drought-tolerant vegetative landscapes or regulate the type, number, and placement of drought-tolerant plantings and hardscapes that may be installed on a unit owner's property or on a limited common element or other property for which the unit owner is responsible.

    (II) This paragraph (i) does not supersede any subdivision regulation of a county, city and county, or other municipality.

(j) (I) The use of a rain barrel, as defined in section 37-96.5-102 (1), C.R.S., to collect precipitation from a residential rooftop in accordance with section 37-96.5-103, C.R.S.

    (II) This paragraph (j) does not confer upon a resident of a common interest community the right to place a rain barrel on property or to connect a rain barrel to any property that is:

    (A) Leased, except with permission of the lessor;

        (B)   A common element or a limited common element of a common interest community;

        (C)   Maintained by the unit owners' association for a common interest community; or

        (D)   Attached to one or more other units, except with permission of the owners of the other units.

    (III)   A common interest community may impose reasonable aesthetic requirements that govern the placement or external appearance of a rain barrel.

(1.5)   Notwithstanding any provision in the declaration, bylaws, or rules and regulations of the association to the contrary, an association shall not effectively prohibit renewable energy generation devices, as defined in section 38-30-168.

(2)   Notwithstanding any provision in the declaration, bylaws, or rules and regulations of the association to the contrary, an association shall not require the use of cedar shakes or other flammable roofing materials.

§ 38-33.3-106.7, C.R.S. *Unreasonable restrictions on energy efficiency measures – definitions.*

(1)   (a)   Notwithstanding any provision in the declaration, bylaws, or rules and regulations of the association to the contrary, an association shall not effectively prohibit the installation or use of an energy efficiency measure.

    (b)   As used in this section, "energy efficiency measure" means a device or structure that reduces the amount of energy derived from fossil fuels that is consumed by a residence or business located on the real property. "Energy efficiency measure" is further limited to include only the following types of devices or structures:

        (I)   An awning, shutter, trellis, ramada, or other shade structure that is marketed for the purpose of reducing energy consumption;

        (II)   A garage or attic fan and any associated vents or louvers;

        (III)   An evaporative cooler;

        (IV)   An energy-efficient outdoor lighting device, including without limitation a light fixture containing a coiled or straight fluorescent light bulb, and any solar recharging panel, motion detector, or other equipment connected to the lighting device; and

        (V)   A retractable clothesline.

(2)   Subsection (1) of this section shall not apply to:

    (a)   Reasonable aesthetic provisions that govern the dimensions, placement, or external appearance of an energy efficiency measure. In creating reasonable aesthetic provisions, common interest communities shall consider:

        (I)   The impact on the purchase price and operating costs of the energy efficiency measure;

        (II)   The impact on the performance of the energy efficiency measure; and

        (III)   The criteria contained in the governing documents of the common interest community.

    (b)   Bona fide safety requirements, consistent with an applicable building code or recognized safety standard, for the protection of persons and property.

(3)   This section shall not be construed to confer upon any property owner the right to place an energy efficiency measure on property that is:

    (a)   Owned by another person;

(b)   Leased, except with permission of the lessor;

(c)   Collateral for a commercial loan, except with permission of the secured party; or

(d)   A limited common element or general common element of a common interest community.

§ 38-33.3-106.8, C.R.S. Unreasonable restrictions on electric vehicle charging systems – legislative declaration – definitions.

(1)   The general assembly finds, determines, and declares that:

(a)   The widespread use of plug-in electric vehicles can dramatically improve energy efficiency and air quality for all Coloradans and should be encouraged wherever possible;

(b)   Most homes in Colorado, including the vast majority of new homes, are in common interest communities;

(c)   The primary purpose of this section is to ensure that common interest communities provide their residents with at least a meaningful opportunity to take advantage of the availability of plug-in electric vehicles rather than create artificial restrictions on the adoption of this promising technology; and

(d)   The general assembly encourages common interest communities not only to allow electric vehicle charging stations in accordance with this section, but also to apply for grants from the electric vehicle grant fund, created in section 24-38.5-103, C.R.S., or otherwise fund the installation of charging stations on common property as an amenity for residents and guests.

(2)   Notwithstanding any provision in the declaration, bylaws, or rules and regulations of the association to the contrary, and except as provided in subsection (3) or (3.5) of this section, an association shall not:

(a)   Prohibit a unit owner from using, or installing at the unit owner's expense for the unit owner's own use, a level 1 or level 2 electric vehicle charging system on or in a unit; or

(b)   Assess or charge a unit owner any fee for the placement or use of an electric vehicle charging system on or in the unit owner's unit; except that the association may require reimbursement for the actual cost of electricity provided by the association that was used by the charging system or, alternatively, may charge a reasonable fee for access. If the charging system is part of a network for which a network fee is charged, the association's reimbursement may include the amount of the network fee. Nothing in this section requires an association to impose upon a unit owner any fee or charge other than the regular assessments specified in the declaration, bylaws, or rules and regulations of the association.

(3)   Subsection (2) of this section does not apply to:

(a)   Bona fide safety requirements, consistent with an applicable building code or recognized safety standard, for the protection of persons and property;

(b)   A requirement that the charging system be registered with the association within thirty days after installation; or

(c)   Reasonable aesthetic provisions that govern the dimensions, placement, or external appearance of an electric vehicle charging system.

(3.5) This section does not apply to a unit, or the owner thereof, if the unit is a time share unit, as defined in section 38-33-110 (7).

(4)   An association shall consent to a unit owner's placement of an electric vehicle charging system on a limited common element parking space, carport, or garage owned by the unit owner or otherwise assigned to the owner in the declaration or other recorded document if:

(a) Notwithstanding any existing ban on electric vehicle charging systems, the system otherwise complies with the declaration, bylaws, and rules and regulations of the association; and

(b) The unit owner agrees in writing to:

   (I) Comply with the association's design specifications for the installation of the system;

   (II) Engage the services of a duly licensed and registered electrical contractor familiar with the installation and code requirements of an electric vehicle charging system;

   (III) Bear the expense of installation, including costs to restore any common elements disturbed in the process of installing the system; and

   (IV) (A) Provide, within the time specified in sub-subparagraph (B) of this subparagraph (IV), a certificate of insurance naming the association as an additional insured on the homeowner's insurance policy for any claim related to the installation, maintenance, or use of the system or, if the system is located on a common element, reimbursement to the association for the actual cost of any increased insurance premium amount attributable to the system, notwithstanding any provision to the contrary in the association's declaration, bylaws, or rules and regulations.

   (B) A certificate of insurance under sub-subparagraph (A) of this subparagraph (IV) must be provided within fourteen days after the unit owner receives the association's consent for the installation. Reimbursement for an increased insurance premium amount under sub-subparagraph (A) of this subparagraph (IV) must be provided within fourteen days after the unit owner receives the association's invoice for the amount attributable to the system.

(5) If the association consents to a unit owner's installation of an electric vehicle charging system on a limited common element, including a parking space, carport, or garage stall, then, unless otherwise specified in a written contract or in the declaration, bylaws, or rules and regulations of the association:

(a) The unit owner, and each successive unit owner with exclusive rights to the limited common element where the charging system is installed, is responsible for any costs for damages to the system, any other limited common element or general common element of the common interest community, and any adjacent units, garage stalls, carports, or parking spaces that arise or result from the installation, maintenance, repair, removal, or replacement of the system;

(b) Each successive unit owner with exclusive rights to the limited common element shall assume responsibility for the repair, maintenance, removal, and replacement of the charging system until the system has been removed;

(c) The unit owner and each successive unit owner with exclusive rights to the limited common element shall at all times have and maintain an insurance policy covering the obligations of the unit owner under this subsection (5), is subject to all obligations specified under subparagraph (IV) of paragraph (b) of subsection (4) of this section, and shall name the association as an additional insured under the policy; and

(d) The unit owner and each successive unit owner with exclusive rights to the limited common element is responsible for removing the system if reasonably necessary or convenient for the repair, maintenance, or replacement of the limited common elements or general common elements of the common interest community.

(6) A charging system installed at the unit owner's cost is property of the unit owner. Upon sale of the unit, if the charging system is removable, the unit owner may either remove it or sell it to

the buyer of the unit or to the association for an agreed price. Nothing in this subsection (6) requires the buyer or the association to purchase the charging system.

(7) As used in this section:

    (a) "Electric vehicle charging system" or "charging system" means a device that is used to provide electricity to a plug-in electric vehicle or plug-in hybrid vehicle, is designed to ensure that a safe connection has been made between the electric grid and the vehicle, and is able to communicate with the vehicle's control system so that electricity flows at an appropriate voltage and current level. An electric vehicle charging system may be wall-mounted or pedestal style and may provide multiple cords to connect with electric vehicles. An electric vehicle charging system must be certified by underwriters laboratories or an equivalent certification and must comply with the current version of article 625 of the national electrical code.

    (b) "Level 1" means a charging system that provides charging through a one-hundred-twenty volt AC plug with a cord connector that meets the SAE international J1772 standard or a successor standard.

    (c) "Level 2" means a charging system that provides charging through a two-hundred-eight to two-hundred-forty volt AC plug with a cord connector that meets the SAE international J1772 standard or a successor standard.

(8) This section applies only to residential units.

§ 38-33.3-107, C.R.S. Eminent domain.

(1) If a unit is acquired by eminent domain or part of a unit is acquired by eminent domain leaving the unit owner with a remnant which may not practically or lawfully be used for any purpose permitted by the declaration, the award must include compensation to the unit owner for that unit and its allocated interests whether or not any common elements are acquired. Upon acquisition, unless the decree otherwise provides, that unit's allocated interests are automatically reallocated to the remaining units in proportion to the respective allocated interests of those units before the taking. Any remnant of a unit remaining after part of a unit is taken under this subsection (1) is thereafter a common element.

(2) Except as provided in subsection (1) of this section, if part of a unit is acquired by eminent domain, the award must compensate the unit owner for the reduction in value of the unit and its interest in the common elements whether or not any common elements are acquired. Upon acquisition, unless the decree otherwise provides:

    (a) That unit's allocated interests are reduced in proportion to the reduction in the size of the unit or on any other basis specified in the declaration; and

    (b) The portion of allocated interests divested from the partially acquired unit is automatically reallocated to that unit and to the remaining units in proportion to the respective interests of those units before the taking, with the partially acquired unit participating in the reallocation on the basis of its reduced allocated interests.

(3) If part of the common elements is acquired by eminent domain, that portion of any award attributable to the common elements taken must be paid to the association. Unless the declaration provides otherwise, any portion of the award attributable to the acquisition of a limited common element must be equally divided among the owners of the units to which that limited common element was allocated at the time of acquisition. For the purposes of acquisition of a part of the common elements other than the limited common elements under this subsection (3), service of process on the association shall constitute sufficient notice to all unit owners, and service of process on each individual unit owner shall not be necessary.

(4) The court decree shall be recorded in every county in which any portion of the common interest community is located.

(5)   The reallocations of allocated interests pursuant to this section shall be confirmed by an amendment to the declaration prepared, executed, and recorded by the association.

§ 38-33.3-108, C.R.S. Supplemental general principles of law applicable.

The principles of law and equity, including, but not limited to, the law of corporations and unincorporated associations, the law of real property, and the law relative to capacity to contract, principal and agent, eminent domain, estoppel, fraud, misrepresentation, duress, coercion, mistake, receivership, substantial performance, or other validating or invalidating cause supplement the provisions of this article, except to the extent inconsistent with this article.

§ 38-33.3-109, C.R.S. Construction against implicit repeal.

This article is intended to be a unified coverage of its subject matter, and no part of this article shall be construed to be impliedly repealed by subsequent legislation if that construction can reasonably be avoided.

§ 38-33.3-110, C.R.S. Uniformity of application and construction.

This article shall be applied and construed so as to effectuate its general purpose to make uniform the law with respect to the subject of this article among states enacting it.

§ 38-33.3-111, C.R.S. Severability.

If any provision of this article or the application thereof to any person or circumstances is held invalid, the invalidity shall not affect other provisions or applications of this article which can be given effect without the invalid provisions or application, and, to this end, the provisions of this article are severable.

§ 38-33.3-112, C.R.S. Unconscionable agreement or term of contract.

(1)   The court, upon finding as a matter of law that a contract or contract clause relating to a common interest community was unconscionable at the time the contract was made, may refuse to enforce the contract, enforce the remainder of the contract without the unconscionable clause, or limit the application of any unconscionable clause in order to avoid an unconscionable result.

(2)   Whenever it is claimed, or appears to the court, that a contract or any contract clause relating to a common interest community is or may be unconscionable, the parties, in order to aid the court in making the determination, shall be afforded a reasonable opportunity to present evidence as to:

(a)   The commercial setting of the negotiations;

(b)   Whether the first party has knowingly taken advantage of the inability of the second party reasonably to protect such second party's interests by reason of physical or mental infirmity, illiteracy, or inability to understand the language of the agreement or similar factors;

(c)   The effect and purpose of the contract or clause; and

(d)   If a sale, any gross disparity at the time of contracting between the amount charged for the property and the value of that property measured by the price at which similar property was readily obtainable in similar transactions. A disparity between the contract price and the value of the property measured by the price at which similar property was readily obtainable in similar transactions does not, of itself, render the contract unconscionable.

§ 38-33.3-113, C.R.S. Obligation of good faith.

Every contract or duty governed by this article imposes an obligation of good faith in its performance or enforcement.

§ 38-33.3-114, C.R.S. Remedies to be liberally administered.

(1)   The remedies provided by this article shall be liberally administered to the end that the aggrieved party is put in as good a position as if the other party had fully performed. However, consequential, special, or punitive damages may not be awarded except as specifically provided in this article or by other rule of law.

(2)   Any right or obligation declared by this article is enforceable by judicial proceeding.

§ 38-33.3-115, C.R.S. Applicability to new common interest communities.

Except as provided in section 38-33.3-116, this article applies to all common interest communities created within this state on or after July 1, 1992. The provisions of sections 38-33-101 to 38-33-109 do not apply to common interest communities created on or after July 1, 1992. The provisions of sections 38-33-110 to 38-33-113 shall remain in effect for all common interest communities.

§ 38-33.3-116, C.R.S. Exception for new small cooperatives and small and limited expense planned communities.

(1)   If a cooperative created in this state on or after July 1, 1992, but prior to July 1, 1998, contains only units restricted to nonresidential use or contains no more than ten units and is not subject to any development rights, it is subject only to sections 38-33.3-105 to 38-33.3-107, unless the declaration provides that this entire article is applicable. If a planned community created in this state on or after July 1, 1992, but prior to July 1, 1998, contains no more than ten units and is not subject to any development rights or if a planned community provides, in its declaration, that the annual average common expense liability of each unit restricted to residential purposes, exclusive of optional user fees and any insurance premiums paid by the association, may not exceed four hundred dollars, as adjusted pursuant to subsection (3) of this section, it is subject only to sections 38-33.3-105 to 38-33.3-107, unless the declaration provides that this entire article is applicable.

(2)   If a cooperative or planned community created in this state on or after July 1, 1998, contains only units restricted to nonresidential use, or contains no more than twenty units and is not subject to any development rights, it is subject only to sections 38-33.3-105 to 38-33.3-107, unless the declaration provides that this entire article is applicable. If a planned community created in this state after July 1, 1998, provides, in its declaration, that the annual average common expense liability of each unit restricted to residential purposes, exclusive of optional user fees and any insurance premiums paid by the association, may not exceed four hundred dollars, as adjusted pursuant to subsection (3) of this section, it is subject only to sections 38-33.3-105 to 38-33.3-107, unless the declaration provides that this entire article is applicable.

(3)   The dollar limitation set forth in subsections (1) and (2) of this section shall be increased annually on July 1, 1999, and on July 1 of each succeeding year in accordance with any increase in the United States department of labor bureau of labor statistics final consumer price index for the Denver-Boulder consolidated metropolitan statistical area for the preceding calendar year. The limitation shall not be increased if the final consumer price index for the preceding calendar year did not increase and shall not be decreased if the final consumer price index for the preceding calendar year decreased.

§ 38-33.3-116.3, C.R.S. Large planned communities – exemption from certain requirements.

(1) A planned community shall be exempt from the provisions of this article as specified in subsection (3) of this section or as specifically exempted in any other provision of this article, if, at the time of recording the affidavit required pursuant to subsection (2) of this section, the real estate upon which the planned community is created meets both of the following requirements:

   (a) It consists of at least two hundred acres;

   (b) It is approved for development of at least five hundred residential units, excluding any interval estates, time-share estates, or time-span estates but including any interval units created pursuant to sections 38-33-110 and 38-33-111, and at least twenty thousand square feet of commercial use.

   (c) (Deleted by amendment, L. 95, p. 236, § 2, effective July 1, 1995.)

(2) For an exemption authorized in subsection (1) of this section to apply, the property must be zoned within each county in which any part of such parcel is located, and the owner of the parcel shall record with the county clerk and recorder of each county in which any part of such parcel is located an affidavit setting forth the following:

   (a) The legal description of such parcel of land;

   (b) A statement that the party signing the affidavit is the owner of the parcel in its entirety in fee simple, excluding mineral interests;

   (c) The acreage of the parcel;

   (d) The zoning classification of the parcel, with a certified copy of applicable zoning regulations attached; and

   (e) A statement that neither the owner nor any officer, director, shareholder, partner, or other entity having more than a ten-percent equity interest in the owner has been convicted of a felony within the last ten years.

(3) A large planned community for which an affidavit has been filed pursuant to subsection (2) of this section shall be exempt from the following provisions of this article:

   (a) Section 38-33.3-205 (1) (e) to (1) (m);

   (b) Section 38-33.3-207 (3);

   (c) Section 38-33.3-208;

   (d) Section 38-33.3-209 (2) (b) to (2) (d), (2) (f), (2) (g), (4), and (6);

   (e) Section 38-33.3-210;

   (f) Section 38-33.3-212;

   (g) Section 38-33.3-213;

   (h) Section 38-33.3-215;

   (i) Section 38-33.3-217 (1);

   (j) Section 38-33.3-304.

(4) Section 38-33.3-217 (4) shall be applicable as follows: Except to the extent expressly permitted or required by other provisions of this article, no amendment may create or increase special declarant rights, increase the number of units or the allocated interests of a unit, or the uses to which any unit is restricted, in the absence of unanimous consent of the unit owners.

(5) (a) The exemption authorized by this section shall continue for the large planned community so long as the owner signing the affidavit is the owner of the real estate described in subsection (2) of this section; except that:

(I)   Upon the sale, conveyance, or other transfer of any portion of the real estate within the large planned community, the portion sold, conveyed, or transferred shall become subject to all the provisions of this article;

(II)   Any common interest community created on some but not all of the real estate within the large planned community shall be created pursuant to this article; and

(III)   When a planned community no longer qualifies as a large planned community, as described in subsection (1) of this section, the exemptions authorized by this section shall no longer be applicable.

(b)   Notwithstanding the provisions of subparagraph (III) of paragraph (a) of this subsection (5), all real estate described in a recorded declaration creating a large planned community shall remain subject to such recorded declaration.

(6)   The association established for a large planned community shall operate with respect to large planned community-wide matters and shall not otherwise operate as the exclusive unit owners' association with respect to any unit.

(7)   The association established for a large planned community shall keep in its principal office and make reasonably available to all unit owners, unit owners' authorized agents, and prospective purchasers of units a complete legal description of all common elements within the large planned community.

§ 38-33.3-117, C.R.S. Applicability to preexisting common interest communities.

(1)   Except as provided in section 38-33.3-119, the following sections apply to all common interest communities created within this state before July 1, 1992, with respect to events and circumstances occurring on or after July 1, 1992:

(a)   38-33.3-101 and 38-33.3-102;

(b)   38-33.3-103, to the extent necessary in construing any of the other sections of this article;

(c)   38-33.3-104 to 38-33.3-111;

(d)   38-33.3-114;

(e)   38-33.3-118;

(f)   38-33.3-120;

(g)   38-33.3-122 and 38-33.3-123;

(h)   38-33.3-203 and 38-33.3-217 (7);

(i)   38-33.3-302 (1)(a) to (1)(f), (1)(j) to (1)(m), and (1)(o) to (1)(q);

(i.5)   38-33.3-221.5;

(i.7)   38-33.3-303 (1)(b) and (3)(b);

(j)   38-33.3-311;

(k)   38-33.3-316;

(k.5)   38-33.3-316.3; and

(*l*)   38-33.3-317, as it existed prior to January 1, 2006, 38-33.3-318, and 38-33.3-319.

(1.5) Except as provided in section 38-33.3-119, the following sections apply to all common interest communities created within this state before July 1, 1992, with respect to events and circumstances occurring on or after January 1, 2006:

(a)   (Deleted by amendment, L. 2006, p. 1217, §3, effective May 26, 2006.)

(b)   38-33.3-124;

(c)   38-33.3-209.4 to 38-33.3-209.7;

(d)   38-33.3-217 (1);

(e)   (Deleted by amendment, L. 2006, p. 1217, §3, effective May 26, 2006.)

(f)   38-33.3-301;

(g)   38-33.3-302 (3) and (4);

(h)   38-33.3-303 (1)(b), (3)(b), and (4)(b);

(i)   38-33.3-308 (1), (2)(b), (2.5), and (4.5);

(j)   38-33.3-310 (1) and (2);

(k)   38-33.3-310.5;

(*l*)   38-33.3-315 (7);

(m)   38-33.3-317; and

(n)   38-33.3-401.

(1.7) Except as provided in section 38-33.3-119, section 38-33.3-209.5 (1)(b)(IX) shall apply to all common interest communities created within this state before July 1, 1992, with respect to events and circumstances occurring on or after July 1, 2010.

(1.8) Except as provided in section 38-33.3-119, section 38-33.3-303 (4)(a) applies to all common interest communities created within this state before July 1, 1992, with respect to events and circumstances occurring on or after July 1, 2017.

(1.9) Notwithstanding any other provision of law, section 38-33.3-303.5 applies to all common interest communities created within this state on, before, or after July 1, 1992, with respect to events and circumstances occurring on or after September 1, 2017.

(2)   The sections specified in paragraphs (a) to (j) and (l) of subsection (1) of this section shall be applied and construed to establish a clear, comprehensive, and uniform framework for the operation and management of common interest communities within this state and to supplement the provisions of any declaration, bylaws, plat, or map in existence on June 30, 1992. Except for section 38-33.3-217 (7), in the event of specific conflicts between the provisions of the sections specified in paragraphs (a) to (j) and (l) of subsection (1) of this section, and express requirements or restrictions in a declaration, bylaws, a plat, or a map in existence on June 30, 1992, such requirements or restrictions in the declaration, bylaws, plat, or map shall control, but only to the extent necessary to avoid invalidation of the specific requirement or restriction in the declaration, bylaws, plat, or map. Sections 38-33.3-217 (7) and 38-33.3-316 shall be applied and construed as stated in such sections.

(3)   Except as expressly provided for in this section, this article shall not apply to common interest communities created within this state before July 1, 1992.

(4)   Section 38-33.3-308 (2) to (7) shall apply to all common interest communities created within this state before July 1, 1995, and shall apply to all meetings of the executive board of such a community or any committee thereof occurring on or after said date. In addition, said section 38-33.3-308 (2) to (7) shall apply to all common interest communities created on or after July 1, 1995, and shall apply to all meetings of the executive board of such a community or any committee thereof occurring on or after said date.

§ 38-33.3-118, C.R.S. Procedure to elect treatment under the "Colorado Common Interest Ownership Act".

(1)   Any organization created prior to July 1, 1992, may elect to have the common interest community be treated as if it were created after June 30, 1992, and thereby subject the common interest community to all of the provisions contained in this article, in the following manner:

(a)   If there are members or stockholders entitled to vote thereon, the board of directors may adopt a resolution recommending that such association accept this article and directing that the question of acceptance be submitted to a vote at a meeting of the members or stockholders entitled to vote thereon, which may be either an annual or special meeting.

The question shall also be submitted whenever one-twentieth, or, in the case of an association with over one thousand members, one-fortieth, of the members or stockholders entitled to vote thereon so request. Written notice stating that the purpose, or one of the purposes, of the meeting is to consider electing to be treated as a common interest community organized after June 30, 1992, and thereby accepting the provisions of this article, together with a copy of this article, shall be given to each person entitled to vote at the meeting within the time and in the manner provided in the articles of incorporation, declaration, bylaws, or other governing documents for such association for the giving of notice of meetings to members. Such election to accept the provisions of this article shall require for adoption at least sixty-seven percent of the votes that the persons present at such meeting in person or by proxy are entitled to cast.

(b) If there are no persons entitled to vote thereon, the election to be treated as a common interest community under this article may be made at a meeting of the board of directors pursuant to a majority vote of the directors in office.

(2) A statement of election to accept the provisions of this article shall be executed and acknowledged by the president or vice-president and by the secretary or an assistant secretary of such association and shall set forth:

(a) The name of the common interest community and association;

(b) That the association has elected to accept the provisions of this article;

(c) That there were persons entitled to vote thereon, the date of the meeting of such persons at which the election was made to be treated as a common interest community under this article, that a quorum was present at the meeting, and that such acceptance was authorized by at least sixty-seven percent of the votes that the members or stockholders present at such meeting in person or by proxy were entitled to cast;

(d) That there were no members or stockholders entitled to vote thereon, the date of the meeting of the board of directors at which election to accept this article was made, that a quorum was present at the meeting, and that such acceptance was authorized by a majority vote of the directors present at such meeting;

(e) (Deleted by amendment, L. 93, p. 645, § 7, effective April 30, 1993.)

(f) The names and respective addresses of its officers and directors; and

(g) If there were no persons entitled to vote thereon but a common interest community has been created by virtue of compliance with section 38-33.3-103 (8), that the declarant desires for the common interest community to be subject to all the terms and provisions of this article.

(3) The original statement of election to be treated as a common interest community subject to the terms and conditions of this article shall be duly recorded in the office of the clerk and recorder for the county in which the common interest community is located.

(4) Upon the recording of the original statement of election to be treated as a common interest community subject to the provisions of this article, said common interest community shall be subject to all provisions of this article. Upon recording of the statement of election, such common interest community shall have the same powers and privileges and be subject to the same duties, restrictions, penalties, and liabilities as though it had been created after June 30, 1992.

(5) Notwithstanding any other provision of this section, and with respect to a common interest community making the election permitted by this section, this article shall apply only with respect to events and circumstances occurring on or after July 1, 1992, and does not invalidate provisions of any declaration, bylaws, or plats or maps in existence on June 30, 1992.

§ 38-33.3-119, C.R.S. Exception for small preexisting cooperatives and planned communities.

If a cooperative or planned community created within this state before July 1, 1992, contains no more than ten units and is not subject to any development rights, or if its declaration limits its annual common expense liability to the amount specified in section 38-33.3-116 (1), then it is subject only to sections 38-33.3-105 to 38-33.3-107 unless the declaration is amended in conformity with applicable law and with the procedures and requirements of the declaration to take advantage of the provisions of section 38-33.3-120, in which case all the sections enumerated in section 38-33.3-117 apply to that planned community.

§ 38-33.3-120, C.R.S. Amendments to preexisting governing instruments.

(1)   In the case of amendments to the declaration, bylaws, or plats and maps of any common interest community created within this state before July 1, 1992, which has not elected treatment under this article pursuant to section 38-33.3-118:

    (a)   If the substantive result accomplished by the amendment was permitted by law in effect prior to July 1, 1992, the amendment may be made either in accordance with that law, in which case that law applies to that amendment, or it may be made under this article; and

    (b)   If the substantive result accomplished by the amendment is permitted by this article, and was not permitted by law in effect prior to July 1, 1992, the amendment may be made under this article.

(2)   An amendment to the declaration, bylaws, or plats and maps authorized by this section to be made under this article must be adopted in conformity with the procedures and requirements of the law that applied to the common interest community at the time it was created and with the procedures and requirements specified by those instruments. If an amendment grants to any person any rights, powers, or privileges permitted by this article, all correlative obligations, liabilities, and restrictions in this article also apply to that person.

(3)   An amendment to the declaration may also be made pursuant to the procedures set forth in section 38-33.3-217 (7).

§ 38-33.3-120.5, C.R.S. Extension of declaration term.

(1)   If a common interest community has a declaration in effect with a limited term of years that was recorded prior to July 1, 1992, and if, before the term of the declaration expires, the unit owners in the common interest community have not amended the declaration pursuant to section 38-33.3-120 and in accordance with any conditions or fixed limitations described in the declaration, the declaration may be extended as provided in this section.

(2)   The term of the declaration may be extended:

    (a)   If the executive board adopts a resolution recommending that the declaration be extended for a specific term not to exceed twenty years and directs that the question of extending the term of the declaration be submitted to the unit owners, as members of the association; and

    (b)   If an extension of the term of the declaration is approved by vote or agreement of unit owners of units to which at least sixty-seven percent of the votes in the association are allocated or any larger percentage the declaration specifies.

(3)   Except for the extension of the term of a declaration as authorized by this section, no other provision of a declaration may be amended pursuant to the provisions of this section.

(4)   For any meeting of unit owners at which a vote is to be taken on a proposed extension of the term of a declaration as provided in this section, the secretary or other officer specified in the bylaws shall provide written notice to each unit owner entitled to vote at the meeting stating that the purpose, or one of the purposes, of the meeting is to consider extending the term of the

declaration. The notice shall be given in the time and manner specified in section 38-33.3-308 or in the articles of incorporation, declaration, bylaws, or other governing documents of the association.

(5)   The extension of the declaration, if approved, shall be included in an amendment to the declaration and shall be executed, acknowledged, and recorded by the association in the records of the clerk and recorder of each county in which any portion of the common interest community is located. The amendment shall include:

(a)   A statement of the name of the common interest community and the association;

(b)   A statement that the association has elected to extend the term of the declaration pursuant to this section and the term of the approved extension;

(c)   A statement that indicates that the executive board has adopted a resolution recommending that the declaration be extended for a specific term not to exceed twenty years, that sets forth the date of the meeting at which the unit owners elected to extend the term of the declaration, and that declares that the extension was authorized by a vote or agreement of unit owners of units to which at least sixty-seven percent of the votes in the association are allocated or any larger percentage the declaration specifies;

(d)   A statement of the names and respective addresses of the officers and executive board members of the association.

(6)   Upon the recording of the amendment required by subsection (5) of this section, and subject to the provisions of this section, a common interest community is subject to all provisions of the declaration, as amended.

§ 38-33.3-121, C.R.S. Applicability to nonresidential planned communities.

This article does not apply to a planned community in which all units are restricted exclusively to nonresidential use unless the declaration provides that the article does apply to that planned community. This article applies to a planned community containing both units that are restricted exclusively to nonresidential use and other units that are not so restricted, only if the declaration so provides or the real estate comprising the units that may be used for residential purposes would be a planned community in the absence of the units that may not be used for residential purposes.

§ 38-33.3-122, C.R.S. Applicability to out-of-state common interest communities.

This article does not apply to common interest communities or units located outside this state.

§ 38-33.3-123, C.R.S. Enforcement – limitation.

(1)   (a)   If any unit owner fails to timely pay assessments or any money or sums due to the association, the association may require reimbursement for collection costs and reasonable attorney fees and costs incurred as a result of such failure without the necessity of commencing a legal proceeding.

(b)   For any failure to comply with the provisions of this article or any provision of the declaration, bylaws, articles, or rules and regulations, other than the payment of assessments or any money or sums due to the association, the association, any unit owner, or any class of unit owners adversely affected by the failure to comply may seek reimbursement for collection costs and reasonable attorney fees and costs incurred as a result of such failure to comply, without the necessity of commencing a legal proceeding.

(c)   In any civil action to enforce or defend the provisions of this article or of the declaration, bylaws, articles, or rules and regulations, the court shall award reasonable attorney fees, costs, and costs of collection to the prevailing party.

(d)   Notwithstanding paragraph (c) of this subsection (1), in connection with any claim in which a unit owner is alleged to have violated a provision of this article or of the declaration, bylaws, articles, or rules and regulations of the association and in which the court finds that the unit owner prevailed because the unit owner did not commit the alleged violation:

    (I)   The court shall award the unit owner reasonable attorney fees and costs incurred in asserting or defending the claim; and

    (II)   The court shall not award costs or attorney fees to the association. In addition, the association shall be precluded from allocating to the unit owner's account with the association any of the association's costs or attorney fees incurred in asserting or defending the claim.

(e)   A unit owner shall not be deemed to have confessed judgment to attorney fees or collection costs.

(2)   Notwithstanding any law to the contrary, no action shall be commenced or maintained to enforce the terms of any building restriction contained in the provisions of the declaration, bylaws, articles, or rules and regulations or to compel the removal of any building or improvement because of the violation of the terms of any such building restriction unless the action is commenced within one year from the date from which the person commencing the action knew or in the exercise of reasonable diligence should have known of the violation for which the action is sought to be brought or maintained.

§ 38-33.3-124, C.R.S. Legislative declaration – alternative dispute resolution encouraged – policy statement required.

(1)   (a)   (I)   The general assembly finds and declares that the cost, complexity, and delay inherent in court proceedings make litigation a particularly inefficient means of resolving neighborhood disputes. Therefore, common interest communities are encouraged to adopt protocols that make use of mediation or arbitration as alternatives to, or preconditions upon, the filing of a complaint between a unit owner and association in situations that do not involve an imminent threat to the peace, health, or safety of the community.

    (II)   The general assembly hereby specifically endorses and encourages associations, unit owners, managers, declarants, and all other parties to disputes arising under this article to agree to make use of all available public or private resources for alternative dispute resolution, including, without limitation, the resources offered by the office of dispute resolution within the Colorado judicial branch through its web site.

(b)   On or before January 1, 2007, each association shall adopt a written policy setting forth its procedure for addressing disputes arising between the association and unit owners. The association shall make a copy of this policy available to unit owners upon request.

(2)   (a)   Any controversy between an association and a unit owner arising out of the provisions of this article may be submitted to mediation by agreement of the parties prior to the commencement of any legal proceeding.

(b)   The mediation agreement, if one is reached, may be presented to the court as a stipulation. Either party to the mediation may terminate the mediation process without prejudice.

(c)   If either party subsequently violates the stipulation, the other party may apply immediately to the court for relief.

(3)   The declaration, bylaws, or rules of the association may specify situations in which disputes shall be resolved by binding arbitration under the uniform arbitration act, part 2 of article 22 of title 13, C.R.S., or by another means of alternative dispute resolution under the "Dispute Resolution Act", part 3 of article 22 of title 13, C.R.S.

A. Creation, Alteration, and Termination

§ 38-33.3-201, C.R.S. Creation of common interest communities.

(1) A common interest community may be created pursuant to this article only by recording a declaration executed in the same manner as a deed and, in a cooperative, by conveying the real estate subject to that declaration to the association. The declaration must be recorded in every county in which any portion of the common interest community is located and must be indexed in the grantee's index in the name of the common interest community and in the name of the association and in the grantor's index in the name of each person executing the declaration. No common interest community is created until the plat or map for the common interest community is recorded.

(2) In a common interest community with horizontal unit boundaries, a declaration, or an amendment to a declaration, creating or adding units shall include a certificate of completion executed by an independent licensed or registered engineer, surveyor, or architect stating that all structural components of all buildings containing or comprising any units thereby created are substantially completed.

§ 38-33.3-202, C.R.S. Unit boundaries.

(1) Except as provided by the declaration:

   (a) If walls, floors, or ceilings are designated as boundaries of a unit, all lath, furring, wallboard, plasterboard, plaster, paneling, tiles, wallpaper, paint, and finished flooring and any other materials constituting any part of the finished surfaces thereof are a part of the unit, and all other portions of the walls, floors, or ceilings are a part of the common elements.

   (b) If any chute, flue, duct, wire, conduit, bearing wall, bearing column, or other fixture lies partially within and partially outside the designated boundaries of a unit, any portion thereof serving only that unit is a limited common element allocated solely to that unit, and any portion thereof serving more than one unit or any portion of the common elements is a part of the common elements.

   (c) Subject to the provisions of paragraph (b) of this subsection (1), all spaces, interior partitions, and other fixtures and improvements within the boundaries of a unit are a part of the unit.

   (d) Any shutters, awnings, window boxes, doorsteps, stoops, porches, balconies, and patios and all exterior doors and windows or other fixtures designed to serve a single unit, but located outside the unit's boundaries, are limited common elements allocated exclusively to that unit.

§ 38-33.3-203, C.R.S. Construction and validity of declaration and bylaws.

(1) All provisions of the declaration and bylaws are severable.

(2) The rule against perpetuities does not apply to defeat any provision of the declaration, bylaws, or rules and regulations.

(3) In the event of a conflict between the provisions of the declaration and the bylaws, the declaration prevails, except to the extent the declaration is inconsistent with this article.

(4) Title to a unit and common elements is not rendered unmarketable or otherwise affected by reason of an insubstantial failure of the declaration to comply with this article. Whether a substantial failure impairs marketability is not affected by this article.

§ 38-33.3-204, C.R.S. Description of units.

A description of a unit may set forth the name of the common interest community, the recording data for the declaration, the county in which the common interest community is located, and the identifying number of the unit. Such description is a legally sufficient description of that unit and all rights, obligations, and interests appurtenant to that unit which were created by the declaration or bylaws. It shall not be necessary to use the term "unit" as a part of a legally sufficient description of a unit.

§ 38-33.3-205, C.R.S. Contents of declaration.

(1)   The declaration must contain:

    (a)   The names of the common interest community and the association and a statement that the common interest community is a condominium, cooperative, or planned community;

    (b)   The name of every county in which any part of the common interest community is situated;

    (c)   A legally sufficient description of the real estate included in the common interest community;

    (d)   A statement of the maximum number of units that the declarant reserves the right to create;

    (e)   In a condominium or planned community, a description, which may be by plat or map, of the boundaries of each unit created by the declaration, including the unit's identifying number; or, in a cooperative, a description, which may be by plat or map, of each unit created by the declaration, including the unit's identifying number, its size or number of rooms, and its location within a building if it is within a building containing more than one unit;

    (f)   A description of any limited common elements, other than those specified in section 38-33.3-202 (1) (b) and (1) (d) or shown on the map as provided in section 38-33.3-209 (2) (j) and, in a planned community, any real estate that is or must become common elements;

    (g)   A description of any real estate, except real estate subject to development rights, that may be allocated subsequently as limited common elements, other than limited common elements specified in section 38-33.3-202 (1) (b) and (1) (d), together with a statement that they may be so allocated;

    (h)   A description of any development rights and other special declarant rights reserved by the declarant, together with a description sufficient to identify the real estate to which each of those rights applies and the time limit within which each of those rights must be exercised;

    (i)   If any development right may be exercised with respect to different parcels of real estate at different times, a statement to that effect together with:

        (I)   Either a statement fixing the boundaries of those portions and regulating the order in which those portions may be subjected to the exercise of each development right or a statement that no assurances are made in those regards; and

        (II)   A statement as to whether, if any development right is exercised in any portion of the real estate subject to that development right, that development right must be exercised in all or in any other portion of the remainder of that real estate;

    (j)   Any other conditions or limitations under which the rights described in paragraph (h) of this subsection (1) may be exercised or will lapse;

    (k)   An allocation to each unit of the allocated interests in the manner described in section 38-33.3-207;

(*l*)   Any restrictions on the use, occupancy, and alienation of the units and on the amount for which a unit may be sold or on the amount that may be received by a unit owner on sale, condemnation, or casualty loss to the unit or to the common interest community or on termination of the common interest community;

(m)   The recording data for recorded easements and licenses appurtenant to, or included in, the common interest community or to which any portion of the common interest community is or may become subject by virtue of a reservation in the declaration;

(n)   All matters required by sections 38-33.3-201, 38-33.3-206 to 38-33.3-209, 38-33.3-215, 38-33.3-216, and 38-33.3-303 (4);

(o)   Reasonable provisions concerning the manner in which notice of matters affecting the common interest community may be given to unit owners by the association or other unit owners;

(p)   A statement, if applicable, that the planned community is a large planned community and is exercising certain exemptions from the "Colorado Common Interest Ownership Act" as such a large planned community;

(q)   In a large planned community:

      (I)   A general description of every common element that the declarant is legally obligated to construct within the large planned community together with the approximate date by which each such common element is to be completed. The declarant shall be required to complete each such common element within a reasonable time after the date specified in the declaration, unless the declarant, due to an act of God, is unable to do so. The declarant shall not be legally obligated with respect to any common element not identified in the declaration.

      (II)   A general description of the type of any common element that the declarant anticipates may be constructed by, maintained by, or operated by the association. The association shall not assess members for the construction, maintenance, or operation of any common element that is not described pursuant to this subparagraph (II) unless such assessment is approved by the vote of a majority of the votes entitled to be cast in person or by proxy, other than by declarant, at a meeting duly convened as required by law.

(2)   The declaration may contain any other matters the declarant considers appropriate.

(3)   The plats and maps described in section 38-33.3-209 may contain certain information required to be included in the declaration by this section.

(4)   A declarant may amend the declaration, a plat, or a map to correct clerical, typographical, or technical errors.

(5)   A declarant may amend the declaration to comply with the requirements, standards, or guidelines of recognized secondary mortgage markets, the department of housing and urban development, the federal housing administration, the veterans administration, the federal home loan mortgage corporation, the government national mortgage association, or the federal national mortgage association.

§ 38-33.3-206, C.R.S. Leasehold common interest communities.

(1)   Any lease, the expiration or termination of which may terminate the common interest community or reduce its size, must be recorded. In a leasehold condominium or leasehold planned community, the declaration must contain the signature of each lessor of any such lease in order for the provisions of this section to be effective. The declaration must state:

(a)   The recording data for the lease;

(b)   The date on which the lease is scheduled to expire;

(c)   A legally sufficient description of the real estate subject to the lease;

(d)   Any rights of the unit owners to redeem the reversion and the manner whereby those rights may be exercised or state that they do not have those rights;

(e)   Any rights of the unit owners to remove any improvements within a reasonable time after the expiration or termination of the lease or state that they do not have those rights; and

(f)   Any rights of the unit owners to renew the lease and the conditions of any renewal or state that they do not have those rights.

(2)   After the declaration for a leasehold condominium or leasehold planned community is recorded, neither the lessor nor the lessor's successor in interest may terminate the leasehold interest of a unit owner who makes timely payment of a unit owner's share of the rent and otherwise complies with all covenants which, if violated, would entitle the lessor to terminate the lease. A unit owner's leasehold interest in a condominium or planned community is not affected by failure of any other person to pay rent or fulfill any other covenant.

(3)   Acquisition of the leasehold interest of any unit owner by the owner of the reversion or remainder does not merge the leasehold and fee simple interests unless the leasehold interests of all unit owners subject to that reversion or remainder are acquired.

(4)   If the expiration or termination of a lease decreases the number of units in a common interest community, the allocated interests shall be reallocated in accordance with section 38-33.3-107 (1), as though those units had been taken by eminent domain. Reallocations shall be confirmed by an amendment to the declaration prepared, executed, and recorded by the association.

§ 38-33.3-207, C.R.S. Allocation of allocated interests.

(1)   The declaration must allocate to each unit:

(a)   In a condominium, a fraction or percentage of undivided interests in the common elements and in the common expenses of the association and, to the extent not allocated in the bylaws of the association, a portion of the votes in the association;

(b)   In a cooperative, an ownership interest in the association, a fraction or percentage of the common expenses of the association, and, to the extent not allocated in the bylaws of the association, a portion of the votes in the association;

(c)   In a planned community, a fraction or percentage of the common expenses of the association and, to the extent not allocated in the bylaws of the association, a portion of the votes in the association; except that, in a large planned community, the common expenses of the association may be paid from assessments and allocated as set forth in the declaration and the votes in the association may be allocated as set forth in the declaration.

(2)   The declaration must state the formulas used to establish allocations of interests. Those allocations may not discriminate in favor of units owned by the declarant or an affiliate of the declarant.

(3)   If units may be added to or withdrawn from the common interest community, the declaration must state the formulas to be used to reallocate the allocated interests among all units included in the common interest community after the addition or withdrawal.

(4)   (a)   The declaration may provide:

(I)   That different allocations of votes shall be made to the units on particular matters specified in the declaration;

(II)   For cumulative voting only for the purpose of electing members of the executive board;

(III)   For class voting on specified issues affecting the class, including the election of the executive board; and

(IV) For assessments including, but not limited to, assessments on retail sales and services not to exceed six percent of the amount charged for the retail sale or service, and real estate transfers not to exceed three percent of the real estate sales price or its equivalent.

(b) A declarant may not utilize cumulative or class voting for the purpose of evading any limitation imposed on declarants by this article, nor may units constitute a class because they are owned by a declarant.

(c) Assessments allowed under subparagraph (IV) of paragraph (a) of this subsection (4) shall be entitled to the lien provided for under section 38-33.3-316 (1) but shall not be entitled to the priority established by section 38-33.3-316 (2) (b).

(d) Communities with classes for voting specified in the declaration as allowed pursuant to subparagraph (III) of paragraph (a) of this subsection (4) may designate classes of members on a reasonable basis which do not allow the declarant to control the association beyond the period provided for in section 38-33.3-303, including, without limitation, residence owners, commercial space owners, and owners of lodging space and to elect members to the association executive board from such classes.

(5) Except for minor variations due to the rounding of fractions or percentages, the sum of the common expense liabilities and, in a condominium, the sum of the undivided interests in the common elements allocated at any time to all the units shall each equal one if stated as fractions or one hundred percent if stated as percentages. In the event of discrepancy between an allocated interest and the result derived from application of the pertinent formula, the allocated interest prevails.

(6) In a condominium, the common elements are not subject to partition except as allowed for in section 38-33.3-312, and any purported conveyance, encumbrance, judicial sale, or other voluntary or involuntary transfer of an undivided interest in the common elements not allowed for in section 38-33.3-312, that is made without the unit to which that interest is allocated is void.

(7) In a cooperative, any purported conveyance, encumbrance, judicial sale, or other voluntary or involuntary transfer of an ownership interest in the association made without the possessory interest in the unit to which that interest is related is void.

§ 38-33.3-208, C.R.S. Limited common elements.

(1) Except for the limited common elements described in section 38-33.3-202 (1) (b) and (1) (d), the declaration shall specify to which unit or units each limited common element is allocated. That allocation may not be altered without the consent of the unit owners whose units are affected.

(2) Subject to any provisions of the declaration, a limited common element may be reallocated between or among units after compliance with the procedure set forth in this subsection (2). In order to reallocate limited common elements between or among units, the unit owners of those units, as the applicants, must submit an application for approval of the proposed reallocation to the executive board, which application shall be executed by those unit owners and shall include:

(a) The proposed form for an amendment to the declaration as may be necessary to show the reallocation of limited common elements between or among units;

(b) A deposit against attorney fees and costs which the association will incur in reviewing and effectuating the application, in an amount reasonably estimated by the executive board; and

(c) Such other information as may be reasonably requested by the executive board. No reallocation shall be effective without the approval of the executive board. The reallocation shall be effectuated by an amendment signed by the association and by those unit owners between or among whose units the reallocation is made, which amendment shall be recorded as provided in section 38-33.3-217 (3). All costs and attorney fees incurred by the association as a result of the application shall be the sole obligation of the applicants.

(3) A common element not previously allocated as a limited common element may be so allocated only pursuant to provisions in the declaration made in accordance with section 38-33.3-205 (1) (g). The allocations must be made by amendments to the declaration prepared, executed, and recorded by the declarant.

§ 38-33.3-209, C.R.S. Plats and maps.

(1) A plat or map is a part of the declaration and is required for all common interest communities except cooperatives. A map is required only for a common interest community with units having a horizontal boundary. The requirements of this section shall be deemed satisfied so long as all of the information required by this section is contained in the declaration, a map or a plat, or some combination of any two or all of the three. Each plat or map must be clear and legible. When a map is required under any provision of this article, the map, a plat, or the declaration shall contain a certification that all information required by this section is contained in the declaration, the map or a plat, or some combination of any two or all of the three.

(2) In addition to meeting the requirements of a land survey plat as set forth in section 38-51-106, each map shall show the following, except to the extent such information is contained in the declaration or on a plat:

(a) The name and a general schematic plan of the entire common interest community;

(b) The location and dimensions of all real estate not subject to development rights, or subject only to the development right to withdraw, and the location and dimensions of all existing improvements within that real estate;

(c) A legally sufficient description, which may be of the whole common interest community or any portion thereof, of any real estate subject to development rights and a description of the rights applicable to such real estate;

(d) The extent of any existing encroachments across any common interest community boundary;

(e) To the extent feasible, a legally sufficient description of all easements serving or burdening any portion of the common interest community;

(f) The location and dimensions of the vertical boundaries of each unit and that unit's identifying number;

(g) The location, with reference to established data, of the horizontal boundaries of each unit and that unit's identifying number;

(g.5) Any units in which the declarant has reserved the right to create additional units or common elements, identified appropriately;

(h) A legally sufficient description of any real estate in which the unit owners will own only an estate for years;

(i) The distance between noncontiguous parcels of real estate comprising the common interest community; and

(j) The approximate location and dimensions of limited common elements, including porches, balconies, and patios, other than the limited common elements described in section 38-33.3-202 (1) (b) and (1) (d).

(3) (Deleted by amendment, L. 93, p. 648, § 12, effective April 30, 1993.)

(4) (Deleted by amendment, L. 2007, p. 1799, § 1, effective July 1, 2007.)

(5) Unless the declaration provides otherwise, the horizontal boundaries of any part of a unit located outside of a building have the same elevation as the horizontal boundaries of the inside part and need not be depicted on the plats and maps.

(6) Upon exercising any development right, the declarant shall record an amendment to the declaration with respect to that real estate reflecting change as a result of such exercise necessary to conform to the requirements of subsections (1), (2), and (4) of this section or new certifications of maps previously recorded if those maps otherwise conform to the requirements of subsections (1), (2), and (4) of this section.

(7) Any certification of a map required by this article must be made by a registered land surveyor.

(8) The requirements of a plat or map under this article shall not be deemed to satisfy any subdivision platting requirement enacted by a county or municipality pursuant to section 30-28-133, C.R.S., part 1 of article 23 of title 31, C.R.S., or a similar provision of a home rule city, nor shall the plat or map requirements under this article be deemed to be incorporated into any subdivision platting requirements enacted by a county or municipality.

(9) Any plat or map that was recorded on or after July 1, 1998, but prior to July 1, 2007, and that satisfies the requirements of this section in effect on July 1, 2007, is deemed to have satisfied the requirements of this section at the time it was recorded.

§ 38-33.3-209.4, C.R.S. Public disclosures required – identity of association – agent – manager – contact information.

(1) Within ninety days after assuming control from the declarant pursuant to section 38-33.3-303 (5), the association shall make the following information available to unit owners upon reasonable notice in accordance with subsection (3) of this section. In addition, if the association's address, designated agent, or management company changes, the association shall make updated information available within ninety days after the change:

(a) The name of the association;

(b) The name of the association's designated agent or management company, if any, together with the agent's or management company's license number if the agent or management company is subject to licensure under part 10 of article 61 of title 12, C.R.S.;

(c) A valid physical address and telephone number for both the association and the designated agent or management company, if any;

(d) The name of the common interest community;

(e) The initial date of recording of the declaration; and

(f) The reception number or book and page for the main document that constitutes the declaration.

(2) Within ninety days after assuming control from the declarant pursuant to section 38-33.3-303 (5), and within ninety days after the end of each fiscal year thereafter, the association shall make the following information available to unit owners upon reasonable notice in accordance with subsection (3) of this section:

(a) The date on which its fiscal year commences;

(b) Its operating budget for the current fiscal year;

(c) A list, by unit type, of the association's current assessments, including both regular and special assessments;

(d) Its annual financial statements, including any amounts held in reserve for the fiscal year immediately preceding the current annual disclosure;

(e) The results of its most recent available financial audit or review;

(f) A list of all association insurance policies, including, but not limited to, property, general liability, association director and officer professional liability, and fidelity policies. Such list shall include the company names, policy limits, policy deductibles, additional named insureds, and expiration dates of the policies listed.

(g) All the association's bylaws, articles, and rules and regulations;

(h) The minutes of the executive board and member meetings for the fiscal year immediately preceding the current annual disclosure; and

(i) The association's responsible governance policies adopted under section 38-33.3-209.5.

(3) It is the intent of this section to allow the association the widest possible latitude in methods and means of disclosure, while requiring that the information be readily available at no cost to unit owners at their convenience. Disclosure shall be accomplished by one of the following means: Posting on an internet web page with accompanying notice of the web address via first-class mail or e-mail; the maintenance of a literature table or binder at the association's principal place of business; or mail or personal delivery. The cost of such distribution shall be accounted for as a common expense liability.

(4) Notwithstanding section 38-33.3-117 (1.5) (c), this section shall not apply to a unit, or the owner thereof, if the unit is a time-share unit, as defined in section 38-33-110 (7).

§ 38-33.3-209.5, C.R.S. Responsible governance policies – due process for imposition of fines.

(1) To promote responsible governance, associations shall:

(a) Maintain accurate and complete accounting records; and

(b) Adopt policies, procedures, and rules and regulations concerning:

   (I) Collection of unpaid assessments;

   (II) Handling of conflicts of interest involving board members, which policies, procedures, and rules and regulations must include, at a minimum, the criteria described in subsection (4) of this section;

   (III) Conduct of meetings, which may refer to applicable provisions of the nonprofit code or other recognized rules and principles;

   (IV) Enforcement of covenants and rules, including notice and hearing procedures and the schedule of fines;

   (V) Inspection and copying of association records by unit owners;

   (VI) Investment of reserve funds;

   (VII) Procedures for the adoption and amendment of policies, procedures, and rules;

   (VIII) Procedures for addressing disputes arising between the association and unit owners; and

   (IX) When the association has a reserve study prepared for the portions of the community maintained, repaired, replaced, and improved by the association; whether there is a funding plan for any work recommended by the reserve study and, if so, the projected sources of funding for the work; and whether the reserve study is based on a physical analysis and financial analysis. For the purposes of this subparagraph (IX), an internally conducted reserve study shall be sufficient.

(2) Notwithstanding any provision of the declaration, bylaws, articles, or rules and regulations to the contrary, the association may not fine any unit owner for an alleged violation unless:

(a) The association has adopted, and follows, a written policy governing the imposition of fines; and

(b) (I) The policy includes a fair and impartial fact-finding process concerning whether the alleged violation actually occurred and whether the unit owner is the one who should be held responsible for the violation. This process may be informal but shall, at a minimum, guarantee the unit owner notice and an opportunity to be heard before an impartial decision maker.

(II) As used in this paragraph (b), "impartial decision maker" means a person or group of persons who have the authority to make a decision regarding the enforcement of the association's covenants, conditions, and restrictions, including its architectural requirements, and the other rules and regulations of the association and do not have any direct personal or financial interest in the outcome. A decision maker shall not be deemed to have a direct personal or financial interest in the outcome if the decision maker will not, as a result of the outcome, receive any greater benefit or detriment than will the general membership of the association.

(3) If, as a result of the fact finding process described in subsection (2) of this section, it is determined that the unit owner should not be held responsible for the alleged violation, the association shall not allocate to the unit owner's account with the association any of the association's costs or attorney fees incurred in asserting or hearing the claim. Notwithstanding any provision in the declaration, bylaws, or rules and regulations of the association to the contrary, a unit owner shall not be deemed to have consented to pay such costs or fees.

(4) (a) The policies, procedures, and rules and regulations adopted by an association under subparagraph (II) of paragraph (b) of subsection (1) of this section must, at a minimum:

(I) Define or describe the circumstances under which a conflict of interest exists;

(II) Set forth procedures to follow when a conflict of interest exists, including how, and to whom, the conflict of interest must be disclosed and whether a board member must recuse himself or herself from discussing or voting on the issue; and

(III) Provide for the periodic review of the association's conflict of interest policies, procedures, and rules and regulations.

(b) The policies, procedures, or rules and regulations adopted under this subsection (4) must be in accordance with section 38-33.3-310.5.

(5) (a) Notwithstanding any provision of the declaration, bylaws, articles, or rules and regulations to the contrary or the absence of a relevant provision in the declaration, bylaws, articles, or rules or regulations, the association or a holder or assignee of the association's debt, whether the holder or assignee of the association's debt is an entity or a natural person, may not use a collection agency or take legal action to collect unpaid assessments unless the association or a holder or assignee of the association's debt has adopted, and follows, a written policy governing the collection of unpaid assessments. The policy must, at a minimum, specify:

(I) The date on which assessments must be paid to the entity and when an assessment is considered past due and delinquent;

(II) Any late fees and interest the entity is entitled to impose on a delinquent unit owner's account;

(III) Any returned-check charges the entity is entitled to impose;

(IV) The circumstances under which a unit owner is entitled to enter into a payment plan with the entity pursuant to section 38-33.3-316.3 and the minimum terms of the payment plan mandated by that section;

(V) That, before the entity turns over a delinquent account of a unit owner to a collection agency or refers it to an attorney for legal action, the entity must send the unit owner a notice of delinquency specifying:

(A) The total amount due, with an accounting of how the total was determined;

(B)   Whether the opportunity to enter into a payment plan exists pursuant to section 38-33.3-316.3 and instructions for contacting the entity to enter into such a payment plan;

(C)   The name and contact information for the individual the unit owner may contact to request a copy of the unit owner's ledger in order to verify the amount of the debt; and

(D)   That action is required to cure the delinquency and that failure to do so within thirty days may result in the unit owner's delinquent account being turned over to a collection agency, a lawsuit being filed against the owner, the filing and foreclosure of a lien against the unit owner's property, or other remedies available under Colorado law;

(VI)   The method by which payments may be applied on the delinquent account of a unit owner; and

(VII)   The legal remedies available to the entity to collect on a unit owner's delinquent account pursuant to the governing documents of the entity and Colorado law.

(b)   As used in this subsection (5), "entity" means an association or a holder or assignee of the association's debt, whether the holder or assignee of the association's debt is an entity or a natural person.

§ 38-33.3-209.6, C.R.S. Executive board member education.

The board may authorize, and account for as a common expense, reimbursement of board members for their actual and necessary expenses incurred in attending educational meetings and seminars on responsible governance of unit owners' associations. The course content of such educational meetings and seminars shall be specific to Colorado, and shall make reference to applicable sections of this article.

§ 38-33.3-209.7, C.R.S. Owner education.

(1)   The association shall provide, or cause to be provided, education to owners at no cost on at least an annual basis as to the general operations of the association and the rights and responsibilities of owners, the association, and its executive board under Colorado law. The criteria for compliance with this section shall be determined by the executive board.

(2)   Notwithstanding section 38-33.3-117 (1.5) (c), this section shall not apply to an association that includes time-share units, as defined in section 38-33-110 (7).

§ 38-33.3-210, C.R.S. Exercise of development rights.

(1)   To exercise any development right reserved under section 38-33.3-205 (1) (h), the declarant shall prepare, execute, and record an amendment to the declaration and, in a condominium or planned community, comply with the provisions of section 38-33.3-209. The declarant is the unit owner of any units thereby created. The amendment to the declaration must assign an identifying number to each new unit created and, except in the case of subdivision or conversion of units described in subsection (3) of this section, reallocate the allocated interests among all units. The amendment must describe any common elements and any limited common elements thereby created and, in the case of limited common elements, designate the unit to which each is allocated to the extent required by section 38-33.3-208.

(2)   Additional development rights not previously reserved may be reserved within any real estate added to the common interest community if the amendment adding that real estate includes all matters required by section 38-33.3-205 or 38-33.3-206, as the case may be, and, in a condominium or planned community, the plats and maps include all matters required by section

38-33.3-209. This provision does not extend the time limit on the exercise of development rights imposed by the declaration pursuant to section 38-33.3-205 (1) (h).

(3)   Whenever a declarant exercises a development right to subdivide or convert a unit previously created into additional units, common elements, or both:

(a)   If the declarant converts the unit entirely to common elements, the amendment to the declaration must reallocate all the allocated interests of that unit among the other units as if that unit had been taken by eminent domain; and

(b)   If the declarant subdivides the unit into two or more units, whether or not any part of the unit is converted into common elements, the amendment to the declaration must reallocate all the allocated interests of the unit among the units created by the subdivision in any reasonable manner prescribed by the declarant.

(4)   If the declaration provides, pursuant to section 38-33.3-205, that all or a portion of the real estate is subject to a right of withdrawal:

(a)   If all the real estate is subject to withdrawal, and the declaration does not describe separate portions of real estate subject to that right, none of the real estate may be withdrawn after a unit has been conveyed to a purchaser; and

(b)   If any portion of the real estate is subject to withdrawal, it may not be withdrawn after a unit in that portion has been conveyed to a purchaser.

(5)   If a declarant fails to exercise any development right within the time limit and in accordance with any conditions or fixed limitations described in the declaration pursuant to section 38-33.3-205 (1) (h), or records an instrument surrendering a development right, that development right shall lapse unless the association, upon the request of the declarant or the owner of the real estate subject to development right, agrees to an extension of the time period for exercise of the development right or a reinstatement of the development right subject to whatever terms, conditions, and limitations the association may impose on the subsequent exercise of the development right. The extension or renewal of the development right and any terms, conditions, and limitations shall be included in an amendment executed by the declarant or the owner of the real estate subject to development right and the association.

§ 38-33.3-211, C.R.S. Alterations of units.

(1)   Subject to the provisions of the declaration and other provisions of law, a unit owner:

(a)   May make any improvements or alterations to his unit that do not impair the structural integrity, electrical systems, or mechanical systems or lessen the support of any portion of the common interest community;

(b)   May not change the appearance of the common elements without permission of the association; or

(c)   After acquiring an adjoining unit or an adjoining part of an adjoining unit, may remove or alter any intervening partition or create apertures therein, even if the partition in whole or in part is a common element, if those acts do not impair the structural integrity, electrical systems, or mechanical systems or lessen the support of any portion of the common interest community. Removal of partitions or creation of apertures under this paragraph (c) is not an alteration of boundaries.

§ 38-33.3-212, C.R.S. Relocation of boundaries between adjoining units.

(1)   Subject to the provisions of the declaration and other provisions of law, and pursuant to the procedures described in section 38-33.3-217, the boundaries between adjoining units may be relocated by an amendment to the declaration upon application to the association by the owners of those units.

(2) In order to relocate the boundaries between adjoining units, the owners of those units, as the applicant, must submit an application to the executive board, which application shall be executed by those owners and shall include:

(a) Evidence sufficient to the executive board that the applicant has complied with all local rules and ordinances and that the proposed relocation of boundaries does not violate the terms of any document evidencing a security interest;

(b) The proposed reallocation of interests, if any;

(c) The proposed form for amendments to the declaration, including the plats or maps, as may be necessary to show the altered boundaries between adjoining units, and their dimensions and identifying numbers;

(d) A deposit against attorney fees and costs which the association will incur in reviewing and effectuating the application, in an amount reasonably estimated by the executive board; and

(e) Such other information as may be reasonably requested by the executive board.

(3) No relocation of boundaries between adjoining units shall be effected without the necessary amendments to the declaration, plats, or maps, executed and recorded pursuant to section 38-33.3-217 (3) and (5).

(4) All costs and attorney fees incurred by the association as a result of an application shall be the sole obligation of the applicant.

§ 38-33.3-213, C.R.S. Subdivision of units.

(1) If the declaration expressly so permits, a unit may be subdivided into two or more units. Subject to the provisions of the declaration and other provisions of law, and pursuant to the procedures described in this section, a unit owner may apply to the association to subdivide a unit.

(2) In order to subdivide a unit, the unit owner of such unit, as the applicant, must submit an application to the executive board, which application shall be executed by such owner and shall include:

(a) Evidence that the applicant of the proposed subdivision shall have complied with all building codes, fire codes, zoning codes, planned unit development requirements, master plans, and other applicable ordinances or resolutions adopted and enforced by the local governing body and that the proposed subdivision does not violate the terms of any document evidencing a security interest encumbering the unit;

(b) The proposed reallocation of interests, if any;

(c) The proposed form for amendments to the declaration, including the plats or maps, as may be necessary to show the units which are created by the subdivision and their dimensions, and identifying numbers;

(d) A deposit against attorney fees and costs which the association will incur in reviewing and effectuating the application, in an amount reasonably estimated by the executive board; and

(e) Such other information as may be reasonably requested by the executive board.

(3) No subdivision of units shall be effected without the necessary amendments to the declaration, plats, or maps, executed and recorded pursuant to section 38-33.3-217 (3) and (5).

(4) All costs and attorney fees incurred by the association as a result of an application shall be the sole obligation of the applicant.

§ 38-33.3-214, C.R.S. Easement for encroachments.

To the extent that any unit or common element encroaches on any other unit or common element, a valid easement for the encroachment exists. The easement does not relieve a unit owner of liability in case of willful misconduct nor relieve a declarant or any other person of liability for failure to adhere to the plats and maps.

§ 38-33.3-215, C.R.S. *Use for sales purposes.*

A declarant may maintain sales offices, management offices, and models in the common interest community only if the declaration so provides. Except as provided in a declaration, any real estate in a common interest community used as a sales office, management office, or model and not designated a unit by the declaration is a common element. If a declarant ceases to be a unit owner, such declarant ceases to have any rights with regard to any real estate used as a sales office, management office, or model, unless it is removed promptly from the common interest community in accordance with a right to remove reserved in the declaration. Subject to any limitations in the declaration, a declarant may maintain signs on the common elements advertising the common interest community. This section is subject to the provisions of other state laws and to local ordinances.

§ 38-33.3-216, C.R.S. *Easement rights.*

(1) Subject to the provisions of the declaration, a declarant has an easement through the common elements as may be reasonably necessary for the purpose of discharging a declarant's obligations or exercising special declarant rights, whether arising under this article or reserved in the declaration.

(2) In a planned community, subject to the provisions of the declaration and the ability of the association to regulate and convey or encumber the common elements as set forth in sections 38-33.3-302 (1) (f) and 38-33.3-312, the unit owners have an easement:

   (a) In the common elements for the purpose of access to their units; and

   (b) To use the common elements and all other real estate that must become common elements for all other purposes.

§ 38-33.3-217, C.R.S. *Amendment of declaration.*

(1) (a) (I) Except as otherwise provided in subparagraphs (II) and (III) of this paragraph (a), the declaration, including the plats and maps, may be amended only by the affirmative vote or agreement of unit owners of units to which more than fifty percent of the votes in the association are allocated or any larger percentage, not to exceed sixty-seven percent, that the declaration specifies. Any provision in the declaration that purports to specify a percentage larger than sixty-seven percent is hereby declared void as contrary to public policy, and until amended, such provision shall be deemed to specify a percentage of sixty-seven percent. The declaration may specify a smaller percentage than a simple majority only if all of the units are restricted exclusively to nonresidential use. Nothing in this paragraph (a) shall be construed to prohibit the association from seeking a court order, in accordance with subsection (7) of this section, to reduce the required percentage to less than sixty-seven percent.

   (II) If the declaration provides for an initial period of applicability to be followed by automatic extension periods, the declaration may be amended at any time in accordance with subparagraph (I) of this paragraph (a).

   (III) This paragraph (a) shall not apply:

      (A) To the extent that its application is limited by subsection (4) of this section;

      (B) To amendments executed by a declarant under section 38-33.3-205 (4) and (5), 38-33.3-208 (3), 38-33.3-209 (6), 38-33.3-210, or 38-33.3-222;

(C) To amendments executed by an association under section 38-33.3-107, 38-33.3-206 (4), 38-33.3-208 (2), 38-33.3-212, 38-33.3-213, or 38-33.3-218 (11) and (12);

(D) To amendments executed by the district court for any county that includes all or any portion of a common interest community under subsection (7) of this section; or

(E) To amendments that affect phased communities or declarant-controlled communities.

(b) (I) If the declaration requires first mortgagees to approve or consent to amendments, but does not set forth a procedure for registration or notification of first mortgagees, the association may:

(A) Send a dated, written notice and a copy of any proposed amendment by certified mail to each first mortgagee at its most recent address as shown on the recorded deed of trust or recorded assignment thereof; and

(B) Cause the dated notice, together with information on how to obtain a copy of the proposed amendment, to be printed in full at least twice, on separate occasions at least one week apart, in a newspaper of general circulation in the county in which the common interest community is located.

(II) A first mortgagee that does not deliver to the association a negative response within sixty days after the date of the notice specified in subparagraph (I) of this paragraph (b) shall be deemed to have approved the proposed amendment.

(III) The notification procedure set forth in this paragraph (b) is not mandatory. If the consent of first mortgagees is obtained without resort to this paragraph (b), and otherwise in accordance with the declaration, the notice to first mortgagees shall be considered sufficient.

(2) No action to challenge the validity of an amendment adopted by the association pursuant to this section may be brought more than one year after the amendment is recorded.

(3) Every amendment to the declaration must be recorded in every county in which any portion of the common interest community is located and is effective only upon recordation. An amendment must be indexed in the grantee's index in the name of the common interest community and the association and in the grantor's index in the name of each person executing the amendment.

(4) (a) Except to the extent expressly permitted or required by other provisions of this article, no amendment may create or increase special declarant rights, increase the number of units, or change the boundaries of any unit or the allocated interests of a unit in the absence of a vote or agreement of unit owners of units to which at least sixty-seven percent of the votes in the association, including sixty-seven percent of the votes allocated to units not owned by a declarant, are allocated or any larger percentage the declaration specifies. The declaration may specify a smaller percentage only if all of the units are restricted exclusively to nonresidential use.

(b) The sixty-seven-percent maximum percentage stated in paragraph (a) of subsection (1) of this section shall not apply to any common interest community in which one unit owner, by virtue of the declaration, bylaws, or other governing documents of the association, is allocated sixty-seven percent or more of the votes in the association.

(4.5) Except to the extent expressly permitted or required by other provisions of this article, no amendment may change the uses to which any unit is restricted in the absence of a vote or agreement of unit owners of units to which at least sixty-seven percent of the votes in the association are allocated or any larger percentage the declaration specifies. The declaration may specify a smaller percentage only if all of the units are restricted exclusively to nonresidential use.

(5) Amendments to the declaration required by this article to be recorded by the association shall be prepared, executed, recorded, and certified on behalf of the association by any officer of the association designated for that purpose or, in the absence of designation, by the president of the association.

(6) All expenses associated with preparing and recording an amendment to the declaration shall be the sole responsibility of:

   (a) In the case of an amendment pursuant to sections 38-33.3-208 (2), 38-33.3-212, and 38-33.3-213, the unit owners desiring the amendment; and

   (b) In the case of an amendment pursuant to section 38-33.3-208 (3), 38-33.3-209 (6), or 38-33.3-210, the declarant; and

   (c) In all other cases, the association.

(7) (a) The association, acting through its executive board pursuant to section 38-33.3-303 (1), may petition the district court for any county that includes all or any portion of the common interest community for an order amending the declaration of the common interest community if:

      (I) The association has twice sent notice of the proposed amendment to all unit owners that are entitled by the declaration to vote on the proposed amendment or are required for approval of the proposed amendment by any means allowed pursuant to the provisions regarding notice to members in sections 7-121-402 and 7-127-104, C.R.S., of the "Colorado Revised Nonprofit Corporation Act", articles 121 to 137 of title 7, C.R.S.;

      (II) The association has discussed the proposed amendment during at least one meeting of the association; and

      (III) Unit owners of units to which are allocated more than fifty percent of the number of consents, approvals, or votes of the association that would be required to adopt the proposed amendment pursuant to the declaration have voted in favor of the proposed amendment.

   (b) A petition filed pursuant to paragraph (a) of this subsection (7) shall include:

      (I) A summary of:

         (A) The procedures and requirements for amending the declaration that are set forth in the declaration;

         (B) The proposed amendment to the declaration;

         (C) The effect of and reason for the proposed amendment, including a statement of the circumstances that make the amendment necessary or advisable;

         (D) The results of any vote taken with respect to the proposed amendment; and

         (E) Any other matters that the association believes will be useful to the court in deciding whether to grant the petition; and

      (II) As exhibits, copies of:

         (A) The declaration as originally recorded and any recorded amendments to the declaration;

         (B) The text of the proposed amendment;

         (C) Copies of any notices sent pursuant to subparagraph (I) of paragraph (a) of this subsection (7); and

         (D) Any other documents that the association believes will be useful to the court in deciding whether to grant the petition.

(c) Within three days of the filing of the petition, the district court shall set a date for hearing the petition. Unless the court finds that an emergency requires an immediate hearing, the hearing shall be held no earlier than forty-five days and no later than sixty days after the date the association filed the petition.

(d) No later than ten days after the date for hearing a petition is set pursuant to paragraph (c) of this subsection (7), the association shall:

(I) Send notice of the petition by any written means allowed pursuant to the provisions regarding notice to members in sections 7-121-402 and 7-127-104, C.R.S., of the "Colorado Revised Nonprofit Corporation Act", articles 121 to 137 of title 7, C.R.S., to any unit owner, by first-class mail, postage prepaid or by hand delivery to any declarant, and by first-class mail, postage prepaid, to any lender that holds a security interest in one or more units and is entitled by the declaration or any underwriting guidelines or requirements of that lender or of the federal national mortgage association, the federal home loan mortgage corporation, the federal housing administration, the veterans administration, or the government national mortgage corporation to vote on the proposed amendment. The notice shall include:

(A) A copy of the petition which need not include the exhibits attached to the original petition filed with the district court;

(B) The date the district court will hear the petition; and

(C) A statement that the court may grant the petition and order the proposed amendment to the declaration unless any declarant entitled by the declaration to vote on the proposed amendment, the federal housing administration, the veterans administration, more than thirty-three percent of the unit owners entitled by the declaration to vote on the proposed amendment, or more than thirty-three percent of the lenders that hold a security interest in one or more units and are entitled by the declaration to vote on the proposed amendment file written objections to the proposed amendment with the court prior to the hearing;

(II) File with the district court:

(A) A list of the names and mailing addresses of declarants, unit owners, and lenders that hold a security interest in one or more units and that are entitled by the declaration to vote on the proposed amendment; and

(B) A copy of the notice required by subparagraph (I) of this paragraph (d).

(e) The district court shall grant the petition after hearing if it finds that:

(I) The association has complied with all requirements of this subsection (7);

(II) No more than thirty-three percent of the unit owners entitled by the declaration to vote on the proposed amendment have filed written objections to the proposed amendment with the court prior to the hearing;

(III) Neither the federal housing administration nor the veterans administration is entitled to approve the proposed amendment, or if so entitled has not filed written objections to the proposed amendment with the court prior to the hearing;

(IV) Either the proposed amendment does not eliminate any rights or privileges designated in the declaration as belonging to a declarant or no declarant has filed written objections to the proposed amendment with the court prior to the hearing;

(V) Either the proposed amendment does not eliminate any rights or privileges designated in the declaration as belonging to any lenders that hold security interests in one or more units and that are entitled by the declaration to vote on the proposed amendment or no more than thirty-three percent of such lenders have filed written objections to the proposed amendment with the court prior to the hearing; and

(VI) The proposed amendment would neither terminate the declaration nor change the allocated interests of the unit owners as specified in the declaration, except as allowed pursuant to section 38-33.3-315.

(f) Upon granting a petition, the court shall enter an order approving the proposed amendment and requiring the association to record the amendment in each county that includes all or any portion of the common interest community. Once recorded, the amendment shall have the same legal effect as if it were adopted pursuant to any requirements set forth in the declaration.

§ 38-33.3-218, C.R.S. Termination of common interest community.

(1) Except in the case of a taking of all the units by eminent domain, or in the case of foreclosure against an entire cooperative of a security interest that has priority over the declaration, a common interest community may be terminated only by agreement of unit owners of units to which at least sixty-seven percent of the votes in the association are allocated or any larger percentage the declaration specifies. The declaration may specify a smaller percentage only if all of the units in the common interest community are restricted exclusively to nonresidential uses.

(1.5) No planned community that is required to exist pursuant to a development or site plan shall be terminated by agreement of unit owners, unless a copy of the termination agreement is sent by certified mail or hand delivered to the governing body of every municipality in which a portion of the planned community is situated or, if the planned community is situated in an unincorporated area, to the board of county commissioners for every county in which a portion of the planned community is situated.

(2) An agreement of unit owners to terminate must be evidenced by their execution of a termination agreement or ratifications thereof in the same manner as a deed, by the requisite number of unit owners. The termination agreement must specify a date after which the agreement will be void unless it is recorded before that date. A termination agreement and all ratifications thereof must be recorded in every county in which a portion of the common interest community is situated and is effective only upon recordation.

(3) In the case of a condominium or planned community containing only units having horizontal boundaries described in the declaration, a termination agreement may provide that all of the common elements and units of the common interest community must be sold following termination. If, pursuant to the agreement, any real estate in the common interest community is to be sold following termination, the termination agreement must set forth the minimum terms of the sale.

(4) In the case of a condominium or planned community containing any units not having horizontal boundaries described in the declaration, a termination agreement may provide for sale of the common elements, but it may not require that the units be sold following termination, unless the declaration as originally recorded provided otherwise or all the unit owners consent to the sale.

(5) Subject to the provisions of a termination agreement described in subsections (3) and (4) of this section, the association, on behalf of the unit owners, may contract for the sale of real estate in a common interest community following termination, but the contract is not binding on the unit owners until approved pursuant to subsections (1) and (2) of this section. If any real estate is to be sold following termination, title to that real estate, upon termination, vests in the association as trustee for the holders of all interests in the units. Thereafter, the association has all the powers necessary and appropriate to effect the sale. Until the sale has been concluded and the proceeds thereof distributed, the association continues in existence with all the powers it had

before termination. Proceeds of the sale must be distributed to unit owners and lienholders as their interests may appear, in accordance with subsections (8), (9), and (10) of this section, taking into account the value of property owned or distributed that is not sold so as to preserve the proportionate interests of each unit owner with respect to all property cumulatively. Unless otherwise specified in the termination agreement, as long as the association holds title to the real estate, each unit owner and the unit owner's successors in interest have an exclusive right to occupancy of the portion of the real estate that formerly constituted the unit. During the period of that occupancy, each unit owner and the unit owner's successors in interest remain liable for all assessments and other obligations imposed on unit owners by this article or the declaration.

(6) (a) In a planned community, if all or a portion of the common elements are not to be sold following termination, title to the common elements not sold vests in the unit owners upon termination as tenants in common in fractional interests that maintain, after taking into account the fair market value of property owned and the proceeds of property sold, their respective interests as provided in subsection (10) of this section with respect to all property appraised under said subsection (10), and liens on the units shift accordingly.

(b) In a common interest community, containing units having horizontal boundaries described in the declaration, title to the units not to be sold following termination vests in the unit owners upon termination as tenants in common in fractional interests that maintain, after taking into account the fair market value of property owned and the proceeds of property sold, their respective interests as provided in subsection (10) of this section with respect to all property appraised under said subsection (10), and liens on the units shift accordingly. While the tenancy in common exists, each unit owner and the unit owner's successors in interest have an exclusive right to occupancy of the portion of the real estate that formerly constituted such unit.

(7) Following termination of the common interest community, the proceeds of any sale of real estate, together with the assets of the association, are held by the association as trustee for unit owners and holders of liens on the units as their interests may appear.

(8) Upon termination of a condominium or planned community, creditors of the association who obtain a lien and duly record it in every county in which any portion of the common interest community is located are to be treated as if they had perfected liens on the units immediately before termination or when the lien is obtained and recorded, whichever is later.

(9) In a cooperative, the declaration may provide that all creditors of the association have priority over any interests of unit owners and creditors of unit owners. In that event, upon termination, creditors of the association who obtain a lien and duly record it in every county in which any portion of the cooperative is located are to be treated as if they had perfected liens against the cooperative immediately before termination or when the lien is obtained and recorded, whichever is later. Unless the declaration provides that all creditors of the association have that priority:

(a) The lien of each creditor of the association which was perfected against the association before termination becomes, upon termination, a lien against each unit owner's interest in the unit as of the date the lien was perfected;

(b) Any other creditor of the association who obtains a lien and duly records it in every county in which any portion of the cooperative is located is to be treated upon termination as if the creditor had perfected a lien against each unit owner's interest immediately before termination or when the lien is obtained and recorded, whichever is later;

(c) The amount of the lien of an association's creditor described in paragraphs (a) and (b) of this subsection (9) against each unit owner's interest must be proportionate to the ratio which each unit's common expense liability bears to the common expense liability of all of the units;

(d)   The lien of each creditor of each unit owner which was perfected before termination continues as a lien against that unit owner's unit as of the date the lien was perfected; and

(e)   The assets of the association must be distributed to all unit owners and all lienholders as their interests may appear in the order described above. Creditors of the association are not entitled to payment from any unit owner in excess of the amount of the creditor's lien against that unit owner's interest.

(10)   The respective interests of unit owners referred to in subsections (5) to (9) of this section are as follows:

(a)   Except as provided in paragraph (b) of this subsection (10), the respective interests of unit owners are the combined fair market values of their units, allocated interests, any limited common elements, and, in the case of a planned community, any tenant in common interest, immediately before the termination, as determined by one or more independent appraisers selected by the association. The decision of the independent appraisers shall be distributed to the unit owners and becomes final unless disapproved within thirty days after distribution by unit owners of units to which twenty-five percent of the votes in the association are allocated. The proportion of any unit owner's interest to that of all unit owners is determined by dividing the fair market value of that unit owner's unit and its allocated interests by the total fair market values of all the units and their allocated interests.

(b)   If any unit or any limited common element is destroyed to the extent that an appraisal of the fair market value thereof prior to destruction cannot be made, the interests of all unit owners are:

(I)   In a condominium, their respective common element interests immediately before the termination;

(II)   In a cooperative, their respective ownership interests immediately before the termination; and

(III) In a planned community, their respective common expense liabilities immediately before the termination.

(11)   In a condominium or planned community, except as provided in subsection (12) of this section, foreclosure or enforcement of a lien or encumbrance against the entire common interest community does not terminate, of itself, the common interest community. Foreclosure or enforcement of a lien or encumbrance against a portion of the common interest community other than withdrawable real estate does not withdraw that portion from the common interest community. Foreclosure or enforcement of a lien or encumbrance against withdrawable real estate does not withdraw, of itself, that real estate from the common interest community, but the person taking title thereto may require from the association, upon request, an amendment to the declaration excluding the real estate from the common interest community prepared, executed, and recorded by the association.

(12)   In a condominium or planned community, if a lien or encumbrance against a portion of the real estate comprising the common interest community has priority over the declaration and the lien or encumbrance has not been partially released, the parties foreclosing the lien or encumbrance, upon foreclosure, may record an instrument excluding the real estate subject to that lien or encumbrance from the common interest community. The board of directors shall reallocate interests as if the foreclosed section were taken by eminent domain by an amendment to the declaration prepared, executed, and recorded by the association.

§ 38-33.3-219, C.R.S. Rights of secured lenders.

(1)   The declaration may require that all or a specified number or percentage of the lenders who hold security interests encumbering the units approve specified actions of the unit owners or the association as a condition to the effectiveness of those actions, but no requirement for approval may operate to:

(a)   Deny or delegate control over the general administrative affairs of the association by the unit owners or the executive board; or

(b)   Prevent the association or the executive board from commencing, intervening in, or settling any solicitation or proceeding; or

(c)   Prevent any insurance trustee or the association from receiving and distributing any insurance proceeds pursuant to section 38-33.3-313.

§ 38-33.3-220, C.R.S. Master associations.

(1)   If the declaration provides that any of the powers of a unit owners' association described in section 38-33.3-302 are to be exercised by or may be delegated to a master association, all provisions of this article applicable to unit owners' associations apply to any such master association except as modified by this section.

(2)   Unless it is acting in the capacity of an association described in section 38-33.3-301, a master association may exercise the powers set forth in section 38-33.3-302 (1) (b) only to the extent such powers are expressly permitted to be exercised by a master association in the declarations of common interest communities which are part of the master association or expressly described in the delegations of power from those common interest communities to the master association.

(3)   If the declaration of any common interest community provides that the executive board may delegate certain powers to a master association, the members of the executive board have no liability for the acts or omissions of the master association with respect to those powers following delegation.

(4)   The rights and responsibilities of unit owners with respect to the unit owners' association set forth in sections 38-33.3-303, 38-33.3-308, 38-33.3-309, 38-33.3-310, and 38-33.3-312 apply in the conduct of the affairs of a master association only to persons who elect the board of a master association, whether or not those persons are otherwise unit owners within the meaning of this article.

(5)   Even if a master association is also an association described in section 38-33.3-301, the articles of incorporation and the declaration of each common interest community, the powers of which are assigned by the declaration or delegated to the master association, must provide that the executive board of the master association be elected after the period of declarant control, if any, in one of the following ways:

(a)   All unit owners of all common interest communities subject to the master association may elect all members of the master association's executive board.

(b)   All members of the executive boards of all common interest communities subject to the master association may elect all members of the master association's executive board.

(c)   All unit owners of each common interest community subject to the master association may elect specified members of the master association's executive board.

(d)   All members of the executive board of each common interest community subject to the master association may elect specified members of the master association's executive board.

§ 38-33.3-221, C.R.S. Merger or consolidation of common interest communities.

(1) Any two or more common interest communities of the same form of ownership, by agreement of the unit owners as provided in subsection (2) of this section, may be merged or consolidated into a single common interest community. In the event of a merger or consolidation, unless the agreement otherwise provides, the resultant common interest community is the legal successor, for all purposes, of all of the preexisting common interest communities, and the operations and activities of all associations of the preexisting common interest communities are merged or consolidated into a single association that holds all powers, rights, obligations, assets, and liabilities of all preexisting associations.

(2) An agreement of two or more common interest communities to merge or consolidate pursuant to subsection (1) of this section must be evidenced by an agreement prepared, executed, recorded, and certified by the president of the association of each of the preexisting common interest communities following approval by owners of units to which are allocated the percentage of votes in each common interest community required to terminate that common interest community. The agreement must be recorded in every county in which a portion of the common interest community is located and is not effective until recorded.

(3) Every merger or consolidation agreement must provide for the reallocation of the allocated interests in the new association among the units of the resultant common interest community either by stating the reallocations or the formulas upon which they are based.

§ 38-33.3-221.5, C.R.S. Withdrawal from merged common interest community

(1) A common interest community that was merged or consolidated with another common interest community, or is party to an agreement to do so pursuant to section 38-33.3-221, may withdraw from the merged or consolidated common interest community or terminate the agreement to merge or consolidate, without the consent of the other common interest community or communities involved, if the common interest community wishing to withdraw meets all of the following criteria:

(a) It is a separate, platted subdivision;

(b) Its unit owners are required to pay into two common interest communities or separate unit owners' associations;

(c) It is or has been a self-operating common interest community or association continuously for at least twenty-five years;

(d) The total number of unit owners comprising it is fifteen percent or less of the total number of unit owners in the merged or consolidated common interest community or association;

(e) Its unit owners have approved the withdrawal by a majority vote and the owners of units representing at least seventy-five percent of the allocated interests in the common interest community wishing to withdraw participated in the vote; and

(f) Its withdrawal would not substantially impair the ability of the remainder of the merged common interest community or association to:

(I) Enforce existing covenants;

(II) Maintain existing facilities; or

(III) Continue to exist.

(2) If an association has met the requirements set forth in subsection (1) of this section, it shall be considered withdrawn as of the date of the election at which its unit owners voted to withdraw.

§ 38-33.3-222, C.R.S. Addition of unspecified real estate.

In a common interest community, if the right is originally reserved in the declaration, the declarant, in addition to any other development right, may amend the declaration at any time during as many years as are specified in the declaration to add additional real estate to the common interest community without describing the location of that real estate in the original declaration; but the area of real estate added to the common interest community pursuant to this section may not exceed ten percent of the total area of real estate described in section 38-33.3-205 (1) (c) and (1) (h), and the declarant may not in any event increase the number of units in the common interest community beyond the number stated in the original declaration pursuant to section 38-33.3-205 (1) (d), except as provided in section 38-33.3-217 (4).

§ 38-33.3-223, C.R.S. Sale of unit – disclosure to buyer. (Repealed)

§ 38-33.3-301, C.R.S. Organization of unit owners' association.

A unit owners' association shall be organized no later than the date the first unit in the common interest community is conveyed to a purchaser. The membership of the association at all times shall consist exclusively of all unit owners or, following termination of the common interest community, of all former unit owners entitled to distributions of proceeds under section 38-33.3-218, or their heirs, personal representatives, successors, or assigns. The association shall be organized as a nonprofit, not-for-profit, or for-profit corporation or as a limited liability company in accordance with the laws of the state of Colorado; except that the failure of the association to incorporate or organize as a limited liability company will not adversely affect either the existence of the common interest community for purposes of this article or the rights of persons acting in reliance upon such existence, other than as specifically provided in section 38-33.3-316. Neither the choice of entity nor the organizational structure of the association shall be deemed to affect its substantive rights and obligations under this article.

§ 38-33.3-302, C.R.S. Powers of unit owners' association.

(1) Except as provided in subsections (2) and (3) of this section, and subject to the provisions of the declaration, the association, without specific authorization in the declaration, may:

    (a) Adopt and amend bylaws and rules and regulations;

    (b) Adopt and amend budgets for revenues, expenditures, and reserves and collect assessments for common expenses from unit owners;

    (c) Hire and terminate managing agents and other employees, agents, and independent contractors;

    (d) Institute, defend, or intervene in litigation or administrative proceedings in its own name on behalf of itself or two or more unit owners on matters affecting the common interest community;

    (e) Make contracts and incur liabilities;

    (f) Regulate the use, maintenance, repair, replacement, and modification of common elements;

    (g) Cause additional improvements to be made as a part of the common elements;

    (h) Acquire, hold, encumber, and convey in its own name any right, title, or interest to real or personal property, subject to the following exceptions:

        (I) Common elements in a condominium or planned community may be conveyed or subjected to a security interest only pursuant to section 38-33.3-312; and

        (II) Part of a cooperative may be conveyed, or all or part of a cooperative may be subjected to a security interest, only pursuant to section 38-33.3-312;

(i)   Grant easements, leases, licenses, and concessions through or over the common elements;

(j)   Impose and receive any payments, fees, or charges for the use, rental, or operation of the common elements other than limited common elements described in section 38-33.3-202 (1) (b) and (1) (d);

(k)   (I)   Impose charges for late payment of assessments, recover reasonable attorney fees and other legal costs for collection of assessments and other actions to enforce the power of the association, regardless of whether or not suit was initiated, and, after notice and an opportunity to be heard, levy reasonable fines for violations of the declaration, bylaws, and rules and regulations of the association.

         (II)   The association may not levy fines against a unit owner for violations of declarations, bylaws, or rules of the association for failure to adequately water landscapes or vegetation for which the unit owner is responsible when water restrictions or guidelines from the local water district or similar entity are in place and the unit owner is watering in compliance with such restrictions or guidelines. The association may require proof from the unit owner that the unit owner is watering the landscape or vegetation in a manner that is consistent with the maximum watering permitted by the restrictions or guidelines then in effect.

(*l*)   Impose reasonable charges for the preparation and recordation of amendments to the declaration or statements of unpaid assessments;

(m)   Provide for the indemnification of its officers and executive board and maintain directors' and officers' liability insurance;

(n)   Assign its right to future income, including the right to receive common expense assessments, but only to the extent the declaration expressly so provides;

(o)   Exercise any other powers conferred by the declaration or bylaws;

(p)   Exercise all other powers that may be exercised in this state by legal entities of the same type as the association; and

(q)   Exercise any other powers necessary and proper for the governance and operation of the association.

(2)   The declaration may not impose limitations on the power of the association to deal with the declarant that are more restrictive than the limitations imposed on the power of the association to deal with other persons.

(3)   (a)   Any managing agent, employee, independent contractor, or other person acting on behalf of the association shall be subject to this article to the same extent as the association itself would be.

       (b)   Decisions concerning the approval or denial of a unit owner's application for architectural or landscaping changes shall be made in accordance with standards and procedures set forth in the declaration or in duly adopted rules and regulations or bylaws of the association, and shall not be made arbitrarily or capriciously.

(4)   (a)   The association's contract with a managing agent shall be terminable for cause without penalty to the association. Any such contract shall be subject to renegotiation.

       (b)   Notwithstanding section 38-33.3-117 (1.5) (g), this subsection (4) shall not apply to an association that includes time-share units, as defined in section 38-33-110 (7).

§ 38-33.3-303, C.R.S. Executive board members and officers – powers and duties – reserve funds – reserve study – audit.

(1)   (a)   Except as provided in the declaration, the bylaws, or subsection (3) of this section or any other provisions of this article, the executive board may act in all instances on behalf of the association.

(b) Notwithstanding any provision of the declaration or bylaws to the contrary, all members of the executive board shall have available to them all information related to the responsibilities and operation of the association obtained by any other member of the executive board. This information shall include, but is not necessarily limited to, reports of detailed monthly expenditures, contracts to which the association is a party, and copies of communications, reports, and opinions to and from any member of the executive board or any managing agent, attorney, or accountant employed or engaged by the executive board to whom the executive board delegates responsibilities under this article.

(2) Except as otherwise provided in subsection (2.5) of this section:

(a) If appointed by the declarant, in the performance of their duties, the officers and members of the executive board are required to exercise the care required of fiduciaries of the unit owners.

(b) If not appointed by the declarant, no member of the executive board and no officer shall be liable for actions taken or omissions made in the performance of such member's duties except for wanton and willful acts or omissions.

(2.5) With regard to the investment of reserve funds of the association, the officers and members of the executive board shall be subject to the standards set forth in section 7-128-401, C.R.S.; except that, as used in that section:

(a) "Corporation" or "nonprofit corporation" means the association.

(b) "Director" means a member of the association's executive board.

(c) "Officer" means any person designated as an officer of the association and any person to whom the executive board delegates responsibilities under this article, including, without limitation, a managing agent, attorney, or accountant employed by the executive board.

(3) (a) The executive board may not act on behalf of the association to amend the declaration, to terminate the common interest community, or to elect members of the executive board or determine the qualifications, powers and duties, or terms of office of executive board members, but the executive board may fill vacancies in its membership for the unexpired portion of any term.

(b) Committees of the association shall be appointed pursuant to the governing documents of the association or, if the governing documents contain no applicable provisions, pursuant to section 7-128-206, C.R.S. The person appointed after August 15, 2009, to preside over any such committee shall meet the same qualifications as are required by the governing documents of the association for election or appointment to the executive board of the association.

(4) (a) (I) Within ninety days after adoption of a proposed budget for the common interest community, the executive board shall mail, by first-class mail, or otherwise deliver, including posting the proposed budget on the association's website, a summary of the budget to all the unit owners and shall set a date for a meeting of the unit owners to consider the budget. The meeting must occur within a reasonable time after mailing or other delivery of the summary, or as allowed for in the bylaws. The executive board shall give notice to the unit owners of the meeting as allowed for in the bylaws.

(II) (A) Unless the declaration requires otherwise, the budget proposed by the executive board does not require approval from the unit owners and it will be deemed approved by the unit owners in the absence of a veto at the noticed meeting by a majority of all unit owners, or if permitted in the declaration, a majority of a class of unit owners, or any larger percentage specified in the declaration, whether or not a quorum is present. If the proposed budget is vetoed, the periodic budget last proposed by the executive board and not vetoed by the unit owners must be continued until a subsequent budget proposed by the executive board is not vetoed by the unit owners.

(B)   This subsection (4)(a)(II) shall not apply to any common interest community formed prior to July 1, 1992, if the declaration sets a maximum assessment amount or limits the increase in an annual budget to a specific amount and the budget proposed by the executive board does not exceed the maximum amount or limits set in the declaration.

(b)   (I)   At the discretion of the executive board or upon request pursuant to subparagraph (II) or (III) of this paragraph (b) as applicable, the books and records of the association shall be subject to an audit, using generally accepted auditing standards, or a review, using statements on standards for accounting and review services, by an independent and qualified person selected by the board. Such person need not be a certified public accountant except in the case of an audit. A person selected to conduct a review shall have at least a basic understanding of the principles of accounting as a result of prior business experience, education above the high school level, or bona fide home study. The audit or review report shall cover the association's financial statements, which shall be prepared using generally accepted accounting principles or the cash or tax basis of accounting.

(II)   An audit shall be required under this paragraph (b) only when both of the following conditions are met:

(A)   The association has annual revenues or expenditures of at least two hundred fifty thousand dollars; and

(B)   An audit is requested by the owners of at least one-third of the units represented by the association.

(III)   A review shall be required under this paragraph (b) only when requested by the owners of at least one-third of the units represented by the association.

(IV)   Copies of an audit or review under this paragraph (b) shall be made available upon request to any unit owner beginning no later than thirty days after its completion.

(V)   Notwithstanding section 38-33.3-117 (1.5) (h), this paragraph (b) shall not apply to an association that includes time-share units, as defined in section 38-33-110 (7).

(5)   (a)   Subject to subsection (6) of this section:

(I)   The declaration, except a declaration for a large planned community, may provide for a period of declarant control of the association, during which period a declarant, or persons designated by such declarant, may appoint and remove the officers and members of the executive board. Regardless of the period of declarant control provided in the declaration, a period of declarant control terminates no later than the earlier of sixty days after conveyance of seventy-five percent of the units that may be created to unit owners other than a declarant, two years after the last conveyance of a unit by the declarant in the ordinary course of business, or two years after any right to add new units was last exercised.

(II)   The declaration for a large planned community may provide for a period of declarant control of the association during which period a declarant, or persons designated by such declarant, may appoint and remove the officers and members of the executive board. Regardless of the period of declarant control provided in the declaration, a period of declarant control terminates in a large planned community no later than the earlier of sixty days after conveyance of seventy-five percent of the maximum number of units that may be created under zoning or other governmental development approvals in effect for the large planned community at any given time to unit owners other than a declarant, six years after the last conveyance of a unit by the declarant in the ordinary course of business, or twenty years after recordation of the declaration.

(b)   A declarant may voluntarily surrender the right to appoint and remove officers and members of the executive board before termination of the period of declarant control, but, in that event, the declarant may require, for the duration of the period of declarant control, that specified actions of the association or executive board, as described in a recorded instrument executed by the declarant, be approved by the declarant before they become effective.

(c)   If a period of declarant control is to terminate in a large planned community pursuant to subparagraph (II) of paragraph (a) of this subsection (5), the declarant, or persons designated by the declarant, shall no longer have the right to appoint and remove the officers and members of the executive board unless, prior to the termination date, the association approves an extension of the declarant's ability to appoint and remove no more than a majority of the executive board by vote of a majority of the votes entitled to be cast in person or by proxy, other than by the declarant, at a meeting duly convened as required by law. Any such approval by the association may contain conditions and limitations. Such extension of declarant's appointment and removal power, together with any conditions and limitations approved as provided in this paragraph (c), shall be included in an amendment to the declaration previously executed by the declarant.

(6)   Not later than sixty days after conveyance of twenty-five percent of the units that may be created to unit owners other than a declarant, at least one member and not less than twenty-five percent of the members of the executive board must be elected by unit owners other than the declarant. Not later than sixty days after conveyance of fifty percent of the units that may be created to unit owners other than a declarant, not less than thirty-three and one-third percent of the members of the executive board must be elected by unit owners other than the declarant.

(7)   Except as otherwise provided in section 38-33.3-220 (5), not later than the termination of any period of declarant control, the unit owners shall elect an executive board of at least three members, at least a majority of whom must be unit owners other than the declarant or designated representatives of unit owners other than the declarant. The executive board shall elect the officers. The executive board members and officers shall take office upon election.

(8)   Notwithstanding any provision of the declaration or bylaws to the contrary, the unit owners, by a vote of sixty-seven percent of all persons present and entitled to vote at any meeting of the unit owners at which a quorum is present, may remove any member of the executive board with or without cause, other than a member appointed by the declarant or a member elected pursuant to a class vote under section 38-33.3-207 (4).

(9)   Within sixty days after the unit owners other than the declarant elect a majority of the members of the executive board, the declarant shall deliver to the association all property of the unit owners and of the association held by or controlled by the declarant, including without limitation the following items:

(a)   The original or a certified copy of the recorded declaration as amended, the association's articles of incorporation, if the association is incorporated, bylaws, minute books, other books and records, and any rules and regulations which may have been promulgated;

(b)   An accounting for association funds and financial statements, from the date the association received funds and ending on the date the period of declarant control ends. The financial statements shall be audited by an independent certified public accountant and shall be accompanied by the accountant's letter, expressing either the opinion that the financial statements present fairly the financial position of the association in conformity with generally accepted accounting principles or a disclaimer of the accountant's ability to attest to the fairness of the presentation of the financial information in conformity with generally accepted accounting principles and the reasons therefor. The expense of the audit shall not be paid for or charged to the association.

(c)   The association funds or control thereof;

(d)   All of the declarant's tangible personal property that has been represented by the declarant to be the property of the association or all of the declarant's tangible personal property that is necessary for, and has been used exclusively in, the operation and enjoyment of the common elements, and inventories of these properties;

(e)   A copy, for the nonexclusive use by the association, of any plans and specifications used in the construction of the improvements in the common interest community;

(f)   All insurance policies then in force, in which the unit owners, the association, or its directors and officers are named as insured persons;

(g)   Copies of any certificates of occupancy that may have been issued with respect to any improvements comprising the common interest community;

(h)   Any other permits issued by governmental bodies applicable to the common interest community and which are currently in force or which were issued within one year prior to the date on which unit owners other than the declarant took control of the association;

(i)   Written warranties of the contractor, subcontractors, suppliers, and manufacturers that are still effective;

(j)   A roster of unit owners and mortgagees and their addresses and telephone numbers, if known, as shown on the declarant's records;

(k)   Employment contracts in which the association is a contracting party;

(*l*)   Any service contract in which the association is a contracting party or in which the association or the unit owners have any obligation to pay a fee to the persons performing the services; and

(m)   For large planned communities, copies of all recorded deeds and all recorded and unrecorded leases evidencing ownership or leasehold rights of the large planned community unit owners' association in all common elements within the large planned community.

§ 38-33.3-303.5, C.R.S. Construction defect actions – disclosure – approval by unit owners – definitions – exemptions.

(1)   (a)   Before the executive board, pursuant to section 38-33.3-302 (1)(d), institutes a construction defect action, the executive board shall comply with this section.

     (b)   For the purposes of this section only:

       (I)   "Construction defect action":

         (A)   Means any civil action or arbitration proceeding for damages, indemnity, subrogation, or contribution brought against a construction professional to assert a claim, counterclaim, cross-claim, or third-party claim for damages or loss to, or the loss of use of, real or personal property or personal injury caused by a defect in the design or construction of an improvement to real property, regardless of the theory of liability; and

         (B)   Includes any related, ancillary, or derivative claim, and any claim for breach of fiduciary duty or an act or omission of a member of an association's executive board, that arises from an alleged construction defect or that seeks the same or similar damages.

       (II)   "Construction professional" has the meaning set forth in section 13-20-802.5 (4).

(c) **Meeting to consider commencement of construction defect action – disclosures – required terms.**

    (I)   The executive board shall mail or deliver written notice of the anticipated commencement of the construction defect action to each unit owner at the owner's last-known address described in the association's records and to the last-known address of each construction professional against whom a construction defect action is proposed; except that this notice requirement does not apply to:

        (A)   Construction professionals identified after the notice is mailed; or

        (B)   Joined parties in a construction defect action previously approved by owners pursuant to subsection (1)(d) of this section.

    (II)   The notice given pursuant to this subsection (1)(c) must call a meeting of the unit owners, which must be held no less than ten days and no more than fifteen days after the mailing date of the notice, to consider whether to bring a construction defect action. A failure to hold the meeting within this time period voids the subsequent vote. A quorum is not required at the meeting. In no event shall the time period for providing the notice required pursuant to subsection (1)(c)(I) of this section, holding the meeting required pursuant to this subsection (1)(c)(II), and voting as required by subsection (1)(d) of this section exceed ninety days. The notice must state that:

        (A)   The conclusion of the meeting initiates the voting period, during which the association will accept votes for and against proceeding with the construction defect action. The disclosure and voting period shall end ninety days after the mailing date of the meeting notice or when the association determines that the construction defect action is either approved or disapproved, whichever occurs first.

        (B)   The construction professional against whom the construction defect action is proposed will be invited to attend and will have an opportunity to address the unit owners concerning the alleged construction defect; and

        (C)   The presentation at the meeting by the construction professional or the construction professional's designee or designees may, but is not required to, include an offer to remedy any defect in accordance with section 13-20-803.5 (3) of the "Construction Defect Action Reform Act".

    (III)   The notice given pursuant to this subsection (1)(c) must also contain a description of the nature of the construction defect action, which description identifies alleged defects with reasonable specificity, the relief sought, a good-faith estimate of the benefits and risks involved, and any other pertinent information. The notice shall also include the following disclosures:

        1.   The alleged construction defects might result in increased costs to the association in maintenance or repair or cause an increase in assessments or special assessments to cover the cost of repairs.

        2.   If the association does not file a claim before the applicable legal deadlines, the claim will expire.

        3.   Until the alleged defects are repaired, sellers of units within the common interest community might owe unit buyers a duty to disclose known defects.

        4.   The executive board (intends to enter) (has entered) into a fee arrangement with the attorneys representing the association, under which (the attorneys will be paid a contingency fee equal to _____ percent of the (net) (gross) recovery of the amount the association recovers from the defendant(s)) (the

association's attorneys will be paid (an hourly fee of $_____) (a fixed fee of $_____)).

5.   In addition to attorney fees, the association may incur up to $_____ for legal costs, including expert witnesses, depositions, and filing fees. The amount will not be exceeded without the executive board's further written authority. If the association does not prevail on its claim, the association may be responsible for paying these legal expenses.

6.   If the association does not prevail on its claim, the association may be responsible for paying its attorney fees.

7.   If the association does not prevail on its claim, a court or arbitrator sometimes awards costs and attorney fees to the opposing party. Should that happen in this case, the association may be responsible for paying the opposing party's costs and fees as a result of such award.

8.   There is no guarantee that the association will recover enough funds to repair the claimed construction defect(s). If the claimed defects are not repaired, additional damage to property and a reduction in the useful life of the common elements might occur.

9.   Until the claimed construction defects are repaired, or until the construction defect claim is concluded, the market value of the units in the association might be adversely affected.

10.   Until the claimed construction defect(s) are repaired, or until the construction defect(s) claim is concluded, owners in the association might have difficulty refinancing and prospective buyers might have difficulty obtaining financing. In addition, certain federal underwriting standards or regulations prevent refinancing or obtaining a new loan in projects where a construction defect is claimed, and certain lenders as a matter of policy will not refinance or provide a new loan in projects where a construction defect is claimed.

(IV)   The association shall maintain a verified owner mailing list that identifies the owners to whom the association mailed the notice required pursuant to this subsection (1)(c). The verified owner mailing list shall include, for each owner, the address, if any, to which the association mailed the notice required pursuant to this subsection (1)(c). The association shall provide a copy of the verified owner mailing list to each construction professional who is sent a notice pursuant to this subsection (1)(c) at the owner meeting required under subsection (1)(c)(II) of this section. The owner mailing list shall be deemed verified if a specimen copy of the mailing list is certified by an association officer or agent. If the association commences a construction defect action against any construction professional, the association shall file its verified owner mailing list and records of votes received from owners during the voting period with the appropriate forum under seal.

(V)   The substance of a proposed construction defect action may be amended or supplemented after the meeting, but an amended or supplemented claim does not extend the voting period. The executive board shall give notice to unit owners of any amended or supplemented claim and shall maintain records of its communications with unit owners. Owner approval pursuant to subsection (1)(d) of this section is not required for amendments or supplements to a construction defect action made after the notice pursuant to this subsection (1)(c) is sent.

(d)   **Approval by unit owners – procedures.**

(I)   (A)   Notwithstanding any provision of law or any requirement in the governing documents, the executive board may initiate the construction defect action only if authorized within the voting period by owners of units to which a majority of votes in the association are allocated. Such approval is not required for an association to proceed with a construction defect action if the alleged construction defect pertains to a facility that is intended and used for nonresidential purposes and if the cost to repair the alleged defect does not exceed fifty thousand dollars. Such approval is not required for an association to proceed with a construction defect action when the association is the contracting party for the performance of labor or purchase of services or materials.

(B)   Notwithstanding any other provision of law, an owner's vote shall be submitted only once and may be obtained in any written format confirming the owner's vote to approve or reject the proposed construction defect action. The association shall maintain a record of all votes until the conclusion of the construction defect action, including all appeals, if any.

(II)   (A)   Nothing in this section alters the tolling provisions of section 13-20-805.

(B)   All statutes of limitation and repose applicable to claims based on defects described with reasonable specificity in the notice, which may be supplemented or amended pursuant to subsection (1)(c)(IV) of this section, are tolled from the date the notice sent pursuant to subsection (1)(c) of this section is mailed until either the ninety-day voting and disclosure period ends or until the association determines that the construction defect action is either approved or disapproved, whichever occurs first.

(C)   The applicable statutes of limitation and repose that apply to claims based on a defect described in the notice with reasonable specificity are tolled pursuant to this subsection (1)(d)(II) once, and may not extend the statutes of limitation and repose that apply to claims based on that defect for more than a total of ninety days, respectively. If a defect not included in the notice sent pursuant to subsection (1)(c) of this section is the subject of a later vote, tolling pursuant to this subsection (1)(d) applies unless the claim based on that defect is otherwise barred by the statute of limitations or statute of repose.

(III) **Vote count – exclusions.** For purposes of calculating the required majority vote under this subsection (1)(d) only, the following votes are excluded:

(A)   Any votes allocated to units owned by a development party. As used in this subsection (1)(d)(III)(A), "development party" means a contractor, subcontractor, developer, or builder responsible for any part of the design, construction, or repair of any portion of the common interest community and any of that party's affiliates; and "affiliate" includes an entity controlled or owned, in whole or in part, by any person that controls or owns a development party or by the spouse of a development party.

(B)   Any votes allocated to units owned by banking institutions, unless a vote from such an institution is actually received by the association;

(C)   Any votes allocated to units of a product type in which no defects are alleged, in a common interest community whose declaration provides that common expense liabilities are not shared between the product types;

(D)   Any votes allocated to units owned by owners who are deemed nonresponsive. If the status of the nonresponsive unit owners is challenged in court, the court shall consider whether the executive board has made diligent efforts to contact the unit owner regarding the vote and may consider: Whether a mailing was returned as undeliverable; whether the owner appears to be residing at the unit; and whether the association has used other contact information, such as an electronic mail address or telephone number for the owner.

(e) **Notice to construction professional.** At least five business days before the mailing of the notice required by subsection (1)(c) of this section, the association shall notify each construction professional against whom a construction defect action is proposed by mail, at its last-known address, of the date and time of the meeting called to consider the construction defect action pursuant to subsection (1)(c) of this section.

(2) Repealed.

(3) Nothing in this section shall be construed to:

(a) Require the disclosure in the notice or the disclosure to a unit owner of attorney-client communications or other privileged communications;

(b) Permit the notice to serve as a basis for any person to assert the waiver of any applicable privilege or right of confidentiality resulting from, or to claim immunity in connection with, the disclosure of information in the notice; or

(c) Limit or impair the authority of the executive board to contract for legal services, or limit or impair the ability to enforce such a contract for legal services.

(4) **Provisions not severable.** Notwithstanding section 2-4-204, the general assembly finds, determines, and declares that if any provision of this section or its application to any person or circumstance is held invalid, the entire section shall be deemed invalid.

§ 38-33.3-304, C.R.S. Transfer of special declarant rights.

(1) A special declarant right created or reserved under this article may be transferred only by an instrument evidencing the transfer recorded in every county in which any portion of the common interest community is located. The instrument is not effective unless executed by the transferee.

(2) Upon transfer of any special declarant right, the liability of a transferor declarant is as follows:

(a) A transferor is not relieved of any obligation or liability arising before the transfer and remains liable for warranty obligations imposed upon such transferor by this article. Lack of privity does not deprive any unit owner of standing to bring an action to enforce any obligation of the transferor.

(b) If a successor to any special declarant right is an affiliate of a declarant, the transferor is jointly and severally liable with the successor for the liabilities and obligations of the successor which relate to the common interest community.

(c) If a transferor retains any special declarant rights but transfers other special declarant rights to a successor who is not an affiliate of the declarant, the transferor is liable for any obligations or liabilities imposed on a declarant by this article or by the declaration relating to the retained special declarant rights and arising after the transfer.

(d) A transferor has no liability for any act or omission or any breach of a contractual or warranty obligation arising from the exercise of a special declarant right by a successor declarant who is not an affiliate of the transferor.

(3) Unless otherwise provided in a mortgage instrument, deed of trust, or other agreement creating a security interest, in case of foreclosure of a security interest, sale by a trustee under an agreement creating a security interest, tax sale, judicial sale, or sale under bankruptcy or receivership proceedings of any units owned by a declarant or real estate in a common interest community subject to development rights, a person acquiring title to all the property being foreclosed or sold succeeds to only those special declarant rights related to that property held by that declarant which are specified in a written instrument prepared, executed, and recorded

by such person at or about the same time as the judgment or instrument or by which such person obtained title to all of the property being foreclosed or sold.

(4)   Upon foreclosure of a security interest, sale by a trustee under an agreement creating a security interest, tax sale, judicial sale, or sale under bankruptcy act or receivership proceedings of all interests in a common interest community owned by a declarant:

(a)   The declarant ceases to have any special declarant rights; and

(b)   The period of declarant control terminates unless the instrument which is required by subsection (3) of this section to be prepared, executed, and recorded at or about the same time as the judgment or instrument conveying title provides for transfer of all special declarant rights to a successor declarant.

(5)   The liabilities and obligations of persons who succeed to special declarant rights are as follows:

(a)   A successor to any special declarant right who is an affiliate of a declarant is subject to all obligations and liabilities imposed on any declarant by this article or by the declaration.

(b)   A successor to any special declarant right, other than a successor described in paragraph (c) or (d) of this subsection (5) or a successor who is an affiliate of a declarant, is subject to all obligations and liabilities imposed by this article or the declaration:

(I)   On a declarant which relate to the successor's exercise or nonexercise of special declarant rights; or

(II)   On the declarant's transferor, other than:

(A)   Misrepresentations by any previous declarant;

(B)   Warranty obligations on improvements made by any previous declarant or made before the common interest community was created;

(C)   Breach of any fiduciary obligation by any previous declarant or such declarant's appointees to the executive board; or

(D)   Any liability or obligation imposed on the transferor as a result of the transferor's acts or omissions after the transfer.

(c)   A successor to only a right reserved in the declaration to maintain models, sales offices, and signs, if such successor is not an affiliate of a declarant, may not exercise any other special declarant right and is not subject to any liability or obligation as a declarant.

(d)   A successor to all special declarant rights held by a transferor who succeeded to those rights pursuant to the instrument prepared, executed, and recorded by such person pursuant to the provisions of subsection (3) of this section may declare such successor's intention in such recorded instrument to hold those rights solely for transfer to another person. Thereafter, until transferring all special declarant rights to any person acquiring title to any unit or real estate subject to development rights owned by the successor or until recording an instrument permitting exercise of all those rights, that successor may not exercise any of those rights other than the right held by such successor's transferor to control the executive board in accordance with the provisions of section 38-33.3-303 (5) for the duration of any period of declarant control, and any attempted exercise of those rights is void. So long as a successor declarant may not exercise special declarant rights under this subsection (5), such successor declarant is not subject to any liability or obligation as a declarant, other than liability for the successor's acts and omissions under section 38-33.3-303 (4).

(6)   Nothing in this section subjects any successor to a special declarant right to any claims against or other obligations of a transferor declarant, other than claims and obligations arising under this article or the declaration.

§ 38-33.3-305, C.R.S. Termination of contracts and leases of declarant.

(1) The following contracts and leases, if entered into before the executive board elected by the unit owners pursuant to section 38-33.3-303 (7) takes office, may be terminated without penalty by the association, at any time after the executive board elected by the unit owners pursuant to section 38-33.3-303 (7) takes office, upon not less than ninety days' notice to the other party:

    (a) Any management contract, employment contract, or lease of recreational or parking areas or facilities;

    (b) Any other contract or lease between the association and a declarant or an affiliate of a declarant; or

    (c) Any contract or lease that is not bona fide or was unconscionable to the unit owners at the time entered into under the circumstances then prevailing.

(2) Subsection (1) of this section does not apply to any lease the termination of which would terminate the common interest community or reduce its size, unless the real estate subject to that lease was included in the common interest community for the purpose of avoiding the right of the association to terminate a lease under this section or a proprietary lease.

§ 38-33.3-306, C.R.S. Bylaws.

(1) In addition to complying with applicable sections, if any, of the "Colorado Business Corporation Act", articles 101 to 117 of title 7, C.R.S., or the "Colorado Revised Nonprofit Corporation Act", articles 121 to 137 of title 7, C.R.S., if the common interest community is organized pursuant thereto, the bylaws of the association must provide:

    (a) The number of members of the executive board and the titles of the officers of the association;

    (b) Election by the executive board of a president, a treasurer, a secretary, and any other officers of the association the bylaws specify;

    (c) The qualifications, powers and duties, and terms of office of, and manner of electing and removing, executive board members and officers and the manner of filling vacancies;

    (d) Which, if any, of its powers the executive board or officers may delegate to other persons or to a managing agent;

    (e) Which of its officers may prepare, execute, certify, and record amendments to the declaration on behalf of the association; and

    (f) A method for amending the bylaws.

(2) Subject to the provisions of the declaration, the bylaws may provide for any other matters the association deems necessary and appropriate.

(3) (a) If an association with thirty or more units delegates powers of the executive board or officers relating to collection, deposit, transfer, or disbursement of association funds to other persons or to a managing agent, the bylaws of the association shall require the following:

        (I) That the other persons or managing agent maintain fidelity insurance coverage or a bond in an amount not less than fifty thousand dollars or such higher amount as the executive board may require;

        (II) That the other persons or managing agent maintain all funds and accounts of the association separate from the funds and accounts of other associations managed by the other persons or managing agent and maintain all reserve accounts of each association so managed separate from operational accounts of the association;

(III) That an annual accounting for association funds and a financial statement be prepared and presented to the association by the managing agent, a public accountant, or a certified public accountant.

(b) Repealed.

§ 38-33.3-307, C.R.S. Upkeep of the common interest community.

(1) Except to the extent provided by the declaration, subsection (2) of this section, or section 38-33.3-313 (9), the association is responsible for maintenance, repair, and replacement of the common elements, and each unit owner is responsible for maintenance, repair, and replacement of such owner's unit. Each unit owner shall afford to the association and the other unit owners, and to their agents or employees, access through such owner's unit reasonably necessary for those purposes. If damage is inflicted, or a strong likelihood exists that it will be inflicted, on the common elements or any unit through which access is taken, the unit owner responsible for the damage, or expense to avoid damage, or the association if it is responsible, is liable for the cost of prompt repair.

(1.5) Maintenance, repair, or replacement of any drainage structure or facilities, or other public improvements required by the local governmental entity as a condition of development of the common interest community or any part thereof shall be the responsibility of the association, unless such improvements have been dedicated to and accepted by the local governmental entity for the purpose of maintenance, repair, or replacement or unless such maintenance, repair, or replacement has been authorized by law to be performed by a special district or other municipal or quasi-municipal entity.

(2) In addition to the liability that a declarant as a unit owner has under this article, the declarant alone is liable for all expenses in connection with real estate within the common interest community subject to development rights. No other unit owner and no other portion of the common interest community is subject to a claim for payment of those expenses. Unless the declaration provides otherwise, any income or proceeds from real estate subject to development rights inures to the declarant. If the declarant fails to pay all expenses in connection with real estate within the common interest community subject to development rights, the association may pay such expenses, and such expenses shall be assessed as a common expense against the real estate subject to development rights, and the association may enforce the assessment pursuant to section 38-33.3-316 by treating such real estate as if it were a unit. If the association acquires title to the real estate subject to the development rights through foreclosure or otherwise, the development rights shall not be extinguished thereby, and, thereafter, the association may succeed to any special declarant rights specified in a written instrument prepared, executed, and recorded by the association in accordance with the requirements of section 38-33.3-304 (3).

(3) In a planned community, if all development rights have expired with respect to any real estate, the declarant remains liable for all expenses of that real estate unless, upon expiration, the declaration provides that the real estate becomes common elements or units.

§ 38-33.3-308, C.R.S. Meetings.

(1) Meetings of the unit owners, as the members of the association, shall be held at least once each year. Special meetings of the unit owners may be called by the president, by a majority of the executive board, or by unit owners having twenty percent, or any lower percentage specified in the bylaws, of the votes in the association. Not less than ten nor more than fifty days in advance of any meeting of the unit owners, the secretary or other officer specified in the bylaws shall cause notice to be hand delivered or sent prepaid by United States mail to the mailing address of each unit or to any other mailing address designated in writing by the unit owner. The notice of any meeting of the unit owners shall be physically posted in a conspicuous place, to the

extent that such posting is feasible and practicable, in addition to any electronic posting or electronic mail notices that may be given pursuant to paragraph (b) of subsection (2) of this section. The notice shall state the time and place of the meeting and the items on the agenda, including the general nature of any proposed amendment to the declaration or bylaws, any budget changes, and any proposal to remove an officer or member of the executive board.

(2)   (a)   All regular and special meetings of the association's executive board, or any committee thereof, shall be open to attendance by all members of the association or their representatives. Agendas for meetings of the executive board shall be made reasonably available for examination by all members of the association or their representatives.

      (b)   (I)   The association is encouraged to provide all notices and agendas required by this article in electronic form, by posting on a web site or otherwise, in addition to printed form. If such electronic means are available, the association shall provide notice of all regular and special meetings of unit owners by electronic mail to all unit owners who so request and who furnish the association with their electronic mail addresses. Electronic notice of a special meeting shall be given as soon as possible but at least twenty-four hours before the meeting.

          (II)   Notwithstanding section 38-33.3-117 (1.5) (i), this paragraph (b) shall not apply to an association that includes time-share units, as defined in section 38-33-110 (7), C.R.S.

(2.5) (a)   Notwithstanding any provision in the declaration, bylaws, or other documents to the contrary, all meetings of the association and board of directors are open to every unit owner of the association, or to any person designated by a unit owner in writing as the unit owner's representative.

      (b)   At an appropriate time determined by the board, but before the board votes on an issue under discussion, unit owners or their designated representatives shall be permitted to speak regarding that issue. The board may place reasonable time restrictions on persons speaking during the meeting. If more than one person desires to address an issue and there are opposing views, the board shall provide for a reasonable number of persons to speak on each side of the issue.

      (c)   Notwithstanding section 38-33.3-117 (1.5) (i), this subsection (2.5) shall not apply to an association that includes time-share units, as defined in section 38-33-110 (7).

(3)   The members of the executive board or any committee thereof may hold an executive or closed door session and may restrict attendance to executive board members and such other persons requested by the executive board during a regular or specially announced meeting or a part thereof. The matters to be discussed at such an executive session shall include only matters enumerated in paragraphs (a) to (f) of subsection (4) of this section.

(4)   Matters for discussion by an executive or closed session are limited to:

      (a)   Matters pertaining to employees of the association or the managing agent's contract or involving the employment, promotion, discipline, or dismissal of an officer, agent, or employee of the association;

      (b)   Consultation with legal counsel concerning disputes that are the subject of pending or imminent court proceedings or matters that are privileged or confidential between attorney and client;

      (c)   Investigative proceedings concerning possible or actual criminal misconduct;

      (d)   Matters subject to specific constitutional, statutory, or judicially imposed requirements protecting particular proceedings or matters from public disclosure;

      (e)   Any matter the disclosure of which would constitute an unwarranted invasion of individual privacy;

(f)   Review of or discussion relating to any written or oral communication from legal counsel.

(4.5) Upon the final resolution of any matter for which the board received legal advice or that concerned pending or contemplated litigation, the board may elect to preserve the attorney-client privilege in any appropriate manner, or it may elect to disclose such information, as it deems appropriate, about such matter in an open meeting.

(5)   Prior to the time the members of the executive board or any committee thereof convene in executive session, the chair of the body shall announce the general matter of discussion as enumerated in paragraphs (a) to (f) of subsection (4) of this section.

(6)   No rule or regulation of the board or any committee thereof shall be adopted during an executive session. A rule or regulation may be validly adopted only during a regular or special meeting or after the body goes back into regular session following an executive session.

(7)   The minutes of all meetings at which an executive session was held shall indicate that an executive session was held and the general subject matter of the executive session.

§ 38-33.3-309, C.R.S. Quorums.

(1)   Unless the bylaws provide otherwise, a quorum is deemed present throughout any meeting of the association if persons entitled to cast twenty percent, or, in the case of an association with over one thousand unit owners, ten percent, of the votes which may be cast for election of the executive board are present, in person or by proxy at the beginning of the meeting.

(2)   Unless the bylaws specify a larger percentage, a quorum is deemed present throughout any meeting of the executive board if persons entitled to cast fifty percent of the votes on that board are present at the beginning of the meeting or grant their proxy, as provided in section 7-128-205 (4), C.R.S.

§ 38-33.3-310, C.R.S. Voting – proxies.

(1)   (a)   If only one of the multiple owners of a unit is present at a meeting of the association, such owner is entitled to cast all the votes allocated to that unit. If more than one of the multiple owners are present, the votes allocated to that unit may be cast only in accordance with the agreement of a majority in interest of the owners, unless the declaration expressly provides otherwise. There is majority agreement if any one of the multiple owners casts the votes allocated to that unit without protest being made promptly to the person presiding over the meeting by any of the other owners of the unit.

      (b)   (I)   (A)   Votes for contested positions on the executive board shall be taken by secret ballot. This sub-subparagraph (A) shall not apply to an association whose governing documents provide for election of positions on the executive board by delegates on behalf of the unit owners.

                  (B)   At the discretion of the board or upon the request of twenty percent of the unit owners who are present at the meeting or represented by proxy, if a quorum has been achieved, a vote on any matter affecting the common interest community on which all unit owners are entitled to vote shall be by secret ballot.

                  (C)   Ballots shall be counted by a neutral third party or by a committee of volunteers. Such volunteers shall be unit owners who are selected or appointed at an open meeting, in a fair manner, by the chair of the board or another person presiding during that portion of the meeting. The volunteers shall not be board members and, in the case of a contested election for a board position, shall not be candidates.

(D)   The results of a vote taken by secret ballot shall be reported without reference to the names, addresses, or other identifying information of unit owners participating in such vote.

(II)   Notwithstanding section 38-33.3-117 (1.5) (j), this paragraph (b) shall not apply to an association that includes time-share units, as defined in section 38-33-110 (7).

(2)   (a)   Votes allocated to a unit may be cast pursuant to a proxy duly executed by a unit owner. A proxy shall not be valid if obtained through fraud or misrepresentation. Unless otherwise provided in the declaration, bylaws, or rules of the association, appointment of proxies may be made substantially as provided in section 7-127-203, C.R.S.

(b)   If a unit is owned by more than one person, each owner of the unit may vote or register protest to the casting of votes by the other owners of the unit through a duly executed proxy. A unit owner may not revoke a proxy given pursuant to this section except by actual notice of revocation to the person presiding over a meeting of the association. A proxy is void if it is not dated or purports to be revocable without notice. A proxy terminates eleven months after its date, unless it provides otherwise.

(c)   The association is entitled to reject a vote, consent, written ballot, waiver, proxy appointment, or proxy appointment revocation if the secretary or other officer or agent authorized to tabulate votes, acting in good faith, has reasonable basis for doubt about the validity of the signature on it or about the signatory's authority to sign for the unit owner.

(d)   The association and its officer or agent who accepts or rejects a vote, consent, written ballot, waiver, proxy appointment, or proxy appointment revocation in good faith and in accordance with the standards of this section are not liable in damages for the consequences of the acceptance or rejection.

(e)   Any action of the association based on the acceptance or rejection of a vote, consent, written ballot, waiver, proxy appointment, or proxy appointment revocation under this section is valid unless a court of competent jurisdiction determines otherwise.

(3)   (a)   If the declaration requires that votes on specified matters affecting the common interest community be cast by lessees rather than unit owners of leased units:

(I)   The provisions of subsections (1) and (2) of this section apply to lessees as if they were unit owners;

(II)   Unit owners who have leased their units to other persons may not cast votes on those specified matters; and

(III) Lessees are entitled to notice of meetings, access to records, and other rights respecting those matters as if they were unit owners.

(b)   Unit owners must also be given notice, in the manner provided in section 38-33.3-308, of all meetings at which lessees are entitled to vote.

(4)   No votes allocated to a unit owned by the association may be cast.

§ 38-33.3-310.5, C.R.S. Executive board – conflicts of interest – definitions.

(1)   Section 7-128-501, C.R.S., shall apply to members of the executive board; except that, as used in that section:

(a)   "Corporation" or "nonprofit corporation" means the association.

(b)   "Director" means a member of the association's executive board.

(c)   "Officer" means any person designated as an officer of the association and any person to whom the board delegates responsibilities under this article, including, without limitation, a managing agent, attorney, or accountant employed by the board.

§ 38-33.3-311, C.R.S. Tort and contract liability.

(1) Neither the association nor any unit owner except the declarant is liable for any cause of action based upon that declarant's acts or omissions in connection with any part of the common interest community which that declarant has the responsibility to maintain. Otherwise, any action alleging an act or omission by the association must be brought against the association and not against any unit owner. If the act or omission occurred during any period of declarant control and the association gives the declarant reasonable notice of and an opportunity to defend against the action, the declarant who then controlled the association is liable to the association or to any unit owner for all tort losses not covered by insurance suffered by the association or that unit owner and all costs that the association would not have incurred but for such act or omission. Whenever the declarant is liable to the association under this section, the declarant is also liable for all expenses of litigation, including reasonable attorney fees, incurred by the association. Any statute of limitation affecting the association's right of action under this section is tolled until the period of declarant control terminates. A unit owner is not precluded from maintaining an action contemplated by this section by being a unit owner or a member or officer of the association.

(2) The declarant is liable to the association for all funds of the association collected during the period of declarant control which were not properly expended.

§ 38-33.3-312, C.R.S. Conveyance or encumbrance of common elements.

(1) In a condominium or planned community, portions of the common elements may be conveyed or subjected to a security interest by the association if persons entitled to cast at least sixty-seven percent of the votes in the association, including sixty-seven percent of the votes allocated to units not owned by a declarant, or any larger percentage the declaration specifies, agree to that action; except that all owners of units to which any limited common element is allocated must agree in order to convey that limited common element or subject it to a security interest. The declaration may specify a smaller percentage only if all of the units are restricted exclusively to nonresidential uses. Proceeds of the sale are an asset of the association.

(2) Part of a cooperative may be conveyed and all or part of a cooperative may be subjected to a security interest by the association if persons entitled to cast at least sixty-seven percent of the votes in the association, including sixty-seven percent of the votes allocated to units not owned by a declarant, or any larger percentage the declaration specifies, agree to that action; except that, if fewer than all of the units or limited common elements are to be conveyed or subjected to a security interest, then all unit owners of those units, or the units to which those limited common elements are allocated, must agree in order to convey those units or limited common elements or subject them to a security interest. The declaration may specify a smaller percentage only if all of the units are restricted exclusively to nonresidential uses. Proceeds of the sale are an asset of the association. Any purported conveyance or other voluntary transfer of an entire cooperative, unless made in compliance with section 38-33.3-218, is void.

(3) An agreement to convey, or subject to a security interest, common elements in a condominium or planned community, or, in a cooperative, an agreement to convey, or subject to a security interest, any part of a cooperative, must be evidenced by the execution of an agreement, in the same manner as a deed, by the association. The agreement must specify a date after which the agreement will be void unless approved by the requisite percentage of owners. Any grant, conveyance, or deed executed by the association must be recorded in every county in which a portion of the common interest community is situated and is effective only upon recordation.

(4) The association, on behalf of the unit owners, may contract to convey an interest in a common interest community pursuant to subsection (1) of this section, but the contract is not enforceable against the association until approved pursuant to subsections (1) and (2) of this section and executed and ratified pursuant to subsection (3) of this section. Thereafter, the association has

all powers necessary and appropriate to effect the conveyance or encumbrance, including the power to execute deeds or other instruments.

(5)   Unless in compliance with this section, any purported conveyance, encumbrance, judicial sale, or other transfer of common elements or any other part of a cooperative is void.

(6)   A conveyance or encumbrance of common elements pursuant to this section shall not deprive any unit of its rights of ingress and egress of the unit and support of the unit.

(7)   Unless the declaration otherwise provides, a conveyance or encumbrance of common elements pursuant to this section does not affect the priority or validity of preexisting encumbrances.

(8)   In a cooperative, the association may acquire, hold, encumber, or convey a proprietary lease without complying with this section.

§ 38-33.3-313, C.R.S. Insurance.

(1)   Commencing not later than the time of the first conveyance of a unit to a person other than a declarant, the association shall maintain, to the extent reasonably available:

(a)   Property insurance on the common elements and, in a planned community, also on property that must become common elements, for broad form covered causes of loss; except that the total amount of insurance must be not less than the full insurable replacement cost of the insured property less applicable deductibles at the time the insurance is purchased and at each renewal date, exclusive of land, excavations, foundations, and other items normally excluded from property policies; and

(b)   Commercial general liability insurance against claims and liabilities arising in connection with the ownership, existence, use, or management of the common elements, and, in cooperatives, also of all units, in an amount, if any, specified by the common interest community instruments or otherwise deemed sufficient in the judgment of the executive board but not less than any amount specified in the association documents, insuring the executive board, the unit owners' association, the management agent, and their respective employees, agents, and all persons acting as agents. The declarant shall be included as an additional insured in such declarant's capacity as a unit owner and board member. The unit owners shall be included as additional insureds but only for claims and liabilities arising in connection with the ownership, existence, use, or management of the common elements and, in cooperatives, also of all units. The insurance shall cover claims of one or more insured parties against other insured parties.

(2)   In the case of a building that is part of a cooperative or that contains units having horizontal boundaries described in the declaration, the insurance maintained under paragraph (a) of subsection (1) of this section must include the units but not the finished interior surfaces of the walls, floors, and ceilings of the units. The insurance need not include improvements and betterments installed by unit owners, but if they are covered, any increased charge shall be assessed by the association to those owners.

(3)   If the insurance described in subsections (1) and (2) of this section is not reasonably available, or if any policy of such insurance is cancelled or not renewed without a replacement policy therefore having been obtained, the association promptly shall cause notice of that fact to be hand delivered or sent prepaid by United States mail to all unit owners. The declaration may require the association to carry any other insurance, and the association in any event may carry any other insurance it considers appropriate, including insurance on units it is not obligated to insure, to protect the association or the unit owners.

(4)   Insurance policies carried pursuant to subsections (1) and (2) of this section must provide that:

(a)   Each unit owner is an insured person under the policy with respect to liability arising out of such unit owner's interest in the common elements or membership in the association;

(b)   The insurer waives its rights to subrogation under the policy against any unit owner or member of his household;

(c)   No act or omission by any unit owner, unless acting within the scope of such unit owner's authority on behalf of the association, will void the policy or be a condition to recovery under the policy; and

(d)   If, at the time of a loss under the policy, there is other insurance in the name of a unit owner covering the same risk covered by the policy, the association's policy provides primary insurance.

(5)   Any loss covered by the property insurance policy described in paragraph (a) of subsection (1) and subsection (2) of this section must be adjusted with the association, but the insurance proceeds for that loss shall be payable to any insurance trustee designated for that purpose, or otherwise to the association, and not to any holder of a security interest. The insurance trustee or the association shall hold any insurance proceeds in trust for the association unit owners and lienholders as their interests may appear. Subject to the provisions of subsection (9) of this section, the proceeds must be disbursed first for the repair or restoration of the damaged property, and the association, unit owners, and lienholders are not entitled to receive payment of any portion of the proceeds unless there is a surplus of proceeds after the property has been completely repaired or restored or the common interest community is terminated.

(6)   The association may adopt and establish written nondiscriminatory policies and procedures relating to the submittal of claims, responsibility for deductibles, and any other matters of claims adjustment. To the extent the association settles claims for damages to real property, it shall have the authority to assess negligent unit owners causing such loss or benefiting from such repair or restoration all deductibles paid by the association. In the event that more than one unit is damaged by a loss, the association in its reasonable discretion may assess each unit owner a pro rata share of any deductible paid by the association.

(7)   An insurance policy issued to the association does not obviate the need for unit owners to obtain insurance for their own benefit.

(8)   An insurer that has issued an insurance policy for the insurance described in subsections (1) and (2) of this section shall issue certificates or memoranda of insurance to the association and, upon request, to any unit owner or holder of a security interest. Unless otherwise provided by statute, the insurer issuing the policy may not cancel or refuse to renew it until thirty days after notice of the proposed cancellation or nonrenewal has been mailed to the association, and each unit owner and holder of a security interest to whom a certificate or memorandum of insurance has been issued, at their respective last-known addresses.

(9)   (a)   Any portion of the common interest community for which insurance is required under this section which is damaged or destroyed must be repaired or replaced promptly by the association unless:

        (I)   The common interest community is terminated, in which case section 38-33.3-218 applies;

        (II)   Repair or replacement would be illegal under any state or local statute or ordinance governing health or safety;

        (III)   Sixty-seven percent of the unit owners, including every owner of a unit or assigned limited common element that will not be rebuilt, vote not to rebuild; or

        (IV)   Prior to the conveyance of any unit to a person other than the declarant, the holder of a deed of trust or mortgage on the damaged portion of the common interest community rightfully demands all or a substantial part of the insurance proceeds.

        (b)   The cost of repair or replacement in excess of insurance proceeds and reserves is a common expense. If the entire common interest community is not repaired or replaced, the insurance proceeds attributable to the damaged common elements must be used to restore the damaged area to a condition compatible with the remainder of the common interest community, and, except to the extent that other persons will be distributees, the insurance proceeds attributable to units and limited common elements that are not rebuilt must be distributed to the owners of those units and the owners of the units to which those limited common elements were allocated, or to lienholders, as their interests may appear, and the remainder of the proceeds must be distributed to all the unit owners or lienholders, as their interests may appear, as follows:

(I)   In a condominium, in proportion to the common element interests of all the units; and

(II)   In a cooperative or planned community, in proportion to the common expense liabilities of all the units; except that, in a fixed or limited equity cooperative, the unit owner may not receive more of the proceeds than would satisfy the unit owner's entitlements under the declaration if the unit owner leaves the cooperative. In such a cooperative, the proceeds that remain after satisfying the unit owner's obligations continue to be held in trust by the association for the benefit of the cooperative. If the unit owners vote not to rebuild any unit, that unit's allocated interests are automatically reallocated upon the vote as if the unit had been condemned under section 38-33.3-107, and the association promptly shall prepare, execute, and record an amendment to the declaration reflecting the reallocations.

(10)   If any unit owner or employee of an association with thirty or more units controls or disburses funds of the common interest community, the association must obtain and maintain, to the extent reasonably available, fidelity insurance. Coverage shall not be less in aggregate than two months' current assessments plus reserves, as calculated from the current budget of the association.

(11)   Any person employed as an independent contractor by an association with thirty or more units for the purposes of managing a common interest community must obtain and maintain fidelity insurance in an amount not less than the amount specified in subsection (10) of this section, unless the association names such person as an insured employee in a contract of fidelity insurance, pursuant to subsection (10) of this section.

(12)   The association may carry fidelity insurance in amounts greater than required in subsection (10) of this section and may require any independent contractor employed for the purposes of managing a common interest community to carry more fidelity insurance coverage than required in subsection (10) of this section.

(13)   Premiums for insurance that the association acquires and other expenses connected with acquiring such insurance are common expenses.

§ 38-33.3-314, C.R.S. Surplus funds.

Unless otherwise provided in the declaration, any surplus funds of the association remaining after payment of or provision for common expenses and any prepayment of or provision for reserves shall be paid to the unit owners in proportion to their common expense liabilities or credited to them to reduce their future common expense assessments.

§ 38-33.3-315, C.R.S. Assessments for common expenses.

(1)   Until the association makes a common expense assessment, the declarant shall pay all common expenses. After any assessment has been made by the association, assessments shall be made no less frequently than annually and shall be based on a budget adopted no less frequently than annually by the association.

(2)   Except for assessments under subsections (3) and (4) of this section and section 38-33.3-207 (4) (a) (IV), all common expenses shall be assessed against all the units in accordance with the allocations set forth in the declaration pursuant to section 38-33.3-207 (1) and (2). Any past-

due common expense assessment or installment thereof shall bear interest at the rate established by the association not exceeding twenty-one percent per year.

(3)   To the extent required by the declaration:

(a)   Any common expense associated with the maintenance, repair, or replacement of a limited common element shall be assessed against the units to which that limited common element is assigned, equally, or in any other proportion the declaration provides;

(b)   Any common expense or portion thereof benefiting fewer than all of the units shall be assessed exclusively against the units benefited; and

(c)   The costs of insurance shall be assessed in proportion to risk, and the costs of utilities shall be assessed in proportion to usage.

(4)   If any common expense is caused by the misconduct of any unit owner, the association may assess that expense exclusively against such owner's unit.

(5)   If common expense liabilities are reallocated, common expense assessments and any installment thereof not yet due shall be recalculated in accordance with the reallocated common expense liabilities.

(6)   Each unit owner is liable for assessments made against such owner's unit during the period of ownership of such unit. No unit owner may be exempt from liability for payment of the assessments by waiver of the use or enjoyment of any of the common elements or by abandonment of the unit against which the assessments are made.

(7)   Unless otherwise specifically provided in the declaration or bylaws, the association may enter into an escrow agreement with the holder of a unit owner's mortgage so that assessments may be combined with the unit owner's mortgage payments and paid at the same time and in the same manner; except that any such escrow agreement shall comply with any applicable rules of the federal housing administration, department of housing and urban development, veterans' administration, or other government agency.

§ 38-33.3-316, C.R.S. Lien for assessments.

(1)   The association, if such association is incorporated or organized as a limited liability company, has a statutory lien on a unit for any assessment levied against that unit or fines imposed against its unit owner. Unless the declaration otherwise provides, fees, charges, late charges, attorney fees, fines, and interest charged pursuant to section 38-33.3-302 (1) (j), (1) (k), and (1) (l), section 38-33.3-313 (6), and section 38-33.3-315 (2) are enforceable as assessments under this article. The amount of the lien shall include all those items set forth in this section from the time such items become due. If an assessment is payable in installments, each installment is a lien from the time it becomes due, including the due date set by any valid association's acceleration of installment obligations.

(2)   (a)   A lien under this section is prior to all other liens and encumbrances on a unit except:

(I)   Liens and encumbrances recorded before the recordation of the declaration and, in a cooperative, liens and encumbrances which the association creates, assumes, or takes subject to;

(II)   A security interest on the unit which has priority over all other security interests on the unit and which was recorded before the date on which the assessment sought to be enforced became delinquent, or, in a cooperative, a security interest encumbering only the unit owner's interest which has priority over all other security interests on the unit and which was perfected before the date on which the assessment sought to be enforced became delinquent; and

(III)   Liens for real estate taxes and other governmental assessments or charges against the unit or cooperative.

(b)   Subject to paragraph (d) of this subsection (2), a lien under this section is also prior to the security interests described in subparagraph (II) of paragraph (a) of this subsection (2) to the extent of:

    (I)   An amount equal to the common expense assessments based on a periodic budget adopted by the association under section 38-33.3-315 (1) which would have become due, in the absence of any acceleration, during the six months immediately preceding institution by either the association or any party holding a lien senior to any part of the association lien created under this section of an action or a nonjudicial foreclosure either to enforce or to extinguish the lien.

    (II)   (Deleted by amendment, L. 93, p. 653, § 21, effective April 30, 1993.)

(c)   This subsection (2) does not affect the priority of mechanics' or materialmen's liens or the priority of liens for other assessments made by the association. A lien under this section is not subject to the provisions of part 2 of article 41 of this title or to the provisions of section 15-11-202, C.R.S.

(d)   The association shall have the statutory lien described in subsection (1) of this section for any assessment levied or fine imposed after June 30, 1992. Such lien shall have the priority described in this subsection (2) if the other lien or encumbrance is created after June 30, 1992.

(3)   Unless the declaration otherwise provides, if two or more associations have liens for assessments created at any time on the same property, those liens have equal priority.

(4)   Recording of the declaration constitutes record notice and perfection of the lien. No further recordation of any claim of lien for assessments is required.

(5)   A lien for unpaid assessments is extinguished unless proceedings to enforce the lien are instituted within six years after the full amount of assessments become due.

(6)   This section does not prohibit actions or suits to recover sums for which subsection (1) of this section creates a lien or to prohibit an association from taking a deed in lieu of foreclosure.

(7)   The association shall be entitled to costs and reasonable attorney fees incurred by the association in a judgment or decree in any action or suit brought by the association under this section.

(8)   The association shall furnish to a unit owner or such unit owner's designee or to a holder of a security interest or its designee upon written request, delivered personally or by certified mail, first-class postage prepaid, return receipt, to the association's registered agent, a written statement setting forth the amount of unpaid assessments currently levied against such owner's unit. The statement shall be furnished within fourteen calendar days after receipt of the request and is binding on the association, the executive board, and every unit owner. If no statement is furnished to the unit owner or holder of a security interest or his or her designee, delivered personally or by certified mail, first-class postage prepaid, return receipt requested, to the inquiring party, then the association shall have no right to assert a lien upon the unit for unpaid assessments which were due as of the date of the request.

(9)   In any action by an association to collect assessments or to foreclose a lien for unpaid assessments, the court may appoint a receiver of the unit owner to collect all sums alleged to be due from the unit owner prior to or during the pending of the action. The court may order the receiver to pay any sums held by the receiver to the association during the pending of the action to the extent of the association's common expense assessments.

(10)   In a cooperative, upon nonpayment of an assessment on a unit, the unit owner may be evicted in the same manner as provided by law in the case of an unlawful holdover by a commercial tenant, and the lien may be foreclosed as provided by this section.

(11) The association's lien may be foreclosed by any of the following means:

(a) In a condominium or planned community, the association's lien may be foreclosed in like manner as a mortgage on real estate; except that the association or a holder or assignee of the association's lien, whether the holder or assignee of the association's lien is an entity or a natural person, may only foreclose on the lien if:

   (I) The balance of the assessments and charges secured by its lien, as defined in subsection (2) of this section, equals or exceeds six months of common expense assessments based on a periodic budget adopted by the association; and

   (II) The executive board has formally resolved, by a recorded vote, to authorize the filing of a legal action against the specific unit on an individual basis. The board may not delegate its duty to act under this subparagraph (II) to any attorney, insurer, manager, or other person, and any legal action filed without evidence of the recorded vote authorizing the action must be dismissed. No attorney fees, court costs, or other charges incurred by the association or a holder or assignee of the association's lien in connection with an action that is dismissed for this reason may be assessed against the unit owner.

(b) In a cooperative whose unit owners' interests in the units are real estate as determined in accordance with the provisions of section 38-33.3-105, the association's lien must be foreclosed in like manner as a mortgage on real estate; except that the association or a holder or assignee of the association's lien, whether the holder or assignee of the association's lien is an entity or a natural person, may only foreclose on the lien if:

   (I) The balance of the assessments and charges secured by its lien, as defined in subsection (2) of this section, equals or exceeds six months of common expense assessments based on a periodic budget adopted by the association; and

   (II) The executive board has formally resolved, by a recorded vote, to authorize the filing of a legal action against the specific unit on an individual basis. The board may not delegate its duty to act under this subparagraph (II) to any attorney, insurer, manager, or other person, and any legal action filed without evidence of the recorded vote authorizing the action must be dismissed. No attorney fees, court costs, or other charges incurred by the association or a holder or assignee of the association's lien in connection with an action that is dismissed for this reason may be assessed against the unit owner.

(c) In a cooperative whose unit owners' interests in the units are personal property, as determined in accordance with the provisions of section 38-33.3-105, the association's lien must be foreclosed as a security interest under the "Uniform Commercial Code", title 4, C.R.S.

§ 38-33.3-316.3, C.R.S. Collections – limitations.

(1) In collecting past-due assessments and other delinquent payments under this article, an association or a holder or assignee of the association's debt, whether the holder or assignee of the association's debt is an entity or a natural person, shall:

(a) Adopt and comply with a collections policy that meets the requirements of section 38-33.3-209.5 (5); and

(b) Make a good-faith effort to coordinate with the unit owner to set up a payment plan that meets the requirements of this section; except that:

   (I) This section does not apply if the unit owner does not occupy the unit and has acquired the property as a result of:

      (A) A default of a security interest encumbering the unit; or

      (B) Foreclosure of the association's lien; and

(II)   The association or a holder or assignee of the association's debt is not obligated to negotiate a payment plan with a unit owner who has previously entered into a payment plan under this section.

(2)   A payment plan negotiated between the association or a holder or assignee of the association's debt, whether the holder or assignee of the association's debt is an entity or a natural person, and the unit owner pursuant to this section must permit the unit owner to pay off the deficiency in equal installments over a period of at least six months. Nothing in this section prohibits an association or a holder or assignee of the association's debt from pursuing legal action against a unit owner if the unit owner fails to comply with the terms of his or her payment plan. A unit owner's failure to remit payment of an agreed-upon installment, or to remain current with regular assessments as they come due during the six-month period, constitutes a failure to comply with the terms of his or her payment plan.

(3)   For purposes of this section, "assessments" includes regular and special assessments and any associated fees, charges, late charges, attorney fees, fines, and interest charged pursuant to section 38-33.3-315 (2).

§ 38-33.3-316.5, C.R.S. Time share estate – foreclosure – definitions.

(1)   As used in this section, unless the context otherwise requires:

(a)   "Junior lienor" has the same meaning as set forth in section 38-38-100.3 (12), C.R.S.

(b)   "Obligor" means the person liable for the assessment levied against a time share estate pursuant to section 38-33.3-316 or the record owner of the time share estate.

(c)   "Time share estate" has the same meaning as set forth in section 38-33-110 (5).

(2)   A plaintiff may commence a single judicial foreclosure action pursuant to section 38-33.3-316 (11), joining as defendants multiple obligors with separate time share estates and the junior lienors thereto, if:

(a)   The judicial foreclosure action involves a single common interest community;

(b)   The declaration giving rise to the right of the association to collect assessments creates default and remedy obligations that are substantially the same for each obligor named as a defendant in the judicial foreclosure action;

(c)   The action is limited to a claim for judicial foreclosure brought pursuant to section 38-33.3-316 (11); and

(d)   The plaintiff does not allege, with respect to any obligor, that the association's lien is prior to any security interest described in section 38-33.3-316 (2) (a) (II), even if such a claim could be made pursuant to section 38-33.3-316 (2) (b) (I).

(3)   In a judicial foreclosure action in which multiple obligors with separate time share estates and the junior lienors thereto have been joined as defendants in accordance with this section:

(a)   In addition to any other circumstances where severance is proper under the Colorado rules of civil procedure, the court may sever for separate trial any disputed claim or claims;

(b)   If service by publication of two or more defendants is permitted by law, the plaintiff may publish a single notice for all joined defendants for whom service by publication is permitted, so long as all information that would be required by law to be provided in the published notice as to each defendant individually is included in the combined published notice. Nothing in this paragraph (b) shall be interpreted to allow service by publication of any defendant if service by publication is not otherwise permitted by law with respect to that defendant.

(c) The action shall be deemed a single action, suit, or proceeding for purposes of payment of filing fees, notwithstanding any action by the court pursuant to paragraph (a) of this subsection (3), so long as the plaintiff complies with subsection (2) of this section.

(4) Notwithstanding that multiple obligors with separate time share estates may be joined in a single judicial foreclosure action, unless otherwise ordered by the court, each time share estate foreclosed pursuant to this section shall be subject to a separate foreclosure sale, and any cure or redemption rights with respect to such time share estate shall remain separate.

(5) The plaintiff in an action brought pursuant to this section is deemed to waive any claims against a defendant for a deficiency remaining after the foreclosure of the lien for assessment and for attorney fees related to the foreclosure action.

§ 38-33.3-317, C.R.S. Association records.

(1) In addition to any records specifically defined in the association's declaration or bylaws or expressly required by section 38-33.3-209.4 (2), the association must maintain the following, all of which shall be deemed to be the sole records of the association for purposes of document retention and production to owners:

(a) Detailed records of receipts and expenditures affecting the operation and administration of the association;

(b) Records of claims for construction defects and amounts received pursuant to settlement of those claims;

(c) Minutes of all meetings of its unit owners and executive board, a record of all actions taken by the unit owners or executive board without a meeting, and a record of all actions taken by any committee of the executive board;

(d) Written communications among, and the votes cast by, executive board members that are:

(I) Directly related to an action taken by the board without a meeting pursuant to section 7-128-202, C.R.S.; or

(II) Directly related to an action taken by the board without a meeting pursuant to the association's bylaws;

(e) The names of unit owners in a form that permits preparation of a list of the names of all unit owners and the physical mailing addresses at which the association communicates with them, showing the number of votes each unit owner is entitled to vote; except that this paragraph (e) does not apply to a unit, or the owner thereof, if the unit is a time-share unit, as defined in section 38-33-110 (7);

(f) Its current declaration, covenants, bylaws, articles of incorporation, if it is a corporation, or the corresponding organizational documents if it is another form of entity, rules and regulations, responsible governance policies adopted pursuant to section 38-33.3-209.5, and other policies adopted by the executive board;

(g) Financial statements as described in section 7-136-106, C.R.S., for the past three years and tax returns of the association for the past seven years, to the extent available;

(h) A list of the names, electronic mail addresses, and physical mailing addresses of its current executive board members and officers;

(i) Its most recent annual report delivered to the secretary of state, if any;

(j) Financial records sufficiently detailed to enable the association to comply with section 38-33.3-316 (8) concerning statements of unpaid assessments;

(k) The association's most recent reserve study, if any;

(l) Current written contracts to which the association is a party and contracts for work performed for the association within the immediately preceding two years;

(m) Records of executive board or committee actions to approve or deny any requests for design or architectural approval from unit owners;

(n) Ballots, proxies, and other records related to voting by unit owners for one year after the election, action, or vote to which they relate;

(o) Resolutions adopted by its board of directors relating to the characteristics, qualifications, rights, limitations, and obligations of members or any class or category of members; and

(p) All written communications within the past three years to all unit owners generally as unit owners.

(2) (a) Subject to subsections (3), (3.5), and (4) of this section, all records maintained by the association must be available for examination and copying by a unit owner or the owner's authorized agent. The association may require unit owners to submit a written request, describing with reasonable particularity the records sought, at least ten days prior to inspection or production of the documents and may limit examination and copying times to normal business hours or the next regularly scheduled executive board meeting if the meeting occurs within thirty days after the request. Notwithstanding any provision of the declaration, bylaws, articles, or rules and regulations of the association to the contrary, the association may not condition the production of records upon the statement of a proper purpose.

(b) (I) Notwithstanding paragraph (a) of this subsection (2), a membership list or any part thereof may not be obtained or used by any person for any purpose unrelated to a unit owner's interest as a unit owner without consent of the executive board.

(II) Without limiting the generality of subparagraph (I) of this paragraph (b), without the consent of the executive board, a membership list or any part thereof may not be:

(A) Used to solicit money or property unless such money or property will be used solely to solicit the votes of the unit owners in an election to be held by the association;

(B) Used for any commercial purpose; or

(C) Sold to or purchased by any person.

(3) Records maintained by an association may be withheld from inspection and copying to the extent that they are or concern:

(a) Architectural drawings, plans, and designs, unless released upon the written consent of the legal owner of the drawings, plans, or designs;

(b) Contracts, leases, bids, or records related to transactions to purchase or provide goods or services that are currently in or under negotiation;

(c) Communications with legal counsel that are otherwise protected by the attorney-client privilege or the attorney work product doctrine;

(d) Disclosure of information in violation of law;

(e) Records of an executive session of an executive board;

(f) Individual units other than those of the requesting owner; or

(g) The names and physical mailing addresses of unit owners if the unit is a time-share unit, as defined in section 38-33-110 (7), C.R.S.

(3.5) Records maintained by an association are not subject to inspection and copying, and they must be withheld, to the extent that they are or concern:

(a) Personnel, salary, or medical records relating to specific individuals; or

(b) (I) Personal identification and account information of members and residents, including bank account information, telephone numbers, electronic mail addresses, driver's license numbers, and social security numbers; except that, notwithstanding section 38-33.3-104, a member or resident may provide the association with prior written consent to the disclosure of, and the association may publish to other members and residents, the person's telephone number, electronic mail address, or both. The written consent must be kept as a record of the association and remains valid until the person withdraws it by providing the association with a written notice of withdrawal of the consent. If a person withdraws his or her consent, the association is under no obligation to change, retrieve, or destroy any document or record published prior to the notice of withdrawal.

(II)   As used in this paragraph (b), written consent and notice of withdrawal of the consent may be given by means of a "record", as defined in the "Uniform Electronic Transactions Act", article 71.3 of title 24, C.R.S., if the parties so agree in accordance with section 24-71.3-105, C.R.S.

(4)   The association may impose a reasonable charge, which may be collected in advance and may cover the costs of labor and material, for copies of association records. The charge may not exceed the estimated cost of production and reproduction of the records.

(5)   A right to copy records under this section includes the right to receive copies by photocopying or other means, including the receipt of copies through an electronic transmission if available, upon request by the unit owner.

(6)   An association is not obligated to compile or synthesize information.

(7)   Association records and the information contained within those records shall not be used for commercial purposes.

§ 38-33.3-318, C.R.S. Association as trustee.

With respect to a third person dealing with the association in the association's capacity as a trustee, the existence of trust powers and their proper exercise by the association may be assumed without inquiry. A third person is not bound to inquire whether the association has the power to act as trustee or is properly exercising trust powers. A third person, without actual knowledge that the association is exceeding or improperly exercising its powers, is fully protected in dealing with the association as if it possessed and properly exercised the powers it purports to exercise. A third person is not bound to assure the proper application of trust assets paid or delivered to the association in its capacity as trustee.

§ 38-33.3-319, C.R.S. Other applicable statutes.

To the extent that provisions of this article conflict with applicable provisions in the "Colorado Business Corporation Act", articles 101 to 117 of title 7, C.R.S., the "Colorado Revised Nonprofit Corporation Act", articles 121 to 137 of title 7, C.R.S., the "Uniform Partnership Law", article 60 of title 7, C.R.S., the "Colorado Uniform Partnership Act (1997)", article 64 of title 7, C.R.S., the "Colorado Uniform Limited Partnership Act of 1981", article 62 of title 7, C.R.S., article 1 of this title, article 55 of title 7, C.R.S., article 33.5 of this title, and section 39-1-103 (10), C.R.S., and any other laws of the state of Colorado which now exist or which are subsequently enacted, the provisions of this article shall control.

§ 38-33.3-401, C.R.S. Registration – annual fees.

(1)   Every unit owners' association shall register annually with the director of the division of real estate, in the form and manner specified by the director.

*   (2)   (a)   Except as otherwise provided in subsection (2)(b) of this section, the unit owners' association shall submit with its annual registration a fee in the amount set by the director in accordance with section 12-10-215 and shall include the following information, updated within ninety days after any change:

(I)   The name of the association, as shown in the Colorado secretary of state's records;

(II)   The name of the association's management company, managing agent, or designated agent, which may be the association's registered agent, as shown in the Colorado secretary of state's records, or any other agent that the executive board has designated for purposes of registration under this section;

(III) The physical address of the HOA;

(IV)   A valid address; email address, if any; website, if any; and telephone number for the association or its management company, managing agent, or designated agent; and

(V)   The number of units in the association.

(b)   A unit owners' association is exempt from the fee, but not the registration requirement, if the association:

    (I)   Has annual revenues of five thousand dollars or less; or

    (II)   Is not authorized to make assessments and does not have revenue.

(3)   A registration is valid for one year. The right of an association that fails to register, or whose annual registration has expired, to impose or enforce a lien for assessments under section 38-33.3-316 or to pursue an action or employ an enforcement mechanism otherwise available to it under section 38-33.3-123 is suspended until the association is validly registered pursuant to this section. A lien for assessments previously recorded during a period in which the association was validly registered or before registration was required pursuant to this section is not extinguished by a lapse in the association's registration, but a pending enforcement proceeding related to the lien is suspended, and an applicable time limit is tolled, until the association is validly registered pursuant to this section. An association's registration in compliance with this section revives a previously suspended right without penalty to the association.

(4)   (a)   A registration is valid upon the division of real estate's acceptance of the information required by paragraph (a) of subsection (2) of this section and the payment of applicable fees.

    (b)   An association's registration number, and an electronic or paper confirmation issued by the division of real estate, are prima facie evidence of valid registration.

    (c)   The director of the division of real estate's final determinations concerning the validity or timeliness of registrations under this section are subject to judicial review pursuant to section 24-4-106 (11), C.R.S.; except that the court shall not find a registration invalid based solely on technical or typographical errors.

§ 38-33.3-402. C.R.S. Manager licensing – condition precedent for enforcement of contract terms.

A person that is subject to licensure under part 10 of article 61 of title 12, C.R.S., shall at all times have and maintain a valid license when acting or purporting to act on behalf of the association. The association's agreement to pay a fee for the services of a community manager or to hold harmless or indemnify the community manager for any act or omission in the course of providing those services is void and unenforceable for any period in which the manager's license is expired, suspended, or revoked.

* VII. Colorado Revised Nonprofit Corporation Act

ARTICLE 121. GENERAL PROVISIONS

§ 7-121-101, C.R.S. Short title.

Articles 121 to 137 of this title shall be known and may be cited as the "Colorado Revised Nonprofit Corporation Act".

§ 7-121-102, C.R.S. Reservation of power to amend or repeal.

The general assembly has the power to amend or repeal all or part of articles 121 to 137 of this title at any time and all domestic and foreign nonprofit corporations subject to said articles shall be governed by the amendment or repeal.

§ 7-121-201, C.R.S. Filing requirements.

Part 3 of article 90 of this title, providing for the filing of documents, applies to any document filed or to be filed by the secretary of state pursuant to articles 121 to 137 of this title.

§ 7-121-301, C.R.S. Powers – repeal. (Repealed)

§ 7-121-401, C.R.S. General definitions.

As used in articles 121 to 137 of this title, unless the context otherwise requires:

(1)   (Deleted by amendment, L. 2003, p. 2332, § 280, effective July 1, 2004.)

(2)   "Articles of incorporation" includes amended articles of incorporation, restated articles of incorporation, and other instruments, however designated, on file in the records of the secretary of state that have the effect of amending or supplementing in some respect the original or amended articles of incorporation, and shall also include:

   (a)   For a corporation created by special act of the general assembly or pursuant to general law, which corporation has elected to accept the provisions of articles 121 to 137 of this title, the special charter and any amendments thereto made by special act of the general assembly or pursuant to general law prior to the corporation's election to accept the provisions of said articles;

   (b)   For a corporation formed or incorporated under article 40, 50, or 51 of this title, which corporation has elected to accept the provisions of articles 121 to 137 of this title, the certificate of incorporation or affidavit and any amendments thereto made prior to the corporation's election to accept the provisions of said articles.

(3)   (Deleted by amendment, L. 2003, p. 2332, § 280, effective July 1, 2004.)

(4)   "Board of directors" means the body authorized to manage the affairs of the domestic or foreign nonprofit corporation; except that no person or group of persons are the board of directors because of powers delegated to that person or group of persons pursuant to section 7-128-101 (2).

(5)   "Bylaws" means the code or codes of rules, other than the articles of incorporation, adopted pursuant to articles 121 to 137 of this title for the regulation or management of the affairs of the domestic or foreign nonprofit corporation irrespective of the name or names by which such rules are designated, and includes amended bylaws and restated bylaws.

(6)   "Cash" and "money" are used interchangeably in articles 121 to 137 of this title. Each of these terms includes:

   (a)   Legal tender;

   (b)   Negotiable instruments readily convertible into legal tender; and

(c)   Other cash equivalents readily convertible into legal tender.

(7)   "Class" refers to a group of memberships that have the same rights with respect to voting, dissolution, redemption, and transfer. For the purpose of this section, rights shall be considered the same if they are determined by a formula applied uniformly to a group of memberships.

(8)   (Deleted by amendment, L. 2000, p. 982, § 76, effective July 1, 2000.)

(9)   "Corporation" or "domestic corporation" means a corporation for profit, which is not a foreign corporation, incorporated under or subject to the provisions of articles 101 to 117 of this title.

(10)   "Delegate" means any person elected or appointed to vote in a representative assembly for the election of a director or directors or on other matters.

(11)   (Deleted by amendment, L. 2003, p. 2332, § 280, effective July 1, 2004.)

(12)   "Director" means a member of the board of directors.

(13)   "Distribution" means the payment of a dividend or any part of the income or profit of a corporation to its members, directors, or officers.

(14)   (Deleted by amendment, L. 2003, p. 2332, § 280, effective July 1, 2004.)

(15)   "Effective date of notice" has the meaning set forth in section 7-121-402.

(16)   "Employee" includes an officer but not a director; except that a director may accept duties that make said director also an employee.

(16.5) "Entrance fee" means any fee or charge, including a damage deposit, paid by a person to a residential nonprofit corporation in order to become a resident member. "Entrance fee" does not include regular periodic payments for the purchase or lease of residential real estate or for the day-to-day use of facilities or services.

(17) to (20) (Deleted by amendment, L. 2003, p. 2332, § 280, effective July 1, 2004.)

(21)   "Internal revenue code" means the federal "Internal Revenue Code of 1986", as amended from time to time, or to corresponding provisions of subsequent internal revenue laws of the United States of America.

(22) and (23) (Deleted by amendment, L. 2003, p. 2332, § 280, effective July 1, 2004.)

(24)   "Member" means any person or persons identified as such in the articles of incorporation or bylaws pursuant to a procedure stated in the articles of incorporation or bylaws or by a resolution of the board of directors. The term "member" includes "voting member" and a stockholder in a cooperative housing corporation formed pursuant to section 38-33.5-101, C.R.S.

(25)   "Membership" refers to the rights and obligations of a member or members.

(25.5) "Mutual ditch company" means a nonprofit corporation that complies with article 42 of this title.

(26)   "Nonprofit corporation" or "domestic nonprofit corporation" means an entity, which is not a foreign nonprofit corporation, incorporated under or subject to the provisions of articles 121 to 137 of this title.

(27) to (29) (Deleted by amendment, L. 2003, p. 2332, § 280, effective July 1, 2004.)

(30)   "Receive", when used in reference to receipt of a writing or other document by a domestic or foreign nonprofit corporation, means that the writing or other document is actually received:

(a)   By the domestic or foreign nonprofit corporation at its registered office or at its principal office;

(b)   By the secretary of the domestic or foreign nonprofit corporation, wherever the secretary is found; or

(c)   By any other person authorized by the bylaws or the board of directors to receive such writings, wherever such person is found.

(31) "Record date" means the date, established under article 127 of this title, on which a nonprofit corporation determines the identity of its members. The determination shall be made as of the close of business on the record date unless another time for doing so is stated when the record date is fixed.

(32) (Deleted by amendment, L. 2003, p. 2332, § 280, effective July 1, 2004.)

(32.5) "Residential member" means a member of a residential nonprofit corporation whose status as a member is dependent upon, or whose membership is accorded voting rights as a result of, owning or leasing specified residential real estate.

(33) (Deleted by amendment, L. 2003, p. 2332, § 280, effective July 1, 2004.)

(33.5) (a) Except as otherwise provided in paragraph (b) of this subsection (33.5), "residential nonprofit corporation" means a nonprofit corporation that has residential members.

(b) Notwithstanding paragraph (a) of this subsection (33.5), "residential nonprofit corporation" does not include:

(I) A unit owners' association or any other entity subject to the "Colorado Common Interest Ownership Act", article 33.3 of title 38, C.R.S., regardless of whether it was formed before, on, or after July 1, 1992;

(II) A nursing care facility licensed by the department of public health and environment under section 25-3-101, C.R.S.;

(III) An assisted living residence licensed under section 25-3-101, C.R.S.;

(IV) A life care institution regulated under article 13 of title 12, C.R.S.; or

(V) A continuing care retirement community, as described in section 25.5-6-203, C.R.S., operated by an entity that is licensed or otherwise subject to state regulation.

(34) "Secretary" means the corporate officer to whom the bylaws or the board of directors has delegated responsibility under section 7-128-301 (3) for the preparation and maintenance of minutes of the meetings of the board of directors and of the members and of the other records and information required to be kept by the nonprofit corporation under section 7-136-101 and for authenticating records of the nonprofit corporation.

(35) to (37) (Deleted by amendment, L. 2003, p. 2332, § 280, effective July 1, 2004.)

(38) "Vote" includes authorization by written ballot and written consent.

(39) "Voting group" means all the members of one or more classes of members or directors that, under articles 121 to 137 of this title or the articles of incorporation or bylaws, are entitled to vote and be counted together collectively on a matter. All members or directors entitled by articles 121 to 137 of this title or the articles of incorporation or bylaws to vote generally on the matter are for that purpose a single voting group.

(40) "Voting member" means any person or persons who on more than one occasion, pursuant to a provision of a nonprofit corporation's articles of incorporation or bylaws, have the right to vote for the election of a director or directors. A person is not a voting member solely by virtue of any of the following:

(a) Any rights such person has as a delegate;

(b) Any rights such person has to designate a director or directors; or

(c) Any rights such person has as a director.

§ 7-121-402, C.R.S. Notice.

(1) Notice given pursuant to articles 121 to 137 of this title shall be in writing unless otherwise provided in the bylaws.

(2) Notice may be given in person; by telephone, telegraph, teletype, electronically transmitted, or other form of wire or wireless communication; or by mail or private carrier. The bylaws may provide that if these forms of personal notice are impracticable, notice may be communicated by a newspaper of general circulation in the area where published.

(3) Written notice by a nonprofit corporation to its members, if mailed, is correctly addressed if addressed to the member's address shown in the nonprofit corporation's current record of members. If three successive notices given to a member pursuant to subsection (5) of this section have been returned as undeliverable, no further notices to such member shall be necessary until another address for the member is made known to the nonprofit corporation.

(4) Written notice to a domestic nonprofit corporation or to a foreign nonprofit corporation authorized to transact business or conduct activities in this state, other than in its capacity as a member, is correctly addressed if addressed to the registered agent address of its registered agent or to the domestic or foreign nonprofit corporation or its secretary at its principal office.

(5) Written notice by a nonprofit corporation to its members, if in a comprehensible form, is effective at the earliest of:

(a) The date received;

(b) Five days after its deposit in the United States mail, as evidenced by the postmark, if mailed correctly addressed and with first class postage affixed;

(c) The date shown on the return receipt, if mailed by registered or certified mail, return receipt requested, and the receipt is signed by or on behalf of the addressee;

(d) Thirty days after its deposit in the United States mail, as evidenced by the postmark, if mailed correctly addressed and with other than first class, registered, or certified postage affixed.

(6) Oral notice is effective when communicated if communicated in a comprehensible manner.

(7) Notice by publication is effective on the date of first publication.

(8) If articles 121 to 137 of this title prescribe notice requirements for particular circumstances, those requirements govern. If the articles of incorporation or bylaws prescribe notice requirements not inconsistent with this section or other provisions of articles 121 to 137 of this title, those requirements govern.

(9) A written notice or report delivered as part of a newsletter, magazine, or other publication regularly sent to members shall constitute a written notice or report if addressed or delivered to the member's address shown in the nonprofit corporation's current list of members, or in the case of members who are residents of the same household and who have the same address in the nonprofit corporation's current list of members, if addressed or delivered to one of such members, at the address appearing on the current list of members.

§ 7-121-501, C.R.S. Private foundations.

(1) Except where otherwise determined by a court of competent jurisdiction, a nonprofit corporation that is a private foundation as defined in section 509 (a) of the internal revenue code:

(a) Shall distribute such amounts for each taxable year at such time and in such manner as not to subject the nonprofit corporation to tax under section 4942 of the internal revenue code;

(b) Shall not engage in any act of self-dealing as defined in section 4941 (d) of the internal revenue code;

(c) Shall not retain any excess business holdings as defined in section 4943 (c) of the internal revenue code;

(d)   Shall not make any investments that would subject the nonprofit corporation to taxation under section 4944 of the internal revenue code;

(e)   Shall not make any taxable expenditures as defined in section 4945 (d) of the internal revenue code.

§ 7-121-601, C.R.S. Judicial relief.

(1)   If for any reason it is impractical or impossible for any nonprofit corporation to call or conduct a meeting of its members, delegates, or directors, or otherwise obtain their consent, in the manner prescribed by articles 121 to 137 of this title, its articles of incorporation, or bylaws, then upon petition of a director, officer, delegate, or member the district court for the county in this state in which the street address of the nonprofit corporation's principal office is located, or if the nonprofit corporation has no principal office in this state, the district court for the county in which the street address of its registered agent is located, or if the nonprofit corporation has no registered agent, the district court for the city and county of Denver, may order that such a meeting be called or that a written consent or other form of obtaining the vote of members, delegates, or directors be authorized, in such a manner as the court finds fair and equitable under the circumstances.

(2)   The court shall, in an order issued pursuant to this section, provide for a method of notice reasonably designed to give actual notice to all persons who would be entitled to notice of a meeting held pursuant to articles 121 to 137 of this title, the articles of incorporation, or bylaws and whether or not the method results in actual notice to all such persons or conforms to the notice requirements that would otherwise apply. In a proceeding under this section, the court may determine who the members or directors are.

(3)   The order issued pursuant to this section may dispense with any requirement relating to the holding of or voting at meetings or obtaining votes, including any requirement as to quorums or as to the number or percentage of votes needed for approval, that would otherwise be imposed by articles 121 to 137 of this title, the articles of incorporation, or bylaws.

(4)   Whenever practical, any order issued pursuant to this section shall limit the subject matter of meetings or other forms of consent authorized to items, including amendments to the articles of incorporation or bylaws, the resolution of which will or may enable the nonprofit corporation to continue managing its affairs without further resort to this section; except that an order under this section may also authorize the obtaining of whatever votes and approvals are necessary for the dissolution, merger, or sale of assets.

(5)   Any meeting or other method of obtaining the vote of members, delegates, or directors conducted pursuant to an order issued under this section and that complies with all the provisions of such order is for all purposes a valid meeting or vote, as the case may be, and shall have the same force and effect as if it complied with every requirement imposed by articles 121 to 137 of this title, the articles of incorporation, or bylaws.

(6)   Court ordered meetings may also be held pursuant to section 7-127-103.

ARTICLE 122. INCORPORATION

§ 7-122-101, C.R.S. Incorporators.

One or more persons may act as the incorporator or incorporators of a nonprofit corporation by delivering articles of incorporation to the secretary of state for filing pursuant to part 3 of article 90 of this title. An incorporator who is an individual shall be eighteen years of age or older.

§ 7-122-102, C.R.S. Articles of incorporation.

(1)   The articles of incorporation shall state:

(a)   The domestic entity name for the nonprofit corporation, which domestic entity name shall comply with part 6 of article 90 of this title;

(b)   The registered agent name and registered agent address of the nonprofit corporation's initial registered agent;

(c)   The principal office address of the nonprofit corporation's initial principal office;

(d)   The true name and mailing address of each incorporator;

(e)   Whether or not the nonprofit corporation will have voting members; and

(f)   Repealed.

(g)   Provisions not inconsistent with law regarding the distribution of assets on dissolution.

(2)   The articles of incorporation may but need not state:

(a)   The names and addresses of the individuals who are elected to serve as the initial directors;

(b)   Provisions not inconsistent with law regarding:

(I)   The purpose or purposes for which the nonprofit corporation is incorporated;

(II)   Managing and regulating the affairs of the nonprofit corporation;

(III)   Defining, limiting, and regulating the powers of the nonprofit corporation, its board of directors, and its members, or any class of members; and

(IV)   Whether cumulative voting will be permitted;

(c)   Any provision that under articles 121 to 137 of this title is required or permitted to be stated in the bylaws;

(d)   The characteristics, qualifications, rights, limitations, and obligations attaching to each or any class of members.

(3)   The articles of incorporation need not state any of the corporate powers enumerated in articles 121 to 137 of this title.

(4)   If articles 121 to 137 of this title condition any matter upon the presence of a provision in the bylaws, the condition is satisfied if such provision is present either in the articles of incorporation or the bylaws. If articles 121 to 137 of this title condition any matter upon the absence of a provision in the bylaws, the condition is satisfied only if the provision is absent from both the articles of incorporation and the bylaws.

§ 7-122-103, C.R.S. Incorporation.

(1)   A nonprofit corporation is incorporated when the articles of incorporation are filed by the secretary of state or, if a delayed effective date is stated pursuant to section 7-90-304 in the articles of incorporation as filed by the secretary of state and if a statement of change revoking the articles of incorporation is not filed before such effective date, on such delayed effective date. The corporate existence begins upon incorporation.

(2)   The secretary of state's filing of the articles of incorporation is conclusive that all conditions precedent to incorporation have been met.

§ 7-122-104, C.R.S. Unauthorized assumption of corporate powers.

All persons purporting to act as or on behalf of a nonprofit corporation without authority to do so and without good-faith belief that they have such authority shall be jointly and severally liable for all liabilities incurred or arising as a result thereof.

§ 7-122-105, C.R.S. Organization of nonprofit corporation.

(1)   After incorporation:

(a)   If initial directors are not named in the articles of incorporation, the incorporators shall hold a meeting, at the call of a majority of the incorporators, to adopt initial bylaws, if desired, and to elect a board of directors; and

(b)   If initial directors are named in the articles of incorporation, the initial directors shall hold a meeting, at the call of a majority of the directors, to adopt bylaws, if desired, to appoint officers, and to carry on any other business.

(2)   Action required or permitted by articles 121 to 137 of this title to be taken by incorporators at an organizational meeting may be taken without a meeting if the action is taken in the manner provided in section 7-128-202 for action by directors without a meeting.

(3)   An organizational meeting may be held in or out of this state.

§ 7-122-106, C.R.S. Bylaws.

(1)   The board of directors or, if no directors have been named or elected, the incorporators may adopt initial bylaws. If neither the incorporators nor the board of directors have adopted initial bylaws, the members may do so.

(2)   The bylaws of a nonprofit corporation may contain any provision for managing and regulating the affairs of the nonprofit corporation that is not inconsistent with law or with the articles of incorporation.

§ 7-122-107, C.R.S. Emergency bylaws.

(1)   Unless otherwise provided in the articles of incorporation, the board of directors may adopt bylaws to be effective only in an emergency as defined in subsection (4) of this section. The emergency bylaws, which are subject to amendment or repeal by the members, may include all provisions necessary for managing the nonprofit corporation during the emergency, including:

(a)   Procedures for calling a meeting of the board of directors;

(b)   Quorum requirements for the meeting; and

(c)   Designation of additional or substitute directors.

(2)   All provisions of the regular bylaws consistent with the emergency bylaws shall remain in effect during the emergency. The emergency bylaws shall not be effective after the emergency ends.

(3)   Corporate action taken in good faith in accordance with the emergency bylaws:

(a)   Binds the nonprofit corporation; and

(b)   May not be the basis for imposition of liability on any director, officer, employee, or agent of the nonprofit corporation on the ground that the action was not authorized corporate action.

(4)   An emergency exists for the purposes of this section if a quorum of the directors cannot readily be obtained because of some catastrophic event.

ARTICLE 123. PURPOSES AND POWERS

§ 7-123-101, C.R.S. Purposes and applicability.

(1)   Every nonprofit corporation incorporated under articles 121 to 137 of this title has the purpose of engaging in any lawful business or activity unless a more limited purpose is stated in the articles of incorporation.

(2)   Where another statute of this state requires that corporations of a particular class be formed or incorporated exclusively under that statute, corporations of that class shall be formed or incorporated under such other statute. The corporation shall be subject to all limitations of the other statute.

(3) Where another statute of this state requires nonprofit corporations of a particular class to be formed or incorporated under that statute and also under general nonprofit corporation statutes, such nonprofit corporations shall be formed or incorporated under such other statute and, in addition thereto, under articles 121 to 137 of this title to the extent general nonprofit corporation law is applicable.

(4) Where another statute of this state permits nonprofit corporations of a particular class to be formed or incorporated either under that statute or under the general nonprofit corporation statutes, a nonprofit corporation of that class may at the election of its incorporators be formed or incorporated under articles 121 to 137 of this title. Unless the articles of incorporation of a nonprofit corporation indicate that it is formed or incorporated under another statute, the nonprofit corporation shall for all purposes be considered as formed and incorporated under articles 121 to 137 of this title.

(5) Articles 121 to 137 of this title shall apply to nonprofit corporations of every class, whether or not included in the term "nonprofit corporation" as defined in section 7-121-401 (26), that are formed or incorporated under and governed by other statutes of this state to the extent that said articles are not inconsistent with such other statutes.

(6) Articles 121 to 137 of this title shall apply to any nonprofit corporation formed prior to January 1, 1968, under article 40 or 50 of this title without shares or capital stock and for a purpose for which a nonprofit corporation might be formed under articles 121 to 137 of this title and that elects to accept said articles as provided therein.

(7) Articles 121 to 137 of this title shall apply to any corporation having shares or capital stock and formed under article 40, 50, or 51 of this title, and each nonprofit corporation whether with or without shares or capital stock formed prior to January 1, 1968, under general law or created by special act of the general assembly for a purpose for which a nonprofit corporation may be formed under articles 121 to 137 of this title, but not otherwise entitled to the rights, privileges, immunities, and franchises provided by said articles that elects to accept said articles as provided therein.

(8) A mutual ditch company may elect by a statement in its articles of incorporation that one or more of the provisions of the "Colorado Business Corporation Act", articles 101 to 117 of this title, apply to the mutual ditch company in lieu of one or more of the provisions of articles 121 to 137 of this title.

§ 7-123-102, C.R.S. General powers.

(1) Unless otherwise provided in the articles of incorporation, every nonprofit corporation has perpetual duration and succession in its domestic entity name and has the same powers as an individual to do all things necessary or convenient to carry out its affairs, including the power:

(a) To sue and be sued, complain, and defend in its name;

(b) To have a corporate seal, which may be altered at will, and to use such seal, or a facsimile thereof, including a rubber stamp, by impressing or affixing it or by reproducing it in any other manner;

(c) To make and amend bylaws;

(d) To purchase, receive, lease, and otherwise acquire, and to own, hold, improve, use, and otherwise deal with, real or personal property or any legal or equitable interest in property, wherever located;

(e) To sell, convey, mortgage, pledge, lease, exchange, and otherwise dispose of all or any part of its property;

(f) To purchase, receive, subscribe for, and otherwise acquire shares and other interests in, and obligations of, any other entity; and to own, hold, vote, use, sell, mortgage, lend, pledge, and otherwise dispose of, and deal in and with, the same;

(g) To make contracts and guarantees, incur liabilities, borrow money, issue notes, bonds, and other obligations, and secure any of its obligations by mortgage or pledge of any of its property, franchises, or income;

(h) To lend money, invest and reinvest its funds, and receive and hold real and personal property as security for repayment; except that a nonprofit corporation may not lend money to or guarantee the obligation of a director or officer of the nonprofit corporation;

(i) To be an agent, an associate, a fiduciary, a manager, a member, a partner, a promoter, or a trustee of, or to hold any similar position with, any entity;

(j) To conduct its activities, locate offices, and exercise the powers granted by articles 121 to 137 of this title within or without this state;

(k) To elect or appoint directors, officers, employees, and agents of the nonprofit corporation, define their duties, and fix their compensation;

(l) To pay pensions and establish pension plans, pension trusts, profit sharing plans, and other benefit or incentive plans for any of its current or former directors, officers, employees, and agents;

(m) To make donations for the public welfare or for charitable, religious, scientific, or educational purposes and for other purposes that further the corporate interest;

(n) To impose dues, assessments, admission, and transfer fees upon its members;

(o) To establish conditions for admission of members, admit members, and issue or transfer memberships;

(p) To carry on a business;

(q) To make payments or donations and to do any other act, not inconsistent with law, that furthers the affairs of the nonprofit corporation;

(r) To indemnify current or former directors, officers, employees, fiduciaries, or agents as provided in article 129 of this title;

(s) To limit the liability of its directors as provided in section 7-128-402 (1); and

(t) To cease its corporate activities and dissolve.

(2) Unless permitted by another statute of this state or otherwise permitted pursuant to section 7-123-101 (5), 7-123-101 (7), or 7-137-201, a nonprofit corporation shall not authorize or issue shares of stock.

§ 7-123-103, C.R.S. Emergency powers.

(1) In anticipation of or during an emergency defined in subsection (4) of this section, the board of directors may:

(a) Modify lines of succession to accommodate the incapacity of any director, officer, employee, or agent; and

(b) Relocate the principal office or designate additional offices, or authorize officers to do so.

(2) During an emergency as contemplated in subsection (4) of this section, unless emergency bylaws provide otherwise:

(a) Notice of a meeting of the board of directors need be given only to those directors whom it is practicable to reach and may be given in any practicable manner, including by publication or radio; and

(b) One or more officers of the nonprofit corporation present at a meeting of the board of directors may be deemed to be directors for the meeting, in order of rank and within the same rank in order of seniority, as necessary to achieve a quorum.

(3) Corporate action taken in good faith during an emergency under this section to further the ordinary business affairs of the nonprofit corporation:

(a)   Binds the nonprofit corporation; and

(b)   May not be the basis for the imposition of liability on any director, officer, employee, or agent of the nonprofit corporation on the ground that the action was not authorized corporate action.

(4)   An emergency exists for purposes of this section if a quorum of the directors cannot readily be obtained because of some catastrophic event.

§ 7-123-104, C.R.S. Ultra vires.

(1)   Except as provided in subsection (2) of this section, the validity of corporate action may not be challenged on the ground that the nonprofit corporation lacks or lacked power to act.

(2)   A nonprofit corporation's power to act may be challenged:

(a)   In a proceeding against the nonprofit corporation to enjoin the act. The proceeding may be brought by a director or by a voting member or voting members in a derivative proceeding.

(b)   In a proceeding by or in the right of the nonprofit corporation, whether directly, derivatively, or through a receiver, trustee, or other legal representative, against an incumbent or former director, officer, employee, or agent of the nonprofit corporation; or

(c)   In a proceeding by the attorney general under section 7-134-301.

(3)   In a proceeding under paragraph (a) of subsection (2) of this section to enjoin an unauthorized corporate act, the court may enjoin or set aside the act, if it would be equitable to do so and if all affected persons are parties to the proceeding, and may award damages for loss, including anticipated profits, suffered by the nonprofit corporation or another party because of the injunction.

§ 7-123-105, C.R.S. Actions against nonprofit corporations.

Any other provision of law to the contrary notwithstanding, any civil action permitted under the law of this state may be brought against any nonprofit corporation, and the assets of any nonprofit corporation that would, but for articles 121 to 137 of this title, be immune from levy and execution on any judgment shall nonetheless be subject to levy and execution to the extent that such nonprofit corporation would be reimbursed by proceeds of liability insurance policies carried by it were judgment levied and executed against its assets.

ARTICLE 124. NAME

§ 7-124-101, C.R.S. Corporate name. (Repealed)

§ 7-124-102, C.R.S. Reserved name. (Repealed)

ARTICLE 125. OFFICE AND AGENT

§ 7-125-101, C.R.S. Registered office and registered agent.

Part 7 of article 90 of this title, providing for registered agents and service of process, applies to nonprofit corporations incorporated under or subject to articles 121 to 137 of this title.

ARTICLE 126. MEMBERS AND MEMBERSHIPS

§ 7-126-101, C.R.S. No requirement of members.

A nonprofit corporation is not required to have members.

§ 7-126-102, C.R.S. Admission.

(1)   The bylaws may establish criteria or procedures for admission of members.

(2)   No person shall be admitted as a member without such person's consent.

(3)   A nonprofit corporation may issue certificates evidencing membership therein.

§ 7-126-103, C.R.S. Liability to third parties.

The directors, officers, employees, and members of a nonprofit corporation are not, as such, personally liable for the acts, debts, liabilities, or obligations of a nonprofit corporation.

§ 7-126-104, C.R.S. Consideration.

Unless otherwise provided by the bylaws, a nonprofit corporation may admit members for no consideration or for such consideration as is determined by the board of directors.

§ 7-126-201, C.R.S. Differences in rights and obligations of members.

(1)   Unless otherwise provided by articles 121 to 137 of this title or the bylaws:

    (a)   All voting members shall have the same rights and obligations with respect to voting and all other matters that articles 121 to 137 of this title specifically reserve to voting members; and

    (b)   With respect to matters not so reserved, all members, including voting members, shall have the same rights and obligations.

§ 7-126-202, C.R.S. Transfers.

(1)   Unless otherwise provided by the bylaws, no member of a nonprofit corporation may transfer a membership or any right arising therefrom.

(2)   Where transfer rights have been provided, no restriction on them shall be binding with respect to a member holding a membership issued prior to the adoption of the restriction unless the restriction is approved by the affected member.

§ 7-126-203, C.R.S. Creditor's action against member.

No proceeding may be brought by a creditor to reach the liability, if any, of a member to the nonprofit corporation unless final judgment has been rendered in favor of the creditor against the nonprofit corporation and execution has been returned unsatisfied in whole or in part or unless such proceeding would be useless.

§ 7-126-301, C.R.S. Resignation.

(1)   Unless otherwise provided by the bylaws, a member may resign at any time.

(2)   The resignation of a member does not relieve the member from any obligations the member may have to the nonprofit corporation as a result of obligations incurred or commitments made prior to resignation.

§ 7-126-302, C.R.S. Termination, expulsion, or suspension.

(1)   Unless otherwise provided by the bylaws, no member of a nonprofit corporation may be expelled or suspended, and no membership or memberships in such nonprofit corporation may be terminated or suspended except pursuant to a procedure that is fair and reasonable and is carried out in good faith.

(2)   For purposes of this section, a procedure is fair and reasonable when either:

    (a)   The bylaws or a written policy of the board of directors state a procedure that provides:

(I)   Not less than fifteen days prior written notice of the expulsion, suspension, or termination and the reasons therefor; and

(II)   An opportunity for the member to be heard, orally or in writing, not less than five days before the effective date of the expulsion, suspension, or termination by a person or persons authorized to decide that the proposed expulsion, termination, or suspension not take place; or

(b) It is fair and reasonable taking into consideration all of the relevant facts and circumstances.

(3) For purposes of this section, any written notice given by mail must be given by first-class or certified mail sent to the last address of the member shown on the nonprofit corporation's records.

(4) Unless otherwise provided by the bylaws, any proceeding challenging an expulsion, suspension, or termination, including a proceeding in which defective notice is alleged, must be commenced within one year after the effective date of the expulsion, suspension, or termination.

(5) Unless otherwise provided by the bylaws, a member who has been expelled or suspended may be liable to the nonprofit corporation for dues, assessments, or fees as a result of obligations incurred or commitments made prior to expulsion or suspension.

§ 7-126-303, C.R.S. Purchase of memberships.

Unless otherwise provided by the bylaws, a nonprofit corporation shall not purchase the membership of a member who resigns or whose membership is terminated. If so authorized, a nonprofit corporation may purchase the membership of a member who resigns or whose membership is terminated for the amount and pursuant to the conditions stated in or authorized by its bylaws. No payment shall be made in violation of article 133 of this title.

§ 7-126-304, C.R.S. Residential membership – return of consideration – cessation of periodic payments – time limits – effective date.

(1) Notwithstanding any provision of the articles of incorporation or bylaws to the contrary:

(a) (I) A residential nonprofit corporation shall refund the entrance fee of a residential member to the member or his or her heirs within ninety days after a transfer of the residential membership.

(II) (A) This paragraph (a) applies only to contracts entered into on or after March 11, 2011.

(B) (Deleted by amendment, L. 2012.)

(b) (Deleted by amendment, L. 2012.)

§ 7-126-401, C.R.S. Derivative suits.

(1) Without affecting the right of a member or director to bring a proceeding against a nonprofit corporation or its officers or directors, a proceeding may be brought in the right of a nonprofit corporation to procure a judgment in its favor by:

(a) Any voting member or voting members having five percent or more of the voting power; or

(b) Any director.

(2) In any such proceeding, each complainant shall be a voting member or director at the time of bringing the proceeding.

(3) A complaint in a proceeding brought in the right of a nonprofit corporation must be verified and allege with particularity the demand made, if any, to obtain action by the directors and either

why the complainants could not obtain the action or why they did not make the demand. If a demand for action was made and the nonprofit corporation's investigation of the demand is in progress when the proceeding is filed, the court may stay the suit until the investigation is completed.

(4)   In any action instituted in the right of a nonprofit corporation by one or more voting members, the court having jurisdiction over the matter may, at any time before final judgment, require the plaintiff to give security for the costs and reasonable expenses that may be directly attributable to and incurred by the nonprofit corporation in the defense of such action or may be incurred by other parties named as defendant for which the nonprofit corporation may become legally liable, but not including fees of attorneys. The amount of such security may from time to time be increased or decreased, in the discretion of the court, upon showing that the security provided has or may become inadequate or is excessive. If the court finds that the action was commenced without reasonable cause, the nonprofit corporation shall have recourse to such security in such amount as the court shall determine upon the termination of such action.

(5)   No action shall be commenced in this state by a member of a foreign nonprofit corporation in the right of a foreign nonprofit corporation unless such action is permitted by the law of the state under which such foreign nonprofit corporation is incorporated.

§ 7-126-501, C.R.S. Delegates.

(1)   A nonprofit corporation may provide in its bylaws for delegates having some or all of the authority of members.

(2)   The bylaws may state provisions relating to:

(a)   The characteristics, qualifications, rights, limitations, and obligations of delegates, including their selection and removal;

(b)   Calling, noticing, holding, and conducting meetings of delegates; and

(c)   Carrying on corporate activities during and between meetings of delegates.

ARTICLE 127. MEMBERS' MEETINGS AND VOTING

§ 7-127-101, C.R.S. Annual and regular meetings.

(1)   Unless the bylaws eliminate the requirement for holding an annual meeting, a nonprofit corporation that has voting members shall hold a meeting of the voting members annually at a time stated in or fixed in accordance with the bylaws, or, if not so fixed, at a time and date stated in or fixed in accordance with a resolution of the board of directors.

(2)   A nonprofit corporation with members may hold regular membership meetings at a time and date stated in or fixed in accordance with the bylaws, or, if not so fixed, at a time and date stated in or fixed in accordance with a resolution of the board of directors.

(3)   Annual and regular membership meetings may be held in or out of this state at the place stated in or fixed in accordance with the bylaws, or, if not so stated or fixed, at a place stated or fixed in accordance with a resolution of the board of directors. If no place is so stated or fixed, annual and regular meetings shall be held at the nonprofit corporation's principal office.

(4)   The failure to hold an annual or regular meeting at the time and date determined pursuant to subsection (1) of this section does not affect the validity of any corporate action and does not work a forfeiture or dissolution of the nonprofit corporation.

§ 7-127-102, C.R.S. Special meeting.

(1)   A nonprofit corporation shall hold a special meeting of its members:

(a)   On call of its board of directors or the person or persons authorized by the bylaws or resolution of the board of directors to call such a meeting; or

(b)   Unless otherwise provided by the bylaws, if the nonprofit corporation receives one or more written demands for the meeting, stating the purpose or purposes for which it is to be held, signed and dated by members holding at least ten percent of all the votes entitled pursuant to the bylaws to be cast on any issue proposed to be considered at the meeting.

(2)   If not otherwise fixed under section 7-127-103 or 7-127-106, the record date for determining the members entitled to demand a special meeting pursuant to paragraph (b) of subsection (1) of this section is the date of the earliest of any of the demands pursuant to which the meeting is called, or the date that is sixty days before the date the first of such demands is received by the nonprofit corporation, whichever is later.

(3)   If a notice for a special meeting demanded pursuant to paragraph (b) of subsection (1) of this section is not given pursuant to section 7-127-104 within thirty days after the date the written demand or demands are delivered to a corporate officer, regardless of the requirements of subsection (4) of this section, a person signing the demand or demands may set the time and place of the meeting and give notice pursuant to section 7-127-104.

(4)   Special meetings of the members may be held in or out of this state at the place stated in or fixed in accordance with the bylaws, or, if not so stated or fixed, at a place stated or fixed in accordance with a resolution of the board of directors. If no place is so stated or fixed, special meetings shall be held at the nonprofit corporation's principal office.

(5)   Unless otherwise provided by the bylaws, only business within the purpose or purposes described in the notice of the meeting required by section 7-127-104 (3) may be conducted at a special meeting of the members.

§ 7-127-103, C.R.S. Court-ordered meeting.

(1)   The holding of a meeting of the members may be summarily ordered by the district court for the county in this state in which the street address of the nonprofit corporation's principal office is located or, if the nonprofit corporation has no principal office in this state, by the district court for the county in which the street address of its registered agent is located or, if the nonprofit corporation has no registered agent, by the district court for the city and county of Denver:

(a)   On application of any voting member entitled to participate in an annual meeting if an annual meeting was required to be held and was not held within the earlier of six months after the close of the nonprofit corporation's most recently ended fiscal year or fifteen months after its last annual meeting; or

(b)   On application of any person who participated in a call of or demand for a special meeting effective under section 7-127-102 (1), if:

(I)   Notice of the special meeting was not given within thirty days after the date of the call or the date the last of the demands necessary to require the calling of the meeting was received by the nonprofit corporation pursuant to section 7-127-102 (1) (b), as the case may be; or

(II)   The special meeting was not held in accordance with the notice.

(2)   The court may fix the time and place of the meeting, determine the members entitled to participate in the meeting, fix a record date for determining members entitled to notice of and to vote at the meeting, prescribe the form and content of the notice of the meeting, fix the quorum required for specific matters to be considered at the meeting or direct that the votes represented at the meeting constitute a quorum for action on those matters, and enter other orders necessary or appropriate to accomplish the holding of the meeting.

§ 7-127-104, C.R.S. Notice of meeting.

(1)   A nonprofit corporation shall give to each member entitled to vote at the meeting notice consistent with its bylaws of meetings of members in a fair and reasonable manner.

(2)   Any notice that conforms to the requirements of subsection (3) of this section is fair and reasonable, but other means of giving notice may also be fair and reasonable when all the circumstances are considered.

(3)   Notice is fair and reasonable if:

(a)   The nonprofit corporation notifies its members of the place, date, and time of each annual, regular, and special meeting of members no fewer than ten days, or if notice is mailed by other than first class or registered mail, no fewer than thirty days, nor more than sixty days before the meeting date, and if notice is given by newspaper as provided in section 7-121-402 (2), the notice must be published five separate times with the first such publication no more than sixty days, and the last such publication no fewer than ten days, before the meeting date.

(b)   Notice of an annual or regular meeting includes a description of any matter or matters that must be approved by the members or for which the members' approval is sought under sections 7-128-501, 7-129-110, 7-130-103, 7-130-201, 7-131-102, 7-132-102, and 7-134-102; and

(c)   Unless otherwise provided by articles 121 to 137 of this title or the bylaws, notice of a special meeting includes a description of the purpose or purposes for which the meeting is called.

(4)   Unless otherwise provided by the bylaws, if an annual, regular, or special meeting of members is adjourned to a different date, time, or place, notice need not be given of the new date, time, or place, if the new date, time, or place is announced at the meeting before adjournment. If a new record date for the adjourned meeting is or must be fixed under section 7-127-106, however, notice of the adjourned meeting must be given under this section to the members of record as of the new record date.

(5)   When giving notice of an annual, regular, or special meeting of members, a nonprofit corporation shall give notice of a matter a member intends to raise at the meeting if:

(a)   Requested in writing to do so by a person entitled to call a special meeting; and

(b)   The request is received by the secretary or president of the nonprofit corporation at least ten days before the nonprofit corporation gives notice of the meeting.

§ 7-127-105, C.R.S. Waiver of notice.

(1)   A member may waive any notice required by articles 121 to 137 of this title or by the bylaws, whether before or after the date or time stated in the notice as the date or time when any action will occur or has occurred. The waiver shall be in writing, be signed by the member entitled to the notice, and be delivered to the nonprofit corporation for inclusion in the minutes or filing with the corporate records, but such delivery and filing shall not be conditions of the effectiveness of the waiver.

(2)   A member's attendance at a meeting:

(a)   Waives objection to lack of notice or defective notice of the meeting, unless the member at the beginning of the meeting objects to holding the meeting or transacting business at the meeting because of lack of notice or defective notice; and

(b)   Waives objection to consideration of a particular matter at the meeting that is not within the purpose or purposes described in the meeting notice, unless the member objects to considering the matter when it is presented.

§ 7-127-106, C.R.S. Record date – determining members entitled to notice and vote.

(1) The bylaws may fix or provide the manner of fixing a date as the record date for determining the members entitled to notice of a members' meeting. If the bylaws do not fix or provide for fixing such a record date, the board of directors may fix a future date as such a record date. If no such record date is fixed, members at the close of business on the business day preceding the day on which notice is given, or, if notice is waived, at the close of business on the business day preceding the day on which the meeting is held are entitled to notice of the meeting.

(2) The bylaws may fix or provide the manner of fixing a date as the record date for determining the members entitled to vote at a members' meeting. If the bylaws do not fix or provide for fixing such a record date, the board may fix a future date as such a record date. If no such record date is fixed, members on the date of the meeting who are otherwise eligible to vote are entitled to vote at the meeting.

(3) The bylaws may fix or provide the manner for determining a date as the record date for the purpose of determining the members entitled to exercise any rights in respect of any other lawful action. If the bylaws do not fix or provide for fixing such a record date, the board may fix a future date as the record date. If no such record date is fixed, members at the close of business on the day on which the board adopts the resolution relating thereto, or the sixtieth day prior to the date of such other action, whichever is later, are entitled to exercise such rights.

(4) A record date fixed under this section may not be more than seventy days before the meeting or action requiring a determination of members occurs.

(5) A determination of members entitled to notice of or to vote at a meeting of members is effective for any adjournment of the meeting unless the board of directors fixes a new date for determining the right to notice or the right to vote, which it must do if the meeting is adjourned to a date more than one hundred twenty days after the record date for determining members entitled to notice of the original meeting.

(6) If a court orders a meeting adjourned to a date more than one hundred twenty days after the date fixed for the original meeting, it may provide that the original record date for notice or voting continues in effect or it may fix a new record date for notice or voting.

§ 7-127-107, C.R.S. Action without meeting.

(1) Unless otherwise provided by the bylaws, any action required or permitted by articles 121 to 137 of this title to be taken at a members' meeting may be taken without a meeting if members entitled to vote thereon unanimously agree and consent to such action in writing.

(2) No action taken pursuant to this section shall be effective unless writings describing and consenting to the action, signed by members sufficient under subsection (1) of this section to take the action and not revoked pursuant to subsection (3) of this section, are received by the nonprofit corporation within sixty days after the date the earliest dated writing describing and consenting to the action is received by the nonprofit corporation. Unless otherwise provided by the bylaws, any such writing may be received by the nonprofit corporation by electronically transmitted facsimile or other form of wire or wireless communication providing the nonprofit corporation with a complete copy thereof, including a copy of the signature thereto. Action taken pursuant to this section shall be effective when the last writing necessary to effect the action is received by the nonprofit corporation, unless the writings describing and consenting to the action state a different effective date.

(3) Any member who has signed a writing describing and consenting to action taken pursuant to this section may revoke such consent by a writing signed and dated by the member describing the action and stating that the member's prior consent thereto is revoked, if such writing is received by the nonprofit corporation before the last writing necessary to effect the action is received by the nonprofit corporation.

(4)   Subject to subsection (8) of this section, the record date for determining members entitled to take action without a meeting or entitled to be given notice under subsection (7) of this section of action so taken is the date a writing upon which the action is taken pursuant to subsection (1) of this section is first received by the nonprofit corporation.

(5)   Action taken under this section has the same effect as action taken at a meeting of members and may be described as such in any document.

(6)   In the event voting members are entitled to vote cumulatively in the election of directors, voting members may take action under this section to elect or remove directors only pursuant to section 7-127-208 and only if the required signed writings describing and consenting to the election or removal of the directors are received by the nonprofit corporation.

(7)   In the event action is taken under subsection (1) of this section with less than unanimous consent of all members entitled to vote upon the action, the nonprofit corporation or the members taking the action shall, promptly after all of the writings necessary to effect the action have been received by the nonprofit corporation, give notice of such action to all members who were entitled to vote upon the action. The notice shall contain or be accompanied by the same material, if any, that under articles 121 to 137 of this title would have been required to be given to members in or with a notice of the meeting at which the action would have been submitted to the members for action.

(8)   The district court for the county in this state in which the street address of the nonprofit corporation's principal office is located or, if the nonprofit corporation has no principal office in this state, the district court for the county in which the street address of its registered agent is located or, if the nonprofit corporation has no registered agent, the district court for the city and county of Denver may, upon application of the nonprofit corporation or any member who would be entitled to vote on the action at a members' meeting, summarily state a record date for determining members entitled to sign writings consenting to an action under this section and may enter other orders necessary or appropriate to effect the purposes of this section.

(9)   All signed written instruments necessary for any action taken pursuant to this section shall be filed with the minutes of the meetings of the members.

§ 7-127-108, C.R.S. Meetings by telecommunication.

Unless otherwise provided in the bylaws, any or all of the members may participate in an annual, regular, or special meeting of the members by, or the meeting may be conducted through the use of, any means of communication by which all persons participating in the meeting may hear each other during the meeting. A member participating in a meeting by this means is deemed to be present in person at the meeting.

§ 7-127-109, C.R.S. Action by written ballot.

(1)   Unless otherwise provided by the bylaws, any action that may be taken at any annual, regular, or special meeting of members may be taken without a meeting if the nonprofit corporation delivers a written ballot to every member entitled to vote on the matter.

(2)   A written ballot shall:

(a)   State each proposed action; and

(b)   Provide an opportunity to vote for or against each proposed action.

(3)   Approval by written ballot pursuant to this section shall be valid only when the number of votes cast by ballot equals or exceeds the quorum required to be present at a meeting authorizing the action, and the number of approvals equals or exceeds the number of votes that would be required to approve the matter at a meeting at which the total number of votes cast was the same as the number of votes cast by ballot.

(4)   All solicitations for votes by written ballot shall:

(a)   Indicate the number of responses needed to meet the quorum requirements;

(b)   State the percentage of approvals necessary to approve each matter other than election of directors;

(c)   State the time by which a ballot must be received by the nonprofit corporation in order to be counted; and

(d)   Be accompanied by written information sufficient to permit each person casting such ballot to reach an informed decision on the matter.

(5)   Unless otherwise provided by the bylaws, a written ballot may not be revoked.

(6)   Action taken under this section has the same effect as action taken at a meeting of members and may be described as such in any document.

§ 7-127-201, C.R.S. Members list for meeting and action by written ballot.

(1)   Unless otherwise provided by the bylaws, after fixing a record date for a notice of a meeting or for determining the members entitled to take action by written ballot, a nonprofit corporation shall prepare an alphabetical list of the names of all its members who are entitled to notice of, and to vote at, the meeting or to take such action by written ballot. The list shall show the address of each member entitled to notice of, and to vote at, the meeting or to take such action by written ballot and the number of votes each member is entitled to vote at the meeting or by written ballot.

(2)   If prepared in connection with a meeting of the members, the members list shall be available for inspection by any member entitled to vote at the meeting, beginning the earlier of ten days before the meeting for which the list was prepared or two business days after notice of the meeting is given and continuing through the meeting, and any adjournment thereof, at the nonprofit corporation's principal office or at a place identified in the notice of the meeting in the city where the meeting will be held. The nonprofit corporation shall make the members list available at the meeting, and any member entitled to vote at the meeting or an agent or attorney of a member entitled to vote at the meeting is entitled to inspect the list at any time during the meeting or any adjournment. If prepared in connection with action to be taken by the members by written ballot, the members list shall be available for inspection by any member entitled to cast a vote by such written ballot, beginning on the date that the first written ballot is delivered to the members and continuing through the time when such written ballots must be received by the nonprofit corporation in order to be counted, at the nonprofit corporation's principal office. A member entitled to vote at the meeting or by such written ballot, or an agent or attorney of a member entitled to vote at the meeting or by such written ballot, is entitled on written demand to inspect and, subject to the requirements of section 7-136-102 (3) and the provisions of section 7-136-103 (2) and (3), to copy the list, during regular business hours, at the member's expense, and during the period it is available for inspection.

(3)   If the nonprofit corporation refuses to allow a member entitled to vote at the meeting or by such written ballot, or an agent or attorney of a member entitled to vote at the meeting or by such written ballot, to inspect the members list or to copy the list during the period it is required to be available for inspection under subsection (2) of this section, the district court for the county in this state in which the street address of the nonprofit corporation's principal office is located or, if the nonprofit corporation has no principal office in this state, the district court for the county in which the street address of its registered agent is located, or if the nonprofit corporation has no registered agent in this state, the district court for the city and county of Denver may, on application of the member, summarily order the inspection or copying of the list at the nonprofit corporation's expense and may postpone or adjourn the meeting for which the list was prepared, or postpone the time when the nonprofit corporation must receive written ballots in connection with which the list was prepared, until the inspection or copying is complete.

(4)　If a court orders inspection or copying of the list of members pursuant to subsection (3) of this section, unless the nonprofit corporation proves that it refused inspection or copying of the list in good faith because it had a reasonable basis for doubt about the right of the member or the agent or attorney of the member to inspect or copy the list of members:

　　(a)　The court shall also order the nonprofit corporation to pay the member's costs, including reasonable counsel fees, incurred in obtaining the order;

　　(b)　The court may order the nonprofit corporation to pay the member for any damages the member incurred; and

　　(c)　The court may grant the member any other remedy afforded the member by law.

(5)　If a court orders inspection or copying of the list of members pursuant to subsection (3) of this section, the court may impose reasonable restrictions on the use or distribution of the list by the member.

(6)　Failure to prepare or make available the list of members does not affect the validity of action taken at the meeting or by means of such written ballot.

§ 7-127-202, C.R.S. *Voting entitlement generally.*

(1)　Unless otherwise provided by the bylaws:

　　(a)　Only voting members shall be entitled to vote with respect to any matter required or permitted under articles 121 to 137 of this title to be submitted to a vote of the members;

　　(b)　All references in articles 121 to 137 of this title to votes of or voting by the members shall be deemed to permit voting only by the voting members; and

　　(c)　Voting members shall be entitled to vote with respect to all matters required or permitted under articles 121 to 137 of this title to be submitted to a vote of the members.

(2)　Unless otherwise provided by the bylaws, each member entitled to vote shall be entitled to one vote on each matter submitted to a vote of members.

(3)　Unless otherwise provided by the bylaws, if a membership stands of record in the names of two or more persons, their acts with respect to voting shall have the following effect:

　　(a)　If only one votes, such act binds all; and

　　(b)　If more than one votes, the vote shall be divided on a pro rata basis.

§ 7-127-203, C.R.S. *Proxies.*

(1)　Unless otherwise provided by the bylaws, a member entitled to vote may vote or otherwise act in person or by proxy.

(2)　Without limiting the manner in which a member may appoint a proxy to vote or otherwise act for the member, the following shall constitute valid means of such appointment:

　　(a)　A member may appoint a proxy by signing an appointment form, either personally or by the member's attorney-in-fact.

　　(b)　A member may appoint a proxy by transmitting or authorizing the transmission of a telegram, teletype, or other electronic transmission providing a written statement of the appointment to the proxy, to a proxy solicitor, proxy support service organization, or other person duly authorized by the proxy to receive appointments as agent for the proxy or to the nonprofit corporation; except that the transmitted appointment shall set forth or be transmitted with written evidence from which it can be determined that the member transmitted or authorized the transmission of the appointment.

(3)　An appointment of a proxy is effective against the nonprofit corporation when received by the nonprofit corporation, including receipt by the nonprofit corporation of an appointment transmitted pursuant to paragraph (b) of subsection (2) of this section. An appointment is valid for eleven months unless a different period is expressly provided in the appointment form.

(4) Any complete copy, including an electronically transmitted facsimile, of an appointment of a proxy may be substituted for or used in lieu of the original appointment for any purpose for which the original appointment could be used.

(5) An appointment of a proxy is revocable by the member.

(6) Appointment of a proxy is revoked by the person appointing the proxy:

    (a) Attending any meeting and voting in person; or

    (b) Signing and delivering to the secretary or other officer or agent authorized to tabulate proxy votes either a writing stating that the appointment of the proxy is revoked or a subsequent appointment form.

(7) The death or incapacity of the member appointing a proxy does not affect the right of the nonprofit corporation to accept the proxy's authority unless notice of the death or incapacity is received by the secretary or other officer or agent authorized to tabulate votes before the proxy exercises the proxy's authority under the appointment.

(8) Subject to section 7-127-204 and to any express limitation on the proxy's authority appearing on the appointment form, a nonprofit corporation is entitled to accept the proxy's vote or other action as that of the member making the appointment.

§ 7-127-204, C.R.S. Nonprofit corporation's acceptance of votes.

(1) If the name signed on a vote, consent, written ballot, waiver, proxy appointment, or proxy appointment revocation corresponds to the name of a member, the nonprofit corporation, if acting in good faith, is entitled to accept the vote, consent, written ballot, waiver, proxy appointment, or proxy appointment revocation and to give it effect as the act of the member.

(2) If the name signed on a vote, consent, written ballot, waiver, proxy appointment, or proxy appointment revocation does not correspond to the name of a member, the nonprofit corporation, if acting in good faith, is nevertheless entitled to accept the vote, consent, written ballot, waiver, proxy appointment, or proxy appointment revocation and to give it effect as the act of the member if:

    (a) The member is an entity and the name signed purports to be that of an officer or agent of the entity;

    (b) The name signed purports to be that of an administrator, executor, guardian, or conservator representing the member and, if the nonprofit corporation requests, evidence of fiduciary status acceptable to the nonprofit corporation has been presented with respect to the vote, consent, written ballot, waiver, proxy appointment, or proxy appointment revocation;

    (c) The name signed purports to be that of a receiver or trustee in bankruptcy of the member and, if the nonprofit corporation requests, evidence of this status acceptable to the nonprofit corporation has been presented with respect to the vote, consent, written ballot, waiver, proxy appointment, or proxy appointment revocation;

    (d) The name signed purports to be that of a pledgee, beneficial owner, or attorney-in-fact of the member and, if the nonprofit corporation requests, evidence acceptable to the nonprofit corporation of the signatory's authority to sign for the member has been presented with respect to the vote, consent, written ballot, waiver, proxy appointment, or proxy appointment revocation;

    (e) Two or more persons are the member as cotenants or fiduciaries and the name signed purports to be the name of at least one of the cotenants or fiduciaries and the person signing appears to be acting on behalf of all the cotenants or fiduciaries; or

    (f) The acceptance of the vote, consent, written ballot, waiver, proxy appointment, or proxy appointment revocation is otherwise proper under rules established by the nonprofit corporation that are not inconsistent with the provisions of this subsection (2).

(3) The nonprofit corporation is entitled to reject a vote, consent, written ballot, waiver, proxy appointment, or proxy appointment revocation if the secretary or other officer or agent authorized to tabulate votes, acting in good faith, has reasonable basis for doubt about the validity of the signature on it or about the signatory's authority to sign for the member.

(4) The nonprofit corporation and its officer or agent who accepts or rejects a vote, consent, written ballot, waiver, proxy appointment, or proxy appointment revocation in good faith and in accordance with the standards of this section are not liable in damages for the consequences of the acceptance or rejection.

(5) Corporate action based on the acceptance or rejection of a vote, consent, written ballot, waiver, proxy appointment, or proxy appointment revocation under this section is valid unless a court of competent jurisdiction determines otherwise.

§ 7-127-205, C.R.S. *Quorum and voting requirements for voting groups.*

(1) Members entitled to vote as a separate voting group may take action on a matter at a meeting only if a quorum of those members exists with respect to that matter. Unless otherwise provided in articles 121 to 137 of this title or the bylaws, twenty-five percent of the votes entitled to be cast on the matter by the voting group constitutes a quorum of that voting group for action on that matter.

(2) Once a member is represented for any purpose at a meeting, including the purpose of determining that a quorum exists, the member is deemed present for quorum purposes for the remainder of the meeting and for any adjournment of that meeting, unless otherwise provided in the bylaws or unless a new record date is or shall be set for that adjourned meeting.

(3) If a quorum exists, action on a matter other than the election of directors by a voting group is approved if the votes cast within the voting group favoring the action exceed the votes cast within the voting group opposing the action, unless a greater number of affirmative votes is required by articles 121 to 137 of this title or the bylaws.

(4) An amendment to the articles of incorporation or the bylaws adding, changing, or deleting a quorum or voting requirement for a voting group greater than that specified in subsection (1) or (3) of this section is governed by section 7-127-207 (2).

(5) The election of directors is governed by section 7-127-208.

§ 7-127-206, C.R.S. *Action by single and multiple voting groups.*

(1) If articles 121 to 137 of this title or the bylaws provide for voting by a single voting group on a matter, action on that matter is taken when voted upon by that voting group as provided in section 7-127-205.

(2) If articles 121 to 137 of this title or the bylaws provide for voting by two or more voting groups on a matter, action on that matter is taken only when voted upon by each of those voting groups counted separately as provided in section 7-127-205. One voting group may vote on a matter even though no action is taken by another voting group entitled to vote on the matter.

§ 7-127-207, C.R.S. *Lesser or greater quorum or greater voting requirements.*

(1) The bylaws may provide for a lesser or a greater quorum requirement, or a greater voting requirement for members or voting groups than is provided for by articles 121 to 137 of this title.

(2) An amendment to the articles of incorporation or the bylaws that adds, changes, or deletes a lesser or a greater quorum requirement or a greater voting requirement shall meet the same quorum requirement and be adopted by the same vote and voting groups required to take action under the quorum and voting requirements then in effect or proposed to be adopted, whichever is greater.

§ 7-127-208, C.R.S. Voting for directors – cumulative voting.

(1) If the bylaws provide for cumulative voting for directors by the voting members, voting members may so vote, by multiplying the number of votes the voting members are entitled to cast by the number of directors for whom they are entitled to vote and cast the product for a single candidate or distribute the product among two or more candidates.

(2) Cumulative voting is not authorized at a particular meeting unless:

  (a) The meeting notice or statement accompanying the notice states that cumulative voting will take place; or

  (b) A voting member gives notice during the meeting and before the vote is taken of the voting member's intent to cumulate votes, and if one voting member gives this notice all other voting members participating in the election are entitled to cumulate their votes without giving further notice.

(3) If cumulative voting is in effect, a director may not be removed if the number of votes cast against such removal, or not consenting in writing to such removal, would be sufficient to elect such director if voted cumulatively at an election for such director.

(4) Members may not vote cumulatively if the directors and members are identical.

(5) In an election of multiple directors, that number of candidates equaling the number of directors to be elected, having the highest number of votes cast in favor of their election, are elected to the board of directors. When only one director is being voted upon, the affirmative vote of a majority of the members constituting a quorum at the meeting at which the election occurs shall be required for election to the board of directors.

§ 7-127-209, C.R.S. Other methods of electing directors.

(1) A nonprofit corporation may provide in its bylaws for election of directors by voting members or delegates:

  (a) On the basis of chapter or other organizational unit;

  (b) By region or other geographic unit;

  (c) By preferential voting; or

  (d) By any other reasonable method.

§ 7-127-301, C.R.S. Voting agreements.

(1) Two or more members may provide for the manner in which they will vote by signing an agreement for that purpose.

(2) A voting agreement created under this section is specifically enforceable.

ARTICLE 128. DIRECTORS AND OFFICERS

§ 7-128-101, C.R.S. Requirement for board of directors.

(1) Unless otherwise provided in the articles of incorporation, each nonprofit corporation shall have a board of directors. The board of directors and the directors may be known by any other names designated in the bylaws.

(2) Subject to any provision stated in the articles of incorporation, all corporate powers shall be exercised by or under the authority of, and the business and affairs of the nonprofit corporation managed under the direction of, the board of directors or such other persons as the articles of incorporation provide shall have the authority and perform the duties of a board of directors. To the extent the articles of incorporation provide that other persons shall have the authority and perform the duties of the board of directors, the directors shall be relieved to that extent from such authority and duties.

§ 7-128-102, C.R.S. Qualifications of directors.

A director shall be an individual. The bylaws may prescribe other qualifications for directors. A director need not be a resident of this state or a member of the nonprofit corporation unless the bylaws so prescribe.

§ 7-128-103, C.R.S. Number of directors.

(1)   A board of directors shall consist of one or more directors, with the number stated in, or fixed in accordance with, the bylaws.

(2)   The bylaws may establish, or permit the voting members or the board of directors to establish, a range for the size of the board of directors by fixing a minimum and maximum number of directors. If a range is established, the number of directors may be fixed or changed from time to time within the range by the voting members or the board of directors.

§ 7-128-104, C.R.S. Election, appointment, and designation of directors.

(1)   All directors except the initial directors shall be elected, appointed, or designated as provided in the bylaws. If no method of election, appointment, or designation is stated in the bylaws, the directors other than the initial directors shall be elected as follows:

  (a)   If the nonprofit corporation has voting members, all directors except the initial directors shall be elected by the voting members at each annual meeting of the voting members; and

  (b)   If the nonprofit corporation does not have voting members, all directors except the initial directors shall be elected by the board of directors.

(2)   The bylaws may authorize the election of all or a stated number or portion of directors, except the initial directors, by the members of one or more voting groups of voting members or by the directors of one or more authorized classes of directors. A class of voting members or directors entitled to elect one or more directors is a separate voting group for purposes of the election of directors.

(3)   The bylaws may authorize the appointment of one or more directors by such person or persons, or by the holder of such office or position, as the bylaws shall state.

(4)   For purposes of articles 121 to 137 of this title, designation occurs when the bylaws name an individual as a director or designate the holder of some office or position as a director.

§ 7-128-105, C.R.S. Terms of directors generally.

(1)   The bylaws may state the terms of directors. In the absence of any term stated in the bylaws, the term of each director shall be one year. Unless otherwise provided in the bylaws, directors may be elected for successive terms.

(2)   Unless otherwise provided in the bylaws, the terms of the initial directors of a nonprofit corporation expire at the first meeting at which directors are elected or appointed.

(3)   A decrease in the number of directors or in the term of office does not shorten an incumbent director's term.

(4)   Unless otherwise provided in the bylaws, the term of a director filling a vacancy expires at the end of the unexpired term that such director is filling.

(5)   Despite the expiration of a director's term, a director continues to serve until the director's successor is elected, appointed, or designated and qualifies, or until there is a decrease in the number of directors.

(6)   Repealed.

§ 7-128-106, C.R.S. Staggered terms for directors.

The bylaws may provide for staggering the terms of directors by dividing the total number of directors into any number of groups. The terms of office of the several groups need not be uniform.

§ 7-128-107, C.R.S. Resignation of directors.

(1)   A director may resign at any time by giving written notice of resignation to the nonprofit corporation.

(2)   A resignation of a director is effective when the notice is received by the nonprofit corporation unless the notice states a later effective date.

(3)   Repealed.

(4)   If, at the beginning of a director's term on the board, the bylaws provide that a director may be deemed to have resigned for failing to attend a stated number of board meetings, or for failing to meet other stated obligations of directors, and if such failure to attend or meet obligations is confirmed by an affirmative vote of the board of directors, then such failure to attend or meet obligations shall be effective as a resignation at the time of such vote of the board.

§ 7-128-108, C.R.S. Removal of directors.

(1)   Directors elected by voting members or directors may be removed as follows:

(a)   The voting members may remove one or more directors elected by them with or without cause unless the bylaws provide that directors may be removed only for cause.

(b)   If a director is elected by a voting group, only that voting group may participate in the vote to remove that director.

(c)   Subject to section 7-127-208 (3), a director may be removed only if the number of votes cast to remove the director would be sufficient to elect the director at a meeting to elect directors.

(d)   A director elected by voting members may be removed by the voting members only at a meeting called for the purpose of removing that director, and the meeting notice shall state that the purpose, or one of the purposes, of the meeting is removal of the director.

(e)   An entire board of directors may be removed under paragraphs (a) to (d) of this subsection (1).

(f)   A director elected by the board of directors may be removed with or without cause by the vote of a majority of the directors then in office or such greater number as is stated in the bylaws; except that a director elected by the board of directors to fill the vacancy of a director elected by the voting members may be removed without cause by the voting members, but not the board of directors.

(g)   (Deleted by amendment, L. 2000, p. 983, § 83, effective July 1, 2000.)

(2)   Unless otherwise provided in the bylaws:

(a)   An appointed director may be removed without cause by the person appointing the director;

(b)   The person removing the director shall do so by giving written notice of the removal to the director and to the nonprofit corporation; and

(c)   A removal is effective when the notice is received by both the director to be removed and the nonprofit corporation unless the notice states a later effective date.

(3)   A designated director may be removed by an amendment to the bylaws deleting or changing the designation.

(4)   Repealed.

§ 7-128-109, C.R.S. Removal of directors by judicial proceeding.

(1)   A director may be removed by the district court for the county in this state in which the address of the nonprofit corporation's principal office is located or, if the nonprofit corporation has no principal office in this state, by the district court for the county in which the street address of its registered agent is located, or, if the nonprofit corporation has no registered agent, by the district court for the city and county of Denver, in a proceeding commenced either by the nonprofit corporation or by voting members holding at least ten percent of the votes entitled to be cast in the election of such director's successor, if the court finds that the director engaged in fraudulent or dishonest conduct or gross abuse of authority or discretion with respect to the nonprofit corporation, or a final judgment has been entered finding that the director has violated a duty set forth in part 4 of this article, and that removal is in the best interests of the nonprofit corporation.

(2)   The court that removes a director may bar the director from reelection for a period prescribed by the court.

(3)   If voting members commence a proceeding under subsection (1) of this section, they shall make the nonprofit corporation a party defendant.

(4)   Repealed.

§ 7-128-110, C.R.S. Vacancy on board.

(1)   Unless otherwise provided in the bylaws, if a vacancy occurs on a board of directors, including a vacancy resulting from an increase in the number of directors:

    (a)   The voting members, if any, may fill the vacancy;

    (b)   The board of directors may fill the vacancy; or

    (c)   If the directors remaining in office constitute fewer than a quorum of the board of directors, they may fill the vacancy by the affirmative vote of a majority of all the directors remaining in office.

(2)   Notwithstanding subsection (1) of this section, unless otherwise provided in the bylaws, if the vacant office was held by a director elected by a voting group of voting members:

    (a)   If one or more of the remaining directors were elected by the same voting group of voting members, only such directors are entitled to vote to fill the vacancy if it is filled by directors, and they may do so by the affirmative vote of a majority of such directors remaining in office; and

    (b)   Only that voting group is entitled to vote to fill the vacancy if it is filled by the voting members.

(3)   Notwithstanding subsection (1) of this section, unless otherwise provided in the bylaws, if the vacant office was held by a director elected by a voting group of directors, and if any persons in that voting group remain as directors, only such directors are entitled to vote to fill the vacancy.

(4)   Unless otherwise provided in the bylaws, if a vacant office was held by an appointed director, only the person who appointed the director may fill the vacancy.

(5)   If a vacant office was held by a designated director, the vacancy shall be filled as provided in the bylaws. In the absence of an applicable bylaw provision, the vacancy may not be filled by the board.

(6)   A vacancy that will occur at a specific later date, by reason of a resignation effective at a later date under section 7-128-107 (2) or otherwise, may be filled before the vacancy occurs, but the new director may not take office until the vacancy occurs.

§ 7-128-111, C.R.S. Compensation of directors.

Unless otherwise provided in the bylaws, the board of directors may authorize and fix the compensation of directors.

§ 7-128-201, C.R.S. Meetings.

(1) The board of directors may hold regular or special meetings in or out of this state.

(2) Unless otherwise provided in the bylaws, the board of directors may permit any director to participate in a regular or special meeting by, or conduct the meeting through the use of, any means of communication by which all directors participating may hear each other during the meeting. A director participating in a meeting by this means is deemed to be present in person at the meeting.

§ 7-128-202, C.R.S. Action without meeting.

(1) Unless otherwise provided in the bylaws, any action required or permitted by articles 121 to 137 of this title to be taken at a board of directors' meeting may be taken without a meeting if notice is transmitted in writing to each member of the board and each member of the board by the time stated in the notice:

    (a) Votes in writing for such action; or

    (b) (I) Votes in writing against such action, abstains in writing from voting, or fails to respond or vote; and

        (II) Fails to demand in writing that action not be taken without a meeting.

(2) The notice required by subsection (1) of this section shall state:

    (a) The action to be taken;

    (b) The time by which a director must respond;

    (c) That failure to respond by the time stated in the notice will have the same effect as abstaining in writing by the time stated in the notice and failing to demand in writing by the time stated in the notice that action not be taken without a meeting; and

    (d) Any other matters the nonprofit corporation determines to include.

(3) Action is taken under this section only if, at the end of the time stated in the notice transmitted pursuant to subsection (1) of this section:

    (a) The affirmative votes in writing for such action received by the nonprofit corporation and not revoked pursuant to subsection (5) of this section equal or exceed the minimum number of votes that would be necessary to take such action at a meeting at which all of the directors then in office were present and voted; and

    (b) The nonprofit corporation has not received a written demand by a director that such action not be taken without a meeting other than a demand that has been revoked pursuant to subsection (5) of this section.

(4) A director's right to demand that action not be taken without a meeting shall be deemed to have been waived unless the nonprofit corporation receives such demand from the director in writing by the time stated in the notice transmitted pursuant to subsection (1) of this section and such demand has not been revoked pursuant to subsection (5) of this section.

(5) Any director who in writing has voted, abstained, or demanded action not be taken without a meeting pursuant to this section may revoke such vote, abstention, or demand in writing received by the nonprofit corporation by the time stated in the notice transmitted pursuant to subsection (1) of this section.

(6) Unless the notice transmitted pursuant to subsection (1) of this section states a different effective date, action taken pursuant to this section shall be effective at the end of the time stated in the notice transmitted pursuant to subsection (1) of this section.

(7) A writing by a director under this section shall be in a form sufficient to inform the nonprofit corporation of the identity of the director, the vote, abstention, demand, or revocation of the director, and the proposed action to which such vote, abstention, demand, or revocation relates. Unless otherwise provided by the bylaws, all communications under this section may be transmitted or received by the nonprofit corporation by electronically transmitted facsimile, e-mail, or other form of wire or wireless communication. For purposes of this section, communications to the nonprofit corporation are not effective until received.

(8) Action taken pursuant to this section has the same effect as action taken at a meeting of directors and may be described as such in any document.

(9) All writings made pursuant to this section shall be filed with the minutes of the meetings of the board of directors.

§ 7-128-203, C.R.S. Notice of meeting – rights of residential members.

(1) Unless otherwise provided in articles 121 to 137 of this title or in the bylaws, regular meetings of the board of directors may be held without notice of the date, time, place, or purpose of the meeting.

(2) Unless the bylaws provide for a longer or shorter period, special meetings of the board of directors shall be preceded by at least two days' notice of the date, time, and place of the meeting. The notice need not describe the purpose of the special meeting unless otherwise required by articles 121 to 137 of this title or the bylaws.

(3) Notwithstanding subsections (1) and (2) of this section, and notwithstanding any provision of the articles of incorporation or bylaws to the contrary, the following rules and procedures apply to meetings of the board of directors of a residential nonprofit corporation or any committee of the board:

    (a) (I) (A) All regular and special meetings of the residential nonprofit corporation's board of directors or executive committee, or any committee of the board that is authorized to take final action on the board's behalf, must be open to attendance by all residential members or their representatives. The board shall make agendas for meetings of the board, and agendas for meetings of committees of the board that are authorized to take final action on the board's behalf, reasonably available for examination in advance by all residential members or their representatives. If there is no formal agenda, residential members or their representatives are nonetheless entitled to a general description of the purpose of the meeting and the subject matter that will be discussed.

            (B) The board shall inform all members, at least annually, of the method by which meeting agendas and other information required by sub-subparagraph (A) of this subparagraph (I) will be provided, including the physical location of places where agendas and meeting notices may be posted or the web address where on-line postings may be made. The board shall give at least thirty days' advance notice of any change in the manner or means by which meeting information will be provided.

      (II) The residential nonprofit corporation is encouraged to provide all notices and agendas required by this article in electronic form, by posting on a web site or otherwise, in addition to printed form. If such electronic means are available, the corporation shall provide notice of all regular and special meetings of residential members by electronic mail to all residential members who so request and who furnish the corporation with their electronic mail addresses. Electronic notice of a special meeting must be given as soon as possible but at least twenty-four hours before the meeting.

(b) At an appropriate time determined by the board of directors, but before the board votes on an issue under discussion, the board shall permit residential members or their designated representatives to speak regarding the issue. The board may place reasonable time restrictions on persons speaking during the meeting. If more than one person desires to address an issue and there are opposing views, the board shall provide for a reasonable number of persons to speak on each side of the issue.

(c) The board of directors or any committee of the board may hold an executive or closed-door session and may restrict attendance to board members and such other persons requested by the board during a regular or specially announced meeting or a part thereof. The matters to be discussed at such an executive session may include only matters enumerated in paragraph (d) of this subsection (3).

(d) Matters for discussion by an executive or closed session are limited to:

(I) Matters pertaining to employees of the residential nonprofit corporation or the managing agent's contract or involving the employment, promotion, discipline, or dismissal of an officer, agent, or employee of the corporation;

(II) Consultation with legal counsel concerning disputes that are the subject of pending or imminent court proceedings or matters that are privileged or confidential between attorney and client;

(III) Investigative proceedings concerning possible or actual criminal misconduct;

(IV) Matters subject to specific constitutional, statutory, or judicially imposed requirements protecting particular proceedings or matters from public disclosure;

(V) Any matter the disclosure of which would constitute an unwarranted invasion of individual privacy;

(VI) Review of or discussion relating to any written or oral communication from legal counsel.

(e) Upon the final resolution of any matter for which the board of directors received legal advice or that concerned pending or contemplated litigation, the board may elect to preserve the attorney-client privilege in any appropriate manner, or it may elect to disclose such information, as it deems appropriate, about such matter in an open meeting.

(f) Before the board of directors or any committee of the board convenes in executive session, the chair of the body shall announce the general matter of discussion as enumerated in paragraph (d) of this subsection (3).

(g) The board of directors shall not adopt any change to the residential nonprofit corporation's articles of incorporation or bylaws during an executive session. An articles of incorporation or bylaw change may be validly adopted only during a regular or special meeting or after the board of directors goes back into regular session following an executive session.

(h) The minutes of all meetings at which an executive session was held must indicate that an executive session was held and the general subject matter of the executive session.

§ 7-128-204, C.R.S. Waiver of notice.

(1) A director may waive any notice of a meeting before or after the time and date of the meeting stated in the notice. Except as provided by subsection (2) of this section, the waiver shall be in writing and signed by the director entitled to the notice. Such waiver shall be delivered to the nonprofit corporation for filing with the corporate records, but such delivery and filing shall not be conditions of the effectiveness of the waiver.

(2)   A director's attendance at or participation in a meeting waives any required notice to that director of the meeting unless:

   (a)   At the beginning of the meeting or promptly upon the director's later arrival, the director objects to holding the meeting or transacting business at the meeting because of lack of notice or defective notice and does not thereafter vote for or assent to action taken at the meeting; or

   (b)   If special notice was required of a particular purpose pursuant to section 7-128-203 (2), the director objects to transacting business with respect to the purpose for which such special notice was required and does not thereafter vote for or assent to action taken at the meeting with respect to such purpose.

§ 7-128-205, C.R.S. Quorum and voting.

(1)   Unless a greater or lesser number is required by the bylaws, a quorum of a board of directors consists of a majority of the number of directors in office immediately before the meeting begins.

(2)   The bylaws may authorize a quorum of a board of directors to consist of:

   (a)   No fewer than one-third of the number of directors fixed if the corporation has a fixed board size; or

   (b)   No fewer than one-third of the number of directors fixed or, if no number is fixed, of the number in office immediately before the meeting begins, if a range for the size of the board is established pursuant to section 7-128-103 (2).

(3)   If a quorum is present when a vote is taken, the affirmative vote of a majority of directors present is the act of the board of directors unless the vote of a greater number of directors is required by articles 121 to 137 of this title or the bylaws.

(4)   If provided in the bylaws, for purposes of determining a quorum with respect to a particular proposal, and for purposes of casting a vote for or against a particular proposal, a director may be deemed to be present at a meeting and to vote if the director has granted a signed written proxy to another director who is present at the meeting, authorizing the other director to cast the vote that is directed to be cast by the written proxy with respect to the particular proposal that is described with reasonable specificity in the proxy. Except as provided in this subsection (4) and as permitted by section 7-128-202, directors may not vote or otherwise act by proxy.

(5)   A director who is present at a meeting of the board of directors when corporate action is taken is deemed to have assented to all action taken at the meeting unless:

   (a)   The director objects at the beginning of the meeting, or promptly upon the director's arrival, to holding the meeting or transacting business at the meeting and does not thereafter vote for or assent to any action taken at the meeting;

   (b)   The director contemporaneously requests that the director's dissent or abstention as to any specific action taken be entered in the minutes of the meeting; or

   (c)   The director causes written notice of the director's dissent or abstention as to any specific action to be received by the presiding officer of the meeting before adjournment of the meeting or by the nonprofit corporation promptly after adjournment of the meeting.

(6)   The right of dissent or abstention pursuant to subsection (5) of this section as to a specific action is not available to a director who votes in favor of the action taken.

§ 7-128-206, C.R.S. Committees of the board.

(1)   Unless otherwise provided in the bylaws and subject to the provisions of section 7-129-106, the board of directors may create one or more committees of the board and appoint one or more directors to serve on them.

(2) Unless otherwise provided in the bylaws, the creation of a committee of the board and appointment of directors to it shall be approved by the greater of a majority of all the directors in office when the action is taken or the number of directors required by the bylaws to take action under section 7-128-205.

(3) Unless otherwise provided in the bylaws, sections 7-128-201 to 7-128-205, which govern meetings, action without meeting, notice, waiver of notice, and quorum and voting requirements of the board of directors, apply to committees of the board and their members as well.

(4) To the extent stated in the bylaws or by the board of directors, each committee of the board shall have the authority of the board of directors under section 7-128-101; except that a committee of the board shall not:

(a) Authorize distributions;

(b) Approve or propose to members action that articles 121 to 137 of this title require to be approved by members;

(c) Elect, appoint, or remove any director;

(d) Amend articles of incorporation pursuant to section 7-130-102;

(e) Adopt, amend, or repeal bylaws;

(f) Approve a plan of conversion or plan of merger not requiring member approval; or

(g) Approve a sale, lease, exchange, or other disposition of all, or substantially all, of its property, with or without goodwill, otherwise than in the usual and regular course of business subject to approval by members.

(5) The creation of, delegation of authority to, or action by a committee does not alone constitute compliance by a director with the standards of conduct described in section 7-128-401.

(6) Nothing in this part 2 shall prohibit or restrict a nonprofit corporation from establishing in its bylaws or by action of the board of directors or otherwise one or more committees, advisory boards, auxiliaries, or other bodies of any kind, having such members and rules of procedure as the bylaws or board of directors may provide, in order to provide such advice, service, and assistance to the nonprofit corporation, and to carry out such duties and responsibilities for the nonprofit corporation, as may be stated in the bylaws or by the board of directors; except that, if any such committee or other body has one or more members thereof who are entitled to vote on committee matters and who are not then also directors, such committee or other body may not exercise any power or authority reserved to the board of directors in articles 121 to 137 of this title, in the articles of incorporation, or in the bylaws.

§ 7-128-301, C.R.S. Officers.

(1) Unless otherwise provided in the bylaws, a nonprofit corporation shall have a president, a secretary, a treasurer, and such other officers as may be designated by the board of directors. An officer shall be an individual who is eighteen years of age or older. An officer need not be a director or a member of the nonprofit corporation, unless the bylaws so prescribe.

(2) Officers may be appointed by the board of directors or in such other manner as the board of directors or bylaws may provide. A duly appointed officer may appoint one or more officers or assistant officers if authorized by the bylaws or the board of directors.

(3) The bylaws or the board of directors shall delegate to the secretary or to one or more other persons responsibility for the preparation and maintenance of minutes of the directors' and members' meetings and other records and information required to be kept by the nonprofit corporation under section 7-136-101 and for authenticating records of the nonprofit corporation.

(4) The same individual may simultaneously hold more than one office in the nonprofit corporation.

§ 7-128-302, C.R.S. Duties of officers.

Each officer shall have the authority and shall perform the duties stated with respect to such office in the bylaws or, to the extent not inconsistent with the bylaws, prescribed with respect to such office by the board of directors or by an officer authorized by the board of directors.

§ 7-128-303, C.R.S. Resignation and removal of officers.

(1)   An officer may resign at any time by giving written notice of resignation to the nonprofit corporation.

(2)   A resignation of an officer is effective when the notice is received by the nonprofit corporation unless the notice states a later effective date.

(3)   If a resignation is made effective at a later date, the board of directors may permit the officer to remain in office until the effective date and may fill the pending vacancy before the effective date with the provision that the successor does not take office until the effective date, or the board of directors may remove the officer at any time before the effective date and may fill the resulting vacancy.

(4)   Unless otherwise provided in the bylaws, the board of directors may remove any officer at any time with or without cause. The bylaws or the board of directors may make provisions for the removal of officers by other officers or by the voting members.

(5)   Repealed.

§ 7-128-304, C.R.S. Contract rights with respect to officers.

(1)   The appointment of an officer does not itself create contract rights.

(2)   An officer's removal does not affect the officer's contract rights, if any, with the nonprofit corporation. An officer's resignation does not affect the nonprofit corporation's contract rights, if any, with the officer.

§ 7-128-401, C.R.S. General standards of conduct for directors and officers.

(1)   Each director shall discharge the director's duties as a director, including the director's duties as a member of a committee of the board, and each officer with discretionary authority shall discharge the officer's duties under that authority:

    (a)   In good faith;

    (b)   With the care an ordinarily prudent person in a like position would exercise under similar circumstances; and

    (c)   In a manner the director or officer reasonably believes to be in the best interests of the nonprofit corporation.

(2)   In discharging duties, a director or officer is entitled to rely on information, opinions, reports, or statements, including financial statements and other financial data, if prepared or presented by:

    (a)   One or more officers or employees of the nonprofit corporation whom the director or officer reasonably believes to be reliable and competent in the matters presented;

    (b)   Legal counsel, a public accountant, or another person as to matters the director or officer reasonably believes are within such person's professional or expert competence;

    (c)   Religious authorities or ministers, priests, rabbis, or other persons whose position or duties in the nonprofit corporation, or in a religious organization with which the nonprofit corporation is affiliated, the director or officer believes justify reliance and confidence and who the director or officer believes to be reliable and competent in the matters presented; or

(d)   In the case of a director, a committee of the board of directors of which the director is not a member if the director reasonably believes the committee merits confidence.

(3)   A director or officer is not acting in good faith if the director or officer has knowledge concerning the matter in question that makes reliance otherwise permitted by subsection (2) of this section unwarranted.

(4)   A director or officer is not liable as such to the nonprofit corporation or its members for any action taken or omitted to be taken as a director or officer, as the case may be, if, in connection with such action or omission, the director or officer performed the duties of the position in compliance with this section.

(5)   A director, regardless of title, shall not be deemed to be a trustee with respect to the nonprofit corporation or with respect to any property held or administered by the nonprofit corporation including, without limitation, property that may be subject to restrictions imposed by the donor or transferor of such property.

(6)   A director or officer of a nonprofit corporation, in the performance of duties in that capacity, shall not have any fiduciary duty to any creditor of the nonprofit corporation arising only from the status as a creditor.

(7)   No person shall be liable in contract or tort merely by reason of being a director, officer, or member of a nonprofit corporation that was suspended, declared defunct, administratively dissolved, or dissolved by operation of law, and the business or activities of which have been continued for nonprofit purposes, with or without knowledge of the suspension, declaration, or dissolution, and the business and activities of which have not been wound up.

§ 7-128-402, C.R.S. Limitation of certain liabilities of directors and officers.

(1)   If so provided in the articles of incorporation, the nonprofit corporation shall eliminate or limit the personal liability of a director to the nonprofit corporation or to its members for monetary damages for breach of fiduciary duty as a director; except that any such provision shall not eliminate or limit the liability of a director to the nonprofit corporation or to its members for monetary damages for any breach of the director's duty of loyalty to the nonprofit corporation or to its members, acts or omissions not in good faith or that involve intentional misconduct or a knowing violation of law, acts specified in section 7-128-403 or 7-128-501 (2), or any transaction from which the director directly or indirectly derived an improper personal benefit. No such provision shall eliminate or limit the liability of a director to the nonprofit corporation or to its members for monetary damages for any act or omission occurring before the date when such provision becomes effective.

(2)   No director or officer shall be personally liable for any injury to person or property arising out of a tort committed by an employee unless such director or officer was personally involved in the situation giving rise to the litigation or unless such director or officer committed a criminal offense in connection with such situation. The protection afforded in this subsection (2) shall not restrict other common law protections and rights that a director or officer may have. This subsection (2) shall not restrict the nonprofit corporation's right to eliminate or limit the personal liability of a director to the nonprofit corporation or to its members for monetary damages for breach of fiduciary duty as a director as provided in subsection (1) of this section.

§ 7-128-403, C.R.S. Liability of directors for unlawful distributions.

(1)   A director who votes for or assents to a distribution made in violation of section 7-133-101 or the articles of incorporation is personally liable to the nonprofit corporation for the amount of the distribution that exceeds what could have been distributed without violating said section or the articles of incorporation if it is established that the director did not perform the director's duties in compliance with section 7-128-401. In any proceeding commenced under this section, a director shall have all of the defenses ordinarily available to a director.

(2) A director held liable under subsection (1) of this section for an unlawful distribution is entitled to contribution:

    (a) From every other director who could be held liable under subsection (1) of this section for the unlawful distribution; and

    (b) From each person who accepted the distribution knowing the distribution was made in violation of section 7-133-101 or the articles of incorporation, the amount of the contribution from such person being the amount of the distribution to that person that exceeds what could have been distributed to that person without violating section 7-133-101 or the articles of incorporation.

§ 7-128-501, C.R.S. *Conflicting interest transaction.*

(1) As used in this section, "conflicting interest transaction" means: A contract, transaction, or other financial relationship between a nonprofit corporation and a director of the nonprofit corporation, or between the nonprofit corporation and a party related to a director, or between the nonprofit corporation and an entity in which a director of the nonprofit corporation is a director or officer or has a financial interest.

(2) No loans shall be made by a corporation to its directors or officers. Any director or officer who assents to or participates in the making of any such loan shall be liable to the corporation for the amount of such loan until the repayment thereof.

(3) No conflicting interest transaction shall be void or voidable or be enjoined, set aside, or give rise to an award of damages or other sanctions in a proceeding by a member or by or in the right of the nonprofit corporation, solely because the conflicting interest transaction involves a director of the nonprofit corporation or a party related to a director or an entity in which a director of the nonprofit corporation is a director or officer or has a financial interest or solely because the director is present at or participates in the meeting of the nonprofit corporation's board of directors or of the committee of the board of directors that authorizes, approves, or ratifies the conflicting interest transaction or solely because the director's vote is counted for such purpose if:

    (a) The material facts as to the director's relationship or interest and as to the conflicting interest transaction are disclosed or are known to the board of directors or the committee, and the board of directors or committee in good faith authorizes, approves, or ratifies the conflicting interest transaction by the affirmative vote of a majority of the disinterested directors, even though the disinterested directors are less than a quorum; or

    (b) The material facts as to the director's relationship or interest and as to the conflicting interest transaction are disclosed or are known to the members entitled to vote thereon, and the conflicting interest transaction is specifically authorized, approved, or ratified in good faith by a vote of the members entitled to vote thereon; or

    (c) The conflicting interest transaction is fair as to the nonprofit corporation.

(4) Common or interested directors may be counted in determining the presence of a quorum at a meeting of the board of directors or of a committee which authorizes, approves, or ratifies the conflicting interest transaction.

(5) For purposes of this section, a "party related to a director" shall mean a spouse, a descendent, an ancestor, a sibling, the spouse or descendent of a sibling, an estate or trust in which the director or a party related to a director has a beneficial interest, or an entity in which a party related to a director is a director, officer, or has a financial interest.

ARTICLE 129. INDEMNIFICATION

§ 7-129-101, C.R.S. Indemnification definitions.

As used in this article:

(1) "Director" means an individual who is or was a director of a nonprofit corporation or an individual who, while a director of a nonprofit corporation, is or was serving at the nonprofit corporation's request as a director, officer, partner, member, manager, trustee, employee, fiduciary, or agent of another domestic or foreign entity or of an employee benefit plan. A director is considered to be serving an employee benefit plan at the nonprofit corporation's request if the director's duties to the nonprofit corporation also impose duties on, or otherwise involve services by, the director to the plan or to participants in or beneficiaries of the plan. "Director" includes, unless the context requires otherwise, the estate or personal representative of a deceased director.

(2) "Expenses" includes counsel fees.

(3) "Liability" means the obligation incurred with respect to a proceeding to pay a judgment, settlement, penalty, fine, including an excise tax assessed with respect to an employee benefit plan, or reasonable expenses.

(4) "Nonprofit corporation" includes any domestic or foreign entity that is a predecessor of a nonprofit corporation by reason of a merger or other transaction in which the predecessor's existence ceased upon consummation of the transaction.

(5) "Official capacity" means, when used with respect to a director, the office of director in a nonprofit corporation and, when used with respect to a person other than a director as contemplated in section 7-129-107, the office in a nonprofit corporation held by the officer or the employment, fiduciary, or agency relationship undertaken by the employee, fiduciary, or agent on behalf of the nonprofit corporation. "Official capacity" does not include service for any other domestic or foreign corporation, nonprofit corporation, or other person or employee benefit plan.

(6) "Party" includes a person who was, is, or is threatened to be made a named defendant or respondent in a proceeding.

(7) "Proceeding" means any threatened, pending, or completed action, suit, or proceeding, whether civil, criminal, administrative, or investigative and whether formal or informal.

§ 7-129-102, C.R.S. Authority to indemnify directors.

(1) Except as provided in subsection (4) of this section, a nonprofit corporation may indemnify a person made a party to a proceeding because the person is or was a director against liability incurred in the proceeding if:

    (a) The person's conduct was in good faith; and

    (b) The person reasonably believed:

        (I) In the case of conduct in an official capacity with the nonprofit corporation, that the conduct was in the nonprofit corporation's best interests; and

        (II) In all other cases, that the conduct was at least not opposed to the nonprofit corporation's best interests; and

    (c) In the case of any criminal proceeding, the person had no reasonable cause to believe the conduct was unlawful.

(2) A director's conduct with respect to an employee benefit plan for a purpose the director reasonably believed to be in the interests of the participants in or beneficiaries of the plan is conduct that satisfies the requirement of subparagraph (II) of paragraph (b) of subsection (1) of this section. A director's conduct with respect to an employee benefit plan for a purpose that

the director did not reasonably believe to be in the interests of the participants in or beneficiaries of the plan shall be deemed not to satisfy the requirements of paragraph (a) of subsection (1) of this section.

(3)   The termination of a proceeding by judgment, order, settlement, or conviction or upon a plea of nolo contendere or its equivalent is not, of itself, determinative that the director did not meet the standard of conduct described in this section.

(4)   A nonprofit corporation may not indemnify a director under this section:

(a)   In connection with a proceeding by or in the right of the nonprofit corporation in which the director was adjudged liable to the nonprofit corporation; or

(b)   In connection with any other proceeding charging that the director derived an improper personal benefit, whether or not involving action in an official capacity, in which proceeding the director was adjudged liable on the basis that the director derived an improper personal benefit.

(5)   Indemnification permitted under this section in connection with a proceeding by or in the right of the nonprofit corporation is limited to reasonable expenses incurred in connection with the proceeding.

§ 7-129-103, C.R.S. *Mandatory indemnification of directors.*

Unless limited by its articles of incorporation, a nonprofit corporation shall indemnify a person who was wholly successful, on the merits or otherwise, in the defense of any proceeding to which the person was a party because the person is or was a director, against reasonable expenses incurred by the person in connection with the proceeding.

§ 7-129-104, C.R.S. *Advance of expenses to directors.*

(1)   A nonprofit corporation may pay for or reimburse the reasonable expenses incurred by a director who is a party to a proceeding in advance of final disposition of the proceeding if:

(a)   The director furnishes to the nonprofit corporation a written affirmation of the director's good-faith belief that the director has met the standard of conduct described in section 7-129-102;

(b)   The director furnishes to the nonprofit corporation a written undertaking, executed personally or on the director's behalf, to repay the advance if it is ultimately determined that the director did not meet the standard of conduct; and

(c)   A determination is made that the facts then known to those making the determination would not preclude indemnification under this article.

(2)   The undertaking required by paragraph (b) of subsection (1) of this section shall be an unlimited general obligation of the director but need not be secured and may be accepted without reference to financial ability to make repayment.

(3)   Determinations and authorizations of payments under this section shall be made in the manner specified in section 7-129-106.

§ 7-129-105, C.R.S. *Court-ordered indemnification of directors.*

(1)   Unless otherwise provided in the articles of incorporation, a director who is or was a party to a proceeding may apply for indemnification to the court conducting the proceeding or to another court of competent jurisdiction. On receipt of an application, the court, after giving any notice the court considers necessary, may order indemnification in the following manner:

(a)   If it determines that the director is entitled to mandatory indemnification under section 7-129-103, the court shall order indemnification, in which case the court shall also order the nonprofit corporation to pay the director's reasonable expenses incurred to obtain court-ordered indemnification.

(b) If it determines that the director is fairly and reasonably entitled to indemnification in view of all the relevant circumstances, whether or not the director met the standard of conduct set forth in section 7-129-102 (1) or was adjudged liable in the circumstances described in section 7-129-102 (4), the court may order such indemnification as the court deems proper; except that the indemnification with respect to any proceeding in which liability shall have been adjudged in the circumstances described in section 7-129-102 (4) is limited to reasonable expenses incurred in connection with the proceeding and reasonable expenses incurred to obtain court-ordered indemnification.

§ 7-129-106, C.R.S. Determination and authorization of indemnification of directors.

(1) A nonprofit corporation may not indemnify a director under section 7-129-102 unless authorized in the specific case after a determination has been made that indemnification of the director is permissible in the circumstances because the director has met the standard of conduct set forth in section 7-129-102. A nonprofit corporation shall not advance expenses to a director under section 7-129-104 unless authorized in the specific case after the written affirmation and undertaking required by section 7-129-104 (1) (a) and (1) (b) are received and the determination required by section 7-129-104 (1) (c) has been made.

(2) The determinations required by subsection (1) of this section shall be made:

(a) By the board of directors by a majority vote of those present at a meeting at which a quorum is present, and only those directors not parties to the proceeding shall be counted in satisfying the quorum; or

(b) If a quorum cannot be obtained, by a majority vote of a committee of the board of directors designated by the board of directors, which committee shall consist of two or more directors not parties to the proceeding; except that directors who are parties to the proceeding may participate in the designation of directors for the committee.

(3) If a quorum cannot be obtained as contemplated in paragraph (a) of subsection (2) of this section, and a committee cannot be established under paragraph (b) of subsection (2) of this section, or, even if a quorum is obtained or a committee is designated, if a majority of the directors constituting such quorum or such committee so directs, the determination required to be made by subsection (1) of this section shall be made:

(a) By independent legal counsel selected by a vote of the board of directors or the committee in the manner specified in paragraph (a) or (b) of subsection (2) of this section or, if a quorum of the full board cannot be obtained and a committee cannot be established, by independent legal counsel selected by a majority vote of the full board of directors; or

(b) By the voting members, but voting members who are also directors and who are at the time seeking indemnification may not vote on the determination.

(4) Authorization of indemnification and advance of expenses shall be made in the same manner as the determination that indemnification or advance of expenses is permissible; except that, if the determination that indemnification or advance of expenses is permissible is made by independent legal counsel, authorization of indemnification and advance of expenses shall be made by the body that selected such counsel.

§ 7-129-107, C.R.S. Indemnification of officers, employees, fiduciaries, and agents.

(1)   Unless otherwise provided in the articles of incorporation:

(a)   An officer is entitled to mandatory indemnification under section 7-129-103, and is entitled to apply for court-ordered indemnification under section 7-129-105, in each case to the same extent as a director;

(b)   A nonprofit corporation may indemnify and advance expenses to an officer, employee, fiduciary, or agent of the nonprofit corporation to the same extent as to a director; and

(c)   A nonprofit corporation may also indemnify and advance expenses to an officer, employee, fiduciary, or agent who is not a director to a greater extent, if not inconsistent with public policy, and if provided for by its bylaws, general or specific action of its board of directors or voting members, or contract.

§ 7-129-108, C.R.S. Insurance.

A nonprofit corporation may purchase and maintain insurance on behalf of a person who is or was a director, officer, employee, fiduciary, or agent of the nonprofit corporation, or who, while a director, officer, employee, fiduciary, or agent of the nonprofit corporation, is or was serving at the request of the nonprofit corporation as a director, officer, partner, member, manager, trustee, employee, fiduciary, or agent of any domestic or foreign entity or of any employee benefit plan, against liability asserted against or incurred by the person in that capacity or arising from the person's status as a director, officer, employee, fiduciary, or agent, whether or not the nonprofit corporation would have power to indemnify the person against the same liability under section 7-129-102, 7-129-103, or 7-129-107. Any such insurance may be procured from any insurance company designated by the board of directors, whether such insurance company is formed under the law of this state or any other jurisdiction, including any insurance company in which the nonprofit corporation has an equity or any other interest through stock ownership or otherwise.

§ 7-129-109, C.R.S. Limitation of indemnification of directors.

(1)   A provision treating a nonprofit corporation's indemnification of, or advance of expenses to, directors that is contained in its articles of incorporation or bylaws, in a resolution of its members or board of directors, or in a contract, except an insurance policy, or otherwise, is valid only to the extent the provision is not inconsistent with sections 7-129-101 to 7-129-108. If the articles of incorporation limit indemnification or advance of expenses, indemnification and advance of expenses are valid only to the extent not inconsistent with the articles of incorporation.

(2)   Sections 7-129-101 to 7-129-108 do not limit a nonprofit corporation's power to pay or reimburse expenses incurred by a director in connection with an appearance as a witness in a proceeding at a time when the director has not been made a named defendant or respondent in the proceeding.

§ 7-129-110, C.R.S. Notice to voting members of indemnification of director.

If a nonprofit corporation indemnifies or advances expenses to a director under this article in connection with a proceeding by or in the right of the nonprofit corporation, the nonprofit corporation shall give written notice of the indemnification or advance to the voting members with or before the notice of the next voting members' meeting. If the next voting member action is taken without a meeting at the instigation of the board of directors, such notice shall be given to the voting members at or before the time the first voting member signs a writing consenting to such action.

ARTICLE 130. AMENDMENT OF ARTICLES OF. INCORPORATION AND BYLAWS

§ 7-130-101, C.R.S. Authority to amend articles of incorporation.

(1) A nonprofit corporation may amend its articles of incorporation at any time to add or change a provision that is required or permitted in the articles of incorporation or to delete a provision not required in the articles of incorporation. Whether a provision is required or permitted in the articles of incorporation is determined as of the effective date of the amendment.

(2) A member does not have a vested property right resulting from any provision in the articles of incorporation or the bylaws, including any provision relating to management, control, purpose, or duration of the nonprofit corporation.

§ 7-130-102, C.R.S. Amendment of articles of incorporation by board of directors or incorporators.

(1) Unless otherwise provided in the articles of incorporation, the board of directors may adopt, without member approval, one or more amendments to the articles of incorporation to:

(a) Delete the statement of the names and addresses of the incorporators or of the initial directors;

(b) Delete the statement of the registered agent name and registered agent address of the initial registered agent, if a statement of change changing the registered agent name and registered agent address of the registered agent is on file in the records of the secretary of state;

(b.4) Delete the statement of the principal office address of the initial principal office, if a statement of change changing the principal office address is on file in the records of the secretary of state;

(b.5) Delete the statement of the names and addresses of any or all of the individuals named in the articles of incorporation, pursuant to section 7-90-301 (6), as being individuals who caused the articles of incorporation to be delivered for filing;

(c) Extend the duration of the nonprofit corporation if it was incorporated at a time when limited duration was required by law;

(d) Change the domestic entity name by substituting the word "corporation", "incorporated", "company", or "limited", or an abbreviation of any such word for a similar word or abbreviation in the name, or by adding, deleting, or changing a geographical attribution; or

(e) Make any other change expressly permitted by articles 121 to 137 of this title to be made without member action.

(2) The board of directors may adopt, without member action, one or more amendments to the articles of incorporation to change the entity name, if necessary, in connection with the reinstatement of a nonprofit corporation pursuant to part 10 of article 90 of this title.

(3) If a nonprofit corporation has no members or no members entitled to vote on amendments or no members yet admitted to membership, its incorporators, until directors have been chosen, and thereafter its board of directors, may adopt one or more amendments to the nonprofit corporation's articles of incorporation subject to any approval required pursuant to section 7-130-301. The nonprofit corporation shall provide notice of any meeting at which an amendment is to be voted upon. The notice shall be in accordance with section 7-128-203. The notice shall also state that the purpose, or one of the purposes, of the meeting is to consider a proposed amendment to the articles of incorporation and contain or be accompanied by a copy or summary of the amendment or state the general nature of the amendment. The amendment shall

be approved by a majority of the incorporators, until directors have been chosen, and thereafter by a majority of the directors in office at the time the amendment is adopted.

§ 7-130-103, C.R.S. Amendment of articles of incorporation by board of directors and members.

(1)   Unless articles 121 to 137 of this title, the articles of incorporation, the bylaws, or the members or the board of directors acting pursuant to subsection (5) of this section require a different vote or voting by class, the board of directors or the members representing at least ten percent of all of the votes entitled to be cast on the amendment may propose an amendment to the articles of incorporation for submission to the members.

(2)   For an amendment to the articles of incorporation to be adopted pursuant to subsection (1) of this section:

    (a)   The board of directors shall recommend the amendment to the members unless the amendment is proposed by members or unless the board of directors determines that, because of conflict of interest or other special circumstances, it should make no recommendation and communicates the basis for its determination to the members with the amendment; and

    (b)   The members entitled to vote on the amendment shall approve the amendment as provided in subsection (5) of this section.

(3)   The proposing board of directors or the proposing members may condition the effectiveness of the amendment on any basis.

(4)   The nonprofit corporation shall give notice, in accordance with section 7-127-104, to each member entitled to vote on the amendment of the members' meeting at which the amendment will be voted upon. The notice of the meeting shall state that the purpose, or one of the purposes, of the meeting is to consider the amendment, and the notice shall contain or be accompanied by a copy or a summary of the amendment or shall state the general nature of the amendment.

(5)   Unless articles 121 to 137 of this title, the articles of incorporation, bylaws adopted by the members, or the proposing board of directors or the proposing members acting pursuant to subsection (3) of this section require a greater vote, the amendment shall be approved by the votes required by sections 7-127-205 and 7-127-206 by every voting group entitled to vote on the amendment.

(6)   If the board of directors or the members seek to have the amendment approved by the members by written consent, the material soliciting the approval shall contain or be accompanied by a copy or summary of the amendment.

§ 7-130-104, C.R.S. Voting on amendments of articles of incorporation by voting groups.

(1)   Unless otherwise provided by articles 121 to 137 of this title or the articles of incorporation, if membership voting is otherwise required by articles 121 to 137 of this title, the members of a class who are entitled to vote are entitled to vote as a separate voting group on an amendment to the articles of incorporation if the amendment would:

    (a)   Affect the rights, privileges, preferences, restrictions, or conditions of that class as to voting, dissolution, redemption, or transfer of memberships in a manner different than such amendment would affect another class;

    (b)   Change the rights, privileges, preferences, restrictions, or conditions of that class as to voting, dissolution, redemption, or transfer by changing the rights, privileges, preferences, restrictions, or conditions of another class;

    (c)   Increase or decrease the number of memberships authorized for that class;

(d)   Increase the number of memberships authorized for another class;

(e)   Effect an exchange, reclassification, or termination of the memberships of that class; or

(f)   Authorize a new class of memberships.

(2)   If a class is to be divided into two or more classes as a result of an amendment to the articles of incorporation, the amendment shall be approved by the members of each class that would be created by the amendment.

§ 7-130-105, C.R.S. Articles of amendment to articles of incorporation.

(1)   A nonprofit corporation amending its articles of incorporation shall deliver to the secretary of state, for filing pursuant to part 3 of article 90 of this title, articles of amendment stating:

(a)   The domestic entity name of the nonprofit corporation; and

(b)   The text of each amendment adopted.

(c) to (f) (Deleted by amendment, L. 2005, p. 1217, § 24, effective October 1, 2005.)

§ 7-130-106, C.R.S. Restated articles of incorporation.

(1)   The board of directors may restate the articles of incorporation at any time with or without member action. If the nonprofit corporation has no members and no directors have been elected, its incorporators may restate the articles of incorporation at any time.

(2)   The restatement may include one or more amendments to the articles of incorporation. If the restatement includes an amendment requiring member approval, it shall be adopted as provided in section 7-130-103.

(3)   If the board of directors submits a restatement for member action, the nonprofit corporation shall give notice, in accordance with section 7-127-104, to each member entitled to vote on the restatement of the members' meeting at which the restatement will be voted upon. The notice shall state that the purpose, or one of the purposes, of the meeting is to consider the restatement, and the notice shall contain or be accompanied by a copy of the restatement that identifies any amendment or other change it would make in the articles of incorporation.

(4)   A nonprofit corporation restating its articles of incorporation shall deliver to the secretary of state, for filing pursuant to part 3 of article 90 of this title, articles of restatement stating:

(a)   The domestic entity name of the nonprofit corporation;

(b)   The text of the restated articles of incorporation; and

(c)   (Deleted by amendment, L. 2008, p. 1879, § 8, effective August 5, 2008.)

(d)   If the restatement was adopted by the board of directors or incorporators without member action, a statement to that effect and that member action was not required.

(5)   Upon filing by the secretary of state or at any later effective date determined pursuant to section 7-90-304, restated articles of incorporation supersede the original articles of incorporation and all prior amendments to them.

§ 7-130-107, C.R.S. Amendment of articles of incorporation pursuant to reorganization.

(1)   Articles of incorporation may be amended, without action by the board of directors or members, to carry out a plan of reorganization ordered or decreed by a court of competent jurisdiction under a statute of this state or of the United States if the articles of incorporation after amendment contain only provisions required or permitted by section 7-122-102.

(2)   For an amendment to the articles of incorporation to be made pursuant to subsection (1) of this section, an individual or individuals designated by the court shall deliver to the secretary of state, for filing pursuant to part 3 of article 90 of this title, articles of amendment stating:

(a)   The domestic entity name of the nonprofit corporation;

(b)   The text of each amendment approved by the court;

(c)   The date of the court's order or decree approving the articles of amendment;

(d)   The title of the reorganization proceeding in which the order or decree was entered; and

(e)   A statement that the court had jurisdiction of the proceeding under a specified statute of this state or of the United States.

(3)   This section does not apply after entry of a final decree in the reorganization proceeding even though the court retains jurisdiction of the proceeding for limited purposes unrelated to consummation of the reorganization plan.

§ 7-130-108, C.R.S. Effect of amendment of articles of incorporation.

An amendment to the articles of incorporation does not affect any existing right of persons other than members, any cause of action existing against or in favor of the nonprofit corporation, or any proceeding to which the nonprofit corporation is a party. An amendment changing a nonprofit corporation's domestic entity name does not abate a proceeding brought by or against a nonprofit corporation in its former entity name.

§ 7-130-201, C.R.S. Amendment of bylaws by board of directors or members.

(1)   The board of directors may amend the bylaws at any time to add, change, or delete a provision, unless:

(a)   Articles 121 to 137 of this title or the articles of incorporation reserve such power exclusively to the members in whole or part; or

(b)   A particular bylaw expressly prohibits the board of directors from doing so; or

(c)   It would result in a change of the rights, privileges, preferences, restrictions, or conditions of a membership class as to voting, dissolution, redemption, or transfer by changing the rights, privileges, preferences, restrictions, or conditions of another class.

(2)   The members may amend the bylaws even though the bylaws may also be amended by the board of directors. In such instance, the action shall be taken in accordance with sections 7-130-103 and 7-130-104 as if each reference therein to the articles of incorporation was a reference to the bylaws.

§ 7-130-202, C.R.S. Bylaw changing quorum or voting requirement for members.

(1)   (Deleted by amendment, L. 98, p. 626, § 36, effective July 1, 1998.)

(2)   A bylaw that fixes a lesser or greater quorum requirement or a greater voting requirement for members pursuant to section 7-127-207 shall not be amended by the board of directors.

§ 7-130-203, C.R.S. Bylaw changing quorum or voting requirement for directors.

(1)   A bylaw that fixes a greater quorum or voting requirement for the board of directors may be amended:

(a)   If adopted by the members, only by the members; or

(b)   If adopted by the board of directors, either by the members or by the board of directors.

(2)   A bylaw adopted or amended by the members that fixes a greater quorum or voting requirement for the board of directors may provide that it may be amended only by a stated vote of either the members or the board of directors.

(3)   Action by the board of directors under paragraph (b) of subsection (1) of this section to adopt or amend a bylaw that changes the quorum or voting requirement for the board of directors shall meet the same quorum requirement and be adopted by the same vote required to take action

under the quorum and voting requirement then in effect or proposed to be adopted, whichever is greater.

§ 7-130-301, C.R.S. Approval by third persons.

The articles of incorporation may require an amendment to the articles of incorporation or bylaws to be approved in writing by a stated person or persons other than the board of directors. Such a provision may only be amended with the approval in writing of such person or persons.

§ 7-130-302, C.R.S. Amendment terminating members or redeeming or canceling memberships.

(1)　Any amendment to the articles of incorporation or bylaws of a nonprofit corporation that would terminate all members or any class of members or redeem or cancel all memberships or any class of memberships shall meet the requirements of articles 121 to 137 of this title and this section.

(2)　Before adopting a resolution proposing an amendment as described in subsection (1) of this section, the board of directors of a nonprofit corporation shall give notice of the general nature of the amendment to the members.

ARTICLE 131. MERGER

§ 7-131-101, C.R.S. Merger.

(1)　One or more domestic nonprofit corporations may merge into another domestic entity if the board of directors of each nonprofit corporation that is a party to the merger and each other entity that is a party to the merger adopts a plan of merger complying with section 7-90-203.3 and the members entitled to vote thereon, if any, of each such nonprofit corporation, if required by section 7-131-102, approve the plan of merger.

(2) and (3) (Deleted by amendment, L. 2007, p. 249, § 54, effective May 29, 2007.)

§ 7-131-101.5, C.R.S. Conversion.

A nonprofit corporation may convert into any form of entity permitted by section 7-90-201 if the board of directors of the nonprofit corporation adopts a plan of conversion that complies with section 7-90-201.3 and the members entitled to vote thereon, if any, if required by section 7-131-102, approve the plan of conversion.

§ 7-131-102, C.R.S. Action on plan of conversion or merger.

(1)　After adopting a plan of conversion complying with section 7-90-201.3 or a plan of merger complying with section 7-90-203.3, the board of directors of the converting nonprofit corporation or the board of directors of each nonprofit corporation that is a party to the merger shall also submit the plan of conversion or plan of merger to its members, if any are entitled to vote thereon, for approval.

(2)　If the nonprofit corporation does have members entitled to vote with respect to the approval of a plan of conversion or plan of merger, a plan of conversion or a plan of merger is approved by the members if:

(a)　The board of directors recommends the plan of conversion or plan of merger to the members entitled to vote thereon unless the board of directors determines that, because of conflict of interest or other special circumstances, it should make no recommendation and communicates the basis for its determination to the members with the plan; and

(b)　The members entitled to vote on the plan of conversion or plan of merger approve the plan as provided in subsection (7) of this section.

(3)   After adopting the plan of conversion or plan of merger, the board of directors of the converting nonprofit corporation or the board of directors of each nonprofit corporation party to the merger shall submit the plan of conversion or plan of merger for written approval by any person or persons whose approval is required by a provision of the articles of incorporation of the nonprofit corporation and as recognized by section 7-130-301 for an amendment to the articles of incorporation or bylaws.

(4)   If the nonprofit corporation does not have members entitled to vote on a conversion or merger, the conversion or merger shall be approved and adopted by a majority of the directors elected and in office at the time the plan of conversion or plan of merger is considered by the board of directors. In addition, the nonprofit corporation shall provide notice of any meeting of the board of directors at which such approval is to be obtained in accordance with section 7-128-203. The notice shall also state that the purpose, or one of the purposes, of the meeting is to consider the proposed conversion or merger.

(5)   The board of directors may condition the effectiveness of the plan of conversion or plan of merger on any basis.

(6)   The nonprofit corporation shall give notice, in accordance with section 7-127-104, to each member entitled to vote on the plan of conversion or plan of merger of the members' meeting at which the plan will be voted on. The notice shall state that the purpose, or one of the purposes, of the meeting is to consider the plan of conversion or plan of merger, and the notice shall contain or be accompanied by a copy of the plan or a summary thereof.

(7)   Unless articles 121 to 137 of this title, the articles of incorporation, bylaws adopted by the members, or the board of directors acting pursuant to subsection (5) of this section require a greater vote, the plan of conversion or plan of merger shall be approved by the votes required by sections 7-127-205 and 7-127-206 by every voting group entitled to vote on the plan of conversion or plan of merger.

(8)   Separate voting by voting groups is required on a plan of conversion or plan of merger if the plan contains a provision that, if contained in an amendment to the articles of incorporation, would require action by one or more separate voting groups on the amendment.

§ 7-131-103, C.R.S. Statement of merger or conversion.

(1)   After a plan of merger is approved, the surviving nonprofit corporation shall deliver to the secretary of state, for filing pursuant to part 3 of article 90 of this title, a statement of merger pursuant to section 7-90-203.7. If the plan of merger provides for amendments to the articles of incorporation of the surviving nonprofit corporation, articles of amendment effecting the amendments shall be delivered to the secretary of state for filing pursuant to part 3 of article 90 of this title.

(2)   (Deleted by amendment, L. 2002, p. 1856, § 144, effective July 1, 2002; p. 1721, § 146, effective October 1, 2002.)

(3)   Repealed.

(4)   After a plan of conversion is approved, the converting nonprofit corporation shall deliver to the secretary of state, for filing pursuant to part 3 of article 90 of this title, a statement of conversion pursuant to section 7-90-201.7.

§ 7-131-104, C.R.S. Effect of merger or conversion.

(1)   The effect of a merger shall be as provided in section 7-90-204.

(2)   The effect of a conversion shall be as provided in section 7-90-202.

(3)   Nothing in this title shall limit the common law powers of the attorney general concerning the merger or conversion of a nonprofit corporation.

§ 7-131-105, C.R.S. Merger with foreign entity.

(1)   One or more domestic nonprofit corporations may merge with one or more foreign entities if:

  (a)   The merger is permitted by section 7-90-203 (2);

  (b)   (Deleted by amendment, L. 2007, p. 252, § 59, effective May 29, 2007.)

  (c)   The foreign entity complies with section 7-90-203.7, if it is the surviving entity of the merger; and

  (d)   Each domestic nonprofit corporation complies with the applicable provisions of sections 7-131-101 and 7-131-102 and, if it is the surviving nonprofit corporation of the merger, with section 7-131-103.

(2)   Upon the merger taking effect, the surviving foreign entity of a merger shall comply with section 7-90-204.5.

(3) and (4) (Deleted by amendment, L. 2006, p. 882, § 82, effective July 1, 2006.)

ARTICLE 132. SALE OF PROPERTY

§ 7-132-101, C.R.S. Sale of property.

(1)   Unless the bylaws otherwise provide, a nonprofit corporation may, as authorized by the board of directors:

  (a)   Sell, lease, exchange, or otherwise dispose of all or substantially all of its property in the usual and regular course of business;

  (b)   Mortgage, pledge, dedicate to the repayment of indebtedness, whether with or without recourse, or otherwise encumber all or substantially all of its property whether or not in the usual and regular course of business.

(2)   Unless otherwise provided in the bylaws, approval by the members of a transaction described in this section is not required.

§ 7-132-102, C.R.S. Sale of property other than in regular course of activities.

(1)   A nonprofit corporation may sell, lease, exchange, or otherwise dispose of all, or substantially all, of its property, with or without its good will, other than in the usual and regular course of business on the terms and conditions and for the consideration determined by the board of directors, if the board of directors proposes and the members entitled to vote thereon approve the transaction. A sale, lease, exchange, or other disposition of all, or substantially all, of the property of a nonprofit corporation, with or without its good will, in connection with its dissolution, other than in the usual and regular course of business, and other than pursuant to a court order, shall be subject to the requirements of this section; but a sale, lease, exchange, or other disposition of all, or substantially all, of the property of a nonprofit corporation, with or without its good will, pursuant to a court order shall not be subject to the requirements of this section.

(2)   If a nonprofit corporation is entitled to vote or otherwise consent, other than in the usual and regular course of its business, with respect to the sale, lease, exchange, or other disposition of all, or substantially all, of the property with or without the good will of another entity which it controls, and if the property interests held by the nonprofit corporation in such other entity constitute all, or substantially all, of the property of the nonprofit corporation, then the nonprofit corporation shall consent to such transaction only if the board of directors proposes and the members, if any are entitled to vote thereon, approve the giving of consent.

(3)   For a transaction described in subsection (1) of this section or a consent described in subsection (2) of this section to be approved by the members:

(a)   The board of directors shall recommend the transaction or the consent to the members unless the board of directors determines that, because of conflict of interest or other special circumstances, it should make no recommendation and communicates the basis for its determination to the members at a membership meeting with the submission of the transaction or consent; and

(b)   The members entitled to vote on the transaction or the consent shall approve the transaction or the consent as provided in subsection (6) of this section.

(4)   The board of directors may condition the effectiveness of the transaction or the consent on any basis.

(5)   The nonprofit corporation shall give notice, in accordance with section 7-127-104 to each member entitled to vote on the transaction described in subsection (1) of this section or the consent described in subsection (2) of this section, of the members' meeting at which the transaction or the consent will be voted upon. The notice shall:

(a)   State that the purpose, or one of the purposes, of the meeting is to consider:

(I)   In the case of action pursuant to subsection (1) of this section, the sale, lease, exchange, or other disposition of all, or substantially all, of the property of the nonprofit corporation; or

(II)   In the case of action pursuant to subsection (2) of this section, the nonprofit corporation's consent to the sale, lease, exchange, or other disposition of all, or substantially all, of the property of another entity, which entity shall be identified in the notice, property interests of which are held by the nonprofit corporation and constitute all, or substantially all, of the property of the nonprofit corporation; and

(b)   Contain or be accompanied by a description of the transaction, in the case of action pursuant to subsection (1) of this section, or by a description of the transaction underlying the consent, in the case of action pursuant to subsection (2) of this section.

(6)   Unless articles 121 to 137 of this title, the articles of incorporation, bylaws adopted by the members, or the board of directors acting pursuant to subsection (4) of this section require a greater vote, the transaction described in subsection (1) of this section or the consent described in subsection (2) of this section shall be approved by the votes required by sections 7-127-205 and 7-127-206 by every voting group entitled to vote on the transaction or the consent.

(7)   After a transaction described in subsection (1) of this section or a consent described in subsection (2) of this section is authorized, the transaction may be abandoned or the consent withheld or revoked, subject to any contractual rights or other limitations on such abandonment, withholding, or revocation, without further action by the members.

(8)   A transaction that constitutes a distribution is governed by article 133 and not by this section.

ARTICLE 133. DISTRIBUTIONS

§ 7-133-101, C.R.S. Distributions prohibited.

Except as authorized by section 7-133-102, a nonprofit corporation shall not make any distributions.

§ 7-133-102, C.R.S. Authorized distributions.

(1)   A nonprofit corporation may:

(a)   Make distributions of its income or assets to its members that are domestic or foreign nonprofit corporations;

(b)   Pay compensation in a reasonable amount to its members, directors, or officers for services rendered; and

(c)   Confer benefits upon its members in conformity with its purposes.

(2) Nonprofit corporations may make distributions upon dissolution in conformity with article 134 of this title.

ARTICLE 134. DISSOLUTION

§ 7-134-101, C.R.S. Dissolution by incorporators or directors if no members.

(1) If a nonprofit corporation has no members, a majority of its directors or, if there are no directors, a majority of its incorporators may authorize the dissolution of the nonprofit corporation.

(2) The incorporators or directors in approving dissolution shall adopt a plan of dissolution indicating to whom the assets owned or held by the nonprofit corporation will be distributed after all creditors have been paid.

§ 7-134-102, C.R.S. Dissolution by directors and members.

(1) Unless otherwise provided in the bylaws, dissolution of a nonprofit corporation may be authorized in the manner provided in subsection (2) of this section.

(2) For a proposal to dissolve the nonprofit corporation to be authorized:

(a) The board of directors shall adopt the proposal to dissolve;

(b) The board of directors shall recommend the proposal to dissolve to the members entitled to vote thereon unless the board of directors determines that, because of conflict of interest or other special circumstances, it should make no recommendation and communicates the basis for its determination to the members; and

(c) The members entitled to vote on the proposal to dissolve shall approve the proposal to dissolve as provided in subsection (5) of this section.

(3) The board of directors may condition the effectiveness of the dissolution, and the members may condition their approval of the dissolution, on any basis.

(4) The nonprofit corporation shall give notice, in accordance with section 7-127-104, to each member entitled to vote on the proposal of the members' meeting at which the proposal to dissolve will be voted on. The notice shall state that the purpose, or one of the purposes, of the meeting is to consider the proposal to dissolve the nonprofit corporation, and the notice shall contain or be accompanied by a copy of the proposal or a summary thereof.

(5) Unless articles 121 to 137 of this title, the articles of incorporation, bylaws adopted by the members, or the board of directors acting pursuant to subsection (3) of this section require a greater vote, the proposal to dissolve shall be approved by the votes required by sections 7-127-205 and 7-127-206 by every voting group entitled to vote on the proposal to dissolve.

(6) The plan of dissolution shall indicate to whom the assets owned or held by the nonprofit corporation will be distributed after all creditors have been paid.

§ 7-134-103, C.R.S. Articles of dissolution.

(1) At any time after dissolution is authorized, the nonprofit corporation may dissolve by delivering to the secretary of state, for filing pursuant to part 3 of article 90 of this title, articles of dissolution stating:

(a) The domestic entity name of the nonprofit corporation;

(b) The principal office address of the nonprofit corporation's principal office; and

(c) That the nonprofit corporation is dissolved.

(d) to (f) (Deleted by amendment, L. 2004, p. 1513, § 305, effective July 1, 2004.)

(2) A nonprofit corporation is dissolved upon the effective date of its articles of dissolution.

(3) Articles of dissolution need not be filed by a nonprofit corporation that is dissolved pursuant to section 7-134-401.

§ 7-134-104, C.R.S. Revocation of dissolution. (Repealed)

§ 7-134-105, C.R.S. Effect of dissolution.

(1) A dissolved nonprofit corporation continues its corporate existence but may not carry on any activities except as is appropriate to wind up and liquidate its affairs, including:

(a) Collecting its assets;

(b) Returning, transferring, or conveying assets held by the nonprofit corporation upon a condition requiring return, transfer, or conveyance, which condition occurs by reason of the dissolution, in accordance with such condition;

(c) Transferring, subject to any contractual or legal requirements, its assets as provided in or authorized by its articles of incorporation or bylaws;

(d) Discharging or making provision for discharging its liabilities;

(e) Doing every other act necessary to wind up and liquidate its assets and affairs.

(2) Upon dissolution of a nonprofit corporation exempt under section 501 (c) (3) of the internal revenue code or corresponding section of any future federal tax code, the assets of such nonprofit corporation shall be distributed for one or more exempt purposes under said section, or to the federal government, or to a state or local government, for a public purpose. Any such assets not so disposed of shall be disposed of by the district court for the county in this state in which the street address of the nonprofit corporation's principal office is located, or, if the nonprofit corporation has no principal office in this state, by the district court of the county in which the street address of its registered agent is located, or, if the nonprofit corporation has no registered agent, the district court of the city and county of Denver exclusively for such purposes or to such organization or organizations, as said court shall determine, that are formed and operated exclusively for such purposes.

(3) Dissolution of a nonprofit corporation does not:

(a) Transfer title to the nonprofit corporation's property;

(b) Subject its directors or officers to standards of conduct different from those prescribed in article 128 of this title;

(c) Change quorum or voting requirements for its board of directors or members, change provisions for selection, resignation, or removal of its directors or officers, or both, or change provisions for amending its bylaws or its articles of incorporation;

(d) Prevent commencement of a proceeding by or against the nonprofit corporation in its entity name; or

(e) Abate or suspend a proceeding pending by or against the nonprofit corporation on the effective date of dissolution.

(4) (Deleted by amendment, L. 2003, p. 2347, § 323, effective July 1, 2004.)

(5) A dissolved nonprofit corporation may dispose of claims against it pursuant to sections 7-90-911 and 7-90-912.

§ 7-134-106, C.R.S. Disposition of known claims by notification. (Repealed)

§ 7-134-107, C.R.S. Disposition of claims by publication. (Repealed)

§ 7-134-108, C.R.S. Enforcement of claims against dissolved nonprofit corporation. (Repealed)

§ 7-134-109, C.R.S. Service on dissolved nonprofit corporation – repeal. (Repealed)

§ 7-134-201, C.R.S. Grounds for administrative dissolution. (Repealed)

§ 7-134-202, C.R.S. Procedure for and effect of administrative dissolution. (Repealed)

§ 7-134-203, C.R.S. Reinstatement following administrative dissolution – repeal. (Repealed)

§ 7-134-204, C.R.S. Appeal from denial of reinstatement – repeal. (Repealed)

§ 7-134-205, C.R.S. Continuation as unincorporated association. (Repealed)

§ 7-134-301, C.R.S. Grounds for judicial dissolution.

(1)   A nonprofit corporation may be dissolved in a proceeding by the attorney general if it is established that:

(a)   The nonprofit corporation obtained its articles of incorporation through fraud; or

(b)   The nonprofit corporation has continued to exceed or abuse the authority conferred upon it by law.

(2)   A nonprofit corporation may be dissolved in a proceeding by a director or member if it is established that:

(a)   The directors are deadlocked in the management of the corporate affairs, the members, if any, are unable to break the deadlock, and irreparable injury to the nonprofit corporation is threatened or being suffered;

(b)   The directors or those otherwise in control of the nonprofit corporation have acted, are acting, or will act in a manner that is illegal, oppressive, or fraudulent;

(c)   The members are deadlocked in voting power and have failed, for a period that includes at least two consecutive annual meeting dates, to elect successors to directors whose terms have expired or would have expired upon the election of their successors; or

(d)   The corporate assets are being misapplied or wasted.

(3)   A nonprofit corporation may be dissolved in a proceeding by a creditor if it is established that:

(a)   The creditor's claim has been reduced to judgment, the execution on the judgment has been returned unsatisfied, and the nonprofit corporation is insolvent; or

(b)   The nonprofit corporation is insolvent and the nonprofit corporation has admitted in writing that the creditor's claim is due and owing.

(4)   (a)   If a nonprofit corporation has been dissolved by voluntary action taken under part 1 of this article:

(I)   The nonprofit corporation may bring a proceeding to wind up and liquidate its business and affairs under judicial supervision in accordance with section 7-134-105; and

(II)   The attorney general, a director, a member, or a creditor may bring a proceeding to wind up and liquidate the affairs of the nonprofit corporation under judicial supervision in accordance with section 7-134-105, upon establishing the grounds set forth in subsections (1) to (3) of this section.

(b)   As used in sections 7-134-302 to 7-134-304, a "proceeding to dissolve a nonprofit corporation" includes a proceeding brought under this subsection (4), and a "decree of dissolution" includes an order of court entered in a proceeding under this subsection (4) that directs that the affairs of a nonprofit corporation shall be wound up and liquidated under judicial supervision.

§ 7-134-302, C.R.S. *Procedure for judicial dissolution.*

(1) A proceeding by the attorney general to dissolve a nonprofit corporation shall be brought in the district court for the county in this state in which the street address of the nonprofit corporation's principal office or the street address of its registered agent is located or, if the nonprofit corporation has no principal office in this state and no registered agent, in the district court for the city and county of Denver. A proceeding brought by any other party named in section 7-134-301 shall be brought in the district court for the county in this state in which the street address of the nonprofit corporation's principal office is located or, if it has no principal office in this state, in the district court for the county in which the street address of its registered agent is located, or, if the nonprofit corporation has no registered agent, in the district court for the city and county of Denver.

(2) It is not necessary to make directors or members parties to a proceeding to dissolve a nonprofit corporation unless relief is sought against them individually.

(3) A court in a proceeding brought to dissolve a nonprofit corporation may issue injunctions, appoint a receiver or custodian pendente lite with all powers and duties the court directs, take other action required to preserve the corporate assets wherever located, and carry on the activities of the nonprofit corporation until a full hearing can be held.

§ 7-134-303, C.R.S. *Receivership or custodianship.*

(1) A court in a judicial proceeding to dissolve a nonprofit corporation may appoint one or more receivers to wind up and liquidate, or one or more custodians to manage, the affairs of the nonprofit corporation. The court shall hold a hearing, after giving notice to all parties to the proceeding and any interested persons designated by the court, before appointing a receiver or custodian. The court appointing a receiver or custodian has exclusive jurisdiction over the nonprofit corporation and all of its property, wherever located.

(2) The court may appoint an individual, a domestic entity, or a foreign entity authorized to transact business or conduct activities in this state, or a domestic or foreign nonprofit corporation authorized to transact business or conduct activities in this state as a receiver or custodian. The court may require the receiver or custodian to post bond, with or without sureties, in an amount stated by the court.

(3) The court shall describe the powers and duties of the receiver or custodian in its appointing order which may be amended from time to time. Among other powers the receiver shall have the power to:

   (a) Dispose of all or any part of the property of the nonprofit corporation, wherever located, at a public or private sale, if authorized by the court; and

   (b) Sue and defend in the receiver's own name as receiver of the nonprofit corporation in all courts.

(4) The custodian may exercise all of the powers of the nonprofit corporation, through or in place of its board of directors or officers, to the extent necessary to manage the affairs of the nonprofit corporation in the best interests of its members and creditors.

(5) The court, during a receivership, may redesignate the receiver a custodian and during a custodianship may redesignate the custodian a receiver if doing so is in the best interests of the nonprofit corporation and its members and creditors.

(6) The court from time to time during the receivership or custodianship may order compensation paid and expense disbursements or reimbursements made to the receiver or custodian and such

person's counsel from the assets of the nonprofit corporation or proceeds from the sale of the assets.

§ 7-134-304, C.R.S. *Decree of dissolution.*

(1) If after a hearing the court determines that one or more grounds for judicial dissolution described in section 7-134-301 exist, it may enter a decree dissolving the nonprofit corporation and stating the effective date of the dissolution, and the clerk of the court shall deliver a certified copy of the decree to the secretary of state for filing pursuant to part 3 of article 90 of this title.

(2) After entering the decree of dissolution, the court shall direct the winding up and liquidation of the nonprofit corporation's activities in accordance with section 7-134-105 and the giving of notice to claimants in accordance with sections 7-90-911 and 7-90-912.

(3) The court's order or decision may be appealed as in other civil proceedings.

§ 7-134-401, C.R.S. *Dissolution upon expiration of period of duration.*

(1) A nonprofit corporation shall be dissolved upon and by reason of the expiration of its period of duration, if any, stated in its articles of incorporation.

(2) A provision in the articles of incorporation to the effect that the nonprofit corporation or its existence shall be terminated at a stated date or after a stated period of time or upon a contingency, or any similar provision, shall be deemed to be a provision for a period of duration within the meaning of this section. The occurrence of such date, the expiration of the stated period of time, the occurrence of such contingency, or the satisfaction of such provision shall be deemed to be the expiration of the nonprofit corporation's period of duration for purposes of this section.

§ 7-134-501, C.R.S. *Deposit with state treasurer.*

Assets of a dissolved nonprofit corporation that should be transferred to a creditor, claimant, or member of the nonprofit corporation who cannot be found or who is not legally competent to receive them shall be reduced to cash and deposited with the state treasurer as property presumed to be abandoned under the provisions of article 13 of title 38, C.R.S.

ARTICLE 135. FOREIGN NONPROFIT CORPORATIONS -. AUTHORITY TO CONDUCT ACTIVITIES

§ 7-135-101, C.R.S. *Authority to conduct activities required.*

Part 8 of article 90 of this title, providing for the transaction of business or the conduct of activities by foreign entities, applies to foreign nonprofit corporations.

ARTICLE 136. RECORDS, INFORMATION, AND REPORTS

§ 7-136-101, C.R.S. *Corporate records.*

(1) A nonprofit corporation shall keep as permanent records minutes of all meetings of its members and board of directors, a record of all actions taken by the members or board of directors without a meeting, a record of all actions taken by a committee of the board of directors in place of the board of directors on behalf of the nonprofit corporation, and a record of all waivers of notices of meetings of members and of the board of directors or any committee of the board of directors.

(2) A nonprofit corporation shall maintain appropriate accounting records.

(3)   A nonprofit corporation or its agent shall maintain a record of its members in a form that permits preparation of a list of the name and address of all members in alphabetical order, by class, showing the number of votes each member is entitled to vote.

(4)   A nonprofit corporation shall maintain its records in written form or in another form capable of conversion into written form within a reasonable time.

(5)   A nonprofit corporation shall keep a copy of each of the following records at its principal office:

    (a)   Its articles of incorporation;

    (b)   Its bylaws;

    (c)   Resolutions adopted by its board of directors relating to the characteristics, qualifications, rights, limitations, and obligations of members or any class or category of members;

    (d)   The minutes of all members' meetings, and records of all action taken by members without a meeting, for the past three years;

    (e)   All written communications within the past three years to members generally as members;

    (f)   A list of the names and business or home addresses of its current directors and officers;

    (g)   A copy of its most recent periodic report pursuant to part 5 of article 90 of this title; and

    (h)   All financial statements prepared for periods ending during the last three years that a member could have requested under section 7-136-106.

§ 7-136-102, C.R.S. Inspection of corporate records by members.

(1)   A member is entitled to inspect and copy, during regular business hours at the nonprofit corporation's principal office, any of the records of the nonprofit corporation described in section 7-136-101 (5) if the member gives the nonprofit corporation written demand at least five business days before the date on which the member wishes to inspect and copy such records.

(2)   Pursuant to subsection (5) of this section, a member is entitled to inspect and copy, during regular business hours at a reasonable location stated by the nonprofit corporation, any of the other records of the nonprofit corporation if the member meets the requirements of subsection (3) of this section and gives the nonprofit corporation written demand at least five business days before the date on which the member wishes to inspect and copy such records.

(3)   A member may inspect and copy the records described in subsection (2) of this section only if:

    (a)   The member has been a member for at least three months immediately preceding the demand to inspect or copy or is a member holding at least five percent of the voting power as of the date the demand is made;

    (b)   The demand is made in good faith and for a proper purpose;

    (c)   The member describes with reasonable particularity the purpose and the records the member desires to inspect; and

    (d)   The records are directly connected with the described purpose.

(4)   For purposes of this section:

    (a)   "Member" includes a beneficial owner whose membership interest is held in a voting trust and any other beneficial owner of a membership interest who establishes beneficial ownership.

    (b)   "Proper purpose" means a purpose reasonably related to the demanding member's interest as a member.

(5)   The right of inspection granted by this section may not be abolished or limited by the articles of incorporation or bylaws.

(6)   This section does not affect:

(a)   The right of a member to inspect records under section 7-127-201;

(b)   The right of a member to inspect records to the same extent as any other litigant if the member is in litigation with the nonprofit corporation; or

(c)   The power of a court, independent of articles 121 to 137 of this title, to compel the production of corporate records for examination.

§ 7-136-103, C.R.S. Scope of member's inspection right.

(1)   A member's agent or attorney has the same inspection and copying rights as the member.

(2)   The right to copy records under section 7-136-102 includes, if reasonable, the right to receive copies made by photographic, xerographic, electronic, or other means.

(3)   Except as provided in section 7-136-106, the nonprofit corporation may impose a reasonable charge, covering the costs of labor and material, for copies of any documents provided to the member. The charge may not exceed the estimated cost of production and reproduction of the records.

(4)   The nonprofit corporation may comply with a member's demand to inspect the record of members under section 7-136-102 (2) by furnishing to the member a list of members that complies with section 7-136-101 (3) and was compiled no earlier than the date of the member's demand.

§ 7-136-104, C.R.S. Court-ordered inspection of corporate records.

(1)   If a nonprofit corporation refuses to allow a member, or the member's agent or attorney, who complies with section 7-136-102 (1) to inspect or copy any records that the member is entitled to inspect or copy by said section, the district court for the county in this state in which the street address of the nonprofit corporation's principal office is located or, if the nonprofit corporation has no principal office in this state, the district court for the county in which the street address of its registered agent is located or, if the nonprofit corporation has no registered agent, the district court for the city and county of Denver may, on application of the member, summarily order the inspection or copying of the records demanded at the nonprofit corporation's expense.

(2)   If a nonprofit corporation refuses to allow a member, or the member's agent or attorney, who complies with section 7-136-102 (2) and (3) to inspect or copy any records that the member is entitled to inspect or copy pursuant to section 7-136-102 (2) and (3) within a reasonable time following the member's demand, the district court for the county in this state in which the street address of the nonprofit corporation's principal office is located or, if the nonprofit corporation has no principal office in this state, the district court for the county in which the street address of its registered agent is located or, if the nonprofit corporation has no registered agent, the district court for the city and county of Denver may, on application of the member, summarily order the inspection or copying of the records demanded.

(3)   If a court orders inspection or copying of the records demanded, unless the nonprofit corporation proves that it refused inspection or copying in good faith because it had a reasonable basis for doubt about the right of the member, or the member's agent or attorney, to inspect or copy the records demanded:

(a)   The court shall also order the nonprofit corporation to pay the member's costs, including reasonable counsel fees, incurred to obtain the order;

(b)   The court may order the nonprofit corporation to pay the member for any damages the member incurred;

(c)   If inspection or copying is ordered pursuant to subsection (2) of this section, the court may order the nonprofit corporation to pay the member's inspection and copying expenses; and

(d)   The court may grant the member any other remedy provided by law.

(4)   If a court orders inspection or copying of records demanded, it may impose reasonable restrictions on the use or distribution of the records by the demanding member.

§ 7-136-105, C.R.S. Limitations on use of membership list.

(1)   Without consent of the board of directors, a membership list or any part thereof may not be obtained or used by any person for any purpose unrelated to a member's interest as a member.

(2)   Without limiting the generality of subsection (1) of this section, without the consent of the board of directors a membership list or any part thereof may not be:

(a)   Used to solicit money or property unless such money or property will be used solely to solicit the votes of the members in an election to be held by the nonprofit corporation;

(b)   Used for any commercial purpose; or

(c)   Sold to or purchased by any person.

§ 7-136-106, C.R.S. Financial statements.

Upon the written request of any member, a nonprofit corporation shall mail to such member its most recent annual financial statements, if any, and its most recently published financial statements, if any, showing in reasonable detail its assets and liabilities and results of its operations.

§ 7-136-107, C.R.S. Periodic report to secretary of state.

Part 5 of article 90 of this title, providing for periodic reports from reporting entities, applies to domestic nonprofit corporations and applies to foreign nonprofit corporations that are authorized to transact business or conduct activities in this state.

§ 7-136-108, C.R.S. Statement of person named as director or officer. (Repealed)

§ 7-136-109, C.R.S. Interrogatories by secretary of state. (Repealed)

ARTICLE 137. TRANSITION PROVISIONS

§ 7-137-101, C.R.S. Application to existing corporations.

(1)   (a)   For purposes of this article, "existing corporate entity" means any corporate entity that was in existence on June 30, 1998, and that was incorporated under articles 20 to 29 of this title or elected to accept such articles as provided therein.

(b)   A corporate entity that was either incorporated under or elected to accept articles 20 to 29 of this title and that was suspended or, as a consequence of such suspension, dissolved by operation of law before July 1, 1998, and was eligible for reinstatement or restoration, renewal, and revival on June 30, 1998, shall be deemed to be in existence on that date for purposes of this subsection (1) and shall be deemed administratively dissolved on the date of such suspension for purposes of section 7-134-105.

(c)   A corporate entity that was either incorporated under or elected to accept articles 20 to 29 of this title and that was suspended or, as a consequence of such suspension, dissolved by operation of law before July 1, 1998, and was not eligible for reinstatement or restoration, renewal, and revival on June 30, 1998, shall be treated as a domestic entity as to which a constituent filed document has been filed by, or placed in the records of, the secretary of state and that has been dissolved for purposes of section 7-90-1001.

(2)   Subject to this section, articles 121 to 137 of this title apply to all existing corporate entities subject to articles 20 to 29 of this title.

(3)   Unless the articles of incorporation or bylaws of an existing corporate entity recognize the right of a member to transfer such member's membership interests in such corporate entity, such interests shall be presumed to be nontransferable. However, if the transferability of such interests is not prohibited by such articles of incorporation or bylaws, such transferability may be established by a preponderance of the evidence taking into account any representation made by the corporate entity, the practice of such corporate entity, other transactions involving such interests, and other facts bearing on the existence of the rights to transfer such interests.

(4)   Until the articles of incorporation of an existing corporate entity are amended or restated on or after July 1, 1998, they need not be amended or restated to comply with articles 121 to 137 of this title.

(5)   Unless changed by an amendment to its articles of incorporation, members or classes of members of an existing corporate entity shall be deemed to be voting members for purposes of articles 121 to 137 of this title if such members or classes of members, on June 30, 1998, had the right by reason of a provision of the corporate entity's articles of incorporation or bylaws, or by a custom, practice, or tradition, to vote for the election of a director or directors.

(6)   The bylaws of an existing corporate entity may be amended as provided in its articles of incorporation or bylaws. Unless otherwise so provided, the power to amend such bylaws shall be vested in the board of directors.

§ 7-137-102, C.R.S. Pre-1968 corporate entities – failure to file reports and designate registered agents – dissolution.

(1)   Corporate entities that were formed prior to January 1, 1968, and that did not elect to be governed by articles 20 to 29 of this title and could, if they so elected, elect to be governed by articles 121 to 137 of this title, but that have not done so, are nevertheless reporting entities that are subject to part 5 of article 90 of this title, providing for periodic reports from reporting entities, and are domestic entities that are subject to part 7 of article 90 of this title, providing for registered agents and service of process.

(2)   Every corporate entity that could or has elected to be governed by articles 20 to 29 or 121 to 137 of this title whose articles of incorporation, affidavit of incorporation, or other basic corporate charter, by whatever name denominated, is not on file in the records of the secretary of state shall file a certified copy of such articles of incorporation, affidavit of incorporation, or other basic corporate charter in the office of the secretary of state. Such certified copy may be secured from any clerk or recorder with whom the instrument may be filed or recorded.

(3)   If any corporate entity, formed prior to January 1, 1968, that could elect to be governed by articles 20 to 29 or 121 to 137 of this title, but that has not so elected and has failed to file periodic reports or maintain a registered agent, may be declared delinquent pursuant to section 7-90-902.

(4)   Any corporate entity formed prior to January 1, 1968, that could elect to be governed by articles 20 to 29 of this title, that was suspended or was declared defunct, but not dissolved by operation of law under section 7-20-105 before July 1, 1998, and that was eligible for reinstatement on June 30, 1998, shall be deemed administratively dissolved on the date of such suspension for purposes of section 7-134-105 and may reinstate itself as a nonprofit corporation as provided in part 10 of article 90 of this title.

(5)   Any nonprofit corporate entity formed prior to January 1, 1968, that could elect to be governed by articles 20 to 29 of this title, that was suspended, declared defunct, administratively dissolved, or dissolved by operation of law, and continues to operate for nonprofit purposes and does not wind up its business and affairs, shall be deemed an unincorporated organization that qualifies as a nonprofit association as provided in section 7-30-101.1 for purposes of the

"Uniform Unincorporated Nonprofit Association Act", article 30 of this title, unless such corporate entity is eligible to reinstate itself as a nonprofit corporation as provided in part 10 of article 90 of this title and does so reinstate itself.

§ 7-137-103, C.R.S. Application to foreign nonprofit corporations.

A foreign nonprofit corporation authorized to transact business or conduct activities in this state on June 30, 1998, is subject to articles 121 to 137 of this title but is not required to obtain new authorization to transact business or conduct activities under said articles.

§ 7-137-201, C.R.S. Procedure to elect to accept articles 121 to 137 of this title.

(1)   Any corporate entity with shares of capital stock formed before January 1, 1968, under article 40, 50, or 51 of this title, any corporate entity formed before January 1, 1968, under article 40 or 50 of this title without shares of capital stock, and any corporate entity whether with or without shares of capital stock and formed before January 1, 1968, under any general law or created by any special act of the general assembly for a purpose for which a nonprofit corporation may be formed under articles 121 to 137 of this title may elect to accept said articles in the following manner:

(a)   If there are members or stockholders entitled to vote thereon, the board of directors shall adopt a resolution recommending that the corporate entity accept articles 121 to 137 of this title and directing that the question of acceptance be submitted to a vote at a meeting of the members or stockholders entitled to vote thereon, which may be either an annual or special meeting. The question shall also be submitted whenever one-twentieth of the members or stockholders entitled to vote thereon so request. Written notice stating that the purpose, or one of the purposes, of the meeting is to consider electing to accept said articles shall be given to each member or stockholder entitled to vote at the meeting within the time and in the manner provided in said articles for the giving of notice of meetings to members or stockholders. Such election to accept said articles shall require for adoption at least two-thirds of the votes that members or stockholders present at such meeting in person or by proxy are entitled to cast.

(b)   If there are no members or stockholders entitled to vote thereon, election to accept articles 121 to 137 of this title may be made at a meeting of the board of directors pursuant to a majority vote of the directors in office.

(2)   In effecting acceptance of articles 121 to 137 of this title, the corporate entity shall follow the requirements of the law under which it was formed, its articles of incorporation, and its bylaws so far as applicable.

(3)   If the domestic entity name of the corporate entity accepting articles 121 to 137 of this title is not in conformity with part 6 of article 90 of this title, the corporate entity shall change its domestic entity name to conform with part 6 of article 90 of this title. The adoption of a domestic entity name that is in conformity with said part 6 by the members or stockholders of the corporate entity, and its inclusion in the statement of election to accept articles 121 to 137 as the entity name, shall be the only action necessary to effect the change. The articles of incorporation, affidavit, or other basic organizational charter shall be deemed for all purposes amended to conform to the entity name.

(4)   All corporate entities accepting articles 121 to 137 of this title whose articles of incorporation, affidavits of incorporation, or other basic charters, by whatever names denominated, are not on file in the records of the secretary of state as required by section 7-137-102 (2) shall deliver to the secretary of state, for filing pursuant to part 3 of article 90 of this title, a certified copy of such articles of incorporation, affidavits of incorporation, or other basic charters at the time of delivery of the statement of election to accept articles 121 to 137 of this title.

(5) All corporate entities accepting articles 121 to 137 of this title are reporting entities subject to part 5 of article 90 of this title, providing for periodic reports from reporting entities, and are subject to part 7 of article 90 of this title, providing for registered agents and service of process.

§ 7-137-202, C.R.S. Statement of election to accept articles 121 to 137 of this title.

(1) A statement of election to accept articles 121 to 137 of this title shall state:

    (a) The domestic entity name of the corporate entity;

    (b) A statement by the corporate entity that it has elected to accept said articles and that all required reports have been or will be filed and all fees, taxes, and penalties due to the state of Colorado accruing under any law to which the corporate entity heretofore has been subject have been paid;

    (c) If there are members or stockholders entitled to vote thereon, a statement stating the date of the meeting of such members or stockholders at which the election to accept articles 121 to 137 of this title was made, that a quorum was present at the meeting, and that such acceptance was authorized by at least two-thirds of the votes that members or stockholders present at such meeting in person or by proxy were entitled to cast;

    (d) If there are no members or stockholders entitled to vote thereon, a statement of such fact, the date of the meeting of the board of directors at which election to accept said articles was made, that a quorum was present at the meeting, and that such acceptance was authorized by a majority vote of the directors in office;

    (e) A statement that the corporate entity followed the requirements of the law under which it was formed, its articles of incorporation, and its bylaws so far as applicable in effecting such acceptance;

    (f) and (g) Repealed.

    (h) A statement that any attached copy of the articles of incorporation, affidavit, or other basic corporate charter of the corporate entity is true and correct;

    (i) If the corporate entity has issued shares of stock, a statement of such fact including the number of shares heretofore authorized, the number issued and outstanding, and a statement that all issued and outstanding shares of stock have been delivered to the corporate entity to be canceled upon the acceptance of articles 121 to 137 of this title by the corporate entity becoming effective and that from and after the effective date of said acceptance the authority of the corporate entity to issue shares of stock is terminated; except that this shall not apply to corporate entities formed for the acquisition and distribution of water to their stockholders.

§ 7-137-203, C.R.S. Filing statement of election to accept articles 121 to 137 of this title.

The statement of election to accept articles 121 to 137 of this title shall be delivered to the secretary of state for filing pursuant to part 3 of article 90 of this title.

§ 7-137-204, C.R.S. Effect of certificate of acceptance.

(1) Upon the filing by the secretary of state of the statement of election to accept articles 121 to 137 of this title, the election of the corporate entity to accept said articles shall become effective.

(2) A corporate entity so electing under articles 121 to 137 of this title or corresponding provision of prior law shall have the same powers and privileges and be subject to the same duties, restrictions, penalties, and liabilities as though such corporate entity had been originally formed under said articles and shall also be subject to any duties or obligations expressly imposed upon the corporate entity by a special charter, subject to the following:

(a) If no period of duration is expressly fixed in the articles of incorporation of such corporate entity, its period of duration shall be deemed to be perpetual.

(b) No amendment to the articles of incorporation adopted after such election to accept articles 121 to 137 of this title shall release or terminate any duty or obligation expressly imposed upon any such corporate entity under and by virtue of a special charter or enlarge any right, power, or privilege granted to any such corporate entity under a special charter, except to the extent that such right, power, or privilege might have been included in the articles of incorporation of a corporate entity formed under said articles.

(c) In the case of any corporate entity with issued shares of stock, the holders of such issued shares who surrender them to the corporate entity to be canceled upon the acceptance of said articles by the corporate entity becoming effective shall become members of the corporate entity with one vote for each share of stock so surrendered until such time as the corporate entity by proper corporate action relative to the election, qualification, terms, and voting power of members shall otherwise prescribe.

§ 7-137-301, C.R.S. *Saving provisions.*

(1) Except as provided in subsection (3) of this section, the repeal of any provision of the "Colorado Nonprofit Corporation Act", articles 20 to 29 of this title, does not affect:

(a) The operation of the statute, or any action taken under it, before its repeal;

(b) Any ratification, right, remedy, privilege, obligation, or liability acquired, accrued, or incurred under the provision before its repeal;

(c) Any violation of the provision, or any penalty, forfeiture, or punishment incurred because of the violation, before its repeal; or

(d) Any proceeding or reorganization commenced under the provision before its repeal, and the proceeding or reorganization may be completed in accordance with the provision as if it had not been repealed.

(2) Except as provided in subsection (3) of this section or in sections 7-137-101 (1) (b) and 7-137-102 (4) for the reinstatement, as provided in part 10 of article 90 of this title, of a corporate entity suspended, declared defunct, or administratively dissolved before July 1, 1998, any dissolution commenced under the provision before its repeal may be completed in accordance with the provision as if it had not been repealed.

(3) If a penalty or punishment imposed for violation of any provision of the "Colorado Nonprofit Corporation Act", articles 20 to 29 of this title, is reduced by articles 121 to 137 of this title, the penalty or punishment, if not already imposed, shall be imposed in accordance with said articles.

Chapter 6:
Appraiser Regulation

An * in the left margin indicates a change in the statute, rule, or text since the last publication of the manual.

I. The Colorado Board of Real Estate Appraisers

The Colorado Board of Real Estate Appraisers ("Board") meets every other month and consists of seven members who are appointed by the Governor. The overall objective of the Board is to protect the public. In order to do so, the Colorado legislature has granted the Board rulemaking authority for matters related to the profession of real estate appraisers, and Appraisal Management Companies (AMC). Rules are made after notice and public hearings in which all interested parties may participate.

The Division of Real Estate ("Division") is part of the Department of Regulatory Agencies and is responsible for budgeting, purchasing, and related management functions. The director of the Division is an administrative officer who executes the directives of the Board and is given statutory authority in all matters delegated by the Board. The Board exercises its duties and authority through licensing, certification, and enforcement.

II. Appraiser Licensing and Certification

* In 1990, the legislature passed laws governing the practice of real estate appraisal in Colorado in response to the federal "Financial Institutions Reform, Recovery and Enforcement Act of 1989" ("FIRREA"). This enabling legislation has been amended several times since being adopted. The full text of the statutes, §§ 12-10-601 through 12-10-623, C.R.S., are reprinted in this chapter.

* The Colorado Board of Real Estate Appraisers is composed of three licensed or certified appraisers, one of whom shall have expertise in eminent domain matters; one shall be a county assessor in office; one shall be an officer or employee of a commercial bank experienced in real estate lending; one shall be an officer or employee of an appraisal management company; and one shall be member of the public at large not engaged in any of the businesses represented by the other members of the board. Members of the Board shall hold office for terms of three years. The Board has statutory authority to implement Colorado law in a manner consistent with federal regulations, including rulemaking and imposing discipline for violations of appraiser license law.

* Unless a specific exemption applies, any person acting as a real estate appraiser in this state must be licensed as provided by §§ 12-10-601, *et seq.* Exceptions to the definition of "real estate appraiser" are found in § 12-10-602(9)(b), C.R.S., and include, among others, licensed real estate brokers who perform broker price opinions and competitive market analyses that are not represented as appraisals and are not used for purposes of obtaining financing. Other exceptions are provided for corporations valuing property they own, may purchase or sell, and for appraisers of personal property, water or mineral rights.

* Colorado appraisal licensing and certification law, rules, and practices are reviewed and approved by the Federal Appraisal Subcommittee (ASC). The ASC oversees the real estate

appraisal process as it relates to federally related transactions. The Appraisal Foundation (TAF), a private non-profit appraisal organization, is charged with developing the qualifications for appraisers and standards for appraisals through two of its independent Boards, the Appraisal Qualifications Board (AQB) and the Appraisal Standards Board (ASB). In general, the standards for the development and reporting of an appraisal are those of the Uniform Standards of Professional Appraisal Practice (USPAP) as developed, interpreted, and amended by the ASB. The AQB and ASB have no legislative power, but their recommendations have been adopted via § 12-10-613(1)(g) and Board Rule 11.1.

Federal financial regulatory agencies have developed rules as to the appraiser and appraisal related requirements that must be met for valuation of properties in "federally related transactions." Additional standards are imposed by federal and/or state law for real estate appraisals, in particular, for eminent domain, conservation easements and appraisals used for income tax purposes.

III. Levels of Appraiser Licensure

Colorado appraiser law and Board rules establish four levels of licensure, summarized in more detail below. A license or certification is issued when an individual meets the education, examination, and experience requirements for their level of licensure. The level of licensure determines what properties an appraiser, if competent for the assignment, may appraise.

Licensed Ad Valorem Appraiser: This level of licensure is only utilized for appraiser employees of county tax assessment offices. These individuals may also qualify for and hold a licensed or certified credential.

Licensed Appraiser: The licensed credential allows the appraiser to appraise non-complex 1-4 unit residential properties having a transaction value of less than $1 million and complex 1-4 unit residential properties having a transaction value of less than $250,000. The terms "Complex Residential Property" and "Transaction Value" are defined by Board Rule and the Real Property Appraiser Qualification Criteria of the AQB.

Certified Residential Appraiser: The certified residential credential allows the appraiser to appraise 1-4 unit residential properties without regard to transaction value or complexity. The credential includes the appraisal of vacant or unimproved land that is utilized for 1-4 residential units purposes or for which the highest and best use is for 1-4 residential units, but does not include the appraisal of subdivisions for which a development analysis/appraisal is necessary.

Certified General Appraiser: The certified general credential allows the appraiser to appraise all types of real property.

Colorado does not have trainee or supervisory appraiser classifications and there are no specific requirements for either in statute or Board rule.

IV. Requirements for Appraiser Licensure

In general, there are three requirements that must be met for appraiser licensure: education, examination, and experience. The specific requirements in these areas for the licensed, certified and ad valorem credentials are detailed under Board Rules 2.2, 2.3, 2.4 and 2.9.

V. Continuing Education Requirements

An initial license or certification issued to an appraiser is valid through December 31 of the year issued. Appraisers who obtain their initial license or certification prior to July 1 of any calendar year must complete at least 14 hours of approved appraiser continuing education before December 31. Appraisers who renew their credential will be issued a two-year license and must complete at least 28 hours of approved appraiser continuing education during the two-year renewal cycle.

At a minimum, appraisers must successfully complete the 7-hour National Uniform Standards of Professional Appraisal Practice (USPAP) Update Course every two calendar years. The update course will be credited towards the required 28 hours of continuing education for the renewal cycle. The 15-hour National USPAP course <u>cannot</u> be substituted for the required 7-hour National USPAP update course. Continuing education requirements are more fully detailed in Chapter 7 of the Board Rules.

VI. Appraisal Management Companies

In accordance with the Dodd–Frank Wall Street Reform and Consumer Protection Act, the Colorado legislature passed HB 12-1110 which requires appraisal management companies (AMCs) to be licensed in the state of Colorado as of July 1, 2013. Each appraisal management company must designate a Controlling Appraiser to supervise all licensed activities that occur in the state. The Board of Real Estate Appraisers shall not issue a license to an AMC until the Controlling Appraiser and each individual that owns more than 10% of the company establishes that he or she is truthful and honest and has good moral character and has submitted a set of fingerprints to the Colorado Bureau of Investigations. Each AMC must maintain a surety bond for a minimum of $25,000.

* **Title 12, Article 10, Part 6, Colorado Revised Statutes – Real Estate Appraisers**

* **§ 12-10-601, C.R.S. Legislative declaration.**

* *Editor's note: This section is similar to former §12-61-701 as it existed prior to 2019.*

The general assembly finds, determines, and declares that sections 12-10-602 to 12-10-623 are enacted pursuant to the requirements of the "Real Estate Appraisal Reform Amendments", Title XI of the federal "Financial Institutions Reform, Recovery, and Enforcement Act of 1989", as amended, 12 U.S.C. secs. 3331 to 3351. The general assembly further finds, determines, and declares that sections 12-10-602 to 12-10-623 are intended to implement the requirements of federal law in the least burdensome manner to real estate appraisers and appraisal management companies. Licensed ad valorem appraisers licensed under this article 10 are not regulated by the federal "Real Estate Appraisal Reform Amendments", Title XI of the federal "Financial Institutions Reform, Recovery, and Enforcement Act of 1989", as amended, 12 U.S.C. secs. 3331 to 3351.

* **§ 12-10-602, C.R.S. Definitions.**

* *Editor's note: (1) This section is similar to former §12-61-702 as it existed prior to 2019; except that §12-61-702 (7) and (8) were relocated to §12-10-101 (1) and (2), respectively.*

* *(2) Before its relocation in 2019, this section was amended in SB 19-046. Those amendments were superseded by the repeal and reenactment of this title 12, effective October 1, 2019. For those* *amendments to the former section in effect from March 25, 2019, to October 1, 2019, see SB 19-046, chapter 50, Session Laws of Colorado 2019.*

* *(3) Section 4 of chapter 50 (SB 19-046), Session Laws of Colorado 2019, provides that the act changing this section takes effect October 1, 2019, only if HB 19-1172 becomes law. HB 19-1172 became law and took effect October 1, 2019.*

As used in this part 6, unless the context otherwise requires:

(1)   (a)   "Appraisal", "appraisal report", or "real estate appraisal" means a written or oral analysis, opinion, or conclusion relating to the nature, quality, value, or utility of specified interests in, or aspects of, identified real estate that is transmitted to the client upon the completion of an assignment. These terms include a valuation, which is an opinion of the value of real estate, and an analysis, which is a general study of real estate not specifically performed only to determine value; except that the terms include a valuation completed by an appraiser employee of a county assessor as defined in section 39-1-102 (2).

(b)   The terms do not include an analysis, valuation, opinion, conclusion, notation, or compilation of data by an officer, director, or regularly salaried employee of a financial institution or its affiliate, made for internal use only by the financial institution or affiliate, concerning an interest in real estate that is owned or held as collateral by the financial institution or affiliate and that is not represented or deemed to be an appraisal except to the financial institution, the agencies regulating the financial institution, and any secondary markets that purchase real estate secured loans. An appraisal prepared by an officer, director, or regularly salaried employee of a financial institution who is not licensed or certified under this part 6 shall contain a written notice that the preparer is not licensed or certified as an appraiser under this part 6.

(c)   "Appraisal", "appraisal report", or "real estate appraisal" does not include a federally authorized "waiver valuation", as defined in 49 CFR 24.2 (a)(33), as amended.

(2)   (a)   "Appraisal management company" or "AMC" means, in connection with valuing properties collateralizing mortgage loans or mortgages incorporated into a securitization, any external third party authorized either by a creditor in a consumer credit transaction secured by a consumer's principal dwelling that oversees an appraiser panel or by an underwriter of, or other principal in, the secondary mortgage markets that oversees an appraiser panel to:

(I)   Recruit, select, and retain appraisers;

(II)   Contract with licensed and certified appraisers to perform appraisal assignments;

(III)   Manage the process of having an appraisal performed, including providing administrative duties such as receiving appraisal orders and appraisal reports, submitting completed appraisal reports to creditors and underwriters, collecting fees from creditors and underwriters for services provided, and reimbursing appraisers for services performed; or

(IV)   Review and verify the work of appraisers.

(b)   "Appraisal management company" or "AMC" does not include:

(I)   A corporation, limited liability company, sole proprietorship, or other entity that directly performs appraisal services;

(II)   A corporation, limited liability company, sole proprietorship, or other entity that does not contract with appraisers for appraisal services, but that solely distributes orders to a client-selected panel of appraisers; and

(III)   A mortgage company, or its subsidiary, that manages a panel of appraisers who are engaged to provide appraisal services on mortgage loans either originated by the mortgage company or funded by the mortgage company with its own funds.

(3)   "Board" means the board of real estate appraisers created in section 12-10-603.

(4)   "Client" means the party or parties who engage an appraiser or an appraisal management company for a specific assignment.

(5)   "Consulting services" means services performed by an appraiser that do not fall within the definition of an "independent appraisal" in subsection (7) of this section. "Consulting services" includes marketing, financing and feasibility studies, valuations, analyses, and opinions and conclusions given in connection with real estate brokerage, mortgage banking, and counseling and advocacy in regard to property tax assessments and appeals thereof; except that, if in rendering the services the appraiser acts as a disinterested third party, the work is deemed an independent appraisal and not a consulting service. Nothing in this subsection (5) precludes a person from acting as an expert witness in valuation appeals.

(6)   "Financial institution" means any "bank" or "savings association", as those terms are defined in 12 U.S.C. sec. 1813, any state bank incorporated under title 11, any state or federally chartered credit union, or any company that has direct or indirect control over any of those entities.

(7)   "Independent appraisal" means an engagement for which an appraiser is employed or retained to act as a disinterested third party in rendering an unbiased analysis, opinion, or conclusion relating to the nature, quality, value, or utility of specified interests in or aspects of identified real estate.

(8)   (a)   "Panel" or "appraiser panel" means a network, list, or roster of licensed or certified appraisers approved by an AMC to perform appraisals as independent contractors for the AMC.

       (b)   Appraisers on an AMC's appraiser panel include both:

              (I)   Appraisers accepted by the AMC for consideration for future appraisal assignments in covered transactions or for secondary mortgage market participants in connection with covered transactions; and

              (II)   Appraisers engaged by the AMC to perform one or more appraisals in covered transactions or for secondary mortgage market participants in connection with covered transactions.

       (c)   An appraiser is an independent contractor for purposes of this subsection (8) if the appraiser is treated as an independent contractor by the AMC for purposes of federal income taxation.

(9)   (a)   "Real estate appraiser" or "appraiser" means a person who provides an estimate of the nature, quality, value, or utility of an interest in, or aspect of, identified real estate and includes one who estimates value and who possesses the necessary qualifications, ability, and experience to execute or direct the appraisal of real property.

       (b)   "Real estate appraiser" or "appraiser" does not include:

              (I)   A person who conducts appraisals strictly of personal property;

              (II)   A person licensed as a broker pursuant to part 2 of this article 10 who provides an opinion of value that is not represented as an appraisal and is not used for purposes of obtaining financing;

              (III) A person licensed as a certified public accountant pursuant to article 100 of this title 12, and otherwise regulated, as long as the person does not represent his or her opinions of value for real estate as an appraisal;

              (IV)   A corporation, acting through its officers or regularly salaried employees, when conducting a valuation of real estate property rights owned, to be purchased, or sold by the corporation;

              (V)   A person who conducts appraisals strictly of water rights or of mineral rights;

(VI) A right-of-way acquisition agent, an appraiser who is licensed and certified pursuant to this part 6, or any other individual who has sufficient understanding of the local real estate market to be qualified to make a waiver valuation when the agent, appraiser, or other qualified individual is employed by or contracts with a public entity and provides an opinion of value that is not represented as an appraisal and when, for any purpose, the property or portion of property being valued is valued at twenty-five thousand dollars or less, as permitted by federal law and 49 CFR 24.102 (c)(2), as amended;

(VII) An officer, director, or regularly salaried employee of a financial institution or its affiliate who makes, for internal use only by the financial institution or affiliate, an analysis, evaluation, opinion, conclusion, notation, or compilation of data with respect to an appraisal so long as the person does not make a written adjustment of the appraisal's conclusion as to the value of the subject real property;

(VIII) An officer, director, or regularly salaried employee of a financial institution or its affiliate who makes an internal analysis, valuation, opinion, conclusion, notation, or compilation of data concerning an interest in real estate that is owned or held as collateral by the financial institution or its affiliate; or

(IX) A person who represents property owners as an advocate in tax or valuation protests and appeals pursuant to title 39.

*
§ 12-10-603, C.R.S. Board of real estate appraisers – creation – compensation – immunity – legislative declaration – subject to review – repeal of part.

* *Editor's note: This section is similar to former §12-61-703 as it existed prior to 2019.*

(1) (a) There is hereby created in the division of real estate a board of real estate appraisers consisting of seven members appointed by the governor with the consent of the senate. Of the members, three shall be licensed or certified appraisers, one of whom shall have expertise in eminent domain matters; one shall be a county assessor in office; one shall be an officer or employee of a commercial bank experienced in real estate lending; one shall be an officer or employee of an appraisal management company; and one shall be a member of the public at large not engaged in any of the businesses represented by the other members of the board.

(b) Members of the board shall hold office for terms of three years. In the event of a vacancy by death, resignation, removal, or otherwise, the governor shall appoint a member to fill the unexpired term. The governor has the authority to remove any member for misconduct, neglect of duty, or incompetence.

(2) (a) The board shall exercise its powers and perform its duties and functions under the division of real estate as if transferred to the division by a **type 1** transfer, as defined in the "Administrative Organization Act of 1968", article 1 of title 24.

(b) The general assembly finds, determines, and declares that the organization of the board under the division as a **type 1** agency will provide the autonomy necessary to avoid potential conflicts of interest between the responsibility of the board in the regulation of real estate appraisers and the responsibility of the division in the regulation of real estate brokers and salespersons. The general assembly further finds, determines, and declares that the placement of the board as a **type 1** agency under the division is consistent with the organizational structure of state government.

(3) Each member of the board shall receive the same compensation and reimbursement of expenses as is provided for members of boards and commissions in the division of professions and occupations pursuant to section 12-20-103 (6). Payment for all per diem compensation and

expenses shall be made out of annual appropriations from the division of real estate cash fund provided for in section 12-10-605.

(4) Members of the board, consultants, and expert witnesses are immune from liability in any civil action based upon any disciplinary proceedings or other official acts they performed in good faith pursuant to this part 6.

(5) A majority of the board constitutes a quorum for the transaction of all business, and actions of the board require a vote of a majority of the members present in favor of the action taken.

(6) This part 6 is repealed, effective September 1, 2022. Before the repeal, this part 6 is scheduled for review in accordance with section 24-34-104.

* ## § 12-10-604, C.R.S. Powers and duties of the board – rules.

* *Editor's note: (1) This section is similar to former §12-61-704 as it existed prior to 2019.*

(2) Before its relocation in 2019, this section was amended in HB 19-1264. Those amendments were superseded by the repeal and reenactment of this title 12, effective October 1, 2019. For those amendments to the former section in effect from June 30, 2019, to October 1, 2019, see HB 19-1264, chapter 420, Session Laws of Colorado 2019.

(3) Section 17 of chapter 420 (HB 19-1264), Session Laws of Colorado 2019, provides that the act changing this section takes effect October 1, 2019, only if HB 19-1172 becomes law. HB 19-1172 became law and took effect October 1, 2019.

(1) In addition to all other powers and duties imposed upon it by law, the board has the following powers and duties:

   (a)   (I)   To promulgate and amend, as necessary, rules pursuant to article 4 of title 24 for the implementation and administration of this part 6 and as required to comply with the federal "Real Estate Appraisal Reform Amendments", Title XI of the federal "Financial Institutions Reform, Recovery, and Enforcement Act of 1989", as amended, 12 U.S.C. secs. 3331 to 3351, and with any requirements imposed by amendments to that federal law.

        (II)   The board shall not establish any requirements that are more stringent than the requirements of any applicable federal law.

        (III)   Licensed ad valorem appraisers are not regulated by the federal "Real Estate Appraisal Reform Amendments", Title XI of the federal "Financial Institutions Reform, Recovery, and Enforcement Act of 1989", as amended, 12 U.S.C. secs. 3331 to 3351, but the board shall adopt rules regarding minimum qualifications and standards of practice for licensed ad valorem appraisers.

        (IV)   In any list or registry it maintains, the board shall identify or separately account for any appraisal management company that oversees a panel of more than fifteen certified or licensed appraisers in Colorado, or more than twenty-five in all states in which it does business, within a given year.

   (b)   To charge application, examination, and license and certificate renewal fees established pursuant to section 12-10-215 from all applicants for licensure, certification, examination, and renewal under this part 6. The board shall not refund any fees received from applicants seeking licensure, certification, examination, or renewal.

   (c)   Through the department and subject to appropriations made to the department, to employ administrative law judges, appointed pursuant to part 10 of article 30 of title 24, on a full-time or part-time basis to conduct any hearings required by this part 6;

   (d)   To issue, deny, or refuse to renew a license or certificate pursuant to this part 6;

   (e)   To take disciplinary actions in conformity with this part 6;

(f) To delegate to the director the administration and enforcement of this part 6 and the authority to act on behalf of the board on occasions and in circumstances that the board directs;

(g) (I) To develop, purchase, or contract for any examination required for the administration of this part 6, to offer each examination at least twice a year or, if demand warrants, at more frequent intervals, and to establish a passing score for each examination that reflects a minimum level of competency.

(II) If study materials are developed by a testing company or other entity, the board shall make the materials available to persons desiring to take examinations pursuant to this part 6. The board may charge fees for the materials to defray any costs associated with making the materials available.

(h) In compliance with article 4 of title 24, to make investigations; subpoena persons and documents, which subpoenas may be enforced by a court of competent jurisdiction if not obeyed; hold hearings; and take evidence in all matters relating to the exercise of the board's power under this part 6;

(i) Pursuant to section 1119 (b) of Title XI of the federal "Financial Institutions Reform, Recovery, and Enforcement Act of 1989", Pub.L. 101-73, as amended, to apply, if necessary, for a federal waiver of the requirement relating to certification or licensing of a person to perform appraisals and to make the necessary written determinations specified in that section for purposes of making the application; and

(j) If the board has reasonable cause to believe that a person, partnership, limited liability company, or corporation is violating this part 6, to enter an order requiring the individual or appraisal management company to cease and desist the violation.

(k) Repealed.

(2) The board shall maintain or preserve, for seven years, licensing history records of a person licensed or certified under this part 6. Complaints of record in the office of the board and board investigations, including board investigative files, are closed to public inspection. Stipulations and final agency orders are public record and are subject to sections 24-72-203 and 24-72-204.

§ 12-10-605, C.R.S. Fees, penalties, and fines collected under part 6.

Editor's note: This section is similar to former §12-61-705 as it existed prior to 2019.

All fees, penalties, and fines collected pursuant to this part 6, not including fees retained by contractors pursuant to contracts entered into in accordance with section 12-10-203, 12-10-606, or 24-34-101, shall be transmitted to the state treasurer, who shall credit the same to the division of real estate cash fund, created in section 12-10-215.

§ 12-10-606, C.R.S. Qualifications for licensing and certification of appraisers – continuing education – definitions – rules.

Editor's note: (1) This section is similar to former §12-61-706 as it existed prior to 2019.

(2) Before its relocation in 2019, this section was amended in HB 19-1166. Those amendments were superseded by the repeal and reenactment of this title 12, effective October 1, 2019. For those amendments to the former section in effect from April 18, 2019, to October 1, 2019, see HB 19-1166, chapter 125, Session Laws of Colorado 2019.

(3) Section 78 of chapter 125 (HB 19-1166), Session Laws of Colorado 2019, provides that the act changing this section takes effect October 1, 2019, only if HB 19-1172 becomes law. HB 19-1172 became law and took effect October 1, 2019.

(1) (a) The board shall, by rule, prescribe requirements for the initial licensing or certification of persons under this part 6 to meet the requirements of the "Real Estate Appraisal Reform Amendments", Title XI of the federal "Financial Institutions Reform, Recovery, and

Enforcement Act of 1989", as amended, 12 U.S.C. secs. 3331 to 3351, and shall develop, purchase, or contract for examinations to be passed by applicants. The board shall not establish any requirements for initial licensing or certification that are more stringent than the requirements of any applicable federal law; except that all applicants shall pass an examination offered by the board. If there is no applicable federal law, the board shall consider and may use as guidelines the most recent available criteria published by the Appraiser Qualifications Board of the Appraisal Foundation or its successor organization.

(b) The four levels of appraiser licensure and certification, pursuant to subsection (1)(a) of this section, are defined as follows:

    (I) "Certified general appraiser" means an appraiser meeting the requirements set by the board for general certification.

    (II) "Certified residential appraiser" means an appraiser meeting the requirements set by the board for residential certification.

    (III) "Licensed ad valorem appraiser" means an appraiser meeting the requirements set by the board for ad valorem appraiser certification. Only a county assessor, employee of a county assessor's office, or employee of the division of property taxation in the department of local affairs may obtain or possess an ad valorem appraiser certification.

    (IV) "Licensed appraiser" means an appraiser meeting the requirements set by the board for a license.

(c) A county assessor or employee of a county assessor's office who is a licensed ad valorem appraiser may not perform real estate appraisals outside of his or her official duties.

(d) The board shall transfer persons employed in a county assessor's office or in the division of property taxation in the department of local affairs who are registered appraisers as of July 1, 2013, to the category of licensed ad valorem appraiser. The board shall allow these persons, until December 31, 2015, to meet any additional requirements imposed by the board pursuant to section 12-10-604 (1)(a).

(2) (a) The board shall, by rule, prescribe continuing education requirements for persons licensed or certified as certified general appraisers, certified residential appraisers, or licensed appraisers as needed to meet the requirements of the "Real Estate Appraisal Reform Amendments", Title XI of the federal "Financial Institutions Reform, Recovery, and Enforcement Act of 1989", as amended, 12 U.S.C. secs. 3331 to 3351. The board shall not establish any continuing education requirements that are more stringent than the requirements of any applicable federal law; except that all persons licensed or certified under this part 6 are subject to continuing education requirements. If there is no applicable federal law, the board shall consider and may use as guidelines the most recent available criteria published by the Appraiser Qualifications Board of the Appraisal Foundation or its successor organization.

(b) The board shall, by rule, prescribe continuing education requirements for licensed ad valorem appraisers.

(3) Notwithstanding any provision of this section to the contrary, the criteria established by the board for the licensing or certification of appraisers pursuant to this part 6 shall not include membership or lack of membership in any appraisal organization.

(4) (a) Subject to section 12-10-619 (2), all appraiser employees of county assessors shall be licensed or certified as provided in subsections (1) and (2) of this section. Obtaining and maintaining a license or certificate under either subsection (1) or (2) of this section entitles an appraiser employee of a county assessor to perform all real estate appraisals required to fulfill the person's official duties.

(b)   Appraiser employees of county assessors who are employed to appraise real property are subject to this part 6; except that appraiser employees of county assessors who are employed to appraise real property are not subject to disciplinary actions by the board on the ground that they have performed appraisals beyond their level of competency when appraising real estate in fulfillment of their official duties. County assessors, if licensed or certified as provided in subsections (1) and (2) of this section, are not subject to disciplinary actions by the board on the ground that they have performed appraisals beyond their level of competency when appraising real estate in fulfillment of their official duties.

(c)   The county in which an appraiser employee of a county assessor is employed shall pay all reasonable costs incurred by the appraiser employee of the county assessor to obtain and maintain a license or certificate pursuant to this section.

(5)   The board shall not issue an appraiser's license as referenced in subsection (1)(b)(IV) of this section unless the applicant has at least twelve months' appraisal experience.

(6)   (a)   The board shall not issue a license or certification until the applicant demonstrates that he or she meets the fitness standards established by board rule and submits a set of fingerprints to the Colorado bureau of investigation for the purpose of conducting a state and national fingerprint-based criminal history record check utilizing records of the Colorado bureau of investigation and the federal bureau of investigation. Each person submitting a set of fingerprints shall pay the fee established by the Colorado bureau of investigation for conducting the fingerprint-based criminal history record check to the bureau. Upon completion of the criminal history record check, the bureau shall forward the results to the board. The board shall require a name-based criminal history record check, as defined in section 22-2-119.3 (6)(d), for an applicant who has twice submitted to a fingerprint-based criminal history record check and whose fingerprints are unclassifiable or when the results of a fingerprint-based criminal history record check of an applicant performed pursuant to this subsection (6) reveal a record of arrest without a disposition. The applicant shall pay the costs associated with a name-based criminal history record check. The board may deny an application for licensure or certification based on the outcome of the criminal history record check and may establish criminal history requirements more stringent than those established by any applicable federal law. At a minimum, the board shall adopt the criminal history requirements established by any applicable federal law.

(b)   An applicant for certification as a licensed ad valorem appraiser is not subject to the fingerprinting and criminal background check requirements of subsection (6)(a) of this section.

§ 12-10-607, C.R.S. Appraisal management companies – application for license – exemptions.

Editor's note: (1) This section is similar to former §12-61-707 as it existed prior to 2019.

(2) Before its relocation in 2019, this section was amended in HB 19-1166. Those amendments were superseded by the repeal and reenactment of this title 12, effective October 1, 2019. For those amendments to the former section in effect from April 18, 2019, to October 1, 2019, see HB 19-1166, chapter 125, Session Laws of Colorado 2019.

(3) Section 78 of chapter 125 (HB 19-1166), Session Laws of Colorado 2019, provides that the act changing this section takes effect October 1, 2019, only if HB 19-1172 becomes law. HB 19-1172 became law and took effect October 1, 2019.

(1)   An applicant shall apply for a license as an appraisal management company, or as a controlling appraiser, to the board in a manner prescribed by the board.

(2)   The board may grant appraisal management company licenses to individuals, partnerships, limited liability companies, or corporations. A partnership, limited liability company, or corporation, in its application for a license, shall designate a controlling appraiser who is actively certified in a state recognized by the appraisal subcommittee of the federal financial institutions examination council or its successor entity. The controlling appraiser is responsible for the licensed practices of the partnership, limited liability company, or corporation and all persons employed by the entity. The application of the partnership, limited liability company, or corporation and the application of the appraiser designated by it as the controlling appraiser shall be filed with the board. The board has jurisdiction over the appraiser so designated and over the partnership, limited liability company, or corporation.

(3)   The board shall not issue a license to any partnership, limited liability company, or corporation unless and until the appraiser designated by the partnership, limited liability company, or corporation as controlling appraiser and each individual who owns more than ten percent of the entity demonstrates that he or she meets the fitness standards established by board rule and submits a set of fingerprints to the Colorado bureau of investigation for the purpose of conducting a state and national fingerprint-based criminal history record check utilizing records of the Colorado bureau of investigation and the federal bureau of investigation. Each person submitting a set of fingerprints shall pay the fee established by the Colorado bureau of investigation for conducting the fingerprint-based criminal history record check to the bureau. Upon completion of the criminal history record check, the bureau shall forward the results to the board. The board shall require a name-based criminal history record check, as defined in section 22-2-119.3 (6)(d), for an applicant who has twice submitted to a fingerprint-based criminal history record check and whose fingerprints are unclassifiable or when the results of a fingerprint-based criminal history record check of an applicant performed pursuant to this subsection (3) reveal a record of arrest without a disposition. The applicant shall pay the costs associated with a name-based criminal history record check. The board may deny an application for licensure or refuse to renew a license based on the outcome of the criminal history record check. The board may require criminal history requirements more stringent than those established by any applicable federal law. At a minimum, the board shall adopt the criminal history requirements established by any applicable federal law.

(4)   The board shall not issue a license to any partnership, limited liability company, or corporation if the appraiser designated by the entity as controlling appraiser has previously had, in any state, an appraiser registration, license, or certificate refused, denied, cancelled, surrendered in lieu of revocation, or revoked. A disciplinary action resulting in refusal, denial, cancellation, surrender in lieu of revocation, or revocation relating to a registration, license, or certification as an appraiser registered, licensed, or certified under this part 6 or any related occupation in any other state, territory, or country for disciplinary reasons is prima facie evidence of grounds for denial of a license by the board.

(5)   The board shall not issue a license to any partnership, limited liability company, or corporation if it is owned, in whole or in part, directly or indirectly, by any person who has had, in any state, an appraiser license, registration, or certificate refused, denied, cancelled, surrendered in lieu of revocation, or revoked. A disciplinary action resulting in refusal, denial, cancellation, surrender in lieu of revocation, or revocation relating to a license, registration, or certification as an appraiser licensed, registered, or certified under this part 6 or any related occupation in any other state, territory, or country for disciplinary reasons is prima facie evidence of grounds for denial of a license by the board.

(6)   The board may deny an application for a license for any partnership, limited liability company, or corporation if the partnership, limited liability company, or corporation has previously had a license revoked or surrendered a license in lieu of revocation. A disciplinary action resulting in the surrender in lieu of revocation or the revocation of a license as an appraisal management company under this part 6 or any related occupation in any other state, territory, or country for

disciplinary reasons may be deemed to be prima facie evidence of grounds for denial of a license by the board.

(7) Each appraisal management company must maintain a definite place of business. If the appraisal management company is domiciled in another state, the appraiser designated by the appraisal management company as controlling appraiser is responsible for supervising all licensed activities that occur in Colorado. All licensed actions occurring within the state of Colorado must occur under the name under which the appraisal management company is licensed or its trade name adopted in accordance with Colorado law.

(8) An application that is submitted by an appraisal management company that is:

   (a) A partnership must be properly registered with the Colorado department of revenue or properly filed with the Colorado secretary of state and in good standing, proof of which must be included in the application. If an assumed or trade name is to be used, it must be properly filed with the Colorado department of revenue or filed and accepted by the Colorado secretary of state, proof of which must be included with the application.

   (b) A limited liability company must be properly registered with the Colorado secretary of state and in good standing, proof of which must be included with the application. If an assumed or trade name is to be used, it must be properly filed with the Colorado secretary of state, proof of which must be included with the application.

   (c) A corporation must be registered as a foreign corporation or properly incorporated with the Colorado secretary of state and in good standing, proof of which must be included with the application. If an assumed or trade name is to be used, it must be properly filed with the Colorado secretary of state, proof of which must be included with the application.

(9) Financial institutions and appraisal management company subsidiaries that are owned and controlled by the financial institution and regulated by a federal financial institution regulatory agency are not required to register with or be licensed by the board. This exemption includes a panel of appraisers who are engaged to provide appraisal services and are administered by a financial institution regulated by a federal financial regulatory agency.

* ### § 12-10-608, C.R.S. Errors and omissions insurance – duties of the division – certificate of coverage – group plan made available – rules.

* *Editor's note: This section is similar to former §12-61-708 as it existed prior to 2019.*

(1) Every licensee under this part 6, except an appraiser who is employed by a state or local governmental entity or an inactive appraiser or appraisal management company, shall maintain errors and omissions insurance to cover all activities contemplated under this part 6. The division shall make the errors and omissions insurance available to all licensees by contracting with an insurer for a group policy after a competitive bid process in accordance with article 103 of title 24. A group policy obtained by the division must be available to all licensees with no right on the part of the insurer to cancel any licensee. A licensee may obtain errors and omissions insurance independently if the coverage complies with the minimum requirements established by the division.

(2) (a) If the division is unable to obtain errors and omissions insurance coverage to insure all licensees who choose to participate in the group program at a reasonable annual premium, as determined by the division, a licensee shall independently obtain the errors and omissions insurance required by this section.

   (b) The division shall solicit and consider information and comments from interested persons when determining the reasonableness of annual premiums.

(3) The division shall determine the terms and conditions of coverage required under this section based on rules promulgated by the board. Each licensee shall be notified of the required terms

and conditions at least thirty days before the annual premium renewal date as determined by the division. Each licensee shall file a certificate of coverage showing compliance with the required terms and conditions with the division by the annual premium renewal date, as determined by the division.

(4) In addition to all other powers and duties conferred upon the board by this part 6, the board is authorized and directed to adopt rules it deems necessary or proper to carry out the requirements of this section.

* ## § 12-10-609, C.R.S. Bond required.

* *Editor's note: This section is similar to former §12-61-709 as it existed prior to 2019.*

(1) Before the board issues a license to an applicant for an appraisal management company license, the applicant shall post with the board a surety bond in the amount of twenty-five thousand dollars. A licensed appraisal management company shall maintain the required bond at all times.

(2) The surety bond shall require the surety to provide notice to the board within thirty days if payment is made from the surety bond or if the bond is cancelled.

* ## § 12-10-610, C.R.S. Expiration of licenses – renewal – penalties – fees – rules.

* *Editor's note: (1) This section is similar to former §12-61-710 as it existed prior to 2019.*

* *(2) Before its relocation in 2019, this section was amended in HB 19-1166. Those amendments were superseded by the repeal and reenactment of this title 12, effective October 1, 2019. For those amendments to the former section in effect from April 18, 2019, to October 1, 2019, see HB 19-1166, chapter 125, Session Laws of Colorado 2019.*

* *(3) Section 78 of chapter 125 (HB 19-1166), Session Laws of Colorado 2019, provides that the act changing this section takes effect October 1, 2019, only if HB 19-1172 becomes law. HB 19-1172 became law and took effect October 1, 2019.*

(1) (a) All licenses or certificates expire pursuant to a schedule established by the director and may be renewed or reinstated pursuant to this section. Upon compliance with this section and any applicable rules of the board regarding renewal, including the payment of a renewal fee plus a reinstatement fee established pursuant to subsection (1)(b) of this section, the expired license or certificate shall be reinstated. A real estate appraiser's license or certificate that has not been renewed for a period greater than two years shall not be reinstated, and the person must submit a new application for licensure or certification.

(b) A person who fails to renew his or her license or certificate before the applicable renewal date may have it reinstated if the person submits an application as prescribed by the board:

(I) Within thirty-one days after the date of expiration, by payment of the regular renewal fee;

(II) More than thirty-one days, but within one year, after the date of expiration, by payment of the regular renewal fee and payment of a reinstatement fee equal to one-third of the regular renewal fee; or

(III) More than one year, but within two years, after the date of expiration, by payment of the regular renewal fee and payment of a reinstatement fee equal to two-thirds of the regular renewal fee.

(2) If the federal registry fee collected by the board and transmitted to the federal financial institutions examination council is increased prior to expiration of a license or certificate, the board shall collect the amount of the increase in the fee from the holder of the license or

certificate and forward the amount to the council annually. The federal registry fee does not apply to licensed ad valorem appraisers licensed under this article 10.

(3) (a) If the applicant has complied with this section and any applicable rules of the board regarding renewal, except for the continuing education requirements pursuant to section 12-10-606, the licensee may renew the license on inactive status. An inactive license may be activated if the licensee submits written certification of compliance with section 12-10-606 for the previous licensing period. The board may adopt rules establishing procedures to facilitate reactivation of licenses.

(b) The holder of an inactive license shall not perform a real estate appraisal or appraisal management duties.

(c) The holder of an inactive license shall not hold himself or herself out as having an active license pursuant to this part 6.

(4) At the time of renewal or reinstatement, every licensee, certificate holder, and person or individual who owns more than ten percent of an appraisal management company shall submit a set of fingerprints to the Colorado bureau of investigation for the purpose of conducting a state and national fingerprint-based criminal history record check utilizing records of the Colorado bureau of investigation and the federal bureau of investigation, if the person has not previously done so for issuance of a license or certification by the board. Each person submitting a set of fingerprints shall pay the fee established by the Colorado bureau of investigation for conducting the fingerprint-based criminal history record check to the bureau. The bureau shall forward the results to the board. The board shall require a name-based criminal history record check, as defined in section 22-2-119.3 (6)(d), for an applicant who has twice submitted to a fingerprint-based criminal history record check and whose fingerprints are unclassifiable or when the results of a fingerprint-based criminal history record check of an applicant performed pursuant to this section reveal a record of arrest without a disposition. The applicant shall pay the costs associated with a name-based criminal history record check. The board may refuse to renew or reinstate a license or certification based on the outcome of the criminal history record check.

* ## § 12-10-611, C.R.S. Licensure or certification by endorsement – temporary practice.

* *Editor's note: This section is similar to former §12-61-711 as it existed prior to 2019.*

(1) The board may issue a license or certification to an appraiser by endorsement to engage in the occupation of real estate appraisal to any applicant who has a license or certification in good standing as a real estate appraiser under the laws of another jurisdiction if:

(a) The applicant presents proof satisfactory to the board that, at the time of application for a Colorado license or certificate by endorsement, the applicant possesses credentials and qualifications that are substantially equivalent to the requirements of this part 6; or

(b) The jurisdiction that issued the applicant a license or certificate to engage in the occupation of real estate appraisal has a law similar to this subsection (1) pursuant to which it licenses or certifies persons who are licensed real estate appraisers in this state.

(2) The board may specify, by rule, what constitutes substantially equivalent credentials and qualifications and the manner in which the board will review credentials and qualifications of an applicant.

(3) Pursuant to section 1122 (a) of Title XI of the federal "Financial Institutions Reform, Recovery, and Enforcement Act of 1989", Pub.L. 101-73, as amended, the board shall recognize, on a temporary basis, the license or certification of an appraiser issued by another state if:

(a) The appraiser's business is of a temporary nature; and

(b) The appraiser applies for and is granted a temporary practice permit by the board.

*   ## § 12-10-612, C.R.S. Denial of license or certificate – renewal – definition.

*   *Editor's note: This section is similar to former §12-61-712 as it existed prior to 2019.*

(1)   The board may determine whether an applicant for licensure or certification possesses the necessary qualifications for licensure or certification required by this part 6. The board may consider such qualities as the applicant's fitness and prior professional licensure and whether the applicant has been convicted of a crime. As used in this subsection (1), "applicant" includes any individual who owns, in whole or in part, directly or indirectly, an appraisal management company and any appraiser designated as a controlling appraiser by a partnership, limited liability company, or corporation acting as an appraisal management company.

(2)   If the board determines that an applicant does not possess the applicable qualifications required by this part 6, or the applicant has violated this part 6, rules promulgated by the board, or any board order, the board may deny the applicant a license or certificate or deny the renewal or reinstatement of a license or certificate pursuant to section 12-10-610, and, in such instance, the board shall provide the applicant with a statement in writing setting forth the basis of the board's determination that the applicant does not possess the qualifications or professional competence required by this part 6. The applicant may request a hearing on the determination as provided in section 24-4-104 (9).

*   ## § 12-10-613, C.R.S. Prohibited activities – grounds for disciplinary actions – procedures.

*   *Editor's note: This section is similar to former §12-61-713 as it existed prior to 2019.*

(1)   A real estate appraiser is in violation of this part 6 if the appraiser:

(a)   Has been convicted of a felony or has had accepted by a court a plea of guilty or nolo contendere to a felony if the felony is related to the ability to act as a real property appraiser. A certified copy of the judgment of a court of competent jurisdiction of the conviction or plea is conclusive evidence of the conviction or plea. In considering the disciplinary action, the board shall be governed by the provisions of section 24-5-101.

(b)   Has violated, or attempted to violate, directly or indirectly, or assisted in or abetted the violation of, or conspired to violate this part 6, a rule promulgated pursuant to this part 6, or an order of the board issued pursuant to this part 6;

(c)   Has accepted any fees, compensation, or other valuable consideration to influence the outcome of an appraisal;

(d)   Has used advertising that is misleading, deceptive, or false;

(e)   Has used fraud or misrepresentation in obtaining a license or certificate under this part 6;

(f)   Has conducted an appraisal in a fraudulent manner or used misrepresentation in any such activity;

(g)   Has acted or failed to act in a manner that does not meet the generally accepted standards of professional appraisal practice as adopted by the board by rule. A certified copy of a malpractice judgment of a court of competent jurisdiction is conclusive evidence of the act or omission, but evidence of the act or omission is not limited to a malpractice judgment.

(h)   Has performed appraisal services beyond his or her level of competency;

(i)   Has been subject to an adverse or disciplinary action in another state, territory, or country relating to a license, certificate, or other authorization to practice as an appraiser. A disciplinary action relating to a license or certificate as an appraiser licensed or certified under this part 6 or any related occupation in any other state, territory, or country for disciplinary reasons is prima facie evidence of grounds for disciplinary action or denial of licensure or certification by the board. This subsection (1)(i) applies only to violations based upon acts or omissions in the other state, territory, or country that are also violations of this part 6.

    (j)   Has failed to disclose in the appraisal report the fee paid to the appraiser for a residential real property appraisal if the appraiser was engaged by an appraisal management company to complete the assignment; or

    (k)   Has engaged in conduct that would be grounds for the denial of a license or certification under section 12-10-612.

(2)   If an applicant, a licensee, or a certified person has violated any provision of this section, the board may deny or refuse to renew the license or certificate, or, as specified in subsections (3) and (6) of this section, revoke or suspend the license or certificate, issue a letter of admonition to a licensee or certified person, place a licensee or certified person on probation, or impose public censure.

(3)   When a complaint or an investigation discloses an instance of misconduct by a licensed or certified appraiser that, in the opinion of the board, does not warrant formal action by the board but should not be dismissed as being without merit, the board may send a letter of admonition by certified mail to the appraiser against whom a complaint was made. The letter shall advise the appraiser of the right to make a written request, within twenty days after receipt of the letter of admonition, to the board to begin formal disciplinary proceedings as provided in this section to adjudicate the conduct or acts on which the letter was based.

(4)   The board may start a proceeding for discipline of a licensee or certified person when the board has reasonable grounds to believe that a licensee or certified person has committed any act or failed to act pursuant to the grounds established in subsection (1) of this section or when a request for a hearing is timely made under subsection (3) of this section.

(5)   Disciplinary proceedings shall be conducted in the manner prescribed by the "State Administrative Procedure Act", article 4 of title 24.

(6)   As authorized in subsection (2) of this section, disciplinary actions by the board may consist of the following:

    (a)   **Revocation of a license or certificate.**

        (I)   Revocation of a license or certificate by the board means that the licensed or certified person shall surrender his or her license or certificate immediately to the board.

        (II)   Any person whose license or certificate to practice is revoked is ineligible to apply for a license or certificate issued under this part 6 until more than two years have elapsed from the date of surrender of the license or certificate. A reapplication after the two-year period is treated as a new application.

    (b)   **Suspension of a license or certificate.** Suspension of a license or certificate by the board is for a period to be determined by the board.

    (c)   **Probationary status.** The board may impose probationary status on a licensee or certified person. If the board places a licensee or certified person on probation, the board may include conditions for continued practice that the board deems appropriate to assure that the licensee or certified person is otherwise qualified to practice in accordance with generally accepted professional standards of professional appraisal practice, as specified in board rules, including any or all of the following:

        (I)   A requirement that the licensee or certified person take courses of training or education as needed to correct deficiencies found in the hearing;

        (II)   A review or supervision of his or her practice as may be necessary to determine the quality of the practice and to correct deficiencies in the practice; and

     (III) The imposition of restrictions upon the nature of his or her appraisal practice to assure that he or she does not practice beyond the limits of his or her capabilities.

    (d) **Public censure.** If, after notice and hearing, the director or the director's designee determines that the licensee or certified person has committed any of the acts specified in this section, the board may impose public censure.

(7) In addition to any other discipline imposed pursuant to this section, any person who violates this part 6 or the rules promulgated pursuant to this article 10 may be penalized by the board upon a finding of a violation pursuant to article 4 of title 24 as follows:

    (a) In the first administrative proceeding against a person, a fine of not less than three hundred dollars but not more than five hundred dollars per violation;

    (b) In any subsequent administrative proceeding against a person for transactions occurring after a final agency action determining that a violation of this part 6 has occurred, a fine of not less than one thousand dollars but not more than two thousand dollars.

(8) A person participating in good faith in making a complaint or report or participating in an investigative or administrative proceeding before the board pursuant to this article 10 is immune from any liability, civil or criminal, that otherwise might result by reason of the action.

(9) A licensee or certified person who has direct knowledge that a person has violated this part 6 shall report his or her knowledge to the board.

(10) The board, on its own motion or upon application at any time after the imposition of discipline as provided in this section, may reconsider its prior action and reinstate or restore a license or certificate, terminate probation, or reduce the severity of its prior disciplinary action. The decision of whether to take any further action or hold a hearing with respect to a prior disciplinary action rests in the sole discretion of the board.

*   *§ 12-10-614, C.R.S. Appraisal management companies – prohibited activities – grounds for disciplinary actions – procedures – rules.*

* *Editor's note: This section is similar to former §12-61-714 as it existed prior to 2019.*

(1) The board, upon its own motion, may, and upon a complaint submitted to the board in writing by any person, shall, investigate the activities of a licensed appraisal management company; an appraiser designated as a controlling appraiser by a partnership, limited liability company, or corporation acting as an appraisal management company; or a person or an entity that assumes to act in that capacity within the state. The board, upon finding a violation, may impose an administrative fine not to exceed two thousand five hundred dollars for each separate offense; censure a licensee; place the licensee on probation and set the terms of probation; or temporarily suspend or permanently revoke a license, when the licensee has performed, is performing, or is attempting to perform any of the following acts:

    (a) Failing to:

      (I) Exercise due diligence when hiring or engaging a real estate appraiser to ensure that the real estate appraiser is appropriately credentialed by the board and competent to perform the assignment; and

      (II) In the case of an AMC, establish and comply with processes and controls reasonably designed to ensure that the AMC conducts its appraisal management services in accordance with the requirements of the federal "Truth in Lending Act", 15 U.S.C. sec. 1639e (a) to (i), and regulations adopted pursuant to that act;

    (b) Requiring an appraiser to indemnify the appraisal management company against liability, damages, losses, or claims other than those arising out of the services performed by the appraiser, including performance or nonperformance of the appraiser's duties and obligations, whether as a result of negligence or willful misconduct;

(c)   Influencing or attempting to influence the development, reporting, result, or review of a real estate appraisal or the engagement of an appraiser through coercion, extortion, collusion, compensation, inducement, intimidation, bribery, or in any other manner. This prohibition does not prohibit an appraisal management company from requesting an appraiser to:

    (I)   Consider additional, appropriate property information;

    (II)   Provide further detail, substantiation, or explanation for the appraiser's value conclusion; or

    (III)   Correct errors in the appraisal report.

(d)   Prohibiting an appraiser, in the completion of an appraisal service, from communicating with the client, any intended users, real estate brokers, tenants, property owners, management companies, or any other entity that the appraiser reasonably believes has information pertinent to the completion of an appraisal assignment; except that this subsection (1)(d) does not apply to communications between an appraiser and an appraisal management company's client if the client has adopted an explicit policy prohibiting the communication. If the client has adopted an explicit policy prohibiting communication by the appraiser with the client, communication by an appraiser to the client must be made in writing and submitted to the appraisal management company.

(e)   Altering or modifying a completed appraisal report without the authoring appraiser's knowledge and written consent, and the consent of the intended user, except to modify the format of the report solely for transmission to the client and in a manner acceptable to the client;

(f)   Requiring an appraiser to provide to the appraisal management company access to the appraiser's electronic signature;

(g)   Failing to validate or verify that the work completed by an appraiser who is hired or engaged by the appraisal management company complies with state and federal regulations, including the uniform standards of professional appraisal practice, by conducting an annual audit of a random sample of the appraisals received within the previous year by the appraisal management company. The board shall establish annual appraisal review requirements by rule and shall solicit and consider information and comments from interested persons.

(h)   Failing to make payment to an appraiser within sixty days after completion of the appraisal, unless otherwise agreed or unless the appraiser has been notified in writing that a bona fide dispute exists regarding the performance or quality of the appraisal;

(i)   Failing to perform the terms of a written agreement with an appraiser hired or engaged to complete an appraisal assignment;

(j)   Failing to disclose to an appraiser, at the time of engagement, the identity of the client;

(k)   Using an appraisal report for a client other than the one originally contracted with, without the original client's written consent;

(*l*)   Failing to maintain possession of, for future use or inspection by the board, for a period of at least five years or at least two years after final disposition of any judicial proceeding in which a representative of the appraisal management company provided testimony related to the assignment, whichever period expires last, the documents or records prescribed by the rules of the board or to produce the documents or records upon reasonable request by the board;

(m)   Having been convicted of, or entering a plea of guilty, an Alford plea, or a plea of nolo contendere to, any misdemeanor or felony relating to the conduct of an appraisal, theft, embezzlement, bribery, fraud, misrepresentation, or deceit, or any other like crime under Colorado law, federal law, or the laws of other states. A certified copy of the judgment of a court of competent jurisdiction of the conviction or other official record indicating that a plea was entered is conclusive evidence of the conviction or plea in any hearing under this part 6.

(n)   Having been the subject of an adverse or disciplinary action in another state, territory, or country relating to a license, registration, certification, or other authorization to practice as an appraisal management company. A disciplinary action relating to a registration, license, or certificate as an appraisal management company under this part 6 or any related occupation in any other state, territory, or country for disciplinary reasons is prima facie evidence of grounds for disciplinary action or denial of a license by the board. This subsection (1)(n) applies only to violations based upon acts or omissions in the other state, territory, or country that would violate this part 6 if committed in Colorado.

(o)   Violating the "Colorado Consumer Protection Act", article 1 of title 6;

(p)   Procuring, or attempting to procure, an appraisal management company license or renewing, reinstating, or reactivating, or attempting to renew, reinstate, or reactivate, an appraisal management company license by fraud, misrepresentation, or deceit or by making a material misstatement of fact in an application for a license;

(q)   Knowingly misrepresenting or making false promises through agents, advertising, or otherwise;

(r)   Failing to disclose to a client the fee amount paid to the appraiser hired or engaged to complete the appraisal upon completion of the assignment; or

(s)   Disregarding, violating, or abetting, directly or indirectly, a violation of this part 6, a rule promulgated by the board pursuant to this part 6, or an order of the board entered pursuant to this part 6.

(2)   When a complaint or an investigation discloses an instance of misconduct that, in the opinion of the board, does not warrant formal action by the board but should not be dismissed as being without merit, the board may send a letter of admonition by certified mail, return receipt requested, to the licensee against whom the complaint was made. The letter shall advise the licensee of the right to make a written request, within twenty days after receipt of the letter of admonition, to the board to begin formal disciplinary proceedings as provided in this section to adjudicate the conduct or acts on which the letter was based.

(3)   Disciplinary proceedings must be conducted in the manner prescribed by the "State Administrative Procedure Act", article 4 of title 24.

(4)   If a partnership, limited liability company, or corporation operating under the license of an appraiser designated and licensed as a controlling appraiser by the partnership, limited liability company, or corporation is guilty of any act listed in subsection (1) of this section, the board may suspend or revoke the right of the partnership, limited liability company, or corporation to conduct its business under the license of the controlling appraiser, whether or not the controlling appraiser had personal knowledge of the violation and whether or not the board suspends or revokes the individual license of the controlling appraiser.

(5)   This part 6 does not relieve any person from civil liability or criminal prosecution under the laws of this state.

(6)   A licensee or certified person having direct knowledge that a person or licensed partnership, limited liability company, or corporation has violated this part 6 shall report his or her knowledge to the board.

(7)   The board, on its own motion or upon application, at any time after the imposition of discipline as provided in this section, may reconsider its prior action and reinstate or restore a license, terminate probation, or reduce the severity of its prior disciplinary action. The decision of

whether to take any further action or hold a hearing with respect to the action rests in the sole discretion of the board.

* ## § 12-10-615, C.R.S. Judicial review of final board actions and orders.

* *Editor's note: This section is similar to former §12-61-715 as it existed prior to 2019.*

Final actions and orders of the board under sections 12-10-612, 12-10-613, and 12-10-614 appropriate for judicial review are subject to judicial review in the court of appeals in accordance with section 24-4-106 (11).

* ## § 12-10-616, C.R.S. Unlawful acts – penalties.

* *Editor's note: This section is similar to former §12-61-716 as it existed prior to 2019.*

(1) It is unlawful for a person to:

    (a) Violate section 12-10-613 (1)(c), (1)(e), or (1)(f) or perform a real estate appraisal without first having obtained a license or certificate from the board pursuant to this part 6;

    (b) Accept a fee for an independent appraisal assignment that is contingent upon:

        (I) Reporting a predetermined analysis, opinion, or conclusion; or

        (II) The analysis, opinion, or conclusion reached; or

        (III) The consequences resulting from the analysis, opinion, or conclusion;

    (c) Misrepresent a consulting service as an independent appraisal; or

    (d) Fail to disclose, in connection with a consulting service for which a contingent fee is or will be paid, the fact that a contingent fee is or will be paid.

(2) Any person who violates any provision of subsection (1) of this section commits a class 1 misdemeanor and shall be punished as provided in section 18-1.3-501. Any person who subsequently violates any provision of subsection (1) of this section within five years after the date of a conviction for a violation of subsection (1) of this section commits a class 5 felony and shall be punished as provided in section 18-1.3-401.

* ## § 12-10-617, C.R.S. Appraisal management company license required – violations – injunction.

* *Editor's note: This section is similar to former §12-61-717 as it existed prior to 2019.*

(1) Except as provided in section 12-10-607 (9), it is unlawful for any person, partnership, limited liability company, or corporation to engage in the business of appraisal management in this state without first having obtained a license from the board. The board shall not grant a license to a person, partnership, limited liability company, or corporation until the person, partnership, limited liability company, or corporation demonstrates compliance with this part 6.

(2) The board may apply to a court of competent jurisdiction for an order enjoining an act or practice that constitutes a violation of this part 6, and, upon a showing that a person, partnership, limited liability company, or corporation is engaging or intends to engage in an act or practice that violates this part 6, the court shall grant an injunction, restraining order, or other appropriate order, regardless of the existence of another remedy for the violation. Any notice, hearing, or duration of an injunction or restraining order shall be made in accordance with the Colorado rules of civil procedure.

(3) Any person, partnership, limited liability company, or corporation violating this part 6 by acting as an appraisal management company without having obtained a license or acting as an appraisal management company after the appraisal management company's license has been

revoked or during any period for which the license was suspended is guilty of a misdemeanor and, upon conviction thereof:

(a) If a natural person, shall be punished by a fine of not more than five hundred dollars, or by imprisonment in the county jail for not more than six months, or by both such fine and imprisonment, for the first violation and, for a second or subsequent violation, shall be punished by a fine of not more than one thousand dollars, or by imprisonment in the county jail for not more than six months, or by both such fine and imprisonment; and

(b) If an entity, shall be punished by a fine of not more than five thousand dollars.

* ## § 12-10-618, C.R.S. Injunctive proceedings.

* *Editor's note: This section is similar to former §12-61-718 as it existed prior to 2019.*

(1) The board may, in the name of the people of the state of Colorado, through the attorney general of the state of Colorado, apply for an injunction in any court of competent jurisdiction to perpetually enjoin a person or appraisal management company from committing an act prohibited by this part 6.

(2) Injunctive proceedings under this section are in addition to and not in lieu of penalties and other remedies provided in this part 6.

(3) When seeking an injunction under this section, the board is not required to allege or prove either that an adequate remedy at law does not exist or that substantial or irreparable damage would result from a continued violation.

* ## § 12-10-619, C.R.S. Special provision for appraiser employees of county assessors.

* *Editor's note: This section is similar to former §12-61-719 as it existed prior to 2019.*

(1) Except as provided in subsection (2) of this section, unless a federal waiver is applied for and granted pursuant to section 12-10-604 (1)(i), a person acting as a real estate appraiser in this state shall be licensed or certified as provided in this part 6. No person shall practice without a license or certificate or hold himself or herself out to the public as a licensed or certified real estate appraiser unless licensed or certified pursuant to this part 6.

(2) An appraiser employee of a county assessor who is employed to appraise real property shall be licensed or certified as provided in this part 6 and shall have two years from the date of taking office or the beginning of employment to comply with this part 6.

* ## § 12-10-620, C.R.S. Duties of board under federal law.

* *Editor's note: This section is similar to former §12-61-720 as it existed prior to 2019.*

(1) The board shall:

(a) Transmit to the appraisal subcommittee of the federal financial institutions examination council or its successor entity, no less than annually, a roster listing individuals and appraisal management companies that have received a certificate or license as provided in this part 6;

(b) Collect and transmit, on an annual basis, to the federal financial institutions examination council an annual registry fee, as prescribed by the appraisal subcommittee of the federal financial institutions examination council or its successor entity, from the following individuals and entities:

(I) Individuals and appraisal management companies that are licensed or certified pursuant to this part 6; and

(II) Appraisal management companies that operate as subsidiaries of federally regulated financial institutions; and

(c)   Conduct its business and promulgate rules in a manner consistent with Title XI of the federal "Financial Institutions Reform, Recovery, and Enforcement Act of 1989", as amended, Pub.L. 101-73.

(2)   The board shall not collect or transmit the information required by this section for licensed ad valorem appraisers.

§ 12-10-621, C.R.S. Business entities.

Editor's note: This section is similar to former §12-61-721 as it existed prior to 2019.

(1)   A corporation, partnership, bank, savings and loan association, savings bank, credit union, or other business entity may provide appraisal services if the appraisal is prepared by a certified general appraiser, a certified residential appraiser, or a licensed appraiser. An individual who is not a certified general appraiser, a certified residential appraiser, or a licensed appraiser may assist in the preparation of an appraisal if:

(a)   The assistant is under the direct supervision of a certified or licensed appraiser; and

(b)   The final appraisal document is approved and signed by an individual who is a certified or licensed appraiser.

§ 12-10-622, C.R.S. Provisions found not to comply with federal law null and void – severability.

Editor's note: (1) This section is similar to former §12-61-722 as it existed prior to 2019.

(2) As of publication date, the revisor of statutes has not received the notice referred to in subsection (2).

(1)   If any provision of this part 6 is found by a court of competent jurisdiction or by the appropriate federal agency not to comply with the federal "Financial Institutions Reform, Recovery, and Enforcement Act of 1989", as amended, Pub.L. 101-73, the provision is null and void, but the remaining provisions of this part 6 are valid unless the remaining provisions alone are incomplete and are incapable of being executed in accordance with the legislative intent of this part 6.

(2)   If the regulation of appraisal management companies is repealed from Title XI of the federal "Financial Institutions Reform, Recovery, and Enforcement Act of 1989", as amended, Pub.L. 101-73, the board's jurisdiction over these entities is also repealed. Before the repeal, the division shall review the regulation of appraisal management companies as provided in section 24-34-104. If the board's jurisdiction is repealed, the director shall notify the revisor of statutes of the date of the repeal.

§ 12-10-623, C.R.S. Scope of article – regulated financial institutions – de minimis exemption.

Editor's note: This section is similar to former §12-61-723 as it existed prior to 2019.

(1) (a)   This article 10 does not apply to an appraisal relating to any real-estate-related transaction or loan made or to be made by a financial institution or its affiliate if the real-estate-related transaction or loan is excepted from appraisal regulations established by the primary federal regulator of the financial institution and the appraisal is performed by:

        (I)   An officer, director, or regularly salaried employee of the financial institution or its affiliate; or

        (II)   A real estate broker licensed under this article 10 with whom the institution or affiliate has contracted for performance of the appraisal.

    (b)   The appraisal must not be represented or deemed to be an appraisal except to the financial institution, the agencies regulating the financial institution, and any secondary markets that purchase real estate secured loans. The appraisal must contain a written notice that the preparer is not licensed or certified as an appraiser under this part 6. Nothing in this subsection (1) exempts a person licensed or certified as an appraiser under this part 6 from regulation as provided in this part 6.

(2)   Nothing in this article 10 limits the ability of any federal or state regulator of a financial institution to require the financial institution to obtain appraisals as specified by the regulator.

Chapter 7:
Rules and Regulations for Appraisers

An * in the left margin indicates a change in the statute, rule, or text since the last publication of the manual.

*   Pursuant to § 12-10-604(1)(a), C.R.S., the Colorado Board of Real Estate Appraisers engages in rulemaking to implement Colorado law in a manner consistent with the requirements of Title XI of the federal Financial Institutions Reform, Recovery and Enforcement Act of 1989.

The rulemaking process is set by § 24-4-103, C.R.S., and involves notice to the public, hearing(s), adoption of rules, and publication. General notice is accomplished through filing with the Secretary of State and publication in the Colorado Register. Specific notice is provided by mail to interested parties. To request mailing of rulemaking notices, send a written request for placement on the rulemaking notice list to: Rule Making Notice List, Colorado Board of Appraisers, 1560 Broadway, Suite 925, Denver, CO 80202.

While rulemaking may occur at any time, the Board prefers to adopt new and amended rules in the fall, with January 1 of the next year as the effective date. Rules are published in the Colorado Real Estate Manual.

DEPARTMENT OF REGULATORY AGENCIES
DIVISION OF REAL ESTATE
BOARD OF REAL ESTATE APPRAISERS
4 CCR 725-2

RULES OF THE COLORADO BOARD OF REAL ESTATE APPRAISERS

Ed. Note: For the most current information, please refer to the Division of Real Estate website: www.dora.state.co.us/real-estate

CHAPTER 1: DEFINITIONS

1.1   The Appraisal Foundation (TAF): An organization that is the source of appraisal standards, qualifications, and ethical conduct in all valuation disciplines to assure public trust in the valuation profession.

1.2   Appraisal Qualifications Board (AQB) of TAF: The AQB establishes the minimum education, experience, and examination requirements for real property appraisers to obtain state certifications. In addition, the AQB performs a number of ancillary duties related to real property and personal property appraiser qualifications.

1.3   Appraiser Standards Board (ASB) of TAF: The ASB develops, interprets, and amends the USPAP.

1.4   Examination: The examination(s) developed by or contracted for the Board and issued or approved by the AQB, if applicable.

1.5   FIRREA: The Financial Institutions Reform, Recovery and Enforcement Act of 1989 as amended.

*   1.6   Board: The Colorado Board of Real Estate Appraisers created and further defined pursuant to section 12-10-603, C.R.S.

1.7   Applicant: Any person applying for a license, Credential Upgrade, or Temporary Practice Permit.

*   1.8   Initial License: The first license granted by the Board to an applicant pursuant to section 12-10-606, C.R.S. An applicant may apply for an initial license at any credential level as long as all requirements for such credential level have been met pursuant to these Rules. An initial license is valid through December 31 of the year of issuance.

*   1.9   Colorado Real Estate Appraiser Licensing Act: That portion of Colorado statutes known as sections 12-10-601 through 623, et seq., C.R.S. as amended.

*   1.10   Uniform Standards of Professional Appraisal Practice (USPAP): Those standards of professional practice promulgated by the ASB of TAF. Pursuant to section 12-10-613(1)(g), C.R.S., as amended, the Board adopts, and incorporates by reference in compliance with section 24-4-103(12.5), C.R.S., as the generally accepted standards of professional appraisal practice the Definitions, Preamble, Rules, Standards, and Standards Rules of the USPAP as promulgated by the ASB of TAF on January 30, 1989 and amended through April 5, 2019 and known as the 2020-2021 edition. Amendments to the USPAP subsequent to April 5, 2019 are not included in this Board Rule 1.10. A certified copy of the USPAP is on file and available for public inspection at the Office of the Board at 1560 Broadway, Suite 925, Denver, Colorado 80202. Copies of the USPAP adopted under this Rule may be examined at any state publications depository library. The 2020-2021 edition of the USPAP may be examined at the Internet website of TAF at www.appraisalfoundation.org, and copies may be ordered through that mechanism. TAF may also be contacted at 1155 15th Street, NW, Suite 1111, Washington, DC 20005, or by telephone at (202) 347-7722 or by telefax at (202) 347-7727.

1.11 Board Rules or Rules: Those rules adopted by the Board pursuant to the Colorado Real Estate Appraiser Licensing Act.

1.12 Repealed.

* 1.13 Licensed Appraiser: A person who has been granted a license pursuant to section 12-10-606(1)(b)(IV), C.R.S. as a Licensed Appraiser by the Board as a result of meeting the real estate appraisal education, experience, and examination requirements established by Board Rule 2.2, the AQB, or as a result of licensure through endorsement from another jurisdiction as provided by Chapter 9 of these Rules. The scope of practice for the Licensed Appraiser is limited to, if competent for the assignment, appraisal of non-complex one to four unit residential properties having a transaction value of less than $ 1,000,000 and complex one to four unit residential properties having a transaction value of less than $ 250,000, or as allowed by section12-10-606(4), C.R.S. For non-federally related transactions, the scope of practice may include vacant or unimproved land that is to be used for development for a one to four unit residential property, or vacant or unimproved land for which the highest and best use is a one to four unit residential property. In compliance with Board Rule 1.16, the scope of practice does not include vacant or unimproved land that has the potential for subdivision development for which the subdivision development analysis method of land valuation is necessary and applicable.

* 1.14 Certified Residential Appraiser: A person who has been granted a license pursuant to section 12-10-606(1)(b)(II), C.R.S., as a Certified Residential Appraiser by the Board as a result of meeting the real estate appraisal education, experience, and examination requirements established by Board Rule 2.3, the AQB, or as a result of licensure through endorsement from another jurisdiction as provided by Chapter 9 of these Rules. The scope of practice for the Certified Residential Appraiser is limited to, if competent for the assignment, appraisal of one to four unit residential properties without regard to transaction value or complexity, or as allowed by section 12-10-606(4), C.R.S. Such scope of practice includes vacant or unimproved land that is to be used for development for a one to four unit residential property, or vacant or unimproved land for which the highest and best use is a one to four unit residential property. In compliance with Board Rule 1.16, the scope of practice for a Certified Residential Appraiser does not include vacant or unimproved land that has the potential for subdivision development for which the subdivision development analysis method of land valuation is necessary and applicable.

* 1.15 Certified General Appraiser: A person who has been granted a license pursuant to section 12-10-606(1)(b)(I), C.R.S. as a Certified General Appraiser by the Board as a result of meeting the real estate appraisal education, experience, and examination requirements established by Board Rule 2.4, the AQB, or as a result of licensure through endorsement from another jurisdiction as provided by Chapter 9 of these Rules. The scope of practice for the Certified General Appraiser will be, if competent for the assignment, appraisal of all types of real property.

1.16 Residential Property: Properties comprising one to four residential units; also includes building sites suitable for development to one to four residential units. Residential property does not include land for which a subdivision analysis or appraisal is necessary.

1.17 Non Residential Property: Properties other than those comprised of one to four residential units and building sites suitable for development to one to four residential units. Non-residential property includes, without limitation, properties comprised of five or more dwelling units, farm and ranch, retail, manufacturing, warehousing, office properties, large vacant land parcels, and other properties not within the definition of residential property.

* 1.18 Temporary Practice Permit: A permit issued pursuant to section 12-10-611(3), C.R.S. as amended and Chapter 10 of these Rules allowing an appraiser licensed or certified in another jurisdiction to appraise property in Colorado under certain conditions without obtaining Colorado licensure.

1.19 Title XI, FIRREA: That part of the Financial Institutions Reform, Recovery and Enforcement Act of 1989 known as the Appraisal Reform Amendments, and also known as 12 U.S.C. sections 3331 through 3355, as amended.

1.20 Contingent Fee: Compensation paid to a person who is licensed as a licensed or certified appraiser, as a result of reporting a predetermined value or direction of value that favors the cause of the client, the amount of value opinion, the attainment of a stipulated result, or the occurrence of a subsequent event directly related to the appraiser's opinion and specific to the assignment's purpose. A person licensed as a licensed or certified appraiser employed by a business entity which is compensated by a contingent fee is considered to be compensated by a contingent fee.

1.21 Licensee: A collective term used to refer to a person who has been licensed by the Board as a Licensed Ad Valorem Appraiser, Licensed Appraiser, Certified Residential Appraiser, or Certified General Appraiser.

1.22 Distance Education: Educational methodologies and presentation techniques other than traditional classroom formats, including and without limitation, live teleconferencing, written or electronic correspondence courses, internet on-line learning, video, and audio tapes.

1.23 Complex Residential Property: Properties comprising one to four residential dwelling units, or land suitable for development to one to four residential units exhibiting complex appraisal factors such as atypical form of ownership, atypical size, atypical design characteristics, atypical locational characteristics, atypical physical condition characteristics, landmark designation, non-conforming zoning, lack of appraisal data, and other similar factors. Complex residential property does not include land for which a subdivision analysis or appraisal is necessary.

1.24 Signature: As defined in the USPAP incorporated by reference in Board Rule 1.10, and including all methods of indicating a signature, such as, without limitation, a handwritten mark, digitized image, coded authentication number, stamped impression, embossed or applied seal, or other means.

1.25 Repealed.

1.26 Qualifying Education: Real estate appraisal education courses completed for credit toward the licensing requirements set forth in Chapter 2 of these Rules and meeting the requirements of Chapter 3 of these Rules. Qualifying education courses must be at least fifteen (15) classroom hours in length and must include an examination.

1.27 Continuing Education: Real estate and real estate appraisal related courses completed for credit toward meeting the continuing education requirements set forth in Chapter 7 of these Rules.

1.28 Transaction value: For purposes of these Rules transaction value means:

    A.   For appraisal assignments carried out as part of a loan transaction, the amount of the loan; or

    B.   For appraisal assignments carried out for other than a loan transaction, the market value of the real property interest.

1.29 Appraisal (Valuation) Process: The analysis of factors that create value to develop an opinion of value. Steps in the analytical process are: defining the problem; determining an appropriate scope of work; gathering and analyzing general and specific data; applying the appropriate analyses, procedures and methodology; the application of reconciliation criteria to reach a final defined value opinion; and correctly reporting that opinion in compliance with the USPAP.

1.30 Accredited college, junior college, community college or university: a higher education institution accredited by the Commission on Colleges, a regional or national accreditation association, or an accrediting agency that is recognized by the U. S. Secretary of Education.

1.31 Repealed.

* 1.32 Real Property Appraiser Qualification Criteria: Pursuant to section 12-10-606(1) and (2), C.R.S. as amended, the Board incorporates by reference in compliance with section 24-4-103(12.5), C.R.S., the 2018 Real Property Appraiser Qualification Criteria adopted by the AQB of TAF on February 1, 2018, including the Required Core Curricula, Guide Notes, and Interpretations relating to the real property appraiser classifications described in Board Rules 1.13, 1.14, and 1.15. This Board Rule 1.32 excludes and does not incorporate by reference the following: the trainee real property appraiser classification and qualification requirements, the supervisory appraiser requirements, and supervisory appraiser/trainee appraiser course objectives and outline. A certified copy of the 2018 Real Property Appraiser Qualification Criteria is on file and available for public inspection at the Office of the Board at 1560 Broadway, Suite 925, Denver, Colorado 80202. Copies of the 2018 Real Property Appraiser Qualification Criteria may be examined at the Internet website of TAF at www.appraisalfoundation.org, and copies may be ordered through that mechanism. TAF may also be contacted at 1155 15th Street, NW, Suite 1111, Washington, DC 20005, or by telephone at (202) 347-7722 or telefax at (202) 347-7727. The 2018 Real Property Appraiser Qualification Criteria is effective as of May 1, 2018.

* 1.33 Credential Upgrade: A licensee, who has been granted a license pursuant to section 12-10-606, C.R.S., may submit an application to the Board requesting an upgrade of the licensee's credential if the licensee has completed the real estate appraisal education, experience, and examination requirements as defined in Chapter 2 of these Rules for the credential for which the licensee is applying. If the Board grants the requested credential, the upgraded license will expire on the same date of the licensee's current license cycle prior to the upgrade.

1.34 Draft Appraisal: A draft appraisal must be identified and labeled as a "draft". The purpose of issuing a draft appraisal cannot be to allow the client and/or the intended user(s) to improperly influence the appraiser.

1.35 Amendment: A written modification of any appraisal, which is dated and signed by the appraiser, and delivered to the client. An amendment is a true and integral component of an appraisal. Amendments may also be referred to as correction pages.

1.36 Good Standing: A licensee, appraisal management company, or controlling appraiser must:

* A. Not have been subject to a stipulation and a final agency order or final agency order, the terms of which were completed not less than three years prior, or had a license revoked or permanently surrendered for any of the violations enumerated under sections 12-10-613, 12-10-614, 12-10-616 or 12-10-617, C.R.S. A license will be considered to be in good standing three years following the completion of all terms of an executed stipulation or final agency order.

B. Not have been subject to a stipulation for diversion, the terms of which have not been fully completed. A licensee will be considered to be in good standing once all terms of the stipulation of diversion have been successfully completed.

* 1.37 Licensed Ad Valorem Appraiser: A person who has been granted a license pursuant to section 12-10-606(1)(b)(III), C.R.S., as a Licensed Ad Valorem Appraiser by the Board as a result of meeting the real estate appraisal education and examination requirements established by Board Rule 2.9. A Licensed Ad Valorem Appraiser cannot conduct appraisal assignments outside the scope of the appraiser's official duties as a County Assessor, an employee of a County Assessor's Office, or as an employee with the Division of Property Taxation within the Department of Local Affairs.

1.38 Review Appraiser: An appraiser, who is actively credentialed in a jurisdiction that is in compliance with Title XI, FIRREA, as determined by the ASC as defined in Board Rule 1.42, who performs a review of another appraiser's work subject to USPAP Standard 3. A review appraiser is not required to obtain a Colorado appraiser's license unless the review appraiser arrives at his or her own opinion of value for real property located in Colorado.

1.39 The Course Approval Program (CAP) of TAF: A voluntary program established by the AQB to provide a minimum level of acceptance for real property appraisal education courses satisfying the Real Property Appraiser Qualification Criteria as defined in Board Rule 1.32.

* 1.40 Division of Real Estate (Division): Has the same meaning as set forth in section 12-10-101(2), C.R.S.

* 1.41 Director of the Division (Director): Has the same meaning as set forth in section 12-10-101(1), C.R.S.

1.42 Appraisal Subcommittee (ASC) of the Federal Financial Institutions Examination Council: A subcommittee created within the Federal Financial Institutions Examination Council as a result of Title XI, FIRREA, or its successor entity, to provide oversight of the appraiser regulatory system.

1.43 College Level Examination Program (CLEP): A group of standardized tests created and administered by the College Board to assess college-level knowledge in certain subject areas and provide a mechanism for earning college credits without taking college courses.

* 1.44 Repealed.

* 1.45 Panel Size Threshold: Has the same meaning as pursuant to section 12-10-604(1)(a)(IV), C.R.S.

* 1.46 Panel: Has the same meaning as pursuant to section 12-10-602(8), C.R.S.

* 1.47 Federally Regulated AMC: Has the same meaning as pursuant to section 12-10-607(9), C.R.S.

* 1.48 AMC Registry Fee: The annual fee collected from appraisal management companies that meet the Panel Size Threshold, including state-licensed appraisal management companies and Federally Regulated AMCs, for transmitting to the Appraisal Subcommittee. The fee is calculated by multiplying the number of licensed or certified appraisers who provided an appraisal in connection with a Covered Transaction on the appraisal management company's Panel in Colorado during the Reporting Period by the registry fee as prescribed by the Appraisal Subcommittee.

* 1.49 AMC National Registry: The registry of state-licensed AMCs and Federally Regulated AMCs maintained by the Appraisal Subcommittee.

* 1.50 Reporting Period:

*   A.   For State-licensed AMCs:

*   1.   Applying for initial licensure, the previous twelve (12) month period or the period the appraisal management company has been in business, whichever period is less.

*   2.   Applying for renewal, the twelve (12) month period beginning November 1 of the prior year through October 31 of the year of renewal.

*   3.   Applying for reinstatement of an expired license, the twelve (12) month period beginning November 1 of the year prior to expiration through October 31 of the year of expiration.

*   B.   For Federally Regulated AMCs reporting to the state, the twelve (12) month period beginning November 1 of the prior year through October 31 of the current year.

* 1.51 Consumer Credit: Credit offered or extended to a consumer primarily for personal, family, or household purposes.

* 1.52 Covered Transaction: Any consumer credit transaction secured by the consumer's principal dwelling.

* 1.53 Creditor: A person who regularly extends consumer credit:

*   A.   That is subject to a finance charge or is payable by written agreement in more than four installments (not including a down payment), and to whom the obligation is initially payable, either on the face of the note or contract, or by agreement when there is no note or contract; or

*   B.   If the person extended the credit (other than credit subject to the requirements of high cost mortgages) more than five (5) times for transactions secured by a dwelling in the preceding calendar year. If a person did not meet these numerical standards in the preceding calendar year, the numerical standards will be applied to the current calendar year. A person regularly extends consumer credit if, in any 12-month period, the person originates more than one (1) credit extension that is subject to the requirements of high cost mortgages or one (1) or more such credit extensions through a mortgage broker.

*   1.54   Dwelling: A residential structure that contains one (1) to four (4) units, whether or not that structure is attached to real property. This includes an individual condominium unit, cooperative unit, mobile home, and trailer, if it is used as a residence.

*   1.55   Person: A natural person or an organization, partnership, proprietorship, association, cooperative, estate, trust, or government unit.

*   1.56   Secondary Mortgage Market Participant: A guarantor or insurer of mortgage-backed securities, or an underwriter or issuer of mortgage-backed securities. Secondary mortgage market participant only includes an individual investor in a mortgage-backed security if that investor also serves in the capacity of a guarantor, insurer, underwriter, or issuer for the mortgage-backed security.

CHAPTER 2:   REQUIREMENTS FOR LICENSURE AS A REAL ESTATE APPRAISER

2.1   Repealed.

2.2   An Applicant for licensure as a Colorado Licensed Appraiser must successfully complete the following requirements or the substantial equivalent thereof, as set forth in the Real Property Appraiser Qualification Criteria as defined and incorporated by reference in Board Rule 1.32:

    A.   Real estate appraisal education:

      1.   Basic Appraisal Principles: 30 hours;

      2.   Basic Appraisal Procedures: 30 hours;

      3.   15-Hour National USPAP Course: 15 hours;

      4.   Residential Market Analysis and Highest and Best Use: 15 hours;

      5.   Residential Appraiser Site Valuation and Cost Approach: 15 hours;

      6.   Residential Sales Comparison and Income Approaches: 30 hours; and

      7.   Residential Report Writing and Case Studies: 15 hours.

    B.   Real estate appraisal experience: An Applicant must demonstrate to the satisfaction of the Board that the Applicant completed at least one thousand (1,000) hours of appraisal experience in no fewer than six (6) months, in conformance with the provisions of Chapter 5 of these Rules and all of the Applicant's experience was obtained after January 30, 1989 and in compliance with the USPAP.

    C.   Real estate appraisal examination:

      1.   The prerequisites to taking the Licensed Appraiser examination are:

        a.   One hundred fifty (150) creditable class hours as specified in Board Rule 2.2(A); and

        b.   One thousand (1,000) hours of qualifying experience completed in no fewer than six (6) months.

      2.   After receiving approval from the Board, an Applicant, who is not currently licensed or certified and in good standing in another jurisdiction, has up to twenty-four (24) months to take and pass the Licensed Appraiser examination.

3. An Applicant must successfully complete the Licensed Appraiser examination as provided in Chapter 4 of these Rules. The only alternative to successful completion of the Licensed Appraiser examination is the successful completion of the Certified Residential Appraiser or Certified General Appraiser examination.

2.3 An Applicant for licensure as a Colorado Certified Residential Appraiser must successfully complete the following requirements or the substantial equivalent thereof, as set forth in the Real Property Appraiser Qualification Criteria as defined and incorporated by reference in Board Rule 1.32:

A. Real estate appraisal education:

1. Basic Appraisal Principles: 30 hours;

2. Basic Appraisal Procedures: 30 hours;

3. 15-hour National USPAP Course: 15 hours;

4. Residential Market Analysis and Highest and Best Use: 15 hours;

5. Residential Appraiser Site Valuation and Cost Approach: 15 hours;

6. Residential Sales Comparison and Income Approaches: 30 hours;

7. Residential Report Writing and Case Studies: 15 hours;

8. Statistics, Modeling and Finance: 15 hours;

9. Advanced Residential Applications and Case Studies: 15 hours; and

10. Appraisal Subject Matter Elective: 20 hours.

B. College-level or in lieu of education options:

1. An Applicant for the Certified Residential Appraiser credential must satisfy at least one (1) of the following six (6) options:

a. Hold a Bachelor's Degree in any field of study from an accredited college or university as defined by Board Rule 1.30;

b. Hold an Associate's Degree from an accredited college or university as defined by Board Rule 1.30, in a field of study related to:

i. Business Administration;

ii. Accounting;

iii. Finance;

iv. Economics; or

v. Real Estate.

c. Successful completion of thirty (30) semester hours of college-level courses that cover each of the following specific topic areas and hours:

i. English Composition (3 semester hours);

ii. Macroeconomics (3 semester hours);

iii. Microeconomics (3 semester hours);

iv. Finance (3 semester hours);

v. Algebra, Geometry, or higher mathematics (3 semester hours);

vi. Statistics (3 semester hours);

vii. Computer Science (3 semester hours);

viii. Business Law or Real Estate Law (3 semester hours); and

ix. Two (2) elective courses in any of the topics listed above or in Accounting, Geography, Agricultural Economics, Business Management, or Real Estate (3 semester hours each).

    d. Successful completion of at least thirty (30) semester hours of examinations created and administered by the CLEP, as defined in Board Rule 1.43, from each of the following specific subject matter areas and hours:

       i. College Algebra (3 semester hours);

       ii. College Composition (6 semester hours);

       iii. College Composition Modular (3 semester hours);

       iv. College Mathematics (6 semester hours);

       v. Principles of Macroeconomics (3 semester hours);

       vi. Principles of Microeconomics (3 semester hours);

       vii. Introductory Business Law (3 semester hours); and

       viii. Information Systems (3 semester hours).

    e. Any combination of Board Rule 2.3(B)(1)(c) and Board Rule (B)(1)(d) above that ensures coverage of all topics and hours identified in Board Rule (B)(1)(c).

    f. As an alternative to the college-level education requirements in Board Rule (B)(1)(a through e) above, an Applicant that has held a Licensed Appraiser credential for a minimum of five (5) years may qualify for a Certified Residential Appraiser credential if the Applicant has had no record of any adverse, final, and non-appealable disciplinary action affecting the Licensed Appraiser's legal eligibility to engage in appraisal practice within the five (5) years immediately preceding the date of application for a Certified Residential Appraiser credential.

2. All college-level education must be obtained from a degree-granting institution by the Commission on Colleges, a national or regional accreditation association, or by an accrediting agency that is recognized by the US Secretary of Education.

3. An Applicant with a college degree from a foreign country may have their education evaluated for "equivalency" by one of the following:

    a. An accredited, degree-granting domestic college or university;

    b. A foreign degree credential evaluation service company that is a member of the National Association of Credential Evaluation Services (NACES); or

    c. A foreign degree credential evaluation service company that provides equivalency evaluation reports accepted by an accredited degree- granting domestic college or university or by a state licensing board that issues credentials in another discipline.

C. Real estate appraisal experience: An Applicant for licensure as a Certified Residential Appraiser must demonstrate to the satisfaction of the Board that the Applicant completed at least one thousand five hundred (1,500) hours of appraisal experience in conformance with the provisions of Chapter 5 of these Rules and all of the Applicant's experience was obtained after January 30, 1989 and in compliance with the USPAP. Real estate appraisal experience must have been gained across a period of not less than twelve (12) months.

D. Real estate appraisal examination:

1. The prerequisites to taking the Certified Residential Appraiser examination are:

    a. Two hundred (200) creditable class hours as specified in Board Rule 2.3(A);

    b. Completion of the college-level education requirements as specified in Board Rule 2.3(B); and

    c. One thousand five hundred (1,500) hours of qualifying experience completed in no fewer than twelve (12) months.

2. After receiving approval from the Board, an Applicant, who is not currently licensed or certified and in good standing in another jurisdiction, has up to twenty-four (24) months to take and pass the Certified Residential Appraiser examination.

3. An Applicant must successfully complete the Certified Residential Appraiser examination as provided in Chapter 4 of these Rules. The only alternative to successful completion of the Certified Residential Appraiser examination is the successful completion of the Certified General Appraiser examination.

2.4 An Applicant for licensure as a Colorado Certified General Appraiser must successfully complete the following requirements or the substantial equivalent thereof, as set forth in the Real Property Appraiser Qualification Criteria as defined and incorporated by reference in Board Rule 1.32:

A. Real estate appraisal education:

1. Basic Appraisal Principles: 30 hours;

2. Basic Appraisal Procedures: 30 hours;

3. 15-Hour National USPAP Course: 15 hours;

4. General Appraiser Market Analysis and Highest and Best Use: 30 hours;

5. Statistics, Modeling and Finance: 15 hours;

6. General Appraiser Sales Comparison Approach: 30 hours;

7. General Appraiser Site Valuation and Cost Approach: 30 hours;

8. General Appraiser Income Approach: 60 hours;

9. General Appraiser Report Writing and Case Studies: 30 hours; and

10. Appraisal Subject Matter Electives: 30 hours.

B. College-level education:

1. An Applicant for the Certified General Appraiser credential must hold a Bachelor's degree, or higher, from an accredited college or university as defined by Board Rule 1.30.

2. An Applicant with a college degree from a foreign country may have their education evaluated for "equivalency" by one of the following:

a. An accredited, degree-granting domestic college or university;

b. A foreign degree credential evaluation service company that is a member of the National Association of Credential Evaluation Services (NACES); or

c. A foreign degree credential evaluation service company that provides equivalency evaluation reports accepted by an accredited degree-granting domestic college or university or by a state licensing board that issues credentials in another discipline.

C. Real estate appraisal experience: An Applicant for licensure as a Certified General Appraiser must demonstrate to the satisfaction of the Board that the Applicant completed at least three thousand (3,000) hours of appraisal experience, of which one thousand five hundred (1,500) hours must be in non-residential appraisal work, in conformance with the provisions of Chapter 5 of these Rules and all of the Applicant's experience was obtained after January 30, 1989 and in compliance with the USPAP. Real estate appraisal experience must have been gained across a period of not less than eighteen (18) months.

D. Real estate appraisal examination:

1. The prerequisites to taking the Certified General Appraiser examination are:

a. Three hundred (300) creditable class hours as specified in Board Rule 2.4(A);

       b.   Completion of the college-level education requirements as specified in Board Rule 2.4(B); and

       c.   Three thousand (3,000) hours of qualifying experience, of which no less than one thousand five hundred (1,500) hours must be in non-residential appraisal work, completed in no fewer than eighteen (18) months.

   2.   After receiving approval from the Board, an Applicant, who is not currently licensed or certified and in good standing in another jurisdiction, has up to twenty-four (24) months to take and pass the Certified General Appraiser examination.

   3.   An Applicant must successfully complete the Certified General Appraiser examination as provided in Chapter 4 of these Rules.

2.5   Repealed.

2.6   Repealed.

2.7   Repealed.

2.8   An applicant for licensure as a Colorado Licensed Ad Valorem Appraiser must be a County Assessor, an employee of a County Assessor's Office, or an employee of the Division of Property Taxation in the Department of Local Affairs.

2.9   An applicant for licensure as a Colorado Licensed Ad Valorem Appraiser must successfully complete the following requirements, or the substantial equivalent thereof:

    A.   Real estate appraiser education:

       1.   Introduction to Ad Valorem Mass Appraisal: no less than 35 hours;

       2.   Basic Appraisal Principles: no less than 30 hours;

       3.   Basic Appraisal Procedures: no less than 30 hours; and

       4.   15-Hour National USPAP Course: 15 hours.

    B.   Real Estate Appraisal examination: successful completion of the Ad Valorem Appraiser examination as provided in Chapter 4 of these Rules; and

    C.   Ad Valorem employment: signed certification by the applicant that the applicant is currently a County Assessor, an employee of a County Assessor's Office, or an employee of the Division of Property Taxation in the Department of Local Affairs.

2.10 Repealed.

CHAPTER 3:   STANDARDS FOR REAL ESTATE APPRAISAL QUALIFYING EDUCATION PROGRAMS

3.1   Repealed.

3.2   Qualifying appraisal education must be taken from providers approved by the Board. In order to be approved, qualifying education courses and the providers must meet the following standards at the time it is offered:

    A.   Course content was developed by persons qualified in the subject matter and instructional design;

    B.   Course content is current and corresponds with the common body of knowledge;

    C.   The instructor is qualified with respect to content and teaching methods, and the body of knowledge;

    D.   The number of participants and the physical facilities are consistent with the teaching method;

    E.   An examination is included for measuring the information learned; and

    F.   The educational offering will be developed and communicated in a manner as to promote and maintain a high level of public trust in appraisal practice.

3.3   The following may be approved as providers of qualifying appraisal education provided that the standards set forth in Board Rule 3.2 are maintained and the education providers have complied with all other requirements of the state of Colorado:

A.   Accredited colleges, junior colleges, community colleges or universities as defined in Board Rule 1.30;

B.   Professional appraisal and real estate related organizations;

C.   State or federal government agencies;

D.   Proprietary schools holding valid certificates of approval from the Colorado Division of Private Occupational Schools, Department of Higher Education;

E.   Providers approved by other jurisdictions, provided the jurisdiction's appraiser regulation program is in compliance with Title XI, FIRREA, as determined by the ASC as defined in Board Rule 1.42;

F.   Providers approved under the CAP as defined in Board Rule 1.39; and

G.   Such other providers as the Board may approve upon petition of the provider or the applicant in a form acceptable to the Board.

3.4   On or after January 1, 1991, in order to be approved by the Board, each education provider must maintain for a period of five (5) years from the last course offering, and provide to the Board upon request, information regarding the qualifying education course offerings including, but not limited to the following:

A.   Outline or syllabus;

B.   All texts, workbooks, handouts or other course materials;

C.   Instructors and their qualifications, including selection, training and evaluation criteria;

D.   Course examinations;

E.   Dates and locations of course offerings; and

F.   Student attendance records.

3.5   The number of hours credited must be equivalent to the actual number of contact hours of in-class instruction and testing. An hour of education is defined as at least fifty (50) minutes of instruction out of each 60-minute segment. For distance education, the number of hours credited must be that number of hours allowed by the CAP as defined in Board Rule 1.39.

3.6   Each qualifying education course offering must be at least fifteen (15) hours in duration, include an examination pertinent to the material covered, and be comprised of segments of not less than one (1) classroom hour.

3.7   Qualifying education courses and corresponding examinations must be successfully completed by the applicant. Successful completion means the applicant has attended the offering, participated in course activities, and achieved a passing score on the course examination.

3.8   Repealed.

3.9   It is the applicant's responsibility to verify that a qualifying educational course offering has been approved by the Board, if the applicant wishes to claim credit for the course.

3.10   Repealed.

3.11   Hours of qualifying education accepted in satisfaction of the education requirement of one level of licensure may be applied toward the requirement for another level and need not be repeated. Applicants are responsible for demonstrating coverage of the required topics.

3.12   The following factors must be used to convert accredited college, junior college, community college or university course credits into qualifying education hours:

A.   Semester Credits x 15.00 = Hours

B.   Quarter Credits x 10.00 = Hours

3.13 Applicants must successfully complete qualifying appraisal education which builds upon and augments previous courses. Qualifying education courses which substantially repeat or duplicate other course work in terms of content and level of instruction will not be accepted. The Board will give appropriate consideration to courses where substantive changes in content have occurred.

3.14 To be acceptable for qualifying appraisal education, distance education offerings must incorporate methods and activities that promote active student engagement and participation in the learning process. Among those methods and activities acceptable are written exercises which are graded and returned to the student, required responses to computer based presentations, provision for students to submit questions during teleconferences, and examinations proctored by an independent third party, who is an official approved by the college or university, or by the sponsoring organization. Simple reading, viewing or listening to materials without active student engagement and participation in the learning process is not sufficient to satisfy the requirements of this Board Rule 3.14.

3.15 As to qualifying education courses completed in other jurisdictions with appraiser regulatory programs that are in compliance with Title XI, FIRREA, as determined by the ASC as defined in Board Rule 1.42, the Board will accept the number of hours of education accepted by that jurisdiction.

3.16 To be acceptable for qualifying real estate appraisal education, distance education courses must meet the other requirements of Chapter 3 of these Rules, and must include a written, closed book final examination proctored by an independent third party, or other final examination testing procedure acceptable to the Board. Examples of acceptable examination proctors include public officials who do not supervise the student, secondary and higher education school officials, and public librarians. Failure to observe this requirement may result in rejection of the course and/or course provider by the Board for that applicant, and may result in the Board refusing or withdrawing approval of any courses offered by the provider.

3.17 All qualifying education courses in the USPAP begun on and after January 1, 2003 must be in the form of a course approved under the CAP as defined in Board Rule 1.39, and taught by an instructor certified by the AQB who is also a state certified appraiser.

3.18 Course providers must provide each student who successfully completes a qualifying real estate appraisal education course in the manner prescribed in Board Rule 3.7 a course completion certificate. The Board will not mandate the exact form of course completion certificates; however, the following information must be included:

   A. Name of course provider;

   B. Course title, which must describe topical content, or the Real Property Appraiser Qualification Criteria Core Curriculum module title;

   C. Course number, if any;

   D. Course dates;

   E. Number of approved education hours;

   F. Statement that the required examination was successfully completed;

   G. Course location, which for distance education modalities must be the principal place of business of the course provider;

   H. Name of student; and

   I. For all USPAP courses begun on and after January 1, 2003, the name(s) and AQB USPAP instructor certification number(s) of the instructor(s).

3.19 The provisions of Board Rule 3.3 notwithstanding, qualifying education courses begun on and after January 1, 2004 and offered through distance education modalities must be approved through the CAP as defined in Board Rule 1.39. The Board will not accept distance education courses begun on and after January 1, 2004 that have not been approved through the CAP.

3.20 All qualifying education courses in the USPAP must be presented using the most recent edition and the most recent version of the National USPAP Course (real property) or equivalent as approved by the CAP, with the exception that courses begun in the three (3) months preceding the effective date of a new edition may be presented using the next succeeding USPAP edition and course version, if available from TAF.

3.21 All qualifying education courses begun on or after January 1, 2008 must be approved through the Course Approval Program of the Appraiser Qualifications Board of the Appraisal Foundation, except as otherwise may be approved in advance and in writing by the Director of the Colorado Division of Real Estate (the "Director") on a limited case by case basis where the Director determines that the public would not be served if course approval were required through the Course Approval Program of the Appraiser Qualifications Board of the Appraisal Foundation for a particular course. Course providers seeking approval of qualifying education courses that have not been approved through the Course Approval Program of the Appraiser Qualifications Board of the Appraisal Foundation shall provide the Director with all requested information the Director deems necessary.

3.22 By offering real estate appraiser qualifying education approved by the Board, each provider agrees to comply with the relevant statutes and Board Rules and to permit the Board to audit said courses at any time and at no cost.

3.23 Introduction to Ad Valorem Mass Appraisal courses that have been approved by the Board as qualifying education can be used for credit as appraisal subject matter electives for applicants seeking licensure as a Certified Residential Appraiser or Certified General Appraiser.

3.24 Applicants are required to provide copies of course completion certificates to the Board in accordance with Board Rule 6.1.

CHAPTER 4:   STANDARDS FOR REAL ESTATE APPRAISAL LICENSING EXAMINATIONS

4.1 Any person wishing to apply for any appraiser's license must register for and achieve a passing score on the appropriate level of examination with the testing service designated by the Board. No other examination results will be accepted. The appropriate levels of examination for the respective levels of licensure are as follows:

License Level	Examination
Licensed Ad Valorem Appraiser	Licensed Ad Valorem Appraiser
Licensed Appraiser	Licensed Real Property Appraiser
Certified Residential Appraiser	Certified Residential Appraiser
Certified General Appraiser	Certified General Appraiser

4.2 Examinees must comply with the standards of test administration established by the Board and the testing service.

4.3 A passing score on an examination will be valid for two (2) years from the examination date. Failure to file a complete application within the two (2) year period will result in the examination grade being void.

4.4 Examinations will be given only to duly qualified applicants for an appraiser's license; however, one instructor from each appraisal qualifying education course provider approved pursuant to Board Rule 3.3 may take the examination one time during any twelve (12) month period in order to conduct research for course content.

4.5 Each examination for a license may, as determined by the Board, be a separate examination.

4.6   Examinations developed by or contracted for the Board for licensed and certified appraisers must comply with the Real Property Appraiser Qualification Criteria as defined in Board Rule 1.32, if applicable.

4.7   Repealed.

4.8   Examinees may use financial calculators during the examination process. The memory functions of any such calculator must be cleared by the testing service staff prior to the beginning and after the conclusion of the examination.

CHAPTER 5:   STANDARDS FOR REAL ESTATE APPRAISAL EXPERIENCE

5.1   The quantitative experience requirements must be satisfied by time spent on the appraisal process. Acceptable experience includes appraisal, appraisal review, appraisal consulting, and mass appraisal experience where the appraiser demonstrates proficiency in the development and reporting of the assignment results utilizing recognized appraisal principles and methodology during the appraisal process as defined by Board Rule 1.29. The Board may consider other experience upon petition by the applicant. All experience must be obtained after January 30, 1989 and comply with the USPAP.

5.2   Repealed.

5.3   Reports or file memoranda claimed as evidence of meeting experience requirements must have been prepared in conformance with the edition of the USPAP in effect as of the date of the appraisal report.

5.4   Repealed.

5.5   The Board reserves the right to verify an applicant's or licensee's evidence of appraisal experience by such means as it deems necessary, including, but not limited to requiring the following:

      A.   Submission of a detailed log of appraisal activity on the form or in the manner specified by the Board;

      B.   Submission of appraisal reports, workfiles or file memoranda;

      C.   Employer affidavits or interviews;

      D.   Client affidavits or interviews; and

      E.   Submission of appropriate business records.

5.6   Repealed.

5.7   Repealed.

5.8   There need not be a client in a traditional sense (i.e. a client hiring an appraiser for a business purpose) in order for an appraisal to qualify for experience, but experience gained for work without a traditional client cannot exceed fifty percent (50%) of the total experience requirement. A client may include a government entity or a court of competent jurisdiction.

      Practicum courses that are approved by the CAP or the Board can satisfy the nontraditional client experience requirement. A practicum course must include the generally applicable methods of appraisal practice for the credential level. Content includes, but is not limited to: requiring the student to produce credible appraisals that utilize an actual subject property; performing market research, containing sales analysis; and applying and reporting the applicable appraisal approaches in conformity with the USPAP. Assignments must require problem solving skills for a variety of property types for the credential level. Experience credit will be granted for the actual classroom hours of instruction, and hours of documented research and analysis as awarded from the practicum course approval process.

5.9   Each application for licensure pursuant to Board Rules 2.2, 2.3, or 2.4 must be accompanied by a log of real estate appraisal experience on a form or in the manner specified by the Board. The experience log must include the following:

A.   Type of property;

B.   Date of report;

C.   Address of appraised property;

D.   Description of work performed by the applicant, and scope of review and supervision of the supervising appraiser, if applicable;

E.   Number of actual work hours by the applicant on the assignment;

F.   The signature and state license number of the supervisor, if applicable. Separate experience logs must be maintained for each supervising appraiser, if applicable;

G.   An attestation certifying the accuracy and truthfulness of the information contained within the experience log; and

H.   The applicant's signature.

5.10 Repealed.

5.11 An applicant for licensure as a Colorado Licensed Appraiser, a Colorado Certified Residential Appraiser or a Colorado Certified General Appraiser must demonstrate that the applicant is capable of performing appraisals that are compliant with USPAP. In accordance with Board Rule 5.5, the Board may verify an applicant's appraisal experience by such means as it deems necessary, including but not limited to requiring the applicant to submit a detailed log of appraisal experience, appraisal reports, and/or work files. Staff within the Division or appraisers selected by the Division may review an applicant's appraisal reports and work files to determine whether the applicant is capable of performing appraisals that are compliant with USPAP and in accordance with Board Rule 13.8.

CHAPTER 6:   APPLICATION FOR LICENSURE

6.1   Except as provided under Chapter 9 of these Rules, an applicant must complete and submit an application as follows:

A.   Licensure for a Licensed Appraiser, Certified Residential Appraiser or Certified General Appraiser credential:

1.   An applicant for an initial license must submit a set of fingerprints to the Colorado Bureau of Investigation for the purpose of conducting a state and national criminal history record check prior to submitting an application.

2.   Complete the Board created application and submit the application with the supporting documentation to include: qualifying education course completion certificates, college transcripts, and experience log.

3.   Upon the Board approving the education and experience requirements, a "Letter of Exam Eligibility" will be issued.

4.   After the issuance of the "Letter of Exam Eligibility", schedule the appropriate examination with the examination provider approved by the Board.

5.   After successfully passing the appropriate examination as defined in Board Rule 4.1, submit a copy of the examination results with proof of the required errors and omissions insurance policy as defined in Board Rule 6.10.

6.   An application is deemed complete at the time that all required supporting documentation and fees are received by the Board.

B.   Licensure for a Licensed Ad Valorem Appraiser credential:

1.   Complete the Board created application and submit the application with the supporting documentation to include: qualifying education course completion certificates, a copy of the examination results as defined in Board Rule 4.1 and proof of employment with a qualified employer as defined in Board Rule 1.37.

2. Applicants for a Licensed Ad Valorem Appraiser credential are not required to submit a set of fingerprints for the purpose of conducting a state and national criminal history record check and are also exempt from the errors and omissions insurance requirements.

3. An application is deemed complete at the time that all required supporting documentation and fees are received by the Board.

6.2 Repealed.

6.3 Repealed.

6.4 Repealed.

6.5 Once the application is deemed complete, the Board will timely process the application. The Board reserves the right to require additional information and documentation from an applicant to determine compliance with applicable laws and regulations, and to verify any information and documentation submitted.

* 6.6 Submission of an application does not guarantee issuance of a license, or issuance of a license within a specific period of time. Applicants must observe the provisions of section 12-10-619, C.R.S., and Chapter 12 of these Rules. Applicants will not represent themselves as being licensees of the Board until the license has been issued by the Board.

* 6.7 Pursuant to section 12-10-612(1), C.R.S., an applicant who has been convicted of, entered a plea of guilty to, entered a plea of nolo contendere, or received a deferred judgment and sentence to a crime, must file with his or her application an addendum to the application in a form prescribed by the Board. Such addendum must be supported and documented by, without limitation, the following:

A. Court documents, including original charges, disposition, pre-sentencing report and certification of completion of terms of sentence;

B. Police officer's report(s);

C. Probation or parole officer's report(s);

D. A written personal statement explaining the circumstances surrounding each violation, and including the statement attesting that "I have no other violations either past or pending";

E. Letters of recommendation; and

F. Employment history for the preceding five (5) years.

6.8 Prior to application for licensure, an individual may request that the Board issue a preliminary advisory opinion regarding the possible effect of convictions, pleas of guilt or nolo contendere or deferred judgments and sentences for criminal offenses. A person requesting such an opinion is not an applicant for licensure. The Board may, at its sole discretion, issue such an opinion, which will not be binding on the Board; is not appealable; and will not limit the authority of the Board to investigate a later application for licensure. The issuance of such an opinion will not prohibit a person from submitting an application for licensure. A person requesting such an opinion must do so in a form prescribed by the Board. Such form must be supported and documented by, without limitation, the following:

A. Court documents, including original charges, disposition, pre-sentencing report and certification of completion of terms of sentence;

B. Police officer's report(s);

C. Probation or parole officer's report(s);

D. A written personal statement explaining the circumstances surrounding each violation, and including the statement attesting that "I have no other violations either past or pending";

E.   Letters of recommendation; and

F.   Employment history for the preceding five (5) years.

6.9   Repealed.

6.10 Every active appraiser, or applicant for an active appraiser's credential, must have in effect a policy of errors and omissions insurance to cover all acts requiring a license.

    A.   The Division will enter into a contract with a qualified insurance carrier to make available to all licensees and license applicants a group policy of insurance under the following terms and conditions:

        1.   The insurance carrier is licensed or authorized by the Colorado Division of Insurance to write policies of errors and omissions insurance in this state.

        2.   The insurance carrier maintains an A.M. best rating of "A-" or better.

        3.   The insurance carrier will collect premiums, maintain records and report names of those insured and a record of claims to the Board on a timely basis and at no expense to the Board.

        4.   The insurance carrier has been selected through a competitive bidding process.

        5.   The contract and policy are in conformance with this Board Rule 6.10 and all relevant Colorado statutory requirements.

    B.   The group policy must provide, at a minimum, the following terms of coverage:

        1.   Coverage for all acts for which a real estate appraiser's license is required to the extent of the professional appraisal work the appraiser is permitted by his or her credential level to perform, except those illegal, fraudulent, or other acts which are normally excluded from such coverage.

        2.   That the coverage cannot be canceled by the insurance carrier except for nonpayment of the premium or in the event a licensee becomes inactive, is revoked or an applicant is denied a license.

        3.   The coverage afforded by the policy must not contain exclusions for coverage of claims for damages reasonably expected in connection with professional appraisal services, including, but not limited to, claims for damages made by or on behalf of the Federal Deposit Insurance Corporation (FDIC), the Federal Housing Finance Agency (FHFA), or any other state or federal agency having regulatory authority over a lender or financial institution, and claims arising from failure of a financial institution.

        4.   Pro-ration of premiums for coverage which is purchased during the course of a calendar year but with no provision for refunds of unused premiums.

        5.   Coverage is for not less than $ 100,000 coverage per claim, with an aggregate limit of not less than $ 300,000 per individual, not including costs of investigation and defense.

        6.   A deductible amount for each occurrence of not more than $ 1,000 for claims and no deductible for legal expenses and defense.

        7.   The obligation of the carrier to defend all covered claims and the ability of the insured licensee to select counsel of choice subject to the written permission of the carrier, which must not be unreasonably withheld.

        8.   The ability of a licensee, upon payment of an additional premium, to obtain higher or excess coverage or to purchase additional coverage from the group carrier as may be determined by the carrier.

        9.   The ability of a licensee, upon payment of an additional premium to obtain an extended reporting period of not less than three hundred sixty-five (365) days.

10. A conformity endorsement allowing a Colorado resident licensee to meet the errors and omissions insurance requirement for an active license in another group mandated state without the need to purchase separate coverage in that state.

11. Policy must not be issued or underwritten using a "self-rated" application form. A "self-rated" application is defined as being an application where a policy is issued based on the answers listed on the application with no subsequent underwriter review.

12. Prior acts coverage must be offered to licensees with continuous past coverage.

C. Licensees or applicants may obtain errors and omissions coverage independent of the group plan from any insurance carrier subject to the following terms and conditions:

1. Individual policies must, at a minimum, comply with the following conditions and the insurance carrier must certify compliance in an affidavit issued to the insured licensee or applicant in a form specified by the Board. The insurance carrier agrees to immediately notify the Board of any cancellation or lapse in coverage. Independent individual coverage must provide, at a minimum, the following:

   a. The insurance carrier is in compliance with all applicable rules and statutes set forth by the Colorado Division of Insurance, and, if required, are licensed or authorized to write policies of Errors and Omissions Insurance in this state.

   b. The insurance carrier maintains an A.M. best rating of "A-" or better.

   c. The contract and policy are in conformance with all relevant Colorado statutory requirements.

   d. Coverage includes all acts for which an appraiser's credential is required, except those illegal, fraudulent or other acts which are normally excluded from such coverage.

   e. Coverage cannot be canceled by the insurance provider, except for nonpayment of the premium or in the event the licensee becomes inactive, is revoked or an applicant is denied a license. Cancellation notice must be provided in manner that complies with section 10-4-109.7, C.R.S.

   f. Coverage is for not less than $ 100,000 per claim, with an annual aggregate limit of not less than $ 300,000 per individual, not including costs of investigation and defense.

   g. A deductible amount for each occurrence of not more than $ 1,000 for claims, and no deductible for legal expenses and defense.

   h. The ability of a licensee, upon payment of an additional premium to obtain an extended reporting period of not less than three hundred sixty-five (365) days.

   i. The coverage afforded by the policy must not contain exclusions for coverage of claims for damages reasonably expected in connection with professional appraisal services, including, but not limited to, claims for damages made by or on behalf of the Federal Deposit Insurance Corporation, the Federal Housing Finance Authority, or any other state or federal agency having regulatory authority over a lender or financial institution, and claims arising from the failure of a financial institution.

   j. The policy may not be issued or underwritten using a "self-rated" application. A "self-rated" application is defined as being an application where a policy is issued based on the answers listed on the application with no subsequent underwriter review.

   k. Prior acts coverage must be offered to licensees with continuous past coverage.

2. For firms that carry policies that cover one (1) or more licensees associated with that firm, all requirements listed in Board Rule 6.10(c)(1) will apply, except Board Rule 6.10(c)(1)(F) and (G) will be replaced with the following:

   a. The per claim limit must be not less than $ 1,000,000, not including the costs of investigation and defense.

   b. The aggregate limit must be not less than $ 1,000,000, not including the costs of investigation and defense.

   c. The maximum deductible amount for each occurrence must not exceed $ 10,000 and the provider must look to the insured for payment of any deductible. There must not be a deductible for legal expenses and defense.

* D. Applicants for licensure, activation, renewal, and reinstatement must certify compliance with this Board Rule 6.10 and section 12-10-608, C.R.S. on forms or in a manner prescribed by the Board. Any active licensee who so certifies and fails to obtain errors and omissions coverage or to provide proof of continuous coverage, either through the group carrier or directly to the Board, will be placed on inactive status:

   1. Immediately, if certification of current insurance coverage is not provided to the Board; or

   2. Immediately upon the expiration of any current insurance when certification of continued coverage is not provided.

E. Appraisers employed by a local, state, or federal government entity are exempt from the errors and omissions insurance requirements.

* 6.11 Pursuant to section 12-10-606(6)(a), C.R.S., the Board must establish the fitness standards that an applicant for a license must demonstrate. Therefore, an applicant must demonstrate that he or she does not possess a background that could call into question the public trust. Some of the criteria that the Board may evaluate in determining whether the public trust may be called into question are:

A. Whether the applicant has previously had an appraiser credential revoked;

B. Whether the applicant has previously had a professional license disciplined in any jurisdiction;

C. Whether the applicant has been convicted of, or pled guilty to, entered a plea of nolo contendere to, or received a deferred judgment and sentence to a crime. An applicant will not be eligible for a license if, during at least the five (5) year period immediately preceding the date of application for a license, the applicant has been convicted of, plead guilty to, or entered a plea of nolo contendere to a crime that would call into question the applicant's fitness for licensure; and

D. Whether the applicant has failed to demonstrate that he or she possesses the character necessary to command the confidence of the community and to warrant a determination that the applicant will operate honestly, fairly and efficiently within the scope and purpose of real property appraisal practice.

6.12 If the fees accompanying any application to the Board (including fees for renewals, transfers, etc.) are paid for by check and the check is not immediately paid upon presentment to the bank upon which the check was drawn, or if payment is submitted in any other manner, and payment is denied, rescinded or returned as invalid, the application will be deemed incomplete. The application will only be deemed complete if the Board has received payment of all application fees together with any fees incurred by the Division including the fee required by state fiscal rules for the clerical services necessary for reinstatement within sixty (60) days of the Division mailing notification of an incomplete application.

CHAPTER 7:   CONTINUING EDUCATION REQUIREMENTS

7.1   For initial licenses issued on or after July 1 of any year, there will be no continuing education requirement as a condition of renewal of such initial license that expires December 31 of the year of issuance as defined in Board Rule 1.8. For initial licenses issued before July 1 of any year, there will be an obligation to complete fourteen (14) hours of continuing education as a condition of renewal before the initial license expires on December 31 of the year of issuance as defined in Board Rule 1.8. Continuing education requirements established by Chapter 7 of these Rules will apply to all other license renewals.

7.2   Except as provided under Board Rule 7.1, each licensee applying for renewal of a license must complete twenty-eight (28) hours of real estate appraisal continuing education during the two-year period preceding expiration of the license. All licensees renewing a license at the end of a two-year licensing period must complete the National USPAP Update Courses set forth in Board Rule 7.19. Continuing education requirements must be completed after the effective date of the license to be renewed and prior to the expiration of such license. Upon written request and receipt of the supporting documentation established by the Board, the Board may grant a deferral for continuing education compliance for licensees returning from active military duty. Licensees returning from active military duty may be placed on active status for up to ninety (90) days pending completion of all continuing education requirements established pursuant to Chapter 7 of these Rules.

7.3   Continuing real estate appraisal education must be taken from providers approved by the Board. In order to be approved by the Board, continuing education must meet the following standards:

   A.   It must have been developed by persons qualified in the subject matter and instructional design;

   B.   It must be current;

   C.   The instructor must be qualified with respect to content and teaching methods; and

   D.   The number of participants and the physical facilities are consistent with the teaching method(s).

   The Board, at its discretion, may require an evaluation in a manner determined by the Board of an educational offering to ensure compliance with the above standards. By offering real estate appraisal continuing education approved by the Board, each provider agrees to comply with relevant statutes and Board Rules and to permit Board audit of said courses at any time and at no cost. If the Board determines that the offering fails to comply with the standards set forth above, the Board will notify the provider of such deficiency and work with the provider to correct such deficiency prior to the next class offering. If such deficiency is not corrected, then the Board may withdraw approval of the provider, instructor and/or the class.

7.4   The following may be approved as providers of continuing appraisal education, provided the standards set forth in Board Rule 7.3 are maintained, and provided they have complied with all other requirements of the state of Colorado:

   A.   Accredited colleges, junior colleges, community colleges or universities as defined in Board Rule 1.30;

   B.   Professional appraisal and real estate related organizations;

   C.   State or federal government agencies;

   D.   Proprietary schools holding valid certificates of approval from the Colorado Division of Private Occupational Schools, Department of Higher Education;

   E.   Continuing education completed in other jurisdictions, providers approved by such other jurisdiction, provided that the jurisdiction's appraiser regulation program is in compliance with Title XI, FIRREA, as determined by the ASC as defined in Board Rule 1.42;

F.   The providers of continuing education approved under the CAP as defined in Board Rule 1.39; and

G.   Other providers as the Board may approve upon petition of the education provider or licensee in a form acceptable to the Board.

7.5   Continuing education providers must, at their own expense, maintain for a period of five (5) years from the last course offering, and provide to the Board on request, information regarding the educational offerings including, but not limited to the following:

A.   Outline or syllabus;

B.   All texts, workbooks, handouts or other materials;

C.   Instructors and their qualifications, including selection, training and evaluation criteria;

D.   Examinations (if any);

E.   Dates and locations of offerings; and

F.   Student attendance records;

7.6   Continuing appraisal education must be at least two (2) class hours in duration including examination time (if any). Continuing appraisal education programs and courses are intended to maintain and improve the appraiser's skill, knowledge, and competency. Continuing appraisal education courses and programs may include, without limitation, these real estate and real estate appraisal topics:

A.   Ad valorem taxation;

B.   Arbitration, dispute resolution;

C.   Courses related to the practice of real estate appraisal or consulting;

D.   Development cost estimating;

E.   Ethics and standards of professional practice, USPAP;

F.   Land use planning, zoning;

G.   Management, leasing, timesharing;

H.   Property development, partial interests;

I.   Real estate law, easements, and legal interests;

J.   Real estate litigation, damages, condemnation;

K.   Real estate financing and investment;

L.   Real estate appraisal related computer applications;

M.   Real estate securities and syndication;

N.   Developing opinions of real property value in appraisals that also include personal property and/or business value;

O.   Seller concessions and impact on value;

P.   Energy efficient items and "green building" appraisals; and/or

Q.   Other topics as the Board may approve, upon its own motion or upon petition by the course provider or the licensee in a form acceptable to the Board.

7.7   The Board will award continuing education credit to credentialed appraisers who attend a Board's public meeting in person, under the following conditions:

A.   Credit will be awarded for a single Board meeting per license cycle; and

B.   The meeting must be open to the public and must be a minimum of two (2) hours in length. The total credit cannot exceed seven (7) hours.

7.8   The Board may consider alternatives to continuing real estate appraisal education such as teaching, authorship of textbooks or articles, educational program developments or similar activities for up to one-half of the required continuing education. Licensees desiring continuing education credit for alternative activities must petition the Board for approval in writing and prior to commencement of the alternative activity.

7.9 The act of applying for renewal constitutes a statement that the licensee has complied with the continuing education requirements of the Colorado Real Estate Appraiser Licensing Act and Board Rules. The Board reserves the right to require a licensee to provide satisfactory documentary evidence of completion of continuing appraisal education requirements. The Board may at its option require such submission as part of the renewal process or subsequent to renewal.

7.10 With the exception of the 7-hour National USPAP Update Course(s), or its equivalent, required pursuant to Board Rule 7.19, licensees may complete the required hours of continuing real estate appraisal education at any time during the licensing period preceding expiration.

7.11 An appraiser may repeat courses or programs previously completed, subject to the limitation that no course or program may be repeated more frequently than once every continuing education cycle, which is the same as the appraiser's license cycle. Education in the USPAP, or its AQB-approved equivalent, is not subject to this limitation.

7.12 Continuing real estate appraisal education must be successfully completed by the licensee. Successful completion means attendance at the offering and participation in class activities. Successful completion of courses undertaken through distance education requires compliance with the provisions of Board Rule 7.14. Teaching of continuing real estate appraisal education will constitute successful completion, if also in compliance with Board Rule 7.8; however, credit will be given for only one (1) presentation of a particular offering during each licensing period.

7.13 The number of hours credited will be equivalent to the actual number of contact hours of in-class instruction and testing. An hour of appraisal education and training is defined as at least fifty (50) minutes of instruction out of each 60-minute segment. For distance education offerings, the number of hours credited must be that number of hours allowed by the CAP as defined in Board Rule 1.39.

7.14 Distance education offerings must include methods and activities which promote active student engagement and participation in the learning process. Among those methods and activities acceptable are written exercises which are graded and returned to the student, required responses in computer based presentations, provision for students to submit questions during teleconferences, and examinations proctored by an independent third party. Simple reading, viewing, or listening to materials is not sufficient engagement in the learning process to satisfy the requirements of this Board Rule 7.14.

7.15 As to continuing education completed in other jurisdictions with appraiser regulatory programs that are in compliance with Title XI, FIRREA, as determined by the ASC as defined in Board Rule 1.42, the Board will accept the number of hours of continuing education accepted by that jurisdiction.

7.16 Repealed.

7.17 Repealed.

7.18 Continuing education content must have a clear application to real estate appraisal practice. Motivational courses, personal growth, or self-improvement courses, general business courses and general computing courses are unacceptable to satisfy the continuing education requirements established by these Rules.

7.19 All licensees must successfully complete a 7-hour National USPAP Update Course, or its equivalent, every two (2) calendar years. Such 7-hour National USPAP Update Course must be in the form of a course approved by the AQB, and taught by an instructor certified by the AQB and who is also a state certified appraiser. Equivalency will be determined through the CAP or by an alternate method established by the AQB.

7.20 A licensee who is a resident of a jurisdiction other than the state of Colorado that imposes continuing education requirements consistent with the criteria promulgated by the AQB may comply with the continuing education requirements of Chapter 7 of these Rules by documenting, in a manner prescribed by the Board, compliance with the continuing education requirements of their jurisdiction of residence. In the event the jurisdiction of residence does not impose continuing education requirements consistent with the criteria promulgated by the AQB, the licensee must comply with the continuing education requirements established by Chapter 7 of these Rules.

7.21 A licensee who renews a license subject to a continuing education requirement must retain documentary evidence of compliance with these continuing education requirements for a period of not less than five (5) years after the expiration of the license being renewed.

7.22 Course providers must provide each student who successfully completes a continuing education course in the manner prescribed in Board Rule 7.12 a course completion certificate. The Board will not mandate the exact form of course certificates; however, the following information must be included:

A. Name of course provider;

B. Course title, which must describe topical content;

C. Course number, if any;

D. Course dates;

E. Number of continuing education hours;

F. Statement that the required examination was successfully completed, if an examination is a regular part of the course;

G. Course location, which for distance education modalities must be the principal place of business of the course provider;

H. Name of student; and

I. For USPAP courses begun on and after January 1, 2003, the name and AQB USPAP instructor certification number of the instructor.

7.23 The provisions of Board Rule 7.4 notwithstanding, real estate appraisal continuing education offered through distance education must be approved through the CAP, unless the provider is a government agency that has sought an exemption from the Board.

7.24 Repealed.

7.25 Repealed.

7.26 Upon written notification from the Board, licensees must provide copies of course certificates to the Board. Failure to provide copies of course certificates within the time set by the Board in its notification will be grounds for disciplinary action unless the Board has granted an extension of time for providing the certificates.

CHAPTER 8:   RENEWAL, REINSTATEMENT, INACTIVATION, SURRENDER OR REVOCATION OF LICENSURE

8.1 Repealed.

8.2 Repealed.

8.3 Repealed.

8.4 Repealed.

* 8.5 No holder of an expired license which may be reinstated may apply for a new license of the same type. Such person must reinstate the expired license as provided in section 12-10-610(1), C.R.S., and these Rules. Nothing in this Board Rule 8.5 will act to prevent a person from applying for and receiving a license with higher qualification requirements than those of the expired license.

8.6   All licensees in active or inactive license status must provide the Board with the following information: (1) a current mailing address and phone number for the licensee; (2) a current email address for the licensee if applicable; and (3) such other contact information as may be required by the Board from time to time. Each licensee must inform the Board within ten (10) calendar days of any change in such contact information on a form or in the manner prescribed by the Board. A mailing address for the licensee will be posted on the Division's public website, and it is the licensee's responsibility to inform the Division of any required changes to the mailing address shown for the licensee on the Division's public website. The address shown for the licensee on the Division's public website will be considered the licensee's address of record. A change of mailing address without notification to the Board will result in the inactivation of the appraiser's license.

8.7   Repealed.

8.8   The holder of a license or Temporary Practice Permit may surrender such to the Board. The Board may deem a surrendered license or Temporary Practice Permit as permanently relinquished. Such relinquishment will not remove the holder from the jurisdiction of the Board for acts committed while holding a license or Temporary Practice Permit. A license or Temporary Practice Permit that is relinquished during the pendency of an investigation or a disciplinary action will be reported to the National Registry as having been surrendered in lieu of discipline. A person who relinquishes a license or Temporary Practice Permit may not reinstate the same, but must reapply and meet the current requirements for initial licensure.

8.9   Upon inactivation, revocation, suspension, surrender, relinquishment, or expiration of a license or Temporary Practice Permit, the holder must:

A.   Immediately cease all activities requiring licensure or a Temporary Practice Permit;

B.   In the instance of revocation, suspension, relinquishment, or surrender, immediately return the license document or Temporary Practice Permit to the Board;

C.   Immediately cease all actions which represent the holder to the public as actively being licensed or being the holder of a Temporary Practice Permit, including, without limitation, the use of advertising materials, forms, letterheads, business cards, correspondence, internet website content, statements of qualifications, and the like.

8.10   A licensee who has not completed continuing education requirements established pursuant to Chapter 7 of these rules may not renew or reinstate licensure on inactive status unless the Board determines that extenuating circumstances existed which caused the deficiency in the continuing education requirements. The Board may require a written request and supporting documentation to determine that an extenuating circumstance exists or existed. A licensee desiring to renew or reinstate licensure on inactive status must submit their renewal or reinstatement on an inactive status application to the Board.

8.11   A licensee may, without limitation, renew or reinstate licensure on inactive status for subsequent renewal periods by complying with the requirements of Rule 8.10.

8.12   Repealed.

8.13   Repealed.

8.14   Repealed.

8.15   Repealed.

8.16   Repealed.

8.17   A Licensed Ad Valorem Appraiser must be a County Assessor, an employee of a County Assessor's Office, or an employee of the Division of Property Taxation in the Department of Local Affairs. If a Licensed Ad Valorem Appraiser is no longer a County Assessor, leaves the employ of a County Assessor's Office, or leaves the employ of the Division of Property Taxation within the Department of Local Affairs, the Licensed Ad Valorem Appraiser must notify the Board within three (3) business days in a manner acceptable to the Board. Upon such notification or discovery by the Board, the Licensed Ad Valorem Appraiser will be placed on inactive status. The Licensed Ad Valorem Appraiser will not be returned to active status unless the licensee signs a certification that he or she is currently a County Assessor, an employee of a County Assessor's Office or an employee of the Division of Property Taxation in the Department of Local Affairs and the Board verifies the licensee's employment.

8.18 A licensee desiring to activate an inactive license must complete all required continuing education hours that would have been required if the licensee had been on active status for the entire period of inactivation, including the most recent version of the National USPAP Course or its equivalent as approved by the CAP as defined in Board Rule 1.39.

CHAPTER 9: LICENSURE BY ENDORSEMENT

* 9.1 Pursuant to section 12-10-611(1) and (2), C.R.S., as amended, licensure by endorsement will be subject to the following restrictions and requirements:

    A.   The Board may issue licenses by endorsement only to those persons holding an active license or certificate from another jurisdiction which is substantially equivalent to those described in Board Rules 1.13, 1.14 or 1.15, with qualification requirements substantially equivalent to those in Board Rules 2.2, 2.3 or 2.4, respectively;

    B.   The applicant must be the holder of an active license or certificate in good standing under the laws of another jurisdiction;

    C.   The appraiser regulatory program of the jurisdiction where the applicant holds an active license or certificate in good standing must be compliance with Title XI, FIRREA, as determined by the ASC as defined in Board Rule 1.42;

*   D.   The applicant must apply for licensure by endorsement on a form provided by the Board, pay the specified fees and meet all other Board requirements, including the submission of a set of fingerprints to the Colorado Bureau of Investigation for the purpose of conducting a state and national fingerprint-based criminal history record check as required by section 12-10-606(6)(a), C.R.S. as amended;

    E.   The applicant must apply for and be issued by the Board a license by endorsement prior to undertaking appraisal activities in Colorado that would require licensure in Colorado; and

*   F.   A license issued by endorsement will be subject to the same renewal requirements as a license issued pursuant to section 12-10-606, C.R.S. as amended, and Chapters 7 and 8 of these Rules.

CHAPTER 10: TEMPORARY PRACTICE IN COLORADO

* 10.1 Pursuant to section 12-10-611(2) and (3), C.R.S., as amended, a Temporary Practice permit may be issued to the holder of an active appraiser's license or certificate from another jurisdiction. Such Temporary Practice Permit must be subject to the following restrictions and requirements:

    A.   The applicant must apply for and be issued a Temporary Practice Permit prior to his or her commencement of a real property appraisal in Colorado that is part of a federally related transaction;

    B.   The applicant's business is temporary in nature and the applicant must identify in writing the appraisal assignment(s) to be completed under the Temporary Practice Permit prior to being issued a Temporary Practice Permit;

C. The Temporary Practice Permit will be valid only for the appraisal assignment(s) listed thereon;

D. The applicant must be the holder of an active license or certificate in good standing under the laws of another jurisdiction;

E. The applicant must apply for a Temporary Practice Permit on a form provided by the Board, pay the specified fees, and meet all other Board requirements; and

* F. Pursuant to section 12-10-611(2) and (3), C.R.S., Temporary Practice Permits are available only to persons holding active licensure in another jurisdiction at levels substantially equivalent to those defined in Board Rules 1.13, 1.14, or 1.15. Temporary Practice Permits are not available to persons holding licensure in another jurisdiction at a trainee, apprentice, associate, intern, or other entry level.

10.2 No person may be issued more than two (2) Temporary Practice Permits in any rolling twelve-month period.

10.3 A Temporary Practice Permit issued pursuant to Chapter 10 of these Rules will be valid for the period of time necessary to complete the original assignment(s) listed thereon, including time for client conferences and expert witness testimony. A Temporary Practice Permit issued pursuant to Chapter 10 of these Rules will not be valid for completion of additional or update assignments involving the same property or properties. Additional or update assignments involving the same property or properties are new assignments, thereby requiring a new Temporary Practice Permit or licensure by endorsement as provided in Chapter 9 of these Rules.

CHAPTER 11: STANDARDS OF PROFESSIONAL APPRAISAL PRACTICE

* 11.1 The USPAP was adopted and incorporated by reference in Board Rule 1.10. The 2018-2019 edition of the USPAP, incorporating the amendments made through February 3, 2017 will remain in effect through December 31, 2019. Beginning January 1, 2020, the 2020-2021 edition of the USPAP will be in effect.

* 11.2 A licensee using the services of an unlicensed assistant under the provisions of section 12-10-621, C.R.S. as amended, or the services of another licensee in the preparation of appraisals or other work products will, consistent with the USPAP, supervise each such assistant or licensee in an active, diligent and personal manner. When any portion of the work involves significant real property appraisal assistance, the licensee must describe and summarize the research, analysis and reporting contributions of each such assistant or other licensee within each such report or other work product in a manner specified in USPAP Standard 2.

* 11.3 A licensee performing any consulting services pursuant to section 12-10-602(5), C.R.S., must not represent any analysis, opinion, or conclusions as an independent appraisal assignment. In compliance with sections 12-10-613(1)(g) and 12-10-616(1)(b), (c) and (d), C.R.S, a licensee compensated by a Contingent Fee as defined in Board Rule 1.20, must disclose in a clear and conspicuous manner in any oral report, or the letter of transmittal, summary of salient facts and conclusions, statement of limiting conditions, and certifications of any written report the following:

A. A contingent fee is being paid;

B. The licensee is performing a consulting service and not an independent appraisal; and

C. Any oral or written reports were not required to be compliant with the Ethics Rule of the USPAP.

CHAPTER 12: LICENSE TITLES, LICENSE DOCUMENTS, AND SIGNATURES

12.1 The descriptive license titles defined in Board Rules 1.13, 1.14, 1.15, 1.18, and 1.37 must only be used by persons who hold such Board issued license or Temporary Practice Permit in good standing. The descriptive license titles may only be used by an individual license holder and may not be used by any other person or group of persons, including a corporation, partnership, or other business entity.

12.2 Repealed.

12.3 Repealed.

12.4 In each appraisal report or other appraisal related work product, the license held by the appraiser(s) must be clearly identified by using the license titles defined in Board Rules 1.13, 1.14, 1.15, and 1.37 and including the license number. Such license titles and numbers must be identified wherever the licensee signs, by any means or method, the report or other work product, including, but not limited to the:

A.   Letter of transmittal;

B.   Certification of the appraiser(s); and

C.   Appraisal or other work product report form or document, including addenda thereto.

12.5 Repealed.

12.6 An appraiser practicing in Colorado under authority of a Temporary Practice Permit must identify the state where they hold licensure, the type of license and the license number, and must further state they hold a Temporary Practice Permit and state the permit number in all instances where license type and number are required under Chapter 12 of these Rules.

12.7 The real estate appraiser's license or Temporary Practice Permit document and identification card issued to an initial applicant or licensee will remain the property of the Board. Such document and card must be surrendered to the Board immediately upon demand. The reasons for such demand may include, but are not limited to, suspension, revocation, surrender, or relinquishment.

12.8 When complying with either Board Rule 12.4 or Board Rule 12.6, an appraiser must use the full license or Temporary Practice Permit title in Board Rules 1.13, 1.14, 1.15, 1.18, and 1.37, or must use the appropriate abbreviation as listed below, followed by the license or Temporary Practice Permit number. Use of initials only, such as the alphabetical prefix included with each Board issued number to identify the type of license or Temporary Practice Permit is prohibited except when necessary to comply with federally implanted data collection or reporting requirements (for example FNMA ("Fannie Mae") or FHLMC ("Freddie Mac") implemented policies or guidelines).

Licensed Ad Valorem Appraiser:	Lic. Ad Val App. or Lic. Ad Val Appr.
Licensed Appraiser:	Lic. App. or Lic. Appr.
Certified Residential Appraiser:	Crt. Res. App. or Cert. Res. Appr.
Certified General Appraiser:	Crt. Gen. App. or Cert. Genl. Appr.
Temporary Practice Permit:	Temp. Prac. Pmt.

12.9 Repealed.

12.10 When stating the type of license or Temporary Practice Permit held, and the number thereof, an appraiser may make use of an impression, provided such impression is legible on each copy of the appraisal report or other work product.

12.11 Where appraisal report forms or other work product forms do not allow space for placing the information required by Board Rule 12.4 or Board Rule 12.6 immediately following the name and signature of the appraiser the required information will be placed in the closest reasonable available space on the same page.

12.12 The holder of a license or Temporary Practice Permit in good standing may copy the license or Temporary Practice Permit document for inclusion in an appraisal report or other appraisal work product. Such copy must have the word "COPY" prominently displayed so as to substantially overlay the printed portions of the license or Temporary Practice Permit document.

12.13 The requirements of Chapter 12 of these Rules must be complied with in any electronic copy or transmittal of an appraisal report or other appraisal related work product.

12.14 No holder of a license or Temporary Practice Permit, or any other person, will make or cause to be made or allow to be made, any alteration to a Board-issued license or Temporary Practice Permit document or copy thereof, other than as provided in Board Rule 12.12.

12.15 No licensee may affix or allow to be affixed the name or signature of a licensee to an appraisal report or other appraisal related work product without the express permission of the licensee for that specific assignment, report, or other work product. Licensees must not give blanket permission for affixing their signature to appraisal reports or other work products and may only authorize the use of his or her signature on an assignment-by-assignment basis.

12.16 No licensee will permit, through action or inaction, their name or signature to be affixed to an appraisal report or other appraisal related work product without their first personally examining and approving the final version of such report or other work product.

CHAPTER 13: DISCIPLINARY PROCEDURES

13.1 Complaints alleging violation of the Colorado Real Estate Appraiser Licensing Act or the Board Rules must be in writing on a form or in the manner prescribed by the Board. Nothing in this Board Rule 13.1 will act to prevent the Board from acting upon its own motion to open a complaint.

* 13.2 Pursuant to section 12-10-604(1)(c), C.R.S., and section 24-4-105(3), C.R.S., any disciplinary hearing conducted on behalf of the Board may, at the discretion of the Board, be conducted by an Administrative Law Judge from the Office of Administrative Courts of the Department of Personnel & Administration.

13.3 Repealed.

13.4 When a holder of a Board-issued license or Temporary Practice Permit has received written notification from the Board that a complaint has been filed against the holder, a written response to the Board is required to be submitted by the holder. Failure to submit a written response within the time set by the Board in its notification will be grounds for disciplinary action, unless the Board has granted an extension of time for the response in writing and regardless of the question of whether the underlying complaint warrants further investigation or subsequent action by the Board. The holder's written response must contain the following:

A. A complete and specific answer to the factual recitations, allegations or averments;

B. A complete and specific response to any additional questions, allegations or averments presented in the notification letter;

C. Any documents or records requested in the notification letter; and

D. Any further information relative to the complaint that the holder believes to be relevant or material to the matters addressed in the notification letter.

13.5 The holder of a Board-issued license or Temporary Practice Permit, including an owner of more than ten (10) percent of a licensed appraisal management company, must inform the Board in writing within ten (10) days of any disciplinary action taken by any other state, district, territorial, or provincial real estate appraiser or appraisal management company licensing authority. For purposes of this Board Rule 13.5, disciplinary action may include, without limitation, actions such as fines, required education, probation, suspension, revocation, letters of censure, debarment, required supervision, and the like.

13.6 Pursuant to section 24-34-106, C.R.S., when a licensee is required to complete real estate appraisal education as part of stipulation, final agency order, or stipulation for diversion, no portion of any such courses or programs will be creditable toward continuing education or qualifying education requirements.

* 13.7 Pursuant to sections 12-10-613(1)(a) and (k), C.R.S., a licensee must inform the Board in writing within ten (10) days of conviction of, entering a plea of guilty to, entering a plea of nolo contendere to, or receiving a deferred judgment and sentence to any felony or misdemeanor offense, excluding misdemeanor traffic offenses, municipal code violations or petty offenses. A licensee must inform the Board in writing within ten (10) days of any disciplinary action taken against any professional licenses held by the licensee, excluding the licensee's Colorado appraisal credential. For purposes of this Board Rule 13.7, disciplinary action include, without limitation, actions such as imposition of fines, required or remedial education, probation, suspension, revocation, letters of censure, debarment, mandatory supervision, and the like.

13.8 Board members, Division staff and contractors hired by the Division are not required to comply with USPAP in performance of the official duties that include, but are not limited to:

A. Investigations;

B. Work experience reviews conducted during license application processing;

C. The review or analysis of investigative findings, experience reviews, and/or work product reviews resulting from Board case resolutions; or

D. The review of the appraisal as part of an application.

An investigation or review conducted by staff, a member of the Board or a contractor hired by the Division is not considered an "appraisal review" or an "appraisal" as defined by the USPAP.

13.9 A holder of a Board-issued license or Temporary Practice Permit must respond in writing to any correspondence from the Board requiring a response. The written response must be submitted within the time period provided by the Board. The Board will send such correspondence to the holder's address of record filed with the Board. Failure to submit a timely written response will be grounds for disciplinary action.

13.10 Exceptions and Board Review of Initial Decisions:

A. Written form, service, and filing requirements

1. All designations of record, requests, exceptions, and responsive pleadings ("pleadings") must be in written form, mailed with a certificate of mailing to the Board and the opposing party.

2. All pleadings must be filed with the Board by 5:00 p.m. on the date the filing is due. These Rules do not provide for any additional time for service by mail. Filing is the receipt of a pleading by the Board.

3. Any pleadings must be served on the opposing party by mail or by hand delivery on the date on which the pleading is filed with the Board.

4. All pleadings must be filed with the Board and not the Office of Administrative Courts. Any designations of record, requests, exceptions, or responsive pleadings filed in error with the Office of Administrative Courts will not be considered. The Board's address is:

Colorado Board of Real Estate Appraisers
1560 Broadway, Suite 925
Denver, CO 80202

B. Authority to Review

1. The Board hereby preserves the Board's option to initiate a review of an initial decision on its own motion pursuant to section 24-4-105(14)(a)(ii) and (b)(iii), C.R.S. outside of the thirty (30) day period after service of the initial decision upon the parties without requiring a vote for each case.

2. This option to review will apply regardless of whether a party files exceptions to the initial decision.

C. Designation of Record and Transcripts

1. Any party seeking to reverse or modify the initial decision of the Administrative Law Judge must file with the Board a designation of the relevant parts of the record for review ("designation of record"). Designations of record must be filed with the board within twenty (20) days of the date on which the Board mails the initial decision to the parties' address of record with the Board.

2. Even if no party files a designation of record, the record must include the following:

   a. All pleadings;

   b. All applications presented or considered during the hearing;

   c. All documentary or other exhibits admitted into evidence;

   d. All documentary or other exhibits presented during the hearing;

   e. All matters officially noticed;

   f. Any findings of fact and conclusions of law proposed by any party; and

   g. Any written brief filed.

3. Transcripts: transcripts will not be deemed part of a designation of record unless specifically identified and ordered. Should a party wish to designate a transcript or portion thereof, the following procedures apply:

   a. The designation of record must identify with specificity the transcript or portion thereof to be transcribed. For example, a party may designate the entire transcript, or may identify witness(es) whose testimony is to be transcribed, the legal ruling or argument to be transcribed, or other information necessary to identify a portion of the transcript.

   b. Any party who includes a transcript or a portion thereof as part of the designation of record must order the transcript or relevant portions by the date on which the designation of record must be filed (within twenty (20) days of the date on which the Board mails the initial decision to the parties).

   c. When ordering the transcript, the party must request a court reporter or transcribing service to prepare the transcript within thirty (30) days. The party must timely pay the necessary fees to obtain and file with the Board an original transcription and one (1) copy within thirty (30) days.

   d. The party ordering the transcript must direct the court reporter or transcribing service to complete and file with the Board the transcript and one (1) copy of the transcript within thirty (30) days.

   e. If a party designates a portion of the transcript, the opposing party may also file a supplemental designation of record, in which the opposing party may designate additional portions of the transcript. This supplemental designation of record must be filed with the Board and served on the other party within ten (10) days after the date on which the original designation of record was due.

   f. An opposing party filing a supplemental designation of record must order and pay for such transcripts and portions thereof within the deadlines set forth above. An opposing party must also cause the court reporter to complete and file with the Board the transcript and one (1) copy of the transcript within thirty (30) days.

   g. Transcripts that are ordered and not filed with the Board in a timely manner by the reporter or transcription service due to non-payment, insufficient payment, or failure to direct as set forth above will not be considered by the Board.

D. Filing of Exceptions and Responsive Pleadings

1. Any party wishing to file exceptions must adhere to the following timelines:

   a. If no transcripts are ordered, exceptions are due within thirty (30) days from the date on which the Board mails the initial decision to the parties. Both parties' exceptions are due on the same date.

   b. If transcripts are ordered by either party, the following procedure will apply. Upon receipt of transcripts identified in all designations of record, the Board will mail notification to the parties stating that the transcripts have been received by the Board. Exceptions are due within thirty (30) days from the date on which such notification is mailed. Both parties' exceptions are due on the same date.

2. Either party may file a responsive pleading to the other party's exceptions. All responsive pleadings must be filed within ten (10) days of the date on which the exceptions were filed with the Board. No other pleadings will be considered except for good cause shown.

3. The Board may in its sole discretion grant an extension of time to file exceptions or responsive pleadings, or may delegate the discretion to grant such an extension of time to the Board's designee.

E. Request for Oral Argument

1. All requests for oral argument must be in writing and filed by the deadline for responsive pleadings. Requests filed after this time will not be considered.

2. It is within the sole discretion of the Board to grant or deny a request for oral argument. If oral argument is granted, both parties will have the opportunity to participate.

3. Each side will be permitted ten (10) minutes for oral argument unless such time is extended by the Board or its designee.

13.11 A controlling appraiser must inform the Board in writing within ten (10) days of conviction of, entering a plea of guilty to, entering a plea of nolo contendere, entering an alford plea, or receiving a deferred judgment and sentence to any misdemeanor or felony relating to the conduct of an appraisal, theft, embezzlement, bribery, fraud, misrepresentation, or deceit, or any other like crime under Colorado law, federal law, or the laws of other jurisdictions.

13.12 A controlling appraiser, or an approved designee of a licensed appraisal management company, must inform the Board in writing within ten (10) days when an owner of an appraisal management company, possessing more than ten percent ownership of the licensed entity, has been convicted of, entered a plea of guilty to, entered a plea of nolo contendere, entered an alford plea, or receiving a deferred judgment and sentence to any misdemeanor or felony relating to the conduct of an appraisal, theft, embezzlement, bribery, fraud, misrepresentation, or deceit, or any other like crime under Colorado law, federal law, or the laws of other jurisdictions.

CHAPTER 14: DECLARATORY ORDERS PURSUANT TO SECTION 24-4-105(11), C.R.S.

14.1 Any person may petition the Board for a declaratory order to terminate controversies or to remove uncertainties as to the applicability to the petitioner of any statutory provisions or of any rule or order of the Board.

14.2 The Board will determine, in its discretion and without prior notice to petitioner, whether to rule upon any such petition. If the Board determines that it will not rule upon such a petition, the Board will issue its written order disposing of the same stating the reason for its action. A copy of the order will be provided to the petitioner.

14.3 In determining whether to rule upon a petition filed pursuant to this Rule, the Board will consider the following matters, among others:

A. Whether a ruling on the petition will terminate a controversy or remove uncertainties as to the applicability to petitioner of any statutory provision or rule or order of the Board.

B. Whether the petition involves any subject, question, or issue which is the subject of a formal or informal matter or investigation currently pending before the Board or a court involving one or more of the petitioners.

C. Whether the petition involves any subject, question, or issue which is the subject of a formal or informal matter or investigation currently pending before the Board or a court but not involving any petitioner.

D. Whether the petition seeks a ruling on a moot or hypothetical question or will result in an advisory ruling or opinion.

E. Whether the petitioner has some other adequate legal remedy, other than an action for declaratory relief pursuant to Rule 57, C.R.C.P., which will terminate the controversy or remove any uncertainty as to the applicability to the petitioner of the statute, rule, or order in question.

14.4 Any petition filed pursuant to this Rule must set forth the following:

A. The name and address of the petitioner and whether the petitioner holds a license issued pursuant to the Colorado Real Estate Appraiser Licensing Act.

B. The statute, rule, or order to which the petition relates.

C. A concise statement of all of the facts necessary to show the nature of the controversy or uncertainty and the manner in which the statute, rule, or order in question applies or potentially applies to the petitioner.

14.5 If the Board determines that it will rule on the petition, the following procedures will apply:

A. The Board may rule upon the petition based solely upon the facts presented in the petition. In such a case:

1. Any ruling of the Board will apply only to the extent of the facts presented in the petition and any amendment to the petition.

2. The Board may order the petitioner to file a written brief, memorandum, or statement of position.

3. The Board may set the petition, upon due notice to the petitioner, for a non-evidentiary hearing.

4. The Board may dispose of the petition on the sole basis of the matters set forth in the petition.

5. The Board may request the petitioner to submit additional facts, in writing. In such event, such additional facts will be considered as an amendment to the petition.

6. The Board may take administrative notice of facts pursuant to the Administrative Procedures Act, section 24-4-105(8), C.R.S., as amended, and may utilize its experience, technical competence, and specialized knowledge in the disposition of the petition.

7. If the Board rules upon the petition without a hearing, it will promptly notify the petitioner of its decision.

B. The Board may, in its discretion, set the petition for hearing, upon due notice to petitioner, for the purpose of obtaining additional facts or information or to determine the truth of any facts set forth in the petition or to hear oral argument on the petition. The notice to the petitioner setting such hearing will set forth, to the extent known, the factual or other matters into which the Board intends to inquire. For the purpose of such a hearing, to the extent necessary, the petitioner will have the burden of proving all of the facts stated in the petition, all of the facts necessary to show the nature of the controversy or uncertainty and the manner in which the statute, rule, or order in question applies or potentially applies to the petitioner and any other facts the petitioner desires the Board to consider.

14.6 The parties to any proceeding pursuant to this Rule will be the Board and the petitioner. Any other person may seek leave of the Board to intervene in such a proceeding, and leave to intervene will be granted at the sole discretion of the Board. A petition to intervene will set forth the same matters as required by Board Rule 14.4. Any reference to a "petitioner" in this Rule also refers to any person who has been granted leave to intervene by the Board.

14.7 Any declaratory order or other order disposing of a petition pursuant to this Rule will constitute agency action subject to judicial review pursuant to section 24-4-106, C.R.S., as amended.

CHAPTER 15: REPEALED

15.1 Repealed.

15.2 Repealed.

15.3 Repealed.

15.4 Repealed.

15.5 Repealed.

CHAPTER 16: REPEALED

16.1 Repealed.

16.2 Repealed.

16.3 Repealed.

16.4 Repealed.

CHAPTER 17: LICENSING REQUIREMENTS FOR APPRAISAL MANAGEMENT COMPANIES

17.1 Prior to application for licensure for an appraisal management company or as a controlling appraiser, a person who has been convicted of, entered a plea of guilty to, entered a plea of nolo contendere to, or received a deferred judgment and sentence to a misdemeanor or felony, or any like municipal code violation, may request the Board to issue a preliminary advisory opinion regarding the possible effect of such conduct on an application for licensure. A person requesting such an opinion is not an applicant for licensure. The Board may, at its sole discretion, issue such an opinion, which will not be binding upon the Board; is not appealable; and will not limit the authority of the Board to investigate a later application for licensure. The issuance of such an opinion by the Board will not act to prohibit a person from submitting an application for licensure. A person requesting such an opinion must do so in a form prescribed by the Board. Such form must be supported and documented by, without limitation, the following:

A. Court documents, including original charges, disposition, pre-sentencing report and certification of completion of terms of sentence;

B. Police officer's report(s);

C. Probation or parole officer's report(s);

D. A written personal statement explaining the circumstances surrounding each violation, and including the statement attesting that "I have no other violations either past or pending";

E. Letters of recommendation; and

F.   Employment history for the preceding five (5) years.

* 17.2 Pursuant to section 12-10-607, C.R.S. an applicant for an appraisal management company's or a controlling appraiser's license who has been convicted of, entered a plea of guilty to, entered a plea of nolo contendere to, or received a deferred judgment and sentence to a misdemeanor or a felony, or any other like municipal code violation, must, with his or her application, include an addendum to the application in a form prescribed by the Board. Such addendum must be supported and documented by, without limitation, the following:

A.   Court documents, including original charges, disposition, pre-sentencing report and certification of completion of terms of sentence;

B.   Police officer's report(s);

C.   Probation or parole officer's report(s);

D.   A written personal statement explaining the circumstances surrounding each violation, and including the statement attesting that "I have no other violations either past or pending";

E.   Letters of recommendation; and

F.   Employment history for the preceding five (5) years.

17.3 Initial licenses will expire on December 31 of the year of issuance. All appraisal management company and controlling appraiser licenses expire annually on December 31.

17.4 An appraisal management company must have a controlling appraiser, with an active controlling appraiser's license, to perform services requiring a license. If the controlling appraiser leaves the employment of the appraisal management company, the controlling appraiser or an authorized representative of the appraisal management company must notify the Board within three (3) business days in a manner acceptable to the Board. Upon such notification or discovery by the Board, the license of the appraisal management company will be placed on inactive status unless or until a replacement controlling appraiser has been identified by the appraisal management company and approved by the Board or a temporary controlling appraiser license is timely processed by the Division.

17.5 The controlling appraiser license will be placed on inactive status upon notification to the Board that the controlling appraiser has left the employ of the appraisal management company. The controlling appraiser license will remain on inactive status until the license expires or the controlling appraiser is designated to be the responsible party for an appraisal management company.

17.6 An individual or company license cannot be transferred for use of the licensed name or license for the benefit of another person, partnership, limited liability company, or corporation.

17.7 The controlling appraiser, or an authorized representative, must notify the Board within ten (10) business days of a change in ownership of the appraisal management company that results in a new owner who owns more than ten (10) percent of the entity, or a change in ownership that increases an existing individual's total ownership to more than ten (10) percent.

17.8 The Board may refuse to issue a license to a partnership, limited liability company, or corporation if the name of said corporation, partnership, or limited liability company is the same as that of any person or entity whose license has been suspended or revoked in any jurisdiction or is so similar as to be easily confused with that of the suspended or revoked person or entity by members of the general public.

17.9 No license will be issued to an appraisal management company under a trade name, corporate name, partnership name, or limited liability company name which is identical to another licensed appraisal management company. A license will not be issued to an individual proprietorship that adopts a trade name which includes the following words: corporation, partnership, limited liability company, limited, incorporated, or the abbreviations thereof.

17.10 All applications will contain a certification that the controlling appraiser is responsible for the appraisal management company. All applications will require the appraisal management company to identify at least one authorized representative responsible for contacting the Board when there has been a change in the employment of the controlling appraiser or there is a change in the ownership of the entity.

17.11 When an application for licensure as an appraisal management company is submitted, the controlling appraiser must certify the following:

*   A.   If the appraisal management company is a corporation, that the corporation complies with section 12-10-607(8)(c), C.R.S. and that the controlling appraiser has been authorized by the corporation as the controlling appraiser for the corporation.

*   B.   If the appraisal management company is a partnership, that the partnership complies with section 12-10-607(8)(a), C.R.S. and that the controlling appraiser has been authorized by the partnership as the controlling appraiser for the partnership.

*   C.   If the appraisal management company is a limited liability company, that the company complies with section 12-10-607(8)(b), C.R.S. and that the controlling appraiser has been authorized by the company as the controlling appraiser for the limited liability company.

17.12 An appraisal management company is not required to be domiciled in Colorado in order to obtain a license, if the company maintains a definite place of business in another jurisdiction and is registered as a foreign entity with the Colorado Secretary of State.

17.13 If the appraisal management company has no registered agent registered in Colorado, such registered agent is not located under its registered agent name at its registered agent address, or the registered agent cannot with reasonable diligence be served, the controlling appraiser, on behalf of the appraisal management company, may be served by registered mail or by certified mail, return receipt requested, addressed to the entity at its principal address and to the controlling appraiser's address of record. Service is perfected at the earliest of:

     A.   The date the controlling appraiser receives the process, notice, or demand;

     B.   The date shown on the return receipt, if signed by or on behalf of the controlling appraiser; or

     C.   Five (5) days after mailing.

* 17.14 Applicants for licensure, activation, renewal, or reinstatement as an appraisal management company must certify compliance with section 12-10-609, C.R.S. in a manner prescribed by the Board. The surety bond must:

     A.   Be for a minimum of $ 25,000.00;

     B.   Be in conformance with all relevant Colorado statutory requirements; and

*   C.   Cover acts contemplated for appraisal management companies under part 6 of article 10 of title 12 during the period of licensure by the appraisal management company.

Any licensed appraisal management company that certifies compliance and fails to maintain a surety bond, or to provide proof of continuous coverage, will be placed on inactive status:

     A.   Immediately if a current surety bond is not provided to the Board; or

     B.   Immediately upon the expiration of any current surety bond when certification of continued coverage is not provided.

17.15 An appraisal management company or controlling appraiser whose license has been placed on inactive status must:

     A.   Cease any activities requiring a license.

     B.   Cease all advertising of licensed services.

     C.   If an appraisal management company, inform all clients of the company's license status and inability to provide any services requiring a license.

      D.   If an appraisal management company, ensure that all appraisal fees collected from the client(s) have been accounted for and disbursed pursuant to section 12-10-614(1)(h), C.R.S.

      E.   If an appraisal management company, fees for services requiring a license can be collected for licensed services performed prior to inactivation of the license.

17.16   Licenses will be issued by the Board in a timely manner after the receipt of a complete application, including required fees and all supporting documentation. The Board reserves the right to require additional information and documentation from an applicant in order to determine compliance with applicable laws and regulations, and to verify any information or documentation submitted.

17.17   If the fees accompanying any application to the Board (including fees for renewals, transfers, etc.) are paid for by check and the check is not immediately paid upon presentment to the bank upon which the check was drawn, or if payment is submitted in any other manner, and payment is denied, rescinded, or returned as invalid, the application will be deemed incomplete. The application will only be deemed complete if the Board has received payment of all application fees together with any fees incurred by the Division including the fee required by state fiscal rules for the clerical services necessary for reinstatement within sixty (60) days of the Division mailing notification of an incomplete application.

17.18   A temporary controlling appraiser's license may be issued to a corporation, partnership, or limited liability company to prevent hardship. No application for a temporary controlling appraiser's license will be approved unless the designated individual is a certified appraiser, in good standing. The temporary license is valid for ninety (90) days. Upon application and showing of good cause, the Board may extend a temporary license for one additional ninety (90) day period.

17.19   Applicants for licensure, renewal, or reinstatement as an appraisal management company must complete the following:

      A.   The controlling appraiser must report and certify:

          1.   The number of licensed or certified appraisers that provided an appraisal in connection with a Covered Transaction on the appraisal management company's Panel in Colorado during the Reporting Period;

          2.   The total number of licensed or certified appraisers on the Panel in Colorado, whether or not the appraisers provided an appraisal in connection with a Covered Transaction, during the Reporting Period; and

          3.   The total number of licensed or certified appraisers on the Panel in all states that the appraisal management company is licensed during the Reporting Period.

      B.   Submit to the Division the AMC Registry Fee for appraisal management companies that meet the Panel Size Threshold along with the application for initial licensure, renewal, or reinstatement.

17.20   Federally Regulated AMCs must annually pay the AMC Registry Fee and must report the following information to the Division prior to December 31 of each calendar year:

      A.   Identifying company information to include the legal name, Employer Identification Number (EIN), address, and contact information of the controlling appraiser or company's designee.

      B.   Information related to ownership limitations.

      C.   The controlling appraiser or company's designee must report and certify:

          1.   The number of licensed or certified appraisers that provided an appraisal in connection with a Covered Transaction on the appraisal management company's Panel in Colorado during the Reporting period;

*   2. The total number of licensed or certified appraisers on the Panel in Colorado, whether or not the appraisers provided an appraisal in connection with a Covered Transaction, during the Reporting Period; and

*   3. The total number of licensed or certified appraisers on the Panel in all states during the Reporting Period.

*   D. Submit to the Division the AMC Registry Fee for appraisal management companies that meet the Panel Size Threshold along with the information as set forth in this rule.

CHAPTER 18: PROFESSIONAL STANDARDS – APPRAISAL MANAGEMENT COMPANIES

* 18.1 An appraisal management company must have and follow a written policy in place regarding the annual audit of appraisals completed for Colorado assignments during the previous Reporting Period. The policy must have an effective date and memorialize the dates any modifications are made. The policy must outline, at a minimum, the following:

*   A. Appraisal Selection. The audit sample must be randomly selected and a USPAP Standard 3 Review must be performed on not less than two percent (2%) of all appraisal reports performed by appraisers for the appraisal management company during the previous Reporting Period. A minimum of at least one (1) USPAP Standard 3 Review must be performed for each appraiser who completed a Colorado appraisal assignment during that Reporting Period.

    B. Risk-Based Reviews. If an appraisal management company maintains a risk-based review process, the appraisal management company is required to comply with Board Rule 18.1(A) of these Rules only for those appraisers for whom a USPAP Standard 3 Review was not performed under the risk-based appraisal review process.

    C. Review Criterion. The appraisals must be evaluated for compliance with state and federal regulations, including the USPAP.

    D. Reviewer Qualifications. The individual(s) performing the audit of the appraisals must possess a certified credential in this state or any jurisdiction and be competent to appraise residential real estate.

    E. Appraisal Deficiencies. The appraisal management company must have procedures in place to address material deficiencies that affect the value conclusion or the credibility of the report with the appraiser. Material violations of the USPAP or the Colorado Real Estate Appraiser Licensing Act must be reported to the Board.

The Board may evaluate an appraisal management company's compliance with its own audit policies during an investigation.

18.2 For each Colorado appraisal assignment, an appraisal management company must maintain the following documents or records for a period of at least five (5) years, or at least two (2) years after the final disposition of any judicial proceeding in which a representative of the appraisal management company provided testimony related to the assignment, whichever period expires last:

    A. Contractual agreements with clients.

    B. Any documents associated with the engagement of an appraiser used to appraise Colorado real estate.

    C. All correspondence with a client or an appraiser regarding a specific assignment, including an accounting of payments received from the client and paid to the appraiser.

    D. Appraisals, appraisal reviews, appraisal updates, recertifications of value, certificates of completion, broker price opinions or competitive market analyses, comparable property checks, rent schedules or income analyses, measurements, building sketches, and any client approved forms (Colorado Real Estate only).

*   E.   A list of all licensed or certified appraisers on the appraisal management company's Panel.

        F.   Copies of final appraisal reports reviewed in accordance with Board Rule 18.1, findings and any subsequent correspondence with the appraiser, client, or Board.

*   G.   Copies of all processes and controls pursuant to section 12-10-614(1)(a)(II), C.R.S.

        Records may be maintained in electronic format, but must be produced upon request by the Board and must be in a format that has the continued capability to be retrieved and legibly printed. Upon request by the Board, printed records must be produced.

18.3   For all Colorado appraisal assignments, an appraisal management company must disclose its Colorado license number in writing in the engagement letter with an appraiser.

Chapter 8:
Mortgage Loan Originators

An * in the left margin indicates a change in the statute, rule, or text since the last publication of the manual.

I. Introduction

In 2003, the Department of Regulatory Agencies received a request to initiate a review of the mortgage loan origination industry to determine whether regulation was appropriate. Accordingly, pursuant to § 24-34-104.1(2), C.R.S., a sunrise review was conducted and completed October 14, 2005. In summary, the review addressed Colorado's current regulatory environment with respect to mortgage transactions and the possibility for public harm.

Colorado was one of two states (the other being Alaska) that had no regulatory oversight of mortgage loan originators. The sunrise review also concluded that there was significant risk to consumers, as mortgage financing often represented their largest financial transaction. The review highlighted an inherent conflict of interest between the consumer, who seeks the lowest possible interest rate, and the mortgage loan originator, who receives compensation from higher interest rates. Ultimately, the sunrise review identified a need for regulatory oversight to ensure consumer protection. As a result, the Mortgage Broker Registration Act, House Bill 06-1161, was passed by the Colorado General Assembly in 2006.

The Mortgage Broker Registration Act provided a minimal registration program for mortgage loan originators. Registration required a completed criminal background check, a $25,000 surety bond, a completed application, and payment of the $200 application fee. Due to the wave of foreclosures and the mortgage fraud epidemic, the Colorado General Assembly passed four new mortgage broker bills in the 2007 session. These included House Bill 07-1322, Senate Bill 07-085, Senate Bill 07-216, and Senate Bill 07-203. Governor Bill Ritter, Jr. signed all four bills into law on June 1, 2007. This legislation created a significant change in Colorado's regulatory environment. House Bill 07-1322 contained measures to prevent mortgage fraud and established comprehensive definitions of prohibited conduct for mortgage loan originators. Senate Bill 07-085 prohibited mortgage loan originators from coercing or intimidating appraisers for the purpose of influencing an appraiser's independent judgment. Senate Bill 07-216 established that mortgage loan originators have a duty of good faith and fair dealing in all communications and transactions with a borrower. Finally, Senate Bill 07-203 required the development of a licensure program and the establishment of grounds for disciplinary actions.

*   In July of 2008, Congress passed the Housing and Economic Recovery Act of 2008. A small portion of this Act is Title V – The S.A.F.E. Mortgage Licensing Act, which may also be cited as the Secure and Fair Enforcement for Mortgage Licensing Act of 2008. In summary, this bill sets minimum national licensing standards for mortgage loan originators and requires that all mortgage loan originators be registered on the Nationwide Mortgage Licensing System and Registry. Additionally, this law requires licensure for a few new groups of individuals and loan originators, including: loan originators working for non-profit organizations; loan originators working in chattel financing related to mobile and manufactured housing; loan originators working for affiliates of depositories; and independent contractor loan processors and underwriters. The S.A.F.E. Act was essentially a mandate for states to ensure that their laws are consistent with this federal mandate. Furthermore, the S.A.F.E. Act mandates the development of the Nationwide Mortgage Licensing System and Registry. This registry will benefit Colorado, because it will be possible to track individuals across state lines. In order to adopt provisions defined in the S.A.F.E. Act, the Colorado General Assembly passed House Bill 09-1085 in May of 2009; it became effective August 5, 2009.

In 2009, the Federal Housing and Finance Agency established a policy decision requiring Fannie Mae and Freddie Mac to only purchase mortgage loans if they contained a unique identifier for the individual mortgage loan originator and the mortgage company. Because Colorado, at that time, was one of two states (the other being Hawaii) that did not have any oversight regarding mortgage companies, the Colorado General Assembly acted and passed House Bill 10-1141. This law became effective on August 11, 2010 and requires mortgage companies to be registered on the Nationwide Mortgage Licensing System and Registry. Furthermore, this law established some standards of conduct for mortgage companies, including: document retention; advertising standards; and a prohibition on mortgage companies hiring unlicensed mortgage loan originators. Additionally, this law transforms the Mortgage Loan Originator Program from a director-model program to a board-model program. The defined board consists of five members, three of which must be licensed mortgage loan originators and two that must be members of the public at large not engaged in mortgage loan origination or mortgage lending. The transition to the new Board of Mortgage Loan Originators is an important change for Colorado's Mortgage Loan Originator regulatory program.

Since the inception of the mortgage regulatory program, there have been several laws that have been passed. Additionally, there have been numerous rules that have been promulgated, many of which were adopted on an emergency basis. This regulatory program has seen a consistent change in licensing requirements, standards of conduct, and prohibitions. The mission of the Department of Regulatory Agencies is consumer protection. The Colorado Division of Real Estate now has the tools to protect Colorado consumers and ensure fair competition through aggressive enforcement and responsible implementation.

II. Mortgage Loan Originator Licensing and Mortgage Company Registration Act

Colorado Revised Statutes Title 12, Article 10, Part 7

§ 12-10-701, C.R.S. Short title.

Editor's note: This section is similar to former §12-61-901 as it existed prior to 2019.

The short title of this part 7 is the "Mortgage Loan Originator Licensing and Mortgage Company Registration Act".

§ 12-10-702, C.R.S. Definitions.

Editor's note: This section is similar to former §12-61-902 as it existed prior to 2019.

As used in this part 7, unless the context otherwise requires:

(1)   "Affiliate" means a person who, directly or indirectly, through intermediaries, controls, is controlled by, or is under the common control of another person addressed by this part 7.

(2)   "Affordable housing dwelling unit" means an affordable housing dwelling unit as defined in section 29-26-102.

(3)   "Board" means the board of mortgage loan originators created in section 12-10-703.

(4)   "Borrower" means any person who consults with or retains a mortgage loan originator in an effort to obtain or seek advice or information on obtaining or applying to obtain a residential mortgage loan for himself, herself, or persons including himself or herself, regardless of whether the person actually obtains such a loan.

(5)   "Community development organization" means any community housing development organization or community land trust as defined by the federal "Cranston-Gonzalez National Affordable Housing Act" of 1990 or a community-based development organization as defined by the federal "Housing and Community Development Act of 1974", that is also either a private or public nonprofit organization that is exempt from taxation under section 501 (a) of the federal "Internal Revenue Code of 1986" pursuant to section 501 (c) of the federal "Internal Revenue Code of 1986", 26 U.S.C. sec. 501 (a) and 501 (c), as amended, and that receives funding from the United States department of housing and urban development, Colorado division of housing, Colorado housing and finance authority, or United States department of agriculture rural development, or through a grantee of the United States department of housing and urban development, purely for the purpose of community housing development activities.

(6)   "Depository institution" has the same meaning as set forth in the "Federal Deposit Insurance Act", 12 U.S.C. sec. 1813 (c), and includes a credit union.

(7)   "Dwelling" shall have the same meaning as set forth in the federal "Truth in Lending Act", 15 U.S.C. sec. 1602 (w).

(8)   "Federal banking agency" means the board of governors of the federal reserve system, the comptroller of the currency, the director of the office of thrift supervision, the national credit union administration, or the federal deposit insurance corporation.

(9)   "HUD-approved housing counseling agency" means an agency that is either a private or public nonprofit organization that is exempt from taxation under section 501 (a) of the federal "Internal Revenue Code of 1986" pursuant to section 501 (c) of the federal "Internal Revenue Code of 1986", 26 U.S.C. sec. 501 (a) and 501 (c), as amended, and approved by the United States department of housing and urban development, in accordance with the housing counseling program handbook section 7610.1 and 24 CFR 214.

(10)   "Individual" means a natural person.

(11)   (a)   "Loan processor or underwriter" means an individual who performs clerical or support duties at the direction of, and subject to supervision by, a state-licensed loan originator or a registered loan originator.

         (b)   As used in this subsection (11), "clerical or support duties" includes duties performed after receipt of an application for a residential mortgage loan, including:

                  (I)   The receipt, collection, distribution, and analysis of information commonly used for the processing or underwriting of a residential mortgage loan; and

                  (II)   Communicating with a borrower to obtain the information necessary to process or underwrite a loan, to the extent that the communication does not include offering or negotiating loan rates or terms or counseling consumers about residential mortgage loan rates or terms.

(12)   "Mortgage company" means a person other than an individual who, through employees or other individuals, takes residential loan applications or offers or negotiates terms of a residential mortgage loan.

(13) "Mortgage lender" means a lender who is in the business of making residential mortgage loans if:

    (a) The lender is the payee on the promissory note evidencing the loan; and

    (b) The loan proceeds are obtained by the lender from its own funds or from a line of credit made available to the lender from a bank or other entity that regularly loans money to lenders for the purpose of funding mortgage loans.

(14) (a) "Mortgage loan originator" means an individual who:

        (I) Takes a residential mortgage loan application; or

        (II) Offers or negotiates terms of a residential mortgage loan.

    (b) "Mortgage loan originator" does not include:

        (I) An individual engaged solely as a loan processor or underwriter;

        (II) A person that only performs real estate brokerage or sales activities and is licensed or registered pursuant to part 2 of this article 10, unless the person is compensated by a mortgage lender or a mortgage loan originator;

        (III) A person solely involved in extensions of credit relating to time share plans, as defined in 11 U.S.C. sec. 101 (53D);

        (IV) An individual who is servicing a mortgage loan; or

        (V) A person that only performs the services and activities of a dealer, as defined in section 24-32-3302.

(15) "Nationwide mortgage licensing system and registry" means a mortgage licensing system developed pursuant to the federal "Secure and Fair Enforcement for Mortgage Licensing Act of 2008", 12 U.S.C. sec. 5101 et seq., as amended, to track the licensing and registration of mortgage loan originators and that is established and maintained by:

    (a) The Conference of State Bank Supervisors and the American Association of Residential Mortgage Regulators, or their successor entities; or

    (b) The secretary of the United States department of housing and urban development.

(16) "Nontraditional mortgage product" means a mortgage product other than a thirty-year, fixed-rate mortgage.

(17) "Originate a mortgage" means to act, directly or indirectly, as a mortgage loan originator.

(18) "Person" means a natural person, corporation, company, limited liability company, partnership, firm, association, or other legal entity.

(19) "Quasi-government agency" means an agency that is either a private or public nonprofit organization that is exempt from taxation under section 501 (a) of the federal "Internal Revenue Code of 1986" pursuant to section 501 (c) of the federal "Internal Revenue Code of 1986", 26 U.S.C. sec. 501 (a) and 501 (c), as amended, and was created to operate in accordance with article 4 of title 29 as a public housing authority.

(20) "Real estate brokerage activity" means an activity that involves offering or providing real estate brokerage services to the public, including, without limitation:

    (a) Acting as a real estate agent or real estate broker for a buyer, seller, lessor, or lessee of real property;

    (b) Bringing together parties interested in the sale, purchase, lease, rental, or exchange of real property;

    (c) Negotiating, on behalf of any party, any portion of a contract relating to the sale, purchase, lease, rental, or exchange of real property, other than matters related to financing for the transaction;

(d)   Engaging in an activity for which a person engaged in the activity is required under applicable law to be registered or licensed as a real estate agent or real estate broker; or

(e)   Offering to engage in any activity, or act in any capacity related to the activity, described in this subsection (20).

(21)   "Residential mortgage loan" means a loan that is primarily for personal, family, or household use and that is secured by a mortgage, deed of trust, or other equivalent, consensual security interest on a dwelling or residential real estate upon which is constructed or intended to be constructed a single-family dwelling or multiple-family dwelling of four or fewer units.

(22)   "Residential real estate" means any real property upon which a dwelling is or will be constructed.

(23)   "Self-help housing organization" means a private or public nonprofit organization that is exempt from taxation under section 501 (a) of the federal "Internal Revenue Code of 1986" pursuant to section 501 (c) of the federal "Internal Revenue Code of 1986", 26 U.S.C. sec. 501 (a) and 501 (c), as amended, and that purely originates residential mortgage loans with interest rates no greater than zero percent for borrowers who have provided part of the labor to construct the dwelling securing the loan or that receives funding from the United States department of agriculture rural development section 502 mutual self-help housing program for borrowers that have provided part of the labor to construct the dwelling securing the loan.

(24)   "Servicing a mortgage loan" means collecting, receiving, or obtaining the right to collect or receive payments on behalf of a mortgage lender, including payments of principal, interest, escrow amounts, and other amounts due on obligations due and owing to the mortgage lender.

(25)   "State-licensed loan originator" means an individual who is:

    (a)   A mortgage loan originator or engages in the activities of a mortgage loan originator;

    (b)   Not an employee of a depository institution or a subsidiary that is:

        (I)   Owned and controlled by a depository institution; and

        (II)   Regulated by a federal banking agency;

    (c)   Licensed or required to be licensed pursuant to this part 7; and

    (d)   Registered as a state-licensed loan originator with, and maintains a unique identifier through, the nationwide mortgage licensing system and registry.

(26)   "Unique identifier" means a number or other identifier assigned to a mortgage loan originator pursuant to protocols established by the nationwide mortgage licensing system and registry.

*   § 12-10-703, C.R.S. Board of mortgage loan originators – creation – compensation – enforcement of part after board creation – immunity.

*   *Editor's note: This section is similar to former §12-61-902.5 as it existed prior to 2019.*

(1)   (a)   There is hereby created in the division of real estate a board of mortgage loan originators, consisting of five members appointed by the governor with the consent of the senate.

    (b)   Of the members of the board:

        (I)   Three must be licensed mortgage loan originators. The general assembly encourages the governor to appoint to at least one of these three positions a licensed mortgage loan originator who is an employee or exclusive agent of, or works as an independent contractor for, a Colorado-based mortgage company.

        (II)   Two must be members of the public at large not engaged in mortgage loan origination or mortgage lending.

    (c)   Of the members of the board appointed for terms beginning on and after August 11, 2010, two of the members appointed as mortgage loan originators and one of the members appointed as a member of the public at large shall be appointed for terms of two years, and one of the members appointed as a mortgage loan originator and one of the members appointed as a member of the public at large shall serve for terms of four years. Thereafter, members of the board shall hold office for a term of four years.

(d)   In the event of a vacancy by death, resignation, removal, or otherwise, the governor shall appoint a member to fill the unexpired term. The governor has the authority to remove any member for misconduct, neglect of duty, or incompetence.

(2)   (a)   The board shall exercise its powers and perform its duties and functions under the department as if transferred to the department by a **type 1** transfer, as such transfer is defined in the "Administrative Organization Act of 1968", article 1 of title 24.

(b)   Notwithstanding any other provision of this part 7, on and after the creation of the board by this section, the board shall exercise all of the rule-making, enforcement, and administrative authority of the director set forth in this part 7. The board has the authority to delegate to the director any enforcement and administrative authority under this part 7 that the board deems necessary and appropriate. If the board delegates any enforcement or administrative authority under this part 7 to the director, the director shall only be entitled to exercise such authority as specifically delegated in writing to the director by the board.

(3)   Each member of the board shall receive the same compensation and reimbursement of expenses as those provided for members of boards and commissions in the division of professions and occupations pursuant to section 12-20-103 (6). Payment for all per diem compensation and expenses shall be made out of annual appropriations from the division of real estate cash fund created in section 12-10-215.

(4)   Members of the board, consultants, and expert witnesses shall be immune from suit in any civil action based upon any disciplinary proceedings or other official acts they performed in good faith pursuant to this part 7.

(5)   A majority of the board shall constitute a quorum for the transaction of all business, and actions of the board shall require a vote of a majority of the members present in favor of the action taken.

(6)   (a)   All rules promulgated by the director prior to August 11, 2010, shall remain in full force and effect until repealed or modified by the board. The board shall have the authority to enforce any previously promulgated rules of the director under this part 7 and any rules promulgated by the board.

(b)   Nothing in this section shall affect any action taken by the director prior to August 11, 2010. No person who, on or before August 11, 2010, holds a license issued under this part 7 shall be required to secure an additional license under this part 7, but shall otherwise be subject to all the provisions of this part 7. A license previously issued shall, for all purposes, be considered a license issued by the board under this part 7.

§ 12-10-704, C.R.S. License required – rules.

Editor's note: *(1) This section is similar to former §12-61-903 as it existed prior to 2019.*

(2) Before its relocation in 2019, this section was amended in HB 19-1166. Those amendments were superseded by the repeal and reenactment of this title 12, effective October 1, 2019. For those amendments to the former section in effect from April 18, 2019, to October 1, 2019, see HB 19-1166, chapter 125, Session Laws of Colorado 2019.

(3) Section 78 of chapter 125 (HB 19-1166), Session Laws of Colorado 2019, provides that the act changing this section takes effect October 1, 2019, only if HB 19-1172 becomes law. HB 19-1172 became law and took effect October 1, 2019.

(1)　(a)　Unless licensed by the board and registered with the nationwide mortgage licensing system and registry as a state-licensed loan originator, an individual shall not originate or offer to originate a mortgage or act or offer to act as a mortgage loan originator.

　　　(b)　On and after January 1, 2010, a licensed mortgage loan originator shall apply for license renewal in accordance with subsection (5) of this section every calendar year as determined by the board by rule.

(2)　An independent contractor may not engage in residential mortgage loan origination activities as a loan processor or underwriter unless the independent contractor is a state-licensed loan originator.

(3)　An applicant for initial licensing as a mortgage loan originator shall submit to the board the following:

　　　(a)　A criminal history record check in compliance with subsection (6) of this section;

　　　(b)　A disclosure of all administrative discipline taken against the applicant concerning the categories listed in section 12-10-711 (1)(c); and

　　　(c)　The application fee established by the board in accordance with section 12-10-718.

(4)　(a)　In addition to the requirements imposed by subsection (3) of this section, on or after August 5, 2009, each individual applicant for initial licensing as a mortgage loan originator must have satisfactorily completed:

　　　　　(I)　At least twenty hours of education as administered and approved by the Nationwide Multistate Licensing System and Registry or its successor; and

　　　　　(II)　A written examination approved by the board. For the portion of the examination that represents the state-specific test required in the federal "Secure and Fair Enforcement for Mortgage Licensing Act of 2008", 12 U.S.C. sec. 5101 et seq., as amended, the board may adopt the uniform state test administered through the Nationwide Multistate Licensing System and Registry or its successor.

　　　(b)　The board may contract with one or more independent testing services to develop, administer, and grade the examinations required by subsection (4)(a) of this section and to maintain and administer licensee records. The contract may allow the testing service to recover from applicants its costs incurred in connection with these functions. The board may contract separately for these functions and may allow the costs to be collected by a single contractor for distribution to other contractors.

　　　(c)　The board may publish reports summarizing statistical information prepared by the nationwide mortgage licensing system and registry relating to mortgage loan originator examinations.

(5)　An applicant for license renewal shall submit to the board the following:

　　　(a)　A disclosure of all administrative discipline taken against the applicant concerning the categories listed in section 12-10-711 (1)(c); and

　　　(b)　The renewal fee established by the board in accordance with section 12-10-718.

(6)　(a)　Prior to submitting an application for a license, an applicant shall submit a set of fingerprints to the Colorado bureau of investigation. Upon receipt of the applicant's fingerprints, the Colorado bureau of investigation shall use the fingerprints to conduct a state and national criminal history record check using records of the Colorado bureau of investigation and the federal bureau of investigation. All costs arising from the criminal history record check must be borne by the applicant and must be paid when the set of fingerprints is submitted. Upon completion of the criminal history record check, the bureau shall forward the results to the board. The board shall acquire a name-based criminal history record check, as defined in section 22-2-119.3 (6)(d), for an applicant who has twice submitted to a fingerprint-based criminal history record check and whose fingerprints are unclassifiable or when the results of a fingerprint-based criminal history record check of an applicant performed pursuant to this subsection (6) reveal a record of arrest without a disposition. The applicant shall pay the costs associated with a name-based criminal history record check.

(b) If the board determines that the criminal background check provided by the nationwide mortgage licensing system and registry is a sufficient method of screening license applicants to protect Colorado consumers, the board may, by rule, authorize the use of that criminal background check instead of the criminal history record check otherwise required by this subsection (6).

(7) (a) On and after January 1, 2010, in connection with an application for a license as a mortgage loan originator, the applicant shall furnish information concerning the applicant's identity to the nationwide mortgage licensing system and registry. The applicant shall furnish, at a minimum, the following:

    (I) Fingerprints for submission to the federal bureau of investigation and any government agency or entity authorized to receive fingerprints for a state, national, or international criminal history record check; and

    (II) Personal history and experience, in a form prescribed by the nationwide mortgage licensing system and registry, including submission of authorization for the nationwide mortgage licensing system and registry to obtain:

        (A) An independent credit report from the consumer reporting agency described in the federal "Fair Credit Reporting Act", 15 U.S.C. sec. 1681a (p); and

        (B) Information related to any administrative, civil, or criminal findings by a government jurisdiction.

(b) An applicant is responsible for paying all costs arising from a criminal history record check and shall pay the costs upon submission of fingerprints.

(c) The board shall acquire a name-based criminal history record check, as defined in section 22-2-119.3 (6)(d), for an applicant who has twice submitted to a fingerprint-based criminal history record check and whose fingerprints are unclassifiable or when the results of a fingerprint-based criminal history record check of an applicant performed pursuant to this subsection (7) reveal a record of arrest without a disposition. The applicant shall pay the costs associated with a name-based criminal history record check.

(8) Before granting a license to an applicant, the board shall require the applicant to post a bond as required by section 12-10-717.

(9) The board shall issue or deny a license within sixty days after:

(a) The applicant has submitted the requisite information to the board and the Nationwide Multistate Licensing System and Registry, including the completed application and any necessary supplementary information, the application fee, and proof that the applicant has posted a surety bond and obtained errors and omissions insurance; and

(b) The board receives the completed criminal history record check and all other relevant information or documents necessary to reasonably ascertain facts underlying the applicant's criminal history.

(10) (a) The board may require, as a condition of license renewal on or after January 1, 2009, continuing education of licensees for the purpose of enhancing the professional competence and professional responsibility of all licensees.

(b) Continuing professional education requirements shall be determined by the board by rule; except that licensees shall be required to complete at least eight credit hours of continuing education each year. The board may contract with one or more independent service providers to develop, review, or approve continuing education courses. The contract may allow the independent service provider to recover from licensees its costs incurred in connection with these functions. The board may contract separately for these functions and may allow the costs to be collected by a single contractor for distribution to other contractors.

(11) (a) The board may require contractors and prospective contractors for services under subsections (4) and (10) of this section to submit, for the board's review and approval, information regarding the contents and materials of proposed courses and other documentation reasonably necessary to further the purposes of this section.

(b) The board may set fees for the initial and continuing review of courses for which credit hours will be granted. The initial filing fee for review of materials shall not exceed five hundred dollars, and the fee for continued review shall not exceed two hundred fifty dollars per year per course offered.

(12) The board may adopt reasonable rules to implement this section. The board may adopt rules necessary to implement provisions required in the federal "Secure and Fair Enforcement for Mortgage Licensing Act of 2008", 12 U.S.C. sec. 5101 et seq., as amended, and for participation in the nationwide mortgage licensing system and registry.

(13) In order to fulfill the purposes of this part 7, the board may establish relationships or contracts with the nationwide mortgage licensing system and registry or other entities designated by the nationwide mortgage licensing system and registry to collect and maintain records and process transaction fees or other fees related to licensees or other persons subject to this part 7.

(14) The board may use the nationwide mortgage licensing system and registry as a channeling agent for requesting information from or distributing information to the department of justice, a government agency, or any other source.

§ 12-10-705, C.R.S. Registration required – rules.

Editor's note: This section is similar to former §12-61-903.1 as it existed prior to 2019.

(1) On or after January 1, 2011, each mortgage company shall register with the nationwide mortgage licensing system and registry, unless exempted by rule by the board, and shall renew its registration each calendar year based on the following criteria:

(a) (I) The mortgage company is legally operating in the state of Colorado in accordance with standards determined and administered by the Colorado secretary of state; and

(II) The mortgage company is not legally barred from operating in Colorado.

(b) Sole proprietors, general partnerships, and other mortgage companies not otherwise required to register with the secretary of state shall register using a trade name.

§ 12-10-706, C.R.S. License or registration inactivation.

Editor's note: This section is similar to former §12-61-903.3 as it existed prior to 2019.

(1) The board may inactivate a state license or a registration with the nationwide mortgage licensing system and registry when a licensee has failed to:

(a) Comply with the surety bond requirements of sections 12-10-704 (8) and 12-10-717;

(b) Comply with the errors and omissions insurance requirement in section 12-10-707 or any rule of the board that directly or indirectly addresses errors and omissions insurance requirements;

(c) Maintain current contact information, surety bond information, or errors and omissions insurance information as required by this part 7 or by any rule of the board that directly or indirectly addresses those requirements;

(d) Respond to an investigation or examination;

(e)   Comply with any of the education or testing requirements set forth in this part 7 or in any rule of the board that directly or indirectly addresses education or testing requirements; or

(f)   Register with and provide all required information to the nationwide mortgage licensing system and registry.

§ 12-10-707, C.R.S. Errors and omissions insurance – duties of the board – certificate of coverage – when required – group plan made available – effect – rules.

*   *Editor's note: This section is similar to former §12-61-903.5 as it existed prior to 2019.*

(1)   Every licensee under this part 7, except an inactive mortgage loan originator or an attorney licensee who maintains a policy of professional malpractice insurance that provides coverage for errors and omissions insurance for their activities as a licensee under this part 7, shall maintain errors and omissions insurance to cover all activities contemplated under this part 7. The division shall make the errors and omissions insurance available to all licensees by contracting with an insurer for a group policy after a competitive bid process in accordance with article 103 of title 24. A group policy obtained by the division must be available to all licensees with no right on the part of the insurer to cancel a licensee. A licensee may obtain errors and omissions insurance independently if the coverage complies with the minimum requirements established by the division.

(2)   (a)   If the division is unable to obtain errors and omissions insurance coverage to insure all licensees who choose to participate in the group program at a reasonable annual premium, as determined by the division, a licensee shall independently obtain the errors and omissions insurance required by this section.

      (b)   The division shall solicit and consider information and comments from interested persons when determining the reasonableness of annual premiums.

(3)   The division shall determine the terms and conditions of coverage required under this section based on rules promulgated by the board. Each licensee shall be notified of the required terms and conditions at least thirty days before the annual premium renewal date as determined by the division. Each licensee shall file a certificate of coverage showing compliance with the required terms and conditions with the division by the annual premium renewal date, as determined by the division.

(4)   In addition to all other powers and duties conferred upon the board by this part 7, the board shall adopt such rules as it deems necessary or proper to carry out this section.

§ 12-10-708, C.R.S. License renewal.

*   *Editor's note: This section is similar to former §12-61-903.7 as it existed prior to 2019.*

(1)   In order for a licensed mortgage loan originator to renew a license issued pursuant to this part 7, the mortgage loan originator shall:

(a)   Continue to meet the minimum standards for issuance of a license pursuant to this part 7;

(b)   Satisfy the annual continuing education requirements set forth in section 12-10-704 (10) and in rules adopted by the board; and

(c)   Pay applicable license renewal fees.

(2)   If a licensed mortgage loan originator fails to satisfy the requirements of subsection (1) of this section for license renewal, the mortgage loan originator's license shall expire. The board shall adopt rules to establish procedures for the reinstatement of an expired license consistent with the standards established by the nationwide mortgage licensing system and registry.

§ 12-10-709, C.R.S. Exemptions – definition – rules.

* *Editor's note: This section is similar to former §12-61-904 as it existed prior to 2019.*

(1) Except as otherwise provided in section 12-10-713, this part 7 does not apply to the following, unless otherwise determined by the federal bureau of consumer financial protection or the United States department of housing and urban development:

    (a) With respect to a residential mortgage loan:

        (I) A person, estate, or trust that provides mortgage financing for the sale of no more than three properties in any twelve-month period to purchasers of the properties, each of which is owned by the person, estate, or trust and serves as security for the loan; or

        (II) An individual who acts as a mortgage loan originator, without compensation or gain to the mortgage loan originator, in providing loan financing for not more than three residential mortgage loans in any twelve-month period to a family member of the individual. The board shall define "family member" by rule. For purposes of this exemption only, "compensation or gain" excludes any interest paid under the loan financing provided.

    (b) A bank and a savings association as these terms are defined in the "Federal Deposit Insurance Act", 12 U.S.C. sec. 1811 et seq., as amended, a subsidiary that is owned and controlled by a bank or savings association, employees of a bank or savings association, employees of a subsidiary that is owned and controlled by a bank or savings association, credit unions, and employees of credit unions;

    (c) An attorney who renders services in the course of practice, who is licensed in Colorado, and who is not primarily engaged in the business of negotiating residential mortgage loans;

    (d) A person who:

        (I) Funds a residential mortgage loan that has been originated and processed by a licensed person or by an exempt person;

        (II) Does not solicit borrowers in Colorado for the purpose of making residential mortgage loans; and

        (III) Does not participate in the negotiation of residential mortgage loans with the borrower, except for setting the terms under which a person may buy or fund a residential mortgage loan originated by a licensed or exempt person;

    (e) A loan processor or underwriter who is not an independent contractor and who does not represent to the public that the individual can or will perform any activities of a mortgage loan originator. As used in this subsection (1)(e), "represent to the public" means communicating, through advertising or other means of communicating, or providing information, including the use of business cards, stationery, brochures, signs, rate lists, or other promotional items, that the individual is able to provide a particular service or activity for a consumer.

    (f) To the extent that it is providing programs benefitting affordable housing dwelling units, an agency of the federal government, the Colorado government, or any of Colorado's political subdivisions or employees of an agency of the federal government, of the Colorado government, or of any of Colorado's political subdivisions;

    (g) Quasi-government agencies, HUD-approved housing counseling agencies, or employees of quasi-government agencies or HUD-approved housing counseling agencies;

    (h) Community development organizations or employees of community development organizations;

(i) Self-help housing organizations or employees of self-help housing organizations or volunteers acting as an agent of self-help housing organizations;

(j) A person licensed under part 2 of this article 10 who represents a person, estate, or trust providing mortgage financing under subsection (1)(a) of this section.

(2) The exemptions in subsection (1) of this section shall not apply to persons acting beyond the scope of the exemptions.

(3) The board may adopt reasonable rules modifying the exemptions in this section in accordance with rules adopted by the federal bureau of consumer financial protection or the United States department of housing and urban development.

§ 12-10-710, C.R.S. Originator's relationship to borrower – rules.

***Editor's note:** This section is similar to former §12-61-904.5 as it existed prior to 2019.*

(1) A mortgage loan originator shall have a duty of good faith and fair dealing in all communications and transactions with a borrower. The duty includes, but is not limited to:

(a) The duty to not recommend or induce the borrower to enter into a transaction that does not have a reasonable, tangible net benefit to the borrower, considering all of the circumstances, including the terms of a loan, the cost of a loan, and the borrower's circumstances;

(b) The duty to make a reasonable inquiry concerning the borrower's current and prospective income, existing debts and other obligations, and any other relevant information and, after making the inquiry, to make his or her best efforts to recommend, broker, or originate a residential mortgage loan that takes into consideration the information submitted by the borrower, but the mortgage loan originator shall not be deemed to violate this section if the borrower conceals or misrepresents relevant information; and

(c) The duty not to commit any acts, practices, or omissions in violation of section 38-40-105.

(2) For purposes of implementing subsection (1) of this section, the board may adopt rules defining what constitutes a reasonable, tangible net benefit to the borrower.

(3) A violation of this section constitutes a deceptive trade practice under the "Colorado Consumer Protection Act", article 1 of title 6.

§ 12-10-711, C.R.S. Powers and duties of the board – rules.

***Editor's note:** This section is similar to former §12-61-905 as it existed prior to 2019.*

(1) The board may deny an application for a license, refuse to renew, or revoke the license of an applicant or licensee who has:

(a) Filed an application with the board containing material misstatements of fact or omitted any disclosure required by this part 7;

(b) Within the last five years, been convicted of or pled guilty or nolo contendere to a crime involving fraud, deceit, material misrepresentation, theft, or the breach of a fiduciary duty, except as otherwise set forth in this part 7;

(c) Except as otherwise set forth in this part 7, within the last five years, had a license, registration, or certification issued by Colorado or another state revoked or suspended for fraud, deceit, material misrepresentation, theft, or the breach of a fiduciary duty, and the discipline denied the person authorization to practice as:

(I) A mortgage broker or a mortgage loan originator;

(II) A real estate broker, as defined by section 12-10-201 (6);

(III) A real estate salesperson;

(IV)   A real estate appraiser, as defined by section 12-10-602 (9);

(V)   An insurance producer, as defined by section 10-2-103 (6);

(VI)   An attorney;

(VII) A securities broker-dealer, as defined by section 11-51-201 (2);

(VIII) A securities sales representative, as defined by section 11-51-201 (14);

(IX)   An investment advisor, as defined by section 11-51-201 (9.5); or

(X)   An investment advisor representative, as defined by section 11-51-201 (9.6);

(d)   Been enjoined within the immediately preceding five years under the laws of this or any other state or of the United States from engaging in deceptive conduct relating to the brokering of or originating a mortgage loan;

(e)   Been found to have violated the provisions of section 12-10-721;

(f)   Been found to have violated the provisions of section 12-10-713;

(g)   Not demonstrated financial responsibility, character, and general fitness to command the confidence of the community and to warrant a determination that the individual will operate honestly, fairly, and efficiently, consistent with the purposes of this part 7;

(h)   Not completed the prelicense education requirements set forth in section 12-10-704 and any applicable rules of the board; or

(i)   Not passed a written examination that meets the requirements set forth in section 12-10-704 and any applicable rules of the board.

(2)   The board shall deny an application for a license, refuse to renew, or revoke the license of an applicant or licensee who has:

(a)   (I)   Had a mortgage loan originator license or similar license revoked in any jurisdiction.

(II)   If a revocation is subsequently formally nullified, the license is not revoked for purposes of this subsection (2)(a).

(b)   (I)   At any time been convicted of, or pled guilty or nolo contendere to, a felony in a domestic, foreign, or military court if the felony involved an act of fraud, dishonesty, breach of trust, or money laundering.

(II)   If the individual obtains a pardon of the conviction, the board shall not deem the individual convicted for purposes of this subsection (2)(b).

(c)   Been convicted of, or pled guilty or nolo contendere to, a felony within the immediately preceding seven years.

(3)   The board may investigate the activities of a licensee or other person that present grounds for disciplinary action under this part 7 or that violate section 12-10-720 (1).

(4)   (a)   If the board has reasonable grounds to believe that a mortgage loan originator is no longer qualified under subsection (1) of this section, the board may summarily suspend the mortgage loan originator's license pending a hearing to revoke the license. A summary suspension shall conform to article 4 of title 24.

(b)   The board shall suspend the license of a mortgage loan originator who fails to maintain the bond required by section 12-10-717 until the licensee complies with that section.

(5)   The board or an administrative law judge appointed pursuant to part 10 of article 30 of title 24 shall conduct disciplinary hearings concerning mortgage loan originators and mortgage companies. The hearings shall conform to article 4 of title 24.

(6)   (a)   Except as provided in subsection (6)(b) of this section, an individual whose license has been revoked shall not be eligible for licensure for two years after the effective date of the revocation.

(b)   If the board or an administrative law judge determines that an application contained a misstatement of fact or omitted a required disclosure due to an unintentional error, the board shall allow the applicant to correct the application. Upon receipt of the corrected and completed application, the board or administrative law judge shall not bar the applicant from being licensed on the basis of the unintentional misstatement or omission.

(7)   (a)   The board or an administrative law judge may administer oaths, take affirmations of witnesses, and issue subpoenas to compel the attendance of witnesses and the production of all relevant papers, books, records, documentary evidence, and materials in any hearing or investigation conducted by the board or an administrative law judge. The board may request any information relevant to the investigation, including, but not limited to, independent credit reports obtained from a consumer reporting agency described in the federal "Fair Credit Reporting Act", 15 U.S.C. sec. 1681a (p).

        (b)   Upon failure of a witness to comply with a subpoena or process, the district court of the county in which the subpoenaed witness resides or conducts business may issue an order requiring the witness to appear before the board or administrative law judge; produce the relevant papers, books, records, documentary evidence, testimony, or materials in question; or both. Failure to obey the order of the court may be punished as a contempt of court. The board or an administrative law judge may apply for an order.

        (c)   The licensee or individual who, after an investigation under this part 7, is found to be in violation of a provision of this part 7 shall be responsible for paying all reasonable and necessary costs of the division arising from subpoenas or requests issued pursuant to this subsection (7), including court costs for an action brought pursuant to subsection (7)(b) of this section.

(8)   (a)   If the board has reasonable cause to believe that an individual is violating this part 7, including but not limited to section 12-10-720 (1), the board may enter an order requiring the individual to cease and desist the violations.

        (b)   The board, upon its own motion, may, and, upon the complaint in writing of any person, shall, investigate the activities of any licensee or any individual who assumes to act in such capacity within the state. In addition to any other penalty that may be imposed pursuant to this part 7, any individual violating any provision of this part 7 or any rules promulgated pursuant to this article 10 may be fined upon a finding of misconduct by the board as follows:

            (I)   In the first administrative proceeding, a fine not in excess of one thousand dollars per act or occurrence;

            (II)   In a second or subsequent administrative proceeding, a fine not less than one thousand dollars nor in excess of two thousand dollars per act or occurrence.

        (c)   All fines collected pursuant to this subsection (8) shall be transferred to the state treasurer, who shall credit them to the division of real estate cash fund created in section 12-10-215.

(9)   The board shall keep records of the individuals licensed as mortgage loan originators and of disciplinary proceedings. The records kept by the board shall be open to public inspection in a reasonable time and manner determined by the board.

(10)   The board shall maintain a system, which may include, without limitation, a hotline or website, that gives consumers a reasonably easy method for making complaints about a mortgage loan originator.

(11)   The board shall promulgate rules to allow licensed mortgage loan originators to hire unlicensed mortgage loan originators under temporary licenses. If an unlicensed mortgage loan originator has initiated the application process for a license, he or she shall be assigned a temporary license for a reasonable period until a license is approved or denied. The licensed mortgage

loan originator who employs an unlicensed mortgage loan originator shall be held responsible under all applicable provisions of law, including without limitation this part 7 and section 38-40-105, for the actions of the unlicensed mortgage loan originator to whom a temporary license has been assigned under this subsection (11).

* **§ 12-10-712, C.R.S. Powers and duties of the board over mortgage companies – fines – rules.**

* *Editor's note: This section is similar to former §12-61-905.1 as it existed prior to 2019.*

(1) With respect to mortgage companies, the board may deny an application for registration; refuse to renew, suspend, or revoke the registration; enter cease-and-desist orders; and impose fines as set forth in this section as follows:

    (a) If the board has reasonable cause to believe a person is acting without a license or registration;

    (b) If the mortgage company fails to maintain possession, for future use or inspection by an authorized representative of the board, for a period of four years, of the documents or records prescribed by the rules of the board or to produce the documents or records upon reasonable request by the board or by an authorized representative of the board;

    (c) If the mortgage company employs or contracts with individuals who are required to be licensed pursuant to this part 7 and who are not either:

        (I) Licensed; or

        (II) In the process of becoming licensed; or

    (d) If the mortgage company directs, makes, or causes to be made, in any manner, a false or deceptive statement or representation with regard to the rates, points, or other financing terms or conditions for a residential mortgage loan; engages in bait and switch advertising as that term is used in section 6-1-105 (1)(n); or violates any rule of the board that directly or indirectly addresses advertising requirements.

(2)   (a) The board, upon its own motion or upon the complaint in writing of any person, may investigate the activities of any registered mortgage company or any mortgage company that is acting in a capacity that requires registration pursuant to this part 7.

    (b) The board may fine a mortgage company that has violated this section or any rules promulgated pursuant to this section as follows:

        (I) In the first administrative proceeding, a fine not in excess of one thousand dollars per act or occurrence;

        (II) In a second or subsequent administrative proceeding, a fine not in excess of two thousand dollars per act or occurrence.

    (c) All fines collected pursuant to this section shall be transmitted to the state treasurer, who shall credit them to the division of real estate cash fund created in section 12-10-215.

(3) The board may adopt reasonable rules for implementing this section.

(4) Nothing in this section automatically imputes a violation to the mortgage company if a licensed agent or employee, or an individual agent or employee who is required to be licensed, violates any other provision of this part 7.

* **§ 12-10-713, C.R.S. Disciplinary actions – grounds – procedures – rules.**

* *Editor's note: This section is similar to former §12-61-905.5 as it existed prior to 2019.*

(1) The board, upon its own motion, may, or upon the complaint in writing of any person, shall, investigate the activities of any mortgage loan originator. The board has the power to impose an administrative fine in accordance with section 12-10-711, deny a license, censure a licensee,

place the licensee on probation and set the terms of probation, order restitution, order the payment of actual damages, or suspend or revoke a license when the board finds that the licensee or applicant has performed, is performing, or is attempting to perform any of the following acts:

(a) Knowingly making any misrepresentation or knowingly making use of any false or misleading advertising;

(b) Making any promise that influences, persuades, or induces another person to detrimentally rely on the promise when the licensee could not or did not intend to keep the promise;

(c) Knowingly misrepresenting or making false promises through agents, salespersons, advertising, or otherwise;

(d) Violating any provision of the "Colorado Consumer Protection Act", article 1 of title 6, and, if the licensee has been assessed a civil or criminal penalty or been subject to an injunction under the act, the board shall revoke the licensee's license;

(e) Acting for more than one party in a transaction without disclosing any actual or potential conflict of interest or without disclosing to all parties any fiduciary obligation or other legal obligation of the mortgage loan originator to any party;

(f) Representing or attempting to represent a mortgage loan originator other than the licensee's principal or employer without the express knowledge and consent of that principal or employer;

(g) In the case of a licensee in the employ of another mortgage loan originator, failing to place, as soon after receipt as is practicably possible, in the custody of that licensed mortgage loan originator-employer any deposit money or other money or fund entrusted to the employee by any person dealing with the employee as the representative of that licensed mortgage loan originator-employer;

(h) Failing to account for or to remit, within a reasonable time, any money coming into his or her possession that belongs to others, whether acting as a mortgage loan originator, real estate broker, salesperson, or otherwise, and failing to keep records relative to the money, which records shall contain such information as may be prescribed by the rules of the board relative thereto and shall be subject to audit by the board;

(i) Converting funds of others, diverting funds of others without proper authorization, commingling funds of others with the licensee's own funds, or failing to keep the funds of others in an escrow or a trustee account with a bank or recognized depository in this state, which account may be any type of checking, demand, passbook, or statement account insured by an agency of the United States government, and to keep records relative to the deposit that contain such information as may be prescribed by the rules of the board relative thereto, which records shall be subject to audit by the board;

(j) Failing to provide the parties to a residential mortgage loan transaction with such information as may be prescribed by the rules of the board;

(k) Unless an employee of a duly registered mortgage company, failing to maintain possession, for future use or inspection by an authorized representative of the board, for a period of four years, of the documents or records prescribed by the rules of the board or to produce the documents or records upon reasonable request by the board or by an authorized representative of the board;

(*l*) Paying a commission or valuable consideration for performing any of the functions of a mortgage loan originator, as described in this part 7, to any person who is not licensed under this part 7 or is not registered in compliance with the federal "Secure and Fair Enforcement for Mortgage Licensing Act of 2008", 12 U.S.C. sec. 5101 et seq., as amended;

(m)   Disregarding or violating any provision of this part 7 or any rule adopted by the board pursuant to this part 7; violating any lawful orders of the board; or aiding and abetting a violation of any rule, order of the board, or provision of this part 7;

(n)   Conviction of, entering a plea of guilty to, or entering a plea of nolo contendere to any crime in article 3 of title 18, parts 1 to 4 of article 4 of title 18, article 5 of title 18, part 3 of article 8 of title 18, article 15 of title 18, article 17 of title 18, or any other like crime under Colorado law, federal law, or the laws of other states. A certified copy of the judgment of a court of competent jurisdiction of a conviction or other official record indicating that a plea was entered shall be conclusive evidence of the conviction or plea in any hearing under this part 7.

(o)   Violating or aiding and abetting in the violation of the Colorado or federal fair housing laws;

(p)   Failing to immediately notify the board in writing of a conviction, plea, or violation pursuant to subsection (1)(n) or (1)(o) of this section;

(q)   Having demonstrated unworthiness or incompetency to act as a mortgage loan originator by conducting business in such a manner as to endanger the interest of the public;

(r)   Procuring, or attempting to procure, a mortgage loan originator's license or renewing, reinstating, or reactivating, or attempting to renew, reinstate, or reactivate, a mortgage loan originator's license by fraud, misrepresentation, or deceit or by making a material misstatement of fact in an application for the license;

(s)   Claiming, arranging for, or taking any secret or undisclosed amount of compensation, commission, or profit or failing to reveal to the licensee's principal or employer the full amount of the licensee's compensation, commission, or profit in connection with any acts for which a license is required under this part 7;

(t)   Exercising an option to purchase in any agreement authorizing or employing a licensee to sell, buy, or exchange real estate for compensation or commission except when the licensee, prior to or coincident with election to exercise the option to purchase, reveals in writing to the licensee's principal or employer the full amount of the licensee's profit and obtains the written consent of the principal or employer approving the amount of the profit;

(u)   Fraud, misrepresentation, deceit, or conversion of trust funds that results in the payment of any claim pursuant to this part 7 or that results in the entry of a civil judgment for damages;

(v)   Any other conduct, whether of the same or a different character than specified in this subsection (1), that evinces a lack of good faith and fair dealing;

(w)   Having had a mortgage loan originator's license suspended or revoked in any jurisdiction or having had any disciplinary action taken against the mortgage loan originator in any other jurisdiction. A certified copy of the order of disciplinary action shall be prima facie evidence of the disciplinary action.

(x)   Engaging in any unfair or deceptive practice toward any person;

(y)   Obtaining property by fraud or misrepresentation;

(z)   Soliciting or entering into a contract with a borrower that provides, in substance, that the mortgage loan originator may earn a fee or commission through the mortgage loan originator's best efforts to obtain a loan even though no loan is actually obtained for the borrower;

(aa)   Soliciting, advertising, or entering into a contract for specific interest rates, points, or other financing terms unless the terms are actually available at the time of the solicitation, advertisement, or contract;

(bb) Failing to make a disclosure to a loan applicant or a noninstitutional investor as required by section 12-10-725 and any other applicable state or federal law;

(cc) Making, in any manner, any false or deceptive statement or representation with regard to the rates, points, or other financing terms or conditions for a residential mortgage loan or engaging in bait and switch advertising;

(dd) Negligently making any false statement or knowingly and willfully omitting a material fact in connection with any reports filed by a mortgage loan originator or in connection with any investigation conducted by the division;

(ee) In any advertising of residential mortgage loans or any other applicable mortgage loan originator activities covered by the following federal acts, failing to comply with any requirement of the "Truth in Lending Act", 15 U.S.C. sec. 1601 and Regulation Z, 12 CFR 226 and 12 CFR 1026; the "Real Estate Settlement Procedures Act of 1974", 12 U.S.C. sec. 2601 and Regulation X, 12 CFR 1024 et seq.; the "Equal Credit Opportunity Act", 15 U.S.C. sec. 1691 and Regulation B, 12 CFR 202.9, 202.11, and 202.12 and 12 CFR 1002; Title V, Subtitle A of the "Financial Services Modernization Act of 1999", also known as the "Gramm-Leach-Bliley Act", 15 U.S.C. secs. 6801 to 6809, and the federal trade commission's privacy rules, 16 CFR 313 and 314, mandated by the "Gramm-Leach-Bliley Act"; the "Home Mortgage Disclosure Act of 1975", 12 U.S.C. sec. 2801 et seq. and Regulation C, home mortgage disclosure, 12 CFR 203 and 12 CFR 1003; the "Federal Trade Commission Act" of 1914, 15 U.S.C. sec. 45 (a) and 16 CFR 233; and the "Telemarketing and Consumer Fraud and Abuse Prevention Act", 15 U.S.C. secs. 6101 to 6108, and the federal trade commission's telemarketing sales rule, 16 CFR 310, as amended. The board may adopt rules requiring mortgage loan originators to comply with other applicable state and federal statutes and regulations.

(ff) Failing to pay a third-party provider, no later than thirty days after the recording of the loan closing documents or ninety days after completion of the third-party service, whichever comes first, unless otherwise agreed or unless the third-party service provider has been notified in writing that a bona fide dispute exists regarding the performance or quality of the third-party service; or

(gg) Collecting, charging, attempting to collect or charge, or using or proposing any agreement purporting to collect or charge any fee prohibited by section 12-10-725 or 12-10-726.

(2) Upon request of the board, when any mortgage loan originator is a party to any suit or proceeding, either civil or criminal, arising out of any transaction involving a residential mortgage loan and the mortgage loan originator participated in the transaction in his or her capacity as a licensed mortgage loan originator, the mortgage loan originator shall supply to the board a copy of the complaint, indictment, information, or other initiating pleading and the answer filed, if any, and advise the board of the disposition of the case and of the nature and amount of any judgment, verdict, finding, or sentence that may be made, entered, or imposed therein.

(3) This part 7 shall not be construed to relieve any person from civil liability or criminal prosecution under the laws of this state.

(4) Complaints of record in the office of the board and board investigations, including board investigative files, are closed to public inspection. Stipulations and final agency orders are public record and subject to sections 24-72-203 and 24-72-204.

(5) When a complaint or an investigation discloses an instance of misconduct that, in the opinion of the board, does not warrant formal action by the board but that should not be dismissed as being without merit, the board may send a letter of admonition by certified mail, return receipt requested, to the licensee against whom a complaint was made and a copy of the letter of admonition to the person making the complaint, but the letter shall advise the licensee that the

licensee has the right to request in writing, within twenty days after proven receipt, that formal disciplinary proceedings be initiated to adjudicate the propriety of the conduct upon which the letter of admonition is based. If the request is timely made, the letter of admonition shall be deemed vacated, and the matter shall be processed by means of formal disciplinary proceedings.

(6) All administrative fines collected pursuant to this section shall be transmitted to the state treasurer, who shall credit them to the division of real estate cash fund created in section 12-10-215.

(7) (a) The board shall not consider an application for licensure from an individual whose license has been revoked until two years after the date of revocation.

(b) If an individual's license was suspended or revoked due to conduct that resulted in financial loss to another person, no new license shall be granted, nor shall a suspended license be reinstated, until full restitution has been made to the person suffering the financial loss. The amount of restitution shall include interest, reasonable attorney fees, and costs of any suit or other proceeding undertaken in an effort to recover the loss.

(8) When the board or the division becomes aware of facts or circumstances that fall within the jurisdiction of a criminal justice or other law enforcement authority upon investigation of the activities of a licensee, the board or division shall, in addition to the exercise of its authority under this part 7, refer and transmit the information, which may include originals or copies of documents and materials, to one or more criminal justice or other law enforcement authorities for investigation and prosecution as authorized by law.

* § 12-10-714, C.R.S. Hearing – administrative law judge – review – rules.

* *Editor's note: This section is similar to former §12-61-905.6 as it existed prior to 2019.*

(1) Except as otherwise provided in this section, all proceedings before the board with respect to disciplinary actions and denial of licensure under this part 7, at the discretion of the board, may be conducted by an authorized representative of the board or an administrative law judge pursuant to sections 24-4-104 and 24-4-105.

(2) Proceedings shall be held in the county where the board has its office or in such other place as the board may designate. If the licensee is employed by another licensed mortgage loan originator or by a real estate broker, the board shall also notify the licensee's employer by mailing, by first-class mail, a copy of the written notice required under section 24-4-104 (3) to the employer's last-known business address.

(3) The board, an authorized representative of the board, or an administrative law judge shall conduct all hearings for denying, suspending, or revoking a license or certificate on behalf of the board, subject to appropriations made to the department of personnel. Each administrative law judge shall be appointed pursuant to part 10 of article 30 of title 24. The administrative law judge shall conduct the hearing in accordance with sections 24-4-104 and 24-4-105. No license shall be denied, suspended, or revoked until the board has made its decision.

(4) The decision of the board in any disciplinary action or denial of licensure under this section is subject to judicial review by the court of appeals. In order to effectuate the purposes of this part 7, the board has the power to promulgate rules pursuant to article 4 of title 24.

(5) In a judicial review proceeding, the court may stay the execution or effect of any final order of the board; but a hearing shall be held affording the parties an opportunity to be heard for the purpose of determining whether the public health, safety, and welfare would be endangered by staying the board's order. If the court determines that the order should be stayed, it shall also determine at the hearing the amount of the bond and adequacy of the surety, which bond shall be conditioned upon the faithful performance by the petitioner of all obligations as a mortgage loan originator and upon the prompt payment of all damages arising from or caused by the

delay in the taking effect of or enforcement of the order complained of and for all costs that may be assessed or required to be paid in connection with the proceedings.

(6)   In any hearing conducted by the board or an authorized representative of the board in which there is a possibility of the denial, suspension, or revocation of a license because of the conviction of a felony or of a crime involving moral turpitude, the board or its authorized representative shall be governed by section 24-5-101.

*   ## § 12-10-715, C.R.S. Subpoena – misdemeanor.

*   ***Editor's note:*** *This section is similar to former §12-61-905.7 as it existed prior to 2019.*

(1)   The board or the administrative law judge appointed for hearings may issue subpoenas, as described in section 12-10-711 (7), which shall be served in the same manner as subpoenas issued by district courts and shall be issued without discrimination between public or private parties requiring the attendance of witnesses or the production of documents at hearings.

(2)   Any person who willfully fails or neglects to appear and testify or to produce books, papers, or records required by subpoena, duly served upon him or her in any matter conducted under this part 7, is guilty of a misdemeanor and, upon conviction thereof, shall be punished by a fine of one hundred dollars or imprisonment in the county jail for not more than thirty days for each such offense, or by both such fine and imprisonment. Each day a person so refuses or neglects constitutes a separate offense.

*   ## § 12-10-716, C.R.S. Immunity.

*   ***Editor's note:*** *This section is similar to former §12-61-906 as it existed prior to 2019.*

A person participating in good faith in the filing of a complaint or report or participating in an investigation or hearing before the board or an administrative law judge pursuant to this part 7 shall be immune from any liability, civil or criminal, that otherwise might result by reason of the action.

*   ## § 12-10-717, C.R.S. Bond required – rules.

*   ***Editor's note:*** *This section is similar to former §12-61-907 as it existed prior to 2019.*

(1)   Before receiving a license, an applicant shall post with the board a surety bond in an amount prescribed by the board by rule. A licensed mortgage loan originator shall maintain the required bond at all times. The surety bond may be held by the individual mortgage loan originator or may be in the name of the company by which the mortgage loan originator is employed. The board may adopt rules to further define surety bond requirements.

(2)   The surety shall not be required to pay a person making a claim upon the bond until a final determination of fraud, forgery, criminal impersonation, or fraudulent representation has been made by a court with jurisdiction.

(3)   The surety bond shall require the surety to provide notice to the board within thirty days if payment is made from the surety bond or if the bond is cancelled.

*   ## § 12-10-718, C.R.S. Fees.

*   ***Editor's note:*** *This section is similar to former §12-61-908 as it existed prior to 2019.*

The board may set the fees for issuance and renewal of licenses and registrations under this part 7. The fees shall be set in amounts that offset the direct and indirect costs of implementing this part 7 and section 38-40-105. The money collected pursuant to this section shall be transferred to the state treasurer, who shall credit it to the division of real estate cash fund created in section 12-10-215.

* ### § 12-10-719, C.R.S. Attorney general – district attorney – jurisdiction.

* *Editor's note: This section is similar to former §12-61-909 as it existed prior to 2019.*

The attorney general shall have concurrent jurisdiction with the district attorneys of this state to investigate and prosecute allegations of criminal violations of this part 7.

* ### § 12-10-720, C.R.S. Violations – injunctions.

* *Editor's note: This section is similar to former §12-61-910 as it existed prior to 2019.*

(1)   (a)   Any individual violating this part 7 by acting as a mortgage loan originator in this state without having obtained a license or by acting as a mortgage loan originator after that individual's license has been revoked or during any period for which the license may have been suspended is guilty of a class 1 misdemeanor and shall be punished as provided in section 18-1.3-501; except that, if the violator is not a natural person, the violator shall be punished by a fine of not more than five thousand dollars.

(b)   Each residential mortgage loan negotiated or offered to be negotiated by an unlicensed person shall be a separate violation of this subsection (1).

(2)   The board may request that an action be brought in the name of the people of the state of Colorado by the attorney general or the district attorney of the district in which the violation is alleged to have occurred to enjoin a person from engaging in or continuing the violation or from doing any act that furthers the violation. In such an action, an order or judgment may be entered awarding the preliminary or final injunction as is deemed proper by the court. The notice, hearing, or duration of an injunction or restraining order shall be made in accordance with the Colorado rules of civil procedure.

(3)   A violation of this part 7 shall not affect the validity or enforceability of any mortgage.

* ### § 12-10-721, C.R.S. Prohibited conduct – influencing a real estate appraisal.

* *Editor's note: This section is similar to former §12-61-910.2 as it existed prior to 2019.*

(1)   A mortgage loan originator shall not, directly or indirectly, compensate, coerce, or intimidate an appraiser, or attempt, directly or indirectly, to compensate, coerce, or intimidate an appraiser, for the purpose of influencing the independent judgment of the appraiser with respect to the value of a dwelling offered as security for repayment of a residential mortgage loan. This prohibition shall not be construed as prohibiting a mortgage loan originator from requesting an appraiser to:

(a)   Consider additional, appropriate property information;

(b)   Provide further detail, substantiation, or explanation for the appraiser's value conclusion; or

(c)   Correct errors in the appraisal report.

* ### § 12-10-722, C.R.S. Rule-making authority.

* *Editor's note: This section is similar to former §12-61-910.3 as it existed prior to 2019.*

The board has the authority to promulgate rules as necessary to enable the board to carry out the board's duties under this part 7.

* ### § 12-10-723, C.R.S. Acts of employee – mortgage loan originator's liability.

* *Editor's note: This section is similar to former §12-61-911.5 as it existed prior to 2019.*

An unlawful act or violation of this part 7 upon the part of an agent or employee of a licensed mortgage loan originator shall not be cause for disciplinary action against a mortgage loan originator unless it appears that the mortgage loan originator knew or should have known of the unlawful act or violation or had been negligent in the supervision of the agent or employee.

§ 12-10-724, C.R.S. Dual status as real estate broker – requirements.

Editor's note: This section is similar to former §12-61-912 as it existed prior to 2019.

(1) Unless a mortgage loan originator complies with both subsections (2) and (3) of this section, he or she shall not act as a mortgage loan originator in any transaction in which:

    (a) The mortgage loan originator acts or has acted as a real estate broker or salesperson; or

    (b) Another person doing business under the same licensed real estate broker acts or has acted as a real estate broker or salesperson.

(2) Before providing mortgage-related services to the borrower, a mortgage loan originator shall make a full and fair disclosure to the borrower, in addition to any other disclosures required by this part 7 or other laws, of all material features of the loan product and all facts material to the transaction.

(3) (a) A real estate broker or salesperson licensed under part 2 of this article 10 who also acts as a mortgage loan originator shall carry on the mortgage loan originator business activities and shall maintain the person's mortgage loan originator business records separate and apart from the real estate broker or sales activities conducted pursuant to part 2 of this article 10. The activities shall be deemed separate and apart even if they are conducted at an office location with a common entrance and mailing address if:

    (I) Each business is clearly identified by a sign visible to the public;

    (II) Each business is physically separated within the office facility; and

    (III) No deception of the public as to the separate identities of the broker business firms results.

    (b) This subsection (3) shall not require a real estate broker or salesperson licensed under part 2 of this article 10 who also acts as a mortgage loan originator to maintain a physical separation within the office facility for the conduct of its real estate broker or sales and mortgage loan originator activities if the board determines that maintaining the physical separation would constitute an undue financial hardship upon the mortgage loan originator and is unnecessary for the protection of the public.

§ 12-10-725, C.R.S. Written disclosure of fees and costs – contents – limits on fees – rules.

Editor's note: This section is similar to former §12-61-914 as it existed prior to 2019.

(1) A mortgage loan originator's disclosures must comply with all applicable requirements of:

    (a) The federal "Truth in Lending Act", 15 U.S.C. sec. 1601 et seq., and Regulation Z, 12 CFR 226 and 12 CFR 1026;

    (b) The federal "Real Estate Settlement Procedures Act of 1974", 12 U.S.C. sec. 2601 et seq., and Regulation X, 12 CFR 1024 et seq.;

    (c) The federal "Equal Credit Opportunity Act", 15 U.S.C. sec. 1691 and Regulation B, 12 CFR 202.9, 202.11, and 202.12 and 12 CFR 1002;

    (d) Title V, Subtitle A of the federal "Financial Services Modernization Act of 1999", also known as the "Gramm-Leach-Bliley Act", 15 U.S.C. secs. 6801 to 6809, and the federal trade commission's privacy rules, 16 CFR 313 and 314, adopted in accordance with the federal "Gramm-Leach-Bliley Act";

    (e) The federal "Home Mortgage Disclosure Act of 1975", 12 U.S.C. sec. 2801 et seq., and Regulation C, 12 CFR 203 and 12 CFR 1003, pertaining to home mortgage disclosure;

(f)   The "Federal Trade Commission Act" of 1914, 15 U.S.C. sec. 45 (a), and 16 CFR 233;

(g)   The federal "Telemarketing and Consumer Fraud and Abuse Prevention Act", 15 U.S.C. secs. 6101 to 6108, and the federal trade commission's telemarketing sales rule, 16 CFR 310.

(2)   The board may, by rule, require mortgage loan originators to comply with other mortgage loan disclosure requirements contained in applicable statutes and regulations in connection with making any residential mortgage loan or engaging in other activity subject to this part 7.

*   *§ 12-10-726, C.R.S. Fee, commission, or compensation – when permitted – amount.*

*   *Editor's note: This section is similar to former §12-61-915 as it existed prior to 2019.*

(1)   Except as otherwise permitted by subsection (2) or (3) of this section, a mortgage loan originator shall not receive a fee, commission, or compensation of any kind in connection with the preparation or negotiation of a residential mortgage loan unless a borrower actually obtains a loan from a lender on the terms and conditions agreed to by the borrower and mortgage loan originator.

(2)   If the mortgage loan originator has obtained for the borrower a written commitment from a lender for a loan on the terms and conditions agreed to by the borrower and the mortgage loan originator, and the borrower fails to close on the loan through no fault of the mortgage loan originator, the mortgage loan originator may charge a fee, not to exceed three hundred dollars, for services rendered, preparation of documents, or transfer of documents in the borrower's file that were prepared or paid for by the borrower if the fee is not otherwise prohibited by the federal "Truth in Lending Act", 15 U.S.C. sec. 1601, and Regulation Z, 12 CFR 226, as amended.

(3)   A mortgage loan originator may solicit or receive fees for third-party provider goods or services in advance. Fees for any goods or services not provided shall be refunded to the borrower, and the mortgage loan originator may not charge more for the goods and services than the actual costs of the goods or services charged by the third-party provider.

*   *§ 12-10-727, C.R.S. Confidentiality.*

*   *Editor's note: This section is similar to former §12-61-916 as it existed prior to 2019.*

(1)   Except as otherwise provided in the federal "Secure and Fair Enforcement for Mortgage Licensing Act of 2008", 12 U.S.C. sec. 5111, the requirements under any federal law or law of this state regarding privacy or confidentiality of any information or material provided to the nationwide mortgage licensing system and registry, and any privilege arising under federal or state law, including the rules of any federal or state court with respect to the information or material, shall apply to the information or material after it has been disclosed to the nationwide mortgage licensing system and registry. The information or material may be shared with all state and federal regulatory officials with mortgage industry oversight authority without the loss of privilege or confidentiality protections provided by federal or state law.

(2)   The board may enter into agreements with other government agencies, the Conference of State Bank Supervisors or its successor organization, the American Association of Residential Mortgage Regulators or its successor organization, or other associations representing government agencies as established by rule.

(3)   Information or material that is subject to privilege or confidentiality pursuant to subsection (1) of this section shall not be subject to the following:

    (a)   Disclosure under a federal or state law governing the disclosure to the public of information held by an officer or agency of the federal government or the respective state; or

(b) Subpoena, discovery, or admission into evidence in any private civil action or administrative process, unless with respect to a privilege held by the nationwide mortgage licensing system and registry regarding the information or material, the person to whom the information or material pertains waives the privilege, in whole or in part.

* ### § 12-10-728, C.R.S. Mortgage call reports – reports of violations.

* *Editor's note: This section is similar to former §12-61-917 as it existed prior to 2019.*

(1) The board may require each licensee or registrant to submit to the nationwide mortgage licensing system and registry mortgage call reports, which shall be in the form and contain the information required by the nationwide mortgage licensing system and registry.

(2) The board may report violations of this part 7, enforcement actions, and other relevant information to the nationwide mortgage licensing system and registry.

* ### § 12-10-729, C.R.S. Unique identifier – clearly displayed.

* *Editor's note: This section is similar to former §12-61-918 as it existed prior to 2019.*

Each person required to be licensed or registered shall show his or her or the entity's unique identifier clearly on all residential mortgage loan application forms and any other documents as specified by the board by rule or order.

* ### § 12-10-730, C.R.S. Repeal of part – subject to review.

* *Editor's note: This section is similar to former §12-61-919 as it existed prior to 2019.*

(1) This part 7 is repealed, effective September 1, 2029.

(2) Before the repeal, the licensing of mortgage loan originators and the registration of mortgage companies is scheduled for review in accordance with section 24-34-104. The department shall include in its review of mortgage loan originators and mortgage companies an analysis of the number and types of complaints made about mortgage loan originators and mortgage companies and whether the licensing of mortgage loan originators and the registration of mortgage companies correlates with public protection from fraudulent activities in the residential mortgage loan industry.

III. Standards for Mortgage Lending and Servicing

§ 38-40-101, C.R.S. Mortgage broker fees – escrow accounts – unlawful act – penalty.

(1) Any funds, other than advanced for actual costs and expenses to be incurred by the mortgage broker on behalf of the applicant for a loan, paid to a mortgage broker as a fee conditioned upon the consummation of a loan secured or to be secured by a mortgage or other transfer of or encumbrance on real estate shall be held in an escrow or a trustee account with a bank or recognized depository in this state. Such account may be any type of checking, demand, passbook, or statement account insured by an agency of the United States government.

(2) It is unlawful for a mortgage broker to misappropriate funds held in escrow or a trustee account pursuant to subsection (1) of this section.

(3) The withdrawal, transfer, or other use or conversion of any funds held in escrow or a trustee account pursuant to subsection (1) of this section prior to the time a loan secured or to be secured by mortgage or other transfer of or encumbrance on real estate is consummated shall be prima facie evidence of intent to violate subsection (2) of this section.

(4) Any mortgage broker violating any of the provisions of subsection (2) of this section commits theft as defined in section 18-4-401, C.R.S.

(5)   Any mortgage broker violating any of the provisions of subsection (1) or (2) of this section shall be liable to the person from whom any funds were received for the sum of one thousand dollars plus actual damages caused thereby, together with costs and reasonable attorney fees. No lender shall be liable for any act or omission of a mortgage broker under this section.

(6)   As used in this section, unless the context otherwise requires, "mortgage broker" means a person, firm, partnership, association, or corporation, other than a bank, trust company, savings and loan association, credit union, supervised lender as defined in section 5-1-301 (46), C.R.S., insurance company, federal housing administration approved mortgagee, land mortgagee, or farm loan association or duly appointed loan correspondents, acting through officers, partners, or regular salaried employees for any such entity, that engages in negotiating or offering or attempting to negotiate for a borrower, and for commission, money, or other thing of value, a loan to be consummated and funded by someone other than the one acting for the borrower.

§ 38-40-102, C.R.S. Disclosure of costs – statement of terms of indebtedness. (Repealed)

§ 38-40-103, C.R.S. Servicing of mortgages and deeds of trust – liability for interest or late fees for property taxes.

(1)   (a)   (I)   Any person who regularly engages in the collection of payments on mortgages and deeds of trust for owners of evidences of debt secured by mortgages or deeds of trust shall promptly credit all payments which are received and which are required to be accepted by such person or his agent and shall promptly perform all duties imposed by law and all duties imposed upon the servicer by such evidences of debt, mortgages, or deeds of trust creating or securing the indebtedness.

                (II)   No more than twenty days after the date of transfer of the servicing or collection rights and duties to another person, the transferor of such rights and duties shall mail a notice addressed to the debtor from whom it has been collecting payments at the address shown on its records, notifying such debtor of the transfer of the servicing of his or her debt and the name, address, and telephone number of the transferee of the servicing.

        (b)   The debtor may continue to make payments to the transferor of the servicing of his or her loan until a notice of the transfer is received from the transferee containing the name, address, and telephone number of the new servicer of the loan to whom future payments should be made. Such notice may be combined with the notice required in subparagraph (II) of paragraph (a) of this subsection (1). It shall be the responsibility of the transferor to forward to the transferee any payments received and due after the date of transfer of the loan.

(2)   The servicer of a loan shall respond in writing within twenty days from the receipt of a written request from the debtor or from an agent of the debtor acting pursuant to written authority from the debtor for information concerning the debtor's loan, which is readily available to the servicer from its books and records and which would not constitute the rendering of legal advice. Any such response must include the telephone number of the servicer. The servicer shall not be liable for any damage or harm that might arise from the release of any information pursuant to this section.

(3)   The servicer of a loan shall annually provide to the debtor a summary of activity related to the loan. Such a summary shall contain, but need not be limited to, the total amount of principal and interest paid on the loan in that calendar year.

(4)   The servicer of a loan shall be liable for any interest or late fees charged by any taxing entity if funds for the full payment of taxes on the real estate have been held in an escrow account by such servicer and not remitted to the taxing entity when due.

§ 38-40-103.5, C.R.S. Notice upon transfer of servicing rights – prior servicer's offer to borrower survives transfer – definitions.

(1)   As used in this section:

    (a)   "Borrower" means a person liable under an evidence of debt constituting a residential mortgage loan.

    (b)   "Evidence of debt" has the meaning set forth in section 38-38-100.3 (8).

    (c)   "Holder" means the holder of an evidence of debt constituting a residential mortgage loan.

    (d)   "Residential mortgage loan" has the meaning set forth in section 12-10-702 (21).

    (e)   (I)   "Servicer" means a person who collects, receives, or has the right to collect or receive payments on behalf of a holder, including payments of principal, interest, escrow amounts, and other amounts due on obligations due and owing to the holder.

          (II)   "Servicer" includes:

             (A)   The person or entity to whom payments are to be sent, as listed on the most recent billing statement or payment coupon provided to the borrower; or

             (B)   A subsidiary, affiliate, or assignee of a servicer, however designated, including a person designated as a subservicer.

(2)   A servicer to whom servicing rights for a residential mortgage loan have been sold or transferred by the holder or by a predecessor servicer is subject to, and shall honor, the borrower's acceptance, prior to the sale or transfer of servicing rights, of any offer previously made by the holder or predecessor servicer in connection with a modification of a residential mortgage loan.

(3)   At the time of the transfer or sale of servicing rights for a residential mortgage loan, the transferor or seller shall inform the buyer or transferee of the servicing rights whether a loan modification is pending.

(4)   A contract for the transfer or sale of servicing rights for a residential mortgage loan must obligate the successor servicer to:

    (a)   Accept and continue processing any pending loan modification requests; and

    (b)   Honor any trial and permanent loan modification agreements entered into by the prior servicer.

§ 38-40-104, C.R.S. Cause of action – attorney fees.

(1)   If any applicant or debtor is aggrieved by a violation of section 38-40-102, 38-40-103, or 38-40-103.5 and the violation is not remedied in a reasonable, timely, and good faith manner by the party obligated to do so, and after a good faith effort to resolve the dispute is made by the debtor or borrower, the debtor or borrower may bring an action in a court of competent jurisdiction for any such violation. If the court finds that actual damages have occurred, the court shall award to the debtor or borrower, in addition to actual damages, the amount of one thousand dollars, together with costs and reasonable attorney fees.

(2)   A transferee from a lender is not liable for any act or omission of the lender under section 38-40-102. A transferee of servicing or collection rights is not liable for any act or omission of the transferor of those rights under section 38-40-103 or 38-40-103.5.

§ 38-40-105, C.R.S. Prohibited acts by participants in certain mortgage loan transactions – unconscionable acts and practices – definitions.

(1)　The following acts by any mortgage broker, mortgage originator, mortgage lender, mortgage loan applicant, real estate appraiser, or closing agent, other than a person who provides closing or settlement services subject to regulation by the division of insurance, with respect to any loan that is secured by a first or subordinate mortgage or deed or trust lien against a dwelling are prohibited:

(a)　To knowingly advertise, display, distribute, broadcast, televise, or cause or permit to be advertised, displayed, distributed, broadcast, or televised, in any manner, any false, misleading, or deceptive statement with regard to rates, terms, or conditions for a mortgage loan;

(b)　To make a false promise or misrepresentation or conceal an essential or material fact to entice either a borrower or a creditor to enter into a mortgage agreement when, under the terms and circumstances of the transaction, he or she knew or reasonably should have known of such falsity, misrepresentation, or concealment;

(c)　To knowingly and with intent to defraud present, cause to be presented, or prepare with knowledge or belief that it will be presented to or by a lender or an agent thereof any written statement or information in support of an application for a mortgage loan that he or she knows to contain false information concerning any fact material thereto or if he or she knowingly and with intent to defraud or mislead conceals information concerning any fact material thereto;

(d)　To facilitate the consummation of a mortgage loan agreement that is unconscionable given the terms and circumstances of the transaction;

(e)　To knowingly facilitate the consummation of a mortgage loan transaction that violates, or that is connected with a violation of, section 12-10-713.

(f)　(Deleted by amendment, L. 2009, (HB 09-1085), ch. 303, p. 1638, §4, effective August 5, 2009.)

(1.5)　(Deleted by amendment, L. 2009, (HB 09-1085), ch. 303, p. 1638, §4, effective August 5, 2009.)

(1.7)　(a)　A mortgage broker or mortgage originator shall not commit, or assist or facilitate the commission of, the following acts or practices, which are hereby deemed unconscionable:

(I)　Engaging in a pattern or practice of providing residential mortgage loans to consumers based predominantly on acquisition of the foreclosure or liquidation value of the consumer's collateral without regard to the consumer's ability to repay a loan in accordance with its terms; except that any reasonable method may be used to determine a borrower's ability to repay. This subparagraph (I) shall not apply to a reverse mortgage that complies with article 38 of title 11, C.R.S.

(II)　Knowingly or intentionally flipping a residential mortgage loan. As used in this subparagraph (II), "flipping" means making a residential mortgage loan that refinances an existing residential mortgage loan when the new loan does not have reasonable, tangible net benefit to the consumer considering all of the circumstances, including the terms of both the new and refinanced loans, the cost of the new loan, and the consumer's circumstances. This subparagraph (II) applies regardless of whether the interest rate, points, fees, and charges paid or payable by the consumer in connection with the refinancing exceed any thresholds specified by law.

(III)　Entering into a residential mortgage loan transaction knowing there was no reasonable probability of payment of the obligation by the consumer.

(b)   Except as this subsection (1.7) may be enforced by the attorney general or a district attorney, only the original parties to a transaction shall have a right of action under this subsection (1.7), and no action or claim under this subsection (1.7) may be brought against a purchaser from, or assignee of, a party to the transaction.

(2)   (a)   Except as provided in subsection (5) of this section, if a court, as a matter of law, finds a mortgage contract or any clause of the contract to have been unconscionable at the time it was made, the court may refuse to enforce the contract, or it may enforce the remainder of the contract without the unconscionable clause, or it may so limit the application of any unconscionable clause as to avoid any unconscionable result.

(b)   When it is claimed or appears to the court that the contract or any clause thereof may be unconscionable, the parties shall be afforded a reasonable opportunity to present evidence as to its commercial setting, purpose, and effect, to aid the court in making the determination.

(c)   (I)   In order to support a finding of unconscionability, there must be evidence of some bad faith overreaching on the part of the mortgage broker or mortgage originator such as that which results from an unreasonable inequality of bargaining power or under other circumstances in which there is an absence of meaningful choice on the part of one of the parties, together with contract terms that are, under standard industry practices, unreasonably favorable to the mortgage broker, mortgage originator, or lender.

(II)   This paragraph (c) shall not apply to an unconscionable act or practice under subsection (1.7) of this section.

(3)   A violation of this section shall be deemed a deceptive trade practice as provided in section 6-1-105 (1)(uu), C.R.S.

(4)   The provisions of this section are in addition to and are not intended to supersede the deceptive trade practices actionable at common law or under other statutes of this state.

(5)   No right or claim arising under this section may be raised or asserted in any proceeding against a bona fide purchaser of such mortgage contract or in any proceeding to obtain an order authorizing sale of property by a public trustee as required by section 38-38-105.

*   (6)   The following acts by any real estate agent or real estate broker, as defined in section 12-10-201 (6), in connection with any residential mortgage loan transaction, are prohibited:

(a)   If directly engaged in negotiating, originating, or offering or attempting to negotiate or originate for a borrower a residential mortgage loan transaction, the real estate agent or real estate broker shall not make a false promise or misrepresentation or conceal an essential or material fact to entice either a borrower or lender to enter into a mortgage loan agreement when the real estate agent or real estate broker actually knew or, under the terms and circumstances of the transaction, reasonably should have known of such falsity, misrepresentation, or concealment.

(b)   If not directly engaged in negotiating, originating, or offering or attempting to negotiate or originate for a borrower a residential mortgage loan transaction, the real estate agent or real estate broker shall not make a false promise or misrepresentation or conceal an essential or material fact to entice either a borrower or lender to enter into a mortgage loan agreement when the real estate agent or real estate broker had actual knowledge of such falsity, misrepresentation, or concealment.

(7)   As used in this section, unless the context otherwise requires:

(a)   "Consumer" has the meaning set forth in section 5-1-301, C.R.S.

(b)   "Dwelling" has the meaning set forth in section 5-1-301, C.R.S.

*   (c)   "Mortgage broker" has the same meaning as "mortgage loan originator" as set forth in section 12-10-702 (14).

* (d) "Mortgage lender" has the meaning set forth in section 12-10-702 (13).

* (e) "Mortgage originator" has the same meaning as "mortgage loan originator" as set forth in section 12-10-702 (14).

* (f) "Originate" has the same meaning as "originate a mortgage" as set forth in section 12-10-702 (17).

* (g) "Residential mortgage loan" has the meaning set forth in section 12-10-702 (21).

IV. Loan Fraud

Legislative declaration

(1) The general assembly hereby determines that mortgage lending has a significant effect upon Colorado's economy; an estimated two trillion five hundred billion dollars in mortgage loans were made in the United States in 2005; an estimated eighty percent of reported mortgage fraud involves collusion by industry insiders; and Colorado's per capita incidents of mortgage fraud is one of the ten highest in the nation.

(2) The general assembly hereby declares that the high rates of mortgage fraud in Colorado are unacceptable and that residential mortgage fraud shall not be tolerated. The general assembly further declares that the goals of Colorado law are to deter residential mortgage fraud and to make the victim whole.

§ 18-4-401, C.R.S. Theft.

(9) (a) If a person is convicted of or pleads guilty or nolo contendere to theft by deception and the underlying factual basis of the case involves the mortgage lending process, a minimum fine of the amount of pecuniary harm resulting from the theft shall be mandatory, in addition to any other penalty the court may impose.

(b) A court shall not accept a plea of guilty or nolo contendere to another offense from a person charged with a violation of this section that involves the mortgage lending process unless the plea agreement contains an order of restitution in accordance with part 6 of article 1.3 of this title that compensates the victim for any costs to the victim caused by the offense.

(c) The district attorneys and the attorney general have concurrent jurisdiction to investigate and prosecute a violation of this section that involves making false statements or filing or facilitating the use of a document known to contain a false statement or material omission relied upon by another person in the mortgage lending process.

(d) Documents involved in the mortgage lending process include, but are not limited to, uniform residential loan applications or other loan applications; appraisal reports; HUD-1 settlement statements; supporting personal documentation for loan applications such as W-2 forms, verifications of income and employment, bank statements, tax returns, and payroll stubs; and any required disclosures.

(e) For the purposes of this subsection (9):

(I) "Mortgage lending process" means the process through which a person seeks or obtains a residential mortgage loan, including, without limitation, solicitation, application, or origination; negotiation of terms; third-party provider services; underwriting; signing and closing; funding of the loan; and perfecting and releasing the mortgage.

(II) "Residential mortgage loan" means a loan or agreement to extend credit, made to a person and secured by a mortgage or lien on residential real property, including, but not limited to, the refinancing or renewal of a loan secured by residential real property.

(III) "Residential real property" means real property used as a residence and containing no more than four families housed separately.

§ 13-21-125, C.R.S. Civil actions for theft in the mortgage lending process.

A person who suffers damages as a result of a violation of section 18-4-401, C.R.S., in the mortgage lending process, as defined by section 18-4-401 (9) (e) (I), C.R.S., shall have a private civil right of action against the perpetrator, regardless of whether the perpetrator was convicted of the crime. A claim arising under this section shall not be asserted against a bona fide purchaser of a mortgage contract.

§ 18-5-208, C.R.S. Dual contracts to induce loan.

It is a class 3 misdemeanor for any person to knowingly make, issue, deliver, or receive dual contracts for the purchase or sale of real property. The term "dual contracts", either written or oral, means two separate contracts concerning the same parcel of real property, one of which states the true and actual purchase price and one of which states a purchase price in excess of the true and actual purchase price, and is used, or intended to be used, to induce persons to make a loan or a loan commitment on such real property in reliance upon the stated inflated value.

. . . .

Loan fraud has become one of the largest areas of white-collar crime and is a recurring subject of Commission disciplinary actions. Loan fraud includes falsified loan applications; fictitious income, employment, or deposit verifications; false occupancy claims; undisclosed buyer rebates or credits; and a host of other items, which can be considered dual contracting.

Loan fraud may also result in disbarment by HUD from all federal programs, large fines, and federal prosecution. Since virtually all loan programs are affiliated with the federal government in either the primary or secondary mortgage market, disbarment can mean the end of a career in real estate, appraisal, and lending or related fields.

Chapter 9:
Rules and Regulations for Mortgage Loan Originators and Position Statements

An * in the left margin indicates a change in the statute, rule, or text since the last publication of the manual.

I. Mortgage Loan Originator Rules

DEPARTMENT OF REGULATORY AGENCIES
DIVISION OF REAL ESTATE

RULES REGARDING MORTGAGE LOAN ORIGINATORS
4 CCR 725-3

CHAPTER 1: DEFINITIONS

1.1 Address: The street address, city, state and postal code.

1.2 Adjustable Rate Mortgage: A mortgage in which the teaser rate, payment rate, or interest rate changes periodically and, in some cases, may adjust according to corresponding fluctuations in an index.

1.3 Adjustment Date: The date the teaser rate, payment rate, or interest rate changes on an adjustable rate mortgage.

1.4 Advertisement: Has the same meaning as set forth in 12 C.F.R. §1026.2(a)(2) as incorporated by reference in Board Rule 1.36.

1.5 Bona Fide Nonprofit Organization: An organization that complies with the following criteria:

A. Has the status of tax-exempt organization under Section 501(c)(3) of the Internal Revenue Code of 1986, incorporated by reference in compliance with Section 24-4-103(12.5), C.R.S., and does not include later amendments or editions of the Code. A certified copy of the Code is readily available for public inspection at the offices of the Board of Mortgage Loan Originators at 1560 Broadway Suite 925, Denver, Colorado. The Internal Revenue Code of 1986 may be examined at the internet website of the Internal Revenue Service at www.irs.gov. The Internal Revenue Service may also be contacted at 1999 Broadway, Denver, Colorado 80202 or by telephone at (303) 446-1675;

B. Promotes affordable housing or provides homeownership education, or similar services;

C. Conducts its activities in a manner that serves public and charitable purposes, rather than commercial purposes;

D. Receives funding and revenue and charges fees in a manner that does not incentivize it or its employees to act other than in the best interests of its clients;

E. Compensates its employees to act other than in the best interests of its clients; and

F. Provides or identifies for the borrower residential mortgage loans with terms favorable to the borrower and comparable to mortgage loans and housing assistance provided under the government housing assistance programs.

1.6 Business Day: Has the same meaning as set forth in 12 C.F.R. §1026.2(a)(6) and 12 C.F.R. §1024.2(b) as incorporated by reference in Board Rule 1.36.

1.7 Business Name: The company for which individuals who originate a mortgage, offer to originate a mortgage, act as a mortgage loan originator, or offer to act as a mortgage loan originator are officers, partners, members, managers, owners, exclusive agents, contractors, independent contractors or employees.

1.8 Consumer Credit: may be either closed-end or open-end credit. It is credit that is extended primarily for personal, family, or household purposes. It excludes business and agricultural loans, and loans exceeding $ 25,000 that are not secured by real property or a dwelling. It also must be extended by a "creditor".

1.9 Creditor: Has the same meaning as set forth in 12 C.F.R. §1026.2(a)(17) as incorporated by reference in Board Rule 1.36.

1.10 Employee: An individual whose manner and means of performance of work are subject to the right of control of, or are controlled by, a person, and whose compensation for federal income tax purposes is reported, or required to be reported, on a W-2 form issued by the controlling person.

1.11 Finance Charge: has the same meaning as set forth in 12 C.F.R. §1026.4(a) as incorporated by reference in Board Rule 1.36.

1.12 Fixed Term: The length of time a teaser rate, payment rate, or interest rate, is fixed and will not adjust.

1.13 Good Faith Estimate Disclosure: Is the same disclosure form established in the Real Estate Settlement Procedures Act, specific to Regulation X, Appendix C as incorporated by reference in Board Rule 1.36.

1.14 Housing Finance Agency: An authority that is chartered by the State of Colorado to help meet the affordable housing needs of the residents of Colorado; is supervised directly or indirectly by the state government; is subject to audit and review by the State of Colorado; and whose activities make it eligible to be a member of the National Council of State Housing Agencies.

1.15 HUD Approved Housing Counseling Agency: is an agency which is either a private or public nonprofit organization that is exempt from taxation under Section 501(a) pursuant to Section 501(c), of the Internal Revenue Code of 1996, 26, U.S.C. 501(a) and 501(c), and approved by the U.S. Department of Housing and Urban Development, in accordance with Housing Counseling Program Handbook 7610.1 and Code of Federal Regulations Title 24, Part 214.

1.16 Independent Contractor: An individual who performs his or her duties other than at the direction of and subject to the supervision and instruction of an individual who is licensed by the Board or is not required to be licensed based on one of the following:

A. The individual is lawfully registered with, and maintains a unique identifier through, the Nationwide Mortgage Licensing System and Registry, and who is an employee of:

1. A depository institution;

2. A subsidiary that is:

a. Owned and controlled by a depository institution; and

b. Regulated by a Federal banking agency; or

3. An institution regulated by the Farm Credit Administration; or

B. An individual who is an employee of a federal, state, or local government agency or housing finance agency and who acts as a loan originator only pursuant to his or her official duties as an employee of a federal, state, or local government agency or housing finance agency; or

C. An employee of a bona fie nonprofit organization who acts as a loan originator only with respect to his or her work duties to the bona fide nonprofit organization, and who acts as a loan originator only with respect to residential mortgage loans with terms that are favorable to the borrower.

1.17 Index: The index for an adjustable rate mortgage.

1.18 Initial Adjustment Cap: The limit on how much the interest or payment rate can change at the first adjustment period.

1.19 Interest Rate: The rate used to calculate a borrower's monthly interest payment.

1.20 Life Cap: The limit on how much the interest or payment rate can change over the life of the loan.

1.21 Loan Modification: A temporary or permanent change in one or more of the terms of a mortgagor's existing loan, allows the loan to be reinstated, and often results in a more affordable mortgage payment. The borrower retains ownership of the real property and the mortgage note and the deed of trust remains intact.

1.22 Loan Modifier: An individual who in the course of the person's business, vocation, or occupation offers to assist, provide, or negotiate on behalf of a borrower to facilitate the receipt of a loan modification from the borrower's current mortgage lender, generally for a fee or other thing of value.

1.23 Offering or Negotiating Terms of a Residential Mortgage Loan: To present for consideration to a borrower or prospective borrower particular residential mortgage loan terms, or to communicate directly or indirectly with a borrower, or prospective borrower for the purpose of reaching a mutual understanding about prospective residential mortgage loan terms. An individual's generic referral to or recommendation of a particular lender in and of itself, is not offering or negotiating the terms of a residential mortgage loan.

1.24 Payment Rate: The rate used to determine a borrower's monthly payment.

1.25 Payment Type: Is the principal and interest, interest only or negative amortization.

1.26 Physical Address: The physical location of the property.

1.27 Prepayment Penalty: A fee assessed pursuant to the terms of the loan on a borrower who repays all or part of the principal of a loan before it is due. Prepayment penalties do not include interest payments of thirty (30) days or less that may be assessed pursuant to the terms of some FHA or VA loans. Prepayment penalties for the purpose of this rule do not include termination fees of $ 500.00 or less that are associated with home equity lines of credit.

1.28 Rate: The teaser rate, payment rate or interest rate used to determine a borrower's monthly payment or deferred interest specific to reverse mortgage transactions.

1.29 Application: Has the same meaning as set forth in 12 C.F.R. §1026.2(a)(3) and 12 C.F.R. §1024.2(b) as incorporated by reference in Board Rule 1.36.

1.30 Safe and Secure Manner: Reasonable measures are taken to minimize the risk of loss, damage, or theft.

1.31 Short Sale: The sale of a real property for less than the mortgage loan balance. In the settlement of the short sale transaction the existing mortgage is extinguished. Any deficiency created from the settlement of the transaction may be transformed into a promissory note, charged off, forgiven, or pursued as a judgment against the previous owner.

1.32 Taking a Residential Mortgage Loan Application: The receipt of a residential mortgage loan application by an individual for the purpose of facilitating a decision whether to extend an offer of residential mortgage loan terms to a borrower or prospective borrower, whether the application is received directly or indirectly from the borrower or prospective borrower. An individual's generic referral to or recommendation of a particular lender, in and of itself, is not taking a residential loan application.

1.33 Teaser Rate: A temporary and often low introductory rate on an adjustable rate mortgage.

1.34 Truth-in-Lending Disclosure: Is the same disclosure form established by the Truth in Lending Act, specific to Regulation Z, Appendices H-2, H-3, H-4(a), (b), (c) and (d) as incorporated by reference in Board Rule 1.36.

1.35 Uniform Residential Loan Application: Is the Freddie Mac form 65 or the Fannie Mae form 1003 used in residential loan transactions on properties of four or fewer units.

1.36 TILA-RESPA Integrated Disclosure Rule: means the Consumer Financial Protection Bureau's Integrated Mortgage Disclosures final rule, set forth in 12 C.F.R. § 1024, *et seq.*, the Real Estate Settlement Procedures Act (Regulation X), and in 12 C.F.R. § 1026, *et seq.*, the Truth in Lending Act (Regulation Z), effective October 3, 2015, incorporated by reference in compliance with Section 24-4-103(12.5), C.R.S., and does not include any later amendments or editions of the final rule. A certified copy of the TILA-RESPA Integrated Disclosure rule is readily available for public inspection at the offices of the Board of Mortgage Loan Originators at 1560 Broadway, Suite 925, Denver, Colorado. The TILA-RESPA Integrated Disclosure rule may be examined at the internet website of the Consumer Financial Protection Bureau at www.consumerfinance.gov. The Consumer Financial Protection Bureau may also be contacted at 1700 G Street, NW, Washington, D.C. 20552 or by telephone at (202) 435-7000.

1.37 Repealed (Effective March 17, 2017).

1.38 Colorado Lock-in Disclosure: means the Colorado Lock-in Disclosure form created by the Board of Mortgage Loan Originators. This form is to be used for any loan application or transaction that is not under the authority of the TILA-RESPA Integrated Disclosure Rule as defined and incorporated by reference in Board Rule 1.36. This disclosure may be found on the Division of Real Estate's Website. A mortgage loan originator may use an alternate form if the alternate form includes all information required on the Colorado Lock-in Disclosure form, as determined by the Board.

1.39 Family Member: A person who is related by blood, marriage, civil union, or adoption.

CHAPTER 2: REQUIREMENTS FOR LICENSURE

2.1 An applicant for licensure as a Colorado mortgage loan originator must successfully complete the requirements set forth below:

A. Submit a set of fingerprints for a criminal history check to the Colorado Bureau of Investigations (CBI) within 1 year immediately preceding the date of application;

B. Register with the Nationwide Mortgage Licensing System and Registry in accordance with policies and procedures established by the Nationwide Mortgage Licensing System and Registry. This includes, but is not limited to completion of the correct registration application, authorization for the registry to pull a credit report and payment of any fees associated with registration;

C. Submit fingerprints to the Nationwide Mortgage Licensing System and Registry in accordance with policies and procedures established by the Nationwide Mortgage Licensing System and Registry;

D. Complete the twenty (20) hours of pre-licensing education reviewed and approved by the Nationwide Mortgage Licensing System and Registry or by a company contracted by the Nationwide Mortgage Licensing System and Registry for the review and approval of pre-licensing courses;

   1. Effective March 1, 2016, applicants must also complete two (2) hours of Colorado specific pre-licensing education reviewed and approved by the Nationwide Mortgage Licensing System and Registry or by a company contracted by the Nationwide Mortgage Licensing System and Registry for the review and approval of pre-licensing courses.

2. The two (2) hours of Colorado specific education replaces what was a required general elective within the twenty (20) hours of pre-licensing education.

3. Applicants may also complete the two (2) hours of Colorado specific pre-licensing education as a standalone course outside of the twenty (20) hour pre-licensing education.

4. The two (2) hours of Colorado specific education must have a final examination that covers all major topics covered in the course. Applicants must receive a passing score of seventy-five percent (75%) on the Colorado specific education examination.

5. The twenty (20) hours of pre-licensing education must be satisfactorily completed within the three (3) year period immediately preceding the date of application for licensure.

E. Successful completion of the S.A.F.E. Mortgage Loan Originator examination, developed by the Nationwide Mortgage Licensing System and Registry, consisting of two sections. These two sections include a national component and a Uniform State Test (UST) component. An individual shall pass the test in accordance with policies and procedures developed and administered by the Nationwide Mortgage Licensing System and Registry and in compliance with the S.A.F.E. Mortgage Licensing Act;

* F. Acquisition of a surety bond as required by § 12-10-707, C.R.S. and in accordance with any rule of the Board that directly or indirectly addresses surety bond requirements;

* G. Acquisition of the errors and omissions insurance required by § 12-10-707, C.R.S. and in accordance with any rule of the Board that directly or indirectly addresses errors and omissions insurance requirements;

H. Completion of the Colorado Division of Real Estate specific Mortgage Loan Originator Application; and

I. Payment of the application fee established by the Board and is non-refundable.

2.2 Authority to audit education provider

The Board or the Board's designee may audit any mortgage loan originator courses offered and may request from each education provider or schools offering such courses, all related instructional materials, student attendance records and other information that may be necessary for an audit. Failure to comply with this rule may result in the withdrawal of course approval.

2.3 Retesting

A. An individual may retake a test three (3) consecutive times with each consecutive taking occurring at least thirty (30) days after the preceding test.

B. After failing three (3) consecutive tests, an individual shall wait at least six (6) months before taking the test again.

C. Individuals who fail to maintain a valid license for a period of five (5) years or longer shall retake the test prior to re-application, not taking into account any time during which such individual was licensed.

* 2.4 Temporary authority and Colorado temporary license

* An applicant applying for mortgage loan originator temporary license that is eligible for temporary authority must meet the following requirements:

* A. Submit a set of fingerprints to the Nationwide Multistate Licensing System and Registry (NMLS) in accordance with policies and procedures as established by the NMLS.

* B. Must be eligible for temporary authority with the NMLS in accordance with policies and procedures as established by the NMLS.

* C. Applicant must be employed and sponsored by a Colorado NMLS registered mortgage company.

*   D.   Applicant has not had any of the following:

*   1.   An application for a mortgage loan originator license denied in any jurisdiction;

*   2.   A mortgage loan originator license revoked or suspended in any jurisdiction;

*   3.   Has been subject to, or served with a cease and desist order; and

*   4.   Has been convicted of, or pled guilty or nolo contendere to, a misdemeanor or felony pursuant to sections 12-10-711(1)(b), (2)(b)(I), and (2)(c), C.R.S.

*   E.   Applicant has met either one of the following:

*   1.   Registered in the NMLS as a loan originator for a depository (i.e. bank or savings association) as defined in section 12-10-709(1)(b), C.R.S. during the one (1) year period preceding the date of application for a temporary license; or

*   2.   A license issued as a mortgage loan originator in another jurisdiction during the thirty (30) day period preceding the date of application for a temporary license.

*   F.   Applicant will have seven (7) business days from notice of issuance of temporary authority from the NMLS to submit the Colorado Division of Real Estate's "Mortgage Loan Originator License Application" which includes the following state specific requirements pursuant to section 12-10-711(11), C.R.S.:

*   1.   Submit a set of fingerprints for the purposes of a criminal history check to the Colorado Bureau of Investigations (CBI).

*   2.   Acquisition of a surety bond pursuant to section 12-10-717, C.R.S. and in accordance with any rule of the Board that directly or indirectly addresses surety bond requirements.

*   3.   Acquisition of the errors and omissions insurance pursuant to section 12-10-707, C.R.S. and in accordance with any rule of the Board that directly or indirectly addresses errors and omissions insurance requirements.

*   4.   Applicant must identify the responsible Colorado licensed mortgage loan originator ("Responsible Mortgage Loan Originator") who is responsible for the supervision of the applicant during the time they hold an active mortgage loan originator temporary license.

*   5.   Payment of the non-refundable application fee as established by the Board.

* 2.5   A mortgage loan originator holding a temporary license must be employed and sponsored by a Colorado NMLS registered mortgage company and must be supervised by a Responsible Mortgage Loan Originator licensed in Colorado.

*   A.   The Responsible Mortgage Loan Originator will be held responsible under all applicable provisions of law, including without limitation this Part 7 and § 38-40-105, C.R.S., for the actions of the mortgage loan originator holding a temporary license, and are personally subject to all applicable penalties under the law.

*   B.   Responsible Mortgage Loan Originators must notify the Division of Real Estate, in a manner acceptable to the Board, the beginning and ending dates of supervision for mortgage loan originators holding a temporary license.

*   C.   Responsible Mortgage Loan Originators will be held responsible for the activities of mortgage loan originators holding a temporary license through and including the date of the temporary license expiration or termination of supervision, whichever is sooner.

* 2.6   A mortgage loan originator temporary license will expire on one of the following dates, whichever is sooner:

*   A.   Applicant withdraws their application for a Colorado mortgage loan originator license;

*   B.   The Board denies the applicant's application for a Colorado mortgage loan originator license;

*   C.   The Board approves and issues a Colorado mortgage loan originator license;

*   D.   Supervision termination date between the Responsible Mortgage Loan Originator and the mortgage loan originator holding a temporary license; or

*   E.   One hundred twenty (120) days after the date the applicant was issued a temporary license.

*   2.7   Applicants seeking a temporary license will be granted one (1) mortgage loan originator temporary license providing the applicant meets all of the requirements as set forth in these rules. Additional or extended temporary licenses will be prohibited.

*   2.8   REPEALED (11/24/2019)

*   2.9   Any mortgage loan originator temporary license issued by the Board will have the same force and effect of the license pursuant to section 12-10-701, et seq., C.R.S. for the period of time it is in effect.

*   2.10   Once the applicant fully complies with the terms of the law as determined by the Board, the Board will license the applicant in accordance with section 12-10-704, C.R.S.

2.11   Preliminary advisory opinion

Potential applicants for a state license or a registration through the Nationwide Mortgage Licensing System and Registry may submit information in order for the Board or an authorized representative of the Board to reasonably ascertain the likelihood of license or registration approval through a defined preliminary advisory opinion process.

2.12   Potential applicants may request a preliminary advisory opinion for any of the following reasons:

     A.   If the individual has been convicted, plead guilty or nolo contendere to any crime in a domestic, foreign or military court.

     B.   If the individual has been enjoined in the immediately preceding five (5) years under domestic or foreign laws from engaging in deceptive conduct relating to the origination of a mortgage loan;

     C.   If the individual has had other professional licenses, certifications or registrations issued by Colorado, the District of Columbia, any other states or foreign countries, revoked or suspended for fraud, theft, deceit, material misrepresentations or the breach of a fiduciary duty and such suspension or revocation denied authorization to practices as: a mortgage loan originator or similar license; real estate broker; real estate appraiser; an insurance producer; an attorney; a securities broker-dealer; a securities sales representative; an investment advisor; or an investment advisor representative; or

     D.   If the individual has been assessed a civil or criminal penalty for violating any provision of the Colorado Consumer Protection Act.

2.13   Individuals requesting a preliminary advisory opinion shall complete the Preliminary Advisory Application located on the Division of Real Estate's website.

2.14   Individuals requesting a preliminary advisory opinion shall submit all corresponding, or relevant documents related to any conduct or actions as set forth in Rule 2.12. Incomplete requests will not be processed.

The Board or an authorized representative of the Board may, at any time, request additional information regarding the preliminary advisory opinion request. Such corresponding, relevant or related documents may include, but are not limited to:

     A.   Police officer reports;

     B.   Dispositions documents;

     C.   Court documents;

     D.   Original charges documents;

E.   Stipulated agreements; or

F.   Final Agency Orders.

2.15   individuals requesting a preliminary advisory opinion shall submit a written and signed personal explanation and detailed account of the facts and circumstances.

2.16   Any preliminary advisory opinion shall not be binding on the Board or limit the Board's authority to investigate a future formal application for licensure.

2.17   An individual seeking a preliminary advisory opinion is not an applicant for licensure and the issuance of an unfavorable opinion shall not prevent such individual from making application for licensure pursuant to the Mortgage Loan Originator Licensing Act.

2.18   The Board or an authorized representative of the Board will provide a favorable or an unfavorable opinion.

2.19   Surety bond

Mortgage loan originators are deemed compliant with the surety bond requirement if their surety bond meets the requirements defined in one of the following options:

A.   Mortgage loan originators, at a minimum, may acquire and maintain an individual surety bond if:

     1.   The surety bond is in the amount of $25,000.00;

     2.   The surety bond is in conformance with all relevant Colorado statutory requirements;

     3.   The surety bond is exclusive to covering acts contemplated under current Colorado mortgage loan originator licensing laws;

     4.   The surety bond is not applicable to any conduct or transactions outside the jurisdiction of the Board; and

     5.   The surety bond is identical to the individual surety bond form developed and approved by the Board.

B.   Mortgage loan originators who are W-2 employees or exclusive agents for companies with less than 20 individuals who are required to be licensed pursuant to current Colorado mortgage loan originator licensing laws and who do not work for more than one company, may, at a minimum, operate under their company's surety bond if the surety bond meets the following criteria:

     1.   The surety bond is in the amount of $100,000.00;

     2.   The surety bond is in conformance with all relevant Colorado statutory requirements;

     3.   The surety bond is exclusive to covering acts of all of the company's W-2 employees or exclusive agents contemplated under current Colorado mortgage loan originator licensing laws; and

     4.   The surety bond is identical to the individual surety bond form developed and approved by the Board.

C.   Mortgage loan originators who are W-2 employees or exclusive agents for companies with 20 or more individuals who are required to be licensed pursuant to current Colorado mortgage loan originator licensing laws and who do not work for more than one company, may, at a minimum, operate under a company's surety bond if the surety bond meets the following criteria:

     1.   The surety bond is in the amount of $200,000.00;

     2.   The surety bond is in conformance with all relevant Colorado statutory requirements;

     3.   The surety bond is exclusive to covering acts of all of the company's W-2 employees or exclusive agents contemplated under current Colorado mortgage loan originator licensing laws; and

4. The surety bond is identical to the company surety bond form developed and approved by the Board.

2.20 Regarding company surety bonds, the company shall provide the Board or an authorized representative of the Board with any and all requested surety bonds relevant to Rule 2.19 or current mortgage loan originator license laws and shall verify and provide adequate proof regarding the timeline of employment for each individual operating under such company policy. Failure on the part of the company to provide such information shall result in non-compliance regarding the surety bond requirement for individual licensees operating under such company bond.

2.21 Mortgage loan originators shall be required to provide proof of continuous surety bond coverage and that all required information is current. The mortgage loan originator may update all required information electronically on the Division of Real Estate's website.

2.22 Any licensee who so fails to obtain and maintain a surety bond in accordance with Board Rules or fails to provide proof of continuous coverage shall be subject to disciplinary action.

2.23 Errors and Omissions Insurance

Mortgage loan originators may obtain errors and omissions coverage from the qualified insurance carrier contracted with the Board of Mortgage Loan Originators to offer licensees and license applicants a group policy of insurance or licensees and applicants may obtain errors and omissions coverage independent of the group plan. Mortgage loan originators are deemed compliant with the errors and omissions insurance requirements if their errors and omissions insurance meets the requirements defined in one of the following options:

A. Mortgage loan originators, at a minimum, may acquire and maintain individual errors and omissions insurance in their own name with the following terms of coverage:

1. The contract and policy are in conformance with all relevant Colorado statutory requirements;

2. Coverage includes all acts for which a mortgage loan originator license is required, except those illegal, fraudulent, or other acts which are normally excluded from such coverage;

3. Coverage shall encompass all types of transactions conducted by the mortgage loan originator and shall be in the individual mortgage loan originator's name;

4. Coverage is for not less than $100,000 for each licensed individual per covered claim, with an annual aggregate limit of not less than $300,000 per licensed individual, not including costs of investigation and defense; and

5. Coverage contains a deductible no greater than $1,000, or a deductible no greater than $20,000 for policies that primarily insure reverse mortgage transactions.

6. Prior acts coverage shall be offered to licensees with continuous past coverage.

B. Mortgage loan originators who are employees or exclusive agents for companies with less than 20 individuals who are required to be licensed pursuant to the current Colorado mortgage loan originator licensing laws and who do not work for more than one company, may, at a minimum, operate under the company's errors and omissions insurance policy if the policy meets the following terms of coverage:

1. The contract and policy are in conformance with all relevant Colorado statutory requirements;

2. Coverage includes all acts for which a mortgage loan originator license is required, except those illegal, fraudulent, or other acts which are normally excluded from such coverage;

3. Coverage shall include all activities contemplated under current Colorado mortgage loan originator licensing laws and states this in the policy;

4.   Coverage shall encompass all types of transactions conducted by all of the mortgage loan originators employed at the company or by all mortgage loan originators who are exclusive agents of the company;

5.   Coverage is for not less than $1,000,000 per covered claim, with an annual aggregate limit of not less than $1,000,000, not including costs of investigation and defense; and

6.   Coverage contains a deductible no greater than $50,000.

7.   Prior acts coverage shall be offered to licensees with continuous past coverage.

C.   Mortgage loan originators who are W-2 employees or exclusive agents for companies with 20 or more employees and who do not work for more than one company, may, at a minimum, operate under the company's errors and omissions insurance policy if the policy meets the following terms of coverage:

1.   The contract and policy are in conformance with all relevant Colorado statutory requirements;

2.   Coverage includes all acts for which a mortgage loan originator license is required, except those illegal, fraudulent, or other acts which are normally excluded from such coverage;

3.   Coverage shall include all activities contemplated under current Colorado mortgage loan originator licensing laws and states this in the policy;

4.   Coverage shall encompass all types of transactions conducted by all of the mortgage loan originators employed at the company or by all mortgage loan originators who are exclusive agents of the company;

5.   Coverage shall encompass all types of transactions conducted by all of the mortgage loan originators employed at the company;

6.   Coverage is for not less than $1,000,000 per covered claim, with an annual aggregate limit of not less than $2,000,000 not including costs of investigation and defense; and

7.   Coverage contains a deductible no greater than $100,000.

8.   Prior acts coverage shall be offered to licensees with continuous past coverage.

2.24   Regarding company errors and omissions insurance policies, the company shall provide the Board, or an authorized representative of the Board, with any and all requested errors and omissions insurance policies relevant to Rule 2.23 or current Colorado mortgage loan originator licensing laws and shall verify and provide adequate proof regarding the timeline of employment for each individual operating under such company policy. Failure on the part of the company to provide such information shall result in non-compliance regarding the errors and omissions insurance requirement for individual licensees operating under the company's errors and omissions insurance policy.

2.25   Mortgage loan originators shall be required to provide proof of continuous errors and omissions insurance coverage and that all required information is current. The mortgage loan originator may update all required information electronically on the Division of Real Estate's website.

2.26   Any licensee who so fails to obtain and maintain an errors and omissions insurance coverage in accordance with Board rules or fails to provide proof of continuous coverage shall be subject to disciplinary action.

CHAPTER 3: CONTINUING EDUCATION REQUIREMENTS

3.1   The continuing education requirements for licensed individuals shall begin after issuance of the initial license. Individuals shall complete at least eight (8) hours of continuing education courses, which must include one (1) hour of Colorado specific education, reviewed and approved by the Nationwide Mortgage Licensing System and Registry or by a company contracted to review and approve continuing education courses. The Colorado specific education may replace what was a required general elective within the eight (8) hour continuing education course or may be completed as a standalone course. The continuing education requirements must be completed each calendar year and prior to license and registration renewals or reinstatements.

3.2 Completion of the 20 hours of pre-licensing education approved by the Nationwide Mortgage Licensing System and Registry in the same year in which the license was approved, shall satisfy the continuing education requirements in that calendar year.

3.3 Repealed.

3.4 Repealed.

3.5 Authority to audit education provider

The Board or the Board's designee may audit any Colorado specific education course reviewed and approved by the Nationwide Mortgage Licensing System and Registry or by a company contracted to review and approve continuing education courses. The Board or the Board's designee may request from each education provider or schools offering such courses, all related instructional materials, student attendance records and other information that may be necessary for an audit. Failure to comply with this rule may result in the withdrawal of course approval.

CHAPTER 4: RENEWAL, REINSTATEMENT, INACTIVATION, SUSPENSION, SURRENDER OR REVOCATION OF A LICENSE OR REGISTRATION

4.1 Renewal process for active licensees.

A. There are two existing databases that licensees shall independently renew their license through annually. The two independent databases include:

1. The license database managed by the Division of Real Estate. This database may be located by visiting the Division of Real Estate's website.

2. The registration database managed by the Nationwide Mortgage Licensing System and Registry.

B. Mortgage loan originators renewing, reinstating or re-applying for registration through the Nationwide Mortgage Licensing System and Registry shall do so in accordance with established timelines, policies and procedures set forth by the Nationwide Mortgage Licensing System and Registry. The Nationwide Mortgage Licensing System and Registry may collect fees for the purpose of registration applications, renewal applications, reinstatement applications, credit reports, criminal background checks and for other processes associated with registration through the Nationwide database.

C. The Board shall issue or deny a license renewal or reinstatement application within thirty days after the applicant has submitted all of the information necessary for license renewal or reinstatement and after the Board has received all information necessary to make a determination regarding the applicants' compliance.

D. Regarding the license database managed by the Division of Real Estate, mortgage loan originators may renew or reinstate their license online or may do so by submitting a paper renewal or reinstatement application.

E. For both databases, the license renewal period begins November 1st of each calendar year and ends December 31st of each calendar year. Individuals who renew their license shall only do so if they are compliant with all provisions of the mortgage loan originator licensing act and all Board Rules.

F. All licenses expire at 12 midnight on December 31st of each calendar year if the licensee has not properly renewed their license.

G.   If a license has expired, individuals may choose to reinstate their mortgage loan originator license. The reinstatement period for both databases begins January 1st of each calendar year and ends on the last day of February of each calendar year. Individuals who reinstate their license shall only do so if they are compliant with all provisions of the mortgage loan originator licensing act and all Board Rules.

H.   Individuals who fail to renew or reinstate their license shall re-apply in the manner set forth in Rule 4.3.

I.   All renewal, reinstatement or application fees shall be prescribed by the Board. All fees collected for the purpose of applying for license renewal, reinstatement or re-application are non-refundable.

4.2   Renewal process for inactive licensees.

A.   Individuals with inactive licenses shall renew their license annually in the manner set forth in Rule 4.1. Individuals with inactive licenses are not required to maintain compliant errors and omissions insurance or a compliant surety bond, but they are required to stay current on all continuing education requirements in order to renew their license.

B.   The fee for reinstatement is one and one half times the amount of the current renewal fee.

4.3   Re-application.

A.   Individuals who fail to maintain an active valid license for at least three (3) years must satisfactorily complete the twenty (20) hours of pre-licensing education within the three (3) year period immediately preceding the date of application for licensure.

B.   Individuals who fail to maintain a valid license for a period of up to five (5) years after the date of license expiration and were compliant with the annual continuing education requirements at the time of license expiration must complete the following:

1.   Comply with the requirements set forth in section (A) of this Rule (if applicable);

2.   Register with the Nationwide Mortgage Licensing System and Registry in accordance with policies and procedures established by the Nationwide Mortgage Licensing System and Registry. This includes, but is not limited to completion of the correct registration application, authorization for the registry to pull a credit report and payment of any fees associated with registration;

3.   Submit fingerprints to the Nationwide Mortgage Licensing System and Registry in accordance with policies and procedures established by the Nationwide Mortgage Licensing System and Registry;

4.   Obtain a compliant surety bond in accordance with Section 12-10-717, C.R.S. and Board Rule 2.19;

5.   Obtain compliant errors and omissions insurance in accordance with Section 12-10-707, C.R.S. and Board Rule 2.23; and

6.   Complete the Colorado Division of Real Estate specific application and pay the application fee.

C.   Individuals who fail to maintain a valid license for a period of up to five (5) years after the date of license expiration and who were not compliant with the annual continuing education requirements at the time of license expiration must complete the following:

1.   Comply with all requirements set forth in section (B), subsection (1) to (6) of this Rule, and

2.   Complete at least eight (8) hours of "late" continuing education courses, which must include one (1) hour of Colorado specific education, reviewed and approved by the Nationwide Mortgage Licensing System and Registry or by a company contracted to review and approve continuing education courses;

    D.   Individuals who fail to maintain a valid license for a period of more than five (5) years after the date of license expiration must complete the following:

        1.   Comply with all requirements set forth in section (C), subsection (1) and (2) of this Rule; and

        2.   Retake and successfully pass the S.A.F.E. Mortgage Loan Originator examination, developed by the Nationwide Mortgage Licensing System and Registry, consisting of two sections. These two sections include a national component and a Uniform State Test (UST) component. An individual shall pass the test in accordance with policies and procedures developed and administered by the Nationwide Mortgage Licensing System and Registry and in compliance with the S.A.F.E. Mortgage Licensing Act.

4.4   Individuals who do not have an active license are prohibited from practicing as a mortgage loan originator. Additionally, individuals who do not have an active license are prohibited from engaging in any mortgage related activities which require licensure pursuant to the Colorado mortgage loan originator licensing and Mortgage Company Registration Act, Board rule or as prescribed by Board position statement.

4.5   Renewal process for mortgage companies.

    A.   Mortgage companies shall renew the registration on the Nationwide Mortgage Licensing System and Registry.

    B.   Mortgage companies renewing, reinstating or re-applying for registration through the Nationwide Mortgage Licensing System and registry shall do so in accordance with established timelines, policies and procedures set forth by the Nationwide Mortgage Licensing System and Registry. The Nationwide Mortgage Licensing System and Registry may collect fees for the purpose of registration applications, renewal applications, reinstatement applications, credit reports, criminal background checks and for other processes associated with registration through the Nationwide database.

    C.   The Board shall issue or deny a registration renewal application within thirty days after the applicant has submitted all of the information necessary for license renewal or reinstatement and after the board has received all information necessary to make a determination regarding the applicants' compliance.

    D.   The registration renewal period begins November 1st of each calendar year and ends December 31st of each calendar year. Mortgage companies that renew or reinstate their license shall only do so if they are compliant with all provisions of the mortgage loan originator licensing and mortgage company registration act and all Board rules.

    E.   All registrations expire at 12 midnight on December 31st of each calendar year if the licensee has not properly renewed their license.

    F.   If a license has expired, mortgage companies may choose to reinstate their registration. The reinstatement period for reinstatement begins January 1st of each calendar year and ends on the last day of February of each calendar year. Mortgage companies that reinstate their registration shall only do so if they are compliant with all provisions of the mortgage loan originator licensing and mortgage company registration act and all Board Rules.

    G.   Mortgage companies that fail to renew or reinstate their registration shall re-apply on the Nationwide Mortgage Licensing System and Registry in order for the Division of Real Estate to review their applications and determine whether the mortgage company is compliant with the registration requirements.

    H.   All renewal, reinstatement or application fees shall be prescribed by the Board and are non-refundable.

4.6   Mortgage companies that do not have an approved registration are prohibited from acting through employees or other individuals who takes residential loan applications or offers or negotiates terms of a residential mortgage loan. Additionally, mortgage companies that do not have an approved registration are prohibited from engaging in any mortgage related conduct that requires a registration pursuant to the mortgage loan originator licensing and mortgage company registration act, Board Rule or as prescribed by the Board by Position Statement.

4.7   Mortgage loan originator license inactivation and reactivation

If a mortgage loan originator license or registration is inactivated by the Board of mortgage loan originators or an authorized representative of the Board for one or any combination of the following reasons, the mortgage loan originator shall pay an administrative fee determined by the board in order to reactivate their license:

* A.   The mortgage loan originator has failed or is failing to comply with the surety bond requirements of section 12-10-704(8), C.R.S. Section 12-10-717, C.R.S. or any rule of the Board that directly or indirectly addresses surety bond requirements;

* B.   The mortgage loan originator has failed or is failing to comply with the errors and omissions insurance requirement in Section 12-10-707, C.R.S. or any Rule of the Board that directly or indirectly addresses errors and omissions insurance requirements;

* C.   The mortgage loan originator has failed or is failing to maintain current contact information, surety bond information, or errors and omissions insurance information as required by this Part 7 or by any Rule of the Board that directly or indirectly addresses such requirements;

   D.   The mortgage loan originator has failed or is failing to respond to an investigation or examination;

* E.   The mortgage loan originator has failed or is failing to comply with any of the education or testing requirements set forth in this Part 7 or in any rule of the Board that directly or indirectly addresses education or testing requirements; or

   F.   The mortgage loan originator has failed or is failing to register with and provide all required information to the Nationwide Mortgage Licensing System and Registry.

4.8   Individuals who have an inactive license or registration are prohibited from practicing as a mortgage loan originator. Additionally, individuals who have an inactive license or registration are prohibited from engaging in any mortgage related activities which requires licensure pursuant to the Colorado mortgage loan originator licensing and mortgage company registration act, Board rule or as prescribed by Board position statement.

4.9   In order for an inactive mortgage loan originator license or registration to be reactivated, the individual seeking reactivation shall provide the Division of Real Estate with proof of full compliance with current mortgage loan originator license law.

4.10   The Board has created the mortgage loan originator license reactivation form and this form may be found on the Division of Real Estate's website.

CHAPTER 5: PROFESSIONAL STANDARDS

5.1   Advertising

* Any advertisement of a residential mortgage loan product or rate offered by a mortgage loan originator as that term is defined in § 12-10-702(14), C.R.S., or mortgage company as that term is defined in § 12-10-702(12), C.R.S., shall conform to the following requirements:

   A.   An advertisement shall be made only for such products and terms as are actually available at the time they are offered and, if their availability is subject to any material requirements or limitations, the advertisement shall specify those requirements or limitations;

   B.   The advertisement shall contain the following, each of which must be clearly and conspicuously included in the advertisement;

1. At least one (1) responsible party. The responsible party must be an individual person or a mortgage company. The responsible party must include their registration number that is approved on the Nationwide Mortgage Licensing System and Registry (NMLS);

2. The mortgage company name; and

3. The business phone number of the responsible party.

C. The advertisement shall not appear to be offered by a government agency, a quasi-government agency or the perspective borrower's current lender and/or loan servicer;

D. An advertisement shall not make or omit any statement the result of which would be to present a misleading or deceptive impression to consumers;

E. An advertisement shall otherwise comply with all applicable state and federal disclosure requirements;

F. Advertisements shall incorporate applicable provisions of the final Interagency Guidance on Nontraditional Mortgage Product Risks ("Interagency Guidance") released on September 29, 2006, incorporated by reference in compliance with Section 24-4-103(12.5), C.R.S., and does not include any later amendments or editions of the final guidance. A certified copy of the Interagency Guidance is readily available for public inspection at the offices of the Board of Mortgage Loan Originators at 1560 Broadway, Suite 925, Denver, Colorado. The Interagency Guidance released by the Office of the Comptroller of the Currency, the Board of Governors of the Federal Reserve System, the Federal Deposit Insurance Corporation, the Office of Thrift supervision, and the National Credit Union Administration can be examined at the internet website of the federal register (volume 71, number 192, page 58609-58618) at www.federalregister.gov. Reference copies of the federal register publications may also be found at the Colorado Supreme Court, located at 101 w. Colfax, Denver, Colorado 80202 or by telephone at (303) 837-3720; and

G. The responsible party must retain copies of all advertisements for a period of four (4) years, and provide said copies for inspection by an authorized representative of the Board upon request.

5.2 The requirements set forth in Rule 5.1(b), Subsections one (1) through three (3) shall not apply to:

A. Any advertisement which indirectly promotes a credit transaction and which contains only the name of the mortgage company, the name and title of the mortgage loan originator, the contact information for the mortgage company or the mortgage loan originator, a mortgage company logo, or any license or registration numbers, such as the inscription on a coffee mug, pen, pencil, youth league jersey, sign, business card, or other promotional item; or

B. Any rate sheet, pricing sheet, or similar proprietary information provided to real estate brokers, builders, and other commercial entities that is not intended for distribution to consumers.

5.3 Loan Modifier Licensure

A. Individuals, not otherwise exempt from Part 7, who directly or indirectly take residential loan modification applications or who negotiate, offer, or attempt to negotiate or offer loan modifications are required to be licensed as a Colorado Mortgage Loan Originator.

B. All individuals required to be licensed shall comply with all other provisions of the Colorado Mortgage Loan Originator Licensing Act and all Board Rules.

5.4 Required Use of a Loan Modification Contract

A.   Individuals taking loan modification applications or offering or negotiating loan modifications are required to use a loan modification contract which complies with the Mortgage Loan Originator Licensing Act and the Foreclosure Protection Act.

B.   The Board has created the Colorado Loan Modification Services Contract to ensure compliance with the aforementioned laws. This contract may be found on the Division of Real Estate's website. Loan modifiers shall use this form or an alternate form, if such alternate form clearly includes all information required on the suggested form, as determined by the Board.

C.   The Colorado Loan Modification Services contract prescribed by this rule shall be completed at time of application.

5.5   The Requirements Set Forth in Rules 5.3 and 5.4 Shall Not Apply to:

A.   Employees of HUD approved housing counseling agencies who are providing advice or general information on loan modifications in an ancillary manner relating to their general housing counseling services or duties.

B.   Employees of mortgage loan servicing companies operating on behalf of the borrowers' mortgage lenders.

C.   Licensed Real Estate Brokers engaged in licensed activities when performing services within the defined short sale transactions do not need to maintain a license as a mortgage loan originator. If a real estate broker engages in the activities of providing loan modification services (those not included in the activities of short sales) as defined, loan modification services are defined as outside the scope of licensed real estate broker activities and therefore, separate licensure as a mortgage loan originator is required.

*   D.   An attorney, as set forth in Section 12-10-709(1)(c), C.R.S., who renders services in the course of practice, who is licensed in Colorado, and who is not primarily engaged in the business of negotiating residential mortgage loans or loan modifications is not required to be licensed as a mortgage loan originator, but is required to comply with all non-licensing provisions of current mortgage loan originator law set forth in Sections 12-10-701 through 12-10-726, C.R.S.

5.6   Reasonable Inquiry

A.   A mortgage loan originator shall only recommend appropriate products after reasonable inquiry has been made in order to understand borrower's current and prospective financial status.

B.   Reasonable inquiry requires the mortgage loan originator to interview and discuss current and prospective income, including the income's source and likely continuance, with borrowers, and may not require the mortgage loan originator to verify such income.

C.   A mortgage loan originator has a duty to recommend mortgage products based on the information provided by the borrower.

*   D.   A mortgage loan originator shall be deemed in compliance with this rule and Colorado law, § 12-10-710(1)(b), C.R.S., concerning reasonable inquiry, upon interviewing and discussing, with all applicable borrowers, all sections contained in the uniform residential loan application and upon completion of a tangible net benefit disclosure. The tangible net benefit disclosure is posted on the Division of Real Estate's website.

5.7   Tangible Net Benefit

*   The reasonable, Tangible Net Benefit Standard in § 12-10-710(1)(a), C.R.S., is inherently dependent upon the totality of facts and circumstances relating to a specific transaction. While the refinancing of certain home loans may clearly provide a reasonable, tangible net benefit, others may require closer scrutiny or consideration to determine whether a particular loan provides the requisite benefit to the borrower.

A. When determining reasonable, tangible net benefit, there are many considerations a mortgage loan originator shall take into account and discuss with prospective borrowers. If applicable, the required considerations for a mortgage loan originator determining the requisite benefit shall include, but are not limited to:

1. Lower payments;
2. Condensed amortization schedule;
3. Debt consolidation;
4. Cash out;
5. Avoiding foreclosure;
6. Negative amortization;
7. Balloon payments;
8. Variable rates;
9. Interest only options;
10. Prepayment penalties; and
11. Hybrid mortgage products.

B. The purpose or reason for a purchase or refinance transaction shall be identified by the borrower. A mortgage loan originator shall require that all borrowers describe, in writing, the reasons they are seeking a mortgage loan, a loan modification or to refinance an existing mortgage loan.

1. It is the responsibility of the mortgage loan originator to ensure this information is acquired and accurately documented.

2. Pursuant to § 12-10-710(1), C.R.S., a mortgage loan originator may not have demonstrated a duty of good faith and fair dealing in all communications and transactions with a borrower if it is determined that a mortgage loan originator completed the required purpose or reason for a purchase, loan modification or refinance transaction without consulting the borrower.

5.8 Tangible Net Benefit Disclosure Form

The Board developed a disclosure form regarding reasonable, tangible net benefit. Alternate disclosures are acceptable if they include all information required on the suggested form, as determined by the Board.

A. At the time of completing a loan application the mortgage loan originator shall complete a Tangible Net Benefit Disclosure with the borrower(s).

B. The Tangible Net Benefit Disclosure shall also be completed with the borrower(s) prior to the borrower(s) signing loan closing documents if the reasonable, tangible net benefit has changed.

C. Tangible Net Benefit Disclosures shall be signed by both the mortgage loan originator and the borrowers.

D. A mortgage loan originator shall provide copies of completed disclosure forms to all borrowers within three (3) business days after receipt of a loan application or any moneys from a borrower. Furthermore, the mortgage loan originator must be able to provide proof to the Board or an authorized representative of the Board that the disclosure forms defined in this rule were in fact provided to the borrower within three (3) business days after receipt of a loan application, any moneys from a borrower or any subsequent changes to any loan terms requiring re-disclosure.

5.9 Mortgage Loan Originator and Mortgage Company Duty to Respond and Provide Requested Documents for Investigations

* A. Persons required to be licensed or mortgage companies required to be registered pursuant to §§ 12-10-704 and 12-10-705, C.R.S., shall provide the Board or the Board's representative with all information required by this rule.

   1. Failure to provide all information requested by the Board or an authorized representative of the Board within a timeline established by the Board, or authorized representative of the Board, shall be grounds for disciplinary action and grounds for the imposition of fines unless the Board, or authorized representative of the Board, has granted an extension of time for the response.

      a. The mortgage loan originator and mortgage company may ask for an extension of time to comply if:

         i. The request is done so in writing; and

         ii. The request is received by the Board or authorized representative of the Board prior to the expiration date defined in the notification letter sent by the Board or authorized representative of the Board.

      b. Any and all extensions granted are done so at the discretion of the Board or an authorized representative of the Board.

   2. Failure to provide all requested information shall be grounds for disciplinary action and grounds for the imposition of fines regardless of whether the underlying complaint results in further investigation or subsequent action by the Board.

B. The response from the person shall contain the following:

   1. If requested in the notification letter, the mortgage loan originator shall provide a complete and specific answer to the factual recitations, allegations or averments made in the complaint filed against the licensee, whether made by a member of the public or on the Board's own motion or by an authorized representative of the Board;

   2. The mortgage loan originator shall provide a complete and specific response to all questions, allegations or averments presented in the notification letter; and

   3. Any and all documents or records requested in the notification letter.

C. Mortgage companies shall maintain any and all documents collected, gathered and provided for the purpose of negotiating and originating residential mortgage loans for a period of four years. Additionally, mortgage companies shall maintain any and all documents used for the purpose of soliciting or marketing borrowers that were directed, made or caused to be made by the mortgage company. These documents include but are not limited to:

   1. All uniform residential loan applications (form 1003);

   2. All required state and federal disclosures;

   3. Asset statements;

   4. Income documentation;

   5. Verification of employment;

   6. Verification of deposit;

   7. Lender submission forms;

   8. Advertisements;

   9. Flyers;

   10. HUD-1 settlement statements;

   11. Uniform underwriting and transmittal summary(form 1008); and

   12. Credit report.

D. The mortgage loan originator shall maintain any and all documents used for the purpose of soliciting or marketing borrowers that were directed, made or caused to be made by the mortgage loan originator.

E. All documents required in this rule shall be kept in a safe and secure manner. Electronic storage is acceptable as long as the information is accessible and kept in a safe and secure manner.

5.10 Mortgage Loan Originators Maintaining Current Contact Information and All Information Required for Licensing

A. Individuals required to be licensed as a state licensed loan originator shall maintain all current contact information and all information required for licensing, in a manner acceptable to the Board, including on the Division of Real Estate database and on the Nationwide Mortgage Licensing System and Registry. Failure to maintain the information identified in this rule shall be grounds for disciplinary action.

B. Contact information shall include, but is not limited to:

1. E-mail address;

2. Legal first, middle and last names;

3. Physical home address;

4. Home phone number;

5. Business address;

6. Business phone number; and

7. Business name.

C. Information required for licensing includes, but is not limited to:

1. Surety bond company;

2. Surety bond number;

3. Surety bond effective date;

4. Errors and omissions insurance provider;

5. Errors and omissions policy number;

6. Errors and omissions effective and expiration date; and

7. Convictions, pleas of guilt or nolo contendere for all crimes.

D. Individuals required to be licensed as a state licensed loan originator shall update the Board within thirty (30) days of any changes to the information defined in this rule on both the Division of Real Estate database and on the Nationwide Mortgage Licensing System and Registry.

5.11 Repealed (Effective March 17, 2017).

5.12 Mortgage Loan Originator Agreements

A mortgage loan originator shall have a written correspondent or loan originator agreement with a lender before any solicitation of, or contracting with, any member of the public. A mortgage loan originator is compliant with this rule and Sections 12-10-713(1)(x) and (aa), C.R.S., if they adhere to one of the following requirements:

A. They individually have a written correspondent or loan originator agreement with a lender before any solicitation of, or contracting with, any member of the public;

B. They are an officer, partner, member, exclusive agent, or employee of a company that has a written correspondent or loan originator agreement with a lender before any solicitation of, or contracting with, any member of the public;

C.   They are acting as an independent contractor and maintain a contractual agreement with a company that has a written correspondent or loan originator agreement with a lender before any solicitation of, or contracting with, any member of the public; or

D.   They are an employee of a lender before any solicitation of, or contracting with, any member of the public.

5.13   Repealed (Effective March 17, 2017).

*   5.14   Colorado specific Lock-in Disclosure requirements under Section 12-10-725(2), C.R.S.

A.   The Colorado Lock-in Disclosure form must be used for all transactions not under the authority of the TILA-RESPA Integrated Disclosure Rule and for which the applicable GFE, HUD-1 and Truth-in-Lending Disclosures are used.

B.   The Colorado Lock-in Disclosure form must be disclosed:

    1.   Within three (3) business days after receipt of a loan application and if applicable, contain the following information:

      a.   The cost, terms, duration and conditions of the lock-in agreement;

      b.   Whether a lock-in agreement has been entered;

      c.   Whether the lock-in agreement is guaranteed by the mortgage loan originator; and

      d.   Disclosure must be made if a lock-in agreement has not been entered and that the interest rate and terms are subject to change.

    2.   If, after the initial written disclosure is provided, a mortgage loan originator enters into a lock-in agreement, within three (3) business days thereafter and prior to the borrower signing loan closing documents.

    3.   If, after a mortgage loan originator enters into a lock-in agreement, the annual percentage rate increases from the annual percentage rate disclosed earlier by more than 1/8 of one (1) percentage point, within three (3) business days of such change and prior to the borrower signing loan closing documents.

    4.   If, after the mortgage loan originator enters into a lock-in agreement, there is a change to any of the information provided on the lock-in disclosure form, including but not limited to a lock-in extension.

C.   The Colorado lock-in Disclosure form or alternate form shall be used when disclosing the secured rate of interest for the prospective borrower or disclosing that the interest rate is not secured and is subject to change.

5.15   Repealed.

5.16   Repealed.

5.17   Repealed (Effective March 17, 2017).

5.18   Repealed.

5.19   Repealed.

5.20   Repealed.

*   5.21   Individuals who originate a mortgage or act as a mortgage loan originator are required to keep records of the disclosures, set forth in Sections 12-10-725(1) and (2), C.R.S., and these rules, for a period of five years, for the purposes of inspection by the Board or authorized representative of the Board.

A.   All documents shall be kept in a safe and secure manner. Electronic storage is acceptable as long as the information is accessible and kept in a safe and secure manner.

B.   The company for whom the mortgage loan originator is an officer, partner, contractor, independent contractor, member, exclusive agent or an employee may provide the requested documents to the Board. However, the mortgage loan originator is responsible for compliance with the Board's request and is subject to disciplinary action if the company fails or refuses to provide the requested documentation.

C.   The mortgage loan originator must be able to provide proof to the Board or an authorized representative of the Board that the disclosure forms defined in this rule were in fact provided to the borrower within three (3) business days after receipt of a loan application or any subsequent changes to any loan terms requiring re-disclosure.

5.22   Dual Status Disclosure

The Board prohibits individuals from acting as a mortgage loan originator and a Real Estate Broker, on the same transaction, unless they comply with the requirements set forth in this rule.

A.   Dual status is a material fact to real estate transactions and shall be disclosed to the borrower(s).

B.   The Board has created the Colorado Dual Status Disclosure form to ensure this information is clearly and concisely disclosed. This disclosure may be found on the Division of Real Estate's website. A mortgage loan originator shall use this form or an alternate form, if such alternate form clearly includes all information required on the suggested form, as determined by the Board.

C.   The Colorado Dual Status Disclosure form shall be completed, disclosed, and provided to the borrower within three (3) business days after receipt of a loan application.

D.   Persons who originate a mortgage, offer to originate a mortgage, act as a mortgage loan originator, or offer to act as a mortgage loan originator shall maintain the disclosure form defined by this rule for a period of five years.

E.   The mortgage loan originator must be able to provide proof to the Board or an authorized representative of the Board that the disclosure forms defined in this rule were in fact provided to the borrower within three (3) business days after receipt of a loan application or any subsequent changes to any loan terms requiring re-disclosure.

5.23   Immediate notification of a conviction, plea, or violation required

Pursuant to Sections 12-10-711 and 12-10-713, C.R.S., a mortgage loan originator shall make written notification to the Board of Mortgage Loan Originators within thirty (30) calendar days of any of the following:

A.   A plea of guilty, a plea of nolo contendere or a conviction of any felony or misdemeanor offense under Colorado law, federal law, or the laws of other states, excluding misdemeanor traffic offenses or petty offenses;

B.   A violation, or aiding and abetting a violation, of the Colorado or federal fair housing laws;

C.   Revocation or suspension of any license, registration, or certification issued by Colorado or another state because of fraud, deceit, material misrepresentation, theft, or breach of a fiduciary duty; and

D.   A revocation, suspension, or any other disciplinary action taken against a mortgage loan originator's license in any jurisdiction.

CHAPTER 6: EXCEPTIONS AND BOARD REVIEW OF INITIAL DECISIONS

6.1   Written form, service, and filing requirements

A.   All designations of record, requests, exceptions and responsive pleadings ("pleadings") must be in written form, mailed with a certificate of mailing to the Board.

B.   All pleadings must be received by the Board by 5:00 p.m. On the date the filing is due. A pleading is considered filed upon <u>receipt</u> by the Board. These rules do not provide for any additional time for service by mail.

C. Any pleadings must be served on the opposing party by mail or by hand delivery on the date which the pleading is filed with the Board.

D. All pleadings must be filed <u>with the Board</u> and not with the Office of Administrative Courts. Any designations of record, requests, exceptions or responsive pleadings filed in error with the Office of Administrative Courts will <u>not</u> be considered. The Board's address is:

> Colorado Board of Mortgage Loan Originators
> 1560 Broadway, Suite 925
> Denver, Colorado 80202

6.2 Authority to review

A. The Board hereby preserves the Board's option to initiate a review of an initial decision on its own motion pursuant to § 24-4-105(14)(a)(ii) and (b)(iii), C.R.S. outside of the thirty day period after service of the initial decision upon the parties without requiring a vote for each case.

B. This option to review shall apply regardless of whether a party files exceptions to the initial decision.

6.3 Designation of record and transcripts

A. Any party seeking to reverse or modify the initial decision of the administrative law judge shall file with the Board a designation of the relevant parts of the record for review ("designation of record"). Designations of record must be filed with the Board within <u>twenty days</u> of the date on which the Board mails the initial decision to the parties' address of record with the Board.

B. Within <u>ten days</u> after a party's designation of record is due, any other party may file a supplemental designation of record requesting inclusion of additional parts of the record.

C. Even if no party files a designation of record, the record shall include the following:

1. All pleadings;

2. All applications presented or considered during the hearing;

3. All documentary or other exhibits admitted into evidence;

4. All documentary or other exhibits presented or considered during the hearing;

5. All matters officially noticed;

6. Any findings of fact and conclusions of law proposed by any party; and

7. Any written brief filed.

D. Transcripts: transcripts will not be deemed part of a designation of record unless specifically identified and ordered. Should a party wish to designate a transcript or portion thereof, the following procedures will apply:

1. The designation of record must identify with specificity the transcript or portion thereof to be transcribed. For example, a party may designate the entire transcript, or may identify witness(es) whose testimony is to be transcribed, the legal ruling or argument to be transcribed, or other information necessary to identify a portion of the transcript.

2. Any party who includes a transcript or a portion thereof as part of the designation of record must <u>order</u> the transcript or relevant portions by the date on which the designation of record must be filed (within twenty days of the date on which the Board mails the initial decision to the parties).

3. When ordering the transcript, the party shall request a court reporter or transcribing service to prepare the transcript within thirty days. The party shall timely pay the

necessary fees to obtain and file with the Board an original transcription and one copy within thirty days.

4. The party ordering the transcript shall direct the court report or transcribing service to complete and file with the Board the transcript and one copy of the transcript within thirty days.

5. If a party designates a portion of the transcript, the opposing party may also file a supplemental designation of record, in which the opposing party may designate additional portions of the transcript.

6. An opposing party filing a supplemental designation of record designating additional portions of the transcript must order and pay for such transcripts or portions thereof within the deadlines set forth above. An opposing party must also cause the court reporter to complete and file with the Board the transcript and one copy of the transcript within thirty days.

7. Transcripts that are ordered and not filed with the Board in a timely manner by the reporter or the transcription service due to non-payment, insufficient payment or failure to direct as set forth above will not be considered by the Board.

6.4 Filing of exceptions and responsive pleadings

A. Any party wishing to file exceptions shall adhere to the following timelines:

1. If no transcripts are ordered, exceptions are due within thirty days from the date on which the Board mails the initial decision to the parties. Both parties' exceptions are due on the same date.

2. If transcripts are ordered by either party, the following procedure shall apply. Upon receipt of all transcripts identified in all designations of record and supplemental designations of record, the Board shall mail notification to the parties stating that the transcripts have been received by the Board. Exceptions are due within thirty days from the date on which such notification is mailed. Both parties' exceptions are due on the same date.

B. Either party may file a responsive pleading to the other party's exceptions. All responsive pleadings shall be filed within ten days of the date on which the exceptions were filed with the Board. No other pleadings will be considered except for good cause shown.

C. The Board may in its sole discretion grant an extension of time to file exceptions or responsive pleadings, or may delegate the discretion to grant such an extension of time to the Board's designee.

6.5 Request for oral argument

A. All requests for oral argument must be in writing and filed by the deadline for responsive pleadings.

B. It is within the sole discretion of the Board to grant or deny a request for oral argument. If oral argument is granted, both parties shall have the opportunity to participate.

C. If a request for oral argument is granted, each side shall be permitted ten minutes of oral argument unless such time is extended by the Board or its designee.

CHAPTER 7: *DECLARATORY ORDERS PURSUANT TO SECTION 24-4-105(11), C.R.S.*

7.1 Any person may petition the Board for a declaratory order to terminate controversies or to remove uncertainties as to the applicability to the Petitioner of any statutory provisions or of any rule or order of the Board.

7.2 The Board will determine, in its discretion and without prior notice to Petitioner, whether to entertain any such petition. If the Board decides that it will not entertain such a petition, the

Board shall promptly notify the Petitioner in writing of its decision and the reasons for that decision. A copy of the order shall be provided to the Petitioner.

7.3 In determining whether to entertain a petition filed pursuant to this rule, the Board may consider the following matters, among others:

A. Whether a ruling on the petition will terminate a controversy or remove uncertainties as to the applicability to Petitioner of any statutory provision or rule or order of the Board.

B. Whether the petition involves any subject, question or issue which is the subject of a formal or informal matter or investigation currently pending before the Board or a court involving one or more of the Petitioners.

C. Whether the petition involves any subject, question or issue which is the subject of a formal or informal matter or investigation currently pending before the Board or a court but not involving any Petitioner.

D. Whether the petition seeks a ruling on a moot or hypothetical question or will result in an advisory ruling or opinion.

E. Whether the Petitioner has some other adequate legal remedy, other than an action for declaratory relief pursuant to Rule 57, C.R.C.P., which will terminate the controversy or remove any uncertainty as to the applicability to the Petitioner of the statute, rule or order in question.

7.4 Any petition filed pursuant to this rule shall set forth the following:

*   A. The name and address of the Petitioner and whether the Petitioner holds a license or registration issued pursuant to Section 12-10-701 *et. seq.* C.R.S. (as amended).

B. The statute, rule or order to which the petition relates.

C. A concise statement of all of the facts necessary to show the nature of the controversy or uncertainty and the manner in which the statute, rule or order in question applies or potentially applies to the Petitioner.

D. A concise statement of the legal authorities if any, and such other reasons upon which the Petitioner relies.

E. A concise statement of the declaratory order sought by the Petitioner.

7.5 If the Board determines that it will rule on the petition, the following procedures shall apply:

A. The Board may rule upon the petition without a hearing. In such case:

1. The Board may dispose of the petition on the sole basis of the matters set forth in the petition.

2. The Board may request the Petitioner to submit additional facts in writing. In such event, such additional facts will be considered as an amendment to the petition.

3. Any ruling of the Board will apply only to the extent of the facts presented in the petition and any amendment to the petition.

4. The Board may order the Petitioner to file a written brief, memorandum or statement of position based on the facts set forth in the petition and any amendment to the petition.

5. The Board may take administrative notice of facts pursuant to The Administrative Procedures Act, Section 24-4-105(8), C.R.S. (as amended), and may utilize its experience, technical competence and specialized knowledge in the disposition of the petition.

6. If the Board rules upon the petition without hearing, it shall promptly notify the Petitioner in writing of its decision.

B. The Board may, in its discretion, set the petition for hearing, upon due notice to Petitioner, for the purpose of obtaining additional facts or information or to determine the truth of any facts set forth in the petition or to hear oral argument on the petition. The notice to the Petitioner setting such hearing shall set forth, to the extent known, the factual or other matters into which the Board intends to inquire and whether the hearing will be evidentiary or non-evidentiary in nature. For the purpose of such a hearing, to the extent necessary, the Petitioner shall have the burden of proving all of the facts stated in the petition, all of the facts necessary to show the nature of the controversy or uncertainty and the manner in which the statute, rule or order in question applies or potentially applies to the Petitioner and any other facts the Petitioner desires the Board to consider.

7.6   The parties to any proceeding pursuant to this rule shall be the Board and the Petitioner. Any other person may seek leave of the Board to intervene in such a proceeding, and leave to intervene shall be granted at the sole discretion of the Board. A petition to intervene shall set forth the same matters as required by section 7.4 of this rule. Any reference to a "Petitioner" in this rule also refers to any person who has been granted leave to intervene by the Board.

7.7   Any declaratory order or other order disposing of a petition pursuant to this rule shall constitute agency action subject to judicial review pursuant to Section 24-4-106, C.R.S. (as amended).

CHAPTER 8: NATIONWIDE MORTGAGE LICENSING SYSTEM AND REGISTRY ("NMLS")

8.1   A mortgage loan originator may challenge information entered into the NMLS by the Division. Such challenge must be in writing and must set forth the specific information being challenge and include supporting evidence. The grounds for a challenge shall be limited to the factual accuracy of the information pertaining to the mortgage loan originator's own license record.

8.2   A challenge submitted to appeal the underlying grounds for a disciplinary action will not be considered by the Director.

8.3   The Director, or an authorized representative of the Director, will review all information submitted by the mortgage loan originator and will determine the merits of the challenge. If the Director, or the Director's authorized representative, determines that the information submitted to the NMLS by the Division is factually incorrect, the Division will promptly submit the correct information to the NMLS.

8.4   A mortgage loan originator may appeal the Director's, or the Director's authorized representative's, decision regarding the challenge to the Board of Mortgage Loan Originators within 30 days of the decision being rendered. The decision of the Board regarding a NMLS challenge is subject to judicial review by the court of appeals by appropriate proceedings under Section 24-4-106(11), C.R.S.

8.5   Call Reports

All mortgage companies must submit the NMLS Mortgage Call Report on a calendar quarterly basis, as set forth below, and shall contain such information as the NMLS may require.

A.   A mortgage company must identify the applicable NMLS Mortgage Call Report. This includes, but is not limited to, the standard section and the expanded section of the NMLS Mortgage Call Report. The mortgage company must identify and complete the report on behalf of all employed mortgage loan originators or other mortgage loan originators that operate through their company.

B.   The quarterly report is due within 45 days of the end of the quarter and the financial condition report of the standard section is due annually 90 days from the company's fiscal year end.

C.   Mortgage companies must comply with any rules, policies and procedures relating to the submission of a Mortgage Call Report that are prescribed by the NMLS.

8.6   Failure to properly submit a NMLS Mortgage Call report in a timely manner prescribed by the NMLS shall prevent the mortgage company from renewing their NMLS registration.

1-1-2 *[Repealed effective 1/14/2014]*

1-1-4 *[Repealed effective 1/14/2014]*

1-1-5 *[Repealed effective 1/14/2014]*

1-2-2 *[Repealed effective 1/14/2014]*

1-3-1 *[Repealed effective 1/14/2014]*

1-4-1 *[Repealed effective 1/14/2014]*

1-5-1 *[Repealed effective 1/14/2014]*

3-1-4 *[Repealed effective 1/10/2014]*

* II. Mortgage Loan Originator Position Statements

Position Statement – MB 1.1 [Repealed]

Position Statement – MB 1.2 [Repealed]

Position Statement – MLO 1.3 – Board Position on Individuals Not Required to be Licensed – Supervisors and Support Staff (revised 09/18/2013) – effective 11/14/2013

The Board of Mortgage Loan Originators ("Board") issues this position statement to provide clarification to the mortgage industry regarding when supervisors and support staff of mortgage loan originators are not required to be licensed.

Supervision of Licensed Individuals:

Persons who directly or indirectly supervise mortgage loan originators, defined as those individuals who either take residential loan applications or offer or negotiate terms of a residential mortgage loan, are not required to hold a license if their duties are purely administrative in nature. Administrative tasks include, but are not limited to: setting goals and objectives, overseeing production, delegating duties, and evaluating performance, as long as performance of these tasks does not amount to the taking of a residential mortgage loan application or offering or negotiating the terms of a residential mortgage loan.

Support Staff:

Individuals who perform purely clerical and support tasks under the direction and supervision of a state licensed individual do not fall within the definitions of "originate a mortgage" or "mortgage loan originator." Clerical or support tasks include, but are not limited to:

a. Communicating with a consumer to obtain the information necessary for the processing or underwriting of a loan, to the extent that such communication does not include offering or negotiating loan rates or terms, or counseling consumers about residential mortgage loan rates or terms; and

b. The receipt, collection, distribution and analysis of information common for the processing or underwriting of a residential mortgage loan.

* However, at any time, if the unlicensed persons activities fall outside of administrative, clerical or support in nature and within the definitions of "originate a mortgage" as defined in section 12-10-

702(17), C.R.S., or "mortgage loan originator" as defined in section 12-10-702(14)(a), C.R.S., they are required to be licensed as a Colorado mortgage loan originator.

Position Statement – MLO 1.4 – Mortgage Loan Originator and Mortgage Company Exemptions (revised 09/18/2013)

* The Board of Mortgage Loan Originators has reissued this position statement to provide guidance for all individuals and entities identified under the exemption portion of the Mortgage Loan Originator Licensing and Mortgage Company Registration Act (the "Act"); specifically section 12-10-709, C.R.S., and federal regulations regarding seller financing.

State specific exemption for real estate brokers:

* The Colorado General Assembly passed two bills in 2013 concerning the regulation of mortgage loan originators with new language affecting the exemption portion of the Act. Section 12-10-709, C.R.S., defines all individuals and entities that are exempt or otherwise excused from complying with licensure and registration standards outlined by the Act.

* The first bill, SB 13-118, added exemption language for real estate brokers representing persons providing seller financing for the sale of no more than three residential properties in any twelve month period. Section 12-10-709(1)(j), C.R.S., now includes as exempt:

"A person licensed under part 2 of this article 10 who represents a person, estate, or trust providing mortgage financing under subsection (1)(a) of this section."

* The Board finds it necessary to clarify in what capacity one is acting when representing a person, estate, or trust that is offering seller financing. The Board has taken the position that "represents" denotes in the capacity of a real estate broker as set forth in section 12-10-201(6)(a), C.R.S. As such, persons licensed under part 2 are limited to the real estate brokerage activities as defined in section 12-10-702(20), C.R.S. "Acting in the capacity of a real estate broker" does not include the offering or negotiation of terms and conditions of any proposed financing arrangements with the seller. That activity would fall under the purview of mortgage origination.

* Additionally, the sunset bill for the mortgage loan originators program, SB 13-156, deleted subsection (m) of former 12-61-911(1), C.R.S., thereby removing any uncertainties as to the plain and straightforward intent to exempt all individuals and entities identified in (what are now) sections 12-10-709(1)(b) through (j), C.R.S., from all sections, provisions, and requirements of the Act.

Compliance with federal requirements:

There have been some questions with regard to SB13-118, and how the new exemption created for licensed real estate brokers reconciles with federal licensure requirements. The Secure and Fair Enforcement for Mortgage Licensing Act of 2008 ("S.A.F.E. Act") sets minimum national licensing standards for mortgage loan originators and requires that all mortgage loan originators be registered on the National Mortgage Licensing System and Registry ("NMLS"). The SAFE Act defines "loan originator" as an individual who (I) takes a residential mortgage loan application; and (II) offers or negotiates terms of a residential mortgage loan for compensation or gain. This regulation also describes activities in the residential mortgage process that are excluded from the definition of "loan originator." Activities that are excluded include: those that pertain to administrative or clerical tasks; real estate brokerage activities by individuals licensed or registered by a state to undertake real estate brokerage activities, unless that person is compensated by a loan originator, loan processing or underwriting under the direction and supervision of a state-licensed loan originator or registered loan originator; and those individuals solely involved in extensions of credit relating to timeshare plans. Care should be taken by anyone licensed under part 2 as not to perform any acts that may require licensure under federal licensing requirements.

Position Statement – MLO 1.5 – Loan Modifications (revised 11/20/2013)

Short sale – A short sale is the sale of a real property for less than the mortgage loan balance. In the settlement of the short sale transaction the existing mortgage is extinguished. Any deficiency created from the settlement of the transaction may be transformed into a promissory note, charged off, forgiven, or pursued as a judgment against the previous owner.

Loan modification – A Loan Modification is a permanent change in one or more of the terms of a mortgagor's existing loan, allows the loan to be reinstated, and often results in a more affordable mortgage payment. The borrower retains ownership of the real property and the mortgage note and deed of trust remain intact.

1. Section 12-10-702(17), C.R.S., defines "originate a mortgage" as to act directly or indirectly as a mortgage loan originator. It is the Board's position that individuals offering or negotiating loan modifications are, at a minimum, indirectly acting as mortgage loan originators. Pursuant to section 12-10-704(1)(a), C.R.S., all persons who meet the definition of originate a mortgage are required to be licensed. As a result, persons who directly or indirectly negotiate, originate or offer or attempt to negotiate or originate loan modifications are currently required to be licensed as mortgage loan originators and are required to be licensed as state-licensed loan originators by July 31, 2010.

2. In addition to the licensing requirements, all individuals who directly or indirectly negotiate loan modifications for borrowers are required to comply with all other provisions of Colorado mortgage loan originator licensing law and Board rules. This includes, but is not limited to:

   a. A duty of good faith and fair dealing in all communications and transactions with borrowers;

   b. A prohibition against making any promise that influences, persuades, or induces another person to detrimentally rely on such promise when the licensee could not or did not intend to keep such promise;

   c. A prohibition against soliciting or entering into a contract with a borrower that provides in substance that the mortgage loan originator may earn a fee or commission through the mortgage loan originator's "best efforts" to obtain a loan even though no loan is actually obtained for the borrower; and

   d. If the mortgage loan originator has obtained for the borrower a written commitment from a lender for a loan on the terms and conditions agreed to by the borrower and the mortgage loan originator, and the borrower fails to close on the loan through no fault of the mortgage loan originator, the mortgage loan originator may charge a fee, not to exceed three hundred dollars, for services rendered, preparation of documents, or transfer of documents in the borrower's file that were prepared or paid for by the borrower if the fee is not otherwise prohibited by the federal "Truth in Lending Act", 15 U.S.C. section 1601, and Regulation Z, 12 CFR 226, as amended.

3. The Board's position on this matter shall not be construed to include employees of non-profit HUD-approved housing counseling agencies as long as such individuals receive neither compensation nor anything of value for participation in loan modifications.

4. The Board's position on this matter shall not be construed to include employees of mortgage loan servicing companies operating on behalf of mortgage lenders.

5. Licensed Real Estate Brokers engaged in licensed activities when performing services within the defined short sale transactions do not need to maintain a license as a mortgage loan originator. However, loan modification services as defined in this position statement are considered outside the scope of real estate brokerage activities and as such, separate licensure as a mortgage loan originator is required.

*   6.   As set forth in section 12-10-709(1)(c), C.R.S., an attorney who renders services in the course of practice, who is licensed in Colorado, and who is not primarily engaged in the business of negotiating residential mortgage loans or loan modifications is not required to be licensed as a mortgage loan originator.

     7.   Noncompliance may result in the imposition of any of the sanctions allowable under Colorado law, including, but not limited to:

        a.   Imposition of fines;

        b.   Restitution for any financial loss;

        c.   Refusal to renew a license;

        d.   Refusal to grant a license; and

        e.   Revocation.

Position Statement – MLO 1.7 – Financial Responsibility Requirement

*   The Board's position on this matter is there is a presumption of compliance with the financial responsibility requirement in section 12-10-711(1)(g), C.R.S., for individuals required to be licensed as state-licensed loan originators who have complied with the errors and omissions insurance requirements defined in section 12-10-707, C.R.S., and any Director rule that directly or indirectly addresses errors and omissions insurance requirements and who have complied with the surety bond requirements defined in sections 12-10-704(8) and 12-10-717, C.R.S., and any Board rule that directly or indirectly addresses surety bond requirements.

Position Statement – MLO 1.8 – Real Estate Brokerage Activity

*   The Board is aware that pursuant to the real estate brokers licensing act, specifically § 12-10-401, C.R.S., *et seq.*, licensed Colorado real estate brokers are required to fulfill specific duties and obligations. Many of the duties prescribed by the act address financial matters involved in the contract for a real property transaction. Whether acting as a single agent or a transaction broker, a real estate broker must exercise reasonable skill and care, including but not limited to: 1) accounting for all money and property received in a timely manner; 2) keeping the parties fully informed of the transaction; 3) assisting the parties in complying with the terms and conditions of any contract including closing the transaction; and 4) making disclosures regarding adverse material facts pertaining to a principal's financial ability to perform the terms of the transaction and the buyer's intent to occupy the property as a principal residence. Without the informed consent of all parties, a transaction broker is prohibited from disclosing that a seller or buyer will agree to financing terms other than those offered. A single agent is prohibited from disclosing whether his or her client(s) will agree to financing terms other than those offered, unless the client consents. The Board is also cognizant that real estate brokers advise on fees relating to homeowner's associations, special assessments, appraisals, surveys, inspections, property insurance, and taxes.

*   Pursuant to § 12-10-702(20)(c), C.R.S., the aforementioned activities could be construed as requiring a mortgage loan originator's license since they involve "matters related to financing for the transaction" at the time of contract negotiation. However, the Board has determined these activities are exempt from the mortgage loan originator's licensing act. Specifically, § 12-10-702(14)(a), C.R.S., defines a mortgage loan originator as an individual who "takes a residential loan application" or "offers or negotiates terms of a residential mortgage loan." Real estate brokers engaging in these activities are required to be licensed as a mortgage loan originator.

Position Statement – MLO 1.9 – Mortgage Company Definition Applicability

The Board of mortgage loan originators views the definition of a mortgage company, pursuant to their interpretation of Colorado law, to exclude the following entities:

1. Persons, other than an individual, who meet all of the following requirements:

    a. Funds a residential mortgage loan when the residential mortgage loan application was taken by a licensed or exempt person;

    b. Does not take residential mortgage loan applications or does not offer or negotiate terms of a residential mortgage loan;

    c. Does not solicit borrowers in Colorado for the purpose of making residential mortgage loans; and

    d. Does not participate in the offering or negotiation of residential mortgage loans with the borrower, except for setting the terms under which a person may buy or fund a residential mortgage loan originated by a licensed person;

2. Private mortgage insurance companies that provide contract underwriting services to the lending community; or

3. Lead generating companies that do not, through employees or other individuals, take residential mortgage loan applications or offer or negotiate terms of a residential mortgage loan to prospective borrowers.

The types of entities described in this position statement are determined to be excluded from the definition of a mortgage company and, therefore, are not required to register as Mortgage Companies with the Colorado Board of Mortgage Loan Originators.

Chapter 10
Landmark Case Law

An * in the left margin indicates a change in the statute, rule, or text since the last publication of the manual.

I. Supreme Court Decision on Practice of Law by Brokers

Colorado brokers are allowed to render services to their clients to a greater degree than are brokers in other states. The practicing real estate broker, of necessity, must work closely with practicing lawyers. Each practitioner zealously guards the legal field of his or her endeavor. In Colorado, a real estate broker renders service to his or her client beyond merely procuring a buyer. Colorado brokers should familiarize themselves with the Colorado Supreme Court's decisions in the cases of (1) *Conway-Bogue Realty Investment Co. v. Denver Bar Association*, (2) *Title Guaranty Co. v. Denver Bar Association*, and (3) *Record Abstract & Title Co. v. Denver Bar Association*.

In the case of *Conway-Bogue Realty Investment Co. v. Denver Bar Association*, 312 P.2d 998 (Colo. 1957), the Colorado Supreme Court addressed whether real estate brokers should be enjoined from preparing certain legal documents relating to and affecting real estate and the title thereto (such as receipts and options for purchase, contracts of sale, deeds, deeds of trust, and leases), and from giving advice to the parties regarding the legal effect of the documents.

In rendering its decision, the Colorado Supreme Court stated:

The first question to be determined is:

Does the preparation of receipts and options, deeds, promissory notes, deeds of trust, mortgages, releases of encumbrances, leases, notice terminating tenancies, demands to pay rent or vacate by completing standard and approved printed forms, coupled with the giving of explanation or advice as to the legal effect thereof, constitute the practice of law?

This question we answer in the affirmative.

. . .

The remaining and most difficult question to be determined is:

Should the defendants as licensed real estate brokers (none of whom are licensed attorneys) be enjoined from preparing in the regular course of their business the instruments enumerated above, at the requests of their customers and only in connection with transactions involving sales of real estate, loans on real estate or the leasing of real estate which transactions are being handled by them?

This question we answer in the negative.

. . .

The testimony shows, and there is no effort to refute the same, that there are three counties in Colorado that have no lawyers, ten in each of which there is only one lawyer, seven in each of which there are only two lawyers; that many persons in various areas of the state reside at great distances from any lawyer's office. The testimony shows without contradiction that the practices sought to be enjoined are of at least 50 years uninterrupted duration; that a vast majority of the people of the state who buy, sell, encumber and lease real estate have chosen real estate brokers rather than lawyers to perform the acts herein complained of. Though not controlling, we must make note of the fact that the record is devoid of evidence of any instance in which the public or any member thereof, layman or lawyer has suffered injury by reason of the act of any of the defendants sought to be enjoined. Likewise, though not controlling, we take judicial notice of the fact that the legislature of the state, composed of 100 members from all walks of life and every section of the state, usually called upon by their constituents to adopt legislation designed to eliminate evils and protect the public against practices contrary to the public welfare, has never taken any steps to prevent continuation of the alleged evil which we are now asked to enjoin.

. . .

We feel that to grant the injunctive relief requested, thereby denying to the public the right to conduct real estate transactions in the manner in which they have been transacted for over half a century, with apparent satisfaction, and requiring all such transactions to be conducted through lawyers, would not be in the public interest. The advantages, if any, to be derived by such limitation are outweighed by the conveniences now enjoyed by the public in being permitted to choose whether their brokers or their lawyers shall do the acts or render the service which plaintiffs seeks to enjoin.

Summary of Decision on Practice of Law by Brokers

The following is an excellent summary of the case given by John E. Gorsuch, legal counsel for the Colorado Association of Realtors, quoted from the August 1957 issue of the Colorado Real Estate News:

It should be kept in mind that the Court states that the practices in question do amount to the practice of law. The Court says that it will not enjoin real estate brokers from doing these simple acts, however, under the circumstances indicated, because of the Court's express belief that the public's best interest will be served by continuing the present practice. The present practice, however, means the practice shown by the evidence. In other words, the broker's activity is limited to the following circumstances:

1. His office must be connected with the transaction as broker.

2. There must be no charge for preparing the documents other than the normal commission.

3. The documents must be prepared on commonly used printed, standard, and approved forms.

It is clear from the decision that the broker should not, under any circumstances:

1. Prepare any legal documents as a business, courtesy or favor, for any transaction with which he is not connected as broker, either with or without pay.

2. He should not prepare any documents which cannot be properly prepared on the standard and approved printed form.

3. He clearly should not draw wills, contracts, agreements and so forth, except the initial binder contract or other customary agreements of the type used to bind the transaction or sale.

4. In addition, it would appear in the best interests of the public and also in conformity with the Court's opinion for the broker to:

    a. Always recommend to the purchaser that the title be examined.

    b. Inform the parties that each has a right to have the papers prepared by an attorney of their own choosing.

    c. Advise the parties that each has a right to be represented at the closing by an attorney if they desire.

    d. In spite of the permission to prepare such documents, there will inevitably arise situations in which the legal complications are beyond the knowledge of the broker. In such instances an attorney's assistance should always be sought.

In conclusion, it could be said that the Supreme Court will allow the brokers to prepare these legal documents on standard and approved printed forms by filling in the blanks therein, with information obtained from the usual sources, in transactions with which they are connected as brokers, when they receive no compensation for these acts other than their ordinary commission. It is to the interest of every broker that these limitations be properly recognized and followed so that the Supreme Court would not have a reason to change its opinion at a future date.

The final words of Mr. Gorsuch's summary bear repeating: "It is to the interest of every broker that these limitations be properly recognized and followed so that the Supreme Court would not have a reason to change its opinion at a future date."

With privilege granted, there must be no abuse. The same authority that granted it may take a privilege such as this away. A privilege respected may be retained. A careless regard is not sufficient. There must be a careful determination and application of what is authorized practice of law by a real estate broker.

The court in its decision referred to the use of "standard and approved" forms, but did not elaborate. Consequently, it was necessary to establish what is a STANDARD and what is an APPROVED form.

Any form purchased from a stationery store or a printer may or may not be a "standard and approved" form. The printer is under no obligation to determine what is standard or what is approved. However, a real estate broker may have such an obligation. Therefore, the brokers needed some guidance and support in their determination of what is a standard and approved form.

In the years following the *Conway-Bogue* decision, the business of real estate practice grew rapidly. There appeared to be less and less standardization of legal forms. Each association of brokers, each locality, and even individual brokers used their own forms, often times drafted with personal prejudice.

* The real estate industry became concerned that its privilege to practice law, within the limited sphere, might be abrogated by the court. In 1970, the Colorado Association of Real Estate Boards passed a resolution requesting the Real Estate Commission to approve standard forms and to make their use compulsory. In response to this request, the Real Estate Commission held public hearings on the question. The consensus of opinion drawn from the hearings was almost unanimous: the industry wanted the Commission to use its authority to standardize forms throughout the state. As a result, the Commission in 1971 promulgated and adopted Rule F, (presently known as the Chapter 7 Rules: Use of Standard Forms), which was submitted to the Attorney General. The Attorney General concluded that Rule F was a constitutional exercise of the Commission's rule-making authority.

* These rules cover forms for listing contracts, sales contracts, exchange contracts, disclosure forms, settlement sheets, extension agreements, and counterproposals. At the time of this writing, the rules do not cover forms for business opportunity listing or sales contracts, management agreements, leases, etc. In these areas, the broker must use his or her best judgment.

* In 1993, the legislature gave the Commission statutory authority to promulgate standard forms for use by real estate licensees. (See § 12-10-403(4), C.R.S.)

* In the area of listing and conveyancing covered by these rules, it is to the advantage of the general public and of real estate licensees to use the Commission-approved forms. Much of the wording used in these approved forms has been interpreted by the Colorado Supreme Court and its meaning is known. Other portions have been rewritten to conform to Colorado Supreme Court opinion when older provisions have been found invalid. Economic conditions have also necessitated changes. Changes can also be expected in the Commission-approved forms, but reasonable notice will always be given to licensed brokers.

Companion Decision on Practice of Law

On the same day as *Conway-Bogue*, the Colorado Supreme Court decided the cases of *Title Guaranty Co. v. Denver Bar Association* and *Record Abstract & Title Co. v. Denver Bar Association*, which were taken as companion cases from which one decision was rendered (See 312 P.2d 1011 (Colo. 1957)).

In these two cases, the Denver Bar Association sought to enjoin the title company and the abstract company from preparing certain legal documents for others, giving advice as to their legal effect, and performing other acts that allegedly constituted the unauthorized practice of law.

The court reduced the issues to three:

1. Wherein one of the defendant corporations prepared papers incidental to the making of a loan from funds belonging to the corporation.

The court held that in such a case, the defendant may prepare the notes, deeds of trust, or mortgages incidental to making the loans. The defendant could not be restrained even if at the time of the closing the defendant had a firm commitment for the sale of the loan.

2. In situations where the parties involved in the transaction used an "escrow service" or "closing service" provided by the defendant corporations wherein they draft deeds, promissory notes, trust deeds, mortgages, and receipt and option contracts, and the defendants set a minimum fee and a sliding scale of charges for this service.

The court mentioned that the defendants actively solicited such business, although it was the same service that real estate brokers rendered as an incident of their business and without separate charge. The court held that the defendants were conducting a separate, distinct, and other business, much of which constituted the practice of law and could properly be restrained.

3. The third problem presented was where the defendant's "closing service" was used and the defendant also sold title insurance on the property involved.

The court held that the defendants could be enjoined and that the "escrow service" or "closing service" was not necessary or incidental to the issuance of title insurance. The court further held that the attorneys employed by them were representing the corporation and not the parties involved. The court said in part, "To hold otherwise would be to authorize corporations to practice law for compensation."

The court began its opinion by stating that it should be read and considered in connection with the opinion on the case between the real estate brokers and the lawyers.

II. Licensee Acting on Own Account—Commission Jurisdiction

The Commission staff is often asked whether it can investigate complaints against a licensee where the licensee is not involved as an agent in the transaction. The answer is yes. The Commission can investigate and take disciplinary action against a licensee acting on the licensee's own account where the licensee acts in a dishonest manner. Typical examples are where the licensee/owner does not disclose a known defect, fails to disclose the licensee's licensed status as a purchaser, or provides fraudulent information on a loan application.

Printed in relevant part below is the Colorado Court of Appeals case of *Seibel v. Colorado Real Estate Commission*, 530 P.2d 1290 (Colo. App. 1974) in which the issue of the Commission's jurisdiction over "non-agency" activities arose.

> Ed. Note: The statutes cited in this opinion are now found in §§ 12-10-201 through -411, C.R.S.

*

This appeal raises the question of jurisdiction of the Colorado Real Estate Commission over acts of a broker in negotiating the acquisition of an interest in real estate for his own use. The hearing officer and the Colorado Real Estate Commission, directly, and the district court, by implication, all concluded that the real estate brokers licensing act, (§12-10-201, C.R.S., (formerly 1963, 117-1-1), *et seq.*, and rules adopted by the commission pursuant to that statute do apply to the conduct of licensed brokers in real estate matters relating to actions taken for their own account. We affirm.

Appellant (Seibel) is a licensed real estate broker. Intending to purchase a home owned by persons named Debord for his own use, he signed a receipt and option agreement, proceeding through the listing broker, Roberts. Seibel was not able to close on the agreed date, and accepted return of his deposit.

Several days later, one Arvidson signed a receipt and option agreement relating to the same property, again proceeding through Roberts. Seibel was not aware of this transaction. He personally contacted the Debords and attempted to have them sign a new contract for sale of the property to him. This proposed contract stated that Seibel and Roberts would divide the commission equally. All of the contacts by Seibel with the Debords regarding the second contract were made without the consent or approval of the listing broker.

After Seibel learned of the Arvidson contract, he recorded the original receipt and option agreement. The Debord-Arvidson sale was closed with $500 being placed in escrow to cover the cost of a possible quiet title suit to clear the records of the Seibel contract.

Pursuant to statute, proceedings were held before a hearing officer of the Colorado Real Estate Commission on alleged violations of both the real estate brokers licensing act and a commission rule. The hearing officer found that the commission had jurisdiction, that Seibel was guilty of improper and dishonest dealing in making direct contact with the sellers, that Seibel had violated both former C.R.S. 1963, 117-1-12(1)(t), and Real Estate Commission Rule E-13 (presently known as Rule 6.15), and therefore recommended that his license be suspended for a period of not less than thirty nor more than ninety days.

C.R.S. 1963, 117-1-12(1)(t), proscribes conduct "which constitutes dishonest dealing." Real Estate Commission Rule E-13 specified that: "A real estate broker shall not negotiate a sale, exchange, lease or listing contract of real property directly with an owner for compensation from such owner if he knows that such owner has a written unexpired contract in connection with such property which grants an exclusive right to sell to another broker, or which grants an exclusive agency to another broker."

The Real Estate Commission approved and adopted the findings of the hearing officer, and suspended Seibel's license for a period of thirty days. The district court reversed the commission's finding that Seibel had violated the statute, but affirmed the finding that he had violated Rule E-13. The matter was remanded to the commission to impose whatever penalty the commission felt was warranted for the violation of the rule. The commission thereupon suspended plaintiff's license for ten days, and this appeal followed.

Seibel urges that 1965 Perm. Supp., C.R.S. 1963, 117-1-2(4), provides him a specific exemption from the authority of the commission in this case, since he was attempting to buy the home for his personal use and was not acting as a real estate broker. The pertinent paragraphs of this section state that:

"(a) The terms 'real estate broker' or 'real estate salesman,' as used in this article, shall not apply to any of the following:

. . . .

(e) Any owner of real estate acting personally, or a corporation acting through its officers, or regular salaried employees, in his or its own behalf with respect to property owned or leased by him or it, except as provided in subsection (2) of this section;

(f) Any person, firm, partnership, association acting personally, or a corporation acting through its officers or regular salaried employees, in his or its own behalf as principal in acquiring or in negotiating to acquire any interest in real estate . . . ."

. . .

Considering the statute in light of these principles, we conclude that the purpose of the exemption section of 1965 Perm. Supp., C.R.S. 1963, 117-1-2(4), is to permit an owner of property to sell it, or to permit one to purchase property for his own account without having to procure a real estate license. These paragraphs have no application to the matter of discipline of licensed real estate brokers and salesmen. To interpret the statute as Seibel urges, would be to adopt an illogical and unduly restrictive meaning of the regulatory provisions of the entire statute.

. . . .

Hence, we conclude that where a real estate broker is dealing in real estate for his own account, the Colorado Real Estate Commission has jurisdiction over his acts and can suspend or revoke his license for proven violations of the licensing statute or of the Commission's rules. A broker can no more be allowed to violate the rules of the Real Estate Commission when purchasing property for his own account than he can when purchasing it for a client.

* III. Eckley v. Colorado Real Estate Commission (1988)

* **Case Topics:**
* 1. **Incompetency/Unworthiness as Applied to License Discipline.**
* 2. **Legal Standards: Court Review of Agency Imposed Sanctions.**
* 3. **Offsetting Actions by Other Regulatory Agencies.**

* In 1985, the Colorado Real Estate Commission (the Commission) issued a Final Agency Order (FAO) which adopted an administrative law judge's findings that the Respondent had engaged in incompetent and unworthy conduct, in violation of the Colorado real estate license law. The case was based on the Respondent's brokerage activities involving the sale of a business (a Denver lounge) which included real property. The Respondent appealed the FAO in the Denver District Court, which affirmed the Commission's order. The Respondent then appealed the District Court's Order with the Colorado Court of Appeals; however, because such appeal challenged the constitutionality of specified portions of the real estate license law, the case was transferred to the Colorado Supreme Court – *Eckley v. Colorado Real Estate Commission*, 752 P.2d 68 (Colo. 1988).

*   **1.** <u>Incompetence/Unworthiness as Applied to License Discipline</u>.

*   In the Supreme Court case, the Respondent challenged the real estate license law which allows for discipline based on acts of "incompetency" and unworthiness," by contending that such terms are unconstitutionally vague; however, relying on standards previously established in Colorado case law, the Court disagreed.

*   According to the Court, "Statutory terms need not be defined with mathematical precision in order to pass constitutional muster. . . Instead, the statutory language must strike a balance between two potentially conflicting concerns: it must be specific enough to give fair warning of the prohibited conduct, yet must be sufficiently general to address the problem under varied circumstances and during changing times."

*   As to the term "incompetency," the Court pointed to its own previous rulings which stated that "[c]ompetence indicates the ability to perform ably and above a minimum level of sufficiency" and that "incompetence refers to a demonstrated lack of ability to perform a required duty." Therefore, the Court held that the term "incompetency" as employed in the context of the real estate license law is "sufficiently precise that persons of common intelligence and understanding would not have to guess at its meaning or differ as to its application."

*   As to the term "unworthiness," the Court relied in part on the *Webster's New World Dictionary*, 1599 (College Ed. 1957), in which "unworthiness" is defined as "the quality or state of being unworthy," and where "unworthy" is defined as "not fit, becoming, or suitable." Therefore, according to the Court, "the concept of unworthiness in the context . . . (of the real estate license law) . . . contemplates conduct or behavior in connection with the business of real estate brokerage that demonstrates the actor to be so unfit or unsuitable to act as a real estate broker or salesman as to endanger the interest of the public."

*   The Count further pointed to rulings made in other state courts, including a 1979 Iowa Supreme Court opinion that Iowa's own license law language "proscribing unworthiness or incompetency to act as a real estate broker becomes clear and unequivocal when measured by common understanding and practice in that profession." *Miller v. Iowa Real Estate Comm'n*, 274 N.W.2d 288, 292 (Iowa 1979).

*   **2.** <u>Legal Standards: Court Review of Agency Imposed Sanctions</u>.

*   In his defense, the Respondent further held that the findings of the Commission and the District Court were arbitrary and capricious. In addressing this defense, the Court cited Colorado case law which held that (1) In order for a court to set aside agency action under the Colorado Administrative Procedures Act, on the ground that it was arbitrary and capricious, the court must find that the action is unsupported by any competent evidence; and that (2) Agency action will also be set aside if it is based on findings of basic or evidentiary facts that are "clearly erroneous on the whole record, unsupported by substantial evidence when the record is considered as a whole, or otherwise contrary to law."

*   Upon review of the underlying administrative hearing, the Court found credible evidence in support of the administrative law judge's findings that the Respondent:

*   • Failed to make financial records of the business being purchased available to the buyer, which may have left the seller open to later adverse claims by the buyer (incompetence).

* • Failed to advise purchaser to consult an attorney concerning the complexity of the transaction (unworthiness and incompetency).

* • Completed an earnest money disbursement agreement which failed to show all of the disbursements actually made (i.e., misrepresentations which constituted incompetency and unworthiness).

* • Failed to advise the purchaser that her earnest money deposit would not be fully refundable if the sale could not close (fraudulent concealment which constituted incompetency and unworthiness).

* • Placed the purchaser's $15,000 earnest money deposit into his operating account in instead of a trust account, opining that a "need for haste" in disbursing those funds does not justify or excuse circumvention of the license law requirements (incompetency and unworthiness).

* • Failed to provide a sufficiently detailed closing statement, opining that approval of such document by the buyer's legal counsel did not nullify the license law requirements (incompetency and unworthiness).

* **3.** Offsetting Actions by Other Regulatory Agencies.

* The Respondent argued that the approval of the transfer of ownership of the subject business by the local and state liquor licensing authorities, a process that required submission to those authorities of the various documents by which the sale of the lounge was accomplished, should cure any violation of the real estate licensing statutes and commission rules.

* The Court was unpersuaded by the Respondent's argument, stating that "Liquor licensing authorities are separate entities with separate standards governing their operation. The commission rules and state real estate broker licensing laws are concerned specifically with assuring that real estate transactions are conducted honestly and competently so as to safeguard the interest of the public." The Court further stated that "These statutes and rules clearly govern the appellant's actions here. The appellant's failure to meet the standards prescribed by the relevant statutes and rules may not be vindicated by reference to action by a separate agency."

* The Court affirmed the District Court's judgment affirming the Commission's FAO, and discipline included a one-year term of license suspension.

* # IV. Colorado Real Estate Commission v. Hanegan (1997)

* **Case Topics:**

* **1. Adequate Notice of CE Requirements.**
* **2. Standards for Court Review of Agency Imposed Sanctions.**

* In 1995, an administrative law judge (ALJ) issued a finding that a real estate licensee had violated the Colorado Real Estate License Law by failing to complete a required mandatory continuing education (CE) course during her 1991-94 term of licensure. The ALJ recommended a $50 fine but declined to add the penalty of a public censure. The Real Estate Commission (the Commission) subsequently adopted the ALJ's Findings of Fact and Conclusion of Law, but opted to impose both the fine and public censure.

*   **1.** <u>Adequate Notice of CE Requirements</u>.

*   In rejecting the Respondent's claim that she did not receive adequate advance notice of the course, the ALJ pointed to relevant portions of the existing Colorado Real Estate Manual, as well as several preceding announcements in the Real Estate Commission's quarterly newsletter. In further support, the ALJ noted that of the 3,000 licensees audited for continuing education during 1994, only ten had failed to take the required course.

*   In 1996, when the Respondent appealed the Commission's Final Agency Order, the Colorado Court of Appeals affirmed the Commission's finding of adequate notice, but reversed the penalty of a public censure, concluding that the Commission's findings did not reveal a "reasonable basis in law" for the added penalty of a public censure. *Colorado Real Estate Commission v. Hanegan*, 924 P. 2d 1170 (Colo. App.1996).

*   **2.** <u>Standards for Court Review of Agency Imposed Sanctions</u>.

*   In 1997, the Real Estate Commission brought the matter before the Colorado Supreme Court (*Colorado Real Estate Commission v. Hanegan*, 947 P.2d 933 (Colo. 1997)). The Supreme Court found that while the "reasonable basis" standard is properly applied to a regulatory agency's review of an ALJ's findings of fact and conclusions of law, such standard does not apply to agency imposition of sanctions. According to the Court, the proper standard was to be found in the Colorado Administrative Procedures Act, which provides that the courts may not overturn agency actions unless such actions are "arbitrary, capricious, legally impermissible or an abuse of discretion." In this case, the Supreme Court found that:

*
- The Commission's sanction was clearly within the parameters of the Commission's statutory authority, which authorizes the Commission to impose a variety of penalties, including censure, for any of a long list of violations, including a catch-all category for disregarding or violating any provision of the real estate license law.

*
- The imposition of sanctions is a discretionary function which, if within the statutory authority of an agency, must not be overturned unless that discretion is abused. (The Court further noted that, per established case law, "The issue for the reviewing court is not whether it would reach the same conclusion on the same facts.").

*
- In this case it could not be concluded, based on the established facts, that "public censure bears no relation to the Respondent's conduct or is manifestly excessive in relation to the needs of the public and is thus an abuse of discretion."

*   The Supreme Court accordingly reversed the Court of Appeals' holding and reinstated the terms of the Real Estate Commission's Final Agency Order.

* # V. Colorado Real Estate Commission v. Bartlett (2011)

* **Case Topics:**

*   **1. Convictions of Attempted Crimes – Jurisdiction.**
*   **2. Proof of Rehabilitation.**
*   **3. Appropriate License Discipline.**

* In the case of *Colorado Real Estate Commission v. Bartlett*, 272 P.3d 1099 (Colo. App. 2011), the Colorado Court of Appeals affirmed a 2010 Real Estate Commission (the Commission) Final Agency Order (FAO) for revocation of the Respondent's Colorado real estate broker's license. The FAO was based on the licensee's conviction of an attempted criminal act, as well as his eight-month delay in reporting such to the Commission.

* **1.** Convictions of Attempted Crimes – Jurisdiction.

* The Court found that the plain language of the Colorado real estate license law provided for disciplinary action against a licensee's conviction for conduct including "attempting to perform" one of the criminal acts enumerated within **the license law**. Citing specific provisions of the Colorado Criminal Code, the Court further found that attempt convictions were sufficiently similar to convictions for the crime itself (in this case sexual assault on a child) to be considered "like crime", therefore placing such conduct within the scope of the Commission's disciplinary authority.

* **2.** Proof of Rehabilitation.

* The Court noted that the Colorado real estate license law, in tandem with specified provisions of the Colorado Administrative Procedures Act, provided that when considering license sanctions based on criminal convictions, the Commission must consider not only the offense itself, but whether the individual has been "rehabilitated" and is "ready to accept the responsibilities of a law-abiding and productive member of society."

* Based on the evidence, the Court found that while the Respondent had remained in compliance with his (then) ongoing terms of probation, there were other offsetting factors including, but not limited to, the nature of and extreme circumstances of the crime, the Respondent's delayed disclosure of the conviction, guiding principles of sex offender management, and the Respondent's testimony during the underlying administrative hearing. The Court concurred with the Commission's conclusion that those added factors indicated "a character inconsistent with licensure in a profession that demands scrupulous honesty, strict compliance with the law, and integrity in dealing with others." The Court thus held that the Commission's determination that the Respondent had not been sufficiently rehabilitated was not "arbitrary or capricious, unsupported by substantial evidence, or contrary to law."

* **3.** Appropriate License Discipline.

* The Court recognized the Commission's statutory discretion in deciding sanctions and found that the Commission's order of license revocation in this case was not "arbitrary and capricious." When making that finding, the Court noted that the case record supported the Commission's finding that the Respondent violated two provisions of the Colorado real estate license law (criminal conviction and failure to timely report). The Court further concluded that at the time of the administrative hearing, and despite demonstrated progress with his ongoing probation, the Respondent's character "remained inconsistent with the requirements of licensure."

* In addition, and citing supporting Colorado and federal case law, the Court held that the Commission was not bound to impose an identical discipline in all comparable cases.

* On February 6, 2012, the Colorado Supreme Court denied the Respondent's Petition for Writ of Certiorari regarding this Court of Appeals case.

* VI. McDonnell v. Colorado Real Estate Commission (2015)

* **Case Topics:**

* 1. **Commission Jurisdiction: Non-Brokerage Activities.**
* 2. **Commission's Disciplinary Authority – Specific Prohibited Acts.**
* 3. **Legal Standards: Court Review of Agency Imposed Sanctions.**

* <u>Background</u>: During 2010-11, while serving as president of a homeowners association, and without proper consent or permission, the Respondent wrote four checks totaling $10,000 on the HOA's account payable to himself or to his business (a sports equipment company); and such funds were used for the benefit of the Respondent's business, not for the HOA's benefit. Afterward, when HOA board members reviewed the HOA's financial records and discovered the discrepancies, the Respondent returned the $10,000 and resigned his position as HOA president.

* The Colorado Real Estate Commission (the Commission) investigated the matter and in 2013 charged the Respondent with multiple violations of the Colorado real estate license law. In 2014, after an evidentiary hearing before an administrative law judge, the Commission issued a Final Agency Order (FAO) which adopted in part, and reversed in part, findings made by the ALJ. Then in 2015, the Respondent brought the Commission's FAO before the Colorado Court of Appeals, *McDonnell v. Colorado Real Estate Commission*, 361 P.3d 1138 (Colo. App. 2015). The Court's findings are summarized below.

* 1. <u>Commission Jurisdiction: Non-Brokerage Activities.</u>

* The Respondent maintained that the Commission did not have the authority to sanction him for conduct that does not involve the actual selling, exchanging, buying, renting, or leasing of real estate. The Court disagreed with this assertion, based on the following:

  * Per statutory language, several of the grounds for discipline set forth in the real estate license law do not necessarily require a link to selling, exchanging, buying, renting, or leasing real estate, and do not involve conduct specific to brokers; and those provisions include: (1) knowingly making any misrepresentation; and (2) violation of a Commission rule or regulation in the interests of the public; and (3) certain criminal convictions and failure to so notify the Commission of such; and (4) revocation or suspension of a professional license in Colorado or other state on certain grounds.

  * Colorado case law holds that the existence of such disciplinary provisions demonstrates that the state legislature intended the Commission's sanction authority to extend to a broker's improper conduct outside the real estate context, "particularly when it speaks to the broker's honesty, dignity, or moral character."

  * In *Hart v. Colorado Real Estate Commission*, 702 P.2d 763 (Colo. App. 1985), the Court read the Commission's sanction authority expansively, to include the power to regulate "selling, exchanging, buying, renting, or leasing" real estate, along with the power to discipline brokers "for related [real estate] activities which do not require a license."

  * Broad sanction authority is not uncommon in the context of professional licensure, as demonstrated in established Colorado case law addressing professional licenses other than real estate brokers.

2. Commission's Disciplinary Authority: Specific Prohibited Acts.

The Court addressed the scope of the Commission's disciplinary authority with respect to four prohibited acts, determining that:

- The Colorado license law provision prohibiting failure to timely account for or remit funds belonging to others includes the language "whether acting as real estate brokers or otherwise," which indicates the legislature's intent to discipline brokers for failing to account or remit others' funds, even in non-real estate transactions (emphasis added). The Court further held that the Commission's recordkeeping requirements properly apply to those non-real estate transactions as well.

- The Colorado license law provision prohibiting conversion, diversion or commingling funds of others, as well as unlawful placement of such funds, does not include language that limits discipline to those instances that occur in the context of real estate. The Court further cited Colorado case law in support of its contention that the Respondent's return of the HOA's funds, absent demand, did not excuse the licensee from disciplinary action.

- The Colorado license law provision which provides for license discipline for "[h]aving demonstrated unworthiness or incompetency to act as a real estate broker by conducting business in such a manner as to endanger the interest of the public," does not apply in this case because nothing in the list of unworthy or incompetent practices set forth in the Commission's administrative rules contemplates the Respondent's conduct in this case or any other conduct outside the context of real estate.

- The Colorado license law provides for license discipline for "any other conduct, whether of the same or a different character" than those acts subject to discipline under the license law "which constitutes dishonest dealing." The Court held that the language of this provision plainly states that it applies to "any other conduct" and that there is no additional language in that particular statute, or in the Commission's administrative rules and regulations, which would limit the reach of this position.

The Court further found that although "dishonest dealing" is not defined in Colorado statute or case law, "a court can determine the meaning of an undefined phrase of common usage by ascertaining its usual and ordinary meaning." The Court cited *Black's Law Dictionary* 733 (10th ed. 2014) where a "dishonest act" is defined as "[c]onduct involving bad faith, dishonesty, a lack of integrity, or moral turpitude." Given the evidence in this case, the Court found that the Commission did not err in determining that the Respondent's conduct constituted dishonest dealing, in violation of the license law.

3. Legal Standards: Court Review of Agency Imposed Sanctions.

As to proper sanctions in this case, the Court cited the standards set forth in in *Colorado Real Estate Commission v. Bartlett*, 272 P.3d 1099 (Colo. App. 2011), that "Courts will uphold an agency sanction unless it (1) bears no relation to the proscribed conduct, (2) is manifestly excessive in relation to the needs of the public, or (3) is otherwise a gross abuse of discretion."

* Even considering its reversal of the Commission's finding of "unworthiness or incompetency" in this case, the Court determined that the Commission-ordered sanctions in this case "do not appear excessive, nor do they constitute an abuse of discretion" and therefore affirmed such sanctions.

* VII. Colorado Real Estate Commission v. Vizzi (2019)

* **Case Topics:**

*   1. **Mandatory Duties of Real Estate Brokers.**
*   2. **Federal Antitrust Defense.**
*   3. **Anonymous Complainants and Due Process Rights.**
*   4. **Legal Standards: Court Review of Agency Imposed Sanctions.**

* In 2017, the Colorado Real Estate Commission (the Commission) issued a Final Agency Order (FAO) that adopted the Administrative Law Judge's (ALJ) findings that: (1) the Respondent licensee must fulfill all of the statutory duties that transaction brokers are required to provide to clients; and that (2) the Respondent violated the Colorado real estate license law by entering into listing contracts which essentially disclaimed any responsibility to provide such duties. The ALJ's sanctions included a $2,000 fine and twelve (12) hours of continuing education. The Commission's FAO additionally sought the issuance of public censure.

* In 2019, the Respondent brought the Commission's FAO before the Colorado Court of Appeals (the "Court") for review. *Colorado Real Estate Commission v. Vizzi*, 2019 COA 33, 17CA2388 (Colo. App. 2019). The Court's findings are summarized below.

*   1. <u>Mandatory Duties of Real Estate Brokers.</u>

* During 2013-14 the Respondent contracted to represent three clients in the capacity of a transaction-broker, but in each case the Respondent was to provide unbundled real estate brokerage services in exchange for a flat fee. In one instance, he contracted only to list the client's property on the Multiple Listing Services (MLS); and in the other two instances he contracted only to provide a yard sign, lock box and centralized showing services, and to list the properties on the MLS. Upon review, the Court made the following findings:

* • The Court disagreed with the Respondent's claim that the statutory duties for transaction-brokers are only default, not mandatory duties; and in doing so the Court noted that the real estate license law defines a transaction-broker as " a broker who assists one or more parties throughout a contemplated real estate transaction with communication, interposition, advisement, negotiation, contract terms, and the closing of such real estate transaction without being an agent or advocate for the interests of any party to such transaction." The Court noted that the use of the words "throughout" and "and" indicates that when enacting the law, the legislature intended that transaction-brokers assist in the entire transaction and undertake each of the transaction-broker duties set forth in the license law. Those duties enumerated in §12-10-407(2)(a-d), C.R.S., are numerous and broad and are consistent with the contemplated activities set forth in the definition of a transaction-broker in §12-10-402(8), C.R.S.

* • Citing a further provision of the license law that "[a] transaction-broker shall have the following obligations and responsibilities . . .," and standing on Colorado case law, the Court concluded that absent a clear indication of contrary intent, the word

"shall" in a statute generally indicates that the legislature intended the listed provisions to be mandatory. The public can only engage a real estate broker in the role of a single agent or a transaction-broker. The Court further noted that "The statutes do not say that the public can engage a real estate broker to provide unbundled brokerage services, or in any manner that the broker and customer might find mutually acceptable."

- The Court also addressed the Respondent's reliance on another portion of the license law that provides "[if] the transaction-broker undertakes any obligations or responsibilities in addition to or different from" those set forth in the license law, then "[s]uch obligations or responsibilities shall be disclosed in a writing which shall be signed by the involved parties." While the Respondent maintained that such language permitted a reduction of the mandatory duties, the Court disagreed, concluding that such language allows a broker to take on duties that are additional to the mandatory duties, but does not permit a broker to contract away any of those mandatory duties.

2. Federal Antitrust Defense.

The Respondent argued that "the Commission's enforcement of 'minimum services' does not stem from formal rulemaking or statute" but merely from an "unenforceable position statement" promulgated by a Commission that is "dominated by market participants – three real estate brokers and two representatives of the public at large." Therefore, according to the Respondent, the Commission's minimum services policy runs contrary to federal antitrust laws.

The Court rejected that assertion, based on federal case law which holds that a state agency's actions are considered the actions of the state in its sovereign capacity, and thus shielded from federal antitrust law, as long as: (1) such state has articulated a clear policy to allow the anticompetitive conduct; and (2) the state provides active supervision of [the] anticompetitive conduct.

In this case, the Court found that the "clear articulation" requirement is met by the Colorado real estate license law provisions which define "transaction-broker," and which "sets out the General Assembly's policy goals in regulating transaction-brokers," and which "sets out mandatory obligations for transaction-brokers."

The Court further found that the 'active supervision" requirement is met by the license law provision that defines what constitutes the practice of a real estate broker; and by the provision that authorizes the Commission to investigate and censure licensed real estate brokers for violations of state license laws.

3. Anonymous Complainants and Due Process Rights.

The Respondent maintains that in the underlying administrative court case, the ALJ violated his due process rights by denying his motion to compel disclosure of the identity of the anonymous complainant. The Court rejected this claim, citing the Respondent's failure to demonstrate how the complainant's identity was relevant to his ability to defend against the Commission's charges; and noting that during the administrative case the Respondent was given notice of all evidence which supported the charges against him.

*   **4.**   <u>Legal Standards: Court Review of Agency Imposed Sanctions</u>.

*   With regard to the Commission's added sanction of public censure, the Court cited *Colorado Real Estate Commission v. Hanegan*, 947 P2d. 933 (Colo. 1997), in that "[a]s long as the record as a whole provides sufficient evidence that the penalty is not manifestly excessive in relation to the misconduct and the public need, the penalty will be upheld."

*   In this case, the Court noted that the Commission's addition of a public censure met the above standard, and was therefore proper, based on: (1) finding that the Respondent violated his statutory duties multiple times after the Commissions' December 2010 position statement put him on advance notice that the listing contracts he prepared in 2013 and 2014 were improper; and that (2) the Commission's sanction bore some relation to the Respondent's misconduct and to the needs of the public.

*   On October 7, 2019, the Colorado Supreme Court denied the Respondent's Petition for Writ of Certiorari regarding this Court of Appeals case.

Glossary

abstract of title. a summary or condensation of the essential parts of all recorded instruments which affect a particular piece of real estate, arranged in the order in which they were recorded.

acceleration clause. a clause in a contract by which the time for payment of a debt is advanced, usually making the obligation immediately due and payable, because of the breach of some condition, such as failure to pay an installment when due.

acceptance. an indication by an offeree of willingness to be bound by the terms of the offer.

acknowledgment. a declaration made by a person to a notary public, or other public official authorized to take acknowledgments, that the instrument was executed by the person and that it is a free and voluntary act.

acre foot. a term used in measuring the volume of water, equal to the quantity of water required to cover one acre one foot deep, or 43,560 cu. ft.

administrator. A person appointed by the court to administer the estate of a deceased person who died intestate (without leaving a will).

ad valorem. Latin meaning "according to value"; normally used to describe a tax based on the assessed value of real property.

adverse possession. the right of an occupant of land to acquire a superior title to the real estate against the record owner, where such possession has been actual, notorious, hostile, visible and continuous for the required statutory period (18 years in Colorado). Adverse possession promotes the productive use of land by giving title to the one putting the land to use.

affidavit. a written statement or declaration, sworn to or affirmed before some officer who has authority to administer an oath or affirmation.

agency. a legal relationship resulting from an agreement or contract, either expressed or implied, written or oral, whereby one person, the agent, is employed by another, called the principal, to do certain acts in dealing with a third party.

agent. any person, partnership, association, or corporation authorized or employed by another, called the principal, to act for, on behalf of, and subject to the control of the principal.

alienation. transfer of real property by one person to another.

amenities. in real estate, amenities are features such as location, outlook, or access to a park, lake, highway, view or the like which enhance the desirability of real estate and which contribute to the pleasure and enjoyment of the occupants.

amortization. liquidation or gradual retirement of a financial obligation by periodic installments.

appraisal. in real estate, an estimate of the quality or value of property; also refers to the report setting forth the estimate of value together with the basis for such conclusions.

appropriation. the act(s) involved in the taking and reducing to personal possession of water occurring in a stream or other body of water, and of applying such water to beneficial use.

appropriator. one who diverts and puts to beneficial use the water of a stream or other body of water, under a water right obtained through appropriation.

appurtenance. that which belongs to something else; something adapted to the use of the real property to which it is connected or belongs intended to be a permanent addition to the land. Appurtenances pass with the title to the land, e.g. a house, barn, garage, right-of-way, etc.

assessed valuation. an estimate of value by a unit of government for taxation purposes.

assessment. in real estate, the valuation of property in order to apportion a tax upon it.

assignee. the party to whom a legal right has been assigned or transferred.

assignment. transfer to another of a legal right.

assignor. the party who assigns or transfers a legal right.

attachment. a type of encumbrance, permitted only under special circumstances, which is placed against the real estate of a defendant in a pending law suit for money damages.

attorney's opinion. in real estate, the written opinion of an attorney-at-law regarding the marketability of title to real property based upon an examination of the abstract of title or the records in the county clerk and recorder's office.

animal unit (A.U.). the grazing capacity of land to properly sustain one animal and any offspring for one year.

balance sheet. a statement showing a company's financial position at the end of an accounting period by listing assets, liabilities and owner's equity.

balloon payment. a final lump-sum payment of an installment debt, much larger than all previous installments, and which pays the debt in full prior to its full amortization.

bargain and sale deed. any deed that recites consideration and purports to convey the real estate. A bargain and sale deed with a covenant against the grantor's acts warrants only that he or she has done nothing to harm or cloud the title.

beneficiary. the person who benefits from certain acts, e.g. a will; one receiving benefits, profits or advantage; one for whose benefit a trust is created.

bill of sale. a written instrument by which a person transfers right, title or interest in personal property to another.

blanket mortgage. a mortgage that covers more than one piece of property.

broker. a duly licensed person, firm, partnership, limited liability company, association, or corporation who, in consideration of compensation or with the intent of receiving such compensation, facilitates a real property transaction for another party. (See 12-10-201 C.R.S. for Colorado statutory definition – chapter 1 of this manual.)

building code. local government regulations specifying structural requirements of buildings.

buyer agent. a broker engaged by and representing the buyer in a real estate transaction.

capitalization rate. a percentage rate of change applied in the income approach to value.

cash basis accounting. recognizing revenue and expense when cash is received or disbursed rather than when earned or incurred. A service business not dealing in inventory has the option of using the cash or accrual basis of accounting. Individual taxpayers must use the accrual basis.

cash flow. cash receipts minus cash disbursements from an operation or asset. An annual cash flow statement shows total return after taxes.

caveat emptor. Latin phrase meaning "let the buyer beware.", formerly imposing a duty on the buyer to examine the products or property accepting them "as is".

certificate of reasonable value (CRV). Veterans Administration's certified appraisal of value of real property.

certificate of taxes. a written guaranty of the condition of the taxes on a certain property made by the county treasurer wherein the property is located. Any loss resulting from an error in a tax certificate shall be paid by the county that such treasurer represents.

chapter 7. provision of the 1978 Bankruptcy Reform Act that covers liquidations under a court appointed trustee.

chapter 11. provision of the 1978 Bankruptcy Reform Act that covers reorganizations where the debtor remains in control of the business and its operations.

chattel. property other than real estate, i.e. personal property; an item of movable property.

check. synonym for quadrangle, a 24 mile square tract of land in the Governmental Survey System.

cloud on title. an outstanding claim or encumbrance that affects or impairs title to the property.

cognovit note. one containing a confession of judgment (waiver of due process) by the borrower.

collateral security. some security additional to the personal obligation of the borrower, as a chattel mortgage or trust deed.

Colorado Association of REALTORS® – (C.A.R). the state organization of real estate licensees whose goal is the professional advancement of the real estate industry and whose membership is comprised of local real estate associations or boards.

Colorado Coordinate System. a method of land description based on measurements from the intersection of statutorily defined north-south and east-west axes; applied only in Delta and Ute Counties.

commingling. mixing money belonging to others with personal or business funds. Illegal commingling is using the money of one beneficiary for the benefit of another or failing to maintain such money in identified escrow accounts.

common interest community. real estate described in a declaration which obligates an individual unit owner to pay property tax, insurance premiums, maintenance or improvement on some declared real property owned in common. Ownership does not include a leasehold interest of less than forty years, measured from the date the initial term commences, including renewal options.

common-law. law evolving from usage, custom and judicial interpretation rather than legislated by statute. Common law originated in old English courts.

community property. property acquired by a husband and wife, or either, during marriage, by their industry and not by gift, belonging equally to husband and wife. Community property laws exist in only nine states: AZ, CA, ID, LA, NV, NM, OK, TX and WA.

condemnation. in real property law, the process by which property of a private owner is taken for public use, with compensation to the owner, under the governmental right of eminent domain.

condominium. a common interest community in which portions of the real estate are designated for separate ownership and the remainder of which is distributed for common ownership solely among separate owners. A common interest community is not a condominium unless the undivided interests in the common elements are vested in the unit owners.

consideration. a promise or an act of legal value bargained for and received in return for a promise; one of the essential elements of a contract.

construction mortgage. a short-term loan used to finance the building of a structure.

constructive (or legal) notice. the conclusive presumption that all persons have knowledge of the contents of a recorded instrument.

contract. an agreement, enforceable at law, between two or more competent persons, having a legal purpose, wherein the parties agree to act in a certain manner.

controller. the chief accounting executive of an organization responsible for (1) financial reporting, (2) tax administration, (3) management audits, (4) planning controls and (5) developing accounting systems and procedures.

conventional mortgage. a mortgage securing a loan made by private investors without governmental participation, i.e. not F.H.A.-insured or V.A.-guaranteed.

conversion. unauthorized appropriation of ownership rights over goods or property belonging to another; also altering one form of property to another such as changing a leasehold apartment building to freehold condominium ownership.

conveyance. an instrument in writing by which a person transfers some estate, interest, or title in real estate to another, such as a deed or lease.

covenant. a promise or agreement, usually in writing, to do or not do certain acts; also stipulations in a real estate conveyance document governing use of the property.

cubage. the product of multiplying width x height x depth (or length) of an object.

cubic foot per second. a unit of discharge for measurement of flowing liquid, equal to a flow of one cubic foot per second past a given section. Also called "second-foot".

cul-de-sac. a street which dead-ends in a semi-circle.

curtesy. a common-law life-estate in all of a wife's real property given to the husband upon her death, provided a child was born from their marriage; abolished in Colorado.

customer. a party to a real estate transaction with whom the broker has no brokerage relationship because such party has not engaged or employed a broker.

debenture. bonds issued without specific security and are secured only by the overall equity of the issuer.

declaration. a recorded instrument that defines boundaries and common elements of a condominium and establishes the basic rights and obligations of the owners. It also provides for the creation of an owners' association including a board of directors with authority to collect common expenses and otherwise act for the benefit of all owners.

dedication. transfer of land from private to public use, as streets in a platted subdivision.

deed. a legal instrument in writing, duly executed and delivered, whereby the owner (grantor) conveys to another (grantee) some right, title or interest in or to real estate.

deed restriction. a provision in a deed controlling or limiting the use of the land.

default. omission or failure to perform a legal duty; failure to meet an obligation when due.

defeasible fee (base- or qualified fee). a fee interest in land that is capable of being defeated or terminated upon the happening of a specified event.

deficiency judgment. a lien against borrower's remaining assets in an amount equal to the shortage between a foreclosure sale price less than the indebtedness owed.

depreciation. loss in value due to deterioration from ordinary wear and tear, action of the elements, functional or economic obsolescence.

designated broker. an employing or employed broker designated in writing by an employing broker to serve as a single agent or transaction-broker for a seller, landlord, buyer or tenant in a real estate transaction; does not include a real estate brokerage firm that consists of only one licensed natural person.

devise. a gift of real property by the last will and testament of a donor.

diversion. illegal or unauthorized use of entrusted funds.

documentary fee. a statutory Colorado tax of one cent per one hundred dollars (sale price x .0001) of consideration paid by a person recording an instrument of conveyance with a county clerk and recorder.

donee. receiver of a gift.

donor. giver of a gift.

dower. a common-law estate consisting of a one-third interest in a husband's real property given to his wife upon his death. abolished in Colorado.

due-on-sale clause. a provision in a mortgage or trust deed which allows the lender to call a promissory note due and payable in full immediately upon the sale or transfer of a secured property; allows a lender to raise the interest rate or force other changes in terms upon assumption of the loan.

duress. forcing action or inaction against a person's will.

earnest money. down payment made by a purchaser of real estate as evidence of good faith.

easement. a right or interest in the real property of another; the right to use another's land for a specific purpose, such as a right-of-way.

economic life. the period of time over which improved property may be profitably used.

eminent domain. a governmental right to take private property for public use through the process of condemnation, and with payment of just compensation.

employing broker. a license level qualifying a broker to employ other licensees, requiring two years of active licensed experience, a 24-hour "brokerage administration" course if licensed after December 31, 1996 and passage of the Colorado part of the broker licensing exam if upgrade to broker associate from salesperson was by means of the broker transition course.

encroachment. illegal intrusion of an improvement or other real property onto another's property.

encumbrance. a claim, lien, charge, or liability attached to and binding upon real property, such as a judgment, mortgage, mechanic's lien, lien for unpaid taxes, or right-of-way.

endorsement. signing one's name on a negotiable instrument with intent to transfer ownership; also an addition altering or clarifying coverage of an (title) insurance policy.

equity. the amount of an owner's interest in real estate exceeding its encumbrances.

equity of redemption. see redemption.

escheat. reversion of property to the state when an owner dies without leaving a will or legal heirs to whom the property may pass by lawful descent.

escrow. the state or condition of money or a deed held conditionally by a third party, called the escrow agent, pending the performance or fulfillment of some act or condition.

escrow account. any checking, demand, passbook or statement account insured by an agency of the United States government maintained in a Colorado depository for money that belongs to others.

escrow agreement. a written agreement whereby a grantor, promissor or obligor delivers certain instruments or property to an escrow agent, to be held until the happening of a contingency or performance of a condition, and then to be delivered to the grantee, promisee or obligee.

estate. the degree, quantity, nature and extent of a person's interest in real property; such as a fee simple absolute estate, or an estate for years.

estate (tenancy) at sufferance. an estate in land arising when the tenant wrongfully holds over after the expiration of the tenant's term; the landlord has the choice of evicting the tenant as a trespasser or accepting such tenant for a similar term and under the conditions of the tenant's previous holding.

estate (tenancy) at will. an interest in land terminable at the will of either the tenant or landlord.

estate (tenancy) for years. an interest in land for a fixed period of time, e.g. one day or 99 years.

estate from period-to-period (periodic tenancy). An interest in land with no contract date of termination. The rental period (week, month or year, etc.) renews by payment of the contract rent.

et al. Latin abbreviation for "et allus", meaning "and others".

et ux. Latin abbreviation for "et uxor", meaning "and wife".

eviction. dispossession by process of law; the act of depriving a person of the possession of land pursuant to a court judgment.

exclusive agency listing. a listing whereby the owner engages a real estate brokerage as sole broker for a specified period of time, while retaining the right to sell the property to a buyer that the owner finds without paying the broker a commission.

exclusive right-to-sell listing. a listing whereby the owner engages one real estate brokerage as sole broker for a specified period of time, entitling the broker to a commission regardless of who sells the property, including the owner.

execution. a writ issued by a court to the sheriff directing seizure and sale of a property to satisfy a debt; the act of signing a contract; completion of the terms of a contract.

executor. the person named in a will to carry out its provisions.

"fannie mae". The pronunciation of "FNMA" (Federal National Mortgage Association). provides a market for government secured mortgages held by primary lenders and provides them with a ready market so as to permit a greater turnover of money for loans.

fee simple absolute (fee or fee simple). the most comprehensive ownership of real property under law; the largest bundle of ownership rights possible.

fee tail. an estate in land which cannot be conveyed but which must descend to the heirs of the holder; abolished in Colorado.

F.H.A.-insured mortgage. a mortgage under which the Federal Housing Administration insures approved lenders against loan default.

fiduciary. a person in a position of trust relative to another party; confidential, as in a fiduciary relationship between an agent and the principal.

fixture. an article of personal property installed in or attached to land or an improvement in a permanent manner, so that it is considered a part of the real estate.

foreclosure. termination of property rights due to some default by the borrower; a judicial or public trustee process whereby secured property is sold to satisfy a debt.

grantee. a person to whom real estate is conveyed; the buyer.

grantor. a person who conveys real estate; the seller.

grazing district. an administrative subdivision of the range lands under the jurisdiction of the Bureau of Land Management, established pursuant to section 3 of the Taylor Grazing Act to facilitate management of BLM forage resources.

grazing lease section 15. a lease authorizing the use of public lands outside of grazing districts (Taylor Grazing Act) for the grazing of livestock for a specified period of time.

grazing licenses. a permit for the grazing of a set number and class of livestock on a designated area of grazing district lands for a specified time, usually less than one year.

grazing permit. a permit to graze a certain number and class of livestock on a designated area of grazing district lands during specified seasons each year for a period of usually 10 years.

grazing preference. a request to graze certain numbers and classes of livestock upon a national forest for a specified time and subject to rules and regulations adopted by the Forest Service.

gross income multiplier. a number used in the income approach to value used to compare potential desirability of income properties, and calculated by dividing sales price by gross annual income.

ground water. a pervious formation with sides and bottom of relatively impervious material, in which ground water is held or retained; also called subsurface water basin.

holdover tenant. one who fails to vacate leased property after the lease has expired.

homeowners association. an association or unit owners association formed as part of a common interest community.

homestead exemption. a/k/a "homestead" or "homestead right"; a fixed, statutory sum exempt from execution by creditors, and intended to protect a family home from foreclosure or sale for debts.

indemnify. to insure; to secure against loss.

independent broker. a license level qualifying a broker to work without the supervision of an employing broker, requiring two years of active licensed experience, and if upgrade to broker associate was by means of the broker transition course, passage of the Colorado part of the broker licensing exam.

installment land contract (ILC), also land contract, or installment contract; an agreement for the purchase of real estate on an installment basis, whereby the deed is withheld until all or a specified portion of the purchase price is paid.

inter alia. Latin meaning "among other things".

intestate. Dying without leaving a valid will.

joint tenancy. a type of co-ownership of real property featuring a right of survivorship and four unities (time, title, interest and possession).

judgment. final declaration of the rights of the parties by a court.

land. real property; all below the surface, the surface and the airspace above it, and that which is affixed to it permanently; synonymous with "real property", "realty", and "real estate"; often used to mean only the unimproved surface of the earth.

land economics. the production, distribution and consumption of wealth deriving from land classification and use.

landlord. an owner who has leased an estate-in-land to a tenant.

landlord agent. a broker engaged by and representing a landlord as an agent in a leasing transaction.

lease. an agreement under which a tenant receives possession and use of real property for a certain period of time and the landlord receives the payment of rent and/or the performance of other conditions.

leasehold. an estate or right in real property held under a lease.

legal description. a description recognized by law that is sufficient to locate and identify a property without oral testimony.

lessee. party who possesses an estate in realty under a lease; commonly referred to as tenant.

lessor. party who conveys a right or estate in realty to a lessee under a lease; commonly referred to as landlord.

lien. a right given by law to a creditor to have a debt or charge satisfied out of the value of real or personal property belonging to the debtor.

life estate. an estate or interest in real property held for the duration of the life of some certain person.

limited agent. an agent whose duties and obligations to a principal are only those set forth in C.R.S. 12-10-404 or 12-10-405, with any additional duties and obligations agreed to pursuant to section 12-10-403 (5).

lis pendens. a filing against specific property, giving public notice that an action at law is pending that may affect the title to the land.

listing. an agreement or contract of employment, either oral or written, whereby the owner authorizes the real estate broker to sell, exchange or lease real estate.

marketable (merchantable) title. a title free from reasonable doubt of defect; which can be readily sold or mortgaged to a reasonably prudent person; a title free from material defects or grave doubts and reasonably free from potential litigation.

market value. the price which a ready and able buyer, not forced to buy, would pay and which a ready and willing seller, not forced to sell, would accept, assuming that both parties are fully informed, act reasonably, and have sufficient time to consider the transaction with due care.

mechanics' lien. a lien created by statute which exists against real property in favor of persons who have performed work or furnished materials for the improvement of the real estate.

metes and bounds. a method of describing or locating real property; metes are measures of length and bounds are boundaries. This method starts from a well-marked point of beginning and follows the boundaries of the land until it returns once more to the point of beginning.

mill. one-tenth of a cent; a tax rate of one mill on the dollar or one-tenth of one percent of the assessed value of a property. (assessed value x .001)

mortgage. a conditional conveyance of property as security for the payment of a debt or the fulfillment of some obligation. Upon payment of the debt or performance of the obligation, a mortgage automatically becomes void.

mortgagee. the party (lender) to whom property is conveyed under a mortgage as security for the repayment of a loan or fulfillment of some obligation.

mortgagor. the party who gives a mortgage (borrower) conveying interest in the property to the lender as security for the obligation to repay a loan or fulfill some obligation.

multiple listing service (MLS). a marketing arrangement among real estate brokers whereby a seller authorizes the listing broker to share information and a pre-determined portion of a commission to any broker cooperating in the sale of the property.

mutual assent (meeting of the minds). agreement of the parties to the contract, mutually consenting to be bound by its exact terms; an essential contract element.

National Association of REALTORS©, (N.A.R.). a national association of real estate personnel whose goal is the professional advancement of the real estate industry and whose membership is comprised of state and local real estate associations or boards.

national forest. a forest or watershed reservation administered by the Forest Service, United States Department of Agriculture.

negotiable instrument. a written instrument containing a promise of payment, which can be endorsed from one person to another.

net listing. a listing contract whereby the owner is to receive a certain net price, with the broker receiving any excess over and above the net price as commission.

note. a written instrument acknowledging a debt and promising payment.

obsolescence. impairment of desirability and usefulness of the property resulting from economic, functional, physical, fashion, or other changes.

offer. to present for sale; or a proposal presented for acceptance or rejection which, if accepted, will form a binding contract.

offeree. one to whom an offer is made.

offeror. one who makes an offer.

open listing. a non-exclusive employment agreement in which an owner retains the right to list the property with other brokers.

option. a temporary right for a specified time, and for which a consideration is paid, during which an optionee may purchase or lease property at a set price.

optionee. one who requests, receives or stands to benefit from an option.

optionor. one who grants an option to another, usually the land owner.

party wall. a wall erected on a line between adjoining properties for the use of both properties.

patent. an instrument of conveyance of government-owned land to an individual.

percentage lease. A commercial lease of property in which the rent is based upon a percentage of the sales volume derived from the leased premises.

percolation (perc) test. determines if soil will take sufficient water seepage for use of a septic tank.

periodic tenancy. see estate from period-to-period.

personal property. all that is not real property; items of a temporary or movable nature.

personalty. synonym for personal property.

plat. a parcel or plot of land; also a method of land description referring to a recorded map (plat) of a subdivision or town which lays out boundaries, streets, easements etc.

police power. governmental right to enact legislation deemed necessary to protect and promote the health, safety and general welfare of the public. (License law is supported by this legal theory.)

power of attorney. a legal instrument authorizing another person to act in place of the person drawing the instrument.

principal. a person, partnership, association or corporation who authorizes or employs another, called the agent, to do certain acts on behalf of the principal.

principal note. a promissory note secured by the mortgage or trust deed.

property. anything which may be owned and its bundle of ownership rights; the right to use, possess, enjoy, and dispose of a thing in every legal way and to exclude everyone else from interfering with these rights; generally classified into two groups; personal and real.

public trustee. a county official to whom borrowers convey title to real property by trust deed for the benefit of the beneficiary (lender).

purchase money mortgage. a mortgage given by the purchaser to secure a loan for part or all of the purchase price. Such a mortgage becomes a lien on the property simultaneously with the passing of title, and if immediately recorded becomes prior to any lien against the purchaser.

quadrangle, (check). a square tract of land in the U.S. Governmental Survey System measuring 24 miles on each side.

quiet-title suit. an action in court to remove a defect, cloud or suspicion regarding the owner's legal rights to a parcel of real estate.

quitclaim deed. a deed in which the grantor warrants nothing, conveying only the grantor's present interest in the real estate, if any.

range. a six-mile wide strip of land that runs in a north-south direction. Ranges are determined by government survey and are numbered in numerical order east or west of a principal meridian.

real estate. real property, realty, land.

real property. land; the surface of the earth and whatever is erected, growing upon, or affixed to the land; including that which is below it and the airspace above it. synonymous with "land", "realty", and "real estate".

REALTOR®. a registered trade name exclusive to members of the National Association of REALTORS®.

realty. real property, land, real estate.

receiver. a court-appointed custodian who holds property pending final disposition of the matter before the court.

recording. entering an instrument in a book of public record in the office of the county clerk and recorder. recording constitutes "constructive" notice to all persons of the rights or claims contained in the instrument.

Rectangular Survey System. see U.S. Government Survey System.

redemption. the right of an owner to redeem or reclaim real estate by paying the debt or charge (such as mortgage or tax lien) after default, together with interest and costs. Specifically, **equity of redemption** is the right to redeem the property after default but before foreclosure. **Statutory right-of-redemption** refers to the right to redeem the property <u>after</u> foreclosure, or other enforcement action, within a certain time specified by statute. In Colorado, a mortgagor has a statutory right to redeem property any time within 75 days (residential) or six months (agricultural)) after foreclosure or three years after a tax sale.

release. the relinquishment or surrender of a right, claim, or interest.

release of lien. the discharge or release of specific property from the charge or lien of a judgment, mortgage or other claim.

restrictive covenant. a clause in a deed limiting the use of a property.

right of survivorship. a characteristic of joint-tenancy whereupon the death of one tenant triggers an automatic and immediate transfer of the decedent's property rights equally among the surviving tenant(s).

right-of-way. an easement or right to pass over another's land; also the strip of land used as roadbed by a railroad or used for a public purpose by other public utilities.

salesperson. an inactive license status in Colorado; in other jurisdictions, a license level authorized to perform real estate activity on behalf of a licensed real estate broker.

seisin. actual possession of real estate by a freehold estate owner; a typical warranty deed covenant.

seller agent. a broker engaged by and representing the seller in a real estate transaction.

single agent. a broker engaged by and representing only one party, i.e. buyer, seller, tenant or landlord in a real estate transaction.

special assessment. a tax against real property made by a unit of government to cover the proportionate cost of an improvement, such as a street or sewer.

special warranty deed. a deed in which the grantor warrants title only against defects arising during the grantor's ownership.

specific performance. a remedy compelling a party to perform or carry out the terms of a valid, existing contract.

state lease. an agreement between the state of Colorado and other parties for the use of lands under the jurisdiction of the State Board of Land Commissioners for grazing, agriculture and other lawful purposes.

statutory right of redemption. see redemption.

subordination clause. a clause in a mortgage or lease stating that the rights of the holder shall be secondary to a subsequent encumbrance or right of another person.

surrender. in leases, the cancellation of a lease by mutual consent of lessor and lessee.

survey. the measurement of a parcel of land and its characteristics.

Taylor Grazing Act. see grazing district.

tenancy at sufferance. see estate at sufferance.

tenancy at will. see estate at will.

tenancy-in-common. a type of co-ownership of an estate in land entitling each tenant to full possession of the property (unity of possession) regardless of proportionate share owned; tenancy-in-common contains no right of survivorship.

tenant agent. a broker engaged by and representing the tenant in a leasing transaction.

testate. a condition of death characterized by the decedent having left a valid will.

time-share. an interval interest in real estate which limits ownership or occupancy rights to specified time periods. Ownership may be either fee simple (deeded) or "right-to-use" (contractual or membership). In Colorado, time-share sales are subject to license law.

title. in real property, the right, or evidence of the right, to ownership.

title insurance. indemnification of a policyholder from loss due to a title defect, provided the loss does not result from a defect excluded by the policy provisions.

Torrens system. a system by which the registrar of Torrens (i.e. clerk and recorder) keeps and maintains title records pertaining to real property located in the county.

tort. a negligent or intentional wrong done to another for which the law will grant money damages in a civil action.

transaction-broker. a broker who assists one or more parties throughout a contemplated real estate transaction with communication, interposition, advisement, negotiation, contract terms, and the closing without being an agent or advocate for the interests of any party.

treasurer. a county official responsible for property tax administration; a chief executive in a firm responsible for (1) obtaining operating capital, (2) investor relations, (3) short-term financing, (4) banking policies, (5) asset custody, (6) credit and collections, (7) investment analysis, and (8) risk management.

treasurer's deed. a deed for property sold at public sale by the county for non-payment of taxes by the owner.

trust deed. a loan security instrument by which a borrower conveys title to a (usually public) trustee, to be held for the protection of a lender as security for the repayment of the debt. Upon payment of the debt a trust deed must be specifically released by the trustee.

United States Government (or Rectangular) Survey System (GSS). a land description method based on reference to governmental surveys.

usury. charging more than the legal rate of interest for the use of money.

V.A.-guaranteed mortgage. a mortgage backed by a Veterans Administration guarantee to the lender for a percentage of the loan amount.

vendee. buyer.

vendor. seller.

vicarious liability. a principal's liability for an agent's acts performed within the scope of the agency; specifically excluded by Colorado statute from a principal's liability unless the act or omission was approved, directed or ratified.

waiver. abandonment of some claim or right.

warranty deed, (general warranty deed). a deed in which the grantor warrants or guarantees the title to real property against defects during the grantor's ownership and as far back as a chain-of-title can be established.

writ of execution. a court order directing an officer of the court, usually the sheriff, to carry out the judgment or decree of the court.

Topical Index

Topical Index

Chapter

vacation clubs (see subdivisions)